BUFFALO BILL'S AMERICA

BUFFALO BILL'S AMERICA

William Cody and the Wild West Show

LOUIS S. WARREN

ALFRED A. KNOPF, NEW YORK, 2005

THIS IS A BORZOI BOOK
PUBLISHED BY ALFRED A. KNOPF

Published in the United States by Alfred A. Knopf,
a division of Random House, Inc., New York,
and in Canada by Random House of Canada Limited, Toronto.
www.aaknopf.com

Knopf, Borzoi Books, and the colophon are registered trademarks of Random House, Inc.

Grateful acknowledgment is made to Liveright Publishing Corporation for permission to
reprint the lines from "Buffalo Bill's" copyright 1923, 1951, © 1991 by the Trustees for the
E. E. Cummings Trust. From *Complete Poems: 1904–1962* by E. E. Cummings, edited by
George J. Firmage. Copyright © 1976 by George James Firmage. Reprinted by permission.

Drawings by Spring M. Warren.

Library of Congress Cataloging-in-Publication Data
Warren, Louis S.
Buffalo Bill's America : William Cody and the Wild West show / Louis S. Warren.—1st ed.
p.   cm.
Includes bibliographical references and index.
ISBN 0-375-41216-6
1. Buffalo Bill, 1846–1917.   2. Pioneers—West (U.S.)—Biography.
3. Frontier and pioneer life—West (U.S.)   4. Entertainers—United States—Biography.
5. Buffalo Bill's Wild West.   6. West (U.S.)—Biography.   I. Title.
F594.B94W37 2005
978'02'092—dc22
[B]
2004063280

Manufactured in the United States of America
Published October 14, 2005
Second Printing, October 2005
First Edition

Once more, for Spring

CONTENTS

PART THREE

INTRODUCTION

He was the most famous American of his age, when practically everyone knew his story: a child of the frontier, he grew up by turns Pony Express rider, prospector, trapper, Civil War soldier, professional buffalo hunter, Indian fighter, and cavalry scout. For all his western upbringing, his greatest success would take him far from the Plains. At twenty-three he was a dime novel hero; at twenty-six he was starring as himself in New York theatrical dramas about his life. An early pioneer of the frontier melodrama, he spent over a decade on the stage before he invented the Wild West show and took it on tour for the first time in 1883. Venturing to Europe in 1887, he and the show were a sensation, and the man who embodied the frontier became an icon along the glittering promenades of Paris, London, and Milan. By the time he was fifty-four, in 1900, he was the subject of a vast literature: fictionalized biographies by the score, dime novels, dramatic criticism, puff pieces extolling the heroism of Buffalo Bill Cody.

His life and career straddled enormous expanses of geographic space. Born near Leclaire, Iowa, he migrated westward to Kansas, Nebraska, and then Wyoming. The western curve of his settlements described the trajectory of American expansion. Remarkably, even the dates of his birth and death bracket the ascendant arc of American power. Born in 1846, the year that the United States went to war against Mexico and became a continental nation, he died in 1917, the year his country entered World War I and took the faltering steps that would culminate in the Atlantic alliance.

In his waning years, he was known to say that he "stood between savagery and civilization most all of my early days."[1] Ironically, if he was a guardian of white American supremacy, in his most successful years he also bridged vast cultural gulfs. Parting company with European and eastern wealth and aristocracy at the end of each show season, he would return to the West, first his ranch in North Platte, Nebraska, later the town he founded at Cody, Wyoming. He moved with consummate ease among the aristocrats who flocked to his show, the genuine cowboys, Mexicans, and Indians who populated it, and the rural white westerners who settled around the ranches where he waited out his off-season and became a benefactor to community churches and schools.

In many ways, he seemed to hold the contradictions of a rapidly modernizing world together through the force of his personality. In a time when America represented the future of the modern world in its exploding cities and its industrial power, Buffalo Bill brought together the wild, primitive past of the American frontier—buffalo, elk, staged prairie fires, real Indians—and the astonishing promise of a technological future, in his show's modern gunplay, its glowing electric lights and brilliantly colored publicity. He represented the coming together of old and new, nature and culture, the past and the future. He straddled the yawning chasms between worlds, and in so doing, rose to greater heights of fame than any American could have dreamed. He became the nation's brightest star.

More even than Charles Lindbergh or Charlie Chaplin, or other world-famous celebrities of the early twentieth century, the name of Buffalo Bill Cody still resonates in the imagination of Americans and people the world over. It is hard to overstate the impact he had on his audiences. Simply by riding into an arena on horseback he could make the crowds gasp. A seemingly simple sight—a man on a horse—became something much more: a visionary encounter, a simultaneous celebration of the past and future, even an apotheosis. Part of it was the way he rode, so much at one with the animal that the word "centaur" sprang to the lips of his admirers. Part of it was the way he offered his audiences a projection of their own fantasies. His show publicity made the most of his virtual organic connection with the horse. Where the appearance of a monster on the cultural scene is usually a dreadful portent, Buffalo Bill seemed to be both monstrous—half man, half horse—and wondrous. When he died, E. E. Cummings recalled the specter of this horse-man as he rode fast around a ring, blasting amber balls from the air with his Winchester rifle.

> *Buffalo Bill's*
> *defunct*
> > *who used to*
> > *ride a watersmooth-silver*
> > > > > *stallion*
> *and break onetwothreefourfive pigeonsjustlike that*
> > > > > *Jesus*
> *he was a handsome man.*[2]

For generations of Americans and Europeans, Buffalo Bill defined the meaning of American history and American identity. From California to Maine, and from Wales to Ukraine, crowds who came to see Buffalo Bill's Wild West show spoke so widely and fervently about it for years afterward that it became a defining cultural memory—or dream—of America.

But if no American rose to greater heights than Buffalo Bill did, it seems that few have fallen further. The world's highest-paid performer and best-loved American died almost penniless in Denver in 1917. He was celebrated through the 1960s in American film, most prominently by Joel McCrea in *Buffalo Bill*, and Charlton Heston in *Pony Express*. But thereafter his country's memory of him became something less than golden. Where the frontier centaur was wonderful to nineteenth-century Americans, to the generation raised on Vietnam he became, like so many frontiersmen, a very different kind of monster. For many, his role in wars against American Indians and in the near extermination of the buffalo made him a figure of revulsion. In Arthur Penn's 1970 film, *Little Big Man*, his character made a cameo appearance as a crass destroyer of Indian lifeway and a grasping materialist. In 1972, in Robert Altman's *Buffalo Bill and the Indians*, Paul Newman portrayed him as a liar, a drunkard, a coward, and a con man. In 1991, his name was taken to much darker realms in Jonathan Demme's *Silence of the Lambs*, a film in which a psychotic killer of women is dubbed "Buffalo Bill" because, as one FBI agent explains, "He skins his humps." From demigod to vampire, culture hero to serial killer, William Cody's career has been as strange in death as it was in life.

But who was he? In recent decades, few scholars have pursued that question. To be sure, illustrated biographies, cultural studies of his show, and coffee-table celebrations of Buffalo Bill and his Wild West continue to roll off the presses at a gallop. But when these books veer into biography, they often take one of two approaches. Either they recount earlier writers with minor revisions, if any, or they weigh in on one side or the other of a single question: Was he a hero, or was he a charlatan? Variations on this theme— Was he a real Indian fighter, or was he a showman? Was he an honest man, or a liar?—weave through a vast Cody literature.

In one sense, this is hardly surprising. After all, what other question can we possibly ask about Buffalo Bill Cody, who made it ever so difficult to tell where reality stopped and representation began? Never was his prowess at fusing life and art greater than in the summer of 1876, when he took leave from the stage to scout for the army. Weeks into the campaign, he learned that George Armstrong Custer and most of his command had fallen before the Sioux and Cheyenne on the banks of the Little Big Horn River. Soon thereafter, dressed in a black velvet stage costume, he swooped into a skirmish with a Cheyenne war party, killing and scalping a Cheyenne subchief named Yellow Hair, whose name was mistranslated in publicity as Yellow Hand. Within months, Cody was reenacting the episode in a play he commissioned, taking this "first scalp for Custer" before packed houses from New York to St. Louis, wearing the same stage velvet and waving the real scalp at the drama's climax. For the rest of his life, he explained the sanguinary episode as a demonstration of his grief for the death of his personal friend, George Custer.

That the authenticity of such a man should become a subject of historical inquiry might be a foregone conclusion. The most enduring biography of Cody, and the last attempt at a comprehensive reevaluation of his life, is Don Russell's *Lives and Legends of Buffalo Bill*, which appeared in 1960. Russell took up the cudgel on Cody's behalf, beating back almost a half century of Buffalo Bill debunkers with a study that shored up the old showman as the "real thing," a Pony Express rider, buffalo hunter, and a skilled scout and Indian fighter who never claimed a military honor he did not actually have (he *did* win a Congressional Medal of Honor in 1872) and who failed to claim some that were rightly his.[3]

Cody's accomplishments were impressive in many ways (that Medal of Honor was real). But as becomes clear in pages to come, we must be cautious with his Pony Express adventures, his alleged bond with the fallen Custer, and many other stories he told in his ongoing effort to evoke himself as the paragon of frontier mastery

Still, by itself, separating truth from fiction in the Buffalo Bill myth is not enough, for Cody's audiences often suspected that his biographical claims had an ambiguous relationship with the truth. Indeed, perhaps the most striking thing about Russell's book and about my challenge to it, and about all the other contributions to the vigorous Buffalo Bill debate, is how much they echo arguments that were in progress during Cody's own life. Modern writers and readers may believe themselves to be more sophisticated than Cody's contemporaries, but, in fact, questions about whether Buffalo Bill was real or fake began to circulate with the young man's arrival in the public eye. Rather than quash these disputes, the savvy performer often encouraged them as a means to keep the attention of his audience.[4]

This aspect of Cody's method has been elusive, partly, and paradoxically, because of the remarkably productive ways scholars of the American West have contrasted real events, or history, against popular ideas of those events, or myth. This is necessary, important work, which has provided us with insights too numerous to count, and without which our sense of the past would be deeply impoverished.[5]

But grasping the artistry and the origins of Buffalo Bill requires a slightly different tack. This book explores Cody's real achievements, but also his many fabrications, less with an air of categorizing Cody as real or fake than to understand how and why he mixed the two. Contemporary arguments over Cody's truthfulness or heroism (or lack thereof) mirrored much wider debates about the meaning of the Far West, and the trustworthiness of the organs of popular culture through which most Americans learned about it: newspapers, advertising, literature, painting, and theater. William Cody's method of promoting his real achievements was to mingle them with colorful fictions, making his own life and myth almost (but not quite) indistinguishable to a public that was sometimes awestruck, sometimes skeptical, but almost invariably amused by his artistic pose as the real embodiment of public fantasy.

I am much indebted in the following chapters to the many scholars who have probed the cultural meaning of Buffalo Bill's Wild West show.[6] But for all their contributions, most cultural studies scholars venture into symbolic and cultural explorations of the show's meaning without seriously examining the earlier frontier and theatrical occupations of its creator. One underlying assumption of such treatments is that the frontier West was divorced—or separated—from the world of popular culture and entertainments. Often, this reinforces the mistaken view that Cody was merely the creation of skilled eastern publicists, and leaves a most intriguing set of questions unanswered. How is it that a frontiersman became the world's most popular showman? Was the West a necessary arena for developing ideas of American entertainment and popular culture? Was there some sense in which the West provided Cody the requisite context for mixing life, myth, and performance?

How Cody adapted and reconciled life to story, and vice versa, is the central question of this book. In recent years, various scholars have examined the ways people shape their lives to fit stories they carry in their heads.[7] As we shall see, Cody's experience on the Great Plains was seminal to his realization that even his young life could be a story, lived for the amusement of a public. Incongruous as it may seem, scouting and hunting were paths to show business, and Cody's development of a show persona reflected many of the lessons he learned in the Indian wars and on the buffalo range. He was a genuine hunter and fighter (if not quite the hunter and fighter he said he was), but he was also an intuitive performance genius who borrowed readily from a popular theory of history, "the progress of civilization," to turn himself into the "representative man" who had "passed through every stage" of frontier development.[8] Through this process, he became an American artist of originality and remarkable vision, on a par with contemporaries and successors such as P. T. Barnum, D. W. Griffith, Eugene O'Neill, and even Orson Welles. How he came to this, from such humble western beginnings, is a major part of the story this book tells.

William Cody was notoriously enigmatic. His private life, and its relation to his performance career, has eluded most scholars. A key feature of
my approach is to explore the most intimate social bond in Cody's life, his
marriage, which began during his time in frontier Kansas and continued
through all his years in show business. Having a respectable family was fundamental to Cody's appeal for his earliest entertainment patrons. As he
developed a public image as defender of the white family, his private life as
patriarch of a real family became wedded to his authenticity. Thus the tensions and divisions within that marriage, which was often troubled, offer us
a valuable, and seldom seen, window into the personal cost of maintaining
the illusion of a life lived in accordance with national myth. Although few
remember it today, Buffalo Bill Cody sued his wife for divorce in 1904, with
calamitous results. The testimony from this courtroom drama provides rare
insight into just how commingled public and private life became for the
most public of Americans, while illuminating both the opportunities his lifelong performance offered him, and the constraints it ultimately imposed.

For all the energy and ink I have devoted to explaining how Cody located
himself in a national story, learning to perform it on the stage and off, I am
equally intrigued by the question of how and why some of America's most
marginalized peoples, including poor cowboys and even poorer Indians,
carved out a place for themselves in Cody's story. This phenomenon was
central to Cody's success. Buffalo Bill's Wild West show could not have
functioned had it not become the destination for dozens of Pawnee Indians,
and subsequently for hundreds of Lakota Sioux (including Sitting Bull, who
toured with the show in 1885). Just as important was the show's appeal to
American cowboys, Mexicans vaqueros, women (including not only Annie
Oakley but Indian women, too), and, later, Cossacks, gauchos, and others.
These show performers necessarily shaped Cody's performance imagination, leading him to reshape his personal mythology and his life story
accordingly.

Why would Indians join the Wild West show, where they reenacted their
own defeat? For that matter, what led real cowboys and all the other "frontier types" on display in the arena to drop their day-to-day lives and tour
with a traveling amusement? Who was Annie Oakley, and how did her own
leap into the Wild West show shore up her own career and the profile of the
show?

On the simplest level, all the show's entertainers needed the money.
Other scholars, notably George Moses, have argued that Indians saw the
show as a means to perpetuate their traditional culture.[9] In this and in other
ways, for Indians as for other cast members, the show's nostalgic celebration
of a mythical, vanished frontier became a limited means to a better future
West. Wild West show performance offered Indian and non-Indian alike a

host of opportunities for earning money, making political connections, learning new skills, and being or becoming American, a process cast members could be profoundly uneasy about. The Wild West show was partly a product of investor capital and Cody's genius. But it was also the product of a potent alchemy, in which the limited options facing rural whites, Mexicans, and Indians combined with their longings, which were as limitless as the western horizon.

Of course, just as the show could not happen without the cast, it was also impossible without the audience. We shall explore who they were, and how show acts appealed to them. For all the thrill of watching the drama in the arena, the camp of the Wild West show became its premier attraction, with hundreds of cowboys, Indians, Mexicans, and later Cossacks, Arabs, Germans, and others living in a mobile village under the management and direction of a frontiersman. This traveling show community, which required three trains to move the cast, props, animals, and equipment, including electric generators and a traveling kitchen, was more racially integrated than any real western town.

To many urban dwellers, it looked oddly familiar. The late nineteenth century saw a vast expansion in the U.S. population, much of it fueled by immigration from eastern and southern Europe. By the 1890s, the need to sell tickets to this increasingly diverse, ethnically divided public inspired Cody to expand and complicate his show drama, and its historical myths, by incorporating phalanxes of new riders from Eurasia and the Americas. As we shall see, his efforts in this direction were in some ways analogous to those of American historians, notably Frederick Jackson Turner, who sought to expand the nation's historical consciousness beyond the eastern seaboard, and to incorporate at least a limited range of non-English immigrants in national histories and myths.

Thus, Buffalo Bill's show community became a touchstone for Americans seeking to understand their own rapidly urbanizing, racially conflicted, industrial communities and country, and for Europeans contemplating a host of concerns, including industrialism, colonialism, race progress, and race decay.

Buffalo Bill's Wild West show inspired much criticism as well as elation, and it allowed its audiences to contemplate the downside of progress, and the dark possibilities of Cody's ambition. Buffalo Bill, the icon of heroism, was also a harbinger of American expansion, which Europeans did not always welcome. As we shall see, *Silence of the Lambs* was not the first time that an artist imagined Buffalo Bill as vampire.

This is a book, then, about how a man crafted a life and a story to reflect and express one another. It is also a story of how the entertainment he devised allowed others to join him in fitting life to story, story to life, and the many ways the resulting spectacle resonated with a vast transatlantic public. Throughout, I borrow a technique from recent scholarly biographies that situate their subjects in changing social and political contexts, to read the life as, in part, an expression of its era.[10] Thus we shall explore William Cody and the communities he created or moved through, from frontier Kansas to the Wild West show and beyond. Examining Cody on the Plains and on the road in this manner illuminates not only his actual accomplishments, but also the sources of his entertainment inspiration. At the same time, it reveals the simultaneous development of his life narrative and his potent show business product, and the many congruences and conflicts between them.

This book is divided in three parts. Part I explores the origins of the Wild West show in William Cody's life on the Great Plains, particularly in the Indian wars. Part II explores his development of frontier melodrama in the theater, and the origins and meaning of his Wild West show. Although modern Americans take for granted the appeal of western mythology, it was no simple proposition to stage western history for the amusement of paying audiences in the early 1880s. Learning from the experience of cast members, who did much to educate the show's management about how to succeed, Cody and his partners worked hard to create a show that both explained America's place in the universe and tied it to Cody as a real westerner who lived his country's seminal adventures.

Part III, the book's final section, explores the decline of William Cody and America's signature entertainment after 1900, when his life increasingly diverged from notions of American progress. His divorce trial presaged the failure of his biggest business ventures, the town of Cody (which succeeded only at the expense of its most famous founder), his mines in Arizona, and ultimately the Wild West show itself. The book closes with an explanation of why the strategies that had won him so much adoration and so much cash should fail him late in life.

Cody persuaded many that his entertainment was genuine in part by refusing to call it a show at all. Its official name was "Buffalo Bill's Wild West," as if it were a real place. This was a ruse to draw reluctant spectators, of course. But the semblance of reality owed much to the apparent bond between his arena full of charging horses and his real life, which began— he said—in a fast-paced drama of Pony Express adventure. We begin our story, then, with the child Will Cody and his legendary connection to the pony line.

PART ONE

CHAPTER ONE

Pony Express

The Former Pony Post rider will show how the Letters and Telegrams of the Republic were distributed across the immense Continent previous to the railways and the telegraph.[1]

LIKE EVERY OTHER frontier reenactment in the Wild West show, the Pony Express was a chapter in the life of its hero and his country. Before audiences of thousands, the horseman—not Cody himself, but another "Former Pony Post" rider—raced "down to the grand stand at a gallop," wrote one ecstatic viewer, "checked his pony within a length, and almost before it was at standstill the rider was on the ground, the bag on another pony, and the man galloping off at full speed, in less time than it would take an ordinary man to dismount."[2] It was a showstopper.

Of course Buffalo Bill rode the Pony Express. Everyone who perused the sixty or so printed pages of Wild West show programs could read it for themselves. "William F. Cody was born in Scott County, Iowa. He removed at an early age to Kansas, and was employed as a herder, wagonmaster, and pony express rider."[3]

The more curious might buy a copy of Buffalo Bill's autobiography, also for sale at the Wild West show. There they could read the story in detail. Left fatherless at an early age, the young Kansas boy ventured out to make money for his bereaved mother, five sisters, and infant brother. Between his eleventh birthday, in 1857, and his fifteenth, in 1861, he freighted wagons over the plains with rough teamsters, befriended Wild Bill Hickok, was captured by enemy Mormons in the government's abortive war against polygamy, survived a starvation winter at Fort Bridger, skirmished with some Indians and befriended others, prospected for gold in Colorado, and trapped beaver on the Plains.[4]

But of all the boyhood adventures William Cody claimed, those on the Pony Express were the most astonishing, and the most famous. On his way back to Kansas after failing to find gold at Pikes Peak, the thirteen-year-old boy ambled into the Pony Express station at Julesberg, Colorado, where he talked his way into his first Pony Express job. His mother feared it would kill him. "She was right about this, as fifteen miles an hour on horseback would, in a short time, shake any man 'all to pieces'; and there were but very few, if any, riders who could stand it for a great length of time." But young Will Cody took up his forty-five-mile route, and "stuck to it for two months," before he returned to Kansas to be with his mother, who had fallen ill.[5]

After she recovered, the boy and a friend tried their hand at trapping beaver up the remote reaches of the Republican River, in western Kansas. They lost an ox, and so were unable to move their wagon when Cody slipped on the ice and broke his leg. Left behind while his friend went for a replacement ox team, the young boy spent a month alone, and avoided being killed by a Sioux war party only because its leader, Chief Rain-in-the-Face, remembered meeting the young Will Cody at Fort Laramie the previous year.[6]

The following summer, in 1860, when he was fourteen, Cody returned to Pony Express riding again, and his adventures made his previous escapades seem pale in comparison. Warned that "it will soon shake the life out of you," he took up the most dangerous length of the Pony Express route, the Sweetwater Division. This section was under the supervision of John Slade, a notorious killer, but Cody recalled the man as civil, even kind, in his autobiography.

> "My boy, you are too young for a pony-express rider. It takes men for that business."
>
> "I rode two months last year on Bill Trotter's division, sir, and filled the bill then; and I think I am better able to ride now," said I.
>
> "What! are you the boy that was riding there, and was called the youngest rider on the road?"
>
> "I am the same boy," I replied, confident that everything was now all right for me.[7]

The boy proved himself more than equal to the man-size job. Arriving at the end of his seventy-six-mile stretch of road one day, he discovered that the rider to whom he was to pass the specially designed saddlebag, or *mochila*, had been killed in a drunken brawl the night before. Cody "did not hesitate for a moment to undertake an extra ride of eighty-five miles to Rocky Ridge," where he arrived on time. "I then turned and rode to Red Buttes, my starting place, accomplishing on the round trip a distance of 322 miles," which would go down in history as one of the longest Pony Express rides ever.

Shortly afterward, he outran an Indian attack, making a twenty-four-mile run on one horse. Not much later, the Indians attacked a company stagecoach between Split Rock and Three Crossings, and managers suspended the pony service. During this lull, the young Cody set out with his friend Wild Bill Hickok and a group of forty men "who had undergone all kinds of hardships and braved every danger" to pursue the Indians and recover stolen horses. They found the Indian encampment up the Powder River, raided it, and returned "with all of our own horses and about one hundred captured Indian ponies."[8]

Ever since 1879, when William Cody first published his life story, this childhood saga has been a favorite of the American public. The Wild West show reprised it over and over again, the high-speed Pony Express scene in Buffalo Bill's Wild West inscribing an almost indelible bond between young America and the child Will Cody. The pony was featured in the show's debut in 1883, and audiences from Omaha to New York, Sarasota to Paris, thrilled to the display every year thereafter until the show ended in 1916.

Cody's boyhood story of horseback days, of a boy who enters a man's world too early, was a familiar one in some respects. Young Will, the story's hero, is the victim of bad circumstances, but raises himself up through hard work, ambition, and good luck, meeting powerful men such as Chief Rain-in-the-Face, Wild Bill Hickok, and John Slade, who patronize his efforts. Like a western version of Horatio Alger's *Ragged Dick*, which had first appeared twelve years earlier, Cody's life story was an exhortation to the sons of the middle class. It inspired faith in the stage star, Buffalo Bill Cody, as a genuine western figure and a respectable, middle-class icon for the urban middle classes who were its intended audience. It extolled family, hard work, and willingness to take risks—all virtues of the middle-class family in the industrial age. "Mr. Cody tells his story in a simple, unaffected style that commands belief," wrote one reviewer, "and it is about as full of incident and adventure as its pages will allow." The book was respectable, too, not like dime novels which corrupted the nation's youth with romantic tales of theft and bloodshed. The reviewer doubted that "the perusal of the book will lure a single boy to run away from school, steal a revolver and tramp to the border, for somehow the men who know what frontier life really is always give the impression that there is a great deal of downright hard work about the borderer's life."[9]

What if you wanted to know more about those Pony Express adventures? The problem was there was not much to read on the subject other than Buffalo Bill's autobiography and show programs. The freighting firm of Russell, Majors, and Waddell created the Pony Express to carry mail between Saint Joseph, Missouri, and Sacramento, California, in 1860. The service was wildly popular, especially in California, where it was memorialized in heroic tributes even as it began.

But it lasted only eighteen months. When it ended, in 1861, the Civil

War had erupted. The epic clash of North and South at Shiloh, Gettysburg, and the Wilderness absorbed the energies of almost every American historian for the next three decades. Few attempted unpacking the West until the 1880s. Nobody wrote a book-length history of the Pony Express until after 1900.[10]

In the meantime, Buffalo Bill's Wild West show became the primary keeper of the pony legend. By the 1890s, when William Lightfoot Visscher began gathering material for his history of the Pony Express, the business records of Russell, Majors, and Waddell had long since vanished, and Buffalo Bill's Wild West show had been promoting William Cody's version of the pony's history for the better part of two decades. Cody was the world's most renowned showman and westerner, and had made himself far and away the most famous rider of the legendary pony line. He was also a personal friend of Visscher's. When the journalist's *Thrilling and Truthful History of the Pony Express* appeared in 1908, it was less history than hagiography, a devotional recounting of the heroic lives of saints.[11] The author repeated Cody's stories without any criticism.

Since then, every scholarly history of the Pony Express has mentioned Buffalo Bill's adventures. Every generation of Americans has thrilled to them in a succession of children's books and movies which have retold his Pony Express days as wholesome, outdoor, familial inspiration to American youth. To this day, William F. Cody's stature as the most famous Pony Express rider of them all remains largely unchallenged.

Only the most devoted reader knows about the doubters. Some who knew Cody said he was lying even in the 1880s. A few historians mention in footnotes or even in the text of their books that his stories are impossible to verify. A tiny minority have suggested he made the whole thing up.[12]

Against these whispers, Cody biographers advance the standard of the trustworthy guide. The most famous of these, Don Russell, long ago concluded that Buffalo Bill mostly told the truth. Cody's account is full of genuine figures from the Pony Express, and he pinpoints locations of Indian battles with descriptions that are often accurate. How could he have known so much if he was not there? Besides, William Cody won the Medal of Honor for Indian fighting in 1872. He was already a wealthy man and a stage star when he put the story in his autobiography in 1879. He had no reason to lie.[13]

How much of the story was true? The search for answers is illuminating in two ways. On the one hand, it may lead us to matters of fact, about what really happened to the boy William Cody. On the other hand, poring over

Cody's stories, true and false, can point the way to deeper truths. A man lies to mislead. But, as any detective can tell you, the most deceptive liar reveals a great deal about himself through his choice of untruths. Lies cover the teller's tracks, but they also betray how he thinks. The line between truth and fiction in William Cody's childhood story is less a boundary marker between the serious and the trivial than a pathway to a deeper understanding of the man and his age.

WHAT WE KNOW of Cody's childhood comes largely from two sources: his own autobiography, which he published in 1879, when he was already a theatrical star, and the memoirs of his elder sister, Julia, which she didn't pen till the early 1900s.[14] The veracity of his autobiography is a constant source of debate. Written in Rochester, New York, during his off-season from the theater, it was a long press release meant to enhance his already formidable star qualities. Cody shaped his life story to meet public expectations and desires. Every single one of the book's claims must be treated with care.

The question of its authorship endures. A coterie of press agents and dime novelists churned out revised editions of the Cody autobiography periodically through 1920. During the same period, dozens of ghostwritten dime novels appeared under Buffalo Bill's authorship. Many critics have lumped Cody's 1879 autobiography with the novels, as the hokum of some advance man or another. But if the pages of some later editions are purple with hack writers' clichés, the prose in this first edition of his life story is markedly restrained (as reviewers noted at the time). Moreover, it is full of what we know to be Cody's own phrasing and tone. It contains a great deal of truth that only Cody knew. If he did not write it, he dictated it. For all its many fictions, it stands as Buffalo Bill Cody's own story of his life from childhood to the age of thirty-three.[15]

Julia Cody's memoirs offer some correctives to her brother's fantasies, but she was understandably reluctant to contradict him. In many cases, neither sibling was entirely truthful. Reading these two accounts against one another, and weighing them against the handful of other evidence we can muster, we begin to discern real events of his childhood under the quilting of fiction which covered them.

William Cody, hero of the Indian wars, did outrun murderous enemies as a boy. But they were not Indians. He did carry messages, but not the U.S. mail. He had his first taste of combat as a very young man, but when he first sighted down a rifle barrel at a man, it was likely not at any Sioux or Cheyenne. The West of the boy William Cody was riven by war on families, in which homes burned, and families were threatened, scattered, or worse. War defined his life from the time he was eight until he was about thirty. And in war he learned, above all else, the vulnerability of family and home.

William Frederick Cody was born near Leclaire, Iowa, on February 26, 1846. His father, Isaac Cody, had been born in Canada and at the age of seventeen had settled in Ohio with his parents and siblings. He was already a widower when he met and married Mary Laycock in Cincinnati in 1840. Soon after, the couple, with Isaac's daughter from an earlier marriage, Martha, moved to Iowa in search of new opportunities. William Cody was the third child of Isaac and Mary, having been preceded by a brother, Sam, in 1841, and a sister, Julia, in 1843. By 1853, there were seven children at home, including the two brothers and a total of five sisters: Martha, Julia, Eliza Alice, Laura Ella (often called Helen), and Mary Hannah, called May.[16] In Iowa, Isaac Cody managed large farms for absentee owners, and ran a stage business between Davenport and Chicago. The children recalled their father as a traveling man who returned home between trips ferrying passengers across the wide prairie. Sometimes the young Codys stood on the riverbank, watching as Isaac's brightly colored wagon passed by on its way to or from Chicago. The constant search for new opportunities led Isaac to consider joining the gold rush to California. He changed his mind when he heard tales of woe from returning emigrants and was unable to finance the trip.[17] Instead, he and Mary Cody settled on a move to Kansas Territory. Their decision may have been motivated in part by the death of their eldest son, Sam, crushed beneath a bucking mare in 1853, at the age of twelve.

Thus, William Cody's earliest memories entwined family and westward expansion. The Codys ventured to Kansas in 1854, even before Congress opened the territory for settlement. They were comparatively well-off, and they stood out from other immigrants. Julia Cody remembered that the family had "as nice an outfit as ever came acrost to Kansas Territory." There were two wagons, a large four-horse outfit filled with family belongings and a smaller two-horse carriage to convey the family. There were two extra horses, and a hired man to assist Mr. Cody in the driving. The family "did not camp as most Emigrants did," but stopped each night "at the best Hotels," where maids helped put the Cody children to bed.[18]

The streams and grassy hills of eastern Kansas seemingly promised a bright future for the Codys. The family located a verdant claim in the Salt Creek Valley, where the children would have many days of gathering wild berries and herding livestock across meadows. True, there was a political cloud on the horizon. Congress had dodged the controversial issue of slavery in Kansas by leaving it to local settlers to decide the issue for their own state. But for the Codys, it was easy to overlook the looming threat of the slavery conflict, at least for the time being.

In many respects, Isaac Cody was a traditional American frontiersman. An experienced surveyor, he was both a settler and a land speculator. In December 1854, he joined several other emigrants in founding the town of Grasshopper Falls (eventually renamed Valley Falls). He spent much time helping newly settled families locate farmlands near the new town site, and in assisting his partners in the construction of a mill.[19] By 1855, there were over 8,500 new settlers in eastern Kansas. Over 90,000 more would arrive by 1861. With Grasshopper Falls drawing ever more residents who would pay to use the mill of which Isaac was part owner, the Cody family's future looked bright indeed.[20]

Then the storm burst. Isaac Cody was a Free Soil Democrat, holding that neither slavery nor black people should be allowed in Kansas. It was soon clear that his family was going to have trouble with their pro-slavery neighbors. Almost immediately after their arrival, Isaac Cody attended a community meeting, at which he joined his neighbors in creating the Salt Creek Squatters Association. Such associations were a tradition in newly settled areas, where they adjudicated claim disputes, often shoring up claims of prior arrivals against interlopers or claim jumpers.[21]

But pro-slavery settlers dominated the Salt Creek Squatters Association. Even though Isaac Cody was a member of the thirteen-man "vigilance" committee that was appointed to enforce the will of the association, he chafed at the resolutions which the group passed at their first meeting, announcing that in the event of disputes, they would not uphold the claims of anti-slavery settlers. In other words, the Salt Creek Squatters Association existed to guarantee the claims of pro-slavery immigrants against anti-slavery or "Free State" rivals.[22]

The Codys' pro-slavery neighbors had strong ties to kindred spirits in the neighboring slave state of Missouri, and they held meetings which drew like-minded crowds. On July 4, 1854, they hosted an Independence Day gathering and invited many of the local Cherokee, Delaware, and Kickapoo Indians, as well as pro-slavery settlers. Julia Cody remembered this as a festive meeting, at which the whites had a long banquet table, with Independence Day addresses, and the Indians "gave their war dances, Horse or Pony races, played at their different Games, and it was the most wonderful Picnic I ever seen."[23]

Eleven-year-old Julia and eight-year-old Will apparently did not remember, or did not notice, the political heat in the air. The meeting had been advertised in pro-slavery quarters as a "General Territorial Convention." It was well attended by Missourians, and it made Isaac and Mary Cody nervous about their future in the Salt Creek Valley. The Indians who so entertained Julia and William Cody likely held their own views on the disposition of slavery in Kansas. Many of them were displaced from the East themselves, and there were many slaveholders among the Cherokees, who had been driven out of Georgia and Tennessee only a generation before. The Civil War would fracture Indian communities as badly as it did those of whites. Independence Day invitations to local Indians may have been an attempt to bring them over to the pro-slavery side. In any case, the theatrics of their dances distracted the children from the gathering neighborhood tensions.[24]

By September, the Salt Creek Squatters Association was denouncing the activities of abolitionists, and questioning whether the Cody family could be allowed to stay in Salt Creek. On September 18, 1854, at a meeting to adjudicate a claim dispute in which Cody was involved, a pro-slavery agitator named Charles Dunn sank a knife in Isaac Cody's side.[25]

The pro-slavery press exulted in the violence. "A Mr. Cody, a noisy abolitionist, living near Salt Creek, in Kansas Territory, was severely stabbed, while in a dispute about a claim with Mr. Dunn, on Monday last week. Cody is severely hurt, but not enough it is feared to cause his death. The settlers on Salt Creek regret that his wound is not more dangerous, and all sustain Mr. Dunn in the course he took."[26]

The traumatized family raced Isaac Cody to his brother Elijah's, across the border in Weston, Missouri. Julia recalled that the family felt "terribul," and that eight-year-old Will wept and called out, "I wish I was a man; I would just love to kill all of those Bad men that want to kill my Father, and I will when I get big." The knife had grazed Isaac's lung. Three weeks passed before he could move about. As Julia remembered, he "was never strong from that day, just able to get around; had to ride as he could not walk any distance."[27]

The stabbing of Isaac coincided with a regional surge in violence over the slavery issue. William Cody later recalled that his father "shed the first blood in the cause" of a free Kansas, and that with that stabbing came "the beginning of the Kansas troubles."[28] "From that time the Border War began," wrote Julia, with pro-slavery partisans pouring "into the Territory by the Hundreds" from Missouri.[29]

Unlike the official violence of the Civil War, with its huge armies under government command, the so-called Bleeding Kansas troubles brought unofficial, paramilitary violence between Free Kansas partisans and advocates of slavery, most of them from Missouri. Both sides perpetrated atrocities. But prior to 1858, when anti-slavery forces consolidated control, pro-slavery Missourians held the upper hand, with frequent raids into Kansas to intimidate and murder anti-slavery settlers.[30]

The Cody home was only one of many to suffer their wrath. Death threats against Isaac Cody began the minute he returned home after the stabbing, and continued for the next two years. One night, "a body of armed men, mounted on horses, rode up to our house and surrounded it," wrote William Cody. Isaac escaped by dressing in Mary's clothes and passing between the murderous horsemen on his way out into the cornfield, where he hid for days before escaping to Leavenworth.[31]

Throughout the Bleeding Kansas period, attacking homes was the primary method of waging war. Threats against Isaac were joined by violence against home and farm. In the spring of 1855, the family cut and stacked tons of hay to sell to the army post at Leavenworth. Before Isaac could move the hay, pro-slavery neighbors torched it. Isaac Cody wept, and his daughter Julia was still sorrowful as she recalled the event, many years later. "In less than one hour the 3,000 Ton of Hay was in a Blaze. All we could do was look at it."[32]

Pro-slavery raiders also stole family livestock, especially their horses, without which settlers could not ride for help, escape the next onslaught, or get to work at neighboring farms or towns. When a pro-slavery party visited the Cody house in 1855, Isaac evaded them again. But they took nine-year-old Will's horse, Prince: "The loss of my faithful pony nearly broke my heart and bankrupted me in business, as I had nothing to ride."[33] Julia Cody remembered that when they stole her horse, "I was left without anything to ride for the cows, or to go to the store, or anything. We felt all broke up. . . ." The raiders stole some of Isaac Cody's best horses as well, "and they stole all of Father's machinery, such as [the] mowing machine, rakes, and everything." They even "took our small wagon and Plow."[34] As at the Codys', so throughout eastern Kansas. Raiders from both sides burned businesses, destroyed farm fields, and broke down fences and barns.

The region's violence grew most extreme after mid-1856, when pro-slavery "border ruffians" from Missouri plundered the town of Lawrence, killing one man and looting shops by the score. Several nights later, an abolitionist mob led by John Brown and two of his sons knocked at the doors of a small pro-slavery settlement on Pottawatomie Creek. Taking five men out of their homes, ignoring the pleas of their desperate families, Brown's party shot, stabbed, and dismembered their victims.[35]

John Brown sought slavery's abolition. The Codys, like most Kansas settlers, wanted only a ban on slavery in Kansas. Nonetheless, pro-slavery forces lumped them all together as "abolitionists," and they suffered fearsome retribution for Brown's raid. The Cody family's sense of vulnerability during this time of terror was compounded by Isaac Cody's frequent lengthy absences. Like many Kansas men, he moved from place to place, not daring to return to his family for fear of being murdered. When he did come home, he often brought Free State crowds with him. The Cody home became the

site of Free Kansas rallies, complete with speeches by visiting Free Soil candidates, angering the pro-slavery neighbors all the more. An election in
1855 gave control of the first territorial legislature to pro-slavery settlers.
Free State voters, infuriated by blatant fraud and intimidation at the polls,
refused to recognize the territorial government and elected their own legislature, which met at Topeka to petition the U.S. Congress for admission to
the Union as a free state. Isaac Cody won a seat in the Topeka legislature,
railing against the armies of drunken "Pukes" who were stealing Kansas
elections by arriving en masse from Missouri and casting votes as Kansas
residents. He may have been an agent to recruit settlers for the Free State
cause in Kansas. His town of Grasshopper Falls was a center of Free State
activity.[36]

Isaac Cody's absence required the family to make their way without him
much of the time, and to contemplate the terrifying possibility of losing him
forever. A family that lost its primary breadwinner easily slipped into
poverty, and there was no social safety net beyond the goodwill of neighbors, whom the Codys understandably mistrusted. All the while, the open
hostility of pro-slavery factions reinforced the family's constant sense of
impending destruction. As Will Cody put it in his autobiography many
years later, "We were almost daily visited by some of the pro-slavery men,
who helped themselves to anything they saw fit, and frequently compelled
my mother and sisters to cook for them, and to otherwise submit to a great
deal of bad treatment." And always, there were more threats against the life
of Isaac Cody. "Hardly a day passed without some of them inquiring 'where
the old man was,' saying they would kill him on sight."[37]

On the rare occasions when they saw him, the family's fears for him only
grew. Julia Cody recalled that "whenever Father came home he had to come
in after Dusk and leave before it was light." Weakness and illness, which the
family attributed to his wound, often compelled his return. At such times,
Julia wrote, "we had to be on the watch all the time. . . ."[38] Once, when Isaac
Cody was sick and confined to bed upstairs, Will and Julia stood guard over
their father with a gun and an ax as a murderous pro-slavery partisan sat in
their kitchen. Mary Cody prepared the man a meal, all the while claiming
her husband had last been heard from at Topeka. The man sharpened his
knife on a whetstone, vowing to kill that "damned abolitionist husband" of
hers.[39]

In many other ways, the Cody children made extraordinary sacrifices and
took horrifying chances. In the summer of 1856, a friendly neighbor
brought word that men were waiting to ambush Isaac Cody on his return
from Grasshopper Falls. Children rarely became targets in the border troubles, and even during the most violent periods, Will and Julia traveled thirty
miles or more on horseback to move cattle or run family errands. Ten-year-

old Will Cody was in bed with influenza when his mother received news of the plot to kill Isaac. The boy arose and clambered onto a horse. Taking a letter from his mother warning Isaac not to return in the near future, he set out for Grasshopper Falls. He made it eight miles, to Stranger Creek, when he noticed he was being pursued by a group of horsemen. As he later recounted the incident, one of the men said, "That is the damned abolition-ist boy. Let's go for him."[40]

The boy put his heels to his horse, and for nine more miles the men chased the sick and terrified child. He finally reined up at the home of a fam-ily friend named Hewitt. The would-be assassins turned and fled. The boy told the man what had happened, and expressed his desire to continue to Grasshopper Falls. Hewitt feared the horse would die without rest, and he was concerned for Will Cody, too. The animal was covered in lather, and flecked with the boy's vomit.

Fortuitously, Hewitt himself had just returned from Grasshopper Falls. He had spoken to Isaac Cody, who told him that he would not be returning home for a few more days. Hewitt put the boy to bed. When he awoke, Will Cody insisted on carrying the message to Isaac anyway. It was a rare oppor-tunity to spend two weeks with his father, who was among friends at Grasshopper Falls, notably the Free State militia of the militant Jim Lane.[41]

Isaac Cody's condition soon worsened again. To recuperate in safety, he traveled to Ohio, where he visited with relatives. After returning from this trip he was followed by many new emigrants. Being a "locator," a man who could read survey lines and claim locations for settlers, his home was a bea-con for new arrivals. Numbers of them could be found there at any time, sometimes seated at the kitchen table, their tents pitched in the front yard.[42] In this small but very noticeable way, the westward expansion of the United States moved through the home of Isaac Cody. Amidst the swirling violence which threatened to demolish that home, he remained its link both to the money they needed and to the expanding West. Patriarch of the family, founder of the town of Grasshopper Falls, Isaac Cody was both a family bul-wark and the center of a rapidly expanding Free Kansas community.

Then, in the spring of 1857, Isaac Cody fell ill again, and finally died.[43] For William and Julia Cody, his passing was a catastrophe. Both children mention his death only briefly, as if it was too painful a memory to explain. Financially, the loss was devastating. Martha, Isaac's daughter by his first marriage, had married and moved out. But Isaac's death left Mary Cody to fend for herself, young Will, four girls, and another son, Charles, who was but an infant.

The economic trial was complicated by the region's rising tensions. Although some historians estimate that only a hundred Kansans died as a direct result of the slavery fight, the violence went far beyond simple murder. Beatings and death threats were pervasive. Not far from the Cody claim was the base of the Kickapoo Rangers, a paramilitary gang hell-bent on driving Free Soil settlers from eastern Kansas, and whose members included Charles Dunn, their father's attacker.[44]

Amidst the continuing fury of this unofficial war, Mary Cody faced what was probably the greatest challenge of her life. Like other young widows, she was constrained by a society that required a woman of good reputation to work at home. Farm women made sizable contributions to their families' economic well-being, but they did not usually take up wage labor. Such activities were for lower-class women, or women of dubious reputation. As Julia recalled, "Now Brother Willie and I would get out together and plan what he must do to help take care of Mother and the 3 sisters and little brother Charlie. . . ."[45] William was barely eleven, but he was the only male capable of outdoor work. He became the family's primary wage earner.

From boyhood, then, William Cody was drawn into a commercial revolution that was sweeping the Plains, and which was impossible to ignore around Leavenworth. Kansas was a western territory, but it was no backwater. Most early settlements were trail towns, along migration routes where the ubiquitous travelers—emigrants, tourists, salesmen, surveyors, and soldiers, to name a few—created a lively commerce. Residents prospered by selling supplies by the trails. When trails shifted, townspeople on occasion jacked up whole towns and moved them on rollers to new settings where they could better exploit the trade of passing pioneers.[46]

Leavenworth, at the junction of the Missouri River and various routes west, was the biggest trail town of all. Some paths actually predated the town. Wagons carrying goods had been plying the Santa Fe Trail between Missouri and northern New Mexico since 1821. By 1855, $5 million in commerce was making its way along the Santa Fe Trail each year, and Leavenworth was only a short distance north of Independence, Missouri, the trail's eastern terminus.[47] Still another trail wound west as handfuls of emigrants to Oregon, and more Mormons bound for Utah, began trundling up the Platte River road in the 1840s. Then, in California, in 1848, John Marshall reached for a glittering nugget in John Sutter's mill race. In the next five years, some 165,000 people traveled this westerly route to seek their share of the gold rush.[48]

From the day in 1854 that Leavenworth was founded along the Platte River road to California, passersby dwarfed the resident population, and as migrations increased, so did the town's economy. Between 1854 and 1860, 80,000 emigrants passed near or through Leavenworth on their way to California.[49] Many of them traveled in small groups from various points to the east, and then stopped in eastern Kansas, where they organized into wagon trains and waited for the spring grass to mature enough to feed the livestock on the Plains crossing. Julia Cody later recalled that when the Cody family arrived in the Salt Creek Valley of Kansas in 1854, "it was filled with Trains and cattle and mules running around. There must have been Hundreds of White covered wagons waiting there to make up their Trains and start West." Little Will Cody "got just wild with Excitement" and said, "Oh, my, that is what I am going to do as soon as we get moved over here in this beautifull place."[50]

The continual cavalcade through Leavenworth increased yet again, in even more dramatic fashion, with another gold strike, this time in Colorado, in 1858. Before then, there had been only the sparsest white settlement along the Platte River road, mostly at trading posts, where traders solicited Indian commerce in buffalo robes and beaver hide. Suddenly, in the spring of 1859 alone, over 100,000 emigrants headed to the Colorado mines.[51]

California and Utah had been so far away that only the most valuable and nonperishable goods could be supplied overland. But Denver was only six hundred miles away, and as the center of the new emigration, it rapidly developed a consumer market which had to be provisioned by wagon. Teamsters drove more than 15 million pounds of goods to Denver in 1860. By 1866, over 100 million pounds of goods found their way to the Queen City of the Rockies, and much of it passed through the vicinity of Leavenworth.[52]

As important as supplying Denver was satisfying the wants and needs of emigrants. By 1860, there were primitive hotels along the entire route, so that one could journey from Leavenworth to Denver in virtually any kind of weather without ever sleeping under the stars. Road ranches, whiskey holes, and general provisioners sprung up along the main routes. From their adobe hovels, tents, or frame houses, these entrepreneurs offered a wide range of consumer commodities: wheel rims, ax handles, clothes, hats, matches, whiskey, horseshoes, tobacco, baking supplies, liniments, and more, all of which had to be hauled out to these trailside outposts on freight wagons.[53]

So emigrant wagons and freight-hauling "prairie schooners" crowded onto the trails alongside a burgeoning form of passenger transport, stagecoaches. By 1857, stages already ran from Leavenworth north into Nebraska Territory along the Platte River, to Kearny and on to Laramie. Stimulated by the surge of emigrants to the Colorado goldfields, in 1859 Leavenworth's premier transport capitalist, William Russell, joined up with a new partner and created the Leavenworth and Pikes Peak Express, running a faster, more direct route (it took about a week) between Leavenworth and Denver via the Smoky Hill River in western Kansas. Russell and his partners expended vast sums to lay out the route and build the twenty-seven stage stations needed along the way, and the new, more direct connection thrilled emigrants with its possibilities. In Denver, the arrival of the new company's first stage on May 7 was greeted with all the joy that three hundred residents could muster. But their party at the foot of the Rockies was eclipsed by the huge celebration in Leavenworth when the stage returned on May 20. Banner headlines announcing the linkage to the Colorado mines were followed by two days of parades, dinners, and bloviating speeches.[54]

Kansas settlers could not ignore the prodigious expansion of Leavenworth's freight and transport industry, especially Russell, Majors, and Waddell. The company was said to employ 6,000 teamsters and 45,000 oxen. One historian calls Russell, Majors, and Waddell "the Mayflower Van Line of their time," and however many people they really employed, their facilities were awesome in 1859. That year, one traveler extolled their Leavenworth company yard: "Such acres of wagons! such pyramids of axeltrees! such herds of oxen! such regiments of drivers and employees!"[55]

These developments were not lost on the Cody family. Isaac had not only driven a stage between Chicago and Davenport, he also conducted various side businesses with Russell and Majors before his death.[56] Leavenworth was only a few miles from the family home. Trains of two dozen or more freight wagons were a frequent impressive sight. Teams of up to twenty oxen hauled wagons, with iron-covered wheels as tall as a man, loaded with up to seven thousand pounds of goods. Each train was accompanied by a small herd of horses, necessary for herding the extra oxen. Prairie schooners dwarfed emigrant wagons. From miles away, their canvas-covered bows bulked over the horizon like the sails of a ship on the sea. The teamsters who drove these outfits swaggered beside the wagons, and their mastery of the long whips they cracked over the backs of animals, and of an extraordinary lexicon of profanity, made them both frightening and alluring to children who watched them pass.[57]

Will Cody soon sought work in the industry. As Mary Cody rented out rooms in the family home to bring in cash, and Julia did "all of the heavy work" of milking and tending the farm, young Will Cody started out as an ox-team driver for a neighbor who was hauling his hay to Leavenworth for sale. The eleven-year-old boy earned a daily wage for several weeks, at the end of which he handed the money over to his mother. Soon after, he went to work as a messenger boy for Russell and Majors (shortly before it became Russell, Majors, and Waddell) carrying messages on horseback from their office in Leavenworth town to the telegraph office at Fort Leavenworth, three miles away.[58]

As difficult as this sorrowful time was for the family, none of the Cody children's activities were unusual enough to distinguish them from their neighbors. Indeed, if most farm women worked out of their own homes in the 1850s, their children were often found in the rural workplace. From nine or ten (and sometimes younger), children hired out to other settlers to bring in the harvest, drive horses, or herd cattle or sheep, in exchange for cash or services. In frontier towns, children worked as bootblacks, newspaper salesmen, or clerks in town businesses. In these circumstances, sons and daughters who were not yet teenagers often lived miles from home for at least part of the year. Freighting outfits on well-established, well-protected trails sometimes hired boys as "cavallard" drivers, who tended the dozens of extra horses that traveled with them. There were dangers in such work, and adventure, too. Sometime in 1858, twelve-year-old Will Cody was a cavallard driver for a wagon train headed by John Willis, traveling along the Platte River road to Fort Laramie. Willis wrote to Cody in 1897, recalling "the time the Buffalo run through the train and stampeded the teams and you stoped the stampede."[59] But as exciting and dramatic as such events look to us, they were routine to nineteenth-century Americans. Indeed, Will Cody probably was not the only child employed at many of his jobs.[60]

Like Willis, many employers did not scruple to hire children even for dangerous labor. In eastern states, children were often maimed and killed at work in coal mines, steel factories, and cotton mills. Given the widespread reliance on child labor, and young Will Cody's experience as a horse drover on the trail to Laramie, some of the other boyhood yarns in his autobiography might seem true. Could he have gone to the Mormon War, as he claimed? The story corresponds with historical events. There was indeed an 1857 expedition to supply the U.S. Army column sent to prevent a threatened Mormon rebellion. The column left from Leavenworth. Their wagons were captured by the Mormons and burned, just as Cody recalled, and the teamsters did endure a terrible winter at Fort Bridger while they waited for the snow to clear so they could return home.[61] Could young Will Cody have been there?

The answer is no. In his account, Cody claimed to have made two separate trips to supply troops in Utah, the first with a herd of cattle that was stampeded by Indians, forcing him to return and begin the second in a wagon train later that summer. Military records show there was a cattle herd scattered by Indians, and a wagon train that followed it. But the same records indicate the cattle herd left Leavenworth only a week before the wagon train. Indians scattered the cattle after the wagons had set out. The boy could not have seen both the scattering of the herd and the beginning of the wagon train's journey.[62] Cody wrote that after the Mormons burned the wagons, he survived the winter with other members of the Utah Expedition at Fort Bridger, in today's Wyoming, in the spring of 1858. But his sister Julia recalled him being in school with her that spring. When William Cody read this recollection in her memoirs, in 1911, he did not disagree. "Say that write up of yours was fine," he wrote his sister. "You have a wonderful memory."[63]

His autobiography next regaled his readers with an account of prospecting in Colorado in 1859. The story is impossible to substantiate, but he claimed to have rafted down the Platte River on his return, something that would have been next to impossible during the river's low season. If he trapped furs in Kansas soon thereafter, as he claims, his account of meeting a Sioux war party in the winter of 1859–60 smacks of fantasy. In 1879, when this adventure first appeared in print, Custer had been dead for only three years, and Rain-in-the-Face was widely believed to be his killer (thanks to a poem on the subject by Henry Wadsworth Longfellow). If Cody's story were true, its Rain-in-the-Face would have to have been the father of the alleged Custer assailant, but his name called up the potent Custer image, which was still fresh in the minds of Cody's readers. This alone explains why Cody told the story. But could it be true? Not likely. The appearance of Rain-in-the-Face with a war party in deep snow at the dead of winter is highly improbable. At precisely such times, Plains Indians generally avoided long-distance travel and warfare. Snow and cold were too severe, and a man of Rain-in-the-Face's stature was unlikely to lead any warriors who proposed such foolishness.

What truth is there to Cody's teenage odyssey? As far as we can tell, he was indeed a boyhood teamster, who at the age of fourteen drove a wagon to Denver. In the summer of 1860, his uncle Elijah, a prominent merchant, moved there from Missouri. Nephew Will went along to drive a wagon of goods. We know this because Arthur "Pat" Patterson, a fifteen-year-old neighbor and friend of young Will Cody, went to Colorado on this very journey as a teamster, and both he and Cody would later recall having made that journey together. The boys waited out the winter in Denver. Will Cody needed money, and it seems likely he tried his hand at prospecting and possibly trapping, two common ways of making extra cash. Somehow, he broke his leg during the trip. He returned home with his friend Pat Patterson, in the summer or fall of 1860, not on a raft but by hiring himself out as a teamster again.[64]

Cody's Utah war and Rain-in-the-Face stories were fictions. So, too, were his Pony Express adventures. Cody claimed to have ridden for the Pony Express for two separate periods, the first in late 1859, out of Julesberg, Colorado. But none of the stations he lists as his stops correspond to stations on that section of the trail. The men he says hired him actually did work for the Pony Express, but they could not have hired him, because they either ranked too low on the corporate hierarchy or were not on that section of the Pony Express line during this time. More to the point, the Pony Express functioned for only eighteen months, beginning in April 1860. Nobody was a Pony Express rider in 1859.[65]

His second stretch as a pony rider, from summer 1860 until spring 1861, was allegedly along the Sweetwater Division, where Indian attacks forced a temporary closure of the line, and Cody says he went with Wild Bill

Hickok's raiding party to reclaim horses from the Sioux on Powder River. Some of the events Cody describes actually happened—but not to him. A station keeper along the transport line, at Gilbert's Station, was killed, just as Cody recounts, but the killing happened in 1859, before the Pony Express began. There was an Indian attack on a stagecoach which did close down the line for six weeks, and the names of passenger casualties even correspond to the names in Cody's account. But it did not happen until April 1862, long after the Pony Express was discontinued. Cody claimed that he joined Wild Bill Hickok's retaliatory raid in 1861. But that year, Hickok was a stock tender at a station in faraway Rock Creek, eastern Nebraska, where he was recovering from an injury which prevented him from doing much of anything.[66]

Cody's pony tale begins to look ragged under investigation, and other eyewitnesses fail to curry it. Julia Cody wrote her memoirs in the early 1900s, when her brother's Pony Express adventures were renowned around the world. She dismisses them with this summary: "he hired to go out and Ride the Pony Express, and he made the longest Ride of any of the others. They sayed he was the youngest one and the Lightest and swiftest rider, and seemed to understand the Country, and the Rouffians and how to handle them."[67] That is all. No details to suggest he really rode for the Pony Express, not even a repetition of one of his stories.

There are three alleged eyewitnesses who claimed to have met Cody on his Pony Express route. One, Edward Ayer, a prominent collector of western Americana, told a story in the 1920s, about getting to know the boy rider during a month's travel along the Platte River in 1860, as Ayer's wagon train journeyed to California. But there are some problems in this story. The wagon route was on the north bank of the Platte; the Pony Express route on the south bank. Riders had deadlines and did not stop to chat. Not even the slowest oxen could keep a wagon train in one rider's assigned section of the trail for a month.[68]

Another eyewitness, Charlie Becker, was a Pony Express rider who recalled meeting Cody both at Fort Bridger and then afterward as a Pony Express rider. But Becker, whose account was not recorded until sometime after 1900, recalls he and Cody became good friends and comrades, serving next to each other on the route for the entire year and a half the pony line was in existence. Even Cody himself wrote that he served in two different sections, and neither for very long. Like Ayer, Becker seems to have embroidered himself into Cody's mythology, decades after the showman wrote his autobiography and long after he had become the embodiment of America's frontier myth.[69]

The third eyewitness is perhaps most revealing. In 1893, Cody paid Alexander Majors, the sole survivor of the Russell, Majors, and Waddell partnership, to write his autobiography. Cody's press agent wrote a preface for it, and his ghostwriter took a hand in the work, too. The book, *Seventy Years on the Frontier*, went on sale at Buffalo Bill's Wild West show that summer, appearing alongside Cody's own autobiography at the bookstall on the showgrounds in Chicago. Royalties went to Majors.

Cody sponsored the book out of kindness. Majors had been a friend of Isaac Cody's. Not long after Isaac died, Mary Cody took her son Will to Majors's office in Leavenworth, and asked a favor. Could he employ the boy? Majors looked at twelve-year-old Will Cody, and he asked no questions—just gave him a job carrying dispatches along the three miles of road between the telegraph station and company offices in Leavenworth.

Now, in 1893, the old man was broke and alone. Cody offered him help. One might expect Majors would oblige Cody's generosity by conjuring up some fabulous adventures for the young Buffalo Bill. But despite the fact that Cody hired Prentiss Ingraham, a voluble dime novelist, to ghostwrite for Majors, and even though Cody paid for the book's publication, Majors was unable to recall any specific feats of Cody's supposed Pony Express riding other than the ones that appear in Cody's own 1879 autobiography.[70]

What was Cody doing if he was not riding the Pony Express in 1860 and 1861? Three other, independent accounts, one by his sister, one by a former teacher, and one actually by himself, all agree: he was in school. Julia wrote, and William Cody confirmed, that he was taught by Valentine Devinny, a teacher who later recalled Cody being a particularly determined ballplayer. Devinny moved to Leavenworth only in the fall of 1860, and left for Colorado sometime in 1862.

The first year Devinny taught at Leavenworth, the Pony Express had begun. The route started in Saint Joseph, Missouri, and passed through northeastern Kansas, to the north of Leavenworth. At the moment Mr. Devinny took up the chalk before a roomful of expectant pupils, young men were stationed at points across the Plains, waiting to carry the mail over trail sections that were seventy-five to a hundred miles long. Their rides were so punishing that they often arrived with blood flowing from noses and gums. Couriers slept on their horses; snow buried the trails. The few authentic accounts that survive describe the agony of forty-below winter blasts and horses (not to mention riders) on the verge of death. Pony Express riders did not take days off for school. William Cody could not have been in Devinny's classroom and riding for the Pony Express at the same time.[71]

If young Will wasn't on the Pony Express, why did no contemporaries debunk his fabulous story? What of his partner in the trapping expedition to Colorado, Dave Harrington? The feared John Slade? Wild Bill Hickok? Together they illustrate William Cody's remarkable talent for choosing witnesses. For if they might once have deflated some of the celebrity's more extravagant lies, by 1879, when the book appeared, it was impossible. They were all dead.

Cody's childhood Mormon-and-Indian-fighting, prospecting, Pony Express–riding, Hickok-knowing, bullwhacking saga was the foundation of his mythic western persona. These glittering ornaments of western youth tied William Cody firmly to the expanding West of the pre–Civil War period, making him an "old-timer" rather than a greenhorn interloper, authenticating his stage performance as "Buffalo Bill" in 1879 and ever after.

But if we know he packed his childhood story with untruths, what do those fabrications tell us about him? About why he told the tales he did? About his rationale for making himself part of the largely forgotten Utah Expedition, and the failed business enterprise of the Pony Express?

Americans of Cody's day were generally concerned about the survival of families in their rapidly changing country. As a performer in theatrical melodrama—a genre that fixated on threats to the family—Cody was profoundly aware that heroism in family defense had popular appeal. Given the constant ordeal of defending Isaac from his many enemies, it was even fitting that so many of Cody's autobiographical fictions, from his Mormon War adventures to the Pony Express saga, reflect an ardent defense of family. From the 1840s until 1900, many Americans perceived polygamous Mormons as a threat to monogamous marriage. Novels and "historical" accounts portrayed them as liars, murderers, and, especially, as kidnappers of virgins to serve as concubines for lecherous church patriarchs. Prior to the Civil War, northern reformers labeled polygamy and slavery as "the twin relics of barbarism" which it was the duty of civilization to banish. In 1857, Mormon militiamen massacred a wagon train of emigrants at Mountain Meadows, in southern Utah. The event was shrouded in secrecy. The U.S. government did not achieve a conviction in the case until 1877, when they tried—and shot—the Mormon elder John D. Lee for masterminding the crime.[72]

Lee's sensational trial renewed America's long-standing anti-Mormonism, and in 1877, Buffalo Bill took advantage of the furor by commissioning a new play, *May Cody, or Lost and Won*. In the drama, his sister May Cody was abducted by Mormons and rescued by Buffalo Bill. Two years later, as Cody wrote his life story for publication, he inscribed himself back into the 1857 Mormon War as a way of claiming the play as an authentic reflection of his real life, with the boy Will Cody facing off against the notoriously antimonogamy religious sect. The story in his autobiography was packed full of authentic details, and placed Indian attacks, cattle herds, and wagon trains in places that correspond with the historical record, so that biographers and historians have long concluded that Cody must have been on the Utah Expedition as a child.[73]

But if his story was so credible, it was because it illustrates William Cody's remarkable talent for grafting details of other people's tales onto his own. Cody was a gifted storyteller, and as such he knew that one of the most effective ways of making a fiction credible is to slather it in seemingly nonessential, truthful details. Repeated genuine details in a story pile up in the reader's—or the listener's—imagination, collectively whispering, "We are the real." The technique is so widely used that the scholar Roland Barthes has given it a name: the "reality effect."[74]

Cody learned the reality effect from other storytellers, and we shall see more in the chapters ahead about how he learned to construct his elaborate fictions. But for now, we may observe that as a messenger boy and drover for the West's biggest transport firm and as a teenage teamster himself, fireside retellings of adventure on the western trails were a regular feature of his upbringing. His account of the Mormon War and the winter at Fort Bridger is remarkably similar to the one recounted by John Y. Nelson, an old trail guide, buffalo hunter, and teamster who also claimed to have been on the Utah Expedition and to have spent the same winter at Fort Bridger that Cody did. Nelson befriended Cody in the 1860s and toured with his dramatic troupe as translator for the two Sioux Indians who joined the theatrical show on its tours of the East and Midwest, beginning in 1877—the same year that Buffalo Bill's anti-Mormon drama, *May Cody, or Lost and Won*, debuted.[75]

If the Mormon drama of Cody's autobiography reflected popular anxieties about the sanctity of marriage, the Pony Express was an even more useful symbol. In American popular reckoning, the Pony Express assumed heroic stature for various reasons. The replacement of people by machines had been a familiar characteristic of American progress at least since the industrial looms of Lowell, Massachusetts, began to replace the weaver by the hearth in the 1810s, and it became increasingly evident throughout rural America as McCormick's reapers began replacing family labor in the 1840s.[76]

Mechanization was both celebrated and condemned, but whatever one's feelings on the advent of technology, it was increasingly inevitable as the nineteenth century wore on, even in frontier mail delivery. When the Pony Express began in 1860, westbound mail traveled by train to Saint Joseph, Missouri, where the tracks ended. There the letters passed to a waiting rider.

But at a rate of $5 per half-ounce, only the most urgent messages went by Pony Express. Regular correspondence went by ship or by creaking coach and wagon on a longer, more southerly route. Faster, more economical delivery would come with the transcontinental railroad, a development long anticipated, and long delayed by congressional fighting over proposed northern and southern routes.

With the departure of the South from Congress, workers would soon begin laying track west again. But long before they completed that job, another machine emerged to carry the most important correspondence between California and the eastern states: the telegraph. A line of poles connected by wire sprouted westward from Saint Joseph beginning the summer of 1861. The riders of the Pony Express were in a sense advance couriers for the train, but even more for the telegraph, the technology that replaced them with the completion of the transcontinental telegraph line in 1861, an achievement that finally destroyed whatever segment of the market remained for the messengers of Russell, Majors, and Waddell. Pony Express riders symbolized not only rugged strength and courage, but the anachronism of organic workers—animals and people—and their heroic endurance as they prepared the ground for the machine. The *Sacramento Bee* eulogized the pony soon after the last rider dismounted. "Thou wert the pioneer of a continent in the rapid transmission of intelligence between its peoples, and have dragged in your train the lightning itself, which, in good time, will be followed by steam communication by rail."[77] As the nineteenth century rolled on, ever more laborers were replaced by an ever wider array of machines, and the horseman as harbinger of technological revolution became ever more apt a symbol for Americans, especially in cities where the Wild West show played to packed stands.

But there was another, surprising reason behind the pony's popularity, one which drew on Cody's experience of boyhood even more directly: the Pony Express represented national unity, in profoundly familial terms. Many were the scribes who evoked the glories of western annexation prior to the war with Mexico, with John O'Sullivan's call to "manifest destiny" being only the most famous. But in reality, the acquisition of the Far West blew the nation apart. The U.S.-Mexican War began the year William Cody was born and ended when he was two. Its most immediate result was the annexation of California and the Far West, but following fast on the heels of that event was the gathering storm over slavery in the new western territories, the fight which took Isaac Cody's life and finally ended only at Appomattox in 1865.

As eastern states grappled over slavery in the West, the West itself became a site of profound familial loss. The gold rush began in 1848, and California's stunning growth made it a state in 1850. But if statehood signified a legal and republican unity, California was very much a place apart, separated from the rest of the nation by 1,500 miles of plain and desert. Suddenly, east-west crossing of the nation required the ordeal of foreign travel. Whether one chose the sea route around the Cape of Good Hope, or a sea-and-land route through Mexico or Panama, or the Overland Trail through Indian country and the Mormon territories, alienation was unavoidable.

Getting from one end of the United States to the other now meant sojourn-
ing among Mexicans, Catholics, polygamous Mormons, and half-naked or
all-naked Indians, amid parching deserts, towering mountains, awesome
storms, and wild, desolate country.

The journey was all the more fearful because, in most cases, the routes to
California pulled families apart.[78] Men went ahead intending to send for
families or merely to return rich. Husbands and wives took their kids, pulled
up stakes, and left their beloved extended kin behind. Letters took at least
three weeks to travel the long stagecoach routes between California and
eastern states. If they went by sea, they could go unread for six months.

By the mid-1850s, the growing threat of a southern secession made the
chasm between California and her sister states seem all the more dangerous.
Californians numbered half a million by that time, and they were most conscious of the urgent need for closer bonds with nation and family. In 1856,
they presented the largest petition in the history of the United States Senate, 75,000 signatures on a memorial complaining, "We are now, as it were,
a distant colony." They requested a federally supported wagon road with
army protection from the Mississippi Valley to their new home, so that distant families could join the multitudes of young men toiling in the mines
and domesticate this distant, wild frontier.[79]

Thus, when they remembered the Pony Express, Americans—especially
Californians—recalled it as a reassuring sign amid rumblings of civil war, as
the entity that sealed the bond of union between West and East. To ride the
Pony Express was to heal the nation's troublesome rift, to bring desolate and
broken families together through the fragile connection of correspondence.
Cody never rode for the Pony Express, but it made sense that he wished he
had. If the adventures he recounted were ones he had heard or read elsewhere, he claimed them as his own in part because he was still seeking to be
the bearer of news that could save the family—just as he had sought to be
when he climbed out of a sickbed to straddle a pony and ride to the rescue of
his father.

The stature of the Pony Express increased through its association with
Buffalo Bill's Wild West show, where the union of man and horse headed
west with the mail came to symbolize not only the last redoubt of organic
labor before ascendant technology and the reunited family and nation, but
also the grafting of the Far West onto America. The unruly, racially distinctive Indians, the mixed-blood Mexicans and perfidious Mormons, the savage, weird nature of the mysterious frontier with its vast herds of buffalo and
rumored hot springs, deserts, unending prairie and endless sky—all of these
were now joined to the republic. In no small way, the Pony Express rider
embodied this hybrid conjunction of wilderness and civilization. The young

white man barely in control of the beast beneath him represented America joined to the West's untamed promise and peril. Thus, contemporaries hailed the Pony Express not only as a fast mail service, not just as a man on a horse, but as a horse-man, and sometimes a hippogriff, a mythical beast with the body of a horse, the head of a lion, and the wings of an eagle. Most of all, though, as Donald C. Biggs has noted, descriptions of the Pony Express often fuse the rider and the horse, sometimes explicitly, sometimes by failing to mention the existence of a rider at all. "The image becomes more animal and rather less than human; what truly emerges is the centaur."[80]

Buffalo Bill Cody could not have explained all this. At least, he never did. But intuitively, he understood from a young age that the story of the Pony Express was about much more than delivering mail. Growing up beside the trail to California, he saw the nation moving west, and in his own front yard heard the lamentations of families sundered by emigration to Colorado and exotic, alluring, and faraway California.

One last, seldom-noticed story in his autobiography suggests his connection of the West and the longing for family reunion. Shortly before he staked his claim in Kansas, Isaac Cody took his son Will on a trip to trade with Kickapoo Indians, just inside Kansas Territory. For the eight-year-old boy, the trip not only provided a first glimpse of Indians, but also a chance meeting with a long-lost relative who proved to be the boy's first showman mentor. While camped near the Indian agency (the headquarters of the government's representative to the Kickapoos), father and son saw a herd of horses "approaching from the West, over the California trail," driven by "seven or eight mounted men, wearing sombreros, and dressed in buckskin, with their lariats dangling from their saddles."[81] When one of the horse drovers ventured over to meet Mr. Cody, "my father called to me to come and see a genuine Western man; he was about six feet two inches tall, was well built, and had a light, springy and wiry step. He wore a broad-brimmed California hat, and was dressed in a complete suit of buckskin, beautifully trimmed and beaded." After a cheerful reunion, the westerner assisted young Will in the breaking of the two ponies which Isaac had just bought from the Kickapoos. Then he demonstrated riding tricks which he claimed to have learned as a circus rider in Hawaii, and in California, where he had also been a "bocarro," or vaquero, a Mexican cowboy.[82]

It sounds too good to be true, and perhaps it is, but both Julia and William Cody recalled that the stranger proved to be Horace Billings, a long-lost nephew of Isaac's. Over the summer Billings took the boy with him on short trips out on the Plains to catch wild horses, which they sold for cash at the nearby military post. Billings departed for the Far West that fall.[83]

There is, in fact, nothing intrinsically incredible about William Cody's colorful version of the story. In the early nineteenth century, young men did run away to sea. Hawaii was a major port of call. Many of the first immigrants to gold rush California came from the Hawaiian Islands. There were circuses that toured the goldfields and the Pacific in the 1840s and '50s, and even if Billings had not been in a circus, many people in the West imitated circus riding tricks for amusement. Wild horses were endemic to California and the Southwest. Americans—and Mexicans, and Indians—did venture out to the Plains for horse-capturing, or "mustanging," expeditions, either to capture and break horses, or to trade for Indian horses, which they then drove to the exploding markets of the midwestern frontier. The Santa Fe Trail, the most popular route for this trade, connected the Far Southwest to Saint Joseph, Missouri, and ran near the Kickapoo Indian agency.[84]

But whether or not Billings was a real figure, Cody's story about him suggests how he thought about the West as a place from which fatherly heroes emerged. The man's mastery of horses reassured the young boy, whose older brother had died beneath a volatile mare the year before. When Little Gray, a troublesome horse, began to sprint for home, "Billings stood straight up on his back, and thus rode him into camp. As he passed us he jumped to the ground, allowed the horse to run to the full length of the lariat, when he threw him a complete somersault."[85]

Cody's memory of Billings was of a consummate horseman, a buckskin-clad showman, mentor, and father figure. "Everything that he did, I wanted to do," recalled the theatrical star. "He was a sort of hero in my eyes, and I wished to follow in his footsteps."[86] Those footsteps led both westward and into show business.

The expedition to the Kickapoo Indian agency showed young Will Cody his first Indians, and also a white man who came out of the West over the California trail, having mastered Mexican horsecraft and wild horses, too. The most striking thing about Billings is how much he resembles the future Buffalo Bill Cody himself, a horseman from the West in finely beaded buckskin and a broad-brimmed hat, "six feet two inches tall," and "well built" with a "light, springy and wiry step."

THE FUTURE LAY WEST. And for the young man who turned his eyes that way after the Civil War was over, the memory of Horace Billings, the glorious man who rode out of the West, made it seem a wonderful place indeed. In William Cody's memory, some harbinger of his own future self rode to him across the Plains from California that summer. Isaac Cody would never come home again. But in William Cody's mind, the western trails brought absent father figures back to the family.

When Cody recounted his life story in future years, he told himself into those trails. In 1867, he had the first of several encounters with writer and railroad agent William Webb. In 1873, Webb published a description of Cody as a man who crossed the Plains "twice as a teamster, while a mere boy, and has spent the greater part of his life on it since."[87] The story was true. Cody traveled from Leavenworth to Denver when he was fourteen. He made another trip to Denver in 1863, and raced back to be with his dying mother.[88] He told Webb nothing about the Pony Express.

Two years after Webb's first meeting with Cody, the dime novelist Ned Buntline toured the West and met William Cody, then an army scout. The two men plied each other with drink and western yarns. Buntline soon published the first version of Cody's life story. It was highly fictionalized, but had many real elements of Cody's life, including fights with Charles Dunn and other bushwhackers, and a friendship with Wild Bill Hickok. But it contained nary a mention of the Pony Express.[89]

Cody's fame as a hunting guide and dramatic actor made him the subject of many newspaper interviews in the early 1870s. But he never said anything about being in the Pony Express until 1874. He had been a stage star for a year and a half when he suddenly blurted out to a newspaperman that he "rode the pony express route from St. Jo to San Francisco" in 1860. By the end of the month, he was announcing himself as the *"first rider who started on the route."*[90]

William Cody created the persona of Buffalo Bill not as a western man alone, but as a man who grew up connecting East and West, the Far West and the States, frontier and home. It was California and the Far West that harbored the youthful manliness and wild horse spirit that so entranced the young boy, and journeying out of that West came familial reunion and adulation. In his mind, the trail to the Far West was the path to manhood, and lost family, too. In his memory of his youth, the trails betokened his own ideal future. In his memory, the Wild West show in some sense came to him from over that far horizon.

William Cody's 1879 autobiography did not recount his childhood so much as reinvent it. Much more than a memoir of real events, the book mixed truth and fiction, to cast the child Will Cody as the protagonist of an American myth. The boy came up through hard times by dint of his own energy, hard work, and good luck and great connections. He grew up holding together the nation with the Pony Express, fighting for its families by battling the Mormons. If these were lies, they were skillfully told ones, and there was a method to them. They appealed to his audience, but, just as important, they retained and embellished a genuine aspect of his childhood struggle to defend his family. At eleven years old, he was the eldest surviving male in a family blasted by the border wars, lurching toward poverty, afflicted with the violence of their enemies.

The desperate effort to protect the Cody family from the maelstrom which engulfed them was a burden that passed from Isaac and Mary, neither of whom lived to see its conclusion, to their eldest children, Julia—who was twenty and married when her mother died—and William, who was a mere seventeen.

In recalling the weight of that load, the grown-up William Cody never dwelt on its darkness. He was innately optimistic, a characteristic which served him well in show business. But to understand him, his biography, and the many lies he told about both, we need only recall the boy who rose from a sickbed, leapt to the back of his pony, and outran border ruffians to meet his father at Grasshopper Falls. One of the reasons we may believe this story is because of details Cody left out, which emerged long after, from other sources. When Buffalo Bill told the story in *The Life of Buffalo Bill* in 1879, he said he got away from his pursuers and found his father, having "arrived in ample time to inform him of the approach of his old enemies."[91] He left out details his sister provided: his stop at the neighbor's, the horse covered with vomit, being put to bed by his concerned friend, and the fact that his father turned out not to be in danger. William Cody left out the panic, the illness, his own weakness. He left out the terror.

The Kansas border wars brought terror for many families, and we can only wonder how many boys and girls rode fast horses to warn parents of impending doom. What were they thinking, during these races to save family from destruction? They likely feared falling from the back of the galloping horse at every bump in the road or hidden hole in the fields across which they made their dark and dangerous journeys. Did they fear that they would die? Perhaps they did not want to remember. Perhaps, like William Cody, they wanted to forget the terror, and to remember something else. When he thought of himself on a horse, he wanted to be like his cousin: a genuine western man who mastered this most powerful beast with the natural skill that came from being a westerner. The loss of fathers wreaked havoc on family after family in eastern Kansas in the 1850s, despite the best efforts of their loved ones to protect them. Thus the Wild West show, for all its colorful posters and glamorous Pony Express mythology, has in its origin this genuine scene of heroism: a darkling Kansas meadow and a winding road, the hoofbeats of a galloping horse, a child clinging to its back with a sob of fear in his throat, and terrible loss on his horizon.

CAREFUL READERS will notice something else about Cody's very tall boyhood tales. His autobiography is remarkably truthful until the death of his father, whereupon he launches into his Mormon War adventure. In rapid succession come all the tales of prospecting, Indian fighting, and the Pony Express. After the death of his father, Cody turns our eyes west, distracting us from the dark, briefer tale of another journey he soon took, to the east and the south. By the late 1870s, when Cody sat down to write his autobiography, slavery had been consigned to history. It was no longer a national issue, the way the future of Indians and the West still was. Cody was a preternaturally talented reader of cultural longings, and so he downplayed his participation in the Civil War and its bloody Kansas prelude as southern, part of the past, in favor of advancing himself as a product of the West, the region of the nation's future. If his imaginary boyhood West was so golden, it was in part because it hid from public view, and perhaps from his own mind, the sense of desperation, loss, and the longing for revenge which consumed him upon the death of his father.

CHAPTER TWO

The Attack on the Settler's Cabin

T HE SETTLER RETURNED from his hunt. His wife stepped out the door to greet him. A shout in the near distance. Turning, the settler confronted an Indian racing toward the house, dazzling and fierce in his feathers and war paint. Raising his rifle, the hunter fired and saw the man topple into the dust. An outburst of cries and screams erupted from nearby, and suddenly, the lonesome cabin became the center of a swirling mass of mounted Indian warriors, guns blazing. The settler and his wife retreated through the door, their children helping to load and fire guns through the windows. But the Indians were too many. They came ever closer to the cabin. The war cries were terrifying, the roar of guns and smoke filled the air. They were even closer now. The destruction of the tiny frontier home was only a moment away.

But suddenly—another yell, and the Indians now turned to face the massed guns of a long-haired Buffalo Bill Cody and an entourage of whooping, shooting cowboys! A fierce fight ensued. Indians and cowboys dropped from saddles, their bodies thudding into the dust. But finally, the last of the Indians rode out of sight. As the settler family emerged from the cabin to thank the scout and his cowboy militia, another sound rolled over the home, a roar, as the audience applauded, stamped their feet, and stood.

FOR MOST OF the Wild West show's long life, the climactic finale of the drama was the "Attack on the Settler's Cabin." Figuratively, that lightning-quick courier of the Pony Express and all the other horsemen who charged around the arena, from the drivers of the Deadwood Stage to the families on the wagon train, were bound for the cabin that appeared in the show's final act. They fought Indians and yelled and raced in circles, on their way to this mock family home.

The image of home salvation reinforced the most persistent claim of Buffalo Bill's Wild West show: that Buffalo Bill Cody was the savior of the settler family. The cabin rescue finale was not the only family scene in the show. White families also rode in the wagon train which trundled into the arena, and which was then attacked by Indians, who were, of course, driven off by Buffalo Bill. There was the oddly humorous and elegant scene in which Buffalo Bill, the cowboys, and the show's cowgirls performed a Virginia reel on horseback, a tableau which suggested that settler men and women could join for courting and marriage even on the rough-and-tumble frontier. The family theme ran through acts from which Cody was absent, too. Annie Oakley spent sixteen years with the show, performing as its star shooter, and everybody knew that she was married to Frank Butler, the man who held her targets. They were a handsome, wholesome couple. The fact that she fired a gun at targets in his hands, over and over, without ever so much as grazing him, made them seem somehow weird proof of the marital covenant's protection. Much of the time, the settler's cabin stood in the arena from the show's beginning, positioned slightly toward one end, so that all of the other show acts swirled around it. The audience could tell that the home was where the action would culminate.[1]

Cody cultivated the connection between Buffalo Bill and home defense for his entire public career. It was a major component of his theatrical performances, which began in 1872, and as we have seen, it was a consistent thread in the autobiography of 1879. In one of the book's yarns about the Civil War, the spy William Cody protects the home of a Missouri secessionist from being plundered by Union soldiers, an action which left him "happy in the thought that I had done a good deed, and with no regrets that I had saved from pillage and destruction the home and property of a confederate and his family."[2] The story was undoubtedly fictional (as we shall see), but it suggests that for Cody, family defense even trumped wartime enmity. Such a code of honor no doubt appealed to northern and southern readers alike, longing as they were for national reunion.

Cody did not invent family defense as an entertainment attraction—he merely perfected it. The "Settler's Cabin" finale of Buffalo Bill's Wild West show seems to have been implemented by Nate Salsbury after he became the show's managing partner in 1884. Even then, it was hardly new. White family defense was a consistent motif in popular literature, art, and entertainment throughout the life of the republic. Myriad writers, dramatists, and artists portrayed Indian war as the necessary precursor to family salvation. In inscribing a frontier line between domestic order and savagery, Buffalo Bill's Wild West made Cody himself into a chief bulwark of the American family. In a sense, the arc of Buffalo Bill's life touched earth at one end with the speeding pony, at the other with the family home.

Despite the fact that he never actually drove an Indian war party away from anybody's home, Cody assumed the role of the white family's defender with the natural grace that comes from experience and conviction. If he was not the first to portray frontier warfare as the fight for domestic bliss, his commitment to it reflected some belief in the essential reality of the scene. Indeed, home salvation was much on his mind as a boy.

But the frontiersmen of myth are not domesticated. They straddle the line between civilization and savagery. In his actual life, if Cody was defender of the home, he could also be its assailant. As a teenager, he found that staving off family destruction meant earning money, a challenge which required him to leave his own home repeatedly and for extended periods. In the early 1860s, he was inspired by fellow Kansans who combined the hunt for money with the quest for revenge.

—————

THROUGHOUT the late 1850s, many Free Kansans longed for vengeance against their tormentors in Missouri. When the Civil War erupted on April 12, 1861, they got their chance. In the absence of a strong occupation by either army, the border of Kansas and Missouri exploded in a vast paramilitary conflagration, as competing bands of Union jayhawkers and secessionist bushwhackers embarked on wars of pillage, rapine, and murder. Jayhawker and bushwhacker alike rousted their enemies from their cabins at night and dispensed beatings, mutilations, hangings, and shootings. They stole, savaged, and ruined.[3]

And they burned homes. George Caleb Bingham, a Unionist, described the devastating progress of a leading anti-slavery regiment, the Seventh Kansas Volunteer Cavalry, better known as Jennison's Jayhawkers, on their raid from Kansas to Missouri in 1861. Their "entire route from Independence to Westpoint may be traced by the ruins of the dwellings of our citizens, which were first pillaged and then burned without discrimination or mercy. As they were generally constructed of wood, they are now but heaps of ashes, above which the tall chimneys remain in their solitude." In 1862, Jennison's regiment fell on the town of Dayton, Missouri, and burned forty-six of forty-seven homes. When they reached the partially burned town of Morristown, they burned the rest. One eyewitness, awed by the horror they inflicted near Kingsville, remembered: "I counted one evening, while standing on Brushy Knob, one hundred and sixty houses on fire."[4]

The Bleeding Kansas years had seen house burnings, too, but the increasing frequency and scale of home destruction makes it hard to overstate the impact of the Civil War on settlers along the Kansas-Missouri line. Throughout the United States, and more so on the western border, the premier social institution was the family, and the premier economic, educational, and social welfare establishment was the family home. In a society where federal, state, and local governments were weak, where educational institutions were rudimentary, where a multiplicity of churches competed for the attention of minority churchgoers, the family home was the chief organizing unit. The home was where children were conceived and delivered, where much of their education took place, where they and their parents produced most of the family's wealth, and where they relaxed and enjoyed their lives and one another. As they grew, children would move into homes of their own, and in those homes they would care for aged parents as well as their own progeny. The home thus enfolded the present and future of the family that created it.[5]

All wars destroy families and homes. In the American South, the Civil War would turn on the destruction of cities and the ravaging of rural plantations, and in the process many thousands of homes were damaged or ruined. But the absence of other institutions across much of Kansas made the destruction of homes, and the families they contained, even more poignant and devastating.

One of the ironies of the guerrilla war in Kansas and Missouri was that in firing the homes of their enemies, and in the most extreme cases killing or driving away their families altogether, partisans removed the one institution which constrained boys and men from extended guerrilla forays. With no families to protect, and no family farms to tend, young men were free— or driven—to pursue revenge. Fierce raids by one band of partisans thus gave rise to more partisans in opposition. "Now," one guerrilla concluded, "when you find a dozen, twenty-five, fifty, or one hundred men whose lives have come together in this way, you can understand how they come to be terrors."[6]

Will Cody was fifteen years old in 1861. As far as he and his family were concerned, pro-slavery partisans had murdered Isaac. For years, they had threatened his mother, his sisters, and his little brother, Charlie. And as Kansas jayhawkers took the war to Missouri on their own terms, he rode with them.

By his own account, in 1861, he took up with a gang of horse thieves bent on avenging the losses of Free Kansas settlers by stealing from their pro-slavery neighbors. He left this crowd after his mother objected.[7]

But then, in 1862, he "became one of the red legged scouts," a paramilitary unit dedicated, at least by their own reckoning, to the defense of Kansas, and whose name was derived from the red leather garters they wore to distinguish themselves. The Red Legs did not keep lists of members, or any other records. Boys and men joined and departed as they wished. Cody says he remained with the Red Legs until the spring of 1863. As he recounted, "our field of operations was confined mostly to the Arkansas country and southwestern Missouri. We had many a lively skirmish with the bushwhackers and Younger brothers, and when we were not hunting them, we were generally employed in carrying dispatches between Forts Dodge, Gibson, Leavenworth, and other posts."[8]

Given the fictional nature of his western tales, we must be careful in accepting his claims about the border war. But several clues suggest there is some truth to this account. First, he barely mentions this period at all, choosing not to mythologize it beyond "many a lively skirmish" with the likes of the Younger brothers. He takes little opportunity to embellish what could have been a highly colored narrative.

Second, his sister Julia's memoir confirms his extensive forays with the Red Legs. Unlike the Pony Express stories, which she summarizes in two sentences with no new detail, and in contrast to other adventures where she simply quotes him at length, she offers far more detail on his Red Leg days than he does. Thus, she writes that he was out with "the Red Legged Scouts" throughout much of late 1861, and that, as their mother fell ill again, "he stayed home that winter and went to school most of the time," occasionally leaving "for several days" when "the Scouts sent for him to go out on a Scouting Tour." The association between William Cody and the Red Legs rings of something other than pure fiction.[9]

Biographers typically dismiss these experiences as incidental. But Cody's affiliation with a band guilty of some of the region's most brutal persecutions suggests a dark counterweight to his gleaming boyhood tales of Pony Express heroism. Elvira Scott, of Miami, Missouri, might have seen the sixteen-year-old Will Cody. If so, she was not favorably impressed. The Red Legs "were about the lowest, most desperate looking specimens of humanity it has ever been my lot to witness." Another Missourian described the settler exodus for St. Louis as the Red Legs raided into the countryside. "The roads are lined with movers driven away from thare homes by Red Legs. . . . The Red Legs are desolating the country, they have no respect for any person's political opinions."[10] Red Leg depredations grew so extreme, their exactions of property and lives from innocent civilians so consistent and terrifying, that the provisional governor of Missouri begged President Lincoln to restrain them.[11]

There are some intriguing hints that Cody was with the Red Legs on some of their forays. Some of the most wrenching testimony about Red Leg savagery comes from the region of Lexington, Missouri, where carriage maker Willard Mendenhall wrote that in the spring of 1862, the Red Legs were so uncontrolled, "they appear to be a band of murderers and robers," burning homes and pillaging Unionist and secessionist alike.[12] Was Cody with them? Throughout his adult life, he stood out. Tall, handsome, and with a pronounced sense of style and timing, he was recognizable from an early age, and it may be that Lexington residents noticed him that spring.

After the war, in 1866, while traveling aboard a Missouri River steamboat out of St. Louis, Cody recalled, "There happened to be on board the boat an excursion party from Lexington, Missouri, and those comprising it seemed to shun me, for some reason which I could not account for." When another passenger advised, "They say that you are one of the Kansas jay-hawkers, and one of Jennison's house-burners"—victims of pro-Union guerrillas often lumped their persecutors together as "Jennison's" soldiers—Cody confirmed that he "was in Kansas during the border ruffian war." Then, almost as an afterthought, he mused, "Perhaps these people know who I am. . . ."[13]

The Red Legs were unsalaried guerrillas. They supported themselves through the theft and sale of their victims' belongings. Indeed, Red Legs often chose targets for their property, not their politics. Pro-Union settlers frequently complained that jayhawkers, and the Red Legs in particular, stole their property as if they were secessionists. But there was little to be done. No lawmen dared stop them. During the Civil War, the towns of Leavenworth and Lawrence served as Red Leg entrepôts, where they auctioned stolen goods with impunity, in the open street.[14]

Looting and sale of goods reflected the hunger for cash not just of the Red Legs, but of Kansans generally. Modern nostalgia for subsistence farmers has created a powerful mythology of settler independence, but in reality, by 1850 almost all westerners were entangled in market relations to some degree. Isaac Cody's stints as stagecoach owner, salaried farm manager, mill owner, land speculator, and hay contractor for the army suggest a dedication less to raising crops than to raising cash. His farm was just one of many businesses he ran. The farm equipment stolen from his home by bushwhackers included modern technological implements, such as the plow, mow, and hay rake, all of which were bought with specie. Like other rural families, the Codys produced some food for the family table, but increasingly they required cash to buy new farm technology which allowed them to cultivate larger parcels, grow more surplus crops, and buy more consumer goods. Kansas during the Civil War was home to a people always in need of money, and the Cody family, which had been comparatively well off, perhaps needed it more than most.[15]

Indeed, the moneymaking ethic so prevalent on the Kansas frontier seems to have been especially strong among the Cody children, particularly Julia and Will. As Julia put it, "I don't think there ever was 2 children that had more Responsibility than we did."[16] The absence of Isaac Cody's income left them with a large and ever present need for money to provide for their young siblings, and the insistence on making money above other needs could extend to the most intimate family relations. In 1862, Julia Cody decided to marry. In her conversations with husband-to-be Al Goodman, she said, "I would tell him to let's Talk Business, not love for my marrying was a Business Proposition. . . ."[17]

The allure of the Red Legs for a boy in need of money was considerable. The shreds of evidence for the teenage William Cody's activities in this period suggest that he, like the Red Legs, "confiscated" property for commercial gain. He "took it for granted that as Missouri was a slave state the inhabitants must all be secessionists, and therefore our enemies." Since he had "a longing and revengeful desire to retaliate upon the Missourians for the brutal manner in which they had treated and robbed my family," stealing Missouri horses was a way of "getting back our own, or the equivalent, from the Missourians."[18]

Cody mingled his stolen Missouri horses with others closer to home. In May of 1862—during the very period in which William Cody says he was with the Red Legs—Mary Cody returned at least two horses to the Union army's Third Wisconsin Cavalry, near Leavenworth. According to her sworn affidavit, the horses were found to have strayed from the post, and they were brought to her by son William Cody. Military authorities demanded to know where he was. "Absent," she told them. Mary Cody visited the fort twice for this purpose, and for her trouble was paid a $2 bounty on each horse.[19] Was William Cody merely returning loose horses he rounded up? Did he confiscate them from a secessionist who had stolen them in the first place? Or was he, like so many Red Legs, stealing horses from Unionist and secessionist alike, and making a little money by returning them for the bounty? Did he hand them over to his mother so she could protect him from suspicion? Was his mother, who disapproved of his jayhawking, returning stolen horses he had left in her care? If he was not stealing horses, why did Mary Cody refuse to reveal her son's whereabouts? Eventually, Union army patrols pursued jayhawkers and Red Legs because their thieving lowered regional support for the anti-slavery cause. Cody recalled that his first forays into horse theft ended when "government officials" finally "put detectives upon our track, and several of the party were arrested." Were those officials pursuing the band because they stole government horses?[20]

Whoever the victims of his thievery were, Cody was now fatherless and adrift in a world where targeted violence—anti-slavery or pro-slavery— easily spread into general violence against anybody who had property or was in the way. Among the partisans along the Kansas-Missouri border were any number of criminals who worked both sides of the conflict, robbing and killing secessionist and Unionist alike. Whether he served as partisan or mostly as an observer, Cody rode through the same social chaos that spawned the James, Dalton, and Younger brothers of future outlaw infamy, not to mention bloody Confederate murderers like William Quantrill,

William "Bloody Bill" Anderson, and, on the other side, the insatiably murderous Union partisan, Charles "Doc" Jennison.[21]

The temptation to borrow a few Union horses and return them for the money must have been considerable. We cannot know if Cody burned houses, as some Missourians alleged, but he rode with men who did. And however he did it, he made money. As his sister Julia recalled of his time with the Red Legs, "the money that Willie Brought Home and gave to Mother was a big help."[22]

Mimicking the pattern set by Isaac Cody, and in keeping with practices of many men of fighting age during the war, young Will Cody was frequently abroad for prolonged periods. The long period of violence imposed such severe strain on the civil order that child rearing and family bonds generally were difficult to achieve or sustain. The gangs of armed men who roamed the countryside were renowned for drunkenness and debauchery in Kansas towns. White and black refugees from Missouri, and anti-slavery Indians routed out of Indian territory to the south, poured into the towns of Leavenworth, Lawrence, and Atchison, contributing to a profound sense of social disorder and anomie. The refugees included or attracted large numbers of prostitutes, vagrants, pickpockets, and thieves. Soldiers and settlers walked the streets among teamsters, steamboat sailors, Mexican traders, Indians, fugitive slaves, and any number of outlaws and killers who styled themselves Free State militiamen, many of whom packed the towns' numerous saloons, bordellos, and gambling halls.[23] The relentless violence of this society shocked even enthusiastic brawlers like James Butler Hickok, later known as Wild Bill, who wrote to his sister from Kansas in 1858, "You dont [k]no[w] what a Country this is for drinking and fighting . . . this is no place for women and children. . . ."[24]

In Leavenworth and elsewhere, bands of men wearing red leather garters were a frequent, intimidating sight on the streets. Cody's prosaic, brief descriptions of town visits during his Red Leg days have an undercurrent of menace. "Whenever we were in Leavenworth we had a festive time. We usually attended all the balls in full force, and 'ran things' to suit ourselves."[25] Whether he was actually a Red Leg or not, he knew Leavenworth and its wartime dissipation intimately.

In November 1863, William Cody returned home to tend his ailing mother, but soon thereafter Mary Cody died. William Cody was bereft. In his autobiography, he recalled taking himself back to Leavenworth for two months, during which time he became "a very 'hard case,' " drinking himself to the point of "dissipation" in the town's unsavory wartime society. The loss of his mother, "whom I had so tenderly loved," meant another severing of family bonds. The alienation was complete when he awoke one morning, "after having been under the influence of bad whisky," and found himself a soldier in the Seventh Kansas Volunteer Cavalry, the regiment better known as Jennison's Jayhawkers.[26]

Cody's career with the Seventh Kansas was remarkable for its lack of distinction. The regiment fought mostly in the Old Southwest, helping to crush Nathan Bedford Forrest in Mississippi and General Sterling Price in Missouri. His service record reveals almost nothing of his duties during this time, although the Seventh Kansas Volunteers saw fierce combat at Tupelo, and Cody must have been there. He later claimed he was a scout and a spy, and that he renewed his acquaintance with Wild Bill Hickok while both were spying. We should remain doubtful of these tales. For one thing, they are mere copies of stories that were widely circulated about Hickok at the time. For another, spying and scouting seem unlikely postings for Cody, a soldier who—according to official records—was ordered to serve as a hospital orderly in January 1865, and who four weeks later took up a cushy post as messenger for an office of the Freedmen's Bureau in St. Louis.[27]

The heroism of protecting family must have seemed all the more important to him by war's end, when he journeyed back to his own family in Kansas. His little brother, Charlie, was sick, and the boy died in October 1865. The family's sadness only accented the sorrow visited on the region by the recent conflict. The fearsome war on the home which had absorbed Cody's energies had also engulfed the countryside. There were so few people across the once thickly populated farmlands of Missouri that much of the state was silent. One traveler recorded a journey from one town to another in which he "did not pass one house," and in truth, "there was neither town nor village" to be found in the entire county. The population of another county had sunk to six families.[28] In western Missouri, one returning exile recounted that "for miles and miles, we saw nothing but lone chimneys to mark the spots where happy homes stood. It seemed like a vast cemetery—not a living thing to break the silence."[29] On the Kansas side of the line, the scene was much the same. When they remembered the war, the people of Kansas and Missouri would be horrified not just by the violence, the vengefulness of the partisans, or the destruction of property. As one journalist reflected, this "most alarming picture of war that can be painted" was the consequence of "the frightful spirit of hate and revenge" with which partisans continually hunted one another, "resulting in the most fearful loss and breaking up of family ties."[30]

The war on the family home was the definitive experience of William Cody's young life. In it, he was, like so many others, both victim and perpetrator. The man who experienced real war on a home front as casualty and victor would spend most of his adult life trying to become a builder of family and community, and representing himself as the savior of the white family home. The Wild West show cut a swath through American entertainments for three decades beginning in the 1880s, and most of its audience were northerners and urbanites who did not live in Kansas or the South. They did not lose homes in the Civil War. Their sense of vulnerability about home and family had many other sources, from exploding slums in America's cities to labor unrest that came close to insurrection. William Cody understood those anxieties intuitively, and he knew that his simulated attack on a settler's cabin gave them a sense of participation in the show's drama.

Buffalo Bill Cody himself never drove Indians away from a cabin. But he had certainly defended a home from savage attack, and longed to wage war on the homes of his enemies from his earliest days.

CHAPTER THREE

The Village . . . The Cyclone

THE DESTRUCTION OF a frontier town by the forces of hostile nature first appeared in the Wild West show's 1886 season, in Madison Square Garden. The expectant crowd sat before a mining camp with a row of army tents. "Thunder is crashing and light[n]ing flashing," wrote a reviewer. "Suddenly comes a roar, the tents sway and then are leveled, several dummies are whirled wildly in midair, and the curtain drops on what is supposed to be the terrific destruction of a camp by a cyclone."[1]

The scene evoked the contest between savage nature and "the advance of civilization," which was the Wild West show's main plot.[2] The mock natural disaster—a kind of "Attack on the Settler's Cabin" writ large—was heavy on mechanical special effects. To simulate a tornado, managers dug a trench to a steam generator across Twenty-seventh Street. The generator turned four six-foot-tall industrial fans inside the showplace, which produced a heavy wind—"the first time on record," wrote the stage manager, that "real wind was used as an effect."[3] Stagehands gathered a mountain of leaves and brush from city parks and roadsides, and poured wagonloads of debris in front of the fans, which blew it across the stage, visually accenting the gusts.[4] Of course, in the outdoor arenas where the show usually appeared, these preparations were impossible. So the scene of town destruction was reserved for the comparatively rare indoor venues with suitable infrastructure, the industrial machinery behind the spectacle suggesting the advanced stage of civilization which the town represented. In 1887, in Manchester, England, Buffalo Bill's Wild West moved indoors for the winter, and the town destruction—before a gale measured at over fifty miles per hour—became the show finale, with "legitimate wind effects by the Blackman Air Propeller."[5] In 1907, again at Madison Square Garden, the mountain village collapsed again, this time under an avalanche whose staging remains a mystery.[6]

AT LEAST SINCE John Winthrop invoked the "city on a hill," town building had expressed America's frontier progress. In keeping with this tradition, the Wild West show's towns were the figurative culmination of westward-marching civilization. Cody grew up with such notions, which were widespread on the Plains by the time the Civil War came to a close. When a train pulled into Sheridan, Kansas, in November 1869, a correspondent on board described the new town as "an apparition of civilization amid the solitudes of the Great American Desert."[7]

In fact, despite popular ideas of towns as the endgame of western development, urbanization went hand in hand with frontier expansion. In the transient world of the Far West, to found a town made one a creator of the fixed institutions of governance, domesticity, and capital. The trade and rising real estate prices of towns made them a short path to wealth and respectability for lucky founders. Even in eighteenth-century Kentucky, Daniel Boone, that paragon of frontiersmen and hunters, had joined partners in creating the town of Boonesborough. He never made any money from it, but by the 1850s the founders of such frontier towns as Des Moines, Davenport, and Moline, to say nothing of Chicago, were respected, and sometimes wealthy.[8]

William Cody's exposure to frontier horsemanship, hunting, and Indian fighting fit our modern notions of frontier life, but it comes as something of a surprise to learn this backcountry man came of age amid fervent urbanization. In Kansas, hysteria for town-founding rose and fell with each pulse in the river of emigrants. As the Cody family joined other settlers there in 1854, speculators were founding no fewer than fourteen towns along the steamboat route of the Missouri River, and others farther inland. So eagerly did speculators like Isaac Cody lay out plans for settlements like Grasshopper Falls that humorists warned some land should be reserved for farming "before the whole Territory should be divided into city lots." Kansas emigrants had such faith in town futures that beautifully colored printed deeds to properties in towns-yet-to-exist served as money. According to one observer, shares in cities consisting of a shack or two "sold readily for a hundred dollars." The flutter of land certificates and the clink of gold coin attracted poor men in droves. "Young men who never before owned fifty dollars at once, a few weeks after reaching Kansas possessed full pockets, with town shares by the score." Isaac Cody's speculation in some town was practically a foregone conclusion. After all, even "servant girls speculated in town lots."[9]

The town of Grasshopper Falls was a success. But William Cody's father seems to have known that most town-promotion schemes in the West failed. Competition for emigrant traffic was fierce. Of the fourteen would-be metropolises established along the Missouri River in Kansas, only three survived. Isaac Cody did not let his success run away with him. He even refused an invitation to invest in the new town of Leavenworth.[10]

Not surprisingly, after the Civil War, as hundreds of thousands of new emigrants poured into the state, town creation was much on the minds of Kansas settlers. But now it was complicated by the technology of the railroad. Boosters had been calling for a transcontinental railroad since the 1830s. In 1861, after the South's departure from Congress finally broke the political logjam over the transcontinental route, the Union Pacific Railroad received the contract to lay the tracks from Omaha to the West. Other railroad financiers, led by the western surveyor-hero John C. Frémont, broke ground on a railroad to connect Saint Joseph, Missouri, to Denver by building a direct route through central Kansas. They began at Leavenworth in 1863 and, anticipating a buyout by the larger line to the north, they called their road the Union Pacific Eastern Division, or the UPED (later it would be called the Kansas Pacific).[11]

Of course, settlers followed the rails. Once the well-watered eastern edge of the state was behind them, they entered a more arid, threatening land. Rainfall was relatively sparse. The rolling hills and streams gave way to flatter, short-grass plains, with fewer sources of water, vast herds of buffalo, and large numbers of Indians who were often less than pleased at this invasion of their homelands. In defiance of Indians and the weird Plains environment, towns sprouted along the rails at Ellsworth, Hays, Junction City, and other places.

In the immediate aftermath of the war, William Cody followed those same rail lines on a path that led him both to create a family for himself—his own settler's cabin—and to attempt ensconcing them in a new community of his own design, a town by the railroad. His little family was a shaky proposition, and his domestic life was not helped by the sudden collapse of his village. In a strange foreshadowing of the staged destruction of the Wild West show, the failure of his town looked like a natural disaster. But it was industrial might, not hostile nature, that destroyed it.

Twenty years later, the Wild West show functioned as a kind of traveling community, and its success was a product of the many railroads which allowed its props, its dozens of animals, and its hundreds of people to move from town to town. Just as railroads brought Cody's show to city lots, they carried audiences from the surrounding countryside, usually at special rates negotiated by Cody and his agents. Later, just before the twentieth century began, Cody would turn again to the creation of a more conventional town, this time in arid Wyoming. There, one of the first steps he took was to secure railroad support for his settlement. William Cody learned the need for alliances with railroads, and he did it during the late 1860s, as a consequence of his first attempt to create a frontier community. Here, the entrepreneurial William Cody learned a hard lesson in the power of corporations and the new railroads. It stayed with him all his life.

ANY ASPIRATIONS to becoming a mythic hero were not in evidence upon Cody's return from the Civil War. Back in Leavenworth, he returned to his series of odd jobs and ephemeral business ventures. For a few months he drove a stage for a transport company in western Nebraska, between Kearney and Plum Creek. It was "a cold, dreary road," and in February 1866, bouncing over its muddy ruts in the frigid air, he decided to "abandon staging forever, and marry and settle down." He returned to St. Louis, where he and Louisa Frederici were married on March 6, 1866. Immediately after the wedding at her parents' home, they took the steamboat north and returned to Leavenworth.[12]

Louisa Maude Frederici grew up in the French-speaking quarter of St.

William Cody at eighteen. Courtesy Buffalo Bill Historical Center.

Louisa Frederici Cody, at about the time of her marriage to William Cody. Courtesy Buffalo Bill Historical Center.

Louis. Her father was an Austro-Italian, French-speaking immigrant from Alsace. Her mother may have been an American woman. Louisa Cody claimed she was, and that her maiden name was Smith. But William Cody described her as a German who spoke the language fluently. We know little about Louisa's early association with William Cody, except that they met during the Civil War, and that they had a jocular courtship. Superficially, they seemed well suited to one another. To Cody, she was a dazzling, beautiful woman at home in the largest city he had ever seen. We can only guess at his attractions for her. He was very handsome. He exaggerated his prospects throughout his life, and there is no reason to believe he did otherwise then.[13]

In any case, Louisa was the child of merchants, and she expected a middle-class life when she married William Cody. Almost immediately, she began to have doubts about her choice of a husband and his financial capabilities, both of which would trouble her for the rest of her life, even after he began to make large profits in show business.[14] Moving back to Leavenworth, Cody took along with him a desire to make a new family around him, and to restore to them the life of relative wealth the Codys had lost since the death of Isaac. In this, Louisa was supportive, but she demanded certain guarantees. She wanted no roving plainsman for a husband. He must settle into a paying business.[15]

Hoping to profit from the widening flow of migrants through the region, William Cody rented his mother's old house from its new owners and opened it as a hotel called the Golden Rule House. Four miles west of Leavenworth and near several arteries of western emigration, it was an ideal location for a business that provided emigrant services.[16] Like most of Cody's ventures, this one was a failure, owing in part to his tendency to spend money faster than he made it, a characteristic which was better suited to the nomadic, raiding economy of the jayhawker than to the fixed business he was trying to run.[17]

The strains of the new business pervaded a house already filled with tension between his wife and his sisters. Initially, he and Louisa stayed with his sister Eliza, who was now married to George Myers. When they moved out of the Myerses' house, little sister Helen Cody moved in with them. Although Helen and Louisa got along at first, they eventually quarreled, and the relationship was never close thereafter.

"She was always wanting a home of her own," recalled William Cody of his wife, many years later, "and of course I was young . . . and I didn't know anything about business and I couldn't get a home in a minute."[18] Money problems aggravated their personal differences, especially as Louisa was soon expecting a child. In September, William Cody gave up his lease and abandoned the Golden Rule House. Leaving his pregnant wife in a rented house with his sister Helen, he "started alone for Saline, Kansas, which was then at the end of the track of the Kansas Pacific railway."[19] He was breaking his promise to settle down, and their parting words must have been acrimonious. He would not return to Louisa for the better part of a year. Their first child, a daughter, Arta, was born in December, while he was away.[20]

Thus began the self-exile from his own hearth that characterized most of Cody's adult life. What began right after the Civil War as a marital estrangement became standard when he was touring with his theater company and, after that, the Wild West show. Ironically, the man who became a hero for saving the frontier family home did so primarily by seeking to escape his own troubled house. For Cody, roving as plainsman or showman was usually preferable to the stationary combat of his fireside.

OUT IN WEST KANSAS, at "the end of the tracks," he scrabbled for a livelihood among mostly low-class frontiersmen: down-and-out prospectors, cowhands, buffalo hunters, and teamsters who moved from job to job, with no fixed address. The cash economy of Kansas had been expanding for most of William Cody's life. After the Civil War, a wave of new Kansas emigrants, combined with a dramatic increase in railroad and other investment, fueled spectacular economic growth. The railroad, especially, brought about a tectonic shift in the prairie's social, economic, and natural relations. Nowhere was that fact more apparent than where the rails extended farthest into the frontier. At track's end, thousands of Irish tracklayers, or "gandy dancers," pounded spikes into ties and did the other work of building the railway toward the western horizon. From the other direction came hundreds of bullwhackers from Mexico, the United States, and points unknown, whips cracking beside prairie schooners creaking with tons of Colorado and New Mexico cattle hide, sheep's wool, buffalo robes, and mineral ore, all to be sold at the railroad's western terminus. At the same time, the east-west migration of goods and people swelled with a northerly flow of mostly poor and young cowboys—white, black, Mexican, and mixed-blood Texans—driving huge herds of cattle to these newly minted "cow towns," from which 50,000 animals were shipped east in 1868 alone.[21] On top of all this, black, white, and immigrant soldiers, merchants, laborers, speculators, entertainers, and tourists, the wealthy and those of middling means, came west on the railroad. Settlers followed not long after.

The rivers of mostly male workers—flowing ahead of the train, alongside the prairie schooners, and behind the cattle—converged in one vast lake of loneliness and thirst in the arid plain. Entrepreneurs took advantage. To the north, in Nebraska, the Union Pacific Railroad created a genuine moving town, famously called "Hell on Wheels," where drink, food, and sex could be had for cash, and where card games, shell games, real estate swindles, and a hundred other ways to cheat men of their money proliferated. End-of-the-line social relations were similar even in more permanent towns on the UPED, where boomers waxed rhapsodic about civilization, but other observers were more critical. "The houses" in Ellsworth, remarked one traveler, "are alternately Beer Houses, Whiskey Shops, Gambling houses, Dance houses and Restaurants," wherein patrons consumed large quantities of beer, whiskey, and "tarantula juice."[22]

As Cody later recalled it, when he was testifying in his own divorce trial, the first year away from Louisa he was "railroading and trading and hunting; I went out to make money and I was just looking around for anything that would come along."[23] He spent the winter like many other single men on the Plains: in a "dugout," a hole in an embankment with a crude roof over the top, sharing the dark, dingy space with a man named Alfred Northrup. Early in 1867, he helped a former neighbor from Leavenworth haul goods to open a new store. He mixed his odd jobs with stuttering efforts at founding a business. That summer, a series of drunken, bloody melees between soldiers and railroad workers compelled army officers at Fort Hays to seize the supplies of unlicensed booze merchants. In their dragnet, they confiscated the stores of William Cody, which included, among other things, four gallons of whiskey and three gallons of bitters.[24] The well-known mule-whacker and aspiring saloonkeeper was also a peddler of buffalo meat on the streets of Hays; locals soon took to calling him Buffalo Bill.[25]

The name itself long preceded him. On the Plains, when any number of men were named Bill, appending "Buffalo" as an epithet was a way of distinguishing among them. In the 1860s and '70s there were Buffalo Bills in Texas, Kansas, and Dakota Territory. As early as 1862, an English traveler in Montana would record his meeting with "Buffalo Bill, a personage whom I have hitherto regarded as a myth."[26] The name may have been applied to Cody in derision, as a taunt. But however he earned the moniker, in the long run it was a boon to his notoriety. The name was so endemic to the frontier that upon being introduced to *the* Buffalo Bill, many believed they were meeting a man of wide reputation, even if the Buffalo Bills they had heard about were different men.

In his long absences from home in the 1860s, this Buffalo Bill's career resembled a low-rent version of his father's. Before Isaac Cody's troubles with pro-slavery settlers began, he had been kept away from his family by the demands of his own stage line, and by the burdens of managing large farms for absentee investors and of founding successful towns. William Cody's stints as teamster, whiskey seller, and market hunter were of a lower-class variety.

So, too, was his next venture, when he joined a man named William Rose in a contract to grade track for the UPED.[27] It was hard, dusty work, driving teams of horses behind the scraper blades which pulled up the prairie sod and churned grit into the air. Although he continued to send Louisa money, there was no way she would join him in this peripatetic life, with no fixed home and surrounded by men of low standing and hard disposition.

Then he made an audacious move. In the summer of 1867, he joined with Rose in founding a town along the course of the railroad near Fort Hays. The young men's faith in the advancement of civilization and their own interests, their conviction of the town's permanence and eventual greatness, was expressed in the name Cody chose for it: Rome.[28]

Cody and Rose would soon learn that, where the game of town-founding had been risky in the 1850s, it was even more treacherous for entrepreneurs in the 1860s. Along the wagon roads, travelers could stop at any roadside settlement or outpost that looked promising. Town founders secured their business and recruited new residents by appealing to emigrant needs.

But train passengers could alight only where railroad executives decided to schedule stops, and in this matter they played a rough game. Corporate survival hinged on settling a dependent population of customers along the tracks. Without farmers, merchants, and others to buy space for their freight and seats for themselves, long stretches of track would be too expensive to sustain. Company executives thus took special interest in town sites, exercising near-monopoly control over their selection. The most charming settlement along the path of the railroad, however thriving and complete with businesses, families, churches, and schools, would turn to a ghost town if the railway company failed to schedule a stop there. Indeed, as the railroads extended along the route of older emigrant roadways, preexisting hotels, stores, saloons, and other provisioning stations were forced to find a niche in the railroad's towns or face bankruptcy. In a curious way, the "civilizing" force of the railroad brought greater commerce at concentrated points along the tracks, but it cleared many Plains entrepreneurs from their holdings, leaving open prairie along the old trails where scattered homes and businesses had once stood.[29]

Thus, in the interval between the death of Isaac Cody and the arrival of the railroad in western Kansas, the opportunity to build towns moved out of the hands of entrepreneurs and into the hands of huge corporations. In the East, railroads were built to connect towns. In the West, railroads were built first, and the towns followed. Railroad agents, sent west to locate depots along the intended route of the railway, frequently threatened to pass existing towns by if they did not receive donations of free lots to line their own pockets. Independent town founders who succeeded in getting the railroads to build depots were usually men of considerable means, some of whom bought up every conceivable nearby railroad stop and forced the railroad to build the depot in the town.[30]

To circumvent such tactics, railroad companies such as the Union Pacific and the Central Pacific, fueled by vast sums of investor capital and taxpayer subsidies, organized subsidiary town-building companies. On occasion, when they were bribed enough, they ran the rail line through or beside an existing town. But more often they steered away from settlements so as better to exploit the economic boom the railroad brought with it. At Cheyenne, Wyoming, for example, the Union Pacific established the town, organized the local government, and sold lots only to people who acknowledged the railroad as rightful owner of the property—all before the company even had title to the land.[31]

Railroad power over town creation was perhaps most potently symbolized by the shipping of the physical stuff of new settlements to the frontier. The Union Pacific and other railroads freighted whole towns in pieces, like giant toys. One western traveler reported a train loaded with "frame houses, boards, furniture, palings, old tents, and all the rubbish which makes up one of these mushroom 'cities.' " As it pulled into Cheyenne, "the guard jumped off his van, and seeing some friends on the platform, called out with a flourish, 'Gentlemen, here's Julesburg.' "[32]

Still, even with the might of America's railroad magnates against them, independent speculators frequently tried to horn in on the railroad's town business. Many simply bought and sold lots in towns founded by the railroad. "Thousands of dollars are daily won and lost all along the line by speculating in town lots," wrote one observer. But the boldest speculators would claim acreage for a homestead directly in the path of the railroad. Instead of plowing fields and making farm improvements, as the Homestead Act intended, they laid out a grid of streets, and made public promises that the railroad would build a station there. These "town founders" would then sell lots to other speculators. Deeds for town properties sold and resold at increasingly exorbitant prices as the end of the tracks approached. Their pockets stuffed with coin, the claimants could exercise their option—written into the Homestead Act—to pay the government $1.25 per acre rather than wait five years for their title. The price of lots rose as the railroad came within a day's ride. It rose again as the dust of the scrapers on the rail bed hung like a dull cloud on the horizon. It crashed when, as almost always happened, the rails passed the town by.[33]

Ignoring the risks, Cody and Rose took this ambitious route. Using Rose's teams to grade the site of the new town, they laid out a grid of streets. They offered free lots to anyone who would build on them, although they reserved the corner lots and some other choice locations for themselves. Before long, the town consisted of thirty houses, some stores and saloons, "and one good hotel." The young men thought they were rich.[34] Cody himself opened a store in a wood frame building with a tent roof. To Louisa, he wrote that he had a home, and that he was worth $250,000. In less than two years on the Plains, Cody seemed to have recaptured his middle-class standing, and to have met Louisa's demand that he become a businessman. Soon after, he met his wife and baby girl at the end of the track, and the little family became Romans.[35]

Louisa appears not to have realized that his wealth was paper. Since the town's businesses had yet to attract settlers willing to pay money for land or services, Cody continued his other, less esteemed employments. Most of his income came from hunting buffalo for Goddard Brothers, contractors who supplied meat to the gangs of Irish railroad workers along the UPED. For bringing in twelve buffalo per day, he received $500 a month, a sizable sum. In addition, he had his whiskey-selling enterprise (at least until the officers seized his supply).[36] It was a bold—some might say foolish—leap for a buffalo hunter and whiskey runner to make a grab at founding a town. Nonetheless, Cody wove these divergent business ventures into one another, using the profits from one to underwrite the others.

William Cody's Rome was built in a few days. It collapsed even faster. The railroad sent William Webb, their division agent, ahead of the rails to select the next town site. Many years later, Cody recalled that when Webb arrived in Rome, "I thought I was going to sell him quite a number of lots from the way he was looking the town over." When Cody announced he was off to hunt buffalo, Webb "expressed a desire that he would like to kill a buffalo himself." Cody took him along, and Webb indeed shot a buffalo. The railroad agent "was so delighted and seemed so happy over the killing [of] a buffalo that I thought I would sell him a block when I got back that night."[37]

But Webb was not interested in buying any lots. Instead, he proposed to make a railroad stop in the town, for a heavy price. The next morning, as Cody prepared to go hunting again, Webb "came up to me and he offered me one-twelfth interest in my own town. I thought he had gone daft and I rode off and left him."

Cody was gone for three or four days. On his return, "when I came within sight of where the town of Rome had been when I left there, I discovered that most of the houses had pulled away or gone some place or a cyclone had struck the town, and something was the matter." He could "see people pulling down the houses and I could see a string of teams moving lumber and everything away from the town." Webb had designated a new town, to be called Hays City, several miles to the east. The railroad stop would be there. With lumber and building supplies scarce and expensive, settlers were removing all they could carry and carting it to the new settlement.

Louisa looked "rather blue," Cody recalled. "Where's the $250,000 that you are worth?" she asked. "Well, I told her that I expected it had gone off with the town, that I was busted." Years after, Cody likened Webb to a barbarian: "That little fellow made Rome howl."

William Cody and his family soon followed Rome's other settlers, pulling down their buildings, carting the expensive lumber over to Hays, and rebuilding. For a few weeks he and Louisa again tried to run a hotel in Hays. But his diminished prospects only made their quarrels worse. By fall of 1867, she had taken the baby and gone. This time, she did not go to Leavenworth. She moved back to St. Louis, and into her parents' house.[38]

Rome joined the burgeoning ranks of Kansas ghost towns, which included a Monticello, a Paris, and a Berlin, whose names reflected the grandiose visions of their would-be founders.[39] As Cody watched his little family recede into the distance, he had lost not only his town, but the flesh and blood of his settler's cabin.

BUFFALO BILL'S WILD WEST show would position Cody as the quintessential frontiersman who had "passed through every stage of frontier life." The notion that the frontier developed in "stages" was never more explicit than in the show's first indoor appearance, in 1886. During the summer, Cody and his managing partner, Nate Salsbury, hired Steele Mackaye, a renowned New York dramatist, as stage director for the Madison Square Garden appearances, and charged him with designing an indoor presentation. Mackaye billed it as "A History of American Civilization." He organized it into a series of epochs, each more advanced than the last. The "First Epoch" was "The Primeval Forest." It was followed by "Second Epoch. The Prairie," "Third Epoch. The Cattle Ranch," and finally, "Fourth Epoch. The Mining Camp," during which Cody's stage town blew away.[40]

According to Steele Mackaye's son, Percy, the Wild West show was a formless extravaganza before the great playwright got his hands on it, "the performances, though delightfully fresh and vibrant, were still very sketchy and disjointed, wholly lacking in dramatic form." To address this deficiency, Steele Mackaye invented the separate "epochs" and their sequence. The passage of the frontier to ever higher stages of civilization presaged the most famous theory of western development, put forward in the historian Frederick Jackson Turner's 1893 essay, "The Significance of the Frontier in American History." In a paper delivered to a gathering of historians at the World's Columbian Exposition in Chicago (while Buffalo Bill's Wild West appeared nearby), Turner argued that Americans passed through stages of social evolution on the frontier, from hunter, to herder, to farmer, and then to urban industry and commerce.[41] Although the details of Mackaye's "epochs" differed somewhat from Turner's stages, they were in remarkable concordance. Percy Mackaye was convinced that such sophisticated ideas could not have occurred to William Cody, rustic frontiersman that he was. Writing in 1927, he declared, "The outstanding dramatic ideas embodied" in Buffalo Bill's Wild West "were Steele Mackaye's ideas."[42]

The notion that any grand theories of progress embedded in the Wild West show originated with well-read publicists, not the Wild West showman, echoes through many Cody biographies. But, in fact, settlers usually perceived events on the Great Plains as expressions of stages in the advancement of civilization, to which their own lives were more or less tied. In this respect, Cody's hunting and town-building each had a symbolic importance, and were not separate occupations so much as the beginning and ending of a single story. In 1886, Mackaye's ideas on the subject of stages of development (to say nothing of Turner's in 1893) were only recent derivatives of very old and widely popular political thought. For at least a century, philosophers and popular writers in Europe and America had theorized that all societies advanced through stages of subsistence, and usually these included at least four: hunting, pastoralism, agriculture, and commerce, the last being characterized by peaceful towns and cities. Each stage was a necessary step, and it prepared the ground for the stage that followed. Frontiersmen who stalked wild game represented the first chapter in a progressive narrative of history yet to unfold. Clearing the land of wild animals was a precursor to abundant farm fields and the rise of towns. Hunting was the beginning of the story of civilization.[43]

Such theories had special resonance in the West because they corresponded—or seemed to correspond—to the visible world. In the minds of a great many travelers and commentators, the trail from frontier to metropole led through all phases of civilization. Thomas Jefferson opined that a traveler journeying from the Rocky Mountains to the East Coast would discover, in successive stages, Indian hunters with "no law but that of nature," then Indians who were "in the pastoral state, raising domestic animals, to supply the defects of hunting." Continuing eastward, the traveler would come upon "semi-barbarous citizens" of the United States, followed by "gradual shades of improving man until he would reach his most . . . improved state, in our seaport towns." Such a journey, Jefferson concluded, "is equivalent to a survey, in time, of the progress of man from the infancy of creation to the present day."[44] Numerous other writers agreed. To travel from frontier to town was to journey through time, along the road of progress.

To live between frontier and town, and to bring about the creation of settlements on the Plains, was to partake of progress, to make history. The Codys did not spend long evenings poring over Jefferson or other four-stages theorists. But they were highly attuned to the need for land clearing as a prelude to settlement. The prosperity of the settled East, and indeed of Louisa's own Missouri, had been wrought from wilderness only through the eradication of wildlife and the felling of forests. Partly for this reason, Plains settlers routinely shot every living animal that was not privately owned, training their guns not only on marketable buffalo, elk, and deer, or on vermin wolves and hawks, but also on inedible and unsalable jackrabbits, badgers, porcupines, sparrows, and chickadees.[45] By the 1860s, in popular accounts of every locality, Americans narrated their history as progress through wildlife destruction, the westward march of civilization marked by elimination of game.[46]

In this connection, market hunting was a central feature of the popular ideology of progress. By converting bison to cash, buffalo hunters simultaneously made a civilized commodity out of savage nature, took bison from Indians, and cleared the grassland for domesticated livestock and the next stage of civilization. The ascendance of pastoralism was unmistakable in the vast herds of Texas cattle lowing their way to Kansas railroad depots. Cattle would eventually give way to crops. Homesteaders were already staking out farms along the railway. Surveyors predicted that Kansas would soon become "the great wheat-producing region of the world."[47] As a market hunter, Cody's work assumed mythic proportions as a nearly ritual passage for his society.

From the fall of 1867 through most of 1868, Cody hunted buffalo.[48] He was well-known as "Buffalo Bill" by this time, and the *Hays City Advance* mentioned his hunting exploits occasionally, such as the day in January 1868 when he brought in the carcasses of nineteen animals. Selling the meat at seven cents per pound, he earned $100 per day.[49] He also continued to hunt buffalo for Goddard Bros. until the railroad reached Sheridan.

Killing buffalo and marketing them were some of the most familiar practices in the entire country. Indians had been hunting buffalo, and trading robes, meat, jerky, and other goods to one another, for nine thousand years. Among Americans, there had been a sizable market for buffalo tongues and robes since the 1840s, when Indian hunters brought these commodities to trading posts, from which they were shipped down the Mississippi River to St. Louis and New Orleans. In 1850 alone, some 100,000 buffalo robes passed through St. Louis.[50]

Before the Civil War, rot and insect infestation kept many robes from reaching more distant consumers. But the extension of the railroad onto the prairies of Nebraska, Kansas, and Texas made it possible to bring smoked buffalo tongues and robes to eastern markets with less fear of spoilage, ushering in a revolution which would destroy the last of the great herds, and most of the Indian social customs and traditions which had grown up around them. In the cities and towns of the United States, consumers bundled themselves into buffalo coats and covered their laps with woolly buffalo robes as they set out by sleigh or wagon in frosty winters. The prices for meat and robes in the cities were augmented by the new markets at the army forts and in towns like Hays (and the more ephemeral ones, like Rome) that were rising rapidly across the Plains. Later, in the early 1870s, tanneries would perfect a method for turning buffalo skins into quality leather, touching off the last great surge of bison hunting. But until then, bison hides were only useful when they came from winter coats.[51] For this reason, Cody's market hunting was particularly intensive during the cold months.

In the Wild West show, Cody reenacted a buffalo hunt that featured himself with several cowboys and Indians, all on horseback, firing blank cartridges at a small herd of buffalo wheeling around the arena. There are no eyewitness accounts of Cody's market hunting, but our knowledge of the industry suggests his hunting trips differed considerably from this scene. For one thing, hunting required a support staff of nonhunters, including skinners and butchers. When he was a meat hunter for the UPED, Cody took along a butcher, who drove a wagon to carry the meat. He likely shared the proceeds with a small camp staff throughout his market hunting forays in the late 1860s.[52]

But more significantly, market hunters rarely, if ever, hunted on horseback. It was hard to aim from a moving horse, and other factors made it pointless to try. Buffalo have a superb sense of smell. They have difficulty seeing people on foot, but no trouble seeing horses. Their sense of hearing is acute. A man on horseback was too prominent to get near a herd without the animals thundering into the distance. For this reason, Indian hunters on horseback attacked herds from all sides simultaneously.

Bison herd defenses had several holes, though, which market hunters exploited. The sharp sound of a rifle did not signify a threat unless it was accompanied by the cry of another bison in pain or distress. So most market hunters hid from their quarry by approaching from downwind, then sitting or lying prone. Aiming a large-caliber rifle, sometimes mounted on a tripod for accuracy, they gunned first for the lead cow, the dominant animal in the herd. If their marksmanship was good, the bullet shredded the animal's heart, and she dropped to the ground without making a sound. The herd stayed put or, if another cow moved out to lead the herd, the hunter then killed her. In a short time, the animals would be confused. They stood still, or milled around. The hunter could fire away until the herd moved out of range, which might not be until most of them were dead.[53]

Felling buffalo after buffalo in this way was called a "stand." Most American market hunters were young men, and most of them probably ventured onto the buffalo grounds for brief stints in the fall, during the seasonal lull in farm or ranch work. Their marksmanship was usually inadequate to effect a stand, and the herds were wary enough that the hunters had great difficulty getting close enough to make a kill. After two or three weeks, they might return with only a dozen hides, or less.[54]

Still, in the many Great Plains stands of the late 1860s, sizable parts of herds vanished in the space of hours. Legendary market hunters were known to kill upward of eighty animals in a single day, sitting in one spot. But skinners could process only so many animals before the carcasses spoiled, so most killed no more than thirty. In any case, when the shooting was done, the butchers took over. Cody's butcher removed the back legs and hump. Some took the tongue. Since Cody did a good deal of hunting in the winter of 1867–68, we may presume that he and his butcher also took skins to sell for robes. Once the wagon was full or the quota was met, they returned to camp, leaving the carrion to rot or be eaten by scavengers.[55]

Like that of his fellow market hunters, Cody's buffalo hunting was oriented more toward volume than style, and he likely hunted the animals on foot. His favorite gun for buffalo hunting was a reconditioned .50-caliber rifle that could kill a buffalo at six hundred yards, a Springfield "needle gun" (so named because its new technology of the firing pin reminded early shooters of a needle). Market hunters preferred the gun for its accuracy and its heavy ball, which could render a wounded bison incapable of charging, something hunters on foot had reason to be concerned about.[56] Cody himself calculated that he killed 4,280 buffalo in his eighteen months as a market hunter. Figuring that he had a total of 360 working days in this period, he would have needed to kill fewer than twelve buffalo a day to reach that number. If anything, his total is likely low. Later hide hunters, in the early 1870s, would kill as many in a couple of months.[57]

Modern Americans rarely honor these buffalo hunters, who are commonly remembered as greedy, lowbrow, filthy, and stupid (nowhere more so than in Larry McMurtry's novel *Anything for Billy*, where gangs of drooling hide hunters populate the town of Greasy Corners, New Mexico).[58] But in 1867, market hunters were somewhat respected. They cleared the land for farmers, and, like fur trappers before them, buffalo hunters were expectant capitalists. They risked their own guns, ammunition, wagons, and other gear—to say nothing of wagering their lives against Indian attack—in anticipation of profit. In many places, they bought their supplies on credit from meat-and-hide dealers in nearby towns, in hopes that their success would allow them to pay off the loan and have something left over. From the ranks of buffalo hunters would come any number of town founders, bankers, and other respectable businessmen. When the *Hays City Advance* hailed William Cody's market hunting, it reflected a regional and national approbation of hunters as small businessmen.[59]

And yet, Louisa lost faith. Even if buffalo hunting retained some respectability as a suitable pursuit for a young man, William Cody's fall from town founder to simple buffalo hunter left his wife unhappy. She "made little of my efforts to succeed in life," William Cody remembered long after. She said "that I was a failure and something like that; and we had our little disagreements again. When everything was going all right and I was selling lots of [town] lots," in Rome, "we seemed to get along pretty well; but when things were different and I wasn't getting along very well, things were the other way and we could not get along so well."[60]

In public, Louisa never admitted to any unhappiness in this early period of their marriage. But something caused her to leave. If the couple's personal, intimate conflicts are beyond our knowledge, it seems likely that at least some of her discontent stemmed from her husband's occupation. Frontier hunters played a role in the drama of civilization, but there was a profound difference between men who hunted to create the institutions of civilization—farms, schools, churches, businesses, and towns—and those who hunted to the exclusion of other work. The former were upwardly mobile, their hunting a phase of life which passed with the frontier itself, leaving them established and settled as farmers, merchants, or other businessmen. Traditionally, the latter were low-class, borderline renegades. To Hector St. John de Crèvecoeur, such men "appear to be no better than carnivorous animals of a superior rank, living on the flesh of wild animals, when they can catch them." The temptations of wilderness indolence overwhelmed their better natures. "Once hunters," he warned, "farewell to the plow. The chase renders them ferocious, gloomy, and unsociable."[61]

Similar views appeared in the writings of James Fenimore Cooper and a host of other frontier observers. In this sense, Cody did not simply move into another line of work when he lost his town and turned to buffalo hunting. He slipped backward along the path of civilization. He was no longer a town builder. At best, he was merely a clearer of land for other town builders. All of the respectability that attached to buffalo hunting depended upon its being a *temporary* pursuit. But Cody seemed uninterested in the more permanent occupations he might have taken up. He seems to have abhorred the thought of farming. He claimed no homestead.

Of course, in reality, Cody was not going back in time. For all the rhetoric of civilization's beginnings among primitive hunters who blazed a path for herdsmen and farmers, buffalo hunters were modern men who relied on the railroad, as well as a host of industrial products, including guns and knives. Cody did not subsist on the meat he shot. He lived on his pay from Goddard Brothers, which, at $500 per month, was the largest salary he earned in the 1860s. This would not have been possible without the presence of a corporate sponsor, in this case the UPED. The subsequent careers of Cody's cohorts in the killing fields of the Great Plains may have been less colorful than his, but they were just as modern. Carl Hendricks left Sweden for Kansas in 1870. There he hunted buffalo for a year, then moved on to take up work in a New England steel-wire mill.[62] Bat Masterson was a market hunter in Kansas, gunning for buffalo only a few years after Cody. He became most famous for his career as a gunfighter and lawman, but eventually moved into industrialized publishing. He was a New York sportswriter when he died.[63] Wyatt Earp and Bill Tilghman became legends of frontier law enforcement. Both began as buffalo hunters and ended up in filmmaking, where they sought to mythologize their lives after the example of Buffalo Bill.[64]

But even in its most modern context, the respectability of buffalo hunting was always tenuous. To see white hunters decimating the great herds reassured most Americans about the forward march of progress. But progress seemed so necessary in part because just beneath the surface lay a more complicated and sometimes frightening possibility. Buffalo hunting required absence from the domesticating influence of home, an institution which was disturbingly ephemeral on the frontier anyway. The passions of lonely men, without the restraining and civilizing influence of women, could find unseemly and dangerous outlets on the open prairie. Through the first half of the nineteenth century, American fur trappers (who assumed the same mythic place as initiators of civilization that other hunters did) frequently married into Indian families. Their reasons were as complex as can be imagined, ranging from romantic love and desire for companionship, to ambition for political alliances with powerful Indian families—to say nothing of the help with the processing of furs which Indian women provided.

Most buffalo hunters saw the occupation as strictly seasonal, and temporary, something to be pursued during the down season on the farm or ranch or when other money was not forthcoming. But the more committed followed the example of earlier trappers. Indeed, some were former beaver trappers who moved into the buffalo robe trade as it supplanted the beaver pelt traffic in the 1850s.[65] In Kansas, hunters like Ben Clark and Abner "Sharp" Grover were married to Indian women. Their mixed-race unions placed them outside the bounds of middle-class respectability in the more established settlements, as people with dubious intentions and as race traitors. In fact, throughout the history of the American frontier, such unions predominated only until the arrival of "respectable" white women in sufficient numbers to furnish marriage partners for white men. In other words, the arrival of middle-class white women like Louisa Cody rendered these earlier mixed-race families—and their devotion to market hunting—an anachronism.[66]

Settlers were all too aware that most Plains hunters *were* Indians, and white men who were committed to hunting as an escape from civilization were suspiciously close to them in geography and lifestyle. Indian hunters were the nation's major source of buffalo robes. Particularly at the trading posts on the upper Missouri, but extending well to the south, Indians traded robes for guns and other goods. Sioux, Cheyenne, Osage, Kaw, Comanche, and other Indians supplied the vast majority of the 200,000 robes brought to American trading posts on the Missouri River in 1870.[67]

Americans welcomed bison eradication in part because if the animals did not vanish, then neither would the Indians. In the 1830s, Washington Irving and other commentators warned about the temptations of the hunt for white men, speculating that the Great Plains, then known as the Great

American Desert, would become a kind of American Mongolia, populated only by nomadic, miscegenated herdsmen and hunters, "a great company and a mighty host, all riding upon horses, and warring upon those nations which were at rest, and dwelt peaceably, and had gotten cattle and goods."[68] The idea of a continuing, lucrative Indian trade disturbed Americans with thoughts of ever more white men and boys drawn into the multiracial hunting grounds, tempted away from farm fields, from the influence of home and civilization, by the chase and by Indian women.

Whether these deep cultural anxieties increased the tensions between William and Louisa Cody is impossible to say. But if her concerns stemmed from the multiracial character or transient qualities of buffalo hunting, she likely felt vindicated when this, her husband's most symbolically primitive occupation, failed. When the Kansas Pacific reached Sheridan, Kansas, in May 1868, its corporate coffers were empty. Construction ceased. Goddard Brothers lost their provisioning contract, and Buffalo Bill Cody lost his salary.

In June, at a personal "end of the tracks," he asked Louisa to see him at Leavenworth. She brought baby Arta up from St. Louis. There the couple had a terrible row, so bad that William Cody later recalled, "I didn't think that we would ever have another meeting; we had kind o' mutually agreed that we were not suited to each other; she was as glad to go back to her home as I was to go to the plains."[69] Advancing civilization was no easy task. Cody had lost his home, his family, his town.

But there were other opportunities. Upon his return to Hays, Cody turned his eyes from railroad contracts—grading and buffalo hunting—to military contracting. Army provisioning was a principal source of income for ambitious settlers in Kansas. Isaac Cody himself had contracted to sell hay to the army fort at Leavenworth. Across the West, the army hired civilians to serve as guides, teamsters, and blacksmiths, and in various other capacities.[70]

Among this latter group of civilian hires were temporary "detectives," deputy lawmen whom officers appointed to track down and apprehend deserters and stock thieves whom regular army soldiers were unable to catch. Cody had already attempted to make a business in selling liquor to troops, only to have his goods seized by officers. In March 1868, officers at Fort Hays appointed the well-regarded hunter William Cody to the position of detective after several soldiers stole some army mules and deserted from Fort Hays. The officers who appointed him could not have known how inspired a choice they had made, but Cody did. Who better to catch horse thieves than an experienced horse thief?

This small, obscure job assumes an important place in Cody's story, less for what he accomplished than for the company he kept. On this and on one subsequent detective assignment, Cody rode alongside the deputy U.S. marshal from nearby Junction City. Not much happened on the trail. The two low-ranking lawmen apprehended the deserters and delivered them to authorities later that month.[71]

But as Cody made his way from frontier Kansas to worldwide stardom, the curious, looming figure of that deputy marshal straddled his path. A tall man with a wide hat and two pearl-handled navy revolvers, standing half in shadow, projecting both promise and menace, he was already something of a myth. His name was James Butler Hickok. But he was better known to his friends, and to his many enemies, as Wild Bill.

CHAPTER FOUR

With the Prince of Pistoleers

W ILD WEST SHOW fans knew from show publicity that William Cody rode the western trails with Wild Bill Hickok. Indeed, the friendship of the two men was well-known even before Cody published his autobiography in 1879. The first dime novel featuring Buffalo Bill appeared in 1869, and it presented him as the best friend of "Wild Bill Hitchcock."[1] The two men actually appeared onstage together for one season, in 1873 and '74, performing in a melodrama about rescuing white women from Indians. Some of the generation that brought their children to Buffalo Bill's Wild West in the 1880s and '90s, and some of the show's employees, too, had seen Cody and Hickok together on the stage back in the early '70s. At least they thought they had. Sometimes they saw Cody alone, or with somebody who looked vaguely like Hickok. Cody's theatrical publicity so assiduously played up his connections with Hickok, and so many dime novels placed them together as brothers in arms, that some recalled seeing the two men together, even when Cody appeared without him.[2]

In fact, Cody forged such a strong public memory of his friendship with Wild Bill, and assumed so many of the lawman's symbolic attributes, that the two are often confused down to the present day. In his autobiography, he claimed that he first met Wild Bill Hickok on that expedition to Utah, when a rough teamster struck the boy and "a tall, handsome, magnificently built and powerful young" Hickok thrashed the bully.[3] He said he rode with Hickok against the Sioux as early as 1861, in retaliation for a raid on the stage line. According to Cody, they met again during the Civil War, when Cody served as a spy, just like Wild Bill, and carried secret dispatches from Hickok to his Union superiors. By the time Cody wrote his autobiography, a thrilling tale of Hickok's 1865 escape from Confederate forces had been in print for over a decade. Into his life story, Cody inserted his own, mostly plagiarized version of the event, in which Hickok galloped across a field of imminent battle under a hail of southern bullets to rejoin his Union comrades, with Cody cheering from the sidelines.[4]

All of these tales were fiction. Cody was not on the Utah Expedition, and neither was Hickok. Neither of them was fighting the Sioux in 1861. That year, Hickok became a teamster in the Civil War, and although he did become a spy, Cody did not. Neither was Cody at the battle where Hickok was alleged to have escaped the Confederates.

But Cody continued to link the lives of Buffalo Bill and Wild Bill long after 1879. Others soon helped in his cause. In 1882, one effusive historian recounted the supposed adventures of the two Bills during Lieutenant Colonel George Custer's attack on a Cheyenne village at the Washita River in 1868. "The two daring and intrepid scouts plunged furiously into the midst of the Indians, each with a revolver in either hand, and literally carved their way through the surging mass of redskins, leaving a furrow of dead Indians in their wake." The battle of the Washita was a genuine Custer fight, but neither Hickok nor Cody was there. That did not stop Cody from reprinting the account in Wild West show programs as if it were real, where his audiences could savor the mutually reinforcing heroism of the two Bills under a headline that read "Cody Saves Wild Bill."[5] Other than Cody himself, no figure bulks so large in Cody's own life story as Wild Bill Hickok. None commands our attention as much. The fact that almost all of Cody's Wild Bill stories were fictional makes his energetic recounting of them all the more intriguing. Why work so hard to hitch his wagon to Hickok's star?

Perhaps the most surprising fact is that William Cody's association with Wild Bill Hickok did go back to his boyhood days, before the Civil War. Moreover, Wild Bill's persistent reappearance in Buffalo Bill's childhood stories hints at the roots of Cody's show business imagination. Of all the figures who fired William Cody's ambition to fulfill (or to *seem* to fulfill) popular frontier fantasies, none was greater than Hickok. In the end, none provided a more cautionary tale of the pitfalls awaiting even the most successful. By March 1868, when Cody and Hickok rode out of Hays on the trail of eleven army deserters, Hickok's life was already a show in progress. For Cody, who had grown up admiring Hickok, and who knew him long before he was famous, the passage of his companion from plainsman to culture hero was a subject for some study. Understanding how William Cody became the world-famous Buffalo Bill requires us to examine it, too.

———

BORN TO A FARMING family in Homer, Illinois, in 1837, James Butler Hickok moved to eastern Kansas to claim his own farm in 1856. He was soon swept up in the same violence that engulfed the Cody family. Like them, he joined the Free State cause. For reasons that are unclear, friends took to calling him Wild Bill. He had an early reputation for fearlessness, and quickly became a bodyguard for the radical Free State leader Jim Lane.[6]

Given the close circles of anti-slavery men who congregated in eastern Kansas, it is hard to believe that he did not meet Isaac Cody. When young Will Cody rode into Grasshopper Falls with a note warning his father of a plot to kill him, he found Isaac was with Jim Lane's militia. Hickok might well have been there, too. In any case, Julia Cody recalled that Hickok was a visitor in the Cody home shortly after Isaac died, in 1858 or '59, when Will Cody was only twelve.[7]

Perhaps the boy looked upon him as a hero, a replacement for the father and the older brother he had lost. Hickok was almost a decade older than Cody. He was over six feet tall, with broad shoulders, a narrow waist, and a somber, brooding face. For most of his adult life, he wore his reddish brown hair in ringlets, cascading to his shoulders. Generally, his demeanor was quiet and unobtrusive, but his reputation became entangled with violent episodes which were legendary—or notorious—throughout the region. He became a teamster in the later 1850s, then a stable hand for the Pony Express in Nebraska in 1861. There he was embroiled in a local feud that ended with the killings of three men at Rock Creek Station. He began the Civil War as a teamster, but eventually became a spy for the Union. After Lee's surrender in 1865, he returned to Kansas. He was an excellent tracker, and soon became a government detective at Fort Riley. He was so successful at returning deserters and stolen mules that in short order he became deputy U.S. marshal in Junction City, a job in which he mainly continued searching for stolen government livestock. By 1866, he was scouting for the army and hiring himself out as guide to parties of tourists. In 1867, he guided General Winfield Scott Hancock and Lieutenant Colonel George Custer in pursuit of the Cheyenne. His fearless reputation and his facility with guns and fists earned him respect in powerful places. In 1869 he was sheriff in Hays; in 1871, marshal of Abilene.[8]

By this time, his exploits in law enforcement only added to his already considerable fame. In fact, his elevation to lawman in Abilene was partly a result of wide press coverage, which launched Hickok to national prominence in 1867. It was the same winter that the twenty-one-year-old Cody huddled for warmth in his dugout near Fort Hays, casting here and there for ways of earning the money and status that would reunite his family. In the summer he would be grading track and founding a town. One wonders how long it took him to lay his hands on a copy of the February *Harper's New Monthly Magazine*. Likely not long. Army officers frequently subscribed, and this issue contained an article that was the talk of Kansas.

That month, the self-proclaimed "Journal of Civilization" published an alleged biography of Cody's old friend Hickok. Until now, Hickok had been locally renowned as an always colorful, sometimes gregarious, hard-drinking teamster, trail guide, hunter, and sometime lawman. Suddenly, he was a popular culture icon.

Harper's correspondent George Ward Nichols reported meeting Hickok in Springfield, Missouri. Nichols reported that Hickok had been a Union spy who had escaped death by the narrowest of margins, and now stood out as an energetic white man on a sleepy, backward frontier, where "the most marked characteristic of the inhabitants seemed to be an indisposition to move, and their highest ambition to let their hair and beards grow."[9] In his frequent frontier duels, Nichols's Hickok outdrew and outshot his villainous opponents every time. The writer described Wild Bill shooting from an open window, the plainsman placing six bullets into the center of an "O" the size of a man's heart on a sign fifty yards distant, in "an off-hand way, and without sighting the pistol with his eye." His mastery of animals balanced the technological wizardry of his gunplay. Nell, his black mare, answered to his whistle, dropped to the ground or galloped away at his hand signal, and, at Hickok's command, leapt onto a billiard table in the local saloon. "When she got down from the table," wrote Nichols, "Bill sprang upon her back, dashed through the high wide doorway, and at a single bound cleared the flight of steps and landed in the middle of the street."[10]

Thus Nichols wove the life of the real borderman into a pithy dime novel plot and strung it with the ornaments of popular fantasy, cautioning all the while that he believed every word of what he wrote. It made Hickok famous. *Harper's Monthly* was no pulp magazine. Its readership was solidly middle and upper class, its circulation among the broadest in the nation.[11]

Just as *Harper's Monthly* told Hickok's life like a dime novel, publishers quickly inscribed his ostensibly real adventures back into fiction. Within months of the first Hickok article, publisher Robert M. De Witt released two dime novels about Hickok's alleged exploits.[12] Readers East and West encountered Hickok in these volumes. Even remote settlers ordered De Witt novels through the mail.[13]

In part, Hickok owed his spectacular rise to the ongoing American longing for frontier heroes. Daniel Boone, Davy Crockett, Mike Fink, and Kit Carson were all popularly imagined to be in command of nature, at ease with technology, capable of great violence, but peaceful at heart. In his fanciful rendering of Hickok's life, George Ward Nichols was resurrecting a literary and historical type, the frontiersman, for a post–Civil War readership.

And yet there was something peculiar about Hickok's celebrity. He was not just a border hero, but a figure of popular entertainment. In this sense, he was a vital transition figure between older frontier heroes, backcountry residents who became renowned nationally, and Buffalo Bill, who eventually played to a much wider audience than any of his frontier predecessors.

Unlike any earlier border figure, the railroad made Hickok accessible to at least some portion of the larger public. Perhaps it is not surprising that, after reading of him in dime novels, newspapers, and magazines, many western travelers sought him out. In 1868, a party of railroad tourists met Hickok in Hays, Kansas, and peppered him with questions about the condition of the country. We might imagine these greenhorns to have been awestruck and slack-jawed in the presence of the "real" Hickok. Perhaps some were. But the fact remains that the only tourist who recorded the meeting was at least as amused as he was impressed. The *Harper's Monthly* biography, he winked, was "a romantic but not o'er true history" of Wild Bill.[14]

Indeed, tourists and others often questioned the truthfulness of Hickok's press coverage. Western newspapers not only reported Hickok's exploits, or rumors of them, but also provided a venue for questioning their veracity, and the Hickok treatment in *Harper's Monthly* was the subject of considerable commentary in newspapers and towns across Kansas and Missouri.[15] "James B. Hickok . . . *is* a remarkable man, and is as well known here as Horace Greeley in New York," wrote one Springfield, Missouri, editor. "But Nichols 'cuts it very fat' when he describes Bill's feats in arms."[16]

More than any of his mythic predecessors, Hickok was a beacon for the public because of his relevance to the ongoing debate over how to discern truth in the age of the popular press, the instrument through which most people learned of Hickok and the Far West he inhabited. In a sense, evaluating the gap between Hickok and his press reputation was a kind of game, in which tourists, frontier locals, and Hickok himself readily joined. Since frontier newspapers had wide circulation in more settled regions, where subscriptions flourished among prospective emigrants and speculators, even small local notices of Hickok's doings found a large audience of readers. Wild Bill was many things—spy, scout, Indian fighter, lawman—but he was also an entertainer who purposely worked up his reputation for popular evaluation and enjoyment. As he remarked at the end of the *Harper's Monthly* article, "I'm sort of public property."[17]

Later admirers saw Hickok as a man who abhorred publicity. In truth, he pursued it so avidly that contemporaries joked that his real aspiration was to become a newspaper editor.[18] His stories dazzled George Ward Nichols, author of the article in *Harper's,* as early as 1865. In 1867, he failed to impress the artist and writer Theodore R. Davis (who thought Hickok a blowhard). "Seeing he was not welcome," wrote Davis, the "scout's stay was short." Hickok blustered as he strode away, "Ther's another dodgasted sardine of a newspaper cuss bunken in the sutlers shack what wants my wind, I see you don't!" That "dodgasted sardine of a newspaper cuss" was none other than Henry Morton Stanley (soon to become world famous for "finding" Dr. David Livingstone in Africa, in 1872). Stanley rewarded Hickok's efforts, penning another cloying sketch—"one of the finest examples of that peculiar class known as frontiersman, ranger, hunter, and Indian scout"—for the *St. Louis Missouri Democrat*.[19]

Hickok's aims in this ongoing performance are not entirely clear, but in his early days it enhanced his prospects in law enforcement. He won election to constable of Monticello township, in Kansas, as early as 1858.[20] He was running for sheriff in Springfield when he met George Ward Nichols (he lost), and won his position in Hays after Nichols's article appeared.[21] His press reputation had everything to do with his appointment as marshal in Abilene, where the town's founders sought to present an image of hard-nosed law enforcement to attract the best class of investors.[22] Press publicity was an asset, too, among the military officers who appointed Hickok a scout. New to the country and fighting enemies they little understood, at least some in the army command were pleased to have an acknowledged hero (or, at least, an alleged one) marking their path.

Because tourists often included writers, and because many of them were often prospective settlers, and potential local voters, Hickok complemented his cultivation of the press with an equally vigorous development of himself as a tourist attraction. Most of his encounters with travelers went unrecorded. But in surviving fragments we glimpse his ongoing public performance, a kind of one-man show of a life in progress, and we gain a sense of its allure for his audiences, among them the canny Will Cody.

Along with all their other baggage, tourists, speculators, and potential settlers inevitably carried notions of frontier heroes absorbed from stage plays, the popular press, and the novels of James Fenimore Cooper. Whether or not they believed that buckskin-clad hunters like Hawkeye and Daniel Boone were still to be found on the frontier, Hickok was adept at imitating these frontiersmen of fantasy, adding enough local and contemporary elements to create a convincing imposture, assuming a life story that was part genuine, part invention.[23]

The pose was alluring in part because his stitching of fiction to fact was so close. Hickok not only knew the Plains and its many human and animal denizens, he looked and sounded so much like popular fantasies of someone who did that it was almost eerie. At the same time, he was eager to put it on display. As the railway extended into western Kansas, Hickok routinely stood at the platform awaiting railroad touring parties. It was not a coincidence that correspondents wrote, upon arriving in Hays, "The first man we saw was 'Wild Bill.'"[24]

His masterful pose, combined with his genuine skills as tracker, marksman, hunting guide, and storyteller, made him a subject of tourist speculation and debate when he was but a local figure, before the article in *Harper's Monthly* ever appeared. "He is a picture," wrote a tourist in 1866, "the most

striking object in camp. Six feet, lithe, active, sinewy, daring rider, dead shot
with pistol and rifle, long locks, fine features and mustache, buckskin leg-
gins, red shirt, broad-brimmed hat, two pistols in belt, rifle in hand . . ."
The tourist went on to describe Hickok's fireside autobiography: "Has lived
since he was eleven on the prairies; when a boy, rode Pony Express on the
California route, and during the war was scout and spy. He goes by the name
of Wild Bill, and tells wonderful stories of his horsemanship, fighting and
hair-breadth escapes." Having reprised Hickok's life in this way, the tourist
then inserted his own amused and skeptical review. Wonderful as the
guide's stories were, "we do not, however, feel under any obligation to
believe them all."[25]

Such cautious appraisal of Hickok's imposture proliferated as his reputation grew. In the many press accounts of Wild Bill's fistfights, gunfights,

"The most striking object in camp"—Wild Bill Hickok, c. 1869.
Courtesy Buffalo Bill Historical Center.

hunting exploits, Indian battles, and feuds, there are two persistent features. The first is Wild Bill himself. The second is the author's advice about which parts of these tales are credible and which are not. To read these accounts is to realize that the most enjoyable thing about meeting Wild Bill was not the encounter with an unimpeachably "real" hero but the parsing of truth and fiction in his legend. Tourists and scribes fully expected Hickok to exaggerate his own accomplishments. He accepted money for his services as guide and lawman, but he did not seek direct financial gain from his fictions. Listeners thus received them less as fraud than as entertaining, playful jibes at tourists' half-secret desires for an encounter with an imagined frontier, and a means of providing them with a "real" frontier story to tell on their return. In turn, their audiences of friends and relatives back in St. Louis, Topeka, or Chicago could then debate Hickok's credibility for themselves.

Indeed, in its combination of authentic wonder and media hoax, Hickok's one-man show bore more than a passing resemblance to the era's most popular diversions. By the 1860s, certain forms of trickery had become legitimate entertainment. Nineteenth-century Americans were a people shaken by rapid urbanization and the ascendance of the cash market, which alienated ever more people from familiar networks of kin, community, and trade. The social revolutions brought on by city growth and industrialization spawned myriad questions and anxieties. Americans relocated from home districts to large cities, or to western outposts on the railroad, jostling one another and the millions of foreign immigrants who joined them. How could one tell good people from bad, honest from crooked, in a bustling, polyglot metropolis, or for that matter in a hustling frontier town, where most people were strangers, everyone claimed to be honest, and seemingly everything was for sale?

This last question raised a host of others, for recognizing shoddy goods in an age of mass production was a new and important challenge. The Industrial Revolution brought Americans face-to-face with a slew of manufactured products. Handcrafted products were each distinctive. Mass-produced goods were essentially copies of an "original" design. All were fronted by colorful advertisements making impossible promises for quality and durability. How could one know a good product from a poor one? Telling the difference between the self-made man and the man on the make, fair-made goods and poor imitations, became serious business.[26]

Entertainments intrigue us by their ability to heighten and then resolve our cultural anxieties. So Americans were drawn to attractions which encouraged them to utilize their own analytical razors in the separation of truth and fiction, reality and representation. Among the most popular were what historian James Cook has called "artful deceptions," tricks designed to entertain and even educate by providing the audience with space to dissect fakery, to probe the gaps between representation and real life. These included a host of popular attractions, including a machine that could play brilliant chess (a talented chess player actually hid inside), magicians who could make pocket watches and wallets disappear and then reappear (in a safe, mimetic performance of the pickpockets and confidence men who bedeviled city newcomers), and "trompe l'oeil" or "trick of the eye" paintings, which were so authentic that viewers, kept at a distance by rope barriers, debated for hours whether these were real paintings or merely real objects arranged and lit to resemble paintings.[27]

In 1868, the most famous of the artful deceivers was P. T. Barnum. Hickok never met him. But his entertainments so shaped the era that Hickok—and Cody—could not help but fall under their influence. Barnum called his entertainments "humbug," and they made him a fortune. Beginning in 1835, he attracted gigantic crowds, first with a traveling exhibition of Joice Heth, a Negro woman alleged to be the 161-year-old former nurse to George Washington. In 1842, he brought his "FeeJee Mermaid" to the public. A grotesquely contorted monkey's head and upper limbs sewn to the tail of a fish, the FeeJee Mermaid inspired vigorous audience banter and newspaper debate over how much Barnum's assertions of authenticity could be believed. He followed it with "What Is It?," alternatively called "The Nondescript." The What Is It? was really a black man in a hairy costume, but Barnum presented him as a possible "missing link" between humanity and the animal world. A wide array of visitors to the exhibit leapt into the debate over whether he was real or fake and what it meant either way.

In general, Barnum's exhibits succeeded less by gulling the masses than by inviting them to speculate on the truth and fiction of the displays. He regularly invented scientific testimony to "verify" his exhibits, which he published alongside fake letters from nonexistent experts denouncing his frauds, all to cultivate controversy and expand his audience. He even published a comprehensive account of his humbugs in his own autobiography to provide the wondering crowds with ammunition against him.[28]

Barnum's invitation to debate and argue, and his unwillingness to condescend, were keys to his popularity. He overtly trusted the reasoning powers of everyday Americans, and their ability to come to their own conclusions about his displays. Visitors flocked to his American Museum in New York. There, they debated and argued over where the truth left off and fraud began. They propounded theories about how a given hoax was executed. They left feeling empowered by their own talents at discernment. Uncovering Barnum's tricks was fundamentally a democratic experience. It made ordinary people feel like they were at least the equal of the journalists, scientists, and experts who foolishly endorsed the FeeJee Mermaid and other Barnum exhibits as real. It established them as competent to know the difference between reality and fakery, and therefore to succeed in the modern world, in public life, and in modern market capitalism.[29]

Today, Barnum's name is identified with falsehood, but his humbugs were more than lies. As Barnum and every other successful showman knew, a degree of truth was essential to the most successful deceptions. All of his hoaxes invited audiences to locate a deeper truth beneath the fake surface. In encouraging people to believe that there was a truth to be found, and that it was within their power to reveal it, Barnum's humbugs were essentially optimistic. If the world was a sediment of fakery, it yet rested on bedrock truths, accessible to the common man.[30]

Like Barnum, Hickok was fully aware of his audience's doubts and even cultivated them in certain ways. His pose as dime novel hero was a self-evident ruse, combining popular symbols of frontier identity (buckskin, guns, knife, hat, horse) with fictional adventures (the closest he came to riding for the Pony Express was tending the horses at Rock Creek Station). These he combined with his real biography, and real hunting and fighting skills, to guide tourists *and* entertain them.

Conditioned as we are to think of the nineteenth-century West as "real" and our memory of it as "myth," it is easy to overlook how much the Kansas of young William Cody's day presented observers with a tangled knot of perceptions and realities. If it seems surprising that Kansans like Hickok should be comfortable developing amusements that resonated with eastern cultural fascinations, we must keep in mind that the regional culture of the West was infused with at least as much anxiety about representation and reality as anyplace else in America. East and west, the expansion of cities and mounting dependence on cash markets provoked fascination with the dance of fake and real. The communities where Hickok worked his magic erupted from the Plains like volcanoes of commerce and seething humanity. In time, they would become well-ordered, middle-class bastions. But in the early days, when Hickok sauntered their streets and sidewalks, Leavenworth, Atchison, Abilene, Hays, Junction City, and others heaved with polyglot crowds of merchants, lawyers, fly-by-night doctors, teamsters, market hunters, and prostitutes. The weakness or even absence of town or state authorities, the inchoate social networks, and the mix of languages and races only made their money-hungry economies and cosmopolitan social mix all the more terrifying for the many newcomers who passed through them.[31]

Outside these nascent metropolises, even in remote areas of mostly rural Kansas, cities and their markets reordered every aspect of daily life. Vanishing game, proliferating livestock, advancing ranks of wheat—all reflected the powerful forces of meat and grain markets in Chicago, St. Louis, and Denver. For those markets, hinterland settlers produced commodities like buffalo hides, beef, and grain, and on those same markets they depended for money, with which they bought goods like lamps, plows, seed, and nails through catalogues and mail-order houses. Western settlers were at least as sensitive as any other Americans to fraud in advertising, and possibly more so.[32]

But the allure of frontier imposture like Hickok's—and, for that matter, Cody's—grew not only from developments in the region, but even more from more widely held perceptions and questions about it. By the 1860s, the populace had come to know the frontier as a deceptive mixture of representation and truth, a kind of gigantic artful deception, or a whole series of humbugs. Partly, this was because it was frequently a subject of hoaxes in the press. In 1844, T. B. Thorpe penned a series of sketches, "Letters from the Far West," in which he pretended to be a member of Sir William Drummond Stewart's hunting party exploring the northern Rockies. In fact, Thorpe was a newspaper editor in Louisiana who composed all of his dispatches from thin air. Although he loaded them with tall tales, sly jokes, and puns, newspapers across the country ran his letters as serious correspondence.[33] Other varieties of western hoaxes abounded, and not all were in good fun. Fraudulent reports of mineral strikes, rich soil, and mild climate proliferated, all intended to inflate the stock of bogus mining companies, disingenuous land speculators, and railroad corporations.[34]

Hoaxes and frauds were often elaborate variations on the tall tale, a form of artful deception which was the most popular and enduring means of representing the West. Although not unique to the United States, the American tall tale achieved an attraction and a currency unmatched elsewhere, and by the 1830s—the same decade that Barnum began to stage his hoaxes almost as tall tales made real—Americans could claim it as a national art form.[35] Tall tales were not unique to the frontier. But because they played on the ignorance of their audience, and because they frequently exploited unfamiliar natural settings and animals, they tended to feature frontier and backcountry locales. Thus, the southwestern frontier of Arkansas, Tennessee, and Louisiana spawned many early tall tales of Davy Crockett, Mike Fink, and others.[36]

In the course of the nineteenth century, the locus of the tall tale moved west, across the Mississippi, with the expanding fur trade and the frontier of settlement. Mountain men provided fonts of entertaining tales for eastern audiences beginning in the 1830s. The West was ideal for this form of entertainment, in part because its distinctive and remote geography often meant that seemingly outrageous elements of stories could prove true. When Jim Bridger described the remote northern Rockies as a place of steaming geysers and boiling pools, the editor of the *Kansas City Journal* refused to publish the story for fear it would reveal him as a dupe of the notorious tale spinner. Years later, he apologized to Bridger when it became apparent that at least that feature of his Yellowstone accounts was true.[37] So there was similar willingness to countenance if not quite believe mountain men's colorful accounts of petrified forests, prairie fires that could outrun a horse, and buffalo herds stretching from one horizon to the other. Audiences enjoyed these tales as a kind of performance: fur trapper Joe Meek once paid passage on a steamboat by charging passengers to hear his entertaining stories of the Oregon country.[38]

The frontier Hickok and Cody grew up hearing about, and which tourists went to Kansas looking for, was not just a region, or a place, but a subject in which fact and fiction had been so thoroughly mixed that the very idea of the Far West suggested deception, some of it entertaining. Both Hickok and Cody had roots in the Old Northwest (today's northern Midwest), the region that provided most of the emigrants who made their way along the Overland Trail to California and Oregon in the 1840s and 1850s.[39] The gold rush generated a torrent of fantastic, but sometimes half-true, tales of fist-sized gold nuggets, a climate so mild it was impossible to die in, and a stupendously fertile land where it never snowed. But already the Far West was a region that had to be seen to be understood, a locus of the fabulous and the monstrous. When Hickok and Cody were boys, legends of the circus permeated every rural hamlet, and none were so entrancing as the stories of gigantic beasts with noses that could lift a man's hat from his head or spray a crowd with water. Rural folk were so intrigued that many abandoned work whenever the big top came to town, paying hard-earned money to examine the legendary animals for themselves. By 1849, stories of the gold rush sounded so much like circus legends that journeying west came to be known as "seeing the elephant."[40]

Consequently, that migration west generated a library of trail narratives, in which people who otherwise never kept journals or wrote letters archived their adventures for posterity. By the end of the 1850s, these made up a new genre of American literature, emigrants' own true tales of discovering the "real" West and its many correspondences with or differences from popular images in emigrant guidebooks (many of which were highly dubious), dime novels, newspaper accounts, and rumor. Through these narratives, and throughout the popular understanding of the West itself, coursed a powerful theme of democratic exploration, less of the trail itself—which was well marked even before the gold rush—than of the spaces between western reality and eastern fantasy.

Of course, in the West as in the East, there were real risks which made the discernment of fantasy and reality more than a game. To many emigrants, the trails west led through cholera, Indian attacks, and financial collapse, not to mention loneliness. When the promoter Lansford Hastings assumed the guise of a trail guide, the Donner Party swallowed his bait, and took his "shortcut" across the desert south of the Great Salt Lake. Those who survived endured a cannibal winter in the Sierra Nevada before they ever made it to Sacramento.[41]

According to William Cody, his own father weighed the stories of California riches and decided they came up short. Discussions about what to believe and what to dismiss in the many California accounts swirled through young Will's trailside upbringing.[42] But if the Donner horror and other, less spectacular failures underscored the importance of discerning fakery from authenticity in the West, it also made the line between them even more a subject for legitimate entertainment. By the time Cody was a child and Hickok was a teenager, the region was understood to have a genuine, spectacular nature, looming beneath layers of cultural fraud and hype, like an elephant beneath a giant canvas tent.

After the Civil War, Kansas and the West developed in ways that further heightened public sensitivity to its many deceptions. Despite the Bleeding Kansas violence, between 1854 and 1865, 142,000 settlers arrived in Kansas. In the next fifteen years, they were joined by 850,000 more.[43] These massive displacements and their concomitant revolutionary changes were announced by a deluge of paper, as presses churned out notices of western opportunities real and fraudulent. Hyperbolic land speculation generated an ocean of advertising: real estate posters; multicolored land titles; maps accurate, fantastic, and many shades between; bird's-eye views of western towns, many of which would never approach their depicted size and many others which never existed at all. Railroad companies and their agents distributed pamphlets in most languages across every state and most European countries. They promised fertile soil with plentiful water, but dumped gullible emigrants on vast and arid grassland, many miles from markets or towns. Dishonest brokers sold claims they did not own, described one parcel to buyers and sold them another, or sold the same parcel to numerous customers before skipping town. Deceptions about land made up only one layer of endemic fraud on the frontier, where any number of "honest men" could sell an aspiring immigrant a lucrative mining claim, a paying saloon, even a bridge. Settlers had their own share of tricks. After 1862, the federal government deeded 285 million acres to homesteaders. Half their claims were fraudulent, backed by false identities, fake improvements, or worse.[44]

By the time William Cody was watching Hickok's imposture in Hays, the West not only possessed a heightened anxiety about fakery and a white-hot market for artful deceptions. In the popular mind the West *was* an artful deception, a place to be explored with the same methods, and often the same level of enjoyment, as any humbug. In ways long underappreciated by historians, frontier ideology reinforced popular eagerness to play this game. After all, the border between settlement and wilderness was not only the meeting point of civilization and savagery. It was also where the West—whatever that was—met the printing press, the artist's canvas, and the lithograph machine. The frontier was the junction of American craft and manufacturing (Artifice) and frontier material (Nature). In detecting for themselves the truth about Hickok, and later Cody, tourists sought to trace a frontier line that ran, shifting and inscrutable, between the Fake and the Real.[45]

Barnum himself recognized the inherent value of the frontier line in this regard. Like the FeeJee Mermaid's conjunction of fish and primate, the best hoaxes befuddled normative boundaries, and the mythic line between civilization and savagery expressed almost every kind of normative boundary there was.[46] The entertainer staged several western attractions, including a buffalo hunt in Hoboken, New Jersey, in 1843, but none of them approached the popularity of Joice Heth or the FeeJee Mermaid, perhaps because Barnum was too much the sharp Yankee to be credible as a presenter of frontier wonders.[47]

Hickok, on the other hand, was an authentic frontiersman, who could track and shoot like few others. Informed by dime novel fictions into which his own life was inscribed, he appropriated popular symbols (those guns, that long hair, and the buckskin and moccasins). All of these had been symbolic of "frontierness" in popular imagination at least since James Fenimore Cooper's Leatherstocking sagas, which in turn were inspired by biographies of Daniel Boone and mountain man lore. Long hair and deerskin garments implied connections to untamed nature, wild animals, and Indians, and the getup was so outdated in post–Civil War Kansas that he stood out. Hickok alternated his leather outfit with fashionable dress shirts and pointed boots, as if the ability to exchange buckskin for fine clothing symbolized the frontiersman's essential civility (while simultaneously it naturalized urban menswear, thereby legitimating many urban readers and tourists as potential frontiersmen). Facility with firearms represented the mastery of technology, particularly the machinery of violence through which an enervated white race could be regenerated.[48]

Hickok sharpened his attraction with genuine feats of pistolcraft like those in the Nichols article. Tourist witnesses recounted Hickok's cool skill: hitting a dime edge-on, driving a cork through the neck of a bottle with a bullet, shooting through a chicken's throat without breaking a bone.[49] To the delight of many observers, Wild Bill practiced pistol shooting frequently on the outskirts of whichever town he happened to be in.[50] However good a shot he actually was—and his willingness to shoot for an audience suggests he must have been at least fairly good—posing as a marksman allowed Hickok to assume the mythical hero's clarity of vision and apply the most modern technology to raw frontier nature. It allowed him to be avatar of the encounter between wilderness and civilization, assert his authority as a law-man, and advertise his services as hunting guide and scout, all at the same time.

Working from his bedrock authenticity as a guide, marksman, and law-man, Hickok's style of tourist entertainment included careful crafting of the tall tale. References to these stories are ubiquitous, and although none of the tales themselves survive, reportedly his personal adventures could entrance a circle of visitors for an hour or more. If we assume that he drew from the well of western standards, we can picture him as he spins out his story for a rapt audience (with Cody among them more than once) before ceasing his narration abruptly, leaving himself surrounded, disarmed, and facing imminent death.

After a breathless pause, some greenhorn would feed him the inevitable question: "How did you escape?"

Taking a breath, Hickok would drawl, "I didn't." Another pause. "I was killed."

This kind of leg pulling (a classic mountain man joke) served as fair warning that he was not strictly honest. His biography reinforced that message, especially in his consistent public claims of having been a spy. Spies were of necessity liars, and their ability to change appearance and identity fascinated Americans during and after the Civil War.[51] As one Union spy explained in his 1866 autobiography, espionage "requires an *accomplished liar.*" That is, not a "*habitual liar,*" but one who "can *successfully practice deception.*"[52] For audiences, the allure of the spy figure was partly in the challenge he posed to their faculties of discernment. In no small measure, the claim to have been a spy called into question the veracity of the storyteller, for if he was indeed "an accomplished liar," how could the audience know if he was telling the truth or not?

In important ways, scouting underscored similar messages. Although scouts today are recalled as authentic wilderness figures, through the Civil War they bore a close relationship to spies. Indian scouts were often called spies, because they not only tracked enemy warriors but could creep close enough to listen in on their conversations.[53] Scouts for Union and Confederate forces also were spies, donning enemy uniform or civilian garb to reconnoiter the territory or plant misinformation. Both Hickok and Cody fought along the bloody Kansas-Missouri line. There, the Red Legs and their bushwhacker opponents often took on the guises of one another. Scouting, deception, imposture: these dubious pursuits went hand in hand. Thus, the occupations converged in Hickok's life. Thus, William Cody, seeking to memorialize himself as the West's greatest scout in 1879, fictionalized assignments as a Civil War spy (and Hickok associate) for his artfully deceptive autobiography.

The scout figure had other sources of popular resonance, which we shall explore in the next chapter. But for now we may observe that scouts were not only repositories of knowledge about the wilderness and the enemy, but also spies who were masters of deception and intrigue. Dime novels were jammed with scouts in part because they were marginal, rural people who dominated the story's action, constantly masquerading and changing identities. In this sense, they were both nostalgic icons of a vanishing frontier America and profoundly modern figures whose talents at imposture empowered them to dominate the city, something they frequently did in the dime novels which proliferated toward century's end.

These literary and cultural trends coalesced around Hickok and many others. To be sure, not every scout who found himself represented in the popular press enjoyed the experience. In 1858, Kit Carson guided an army detachment to the camp of a Jicarilla Apache raiding party in hopes of rescuing a captive emigrant, one Mrs. White. The Apaches escaped, and Mrs. White was found dead soon after. But Carson was most troubled by something that turned up in her belongings: "We found a book in the camp, the first of the kind I had ever seen, in which I was represented as a great hero, slaying Indians by the hundred." Carson could only ponder the tragic elements of this misrepresentation: "I have often thought that Mrs. White must have read it, and knowing that I lived near-by, must have prayed for my appearance in order that she might be saved."[54]

Carson, ever a private man, refused to cultivate a public. Others thought trying to make dime novel fantasies into reality was distasteful or outlandish. But the expansion of the press and the extension of the railroad gave many others the chance to assume the pose of frontier hero, and playing to the cultural longings of tourists was pervasive in Kansas by the mid-1860s. One journalist reported his 1867 encounter with a Kansas railroad conductor who, like Hickok, "had much experience in life on the plains." Appropriating symbols of frontier identity, the conductor "always had a rifle by his side and pistols, either about his waist, or where he could conveniently put his hands upon them." Like Hickok, he was "an excellent shot," and he freely mingled experience and imposture, challenging his audience to separate the two. "Indeed, so marvelous were his stories that he was listened to with evident incredulity."[55]

In similar ways, different figures combined elements of frontier identity with real life to create powerful attractions in many railroad towns. Custer's abilities in this regard were so formidable that we will have to explore them at length below. But so too did any number of other men and women. Prior to the completion of the transcontinental railroad in 1869, most tourists and correspondents appear to have been drawn along the line of the Kansas Pacific, through central Kansas on the path to Denver, the center of a lavish gold strike and a vigorous mining community. Travelers could get to the city and return with ease, even before the railroad was complete. Moreover, the cattle towns which served as northern terminuses of various Texas cattle trails lay along the Kansas Pacific. The "KP" thus rolled through the most visible "progressive" landscape in the West, where the "wilderness" was giving way to pasture and mine, and the advent of farmers was imminent. Here, Wild Bill Hickok, William Cody, and other men, including Bat Masterson, plied the line as self-made embodiments of frontier myth.

After 1869, the focus of press attention shifted to the more northerly, newly completed transcontinental line, and so did those men and women who crafted frontier impostures of their own. Hickok, along with Charles "Colorado Charlie" Utter, Moses "California Joe" Milner, and Martha "Calamity Jane" Cannary, moved to the vicinity of Cheyenne, a major stop on the Union Pacific. Eastern reporters venturing to Cheyenne might disembark first at North Platte, Nebraska, where, by 1870, they would find John "Texas Jack" Omohundro, William "Doc" Carver, John Y. Nelson, Charles "Dashing Charlie" Emmett, Charles "The White Chief" Belden, and, of course, William "Buffalo Bill" Cody. All of these men gravitated to this locale in part because of its proximity to the railroad, which guaranteed the flow of writers and tourists who were their partners in formulating public personas. Each of them cultivated journalists and writers who descended from the train. Not coincidentally, every single one of these figures appeared in dime novels, and with the exception of Belden, who was murdered in 1870, all of them went on to careers on the stage and in show business before 1880. Many of them saw their cachet as guides and raconteurs enhanced as a result, and in varying degrees each made a career of appearing before audiences who thrilled at the chance to see the legend, and evaluate its validity for themselves.[56]

Frontier imposture of this order replicated itself in newly opened frontiers throughout the 1870s. The Black Hills were Hickok's last stop on his show of heroic life in progress; in addition to Calamity Jane, James "Captain Jack" Crawford, and other personalities whose achievements were at least as theatrical as real, the region sported ranks of men and boys who were adept at playing the role of frontier hero for tourists. Frontier imposture was an art form that drew heavily on literary fiction, with real people taking on language and shaping (or fabricating) their biographies from fictional stories, and vice versa. But where real people like Hickok inspired the fictions through the 1860s, by the mid-1870s the flow from history to fiction had reversed. Deadwood, South Dakota, became home base for the fictional "Deadwood Dick," protagonist in a raft of dime novels after 1874. Over the next twenty years, at least three men claimed to have been the "real" Deadwood Dick, and such figures, who adopted the identities of fictional westerners from popular novels, became legion.[57]

By the 1860s, no region could match the West as a venue for the staging of attractions and the invention of personas that appealed to popular desires and begged audiences to separate them from reality. The best-known literary treatment of the West in this period, Mark Twain's *Roughing It*, purports to be a factual memoir of a western tour, but it employs so many jokes, tall tales, and fabrications that it challenges the most analytical reader. Published in 1872, it was inspired by Twain's travels in the region between 1861 and 1865. In other words, it was a product of the same West that gave us Wild Bill Hickok and William Cody. Just as Twain rhapsodized about the Pony Express, by 1866 Hickok was telling tourists that he had ridden the pony, a lie which William Cody grafted on to his own life story in 1874. Between the literary adventures of America's greatest nineteenth-century writer and the supposed feats of her "real" western heroes there was a vigorous interchange of symbols, fictions, narrative devices, and outright lies.[58]

The tourists who gathered around Hickok usually came away with a sense that there was some amount of truth entangled with their fantasy West. Something enormous, real, and natural hung in the air when Hickok entered a room and began to tell his tales. Did you see the elephant? Those who met Hickok could say yes. Relatively few Americans would be able to move to the frontier, or to play any role in the great project of annexing the West. But many could travel there over a few days, for a break from work or to survey the opportunities for a farm or a business. Seeking out western characters like Hickok and deciding how much truth was tangled in magazine fictions and in dime novel lore about them were more accessible than almost any other frontier experiences. It is not too much to say that speculating and arguing about figures like Wild Bill Hickok was the frontier experience most available to the American public.

By all accounts, Hickok made his presence known whereever he went. His impact on Cody was profound. From an early age, Hickok was a mentor to Cody, who as a young man claimed Wild Bill as a cousin.[59] By the late 1860s, when both were in Hays, they both wore long hair, and dressed so similarly—buckskin, colorful shirts, and wide sombreros—that even people who knew them both would on occasion mistake one for the other in their memories. Both handed out small, calling card photographs of their longhaired selves to tourists and other potential clients.[60] The younger man sensed that Hickok was getting opportunities he did not have, and he was right. Hickok was already a favorite of General William Tecumseh Sherman. By 1867, he no longer sought work as a scout; it sought him. Those droves of tourists around him had paid train fare for the thrill. Many of them paid for his guiding services, too. Being a guide required shepherding a flock of greenhorns while posing as the frontiersman that dime novels and *Harper's Monthly* taught them to expect, but for a man with the right temperament, it was not difficult. Hickok had found a way to manipulate the national press, the army officer class, and even the tourist public to his own ends. Cody wanted the same.

But Hickok's imposture was a work in progress, and in many ways he eventually proved inferior to Cody at playing the frontiersman of public longing. His violence was problematic, his ascent to dime novel stardom and public renown strewn with the bodies of his opponents, and his imposture too anti-Southern, too sectionalist for a nation aching to heal the wounds of the Civil War.[61] We shall revisit these limitations when we come to the beginnings of William Cody's stage career, a moment when he linked his name publicly to Wild Bill's before he and his old friend became show business rivals and finally parted ways.

In the meantime, Hickok embodied certain elements of the frontier myth that Cody needed and wanted for his own. His early attempts to tie himself to the Hickok legend as Wild Bill's cousin in the 1860s began a decade-long effort to selectively entwine the myth of Buffalo Bill with the legend of Wild Bill. Cody retold many of Hickok's tales as his own adventures. As we have seen, both men claimed to have ridden for the Pony Express, and to have been Civil War spies.

Cody made this enthusiastic borrowing of Hickok's material somewhat more credible by inserting himself alongside Hickok in these tales, as if to protect himself against the charge of trying to substitute himself for Wild Bill. But the result was just that. When Ned Buntline arrived on the Plains in the summer of 1869, he was looking for Wild Bill Hickok, or perhaps Frank North, another legendary scout. Buntline was eager to write a novel about a real-life frontier hero. But North hated publicity, and Hickok was in a churlish mood. Cody, on the other hand, was gregarious and funny, regaling the writer with stories. Since he was claiming Hickok as a blood relative at the time, it seems likely that some of those stories informed the plot of Buntline's novel, in which Buffalo Bill and Wild Bill ride across the prairies as brothers in arms.[62]

When Cody wrote his own autobiography in 1879, he validated the fiction by making himself the protégé of Hickok. In some of the book's more fanciful sections, Wild Bill champions young Buffalo Bill during his fictitious adventures in the Mormon War and in his imaginary fights with Indians on the Pony Express. Cody even recapitulated Nichols's account of Hickok's feats as a Union spy, and added himself as an observer and minor participant in the action (which he certainly was not). He included an entire chapter about Wild Bill's killing of Dave Tutt in Springfield, Missouri, an event which also featured prominently in the Nichols article, without ever inserting himself in the story, as if including this tale of the code duello somehow conveyed its chivalrous legacy to Cody (who was on detached service in St. Louis, courting Louisa, and probably visiting the theater, when the killing occurred). In 1861 Hickok had been in a shoot-out with Jake McCanles and his family. Cody wrote up the killing of Jake McCanles and his "gang" as if it were a sad but inevitable coda to the Civil War rather than an ugly personal dispute over a local woman, all to link himself to Hickok's ability to use violence in defense of honor.

Cody's eager borrowing from the Hickok story was part of his overall technique of sculpting his own persona from the myths that surrounded him. During the early 1870s, when the two men appeared in stage plays about frontier life, their rivalry increased. Cody's mirroring of Hickok's biography irritated the older man, who grew to resent the acolyte's appropriation of his myth.[63] But Hickok was murdered in 1876, and by 1879, his legend was practically a Cody vehicle. Cody's stage publicist, John Burke, tended to the deceased Hickok's reputation, and defended him in the press, because the two scouts were so closely linked in the popular mind that to allow bad press about Hickok would ill betide Cody.[64] By 1879, in his own autobiography, Cody could claim Hickok as a mythic brother, and by telling some Wild Bill stories (the duel with Tutt) and eliding others (his killing of a Seventh Cavalry soldier in a brawl, which forced his departure from Hays in 1870), Cody contained the meaning of the Hickok myth and wrapped it around himself like a cape.[65]

To this day, visitors to the Buffalo Bill Historical Center in Cody, Wyoming, will on occasion exclaim, "Wow, a whole museum for Wild Bill!" The confusion of Buffalo Bill with Wild Bill was Cody's intention from the late 1860s onward. Its endurance is partly a testament to Cody's effectiveness, which was so pronounced that people could be unaware they were different people even when they were both alive. Wild Bill Hickok left Buffalo Bill's stage show after a brief series of joint appearances in 1873 and 1874. Months afterward, Cody was still advertising the performances of Wild Bill—and as long as they had Buffalo Bill to look at, critics seldom noticed the gunfighter's absence.[66] During the 1887 shows of Buffalo Bill's Wild West, in London, General Sherman received Cody's request for a testimonial, to be used in the publicity for the Wild West show, and wrote back that Cody had "guided me honestly and faithfully, in 1865–66, from Fort Riley to Kearny, in Kansas and Nebraska."

Sherman was mistaken. His guide on that trip was Hickok. Cody, not to be put off by a small error of fact, published the testimonial. In later editions of his autobiography, he concocted a whole expedition to go with it.[67]

Cody's willingness to deceive his audiences may have exceeded Hickok's.

The younger man certainly proved more successful at that end of the business than his early mentor ever had. But the development of Buffalo Bill from frontier Kansan to transatlantic media phenomenon was in some ways dependent on the prior emergence of Wild Bill, who blazed much of the early path for him but whose violence made him a more questionable figure than Cody ever was. By blurring the line between Buffalo Bill and Wild Bill Hickok, and obscuring their differences, Cody used his predecessor in frontier imposture to concoct a multilayered public deception and amusement. Audiences and writers who enjoyed debating whether Cody was frontiersman or showman could revel in the chaos of symbols and stories that poured from the merger of the men's exploits. Did Wild Bill invent the Wild West show? Did he really know Buffalo Bill? Buffalo Bill—wasn't he a lawman? Did he kill somebody— an ex-Confederate? A Union soldier? In a gunfight? The real distinctions between the men made Cody the more palatable figure, and his publicists skillfully illuminated those distinctions as the need arose. But after Cody died, only the most devoted fans and scholars knew where Wild Bill and Buffalo Bill diverged—and to them would go the consummate pleasure (mine) of explicating these linked figures to curious audiences of their own (you).

Homage to the Master Showman. William Cody, right, meets with his sister, May Cody Decker, and hotel manager Lew Decker in Cody's office at the Irma Hotel, Cody, Wyoming, c. 1910. On the back wall, in the upper right corner of the photograph, hangs a picture of P. T. Barnum. Courtesy Buffalo Bill Historical Center.

As a young man constructing a public persona, Cody trailed Wild Bill Hickok, reading his sign, aping his moves. He learned from Hickok how to embody not just the balancing of technology and nature that met along the frontier line, but the debate over what was real and what was fake, what was truth and what was fiction, which consumed nearly all discussions of the frontier and the Far West, and modern America, too. By taking such serious questions and turning them into entertainment, Wild Bill was a model for the younger man, who began to carve out his own space as a frontiersman and entertainment figure alongside Hickok, in Hays, in 1868.

CHAPTER FIVE

Guide and Scout

WILLIAM CODY avoided a law enforcement career. But in other ways, his foray into frontier imposture would resemble Hickok's, combining real violence with a self-conscious pose that grafted popular symbols of the frontiersman—especially buckskin, long hair, and modern weapons—to the demanding career of an army scout.

With Louisa no longer on his horizon, he returned to west Kansas alone and searched for work around the forts. Following Hickok's example, he turned to guiding and scouting. In August 1868, Cody served as guide and hunter to the U.S. Tenth Cavalry, a segregated black unit, and his white commanding officer reported that Cody "gets $60 per month and a splendid mule to ride, and is one of the most contented and happy men I ever met."[1] Later that year, in September, he offered his services to the army again. This time he was resacking forage for army livestock at Fort Larned, for $30 per month.[2] Within a week, on the strength of his reputation as a hunter and hunting guide, he had been promoted to scout at $75 per month.[3]

Today, frontier scouts are mythic figures, in no small measure because Buffalo Bill Cody dedicated his career to securing their place in American history. But even in 1867, the term "scout" was resonant with meanings far beyond the duties of the job. As early as the sixteenth century, soldiers detailed to reconnoiter enemy territory were called scouts, from the Middle French *escouter*, "to listen."[4]

Conditioned by generations of Indian conflict, Americans conflated the heroic scout and the "white Indian," a white man who adopted Indian woodcraft and fighting methods, combined them with a heart that remained true to the cause of civilization, and contained all within a white, civilized body.[5] If Indians embodied Nature and Europeans embodied Culture, the white Indian embodied the proper, virtuous mixing of both. He was the essence of American identity. In popular culture, especially in the prolific dime novels which entertained the mass of American readers, frontier scouts from the fictional Hawkeye and Seth Jones to the historical (or historically based) Kit Carson made the American white Indian and scout one of the most popular of protagonists, even before the Civil War.[6]

Throughout its history, the U.S. military utilized different kinds of scouts to serve different needs. Colonial militia units like Roger's Rangers and later militiamen of the republic, like Daniel Boone, became legendary for their ability to fight Indians with Indian methods. In the 1850s and '60s, Kit Carson joined the ranks of these earlier frontier Indian fighters.[7] But white Indian scouts, if they existed, had limited usefulness outside of the Indian wars. Officers struggled to keep scouts under military command and discipline. During the Civil War, the union army generally kept scouting assignments within the ranks of professional soldiers, who took on scout duty as today's soldiers make reconnaissance patrols.

But the U.S. Army found the Great Plains such a confusing and forbidding environment that commanders sought local men to perform a variety of functions that were subsumed under the term "scouting." They were not necessarily knowledgeable about Indians. Scouts were often mere couriers, who carried orders between distant posts. Other duties including guiding troops from one place to another, tracking Indians, hunting game for officers and men as the need arose, and reconnoitering territory. From 1868 until 1872, William Cody made his living by scouting for the army in pursuit of Indians, and guiding tourists and army officers on buffalo hunts. His success at these occupations brought him considerable financial reward, and reunion with Louisa and Arta, who returned to him in 1869. The gathering of his respectable wife and family at Fort McPherson, Nebraska, was no trivial event. As we shall see, the context of his white family made his white Indian act respectable, and helped launch him to fame exceeding that of any other scout.

The veracity of Cody's Indian fighting exploits preoccupied critics and reviewers while he was alive, and it has intrigued historians ever since. In 1960, historian Don Russell published what remains the most comprehensive examination of Cody's career as scout, *The Lives and Legends of Buffalo Bill*. Russell's method of evaluating Cody's accomplishments was seductively simple. After examining the reports, correspondence, and public statements of Cody's commanding officers, Russell concluded that Cody was a superlative scout who actually did perform most of the exploits he later claimed. In fact, he was so modest that he downplayed his achievements. "In an age that is skeptical of heroism," concluded Russell, "anyone who does bother to find out what William F. Cody really amounted to may turn up a record that is impressive in its universal acclaim from a wide variety of sources as well as in its lack of any hint that he ever faltered or blundered."[8]

To be sure, William Cody was an excellent tracker and hunter, and he

proved an exceptionally able fighter in the running skirmishes which typified the Plains wars. But Russell's biography of Cody ignores the scout's
social context, with the result that he fails to see how badly Cody's commanders *wanted*, even needed, to find a hero in the person of Buffalo Bill, and
how hard Cody worked to accommodate them. Cody's success as guide
flowed in part from his early, almost preternatural sense that it was far more
than a job. The occupation was infused with such powerful symbolic meanings that it provided him a kind of stage or arena in which to construct a persona, to master a frontier imposture, akin to Hickok's. To grasp his
transformation from private man to public figure in the Indian wars and on
the hunting grounds, we must understand how his pose reassured, and
sometimes amused, army officers, the men who became his chief cultural
patrons in the early days of his show career. And for that, we must explore
how confusing, even terrifying, the Great Plains was for the Americans who
confronted it after the Civil War.

INDIANS, SOLDIERS, AND SCOUTS

The army came to the Plains, of course, to fight Indians. But America's
advance onto the Plains was only one of several overlapping expansions by
distinct peoples. The acquisition of horses and the advent of American and
European markets for buffalo robes drew various once-horticultural Indians
from their woodland and mountain homes onto the Great Plains after 1700.
Among these were the Lakota, commonly known as the western Sioux. By
1867, they had been occupying an ever-larger swath of the northern and
central Plains for a century and a half. As they did so, they forced aside older
Plains inhabitants, such as the horticultural Arikara, Hidatsa, Mandan, and
Pawnee, as well as eastern Indians who relocated to Kansas in the nineteenth century, such as the Delaware, Osage, and Cherokee. Nomadic peoples benefited from the differential fallout of the great diseases that swept
Indian villages away in this period. As the more sedentary, horticultural peoples reeled from smallpox, measles, and other Eurasian maladies to which
they had no resistance, nomads were more widely dispersed, so less prone to
all-out catastrophe.[9]

Arapaho and Cheyenne joined the Lakota in their expansionist thrust.
They, too, left settled villages in today's Minnesota to seize the buffalo
hunting grounds to the south and west over the course of the nineteenth
century. On the southern Plains, Comanche and Kiowa made analogous
moves, venturing from homelands in the West out onto the plains of
Texas and Kansas. Nomads were not united. The Lakota and Cheyenne, for
example, contested access to the buffalo herds with other, newly nomadic

groups such as the Crow and the Shoshone. But by 1840, many of the nomads—Lakota, Cheyenne, Arapaho, Comanche, and Kiowa—had allied with one another, to combat their common enemies among their beleaguered Plains predecessors.

American expansion into Nebraska and Kansas followed fast on the nomads' triumph. U.S. emigrants venturing to the California and Colorado mines and settlers taking up lands along the route of the emigrant trails and railroads sliced through the heart of their homeland. As early as 1853, authorities reported that Cheyenne were starving because settlers and emigrants had driven away game and the latter's livestock had eaten forage for the former's horses.[10] In 1862, a Sioux warrior, Shan-tag-a-lisk, told an army officer that settler oxen and mules had long since demolished the range along the main emigrant route west. "Your young men and your freighters have driven all the game out, or killed it, so we find nothing in the Platte valley."[11]

Not surprisingly, there was fighting between U.S. forces and the Sioux-Cheyenne alliance by the mid-1850s, which increased in the 1860s, with periodic efforts to make peace. In 1864, a Colorado volunteer militia fell on a peaceful Cheyenne village at Sand Creek, massacring hundreds of men, women, and children. The Plains erupted. Kansas frontier settlements, where aspiring farmers plowed up the buffalo grass and planted fields, were beset by Indian war parties. Out on the sparsely forested Plains, settlers' cabins were often made of sod bricks. These "soddies" were more and more often the target of Indian raids, and between 1865 and 1867, some two hundred settlers and untold numbers of Indians died in these clashes. Another two hundred Americans perished in fights with Sioux and Cheyenne in 1868.[12] In prominent cases, Indian raiders abducted settler women and children, as either hostages, slaves, or potential adoptees. Some women captives became wives, and captors adopted children as their own. By the time Cody took up scouting for the army, the Sioux and Cheyenne, along with the Comanche, Kiowa, and Arapaho, constituted the most fearsome horse warriors the American military had ever faced.[13] The war on the Plains destroyed soddies and tipis and the loving inhabitants of both. Like the earlier war in Cody's life, this one was also, above all, a war against the family home.

IN THE ARMY, scouts became necessary because the soldiers who came to fight the Plains Indians so easily got lost in the strange grassland. The land looked flat. But the mostly treeless expanse actually sloped gradually from east to west, a rolling territory coursed with coulees, or gulleys, which hid streambeds and broken, winding canyons. Seemingly straight paths veered subtly in directions which could lead a party far afield. Few experiences were more frightening than searching for enemy Indians and becoming lost on the Plains in a thunderstorm or a blizzard. Army guides navigated the Plains by following watersheds between places, staying on the higher ridges of this deceptive terrain. "The swell in the surface, which constitutes the main water shed, is termed the 'divide,'" wrote one journalist. "To know the 'divide' and how to follow it constitutes the highest art of the guide."[14]

Generally, that art's chief practitioners were local hunters and traders. Some could read the land well enough to warn troops at what point along the trail an attack was likely to come. Long experience gave local guides facility at discerning distant creatures from the way they moved, a welcome talent since the light of the Plains projected mirages and a thousand other tricks of the eye. In the distance, buffalo looked like horses, which could be mistaken for Indians, who were hard to distinguish from soldiers. In 1867, two unguided detachments of the same U.S. cavalry regiment watched each other suspiciously and at length, each mistaking the other for Indians. They avoided a skirmish only at the very last moment.[15]

Cody earned his military reputation by guiding troops and fighting alongside them during these campaigns. By 1869, he was a well-known Indian fighter whose name was appearing in the popular press. He received the Congressional Medal of Honor in 1872. During his Wild West show career, his programs reprinted a torrent of praise from military officers, among whom numbered many good friends. General Wesley Merritt wrote, "He was cool and capable when surrounded by dangers, and his reports were always free from exaggeration." Major General W. H. Emory wrote that Cody had been "chief guide and hunter" to his command on the North Platte, "and he performed all his duties with marked excellence."

The most sterling accolades came from General Eugene A. Carr, who had worked with "a great many guides, scouts, trailers, and hunters," and judged Cody "king of them all."[16] Mr. Cody, he wrote, "seemed never to tire, and was always ready to go, in the darkest night, or the worst weather." His eyesight was "better than a good field-glass; he is the best trailer I ever heard of, and the best judge of the 'lay of the country.' . . . In a fight, Mr. Cody is never noisy, obstreperous or excited." He was "always in the right place, and his information was always valuable and reliable."[17] By 1887, he was claiming the rank of colonel, and for the rest of his life, friends and associates referred to him as "Colonel Cody."

The militarization of Buffalo Bill's reputation was so complete that it obscured a central fact of Cody's career: for all his military glory, Cody was never *in* the army during the Indian wars.[18] His colonelcy came as an honorary appointment to the Nebraska state militia—the predecessor to the national guard—in 1887, long after the Indian wars were over. The rank was bestowed upon him by John Thayer, the governor of Nebraska, who awarded it at Cody's request, as the entertainer sought to professionalize his ambiguous military record just before his Wild West show embarked for London. (For his part, Thayer was only too happy to appoint Buffalo Bill to his "honorary" staff, as an advertisement for Nebraska.) Although Cody was initially forthright about the commission (he printed it in the 1887 show program), by the early 1890s he had changed its date to *1867* to provide his earlier scouting adventures a professional veneer.[19]

But scouts like Cody were civilians, not soldiers. They were private contractors, who sold their services as guides and messengers to the army, usually on a job-by-job basis. At times, this was a distinction without a difference. In combat, hunkering down in a buffalo wallow with bullets zinging overhead amidst the smell of sweat and fear, scouts were expected to fight and had to obey their ranking officers like any trooper. During the 1860s, Cody fought in nine pitched battles, more than most full-fledged soldiers.[20]

But in day-to-day life, scouts were outside the hierarchy of command which defines military life, politics, and culture. Thus, many years later, just before he died, the army stripped Cody of his Congressional Medal of Honor on the grounds that he had been a civilian scout in 1872 when he won this most coveted award for enlisted men or officers.[21]

The contrast between the working conditions of soldiers and scouts explains why Cody took care to avoid becoming a soldier. As he discovered during his undistinguished career as a private in the Union army in 1864–65, troopers were all but invisible to their commanders, endured paltry and irregular salaries, and had no freedom to take up other occupations. Scouts, on the other hand, reported directly to officers. Their pay varied with experience, skill, and the needs of the army, but Cody started out at $75 a month, four times the pay of an army private. Favorite scouts might stay on the payroll indefinitely. This could bring more tangible benefits. For Cody, being a scout enhanced his availability to serve as a paid hunting guide for visiting tourists and for officers. In short, being a scout offered Cody a chance to cross the class divide that separated mostly educated, middle-class army officers from working-class soldiers.

The financial advantages of this position were augmented by the predatory entrepreneurialism of scouting, which gave it a resemblance to jayhawking. During the 1860s and '70s, he often made gifts of booty, conferring war bonnets and other Indian curios on admirers and visitors, and selling captured horses for extra cash. Writing to friends in the East in 1874, Cody would apprise them of his latest scouting assignment, advising them to "look for those Indian trophys if we have luck enough to capture an Indian village," and promising to "send those buffalo tongues from here tomorrow."[22]

Scouts had more latitude in their private lives, too. On patrol, their actions were constrained by the officer in charge of the expedition. But back at the fort, they could carouse as they liked. They could run other businesses. They did not have to live in the barracks, or even at the post. Soldiers who bolted from the ranks were pursued by army detectives—many of them scouts. But outside of combat, scouts could quit when they wanted. In short, being a scout entitled Cody to a military salary and a position where his talents could come to the notice of the military establishment, while it gave him the freedom to pursue other business ventures, and paid him to ride across the Plains in search of game when he was not looking for Indians.

All these characteristics of the job suited Cody. Where he had consistently failed to attract notice from his commanders during his Civil War years, he soon came to the attention of officers as a scout. His willingness to make long rides through perilous country quickly impressed the commanding general, the Civil War hero Philip Sheridan. Sheridan met Cody when he rode into Fort Hays one day in 1868, bearing dispatches from Fort Larned, sixty-five miles away. The messages informed Sheridan that Comanches and Kiowas were preparing to leave the vicinity of Larned, probably to make war on nearby settlements.[23]

On reading this news, Sheridan sought a courier to take urgent orders to Fort Dodge, ninety-five miles south, for troops to intercept the Kiowas and Comanches. The only men who could perform such duty were local volunteers who knew the country, but as Sheridan recalled in his memoirs, it was hard to find one. The trail to Dodge was "a particularly dangerous route— several couriers having been killed on it," and it proved "impossible to get one of the various 'Petes,' 'Jacks,' or 'Jims' hanging around Hays City to take my communication." But Cody "manfully came to the rescue" and volunteered, despite having just ridden sixty-five miles from Larned. Upon reaching Dodge, he did not rest, but pressed on again, carrying more dispatches back to Fort Larned, completing a run of 350 miles in a total of sixty hours.[24]

Cody's recollection of the ride suggests his Plains savvy and other qualities which contributed to his success, while revealing crucial aspects of scout subculture. Like many of the best scouts, he opted to travel at night to decrease the chances of being seen by Indians. Beginning at Larned, "after eating a lunch and filling a canteen with brandy," he tied one end of a leather thong to his belt, and the other to his mount's bridle. When his horse stepped in a prairie dog hole and Cody fell off several miles along the route, the thong kept the animal close at hand. The scout rode all night to Hays, nearly meeting with disaster when he accidentally stumbled into an Indian village along the way. After resting for two hours at the Perry House in Hays City, Cody accepted Sheridan's offer of "a reward of several hundred dollars" for riding on to Fort Dodge, but first asked for more rest. "It was not much of a rest, however, that I got, for I went over to Hays City again and had 'a time with the boys,' " before pressing on to Dodge, and then to Larned.[25]

Although Buffalo Bill always rode a beautiful horse in the show arena, on the Plains scouts often eschewed horses, because most army mounts were not accustomed to Plains grasses and needed more frequent feeding with hay and oats for long rides. The typical mount of the Plains scout was a mule, an animal with more endurance than the horse. But mules were also notoriously stubborn, and scouts despised them. Thus, on this last leg of his journey, Cody wrote, his mule ran away from him as he was taking a drink at a stream. The animal continued on to Larned, "and kept up a little jog trot just ahead of me, but would not let me come up to him, although I tried it again and again. . . . Mile after mile I kept on after that mule, and every once in a while I indulged in strong language respecting the whole mule fraternity." In sight of Fort Larned, just before dawn, with the danger of Indian attack now remote, Cody opened fire on the recalcitrant animal. "I continued to pour lead into him until I had him completely laid out. Like the great majority of government mules, he was a tough one to kill, and he clung to life with all the tenaciousness of his obstinate nature. He was, without doubt, the toughest and meanest mule I ever saw, and he died hard."[26]

Cody's recounting was full of verve and color and probably half-true at best, but his tale of hard drinking, hard work, and little sleep suggests the titanic energy, and the equally large appetite for drink and good times, which were nearly lifelong traits. Among scouts, nighttime travel, objectionable mules, entrepreneurial zeal, hard liquor, and conviviality were all part and parcel of day-to-day existence. Some of these scout characteristics, particularly the lively party scene, gave commanders fits. But guides and couriers like Cody, who rode hundreds of miles through Indian country on little or no sleep in return for cash bonuses, were indispensable. As Sheridan remembered Cody's legendary ride, "such an exhibition of endurance and courage was more than enough to convince me that his services would be extremely valuable in the campaign." His faith in Cody's prowess was such that he appointed Cody to the position of chief of scouts for the Fifth Cavalry.[27]

Chief of scouts was not a military rank, and it was less a command position than a promise to ask Cody's advice in hiring other scouts and to retain his services in preference to others. His responsibilities took him all over Kansas for the next year, and he saw combat often. In the fall of 1868, Cody accompanied the Fifth Cavalry from Fort Hays north, to the tributaries of the Republican River called Beaver Creek and Prairie Dog Creek. The Fifth was soon in battle when a band of Cheyenne Dog Men under the noted chief Tall Bull attacked. The Dog Men earned their name from the legendary practice of select warriors, who demonstrated their refusal to retreat by dismounting in the midst of battle and plunging into the ground a stake, to which the warrior was tied by an ornamented buffalo-hide sash, the "dog rope." From this position he could not retreat unless another Dog Man pulled the stake and whipped him—"like a dog"—to drive him from battle.[28] Cody was out with a detachment and missed this first fight, but the soldiers and Cody subsequently pursued the Dog Men in a series of running fights across Beaver Creek and north into Nebraska. The number of Cheyenne, Sioux, and Arapaho warriors increased to around five hundred as the moving battle continued through the next week. Then the Indians turned back south again. They scattered, and Cody and the troops lost them at the end of October.[29]

The battalion then moved to Fort Wallace, where Cody helped fend off a Cheyenne attack while out with a hunting party, before moving on to Fort Lyon in Colorado, where they arrived in late November 1868.[30]

CODY HAD ALREADY proved himself a good scout. But was he ever good enough to merit the river of military accolades that flowed through his show programs? If not, why would the military command take such an interest in furthering Cody's show business career? In fact, military commanders who later trumpeted Cody's skills initially proved skeptical, precisely because he was already a showman, self-consciously playing to popular fantasies of white scouts in ways that sometimes grated on officers. Commanders of the Plains army regarded scouts with deep and abiding suspicion. Following the high divides was indeed an art form. But the men who sold their services as guides often showed more talent for the art of deception. In the words of one travel writer, the Great Plains was "infested with numberless charlatans, blazing with all sorts of hunting and fighting titles, and ready at the rustle of greenbacks to act as guides through a land they know nothing about."[31] Some were just plain cowardly, like the " 'Petes,' 'Jacks,' or 'Jims' hanging around Hays City" who refused to carry Sheridan's dispatches. Others were merely incompetent. "Any person who has had much to do with expeditions in Indian country knows how many and how frequent are the applications made to the commanding officer to obtain employment as scouts or guides," wrote George Custer. "Probably one in fifty of the applicants is worthy of attention."[32]

Officers had less authority over the civilians than over soldiers, and were correspondingly reluctant to trust them. In other ways, the pervasive skepticism about frontier guides was a reflection of broader cultural anxieties, some of which sprang from surprisingly urban sources. Specifically, the fear that a fake guide might be posing as an "authentic" tracker to take a client's money and lead him into danger made scouts the rural counterparts of a renowned product of urban decadence, the confidence man. The figure of the confidence man was the bête noire of American moralists for much of the nineteenth century, and although he is normally considered an urban figure, he was a paradoxically prominent symbol lurking in the background of Cody's rise to fame on the Plains.

As the Industrial Revolution enticed and compelled millions of young, rural Americans to move to the city in the nineteenth century, fearful authors penned guidebooks and etiquette manuals warning of savvy criminals who waited at city railroad stations to entrap hale farm youths and blushing country maidens. Advice literature frequently referred to these social predators, who persuaded the naive newcomers of their good intentions, then led them down the darkest alleys of the urban wilderness into gambling, alcoholism, prostitution, and death. In popular accounts, the modus operandi of these malefactors was to convince their victims that their intentions were sincere, to gain their confidence. Thus they came to be known as "confidence men," or, in the vernacular, con artists, and their reputed blandishments defined the writings of urban reformers for much of the nineteenth century.[33]

In later decades Buffalo Bill's Wild West show drew crowds by persuading audiences that the heroic Plains scout would not take their money under false pretenses. William Cody stood in sharp contrast to the con men who ran the tawdry circuses, lewd burlesques, and other immoral entertainments. As the rustic frontiersman new to the city, he seemed the opposite of the confidence man. Instead, Buffalo Bill was a real westerner who provided a rollicking good show of frontier virtue for urban families.

Publicists played a role in constructing this image, but Cody himself intuited the urban fear of confidence men, and how to heighten and assuage it simultaneously, from the very earliest days of his scouting career on the Great Plains. Fear of the con man became the context for Cody's ascent in officer esteem to the position of trustworthy scout, and his exposure to it provided him an education in audience longings, because in the end, the divergent processes of urbanization and frontier settlement provoked closely related anxieties. The frontier, like the city, was where young Americans went to make their fortunes. Thus, after the Civil War, the West proved to be, like New York City, Boston, and Chicago, the destination for hundreds of thousands of disparate emigrants from various rural regions of the country and the world. In frontier Kansas, as in any American metropolis, these immigrants alighted from the railroad. Usually, their first stop was in one of the booming towns, most of which were bereft of extended families, established social networks, or institutions, and rife with "unseemly" mixing of races, unregulated markets, urban decadence, and violence. Kansas cow towns inspired as much reformist zeal as the slums of Gotham. Amidst their confusing mix of German, Irish, Mexican, Jewish, and Yankee residents "bent on debauchery and dissipation," observed one commentator, prostitutes walked the streets with derringers, "monstrous creatures undeserving the name of women." The violence—or threat of violence—was breathtaking. "I verily believe there are men here who would murder a fellow-creature for five dollars."[34]

In these small, scary towns, aspiring frontier guides waited by the train to meet prospective clients, especially tourists and land speculators, whom they approached with promises to lead them to scenic attractions or the best parcels in safety for a most reasonable fee. Small wonder that fearful commentators should think them confidence men who could swindle and debase greenhorns. Small wonder, too, that the figure of the trustworthy frontier scout should ascend to new heights of public appeal.

Cody learned from Hickok's imposture, which exploited these fears masterfully. Waiting at the train platform, Wild Bill was renowned as a man who could protect the tourist or the emigrant from both the violent town and the savage frontier, and his appearance so approached the ideal of the white Indian that tourists could enjoy a debate over how real the pose was. Cody learned to play to the fears and hopes of soldiers and tourists in similar ways. Photos from the late 1860s and early 1870s show him in the costume of the white Indian: buckskin, rifle, and long dark hair. He was about six feet tall and very handsome. Like Hickok, his appearance as a guide borrowed so heavily from fictional representations of the profession that the people who followed him invariably wondered how much they should believe his act.

Thus, when Brevet Major General Eugene Carr first encountered William Cody, in October of 1868, he had his doubts. Carr arrived on the Plains to assume command of the Fifth Cavalry that month, and Cody met him at the train station. "I was loading my baggage when attracted by a man in buckskin, with [a] broad-brimmed hat, sitting on a horse on some rising ground not far from the station," recalled the officer. "There were so many so-called scouts who masqueraded around the railroad stations, mostly fakes and long-bow story tellers to tenderfeet, I thought to myself: 'There is one of those confounded scouts posing.' "[35]

As Carr discovered, Cody possessed very real skills as tracker, fighter, and buffalo hunter. Nonetheless, these were but the grit of truth in the cement of his artful deception, which combined genuine mastery of martial skills with a costume and manner that invited soldiers and settlers to indulge their fantasies of heroic white scouts. Long before he ever set foot on a stage, Cody was playing a role that was both deadly real—killing Cheyenne and Sioux Indians and harrying them from their homes—and presenting himself in ways that reassured, and thereby entertained, a larger public about the heroism of American conquest. The combination of Indian fighter and man who *looked* like an imaginary Indian fighter invited new acquaintances, like General Carr, to ask the same question that audiences would ask for the rest of Cody's life: Is he an entertainer? Or is he an Indian fighter? In the end, guiding offered a means to be both, and it set his feet on the path to much wider showmanship and fame.

But Cody's white Indian pose disguised the superficiality of his knowledge of Indians, which was restricted to a familiarity with their fighting techniques and their standard travel routes, since many of their paths were utilized by frontier settlers and market hunters. He never learned to speak any Indian language. At this point, he had no Indian friends. In fact, he knew next to nothing about what we would call Indian culture. Many other scouts had far more knowledge of the Plains and its inhabitants than Cody did.

But the army's interest in Cody's career was based on much larger, ideological considerations than how much he actually "knew Indians." His pose, when combined with his not inconsiderable tracking and fighting skills, reassured the officers he guided in subtle, powerful ways. If he looked like a hero out of a novel by James Fenimore Cooper (or one of Cooper's many dime novel imitators), his abilities seemed to validate those novels as projections of larger truths about frontier conquest and Americans. If that was the case, then the American conquest of Indians *was* inevitable. And on that score, in 1867 and '68 army men needed all the reassurance they could get. For them, the heroic Buffalo Bill was a boon to the troubled reputation and miserable condition of the U.S. Army in the Indian wars.

THE ARMY'S DREARY WAR

In the 1880s, Buffalo Bill's Wild West show would stage battle scenes in which a united Sioux met a united white cavalry in glorious combat. But at almost every level, these so-called "reenactments" were artful contrivances designed to obscure the real history they represented. The Plains Indian wars were confusing, messy, and terrifying for everyone caught up in them. Throughout the many skirmishes and massacres which constituted their primary drama, the army fought and feuded in the ranks, and any sense of national purpose was almost consistently absent. Witness to the army's dismal season, Cody discovered his usefulness not only as an Indian fighter, but as a symbol of Indian fighting, as a protagonist on whom white officers and other middle-class Americans could hang their own desires and longings.

Grasping the essence of Cody's appeal to the army requires first the debunking of one prominent myth about the history of the American military. Today, it is widely believed that until the Vietnam War, Americans respected, admired, and supported their military. Then critics of the war (mostly on the left) demeaned the armed forces. Only in recent years has the army recovered its now jealously guarded status as one branch of a wildly popular armed service. According to many commentators, today's veneration of the American soldier marks the rightful return of an old tradition.

Beholden to this view, modern Americans are often surprised to learn that in the years that Cody began scouting for the military, Americans were so divided on the issue of fighting Indians, and so dubious of their army's valor, that the campaigns were anything but glorious. Part of the reason lay in public suspicions of the new federal army. From the earliest days of the United States, citizens preferred short-term, all-volunteer, local militias to a permanent military. To many people, a paid, professional military was a threat to the republic, an overly aristocratic institution at odds with democracy, a drain on public finances, and a haven for criminals, layabouts, and others incapable of making a living in commerce.

The wide popularity of the Civil War's Union army was a rare exception to this rule, a shift in perception occasioned by the volunteering of middle-class men who answered the call to save the Union, and temporarily drove darker aspersions about the army into the wilderness. But as Union veterans went back to civilian life after 1865, Americans by and large returned to their traditional anti-army sentiments.[36] After Appomattox, funding for the army vanished. Almost a million soldiers mustered out by the spring of 1866, shrinking the army to 54,000 troops. Soldiers confronted the two great challenges of occupying the defeated South and winning the Indian wars despite worsening shortages of men and matériel. By 1874, Congress was budgeting for only 27,000 soldiers and officers. Recruitment was so poor that the true number of soldiers rarely exceeded 19,000, and these were but poorly provisioned.[37]

The army's post–Civil War missions failed to rouse public esteem. The southern occupation was inglorious, thankless, and contentious, riven with questions about the constitutionality of martial law and the rights of black freedmen and their former owners.

The Indian wars were as controversial as the southern occupation, but for different reasons. Americans were united in the proposition that Indian cultures should disappear, but they fought bitterly over how to effect that end. Frontier settlers tended to be vehemently in favor of massive military force to remove Indians altogether. But these citizens were in the minority. The more numerous easterners were more skeptical of the need for military action. Uncertain of the arability of western lands, they often believed that Indians would gradually diminish before the superior civilization and not require military conquest at all. Echoing these doubts were religious reformers, also based largely in the East, who were newly energized by their successful campaign to rid America of slavery. After the Civil War, they turned their attentions to reforming Indian policy. Seeking to settle and Christianize America's nomadic, pagan Indians, they viewed the army with deep suspicion. Indians needed to know Christian charity and hear the gospel so they could fly to Christ. The last thing the cause of civilization needed was violent ranks of drunken, blaspheming, lecherous soldiers in Indian Country.

Between these competing segments of the electorate, the army occupied a middle ground, less a conquering force than "a frontier constabulary charged with mediating among various foes," in the words of historian Sherry Smith.[38] Their role was to prevent not only massacres of whites by Indians, but massacres of Indians by whites. It was a volunteer militia of Colorado civilians that slaughtered over one hundred women, children, and elderly Cheyenne in the Sand Creek massacre of 1864. The village had been guaranteed federal protection, and the atrocity understandably enraged Cheyenne survivors. It also infuriated federal authorities, by renewing U.S.-Cheyenne hostilities, confounding federal diplomacy, and interrupting the westward flow of settlement and commerce. Throughout the 1860s, the ongoing struggle over Indian policy at the national level meant the army continually sought to justify more expenditures and larger troop deployments, often to congressional committees which were at best ambivalent. Not surprisingly, military people in the latter 1860s and throughout the 1870s felt unsupported, underpaid, and even betrayed by their country.[39]

In his continuing bid for respectability, Cody socialized almost exclusively with officers, most of whom were northern middle-class men like himself.[40] But in doing so, he trod warily over political fault lines which crisscrossed the military and aggravated their difficulties during the Indian wars. Officers extolled higher notions of duty and honor, often professing devotion to an aristocratic code of conduct resembling—and sometimes derived from—Sir Walter Scott's best-selling lore of the Round Table.[41] But the men who wore the epaulets, stars, and shoulder braids were often bitterly factionalized. Many officers sought transfers to the West in 1866, believing they would have more chance to prove themselves in combat on the Plains. Accelerated promotion through brevet ranks was the chief method of rewarding combat valor and the most coveted honor in the Civil War. But even in those relatively rare moments when the army and their

Indian opponents closed on the battlefield, officers were rarely promoted. The War Department did not award brevet ranks in the Indian wars.[42] Moreover, as congressional budgeteers reduced the number of troops, the number of officers' commissions fell into a corresponding decline. Thus, on the Plains, the army had too many young officers with ever fewer chances of promotion. Advancement in rank came mostly when superiors retired or died. Consequently, officers politicked furiously to have rivals disciplined, demoted, transferred, or court-martialed, and the resultant political frictions troubled the entire theater of the West.[43]

Commanders' frustrations were compounded by the theater of combat, for the West offered few opportunities for reversing public scorn. The weird landscape of the Plains was in thrall to weather that veered between parching heat and cold so fierce it froze a man's mouth shut.[44] Reports of Indian attacks were practically continuous, but meeting Sioux or Cheyenne in decisive combat was rare. Indian war parties, even entire villages, usually outran and outsmarted army patrols, separating into small groups and dispersing into the vastness of the Plains which they knew so well. All too often, soldiers had the same experience Lt. Col. George Custer did in 1867, thundering across the Plains in pursuit of an entire Cheyenne village, only to be "discouraged by seeing the broad, well-beaten trail suddenly separate into hundreds of indistinct routes, leading fan-shape in as many different directions."[45] The U.S. Army was better armed, better mounted, and usually larger than the Indian forces. Eventually, these advantages would tell in the army's favor. But in the short term, none of them seemed to make much difference, as Indians repeatedly fought and then fled, leaving army leaders to explain to the newspapers, and to the public, why they had failed to catch Indians yet again.[46]

For officers it was depressing and humiliating. For soldiers, it was worse. The frontier army was plagued by scurvy, rank-and-file boredom, and high rates of desertion, all exacerbated, especially in 1866 and 1867, by the absence of any great victories. General Winfield Scott Hancock ventured out to treat with—and hopefully intimidate—the Cheyenne Dog Men in 1867. He found no warriors willing to meet him in battle, burned the wrong village, provoked more Cheyenne raids, and terrified Cheyenne diplomats who might have helped establish peace. "Hancock's War" was roundly criticized in the national press.[47]

Not surprisingly, soldier morale was low and desertions high. On average, the army lost fully one-fourth of its troops to desertion in the 1870s, and over a longer period, between 1867 and 1891, one-third of the army deserted.[48] There were abundant reasons for discontent: drafty barracks, ill-fitting uniforms and boots, and a dismal diet of pork, hardtack, and coffee, which barely sustained a soldier's health. Troopers could go six months without seeing their wages, which dropped from $16 a month in the Civil War to $13 a month in 1871. They did not rise for the next twenty-seven years.[49]

In the future, the public would remember the grumbling, desertion-prone soldiers not only as enthusiastic subordinates of a united, heroic officer class, but as standard-bearers of a white vanguard. Thus, in 1887, when Cody debuted his reenactment of "Custer's Last Rally" in New York, the presentation of an immaculately uniformed, all-white army in Buffalo Bill's Wild West show reinforced dominant theories about race and civilization. Americans generally saw their westward expansion as the onward march of Anglo-Saxons along the arc they had followed from Britain to the New World centuries before, and which set their Aryan forebears wandering west from the Asian highlands long before that. Civilization was the product of the white race; white people moving to the West would establish it in defiance of their barbarian opponents. Just as the westering Saxons displaced the primitive Celts, so the Anglo-Saxons would defeat the Sioux and Cheyenne.[50]

Perhaps nothing has done more to obscure the complex history of the Plains Indian wars than these simplistic and enduring fantasies of grand racial conflicts. For on the ground, in the real Indian wars, class divisions between officers and troopers often undermined morale and esprit de corps while the ethnic and racial composition of troops confounded notions of clear-cut race war. Prominent fighters in the Plains campaigns included six all-black regiments (with white officers), the so-called Buffalo Soldiers, organized into four infantry regiments and the famed Ninth and Tenth Cavalry.[51]

But other troops, too, complicated ideals of a white man's army. Most soldiers were poor men, and many were immigrants. For the first decade after the Civil War, foreign-born recruits, mostly Irish and German immigrants, comprised 50 percent of the ranks. Almost a third of Custer's Seventh was Irish in 1876, and they were joined by Germans, Italians, and others. In the words of one scholar, the Plains army "was a foreign legion," patched together from Americans, Irish, Germans, French, British, Scandinavians, Italians, and Russians. Legend has it that the Eighth Infantry band in 1880s Montana was imported wholesale from Italy.[52] The Seventh Cavalry band spoke German and, according to Custer, regimental conversation was a "parody of Babel," where "almost every language has its representatives."[53]

Today we might see these disparities as quaint cultural variations. But in the 1860s, they aggravated class frictions between soldiers and their commanders, and they had pronounced implications for the ability of the army to fulfill white racial destiny: at the time, to be "white" meant more than having a pink skin. In the 1860s, "white" men were of Anglo-Saxon descent.

They were Protestant, English-speaking, and usually native-born. Most of all, white men possessed an inherited facility for self-governance, which flowed from the capacity to restrain appetites for violence and sensual pleasures.[54]

Germans, widely known as "Dutch" (from "Deutsch," their term for themselves) were mostly Catholics, and speakers of an alien language. They were tenuously white, at best.

The Irish were even more problematic. In popular reckoning, they were characteristically violent (a trait they displayed in the many strikes that paralyzed American cities), hostile to the rudiments of civilized behavior, and unable to restrain their appetites for liquor or sex. Many critics saw them as threats to the American republic, on a par with newly freed blacks, or savage Indians. Recalling New York's draft riots, one journalist described the noise of the Irish mob as "a howling as of thousands of wild Indians let loose at once."[55]

In this sense, a war that pitted "savage" Irish troopers against "savage" Indians was singularly ironic. Indians were of mysterious origin themselves (there were none in the Bible, after all). Some theorized that the most ardent opponents of the frontier army, the Oglala Sioux, were in fact Irish—as in "O'Gallalla."[56]

Laughable as it may seem, it made a certain kind of cultural sense to white Americans, who had long derided the Irish as savages. Comparisons of Irish to blacks were just as common, and they cut both ways across the racial divide, with Irish pegged as "white negroes" and blacks as "smoked Irish."[57]

By the 1860s, writers had been warning for decades that the prodigious immigration of "the most degenerate races of olden day Europe," including the "Irish, cross-bred German and French, and Italians of even more doubtful stock," would result in political chaos, and the racial decay of American Anglo-Saxondom.[58] In the 1880s and '90s, Buffalo Bill's Wild West "reenactments" of Plains battles depicted an all-white army pitted against a dark Indian menace. But in 1867, when Cody began scouting for the army, its ranks replicated the immigrant hodgepodge which seemed to threaten the Anglo-Saxon republic with racial dissolution. The result was an army riven with racial and class tensions. Irish ascended to racial respectability, to whiteness, by helping to resist and marginalize other nonwhites.[59] So, just as Americans ridiculed Irish immigrants as "savages," Irish soldiers conflated their hostilities to Indians and blacks. George Custer overheard two of his Irish troopers preparing to fire on a furious Sioux charge in 1873:

"Say Teddy, I guess the ball's opened."
"Yis, and by the way thim rid nagurs is comin' it's openin' wid a grand march."[60]

For immigrant troopers anxious to grasp some fragments of elusive whiteness, fighting Indians was only half the battle. They scrambled constantly to put distance between themselves and other "nonwhites" who wore the same uniform. After one particularly grueling 1869 campaign, the all-black Tenth Cavalry nearly went to war against the heavily immigrant Fifth Cavalry. "Men on both sides appeared to be desperate, and it required all my time and careful watching to prevent a terrible conflict," reported the white commander of the Tenth.[61]

Racial dissension in the army was so pronounced that to a limited degree even Indians exploited it. White commanders of the black Tenth Cavalry reported racial taunts "in plain English" by some of the hundreds of Cheyenne warriors who surrounded them on the Solomon River in August 1867. "Come here, come here, you sons of guns; we don't want to fight the niggers, we want to fight you white sons of guns."[62]

Army race tensions were evident throughout Cody's own autobiography, in which he poked fun at black soldiers, mocking their aspirations to "sweep de red debels from off de face ob de earth." In another anecdote, he recalled the night that a camp sentinel "who was an Irishman" bumped his head on a tree limb and insisted that Indians had hit him over the head. "As shure ez me name's Pat Maloney, one of thim rid divils hit me on the head wid a club, so he did."[63]

Frictions between native-born English-speakers and immigrant Germans strained the Cody household. In 1904, Cody recalled an instance from early in his marriage when Louisa took umbrage that he, "not thinking any that her mother was German," began "humming a little song that the soldiers used to sing there about the Dutch." As he told Louisa's lawyers many years later, his thoughtlessness "made Mrs. Cody angry and she give me a good deal of trouble about it."[64]

Whiteness within the frontier army was thus limited, contested, and often the provenance of a minority, and there was little hope for change in the short term. Popular theory, or wishful thinking, had it that the environmental influences of settling the land and sharing in America's abundance of nutrition could "whiten" immigrants, and for this reason many of the ethnic and racial conflicts that roiled the East were supposedly muted on the frontier.[65] But army recruits were often very new to American shores. They were soldiers, not settlers. In fact, settlers despised them. Army rations constituted anything but good food, a fact made abundantly clear by the numbers of troopers who stole into town to buy meals, or filch them. And soldiers, like urban immigrants, were renowned for slovenliness, belligerence, and savage predilection for drink.[66]

Seen in the internally contentious, multiracial context of the frontier army, beleaguered by public hostility and congressional indifference, Cody's popularity with officers begins to make a certain sense. An energetic, courageous, buckskin-clad white scout who could steer troops across the Plains and back again, fighting hostile Indians, would be welcome indeed for the white middle-class commanders of the U.S. Army. But one final feature of Plains warfare upped the currency of Cody's white Indian imposture even more. White scouts, or at least competent ones, were almost impossible to find. Indeed, scouts were perhaps the most troublesome of all civilians for the American army.

While the army pursued Indians in combat, and fantasized about white Indian scouts who could lead them to glory, most of their best scouts were actually Indians. Army scouting parties were predominantly made up of Shoshones, Crows, Arikaras, Pawnees, Osages, Kaws, Cherokees, Delawares, and an assortment of other Indians who opted for the army in the war between expansionist nomads and expansionist Americans. In a reflection of their prominence, no fewer than sixteen Indian scouts won the Congressional Medal of Honor between 1869 and 1890.[67]

As effective as Indian scouts could be, army commanders suspected them of having their own agenda in the Plains wars. Such fears were often misplaced, but not always. Many Indian scouts *were* out to settle old scores against the numerous Sioux and Cheyenne who had displaced them from their Plains homes. At times, Indian scouts' eagerness for combat upset commanders' goals of stealth and reconnaissance, endangering military operations. Thus, Cody was chief of scouts for General Carr's Fifth Cavalry expedition against the Cheyenne in the summer of 1869, during which Carr hoped to track detachments of Cheyenne warriors to the elusive village of Dog Man chief Tall Bull, which he proposed to attack. But the strategy was almost undone by Pawnee auxiliaries who refused to stalk small contingents of Cheyenne and instead attacked them. Tall Bull soon learned of the army's presence. Other officers feared that Indian scouts would commit atrocities against Cheyenne and Sioux opponents, and sometimes their fears were justified.[68] One of the reasons for the hiring of white scouts like Cody was that ideally they could serve as go-betweens for commanders and their Indian scouts, whose techniques and strategies were often mysterious or threatening to the army's own mission.

Equally prominent among scouts were so-called "half-breeds," mixed-blood men descended from white-Indian unions. Among these were French-speaking mixed-bloods like the legendary Baptiste "Little Bat" Garnier, Baptiste "Big Bat" Pourier, Ed Guerrier, Louis Richard, and the Shangrau brothers, Louis and John. Descendants of French traders who married into Indian families as early as the seventeenth century, these French- and Lakota-speaking families were traditionally cultural brokers and conduits between Indian tribes, Europeans, and Americans. But as they lost wealth and influence in the increasingly American nineteenth century, their declining fortunes seemed proof of frontier degeneration and the power of interracial sex to weaken a race that had once been vital.[69]

By their very existence, mixed-blood scouts hinted at uncomfortable facts, at the oft-unspoken transgressions of white Indians who rather than retaining white virtue as they crossed into savagery, became deviant and indulged in interracial sex. The idea was so loaded because popular beliefs equated race with species. Mixed-blood people were infertile hybrids, like the mule, the sterile offspring of a male donkey and a female horse. Thus the term *mulatto*, from the Spanish word for mule (*mulato*), and frequently applied to children of white-black unions, also found wide use on the Plains.[70] Racial theories maintained that sex between "proximate" and "distant" races, between whites and Indians, for example, produced *mulato*-like, degenerate races, prone to infertility, but also possessed of excessive (white) intelligence, in the service of inescapable (dark) savagery.[71] On the frontier, the children of Indian and white unions were "like the mulatto, quasi-mules," in the words of one observer, "untrustworthy, and disposed to every villainy."[72]

Such ideas gained a special purchase after the Civil War. At a time when the South was infused with white hysteria over the supposed need to contain the lust of free black men, the westward edge of the nation was by definition a place where widely divergent races met.[73] Anglo-Saxonists reassured themselves that the white race—and its civilization—were hardened by the bloodletting of frontier war, and in the 1880s and '90s Buffalo Bill's Wild West show reinforced such notions with its triumphalist pageantry of white victory on the Plains. But during the Plains Indian wars, mixed-blood scouts aggravated an old fear of frontier degeneracy, the destabilizing of the white race in lusty entangling of limbs with primitive peoples in the forests and prairies of the American interior. Their very presence called to mind Washington Irving's 1832 warning that on the Plains "may spring up new and mongrel races," the "amalgamation of the 'debris' and 'abrasions' of former races, civilized and savage."[74] In this sense, the frontier held out the possibility that if Americans were to be transformed into a new race, it would be a darker, not a lighter one.

French-speaking mixed-bloods were not the only harbinger of this fate. Much of the West had belonged to Mexico as recently as 1848. Mexican scouts, including Charles Autubees and his sons, from Bent's Fort, in Colorado, guided with Cody in 1868.[75] Mexicans themselves were ubiquitous reminders of the frontier's potential for "unfit amalgamation" of Europeans and Indians, a racial mixture that resulted in Mexico's political weakness and, ultimately, conquest by the racially vigorous United States.[76]

But as much as the imagined specter of the mongrel, miscegenated, monstrous half-breed haunted the westward passage of white America, in

real life, mixed-bloods proved indispensable as scouts. Mixed-blood children were potential translators, because they frequently spoke both English
or French and one or more Indian languages. Raised among Indians, they
often knew the whereabouts of different Indian bands at any time of year.
Tutored by Indian uncles, they learned to track—and fight—like few settlers
could. The long list of mixed-blood men who rode with Cody in the late
1860s grew longer as the wars continued. For the Powder River campaign of
1876, the army hired "every half-breed at Red Cloud or Spotted Tail agency
who could be secured."[77]

Army men might have been able to overlook some of their prejudices
against mixed-blood scouts, if only mixed-blood politics had not been so
conflicted. Mixed-blood men with family on both sides of the Indian wars
did not always flock to the American banner. George Bent, son of American
trader William Bent and his Cheyenne wife, Owl Woman, grew up speaking
Cheyenne and English. Although he was educated at a boarding school in
St. Louis, he chose to live as a Cheyenne, and fought Americans at Sand
Creek and in other battles. His brother, Charley Bent, attended the same
boarding school as George did. He became one of the most fearsome leaders of the Dog Men, taunting and battling American troopers with startling
effect, leading them against Custer's Seventh Cavalry outside Fort Wallace
in the summer of 1867. He became so menacing in American imaginations
that settlers and soldiers reported seeing him at the head of war parties from
Texas to Nebraska.[78] Ed Guerrier was a mixed-blood scout who joined Cody
in scouting for the Fifth Cavalry in 1876. In 1867, he was planning to marry
George and Charley Bent's sister, Julia. He was therefore profoundly
uncomfortable to find himself that summer guiding Custer's Seventh in pursuit of the very village in which Julia was living. Unbeknownst to Custer, he
located the village and warned them away, then steered Custer's troops in
another direction.[79]

The Bent brothers and their brother-in-law Ed Guerrier were just three
of many mixed-bloods who, in the minds of army officers, turned on the
higher civilization. To most Americans, the frontier was the boundary line
between the white and the red, and the army stood in defense of white
homes from Indian raiders who carried white women away into savagery.
But mixed-bloods were proof that the central institution of frontier life, the
family, sometimes straddled racial lines, and that the settler's cabin could be
the hearth of race mixing. The mixed-blood scout—light-skinned, fluent in
English and the enemy language, too—could as easily be a renegade spy.

With so much suspicion to go around, it is not surprising that white
scouts were often tarred with the mixed-blood brush. With a reputation as
frontier confidence men, they made dubious scouts at the best of times. And
if they *could* track Indians, were they white men at all? The best of them

were suspiciously well informed about the ways of these mysterious Plains nomads. Besides, popular beliefs maintained that tracking was the province of dark-skinned people, who were closest to nature. In the words of one army captain, white men "have not the same acute perceptions" in "the art of trailing or tracking men and animals" that characterized "the Indian or the Mexican."[80]

Where the white Indian was often heroic in American literature, he was in fact a notoriously unstable figure, who could be either hero or villain. In the conquest of Kentucky, Daniel Boone, the consummate white Indian hero, faced off not only against the Shawnees, but against Simon Girty and Alexander McKee, two white men who had become Shawnee. The story of that confrontation between the virtuous white Indian and his renegade alter egos inspired thousands of American stories and novels in the nineteenth century.[81] White Indian renegades embodied a dark warning about the frontier's potential to convey savagery to the very white people who were supposed to conquer it. Many Americans suspected that absence from white civilization would eventually overwhelm a person's race loyalty. "Long exile from Christendom and civilization inevitably restores a man to that condition in which God placed him," wrote Herman Melville, "*i.e.* what is called savagery."[82] In Kansas, in the late 1860s, soldiers and civilians alike attributed frequent army defeats to phantom white-men-turned-red, and the Plains was rife with the rumor of renegades.[83]

A reluctance to confront suspicions of being a renegade likely limited the willingness of other scouts to assume the pose of the white Indian. Certainly there were white scouts who, given a greater willingness to play the game, might have matched Cody's rise or even surpassed it. Hickok quit scouting for the army after 1868. But even if he had not, his moodiness with journalists and officers made him unpopular with various commanders, including Carr. After Hickok, the scout best situated to capitalize on his fame as a white Indian was probably Frank North. A resident of Colville, Nebraska, North was a middle-class store owner with a wood frame house and a white wife and family. He was highly unusual, though, in that he spoke fluent Pawnee, a language he learned while working as a clerk at the nearby Pawnee reservation. Beginning in the 1860s, he helped organize and rode with three battalions of Pawnee scouts fighting the Sioux and Cheyenne alongside the army. He was the Pawnees' putative commander, although in reality he appears to have been their translator and liaison to the army command.[84]

North had adventures aplenty on the Pawnee scouts' numerous forays against the Sioux and Cheyenne. He knew Cody well, rode with him more than once, and found his theatrics amusing. He even accompanied the Pawnee veterans in joining Buffalo Bill's Wild West show in 1883, and stayed with the show for two years, until he was injured in the arena. But something held him back. Photographs show him dressed in middle-class jacket and trousers, like a merchant. No buckskin for him. North was already so close to the Pawnees that perhaps he feared a white Indian pose would alienate him from his white neighbors, leery as they were of renegades. Perhaps he was weakened by poor health—his asthma finally killed him in 1885. In any case, he seems never to have understood Indian fighting as anything more than a distasteful, even tragic necessity. In the 1860s, he had little time for frontier imposture. In 1869, dime novelist Ned Buntline read about North in the newspapers, and sought him out at Fort Sedgewick, hoping to write a novel based on his adventures as a "white chief" of the Pawnees. Nobody knows what they said to one another, but according to one colorful (and probably apocryphal) story, North demurred. "If you want a man to fill that bill," he is said to have told Buntline, "he's over there sleeping under the wagon." The man sleeping under the wagon was, of course, William Cody.[85]

Other than Hickok, North, and Cody, there were only a few competent white scouts on the Plains. Among the best of these were Will Comstock, Abner "Sharp" Grover, John Y. Nelson, and Ben Clark. All of these men worked at one time or another with William Cody, or in nearby regiments. All of them came to the Plains as fur trappers and market hunters. All were superb at guiding, scouting, and fighting, and some of them were even drawn to white Indian performance (John Y. Nelson was, after all, a member of Buffalo Bill's Wild West show).

But, significantly, all had "gone native" in ways disturbingly like predecessors on other frontiers. All of them had married, or were rumored to have married, Cheyenne, Sioux, or Comanche wives. All of them spoke English and the language of their Indian families. Their Indian wives, to say nothing of their mixed-blood children, increased the plausibility that they might be spies, making them all the more suspicious to the American public, and to army officers.

Thus, even the best white scouts were a little too Indian to be acceptable in polite company. Although their talents were often appreciated, officers saw these so-called "squaw men" as peculiar at best and treasonous at worst. Until the post–Civil War period, mixed-race families had been common on the Plains. Many of the most successful traders had Indian wives, as we have seen, in part to better their alliances with powerful clients. But as their Indian in-laws lost power, and as middle-class America expanded onto the Plains, middle-class white women increased in number, and white men with Indian wives were shunted aside as racially degenerative vestiges of a bygone era.

The army, in pushing the Sioux and Cheyenne from the Plains and facilitating railroad construction and middle-class settlement, thus helped to marginalize mixed-race families at the same time they exploited the talents of their white patriarchs as scouts and guides. In the process, these men became, at best, quaint relics of an older time, backward white men with Indian ways of thinking. General Carr related that Sharp Grover "was a squaw man and had imbibed some of their [Cheyenne] superstitions."[86] Another Plains witness reported, "No Indian was ever half so superstitious" as Will Comstock. "He had his 'medicine' horse, 'medicine' field-glass, 'medicine' everything, in fact. Even Will's evil-looking dog was 'medicine,' and had a 'medicine' collar. If he had bad luck his 'medicine' was bad, and something must be done to change the condition of things."[87]

Socially retarded throwbacks to a vanishing frontier, "squaw men" rarely climbed into the respectable white middle class after the Civil War. They were also a political threat. Despite their pro-U.S. leanings and, in some cases, army heroics, they could not escape the stigma of renegades.[88] Colonel Richard Irving Dodge denounced them as "ruffians" whose large broods of "half-breed children" were "fed and fostered by the Government," and whose propensity for suborning Indians against the interests of the nation made them a menace. "They are an injury to the country, a detriment to the Indian, and should be abolished."[89]

Scouts' intimacy with Indians and the frontier was thus a double-edged sword. It provided the army with keys to white conquest of the savage wilderness, but simultaneously, it implied the danger of race decline, in which the savagery of the frontier essentially conquered the race, turning white men against civilization. In American cultural thought, men were less subject than women to corruption from interracial sex, but they were not immune to suspicions of weakened racial loyalty. In a sense, scout forays into Indian society and Indian sex raised the same fear that Attack on the Settler's Cabin raised for audiences of Buffalo Bill's Wild West show: the savage capture of civilization.

ONLY THE MOST concerted effort at simplification could reduce the complex and confusing racial dynamics of the Plains conflicts to a white-on-red war. Even during the Plains wars, Cody himself provided a means to do so. He was that rarity, a competent white scout. Even rarer, he had a white wife and a white daughter, although they were far away from him at the moment. Until he could bring the family together again, he was not without prospects in his effort to become a leading army scout. On the one hand, Indian and mixed-blood scouts had skills, including bilingualism, he could not match.

But, on the other, his very ignorance of Indian language protected him from the suspicions swirling around men like Grover and Comstock.

Cody exploited these social assets through an imposture so aggressive and so skillful that it allowed, even invited, commanders to overlook his shortcomings. He obscured his limitations as a tracker by sticking close to the Indians and mixed-bloods in his scouting parties, and accepting credit for their accomplishments. This was no trivial skill. Most white men, after all, were so afraid or scornful of Indians that they kept their distance even from Indian allies. Cody was not self-conscious about riding with them, and he was even curious to watch them work. Thus, in 1869, he followed a Pawnee trailer in pursuit of a Cheyenne band for miles across a grassland where he and the other white scouts could find no trace of the enemy. When the grass gave way to sand, the tracks of the Cheyenne suddenly were visible. The Pawnee's abilities awed Cody: "I take off my hat to him, he is the best I ever saw."[90]

In 1876, officers with General Crook were all but certain that a plume of dust rolling into the distant sky was a huge party of approaching Sioux. Cody bolted from his coterie of Shoshone scouts and dashed toward it, seemingly unafraid. "He's going to reconnoiter," remarked Captain Royall. "That's Bill's style, you know." At that remark, a young Shoshone approached the officers, to tell them what he had already told Cody. "No Sioux," he said. "Heap pony soldier." Sure enough, the men kicking up that dust cloud turned out to be General Terry's cavalry.[91]

Cody's imposture, his artful deception that combined some degree of scout skill with some sleight of hand, allowed officers to go about the serious business of fighting Indians while believing in the superiority of white men, and as his celebrity increased, their views seemed ever more vindicated. In the 1890s, the rising militarism of American society, along with the nostalgic paintings of Frederic Remington, and Cody's own Wild West show, which began to glorify the army as a frontier institution in 1887, would elevate the memory of the U.S. military's western service. In no small measure, the new appreciation stemmed from the whitewash in these popular images, in which the impoverished, multilingual, multihued troopers, and their weird assemblages of Indian, mixed-blood, and bicultural white scouts, too, all became battle-hardened Anglo-Saxons. But the frontier itself was far more confusing than these later images conveyed. In the 1860s and '70s, officers and soldiers of the Plains campaigns had no idea they would ever be so appreciated. Between the end of the Civil War in 1865, and the end of hostilities against the Sioux in 1877, the U.S. military struggled to establish dominance on the Plains, in a context of low morale, high desertion in the ranks, pervasive ethnic and racial frictions, and weak political support at home.

SCOUT HERO OF '69

Following Cody's progress through the campaigns of 1868–69 is difficult, because army documents seldom record the achievements or even the presence of civilian scouts. Most of the testimony to Cody's valor came years later, after he was a famous showman. Nonetheless, sifting the sources carefully we can see how he negotiated the complex multiracial terrain of the army scout's world, and how he began to position himself as the deliverer of an anxious white officer class from a racially corrosive frontier. In the fall of 1868, the Fifth Cavalry joined Sheridan's winter offensive. The general hoped to catch Indian warriors in their winter camps and destroy their horses, stores of food, and weapons, leaving them unable to mount an offensive when warm weather returned. The most notable event of this campaign was Custer's attack on Black Kettle's band of Cheyenne at the Washita River. While Custer and the Seventh Cavalry journeyed to the Washita, Cody guided General Carr and seven troops of Fifth Cavalry from Fort Lyon, in eastern Colorado, southward to the North Canadian River, in western Indian Territory (today's Oklahoma). The seventy-five supply wagons of the Fifth Cavalry were vital support for General William Penrose's Third Cavalry, which had ventured out earlier with scant provisions and was now enduring frigid winter conditions. Tracking through thick snow and freezing cold, Cody led Carr to the Third Cavalry. Upon hearing from straggling soldiers that Penrose's troops were near starvation, Carr ordered Cody ahead with two troops of cavalry and fifty pack mules. Despite fierce cold and still more snow, Cody located the Penrose command on Paloduro Creek, where the Third Cavalry—with Wild Bill Hickok among its scouts—had been on quarter rations for two weeks, and two hundred horses and mules had perished from exhaustion and lack of food.[92]

As much as Cody contributed to Carr's success that fall, at times he displayed the very characteristics of distracting entrepreneurialism, conviviality, and combativeness that troubled commanders where scouts were concerned. The racially mixed crowd of scouts, only nominally under military authority, could be as explosive as the troopers. After leading Carr to Penrose's command, Cody teamed up with Hickok and persuaded a Mexican wagonmaster on a passing beer train to advance them his cargo in exchange for a share of the profits. The two scouts sold the beer "to our boys in pint cups, and as the weather was very cold we warmed the beer by putting the ends of our picket-pins heated red-hot into the cups. The result," recalled Cody, "was one of the biggest beer jollifications I ever had the misfortune to attend." A subsequent spree resulted in a brawl between white scouts, led by Hickok and Cody, and the Mexican and Mexican American scouts, notably the Autubees brothers. Cody said the fight was a result of "a feud" between the "fifteen Mexicans" scouting for Penrose scouts and the white scouts, led by himself.[93] Indeed, the instigation for the fight hinted at the simmering white resentment of degenerate race mingling. Fists flew after Hickok called the Autobees brothers a bunch of "mongrels."[94]

Carr had no intention of letting the scouts repeat the episode. He sent Cody and Hickok to scout for a five-hundred-man detachment marching into the Texas Panhandle in search of Indians. They found none. By the end of the campaign, the troops were suffering from scurvy, and Cody was dispatched to hunt fresh meat. With twenty wagons in tow, Cody searched four days for buffalo before sighting a herd. Stampeding them into a snow-choked arroyo, he killed fifty-five. The next day, he killed forty-one more. In the following two days, he nearly doubled this total again. His shoulder was beaten black and blue by the kick of his rifle, and swollen so badly that he needed help to get his coat on. In February 1869, Cody returned to Fort Lyon with the Fifth Cavalry.[95]

At the end of the campaign, as other scouts were paid off and sent on their way, Carr retained Cody's services. The scout requested a leave to visit his wife in St. Louis, and Carr agreed.[96]

The visit with Louisa went well. Cody later said it was because he was not there long enough to fight with her.[97] But there may have been other reasons for the couple's placidity, among them Cody's recent ascension to the respectable wage of $125 per month.[98]

If his pay increase reflected his success in fighting the Cheyenne, the rapprochement between William and Louisa Cody coincidentally resonated with a primary aim of the Indian wars, to shore up American families threatened by the Indian destruction of their homes, and the abduction of settlers, especially women and children. Even if no white women had been abducted, Americans so imagined Indian men as rapists that the ideology of captive redemption would have motivated hostilities anyway. But enough settlers were abducted by Indians in the combat theater that in the public eye the multihued, squabbling army and its equally diverse, contentious scouts were ironically arrayed in an ongoing defense of white womanhood.

Thus, at the Washita, Custer sought to redeem from Cheyenne captivity one Mrs. Blynn, who was killed in the onslaught.[99] Subsequently, as the war continued through the spring of 1869, the army secured the release of several white women from Indian captivity. George Custer finally caught up with a large contingent of Dog Men, in March 1869, at Sweetwater Creek. After opening negotiations with a number of chiefs, Custer took three of them hostage. He had learned that two white women captives, Anna Morgan and one Mrs. White, were in the village. Custer announced that unless they were returned, and unless all 260 lodges went to the reservation south of the Arkansas River, he would hang the hostages. Ultimately, the Indians handed over the white women, and agreed to go to the reservation.[100]

Meanwhile, farther north, Cody's star continued its rise, in another effort at captive redemption. In May 1869, the Fifth Cavalry moved to Fort McPherson, in Nebraska. Along the way, the regiment fought two skirmishes against Sioux and Cheyenne warriors, with Cody earning extraordinary praise from General Eugene Carr for his tracking and marksmanship, as well as his bravery. According to Carr's report, Cody "displayed great skill in following" the trail, and also "deserves great credit for his fighting in both engagements, his marksmanship being very conspicuous." In June, the secretary of war himself approved Carr's request for a $100 bonus for Cody to honor his service.[101]

The coming battle would be the largest and, militarily, the most consequential of his life. In May of 1869, Cody marched with a battalion of the Fifth Cavalry from Fort Lyon, Colorado, to new headquarters at Fort McPherson, Nebraska. On the way, he saw more fighting at Beaver Creek. The Dog Men were out in force that month. Joined by at least three bands of Sioux and by various Arapaho warriors and their families, they warred across northern Kansas, attacking a crew on the Kansas Pacific, destroying homesteads, killing settlers, and finally carrying off two German immigrant women, Mrs. Maria Weichell and Mrs. Susanna Alderdice, who was abducted with her baby. Although many children, women, and sometimes men were adopted by the Cheyenne after abduction, murder of captives was permissible and even standard when they were in flight from the army. A Cheyenne warrior strangled the Alderdice infant shortly after the abduction. Tall Bull and other leaders of those Dog Men now decided to break for the north. In the Powder River country of Wyoming, they hoped, they would find allies among the Northern Cheyenne and Sioux, and respite from army patrols. Sheridan, knowing that the Dog Men were headed north, sent Carr and the Fifth Cavalry in pursuit.[102]

The Republican River expedition, as it became known, was the largest in the history of Fort McPherson, and amid the unwieldy, contentious mixture of officers, soldiers, white scouts, Indian scouts and auxiliaries, civilian teamsters, wagons, mules, and horses, we get a glimpse of young Cody, chief of scouts, his abilities as Indian fighter and his significance as a symbol for a beleaguered army. We sense, too, how the campaign to turn the weird assemblage of peoples into a unified force through pageantry, drill, and celebration later inspired his development of multiracial traveling amusements.

At fewer than 400 men, the expedition was small for the challenge of fighting the Dog Men. Numerical shortcomings made it ever more dependent on Indian knowledge, guidance, and fighting power: 150 Pawnee scouts, under the nominal command of translator and scout Frank North and his brother, Luther, set out alongside the expedition. Trundling after the command was a heavily overloaded supply train, driven by civilian teamsters. The day before the expedition departed, the Fifth Cavalry paraded at the fort, performing mock charges with sabers glinting in the sun. The Pawnee scouts matched their display, borrowing full dress uniforms and making some mock charges of their own, as if to declare their alliance—and equality—with the U.S. Army.

The formal pageantry over, the Pawnees spent the night in war dances and traditional recitation of personal battle histories. Together, all of these preliminaries were a Wild West show in their own right, with an appreciative audience, too: soldiers and their families, as well as other residents of the fort and dozens of teamsters, all turned out to watch. The next day, under regimental flags and to the accompaniment of the regimental band, this motley assemblage officially known as the Fifth Cavalry—but actually the Fifth Cavalry plus many Pawnees, some white scouts, and a lot of civilians— headed out. Cody, the North brothers, and the Pawnee scouts led the way.[103]

On this journey, as on others, Cody exercised his customary entrepreneurship, as well as the chaotic social latitude of the typical scout. Along with two other civilians, he invested in a wagon of tinned goods to sell to soldiers, and it lumbered along with the other fifty or so wagons which carried the command's provisions. Financially, the venture failed. At least Cody never paid his partner, Eric Ericson, for his share of the investment, something Ericson resented for years afterward.[104]

Keeping order among his scouts would trouble General Carr on this journey as on others. A few nights before the expedition departed, Cody was drinking at the California Exchange Keg House in North Platte, and ended up getting the worst of a fistfight with the saloonkeeper, Dave Perry, a friend with whom Cody subsequently reconciled.[105] On the first night of the march, he and Luther North left the command for a private dinner at Cody's house, back at the fort. A storm broke out on their return, and they were unable to find their way back to the command in the lightning. "Well, we are fine scouts," commented Cody, "lost within three miles of the fort." They had to wait till dawn to find their way back to Carr's troops. Only their good fortune prevented the regiment from needing their services in the meantime.[106]

For Cody, numerous encounters with Cheyenne and Sioux parties began the next week, and the scout's autonomy agitated Carr. A week out, a Sioux raiding party tried to stampede the army mule herd and thereby strand the supply train. Officers were too stunned to give orders. The scouts did not wait for them. Cody leapt onto his horse and pounded after the raiding party, with scouts Frank and Luther North and dozens of Pawnee auxiliaries right behind him. They soon passed Cody, whose mount was exhausted.

Cody caught up with them as they recovered the mules, and two of the Pawnees killed two of the retreating Sioux. The scout party continued the pursuit, in vain, until after dark. When they returned, Carr was furious. Luring soldiers away from the main command was a standard Sioux tactic. Captain William Fetterman had fallen for the trick just three years before, at Fort Phil Kearny, in Wyoming Territory, and he had perished with his entire command of eighty-one men. Careful not to offend Cody, Frank North, or the Pawnees, Carr vented his fury on Luther North, the youngest and most dispensable of the scouts.[107]

Although the command followed the trail of a large village to the North Fork of the Solomon River the next day, the Cheyenne scattered and even the Pawnees could not pick up the trail. For the next ten days, Carr's command wandered through the valley of the Republican River, searching for Indians.[108]

After several more brief skirmishes, Carr ordered a forced march across the Sand Hills to catch up to the retreating Cheyenne. Moving rapidly through abandoned Cheyenne campsites along the way, the command was soon approaching its limits. Grass gave way to yucca and cactus. There was no wood for fires. The horses were exhausted. Selecting only those men whose mounts were still fit for duty—244 cavalry, 50 Pawnee scouts, the North brothers, and William Cody—Carr set out at dawn on July 11 with rations for three days. If they did not find the Cheyenne in that time, the Dog Men would escape.[109]

Cody later wrote that on Carr's order he handpicked "five or six of the best Pawnees," with whom he found the Dog Men's camp. But regimental records credit the Pawnee scouts, not Cody: "The Pawnees with General Carr's column soon reported an Indian village near 'judging from signs.' Ten minutes later the Indian village was discovered." Cody's eagerness to receive credit for the discovery was in keeping with his artful claim to supreme scouting abilities for the rest of his career. But, if the account does not say who first saw the village, all battlefield reports credit the Pawnees for their scouting and fighting; none so much as mentions Cody.[110]

Galloping together in three parallel columns, double file, Carr's command roared into a valley thick with Cheyenne tipis. Although the Pawnee horses were in poorer condition than the cavalry mounts, the Pawnees actually arrived among the Cheyenne lodges first. In a reflection of how much the army depended on Indian scouts and allies to win the Plains wars, Maria Weichell, the only captive to survive the fight, feared she was being rescued from the Cheyenne only to become the captive of other Indians.[111]

The battle was quick. Tall Bull was killed, the Dog Men crushed. By 1879, Cody was claiming that he shot Tall Bull himself, after seeing him "riding a large bay horse, and giving orders to his men in his own language—which I could occasionally understand." Cody recounted how he dashed into a ravine and shot Tall Bull from hiding, then retrieved the splendid horse he was riding. After the battle, he wrote, when he found Tall Bull's wife weeping, "I informed her that henceforth I should call the gallant steed 'Tall Bull,' in honor of her husband." During his Wild West show days, Cody's programs included a pen-and-ink drawing of himself closing in mounted combat with Tall Bull and stabbing him in the chest. Later, cover illustrations showed him shooting Tall Bull off his horse, from a ravine.[112] His stature as the white Indian who tracked down and killed this Plains nemesis grew in the following decades, slathered in realistic detail and his real participation in the battle where the Dog Man fell.[113]

Of course, Cody's account was fanciful. He did not understand Cheyenne, and none of his versions of Tall Bull's demise square with numerous other accounts. After the battle, General Carr interviewed one of Tall Bull's wives. She told him that as the attack began, the chief told his family to escape. "The wife begged him to escape with her, but he shut his ears." He killed his horse (as a sign, like the dog rope, that he would not retreat), and she saw him killed in the fighting.

Other sources suggest truth to this account. Luther North made the dubious claim that his brother, Frank North, shot Tall Bull. But he also recounts the Dog Man was shooting from cover, on foot, in a ravine, at the time he was killed. A Cheyenne painting places Tall Bull on foot, in a ravine, being shot by the Pawnees. For their part, the Pawnees said that it was impossible to tell who killed Tall Bull, because so many men were shooting at him—in a ravine.[114]

In truth, it is doubtful anybody could tell who shot whom amidst the chaos and the howling wind, which was blowing so hard that the Cheyenne did not hear the thunderous cavalry charge until the soldiers were fifty yards from the village. Whoever brought about Tall Bull's death, the capture of his village was a resounding success for the army. For the Dog Men, it was the final catastrophe.[115]

Cody scouted for the Fifth Cavalry several more times that fall, and in one engagement he and Frank North found themselves cut off and in need of rescue by the troups.[116] But these were relatively minor encounters. The 1869 battle of Summit Springs was the largest battle of the Indian wars in which Cody took part. Absent his participation, and his decades-long mythologizing of the event in the Wild West show, it likely would have been a footnote in Plains history, as most Indian battles were. More immediately, Cody's participation and his flashy self-presentation allowed him to catch the attention of visiting dime novelist Ned Buntline, who was at Fort Sedgewick, in Colorado, looking for a scout to write a story about, when the Fifth returned from Summit Springs. Buntline's real name was Edward Z. C. Judson, and he was rumored to be the highest-paid author in America. Six months later, Buntline published the first-ever Buffalo Bill dime novel, *Buffalo Bill: The King of Border Men*, in the story paper *New York Weekly*.

The story had nothing to do with the Summit Springs campaign. It was a romance of Cody's life, and Buntline took the precaution of including "Wild Bill Hitchcock" and several other characters from Hickok's well-known adventures to make Cody's character recognizable as a heroic frontier scout. The plot, in which Buffalo Bill and Wild Bill rescue Will Cody's mother and sisters from white renegades and their Indian allies, bore little resemblance to any of Cody's experiences. It did, however, express popular anxieties about frontier renegades, which permeated urban and frontier communities alike and which formed much of the backdrop to Cody's rise to prominence as a trustworthy, loyal white scout for the troubled army.[117]

Cody's fame as a dime novel hero enhanced his attraction as a hunting guide, and thereafter journalists resorted to romantic, dime novel language to describe him. The genre of serial fiction typically inserted real people, many drawn from newspaper accounts of current events, into fictional plots. Audiences could wonder how much was true and how much was fake in Buntline's "true" story of the western hero, but as much as dime novels resembled artful deceptions, they were properly understood as a form of entertainment journalism, akin to today's television "docudramas." Buffalo Bill Cody's public debut was in a lowbrow story magazine, not the venerable *Harper's New Monthly*, but for all that he was now a press phenomenon.[118]

His fame arrived just in time. After 1869, with the southern Cheyenne defeated and the northern Indians not yet confronted, major hostilities diminished in Kansas. Cody's arrival in the public eye would have been much harder had he begun service as a scout any later.

After Summit Springs, his commanders took the unusual step of keeping him on the payroll even without a mission for him to perform. Carr cashiered all his other scouts. But rather than let Cody go completely, he named him chief herder for Fort McPherson's livestock, and continued to pay him at a higher, scout wage of $75 a month.[119]

Importantly, Cody's starring role as a guide in the campaign that rescued Maria Weichell brought him victory in his private campaign to reunite the Cody family. Soon after the fight at Summit Springs, he persuaded Louisa and baby Arta to move in with him again, since he "was then in a position to take care of them. My salary was not only a good one from the United States Government but I had a share of all the captured stock—captured horses or captured property from the enemy." He also sent for two of his sisters, Helen and May. The Cody family would stay together at Fort McPherson for the next three years.[120]

In many ways, the war in which he fought resembled the border blood-letting of his boyhood in Kansas. Just as Red Legs and bushwhackers burned homes, so, too, did Indians burn farms and the army burn Cheyenne and Sioux lodges. As Cody himself had done in Kansas and Missouri as a teenager, Indian boys and young men fought a vain war in defense of those homes. As the Fifth Cavalry and the Pawnee scouts thundered toward the Cheyenne that day in July 1869, the first Cheyenne to see them was a fifteen-year-old boy tending the village horse herd. With the deftness of a man many years his senior, he turned the herd and drove it right into the village, where the horses provided means of escape for those few who were not killed or captured. The boy had a horse and could have run, but he turned at the village perimeter and made his stand against the Pawnees, who quickly killed him. Years later, Luther North still remembered the boy's courage: "No braver man ever lived than that fifteen-year-old boy."[121]

North, and no doubt Cody, too, saw in such young men the heroic counterparts of themselves, young men who sacrificed all to defend hearth and home. But if Indian warriors and army scouts were not that different (and in some cases they were one and the same), Cody reassured officers because he made it easy to ignore Indians, and to avoid thinking about how familiar their heroism looked, or what that meant for the army's often-unsavory conquest mission.

The struggle for home was central to U.S. Army life, too, and it defined day-to-day social relations in ways that divided officers and enlisted men. At western forts, officers' wives generally constituted a small outpost of middle-class sensibility, fashion, and femininity, with cotillions, teas, dinner parties, and other social engagements that distinguished officer society from that of lower-class enlisted men, fewer of whom were married and whose wives were usually post laundresses or otherwise working class. The presence of a genteel white family in a sense marked the class divide between officers and the men they commanded, who were typically excluded from the vibrant officers' social scene.[122]

The presence of Cody's family ultimately gave him a powerful class connection to army officers. He and Louisa were entitled to free government housing on a par with officers' quarters. But Cody did not put his family in those dreary lodgings. Instead, with newfound riches burning a hole in his pocket and anxious to persuade Louisa to stay with him this time, he ordered the construction of a small house. Modest as it was, it was no rude cabin, and as it took shape it announced the Cody family's arrival among the fort's middle class. It had a picket fence, frame windows, and inside, a carpet.[123] In St. Louis, a sign reading "Louisa Frederici, Dressmaker" had hung in front of the Frederici home. Louisa brought the old sign to Fort McPherson, crossed out "Frederici," wrote in "Cody," and put it proudly in front of her new house. The extra money she earned from taking in sewing would help the little family make ends meet. Three-year-old Arta soon had a new brother, Kit Carson Cody, born on November 26, 1870. A well-heeled southern lady who had recently settled near Fort McPherson occasionally slept over at the Cody home, darning rugs with Louisa, whom she found "quite pleasant in her manner," her home all the more inviting for her "two charming little children."[124]

FRONTIER THEATRICS

Partly because he had now secured middle-class status at the fort, in subsequent years army officers found it ever easier to utilize Cody not just for his considerable skills as scout but as a symbol of their own valor. Our story becomes more tangled here, because after 1869 Cody's military exploits quickly became conflated with his press reputation as a hunter and scout, and with his theatrical career, which began in 1872. Nonetheless, a brief overview suggests how useful Cody became for the army command after the battle of Summit Springs, and how much their patronage reinforced his credibility as a real frontier hero.

In 1869 and for the decade thereafter, officers authenticated Cody's imposture through recommending him to eastern financiers and politicians on hunting excursions, in encouraging and assisting him in planning his first trips to the East, and in decorating him with a Medal of Honor, in 1872. The battle that brought Cody the medal was a small, nameless skirmish, which occurred when he led a detachment of the Third Cavalry to the camp of about a dozen Minneconjou Sioux horse raiders. Cody guided the party "with such skill that he approached the Indian Camp within fifty yards before he was noticed," reported the commander, Captain Charles Meinhold. "The Indians fired immediately upon Mr. Cody and Seargeant Foley. Mr. Cody killed one indian, two others ran towards the main command and were killed."

Cody then noticed a party of six Sioux racing downriver. Captain Meinhold related: "I at once sent Lieutenant Lawson with Mr. Cody and fifteen men in pursuit." With Cody at the front, the party gained on the Sioux until they cut loose two stolen horses, but the warriors escaped. Meinhold commended a number of his soldiers, including two of his sergeants, and one Private William Strayer, "who bravely closed in upon an Indian while he was fired at several times, and wounded him." Summarizing Cody's contribution, Meinhold noted that "Mr. William Cody's reputation for bravery and skill as a guide is so well established that I need not say anything else but that he acted in his usual manner."

Authors who have never faced enemy fire should not discount the heroism of those who have. But as real as Cody's courage was, and as skillful as he was at horseback warfare, this expedition was no masterwork of guiding. In Meinhold's words: "The country I have marched over is so well known that I omit to furnish a map."[125]

More, we have to recall that by this time Cody's "reputation for bravery and skill" was inflated through Ned Buntline's *King of Border Men* and other press accounts. In 1870, six months after Buntline's story appeared, the *New York Times* reported one of Buffalo Bill's recent encounters with Indians who had taken stock from Fort McPherson. According to the correspondent, a company of cavalry from the fort "started in pursuit, without rations, not even stopping for breakfast." After "a hard chase of over sixty miles across a difficult country," the soldiers surprised the Indians, killing three, and recaptured all the stock. "Buffalo Bill was with the party and distinguished himself as usual."[126] In October 1871, newspapers gave wide coverage to a hunting party hosted by General Phil Sheridan, which included prominent New York publishers August Belmont and James Gordon Bennett, and which was guided by Buffalo Bill.[127] The *New York Herald* again hailed "the genial and daring Buffalo Bill," a "hero of the Plains," in January 1872, when he guided for the hunt of the Grand Duke Alexis of Russia and Phil Sheridan. By April 1872, when Cody set out with the Third Cavalry in pursuit of the Minneconjou Sioux, it was virtually impossible to separate the man's "real" talents from his reputation in the media.[128] To some degree, army commanders found in Cody a means to reflect elusive fame and glory onto themselves. Just having him along on a campaign almost guaranteed enthusiastic press coverage.

Upon receiving Meinhold's report, Colonel J. J. Reynolds, commander of the Third Cavalry, submitted the names of the two commended sergeants—Vokes and Foley—along with those of Private William Strayer and scout William Cody for Congressional Medals of Honor. He forwarded the recommendation to General Phil Sheridan, who approved it, as did civilian officials in Washington. In May, all four men received the Medal of Honor.[129]

If the award seems excessive in light of the small battle, this is in part because the Medal of Honor meant something quite different in 1872 than it does today. Conceived during the Civil War as a means of rewarding valor in the Union cause, until 1918 it was the only medal the army dispensed. Valor was not an exclusive requirement. Men who displayed "soldierly qualities," such as following orders, also received it. Thus, Sergeant Leroy

Vokes, who rode with Cody against the Sioux that day, received the Medal of Honor because, in Meinhold's words, "his prompt, intelligent, and cheerful obedience to my orders aided me essentially." The medal bore little of the aura it has today. There was no great ritual attached to it. Honorees received it in the mail, not in a White House ceremony. By 1869, the medal was so widely faked that many were reluctant to claim it.[130] (This helps explain why Cody rarely mentioned it, even in his Wild West show publicity.) Moreover, the award was perfectly in keeping with the army command's increasing resort to Cody as a symbol of their own heroism.

In subsequent years, Cody's presence not only elevated his commanders in the eyes of the public, but in the eyes of their troopers as well. Cody began his stage career in 1872, but he scouted for the army twice thereafter. The first time was in 1874, when he rode alongside several dozen Pawnee scouts during an uneventful campaign into the Big Horn Mountains in today's Wyoming. The expedition proved to be so minor that the commanding officer all but forgot it in his memoirs, and even at the time it paled in comparison to Custer's highly publicized march of that summer, through the Black Hills, where he confirmed the presence of gold on the Great Sioux Reservation and touched off the Indian war that finally got him killed. Cody nonetheless inflated the importance of his own activities as best he could. "The command will number nearly as many men as General Custers and be commanded by Col. Mills we are going in to one of the worst Indian countrys on the plains," wrote Cody to friends in the East. But the tour through the Big Horn Mountains encountered no Indians, and by September the expedition had returned to base, where it was dissolved.[131]

More famous was Cody's last venture with the cavalry, in 1876, as war with the Sioux and Cheyenne commenced again. That summer, Carr requested Cody's appointment as scout. Cody departed his stage show in Taunton, Massachusetts, and headed out to Wyoming Territory, where he rendezvoused with the Fifth Cavalry. Some in the army doubted that the theatrical star could be of any real assistance. Perhaps Carr was betting that Cody's pose would convince the soldiers of their own invulnerability. If so, he was right. Upon seeing Carr and Cody together, "all the boys in the regiment," wrote one trooper, "exchanged confidences and expressed themselves to the effect that with such a leader and scout they could get away with all the Sitting Bulls and Crazy Horses, in the Sioux tribe."[132]

Cody's effectiveness as a scout was undeniable, but his usefulness owed as much to his symbolic value as to his material abilities at tracking and fighting. His artful imposture as white Indian continued to hinge on his ability to ride close enough to Indian scouts—whom he knew how to trust when commanders and soldiers did not—to claim credit for their accomplishments, while he remained unquestionably white in the eyes of civilians and the army. All this helped to make him a potent antidote to fears of low-class scout decadence. One correspondent described the cadre of scouts riding with the Fifth Cavalry, which included a large number of mixed-bloods. "As a class, these men have rather a bad reputation—most of them being dangerous and good-for-nothing rascals, who take to their risky business because it pays well." Among this dubious company, one man stood out. "Cody, however, is an exception, and stands high in the estimation of those he serves."[133]

The Fifth Cavalry received word that up to eight hundred Cheyenne had left the Red Cloud Agency at Fort Robinson, Nebraska, to reinforce Crazy Horse to the north. The command set out to intercept them. On July 7, a cable informed commanders that Custer and five companies of the Seventh Cavalry had fallen at the Little Big Horn River, 150 miles to the northwest. Bent on stopping any more Cheyenne from joining the Sioux who had vanquished Custer, the Fifth continued their march to the east. Finally, on July 17, the Fifth engaged a small party of Cheyenne on Warbonnet Creek (on today's border between Wyoming and Nebraska). The Indians retreated to the reservation almost immediately, in a running skirmish during which no more than three Cheyenne (and possibly only one) were killed.

This small fight became famous around the world, ultimately, because during the engagement Buffalo Bill Cody, dressed in a stage costume of black velvet slashed with scarlet and trimmed with silver buttons, shot and scalped a Cheyenne subchief named Yellow Hair (mistranslated as "Yellow Hand"). The most reliable account suggests that Cody and his opponent met while Cody was on his way to warn two couriers about a potential ambush. He and Yellow Hair encountered each other suddenly, by accident, and the two men fired simultaneously. But that fall, Cody commissioned a stage play based on the event, *The Red Right Hand, or First Scalp for Custer,* in which he and the Cheyenne squared off in a ritualized duel to the death. In 1879, he drafted his own account of the battle in his autobiography, and he was careful to make it correspond to the play's fantasy face-off. According to Cody, on July 17, while scouting for the Fifth, he spied "a large party of Indians." As he watched, a small detachment of Cheyenne, unaware that hundreds of Fifth Cavalry soldiers were secreted behind a nearby ridge, dashed out to ambush two army couriers who were coming up the valley. Cody and a group of soldiers cut them off. "A running fight lasted several minutes, during which we drove the enemy some little distance and killed three of their number. The rest," he recalled, "rode off towards the main body, which had come into plain sight, and halted, upon seeing the skirmish that was going on."

Cody never explained why a "large party of Indians" looking to fight soldiers would stop cold upon seeing a half-dozen soldiers and one bizarrely dressed scout pursuing their kith and kin. But, as he told it, at this point the fleeing Indians suddenly turned to fight. "One of the Indians, who was handsomely decorated with all the ornaments usually worn by a war chief when engaged in a fight, sang out to me, in his own tongue: " 'I know you Pa-he-haska, if you want to fight, come ahead and fight with me.' " The two men charged each other between observant ranks of Cheyenne and Americans, like two knights on a medieval battlefield. They fired simultaneously, Cody's bullet killing the Cheyenne's horse, but his own horse going down at the same moment as it stepped in a prairie dog hole. The men stood and fired at each other again. Yellow Hair missed. Cody did not. "Jerking his war-bonnet off, I scientifically scalped him in about five seconds." The Indians, "not less than two hundred of them," now raced to kill Cody, but the soldiers charged them. "As the soldiers came up I swung the Indian chieftain's top-knot and bonnet in the air, and shouted: *'The first scalp for Custer.'* "[134]

In Cody's highly fictionalized tale, he again dons the mask of the white Indian, pretending (as he did in the case of Tall Bull's killing) to be a white man who understood the language of the Cheyenne, a knight errant who bested them in individual, chivalric contests to which they foolishly challenged him, and who was so notorious among them as to have a Cheyenne name. The fact that Cody wore a stage costume during his real killing and scalping of a Cheyenne man suggests how much he continued to experiment with concocting a persona that closely approximated popular fantasies of Indian fighters.

In reality, the Northern Cheyenne had never faced Cody on the battlefield and likely would not have known him if they had. In 1930, a curious writer sought out Beaver Heart, a Northern Cheyenne warrior who had been at Warbonnet Creek, where he saw his friend Yellow Hair fall. "I have heard the story as related by him regarding the fight, and that fact that Yellow Hair challenged him," said Beaver Heart. "This is not true. Buffalo Bill, whoever he was, could not talk Cheyenne, and Yellow Hair could not talk English or Sioux, and I do not know how these two people could talk to each other."[135]

But Cody's battlefield theatrics and subsequent embellishment of them did more than enhance his own celebrity. They also inflated the significance of a skirmish so minor that other officers, notably General George Crook, accused the commanding officer of wasting army resources for seeking it out. Crook had ordered General Wesley Merritt to bring his forces north so their combined forces could pursue the Lakota who had pummeled Custer's Seventh Cavalry almost to oblivion. And what was the reason for the Fifth's delay? Cody claimed to have seen "a large party of Indians" that day on the Warbonnet. Army partisans wrote (and have written ever since) that eight hundred Cheyenne had broken from their reservation and headed north. But there were only about two hundred Cheyenne on that reservation to begin with, and only a portion of those had left. Nobody at Warbonnet Creek ever saw more than about thirty warriors on July 17. Merritt reported seeing only seven, all of whom fled when more than four hundred soldiers of the Fifth Cavalry roared into the valley on the heels of Cody and the small detachment he accompanied. Merritt, a Civil War veteran who had never fought Indians, was thrilled with his one-sided "victory." But General Eugene Carr, who had been in blazing battles where his command was nearly overrun by Cheyenne, thought the fight on the Warbonnet hardly worth the name. "Wish I could make such a one on such small material," he grumbled to his wife. "There were not over 30 Indians in sight at any time and we had over 400 men. There were a few sacks of flour destroyed, three Indians killed, 12 ponies captured and a few went back to the Agency."[136]

There can be little question that Cody actually killed Yellow Hair that day, although exactly how has been a source of continuing debate and controversy. He was so attuned to popular longings and so adept at the arts of imposture that he thought of himself as both a theatrical and a historical actor even when he was not on the stage. The day after he shot Yellow Hair, he wrote a letter to Louisa, at their home in Rochester, New York: "We have had a fight. I killed Yellow Hand a Cheyenne Chief in a single-handed fight. You will no doubt hear of it through the papers." As soon as he reached Fort Laramie, he informed her, he would "send the war bonnet, shield, bridal, whip, arms and his scalp to Kerngood [Moses Kerngood owned a store in Rochester] to put up in his window." Already, he anticipated that the scalp would enhance his image as an Indian fighter and increase his attraction for theatrical audiences. "I will write to Kerngood to bring it up to the house so you can show it to the neighbors. . . . I have only one scalp I can call my own that fellow I fought single handed in sight of our command and the cheers that went up when he fell was deafening."[137]

Granting that he shot and scalped Yellow Hair, his other material contributions were hardly substantial. Most of the real tracking on the foray was done by the mixed-blood scout, Baptiste "Little Bat" Garnier. For the rest of the expedition, Indian auxiliaries, especially Shoshones and Crows, did most of the scouting. When Merritt's command finally made its rendezvous with George Crook, Cody's tracking abilities were overshadowed by those of Crook's chief of scouts, Frank Grouard. The son of a Mormon missionary and a Polynesian woman, Grouard had spent his childhood in California before being captured and then adopted by the Lakota while working on the Plains in the late 1860s. Grouard fought alongside Sitting Bull's Hunkpapas against the U.S. Army as late as 1873. For reasons that have never been clear, he switched sides in 1874, becoming a remarkably adept army scout. Cody himself remarked that Grouard "knew the country thoroughly," and General Crook once said he would rather lose a third of his command than do without Grouard. Cody, by contrast, had spent his career well to the south, had never been in the Black Hills before, and often stumbled. On his last mission, he carried dispatches to General Alfred Terry through the badlands of the Yellowstone, reaching his destination "after having nearly broken my neck a dozen times."[138]

But Grouard, after all, was a mixed-race man, and white contemporaries questioned his racial loyalties. Well into the twentieth century, writers were still debating whether his Hawaiian ancestry made him a Kanaka scout or a mulatto renegade.[139] Cody's imposture allowed the army command to exploit the talents of Grouard and other mixed-blood and Indian scouts even as they shoved them aside. Indeed, the white Indian's very presence was a source of pride and excitement. "*Buffalo Bill* arrived . . . ," noted General Terry upon seeing Cody approach his command that August.[140]

Officers recounted his exploits and assisted his career in the most unexpected ways. One veteran of the 1876 Sioux campaigns, Major Andrew Burt, penned a play for Cody's stage troupe, *May Cody, or Lost and Won* (in which Cody rescued his sister from Mormons), which the Buffalo Bill Combination performed to great success in 1877–78.[141]

After *May Cody* debuted in Milwaukee, in January 1878, the *Milwaukee Sentinel* asked a local Fifth Cavalry veteran, Captain Charles King, for an article about Buffalo Bill. King was on the cusp of a literary career that would see him produce sixty-nine novels between 1885 and 1909. Through all of them, he carried a torch for the army, whose valor, he believed, was unheralded among ignorant civilians.

King was a drinking buddy of Cody's who had actually written one of the first press accounts of Cody's killing of Yellow Hair, or as he was called, Yellow Hand, penning a brief article for the *New York Herald* a week after the battle. His article for the *Sentinel* foreshadowed his crusade to shore up the army's public image in subsequent decades, and it became a chapter in a small pamphlet, *Campaigning with Crook*, that appeared on newsstands in 1880. In this account, Cody—or, rather, King's stilted version of Cody—takes center stage as the frontier hero leading the valiant Fifth to battle. " 'By Jove! General,' said Cody, sliding down the hill toward his horse, 'now's our chance. Let our party mount here out of sight and we'll cut those fellows off.' "[142] Cody's killing of Yellow Hand became the climax of an adventurous Fifth Cavalry campaign. "I see Buffalo Bill closing on a superbly accoutred warrior. It is the work of a minute; the Indian has fired and missed. Cody's bullet tears through the rider's leg, into his pony's heart, and they tumble in confused heap on the prairie. The Cheyenne struggles to his feet for another shot, but Cody's second bullet crashes through his brain, and the young chief, Yellow Hand, drops lifeless in his tracks."[143]

Of course, the crafty scout was ahead of King all the time. By the time the army man first published this account, in 1879, Cody's reenactment of "The First Scalp for Custer" was already popular theater fare.[144] Cody's adept use of the scrape on Warbonnet Creek to boost his reputation as an Indian fighter allowed King to create a heroic battle for the entire Fifth Cavalry, all from an encounter so small it could hardly be called a battle. Crook, waiting far to the north for reinforcements so he could pursue the Lakota, who badly outnumbered his command, complained that Merritt's march against the phantom Cheyenne actually delayed the pursuit of the Sioux who killed Custer, allowing Sitting Bull and Crazy Horse to escape. Absent Cody's theatrics, no officer would have commemorated it, nor likely remembered it. So it was that King, writing up the event later, played Cody's time with the Fifth for all it was worth: "Buffalo Bill is radiant; his are the honors of the day."[145]

More senior officers, too, exploited Cody's self-presentation as scout-hero. In 1879, as Cody completed his autobiography, not only did General Carr write the preface to it, but General Phil Sheridan wrote a letter of endorsement, on army letterhead, selectively validating the tale. "I have read your book which sketches your life on the plains with much interest *so far as it relates to your intercourse with me*," he announced. "I find it scrupulously correct." The publisher attached the endorsement to the book's front matter; Cody returned Sheridan's favor by dedicating the book to him. Sheridan completed the circle by writing Cody into his memoirs in 1888.[146]

For all of Cody's Wild West show career, old commanders sallied to his arena, partly for the entertainment, and partly for the heroic aura he conferred to them. In return they sometimes supported even his most fictional claims, as we can see in the story of how General Carr finally endorsed Cody's fictional heroics at Summit Springs. General Carr did not attribute the killing of Tall Bull to Cody in his battlefield report of 1869, nor in his preface to Cody's 1879 autobiography (wherein Cody first wrote that he was the legendary Dog Man's killer).

But many years after Summit Springs, in 1906, Cody wrote to the old general about his plans for a reenactment of the Battle of Summit Springs in his show. He graciously asked Carr for his permission to stage the tableau, and for a testimonial of the scout's participation in the real battle. Carr pretended embarrassment, warning Cody to stay "close to facts," and avoid "embroidery."

But he must have been thrilled. The old man had been a decorated, accomplished soldier. During the Civil War's Battle of Pea Ridge he was wounded three times in a day (and won the Congressional Medal of Honor). The Battle of Summit Springs had been his most successful fight in a long and mostly successful career of battling Cheyenne, Sioux, Apaches, and Comanches. But he had been forced into retirement in 1893. Now all but forgotten by the public, he battled the War Department to remove black marks on his record, from a few command decisions he made late in his career, in Arizona.

Suddenly, here was Buffalo Bill wanting to make him a hero in the Wild West show. The showman had even reserved General and Mrs. Carr private seats—he called it the "Royal Box"—for the show's opening in Madison Square Garden, so they went to New York and spent an entire week there. They attended the Wild West show every single day, basking in the adulation of the crowd.

Cody hardly had to embroider his Summit Springs account any further, for Carr did much of the colorful stitching himself. For his testimonial, he wrote that on that fateful day in 1869, Cody arrived on the battlefield of Summit Springs and "saw a chief charging about, and haranguing his men." As he drew closer, "Buffalo Bill shot him off his horse and got the horse." The general's new version corresponded to Cody's account from his own autobiography. Carr's testimonial was reprinted in the Wild West show program, and combined with his attendance at the reenactment, it gave the highly fictional entertainment a stamp of almost unimpeachable authority.[147]

Army officers did more than appreciate Cody. They were instrumental in creating his myth, seeking a place for him in the pantheon of frontier heroes. As his Wild West show career made him more famous than any had imagined possible, the presence of this heroic white Indian in the army's often controversial, frustrating campaigns helped officers to leave the many embarrassing disputes over their policies and careers in the dust of history. By writing themselves into stories of Cody's heroics (and Cody into stories of their failures) they inscribed their names alongside Buffalo Bill's, as saviors of the settler's cabin and American civilization.

Their efforts shaped public perceptions of Cody long after his death in 1917, right down to the present day. The 1920s witnessed a biography and numerous articles debunking Cody's valor. In 1929, an eighty-five-year-old Charles King fired one last salvo for his long-gone friend. Contacted by an enthusiastic Chicago journalist (a former lieutenant in the 342nd Infantry), King regaled the young writer with stories of Buffalo Bill's heroism. The interview appeared under the title "My Friend, Buffalo Bill" in the *Cavalry Journal* in 1932. The author was Don Russell, and he was so inspired by King's account that he dedicated years of his life to a new Cody biography. Published in 1960, the hagiographic and popular *Lives and Legends of Buffalo Bill* endured for decades as the most careful analysis of Cody's real-life battlefield exploits. But in fact Russell accepted at face value almost everything that every officer ever wrote about Cody, without once exploring why officers needed to believe in Cody's mythology, or how Cody exploited their appetite for frontier theatrics.[148]

As early as 1869, Cody had learned to navigate the complicated, confusing world of frontier warfare by combining real tracking and fighting skills with the costumed theatrics of the white Indian. Central to his artful deception was his real and respectable white family and home. Officers felt no need to qualify their praise of a white man who approximated the ideal middle-class family in his private life and the heroic white scout on the battlefield.

But Cody had not learned how to defuse the tension that frayed the bond between him and Louisa. When angered, she could go weeks without speaking to him.[149] If William Cody later remembered the Fort McPherson days as among the more peaceful in his marriage, it was because "I was at home so little of the time." He was, he recalled, "continually scouting and guiding the army" and so many officers wanted to hunt with him that "I had no trouble in getting away from home whenever I chose."[150] These hunting excursions amounted to recreational diversions, but they proved no less important to his development of a frontier imposture as popular entertainment for an audience beyond the army and the Plains, as we shall see in the next chapter.

CHAPTER SIX

Buffalo Hunt

As it was in the Far West of North America—"Buffalo Bill" and Indians.
The last of the only known native herd.[1]

THE WILD WEST show's buffalo hunt reenactment visually inscribed many of Cody's hunting stories. According to his autobiography, in 1869 during the Republican River expedition scouts for the Fifth Cavalry proposed a buffalo hunt. General Carr acquiesced. The Pawnees surrounded a herd, charged it, and killed thirty-two buffalo. Cody claimed that he one-upped the Indians and dazzled them that day. "Let me show your Pawnees how to kill buffalo," he told Frank North. Charging into the herd alone, he downed thirty-six buffalo. "At nearly every shot I killed a buffalo, stringing the dead animals out on the prairie, not over fifty feet apart."[2] By 1883, his hunting prowess on the Republican River had grown. That year's Wild West show programs related that he shot forty-eight buffalo before the awestruck Pawnees.[3]

These and other hunting accounts in the autobiography and in show programs provided the "historical" context for a perennial display of buffalo killing in the show arena. From the opening season of the Wild West show, in 1883, almost to its end in 1916, Buffalo Bill always performed a mock buffalo hunt for spectators. Thundering out from one end of the arena, he was joined by a handful of cowboys and Indians who chased a small captive herd of bison around the arena, guns firing blanks.

For the audience, the buffalo were a reminder of America's wilderness beginnings. The mock hunt also underscored Cody's long-ago reputation as "the champion buffalo-hunter of the plains," and his show publicity made his hunting stories the best known of any contemporary hunter.[4] His language in these tales was unadorned, humorous, and his stories meshed so well with popular fantasies of buffalo hunting that it was easy to believe them.

In fact, Cody constructed these tales with some care. His continuing quest for middle-class respectability made him sensitive to the dubious reputation of professional hunters. For this reason, *The Life of Buffalo Bill* fea-

The reenactment of a buffalo hunt was a standard act of the Wild West show from its earliest days. Courtesy Buffalo Bill Historical Center.

tures plenty of hunting exploits, but little mention of his stint as a market hunter. The book depicts no stands, no guns mounted on tripods, no hunting on foot.

Instead, the autobiography shores up Cody's reputation as an expert hunter who shot all his buffalo from the back of a galloping horse. He told one tale—possibly true—about dazzling a group of supercilious army officers by killing eleven buffalo with twelve shots.[5] He told another about a buffalo-hunting competition against another frontier scout, Will Comstock. Cody's victory over Comstock came from his superior ability to manipulate not just his gun and his horse, but the buffalo, too. "My great *forte* in killing buffaloes from horseback was to get them circling by riding my horse at the head of the herd, shooting the leaders, thus crowding their followers to the left, till they would finally circle round and round."[6] In this manner, he killed sixty-nine buffalo without tiring his faithful horse. Witness to his victory over Comstock was a champagne-drinking crowd of St. Louis ladies and frontier army officers who came out to watch via the railroad. In the 1880s, Wild West show audiences could rest assured that in watching Buffalo Bill perform feats of marksmanship and buffalo chasing, they were following a frontier tradition.[7] The competition story and other, even more embellished vignettes—like the one in which he drove buffalo into an army camp before killing them so he would not need wagons to transport the meat—appeared in show programs for all of Cody's career with the Wild West show.[8]

Measuring these stories against William Cody's real experience, it is tempting to dismiss them as simple fictions. But if Cody's trajectory from Great Plains to great showman seems so peculiar in many ways, there could be no richer source for his later merging of show and history than the buffalo range of the Far West. Even in 1860s Kansas, buffalo hunting was an activity around which swirled a powerful national mythology, a nascent tourist industry, and a vibrant atmosphere of showmanship. How the public came to see buffalo hunting on horseback as a fundamental marker of the frontier, and how Cody came to see himself as a provider of the mounted hunt spectacle, speaks volumes about the origins of his show business imagination. By the early 1870s, before he ever ventured to the East, Cody had completed his passage from utilitarian hunting, in which he killed buffalo for cash, to show hunting, in which he killed buffalo for audiences who paid to see him do it.

In fact, buffalo-hunting competitions like the one he described in his autobiography were common among frontier army officers, and Cody probably participated in more than one. In the 1870s, during his stage career, he issued and responded to hunting challenges in the press. "The challenge issued by Buffalo Bill, through the columns of this paper, to a trial of Buffalo killing, has been accepted by a man at Fort Russell named Knox, formerly a government scout," reported one Nebraska paper in the 1870s. "Mr. Cody will put up a forfeit of $500, the hunt to take place inside of thirty days. The ground has not been selected yet, but Mr. Cody expressed a preference for the range about twenty miles south of here."[9]

Cody's scrappy showdowns on the buffalo range were a way of shoring up his status as a real frontiersman during his years of eastern stage play. But if he participated in the ubiquitous hunting competitions of the Plains, we can yet be certain that few of his hunting exploits unfolded the way he claimed they did. In particular, the Cody-Comstock match hunt never happened, at least not the way Cody says it did. When he wrote that he turned buffalo in a circle or drove them into camp before killing them, he echoed tall tales common in the West, in which hunters herded the unherdable bison before tidily dispatching them. Such fantasies appeared in emigrant guidebooks at least as early as 1845, and by 1890 they appeared in the frontier memoirs of Elizabeth Custer, the widow of Lieutenant Colonel George Custer.[10] Perhaps more to the point, no credible eyewitness to Cody's alleged "herding hunt" has ever emerged.[11]

Indeed, Cody could not have faced off against Comstock when he claims he did. William "Medicine Bill" Comstock, an army scout, was wanted for murder at the time of the alleged competition. Would he have participated in a public contest that was advertised in the press and attended by numerous officers and town ladies? Why has no advertisement, or any other record of this supposedly well attended hunt, ever surfaced?[12] It is suspiciously convenient, and Codyesque, that the story was impossible to verify. By the time Cody began hawking *The Life of Buffalo Bill* in theater lobbies, Comstock himself was long dead.[13]

But, like his Pony Express fictions, the fabricated Cody-Comstock buffalo duel tells us almost as much about Cody as any real episode could. His consistent depiction of himself as a flashy horseback hunter reflects his grasp of hunting ideology common to people who would fill the seats at his show years later. Where hide and meat hunters bragged about their "stands," speed and mobility made mounted buffalo hunting a highly attractive symbol for a very different circle of hunters known as sportsmen, or "sports." Market hunters gauged their skills in volume, sports valued style over substance. In this respect, Cody's tales reflect his exposure to the ethos of sport hunting and of the hunting guide, a new occupation which he took up with great vigor during his days as an army scout, and which played a large role in his self-development as a showman.

From the Daniel Boone of history to the Natty Bumppo of James Fenimore Cooper, the white Indian, noble and natural, was a hunter par excellence. His facility with killing wild beasts was at once a seminal, regenerative bond with his native terrain and a mark of his belonging to the past, the time before progress, before farms and cities and commerce.[14] Like Indians and wild animals, the white Indian would vanish into history as livestock and farms spread over the country. Cody's effort to embody this figure required his crafting of a hunter image specifically to entertain a small but increasingly devoted public, who valued proximity to the white Indian as insurance against their alienation from nature in a rapidly industrializing America. In an important sense, guiding the hunt provided Cody another stage, on which he made a show of merging the figure of the hunter, the agent of American history, with the avatar of American wilderness.

HAVING CEASED SHOOTING buffalo for the Kansas Pacific in 1868, Cody's hunting thereafter was devoted almost exclusively to recreation and the cultivation of tourism. The golden spike that connected the Union Pacific to the Central Pacific, and the East to the West, was not driven until 1869. But as we have seen, tourists ventured west even before that. By 1867, there were hundreds, perhaps thousands of tourists heading to frontier Kansas on the rail line, paying their $10 fare to see the West. Some were wealthy. Most were solidly middle class. They slept in baggage cars, or in their stiff seats, and in cheap boardinghouses when they could find them. They scanned the horizon for Indians—usually in vain—and they stumbled off the train, bleary-eyed and wondering at the bleak and trashy cow towns.

Already, travel writers lamented the way that tourism had desecrated "many a lovely spot" with "the sandwich-papers, orange-peel, and broken bottles of former devotees." For the public that felt likewise, the West was a beacon.[15] These tourists, like those before and after, were in pursuit of the authentic and the natural, searching out signs of "the frontier," the "real West."[16] In Hays and other towns, a whole industry of guiding, provisioning, and meeting the aesthetic demands of excursionists soon emerged. Tourists not only invited local men like Hickok and Cody to strike convincing western poses; they also shaped popular understandings of the natural world. In 1872, Congress legislated the creation of Yellowstone National Park in northwest Wyoming, largely at the insistence of the Northern Pacific Railroad's director, Jay Cooke, who saw in the place a magnificent attraction for tourists (who would, of course, buy tickets on his trains to get there, and accommodation at the hotel he built there).[17]

The unmistakable cultural power of tourists in creating natural attractions extended to hunting. These visitors expected the West to resemble the one they saw in the numerous popular paintings of the period, and which they read about in dime novels, memoirs, and reports of earlier western excursionists, and in newspapers. In some sense, then, the "real West" was where one shot at buffalo. So as trains raced alongside buffalo herds, hundreds of guns blazed from the windows. Surprisingly few animals might fall in such an episode, but one tourist noted that when one old bull collapsed within sight of the tracks, the locomotive wailed to a halt, "and men, women, and children tumbled from the train and joined in the pursuit." They climbed atop the carcass, led cheers for the president and the railroad, and, in this case, pulled the old bull on board the train as a kind of mascot.[18] They behaved much like the party of Ohio excursionists who ventured out with George Custer in 1869 and clipped locks of hair (which they jokingly compared to scalps) from a fallen buffalo, as souvenirs of their frontier experience.[19]

Not surprisingly, railroads advertised buffalo hunts as an inducement to the tourist trade as early as 1868.[20] The following year, a Topeka journalist commented, "Persons from the east are stopping off here every day, hoping to get a chance to immortalize their names by killing buffalo."[21] Trains stopped frequently to allow passengers from Topeka, Omaha, or points east to blast away at the buffalo, while trainmen installed extra cowcatchers on the back of the train to keep at bay the longhorn cattle which milled up to, and even onto, the platform at Abilene and other towns. The replacement of hunting by pastoralism, the march of civilization, was under way. In part, tourists went west to participate in it.[22]

Many fantasized about longer hunting excursions, and for wealthier hunters, full-fledged expeditions were popular. As we have seen, by the 1860s, hunting animals for hides and pelts had only a tenuous acceptability, as a petty-capitalist endeavor for upwardly mobile white men. But meanwhile, other kinds of hunting, especially for recreation, had acquired a new kind of legitimacy as a leisure pursuit. Beginning in the 1830s, and accelerating through the century, industrialization, urbanization, and the growth of the market system created a large, managerial middle class and a smaller upper class of white men who were increasingly self-conscious about their own urbanity and privilege, and about their vulnerability to systems of banking, finance, and salaried living. Where their fathers, or grandfathers, had been independent farmers, they depended on a strange and—as the era's repeated financial panics reminded them—unreliable system of commerce, trade, and cash. At the same time, surging immigration of Irish, German, and other foreign laborers swelled city tenements to bursting. Managers and technicians of the new economy supervised these rough workers, whose alien characteristics and strenuous labor underscored managers' fears about losing touch with farm, field, and forest, the traditional sources of masculinity. For these middle- and upper-class men of the cities, then, an increasingly attractive, powerful antidote to urban decadence was to reconnect with traditional American landscapes and activities, to claim a bond of their own with the American earth, with indigenous Nature.[23]

As an "invented tradition," a revamped practice that conformed to popular ideas of history without actually resembling it too closely, hunting was just the ticket.[24] The problem was that game, especially big game, had long since disappeared from the farm country outside of the middle-class bastions of Chicago, New York, and other cities. Today's abundant deer herds reflect a century of wildlife management and forest stewardship. But in the 1870s, in the East, deer could be found only in the remote Adirondacks and a few other mountain redoubts. So, seizing the image of the frontier hunter as an icon of self-reliance, staving off their fears about being dependent on salaries and dividends and not on nature, and eager to identify themselves with some fundamentally American, ritualized experience to naturalize themselves against the alien classes of immigrant workers who toiled in their factories, wealthy sport hunters from midwestern settlements, and even wealthier ones from the East, followed the game west.

Here their longings intersected with another cultural phenomenon: the emergent appreciation of the Great Plains as a distinctively American landscape. The vast grassland between the Mississippi and the Rockies, along with its buffalo herds and the Indians who hunted them, became popular symbols of American nature and American exceptionalism not long after Lewis and Clark returned with the first official descriptions of the region in 1807.[25] In their ongoing quest to express American natural virtue as an antidote to European corruption, American artists began producing images of Indians killing buffalo from horseback sometime around 1820, and they became a staple of popular press illustration after 1840.[26]

In fact, very few whites hunted buffalo for most of these years, since few of them lived near enough to the prairies to do so. But there were other ways the public absorbed the potent symbolism of the Plains. In 1832, after seventeen years in Europe, Washington Irving "re-naturalized" himself with a Plains buffalo hunt. The same year, painter George Catlin ventured up the Missouri River to record scenes of Indian life. So, too, did the Bavarian explorer-naturalist Prince Maximilian of Wied-Neuwied, with the Swiss artist Karl Bodmer in tow. In 1837, British aristocrat Sir William Drummond Stewart made a similar journey, hiring the American painter Alfred Jacob Miller to document the trek. From these forays emerged some of the most powerful, formative literary and visual images of American nature. The canvases of Catlin, Bodmer, and Miller fueled the fantasies of the increasingly urban and denatured middle classes with their vast herds of bison, the footloose hunters who pursued them, and the Edenic Great Plains stretching beneath the open sky. The images were widely admired, reproduced, and imitated. The bison, America's iconic game animal, was the symbol of wild nature in general. Killing them was not only the first stage in the great march of civilization westward, and therefore necessary; by the mid-nineteenth century it became a fundamentally natural and uniquely American experience, too.

The popular appeal of these images was such that urban showmen soon exploited them. P. T. Barnum staged his mock buffalo hunt in Hoboken, New Jersey, in 1843, and at least one circus owner attempted it in 1856.[27] By the time of the California gold rush in 1849, public longing to assume the pose of the renatured American who killed buffalo from horseback was so pervasive that overland emigrants, most of whom were from areas where game was long extinct and hunting but a memory, eagerly anticipated it. Leaping to their horses at the first sight of buffalo, emigrant men chased pell-mell after the herds, guns blazing, even though these forays more often ended with injured hunters than with meat in camp.[28]

SHOOTING BUFFALO FROM the train was a cheaper option, but it failed to satisfy the core cultural longings for *mounted* buffalo hunting. William Cody became adept at delivering the mounted hunting experience, for the right amount of money. Even before he became an army scout, his reputation among railroad personnel and other local luminaries garnered him some of the nascent guiding business with wealthier hunters. He guided the railroad agent William Webb on a hunt in 1867, and in 1868 he shepherded wealthy St. Louis sports on a hunt out of Hays.[29]

His frontier imposture took shape as he watched these aspiring nimrods attempt their own. They did not hunt like market hunters. To their minds, *proper* hunting was recreational. Those who hunted for a living, who *labored* at it, were rude and uncivilized, like Indians. Sport hunters as a group claimed superiority in part by elevating more difficult, less productive techniques of hunting over customary practices of lower-class subsistence and market gunners, whom sports reviled as "game hogs" and "pot hunters." Thus, in these very years, to hunt deer with torches, and just about every other form of night hunting, came to be excoriated as "unsporting." So, too, were "hounding" deer, "ground swatting" birds instead of shooting them on the wing, and any kind of fishing that did not require a rod and reel. By 1900, the codification of these often contradictory and implicit rules in the nation's law books ensured that as hunting became a highly charged, symbolic pastime for elites and the middle class, it also became a means to wrap their commercial and political power in the cloak of nature.[30]

Most historians place the epicenter of the sport hunting craze in eastern cities at the end of the nineteenth century. But Cody was exposed to it earlier than that, in Kansas, and it had a pronounced effect on how he presented his hunting exploits to the broader public. If he did not intuit the elite preference for shooting buffalo from horseback from popular images of it, he had certainly learned it by the time his town of Rome failed. William Webb, the railroad agent who wrecked the town right after its founder took him hunting, had strong views on the subject of buffalo killing. Webb's account of his Plains tour appeared in 1873, and in it he not only praised Buffalo Bill as "altogether the best guide I ever saw," but also explained to his readers that "horseback hunting" was the "only legitimate way" of taking buffalo. There was, indeed, "little genuine sport" in "stalking" the animals on foot, a practice that "holds the same relation to horseback hunting that 'hand line' fishing does to that with the rod and reel . . . or that killing birds on the ground does to wing-shooting."[31]

Even earlier, in 1868, another writer explained proper buffalo hunting to the public in *Harper's New Monthly Magazine*. Hunting buffalo from horseback was the method "usually adopted by our cavalry officers and the best hunters among the frontiersmen," while stalking was the domain of "colored infantry troops" and "a kind of pot-hunting, that is not entitled to the name of sport."[32] Even Indian hunters were not true sportsmen, for "hunting buffalo is to the Indian a labor rather than a pastime."[33]

But for tourists and guides, the problem with assuming the guise of the mythic mounted buffalo hunter was that it was so exceedingly difficult. Shooting a buffalo from the back of a running horse was considerably more challenging than it looked, requiring practice, one sportsman noted, "to enable one to hit anything smaller than a mammoth." Inexperienced hunters, unable to steady the weapon, fired most of their bullets—sometimes all of them—into the ground or the sky.[34] Among such company, the safest place to be, remarked one guide, "was nearest the buffalo."[35]

The buffalo's strength and power compounded the dangers. The animals could switch directions at full speed. They could stop dead from a full run, hook their horns into a horse and topple it, then gore the hunter, who might already be wounded from the fall or from being trampled by other animals. Second Lieutenant George Armes summarized a typical hunt in 1866: "Sergeant Miller shot his horse through the head during the excitement, and six or eight of the horses fell, and some ran away with their riders."[36] George Custer, astride his wife's favorite horse, pursued his first buffalo for several miles across the prairie only to have the animal turn on him suddenly. Just as Custer fired his pistol, his mount reared, and Custer blew the horse's brains out. The bison turned and trotted away, leaving the Boy General stranded and lost in the middle of Kansas. During his first year on the Plains, he killed two more horses the same way.[37]

Obviously, the cultural importance of hunting from horseback outweighed its effectiveness at killing bison, even as practitioners discovered how hard it was. Their persistence in the sport suggests the strength of sports' attachment to the charged symbolic tableau, the setting of the Great Plains, the quarry of the buffalo, and the mounted hunter, a semiotic triad that simultaneously evoked Plains Indians and implied their decline before an ascendant class (and race) of American sport hunters with modern weapons. Substituting their vacationing selves for laboring Indian men, and the revolver and the rifle for bows and arrows, they transformed the popular iconography of Plains buffalo hunters into a symbol of elite power (thus, buffalo killing was a leisure pursuit) which was at once industrial—thus the gun—and sprung full-blown from nature, from the boundless grassland, and the horse.

Among army officers, from whom Cody learned much about public longings for the white Indian, these social concerns of America's elite were both echoed and pronounced. Like captains of industry who sought to shore up their authority over ranks of immigrant workers, captains of the army commanded ranks of immigrant, black, and working-class soldiers. They underscored their native origins and their natural authority over their troops by hunting buffalo and antelope from horseback. Army policy encouraged mounted hunting excursions as practice for combat against Indians. Hunting helped soldiers to learn the lay of the land, and officers who wanted brief leaves for hunting could often get them if they agreed to draw maps of the country they crossed when they got back.[38] Officers could frequently be seen charging into bison herds with pistols blazing.[39] They competed against one another to see who could kill the most buffalo in a day, and they often sought out hunting guides, like Cody, to help them find the game, kill it, and butcher it.[40]

The traditional mystique of buffalo hunting was decades old by this time. But after the Civil War, it achieved a new purchase in popular imagination in no small measure through the efforts of the very army officer with whom Cody's legend would one day become most entangled: Lieutenant Colonel George Armstrong Custer. A bona fide Civil War hero and Indian fighter, Custer was also an avid hunter who, like Hickok, became a tourist attraction in his own right as the railroad advanced across the Plains. In the summer of 1869, when his Seventh Cavalry was stationed at Fort Hays, literally hundreds of people stepped off the train to gawk at his house, shake his hand, or ask him for hunting advice.

Never one to discount the importance of fans, Custer became a celebrity guide for wealthy tourists and other officers, affecting the long hair and buckskin clothing of the frontier hero. At the same time, his literary abilities made him an accomplished author. From 1867 to 1875, under the pen name "Nomad" (his white Indian identity), he wrote columns on his hunting exploits and Indian fights for *Turf, Field, and Farm*, a sportsman's magazine.[41] By expounding on the attractions of buffalo hunting in print, he helped keep a steady stream of tourist hunters flowing west. To Custer, buffalo hunting was "the most exciting of all American sports."[42] In fact, as a "true, manly sport, buffalo hunting, *par excellence*, stands at the head of the list." Requiring horsemanship, courage, and skill in firearms, it necessitated "a combination of all the attributes necessary in other modes of hunting."[43] And it provided an ersatz army experience for civilian men. In the end, there was "nothing so nearly resembling a cavalry charge as a buffalo chase."[44]

Buffalo hunting was fun for people who were good at it. But beyond their own recreation, Cody and Custer each had other distinct reasons for devoting so much time to it. Cody guided hunters to make a living; Custer did it to enhance his image and to cultivate connections among financiers, politicians, and journalists. In part, the similarities between Custer and Cody could be expected insofar as they sought to fill the same mythic space, the white Indian guide, avatar of wilderness for gentleman hunters. In this respect, as in others, they were competitors, and Cody remained in the Boy

General's shadow. Custer's magazine articles and his memoirs circulated among the army brass. Cody may have read them, but he did not yet possess the skills or the connections to publish his own. Custer, no doubt, was aware of Cody's scouting and hunting exploits. But in his early days Cody's most celebrated hunting parties could not match Custer's. In the summer of 1869, while Cody awaited publication of the first pulp press story about himself, Custer guided a hunting party of two aristocrats from England, 150 tourists from Cleveland, and at least two reporters from the *New York Times* and the *Ohio State Journal*. Spectacular as this hunt was, it was also typical of Custer's self-presentation. To the accompaniment of the regimental band playing "Garryowen"—the very music which signaled a Seventh Cavalry charge on Indian villages—the huge party sallied forth in wagons and carriages, fifteen miles from Fort Hays. "What a party it was!" recalled one participant, a young woman. In her literary sketch, Custer appears as the sportsman's ideal, a white Indian in full costume: "Custer, ahead, was seen to rise in his saddle, with his long hair flying in the wind, his heavily fringed buckskin suit matching the color of his hair. He gave the Indian war-whoop—every horse and dog understood it meant a dash—a run at full gallop."[45]

It was only one of many such Custer forays. In November 1869, Custer guided fifty hunters—various politicians and wealthy industrialists from Michigan, some Seventh Cavalry officers, and a reporter from the *Detroit Post*—in a cavalcade of eight wagons, three ambulances, and numerous extra horses, again accompanied by the Seventh Cavalry band. Wrote Custer: "One of the gentlemen remarked that the scene reminded him of events described as belonging to the feudal ages, when marshaling his retainers some ancient Baron marched forth to battle or the chase."[46]

As Custer obviously understood, guiding for buffalo hunts was a form of showmanship. This fact was never better illustrated than when P. T. Barnum, America's greatest showman, and the impresario of the first staged buffalo hunt in New Jersey twenty-seven years before, arrived at Fort Hays for a real hunt with Custer in the summer of 1870. The officer "received us like princes," wrote Barnum. "He fitted out a company of fifty cavalry, furnishing us with horses, arms, and ammunition."[47] (If he did not also provide the Seventh Cavalry band, perhaps they were out with another party.)

Years later, after Custer died, Cody made the army officer and hunter-hero into a touchstone of his own career. As we have seen, Cody took the "first scalp for Custer" after the battle of the Little Big Horn in 1876. He staged the scene repeatedly in his theatrical career and, later, in the Wild West show, sometimes with a reenactment of "Custer's Last Fight" as a prelude. He shored up his Custer act by speaking glowingly of the fallen general in interviews. And in his 1879 autobiography he explained that his friendship with the martyr of the Little Big Horn went back to 1867, when

"I had my first ride with the dashing and gallant Custer," whom he guided through a sixty-five-mile stretch between Fort Ellsworth and Fort Larned. Custer was so impressed with the young scout's abilities that he promised to "find something for me to do" if ever Cody needed work. "This was the beginning of my acquaintance with General Custer, whom I always admired as a man and as an officer."[48]

But the Custer-Cody friendship was as imaginary as the Comstock match hunt. Cody competed against other hunters, but not against Comstock. He had friendships with army officers, but not with Custer. Although Custer did journey in July 1867 along the route between Ellsworth and Larned, where Cody claimed to be his guide, he went opposite the direction that Cody remembered, and Cody was not along. In fact, there is no record of William Cody ever scouting for Custer. He and Custer shared a patron in General Philip Sheridan, and their paths crossed at Fort Hays, where the Seventh Cavalry was often stationed and where Cody lived between 1867 and 1869. But the only documented meeting between these two men occurred at a Nebraska buffalo hunt, in 1872, a highly publicized, glamorous expedition concocted by General Sheridan for the entertainment of Russia's visiting Grand Duke Alexis.

That Custer and Cody did not renew their acquaintance after 1872 may reflect that each was too much of a showman to tolerate the other's company for long. But there were likely other reasons. Custer was the most controversial officer on the Plains. A West Point graduate whose full-gallop charge into Confederate General J. E. B. Stuart's "Invincibles" at Gettysburg routed the South's most famous cavalry regiment, Custer was a Civil War hero. He underscored his martial valor with a showy bearing. His insistence on carrying a medieval battlefield standard, on camping atop high ridges with campfires blazing, and on such frivolities as a regimental band made him hard to miss. The press loved him, and superiors rewarded him by brevetting him (that is, accelerating his promotion until the war was over) to the rank of major general, the youngest in the Union army, in 1863.[49]

Although his courage was real enough, his self-aggrandizing theatrics served him ill on the Plains. Arriving in Kansas in 1866, he took the Seventh Cavalry on extended fruitless expeditions which the Cheyenne and Sioux easily evaded. In 1867, during a misguided search for Indians in conditions so harsh that dogs died of exhaustion, he found himself powerless to stem the outflow of deserters, thirty-four of whom departed in one day. In frustration, he ordered summary executions of those he caught. Junior officers apprehended several troopers and indeed shot them, killing one. Soon after, Custer's wife arrived in Kansas; setting out to reach her, he force-marched troops on a 155-mile journey in 55 hours. Soldiers' mounts broke down, and when they did, Custer ordered their riders left behind. Sioux warriors caught up with them, killing one and wounding another, before help arrived.[50]

Not surprisingly, Custer was court-martialed for these offenses, and found guilty of violating orders and of abandoning his troops to the enemy. He was suspended from duty for one year, without pay. But in 1868, Sheridan recalled him for the winter campaign, during which he attacked the Cheyenne Chief Black Kettle's village on the Washita River, achieving the army's biggest victory of the Plains campaigns to that point.[51]

Victory on the Washita secured his reputation among admirers. But it failed to mollify his critics. Some charged Custer with attacking the wrong village. Black Kettle was a peace advocate who had survived the Sand Creek Massacre four years before, and the Cheyenne horse thieves Custer was pursuing came from a different band.[52] If that was not enough, the stain of troop abandonment was renewed. During the battle, a subordinate officer, Captain Joel Elliott, led a detachment of eighteen men into a pocket of Cheyenne and Arapaho resistance. As Custer left the Washita, junior officers urged a search for Elliott, but Custer refused to order one. Elliott, of course, was killed, with all his men.[53]

These issues alone would have made Custer a subject of arguments. But there was more. After the Washita, various officers selected concubines from the captives. In this adventure, they were led by Custer, who took a beautiful Cheyenne woman named Monahsetah as his mistress. Various sources, both Cheyenne and American, claim that she had a child by Custer. The shakiness of Custer's marriage was already the stuff of camp gossip. (Rumor had it that notorious "death march" to Fort Hays in 1867 was occasioned by news that Libbie was behaving inappropriately with another officer at Fort Riley. Whether the tale was true or not, the couple was separated during the Christmas season of 1869.) The officer's affair with a Cheyenne captive was widely known among fellow officers—and scouts, too—and fanned the flames of controversy around him.[54]

William Cody worked and lived in Hays when Custer was posted there. He was at the epicenter of the ongoing Custer uproar, and even if he dismissed most of the criticism, it is unlikely he could overlook all the complaints about Custer's vanity, pettiness, and cruelty. Custer ordered poor troopers to have half their heads shaved as a mark of disgrace, or ordered them flogged, or threw them into the deep circular pit he used as a guardhouse in Hays, for offenses as minor as leaving camp for forty-five minutes to buy a tin of fruit (which soldiers frequently did to fend off rampant scurvy).[55]

Custer was a hero to the nation after he died, in part through Cody's adept stitching of the Custer legend onto his own entertainment. But while he lived, George Custer was a polarizing figure. During Cody's career as an army scout, it was almost impossible to know Custer and not take a position

in the many disputes which seemed to blow about him like so many torna-
does. The divisions he created in an already deeply divided army were
unmistakable. "He is the most complete example of a petty tyrant that I have
ever seen," wrote one of his junior officers in 1867.[56] General Eugene Carr,
who commanded the Fifth Cavalry and gave Cody his first commendation
for superlative service in 1869, also disliked George Custer.[57]

All of which explains why Cody wanted so little to do with Custer while
he lived. Whether or not he could tolerate Custer's arrogance, Cody seldom
saw a political fight worth getting involved in unless it directly affected his
own well-being. He blamed bushwhacker cruelty for his family's misery in
eastern Kansas but, at times, he also suggested that his father's own outspo-
kenness needlessly provoked his enemies. Recalling Isaac Cody's stabbing in
1856, Cody remembered, "My father's indiscreet speech at Rively's brought
upon our family all of the misfortunes and difficulties which from that time
befell us."[58] The violence that followed Wild Bill Hickok, Cody's mentor in
frontier imposture, as he publicly challenged lawbreakers to test his mettle,
made him another prime exemplar of the perils awaiting the pugnaciously
outspoken.

Although Cody flirted with politics, he lived his entire adult life trying to
steer clear of the era's fierce partisan battles, which extended from the slavery struggles of his boyhood, through the infamous "stolen election" of
1876, and on to the bitter struggles between Democrats and Republicans at
almost every level of government that continued until 1900. In many ways,
Cody crafted his public persona to transcend such divides, or at least to
ignore them. Indian fighting, as we have seen, inspired debates over what
was just and whether the army should be deployed to fight or not. Custer
galvanized partisans on all sides of such questions. Cody was not an officer,
not a commander, and therefore not accountable for army decisions
(another aspect of scouting that served his purposes). As the entrepreneurial
white Indian, fighter against savagery, and killer of wild animals, he symbolized processes of "land clearing" which were so fundamental to the entire
political and economic system that they inspired much less argument than
"current events" like the gold standard, the tariff, or army corruption.

For his part, Custer himself not only encouraged Cody to keep his distance, but resented Cody's rise to fame and obstructed it when he could.
The only mention of Cody in any Custer correspondence was a derisive reference to the fun Custer and his brother had in tormenting their brother-
in-law, Lieutenant James Calhoun, by suggesting that he attempt a stage
career like Buffalo Bill's under the theatrical name "Antelope Jim."[59] His
most obvious tactic for impugning Cody was to remain silent about Buffalo
Bill in the press, while he extolled rival scouts as the "real" heroes of the
Plains, at the very moment that Cody was entering the public eye. Custer's

jabs were so effective that Cody felt compelled to counter them years after Custer died.

It was just this concern that led Cody, in 1879, to cast the long-dead William Comstock as his legendary opponent in the buffalo-killing contest that never happened. William Comstock once had the makings of a potential media star, like Wild Bill Hickok. In 1868, reporter Theodore R. Davis presented Comstock as a skilled guide and buffalo hunter in *Harper's New Monthly Magazine*, the same middle-class journal that had launched Hickok to national fame the year before.[60] But whatever promise he had was cut short when a Cheyenne attacker killed him later that year. Had he lived, his celebrity would likely not have approached Cody's. He was devoted to Cheyenne culture (his nickname, "Medicine Bill," reflected his eager embrace of Cheyenne "medicine"), spoke fluent Cheyenne, and lived among them. The Cheyenne who killed him likely saw him as a turncoat for his service as a scout for the Seventh Cavalry in 1867.[61]

But Custer exploited Comstock's demise, turning him into the greatest scout the Plains had ever seen. Given that the officer set about this project at the very moment that Cody was ascending to national fame, it is hard to believe it was not a conscious strategy. Custer's account appeared first in the respected *Galaxy* magazine in the early 1870s, and was republished in 1874, in his best-selling memoir, *My Life on the Plains*. The West Point graduate, Civil War hero, and famous Indian fighter left no superlative unturned in pumping the reputation of the dead-and-unchallengeable Comstock, all at the expense of unnamed scout pretenders. "Comstock was the favorite and best known scout on the central plains," claimed Custer. He was also the ideal white Indian. "No Indian knew the country more thoroughly than did Comstock. He was perfectly familiar with every divide, watercourse, and strip of timber for hundreds of miles in either direction. He knew the dress and peculiarities of every Indian tribe, and spoke the languages of many of them. Perfect in horsemanship, fearless in manner, a splendid hunter, and a gentleman by instinct, as modest and unassuming as he was brave," he was, concluded Custer, "the superior of all men who were scouts by profession with whom I had any experience."[62]

Cody, on the other hand, never appeared in any of Custer's voluminous accounts. *My Life on the Plains* appeared two years into Cody's stage career, with his reputation ever more inflated by theatrical reviews and testimonials from his army commanders (but not Custer). In his memoirs, Custer reveled in the company of Comstock and other scouts, including Wild Bill Hickok—"then as now, the most famous scout on the Plains," and "one of the most perfect types of physical manhood I ever saw." He regaled readers with tales of the colorful Moses "California Joe" Milner, and the "squaw man" Ben Clark.[63] But he made not one mention of Cody.

After Custer's martyrdom on the banks of the Little Big Horn in 1876, his published effusions about Comstock (and his silence about Buffalo Bill Cody) represented a potential problem for Buffalo Bill, whose claim to fame as the premier scout hero could be challenged by any of the thousands who read Custer's best seller.

Cody vanquished this threat in a number of ways, including his timely, very theatrical, and brilliantly astute (if bloodthirsty) grab at "the first scalp for Custer" in 1876. But a more subtle maneuver came three years later, when he invented a hunting competition, which looked on paper like any number that were reported in the memoirs of officers and in the press, and in which he positioned the late Will Comstock as a loser. This simple fabrication, inserted in an autobiography which contained a mixture of truth and falsehood so complex that few could detect the difference, was insurance against any continuing threat from Comstock's reputation, or Custer's slight.

———

THE VIGOROUS COMPETITION between Cody and Custer suggests how much buffalo hunting was a realm of commerce and theater, in which the best guides packaged a whole range of signal "frontier experiences" for their clients. The most popular guides provided keys not only to game but to the mystique of wilderness, which they embodied. Of course, where Cody's reputation as a white Indian who was certifiably *white* facilitated his appeal as an army scout, it complemented his career as a hunting guide. White men who were sports, after all, wanted to believe not only that Buffalo Bill was the greatest guide and hunter of all time, but that he represented their own potential for hunting prowess and frontier mastery.

In the 1860s, many sportsmen utilized army connections so they could ride with the U.S. Cavalry, whose commanders were eager—within limits—to cultivate good relations with influential voters and financiers, and who often saw killing buffalo as an indirect way of fighting Indians. Many sport hunters turned to Phil Sheridan, who commanded all the forts west of the Missouri River, for advice about where to hunt and which guide to hire. In turn, he frequently referred them to Cody. The confluence of wealthy hunters, army officers, and frontier scouts gave Cody some of his first press among a social elite he came to admire and which he sought to join. Indeed, Cody's reputation as a hunter and guide grew in concert with his reputation as an Indian fighter, partly because of reports that began to filter through army hunting circles about his skills and his helpful demeanor.

Thus, one year after the Summit Spring fight, in the summer of 1870, General Carr hosted a half-dozen tourist hunters from England and Syra-

cuse, New York, on a buffalo hunting trip into the Republican River country. Along with a trooper escort went scouts William Cody and Luther
North. Later, in December, Cody, Luther North, and Frank North guided
for a combined army-civilian hunting party which included James W.
Wadsworth, a New York congressman, a number of railroad dignitaries, and
several officers from Fort McPherson.[64]

A steady stream of sport hunters kept officers and guides busy, at Fort
McPherson and elsewhere, for much of the 1870s. There were sport hunters
from nearby Omaha in September 1872. Later, Sheridan himself invited the
Earl of Dunraven to hunt buffalo, guided by Cody and Texas Jack Omohundro. George Bird Grinnell went hunting with Omohundro and the North
brothers in the summer of 1872.[65]

Such outings became so common, and constituted such a drag on thinly
stretched military resources, that they emerged as a subject of complaint
among post commanders, particularly those in better hunting grounds.
Modern readers might assume that army families most dreaded news of
Indian hostility. But in 1870, wrote Libbie Custer, she and her husband,
George, would "tremble at every dispatch for fear it announces buffalo
hunters."[66] Requests for guides and protection were hard for officers to

*Cody in 1873–74, as he dressed for scouting missions and
guided hunts. Courtesy Buffalo Bill Historical Center.*

refuse. Many of the businessmen who wanted them were Union army veterans, with personal connections to powerful generals and politicians. Supporting their recreation was a way of earning their support for better army funding in the continuing wrangle between the War Department and other branches of the federal government.[67]

Apparently, Cody saw guiding as a two-pronged business. On the one hand, a guide had to lead his clients to game. He did everything he could to see they bagged their fill of Plains buffalo, antelope, elk, and deer.[68]

But on the other hand, the guide had to be able to bundle a host of other experiences and deliver them in a particular manner. The ideal buffalo hunting guide was an expert not just in finding buffalo but in killing them—in the prescribed manner, of course. Whether he was fashioning his image to the needs of his audience, or indulging cultural longings he shared with other middle-class men of his era, or both, Cody achieved prowess as a mounted hunter that was astonishing, even to the most skilled Plains hunters. In 1870 Luther North, a scout whose resentment of Cody's fame verged on open hostility, watched him kill sixteen buffalo with sixteen shots from the back of a skittish horse, awing an audience of sports. The episode may have been the source for Cody's story of killing thirty-six buffalo (and, later, forty-eight) in one run. According to North, Cody was never known for being a pistol shot, and his marksmanship on foot was only good. But "on horseback he was in a class by himself," his "exhibition" of buffalo killing "the most remarkable I ever saw."[69] North had many friends among the Pawnees, whose language he spoke fluently. According to him, Pawnee hunters, who killed buffalo all their lives and who knew a great hunter when they saw one, also witnessed Cody's string of sixteen kills. To them, wrote North, "his buffalo killing was miraculous."[70]

In addition to providing the spectacle and experience of the mounted hunt, the ideal Plains hunt included at least some manifestation, or sign, of Indians. For many, buffalo hunting was a kind of stand-in for Indian killing. Tourists spoke of buffalo "tribes" and took "scalps" from their hides, and as they embarked on hunting expeditions, they sometimes hoped aloud for a chance to fight Indians, or at least to see them, so they could tell the story on their return.[71]

Such longings were expressions of a common, complex American desire. The proximity of Indians was potentially dangerous, but paradoxically, even as the war on the Plains unfolded, tourists were entranced by them. Over most of the United States, the experience of meeting Indians had retreated from daily life into the dim mists of history. As it did so, Americans became even more drawn to encounters with Indians, who come to stand for something more than just other people. By the early part of the nineteenth century, they were markers of American identity. For the broad middle class, by the 1860s, Indians already embodied the presence of history and authentic nature; they signified freedom from the artifice of modern industrialism, the market, and the city.

Few tourists ever fought Indians, and judging by their actions, they did not need a skirmish to authenticate their frontier experience. General Carr often requested the services of the Pawnee scouts on hunting expeditions to provide both protection from the enemy and the companionship of authentic Indians. But he was not the first to exploit their performance capabilities. In 1866, the Union Pacific railroad hired the first battalion of Pawnee auxiliaries, under the command of white frontiersman Frank North, to defend railroad workers from Sioux and Cheyenne raiding parties. The proximity of the Pawnees to the railroad soon brought them into the tourist business. That year, a party of eminent politicians, journalists, and financiers journeyed to the hundredth meridian, courtesy of the Union Pacific's directors, in celebration of the company's successes. This carefully arranged tour included not only a real, miles-long prairie fire set by excursion managers, but displays of Pawnee war dances, a mock fight between Indians (with some of the Pawnee dressed as Sioux), and a mock Indian attack (again by the Pawnees) on the excursion party itself as they camped outside of Colville, Nebraska.[72]

It is hardly surprising that with experience like this to their credit, many Pawnees would join the Wild West show less than two decades later.[73] For the hundredth meridian excursion was, of course, a show, stage-managed to connect the powerful audience with a sequence of attractions: Indian war dances, battles, an Indian attack, and a prairie fire, all as a kind of primitive counterpoint to the railroad itself, the paragon of technological mastery and the advancement of civilization. Set against the railroad, the attractions suggested a story about the progress of civilization from ancient savagery in the wilderness to modern machines and manufactured comfort. Silas Seymour, who organized the tour, was not by profession a showman. He was an engineer. But cultural longings for prairie fires and Indians as savage signifiers were so pervasive that he had no trouble imagining that his party would enjoy them.

William Cody was nowhere near the Union Pacific line in 1866. He probably did not know about Seymour's show. But he did know about the desires and longings of American tourists on the frontier, for guides and hosts played to them across Kansas and Nebraska. Perhaps he heard about another hunting expedition by some Union Pacific executives in 1867, during which Traveling Bear, a Pawnee scout who accompanied the party, impressed the crowd by shooting an arrow right through a buffalo.[74] Riding with the North brothers and the Pawnees in the late 1860s and the 1870s, Cody had many opportunities to absorb the importance of Indians to sport hunters.

But Indians were not always available or willing to accompany sports, and when they were, guides who hired them had to share the compensation. Also, although proximity to Indians potentially accorded "white Indianness" to guides, recruiting them required more expertise than Cody actually had—thus, Carr's hunt in 1870 depended on the assistance of the Norths. Guides, in other words, were entertainers who delivered the trappings, or aura, of Indianness for their clients. Cody learned, as had other guides, to provide a "safer," cheaper Indian context through his own ostensible expertise in what today we would call Indian culture, a knowledge he conveyed in camp stories.

The few fragments we have of Cody's oral performances suggest that in circles of light around Plains campfires, with audiences of city dudes, he began crafting tales which later appeared in his autobiography and in his lifelong performance of Buffalo Bill's Indian adventures in the press and in the arena. The campfire light focused attention on him as a narrator, creating a kind of open-air auditorium for tall tales, in the performance of which lay seeds of his entire career. Where Hickok's tales urged audiences to debate how much he could be believed, Cody's method was more subtle. His mingling of truth and fiction was so artful that his stories were less obviously fictional than Hickok's. He followed accounts of Indian ambushes with advice about how to avoid Indian attack. "When you are alone, and a party of Indians are discovered, never let them approach you. If in the saddle, and escape or concealment is impossible, dismount, and motion them back with your gun." Such advice—running or hiding is preferable to fighting—was sensible, and seemingly down-to-earth. But at the same time, he exploited his fund of Plains lore by recounting battles fought by other people as well as himself, making himself the hero of more fights than he had seen. "Bill was the hero of many Indian battles," wrote one excursionist Cody guided in the late 1860s. He "had fought savages in all ways and at all hours, on horseback and on foot, at night and in daytime alike."[75]

Just as important as the content of his stories was his artful self-presentation, his attention to props and setting, which was unsurpassed. As one hunter wrote, "Bill was dressed in a buckskin suit, trimmed with fur, and wore a black slouch hat, his long hair hanging in ringlets down his shoulders." His stories of "hunting experiences since he was old enough to ride a horse—for Bill was born and brought up on the Plains—are truly wonderful to hear related, as they are, around our blazing camp fires, and in the presence of all the paraphernalia of frontier life upon the Plains."[76] Between the sun-splashed grassland, across which he chased and shot buffalo looking for all the world like the fantasy hunter out of a painting or a novel, and the flickering circles of campfire light where his audience sat spellbound by his stories, Cody found a stage for an ongoing performance. Here he invented the character of Buffalo Bill, and much of his heroic life story. His open-air show invited clients to project their fantasies onto him, to partake of frontier nature through him, to revel in the inevitable progress he and they together represented: sports and guide united, clearers of the land, savoring the fast-retreating wilderness, rooting themselves in it, even as they swept it away.[77]

THE SOCIAL CHALLENGES of guiding sharpened Cody's development of the hunt spectacle. Guided hunts were exercises in manly bonding, and when they carried off their performance, guides' mystique conveyed a kind of natural aristocracy, a fraternity of hunters, beyond class boundaries. Ideally, the artificial ranks and false privileges of urban life melted away in the wilderness.

But guides walked a fine line between courteous assistance and fawning subservience. They were, after all, hired hands, employees of their clients, who could be condescending and snide. To humiliate a guide was to challenge or discount his wilderness expertise. As such, it was a threat to the entire experience of the hunt. With the hardships of all-day rides and the frustrations of buffalo hunting so common among novices, short tempers abounded. One rude client in a party could undermine the theater of the guided hunt.

At the same time, guides had limited options for responding. They were expected to command their surroundings through displays of wilderness knowledge and hunting prowess, but without making their clients look bad. This was not easy. Many sports could not ride well (some not at all) and many more barely knew one end of a rifle from the other. Since they were on vacation, they expected an enjoyable outing. A guide protected his reputation, and his guiding business, by maintaining both his own superiority as wilderness master and the illusion of fraternal brotherhood among the hunters, and the latter could be as tricky as the former.

The most valuable tool guides had for reining in condescension was the practical joke. By humoring the rest of the party at the expense of its most offensive member, the guide could display his own savvy, while returning the sneering sport to his proper place as a dude, without challenging the class hierarchy.[78] "Cody had all the frontiersman's fondness for practical jokes," wrote one client, who related how the guide instructed one visiting sport to ride through rank grass in pursuit of a buffalo. As a result, the man smelled so bad the party made him ride downwind.[79]

But the most impressive joke was the staged Indian attack, which pushed tourists' longing for "Indian experience" to the very limit, while it reinforced the standing of the guide as white Indian and master of ceremonies on the Great Plains stage. Custer and Cody both resorted to this ruse. In some cases, members of the hunting party in Indian disguise carried off the joke, but Cody's pranks sometimes featured real Indians.[80] In 1871, Cody arranged for the Pawnee scouts to form a mock war party, which "ambushed" himself and a client, one Mr. McCarthy, on whom Cody had been "wishing for several days to play a joke." The Indians raced down a creekbed toward the guide and his client, whooping and shouting, but the attack was more convincing than Cody intended. " 'McCarthy, shall we dismount and fight, or run?' said I." McCarthy, though, "did not wait to reply, but wheeling his horse, started at full speed down the creek, losing his hat and dropping his gun; away he went, never once looking back to see if he was being pursued." Cody rode after him, trying to explain the joke, but to no avail. McCarthy reached camp first. By the time Cody arrived, General Carr was already dispatching the hunt's trooper escort in pursuit of the phantom enemy.[81]

For sports, such tricks underscored how much the party was in the hands of the guide. It made them feel vulnerable, but at the same time reassured them that their guide not only knew the country, but in some ways he commanded it. Their fear revealed their inability to read the signs of real and fake which the guide had mastered so convincingly. In laughing off the humiliation, they shored up their dignity and announced their acceptance of the guide's mastery.

By the early 1870s, Cody developed a guiding style which merged showmanship and hunting in a close weave, which was never more apparent than in his service to General Philip Sheridan's hunting party in September of 1871. The very large and very public hunting party marked a culmination of Cody's guiding career to that date, and in the ways that Cody manipulated his own image we can see his appreciation of the needs of his audience, and his ability to shape his performance to those needs.

Sheridan's party included a group of financiers, lawyers, and newspapermen, among them Henry Davies, an assistant district attorney general for southern New York; James Gordon Bennett, Jr., the editor of the fashionable *New York Herald*; Lawrence Jerome and Leonard Jerome, newspaper-owners-turned-financiers and New York City social lions; Carroll Livingston, a prominent member of the New York Stock Exchange; John G. Heckscher, a New York businessman; Charles Lane Fitzhugh, one of Sheridan's officers who had recently resigned to become a prominent businessman in Pittsburgh; M. Edward Rogers, a Philadelphia businessman; and John Schuyler Crosby, scion of an eminent New York family. The party also included prominent Chicagoans, including Samuel Johnson, whose Pine Street mansion was a chief gathering place for that city's young bachelors; Anson Stager, superintendent of the Central Division of the Western Union Telegraph Company and a close friend of Sheridan's; and Charles L. Wilson, owner of the *Chicago Evening Herald*.[82] One of the most glamorous hunting parties in the history of the Plains, it expressed the confluence between the urban power elite of the East and Midwest, the U.S. Army, and sport hunting on the Great Plains, providing fertile context for Cody's exploration of American culture and political power.

Cody recalled considering his costume carefully. As it was "a nobby and high-toned outfit which I was to accompany, I determined to put on a little style myself."[83] One of the hunters called him "the most striking feature" of the camp's "exciting and attractive" picture that first morning. Riding down from the fort on a white horse, he was, Henry Davies recalled, "Dressed in a suit of light buckskin, trimmed along the seams with fringes of the same leather, his costume lighted by the crimson shirt worn under his open coat, a broad sombrero on his head, and carrying his rifle lightly in one hand, as his horse came toward us on an easy gallop, he realized to perfection the bold hunter and gallant sportsman of the plains."[84]

With his rifle in one hand and mounted on his snowy white horse, he was not just a guide *to* sportsmen, but an icon *of* sportsmen, the buckskin-clad, rifle-toting, mounted buffalo hunter, an updated version of Leatherstocking, and perhaps a more pastoral edition of Hickok. If Cody's entrée was a token of showmanship, it was in keeping with the whole expedition, which was imbued with ceremony, performance, and show. A hundred cavalry escorted the hunters, hauling sixteen wagons of provisions, and three four-horse ambulances for the guns and any hunters who grew weary.[85] Around the campfire at night, Cody told stories about Indians and hunting and acted as judge in the kangaroo court the party held for their entertainment.[86] And, just as important, Cody rode among a buffalo herd and killed an animal from horseback.[87] His skills found a friendly audience. Hugh Davies called him "our guide, philosopher and friend, Buffalo Bill."[88]

Cody's performance in this hunt was in fact his dress rehearsal for a bigger performance, as guide to the hunting party of the visiting Russian Grand Duke Alexis in 1872. Cody partisans usually consider this hunting party a precursor to his Wild West show and an early moment of stardom on a public stage. He met the grand duke on his arrival at North Platte on the Union Pacific, where one columnist's florid description echoes the dime novel language which had catapulted Cody to celebrity after his appearance in Ned Buntline's tale in 1869. "He was seated on a spanking charger, and with his long hair and spangled buckskin suit he appeared in his true character of one feared and beloved by all for miles around. White men and the barbarous

Indians are alike moved by his presence, and none of them dare do aught in word or deed contrary to the rules of law and civilization."[89] Cody rode in advance of the party on their fifty-mile ride to camp at Red Willow Creek: twelve wall tents, festooned with flags. Dinners were banquets with a wide array of game, wines, and champagne.[90] To provide the requisite presence of Indians, Sheridan asked Cody to visit the camp of Brulé Sioux Chief Spotted Tail, inviting him and his warriors to hunt with Sheridan, Custer, and the Grand Duke. Spotted Tail accepted.

Other than relaying the invitation, Cody's only duty was to find buffalo, and once he had accomplished that, there was precious little else for him to do. This was Sheridan's show, and Custer was his star. Throughout, Cody was in Custer's shadow. In the description of one columnist, the general "appeared in his well-known frontier buckskin hunting costume." And Cody? "Buffalo Bill's dress was something similar to Custer's." Alexis, Custer, and Cody ventured out from the camp together on the first morning, attracting "the attention and admiration of every one." But it soon became clear that Custer was the primary guide for Alexis. Cody was but an auxiliary. When Cody located buffalo, "the Duke and Custer charged together," leaving the young guide on the sidelines.[91]

He remained there, by order or by his own preference, for the rest of the hunt. When the party moved out again the next morning, they paused for a photograph in front of the camp, "with the Grand Duke, General Sheridan, and General Custer at the head," followed by the Russian party, American officers and soldiers, and Spotted Tail with his Brulés. There was no mention of Cody.[92]

Sheridan dispatched Cody to find buffalo on the hunt's second day—but it was Custer who found them. "Sheridan gave orders that only the Grand Duke and Custer should ride in advance of himself" as they charged the herd, so the Grand Duke would have first choice of buffalo. The grand duke and Custer together pursued a buffalo cow, which the grand duke killed. With the herd disbanded, Alexis and Custer rode off together again, on a fruitless hunt for more.[93]

That night the Indians performed a dance for the grand duke. Custer flirted brazenly with Spotted Tail's sixteen-year-old daughter (Crazy Horse's cousin). There was a smoke and an exchange of gifts between Sheridan, the grand duke, and Spotted Tail, witnessed by all the party's dignitaries— although press accounts again fail to mention Cody. The next morning, as the grand duke departed for North Platte, he requested photographs of Cody, and of Custer in his buckskin hunting costume. Cody led the party back to the railway station, where he left them.[94] The grand duke had other adventures, charging more herds of buffalo, alongside the redoubtable

Custer, as the train proceeded through Colorado. He shot buffalo from the train, again with Custer, as they returned through Kansas.[95]

Insofar as Cody figured in the grand duke's hunt, he was a bit player. When Custer and the grand duke had their pictures taken in wilderness hunting garb against a painted forest backdrop in a photographic studio, Cody was nowhere to be seen. Years later, when the martyred Custer was a legend, Cody's exile to the margins of this hunt still smarted. For a palliative, he fabricated a publicity photo. He spliced himself into the image of Custer and the grand duke, making the mythic duo into a triumvirate that included Buffalo Bill Cody.[96]

The maneuver suggests the deeper truth of Cody's tangential place among the power elite of the U.S. Army and the major iconic figures in American culture. For all his success, by early 1872, he was still a minor fig-ure, hero of a trash novel, hunting guide, and an occasional scout for the army against an enemy which had largely retreated to the reservations, and whose ultimate defeat now looked more inevitable than ever.

If he was to continue profiting from his position as the white Indian, he would have to make a bold move. Fortunately, another option presented itself. As the hunt with Alexis ended, "General Sheridan took occasion to remind me of an invitation to visit New York which I had received from some of the gentlemen who accompanied the General on the hunt from Fort McPherson to Hays City, in September of the previous year." By Feb-ruary 1872, Cody was bound for New York City, and bigger things.[97]

PART TWO

CHAPTER SEVEN

Theater Star

EARLY IN 1872, Fred G. Maeder, a prominent New York playwright, adapted Ned Buntline's Buffalo Bill dime novel for the stage. *Buffalo Bill* premiered at a working-class haven, the Bowery Theater, in February 1872, starring a noted melodrama actor, J. B. Studley, in the title role. The premiere coincided with Cody's visit to New York. As Cody told it, "I was curious to see how I would look when represented by some one else, and of course I was present on the opening night, a private box having been reserved for me." During the play, Studley stepped out of character to announce that Cody was in the theater. "The audience, upon learning that the real 'Buffalo Bill' was present, gave several cheers between the acts, and I was called on to come out on the stage and make a speech." Cody relented, "and the next moment I found myself standing behind the footlights and in front of an audience for the first time in my life." Not knowing what to say, "I made a desperate effort, and a few words escaped me, but what they were I could not for the life of me tell, nor could any one else in the house."[1]

In a sense, there were two performances that night. In the first, J. B. Studley played Buffalo Bill. In the second, and no less significant, the real Buffalo Bill played the frontier rustic who confronts his own representation in the metropolis. He was following an American tradition, established decades earlier by none other than Davy Crockett. A Tennessean who self-consciously appropriated the symbols of Daniel Boone's myth on his way to a congressional seat in 1827, Crockett had a tall-tale-telling, homespun persona that was a distinctive touch in official Washington, and he became a national celebrity. His political and social trajectory inspired James Kirk Paulding's play, *The Lion of the West*, in which a thinly disguised parody of Crockett named Nimrod Wildfire repeatedly outwits an English snob. Intended as a lampoon of Crockett, the play was received as a celebration of his authenticity and sincerity. After beginning his political career as a hero to Democrats, Crockett soon fell out with Andrew Jackson over the congressman's opposition to the Cherokee removal. In 1831, in the midst of his public feud with the president, Crockett himself attended a performance of

The Lion of the West in Washington, D.C. His presence authenticated the fictional portrayal, and bound the audience's entertainment to frontier history and an ongoing political struggle for the soul of the republic. Allegedly he bowed from his box to the delight of a vocal crowd.[2] Subsequently, *The Lion of the West* was rewritten various times, with one version called *The Kentuckian, or, a Visit to New York*.[3] Thus, even before Crockett's apotheosis at the Alamo, he was a national figure who fused frontier politics, national identity, and popular entertainment. If nobody invoked Crockett at the New York opening of *Buffalo Bill*, it is hard to believe that old theater hands like Buntline and the renowned dramatist Fred Maeder were unaware of the parallels to Crockett's 1831 appearance—and harder still to believe that Buntline in particular was not manipulating the evening to reenact it. Subsequently, the novelist took Cody to Philadelphia to meet with his newly founded Patriotic Order of the Sons of America, a nativist organization for whom Buntline hoped Cody would be a symbol.[4]

In any case, Cody's attendance at the city theater both announced his arrival in the metropolis and, paradoxically, authenticated him—Crockett-like—as a frontiersman.[5] Perhaps with the Tennessean in mind, he toyed with the idea of a political career afterward. A Democrat like his father, he was appointed justice of the peace for a brief tenure at Fort McPherson in 1871. Not long after his return from New York, friends nominated him for a seat in the Nebraska legislature, and he was a candidate in the 1872 elections. In his autobiography and show programs, Cody claimed he won that race, but resigned the seat to go on the stage. In fact, although initial returns showed him winning, the official tally made him a loser by forty-two votes.[6]

This supposed election to the legislature became the source of his title "Honorable," which he emblazoned across his posters and show programs—"The Honorable William F. Cody"—for the rest of his career. His imagined electoral victory placed him in the pantheon of American frontiersmen who rose to civic leadership. If white men were distinguished from savages by their capacity for self-governance, then the humble white frontiersman who rose to elective office was proof both of American upward mobility and of the governing capacity of whiteness itself. Cody's fake political biography, in this sense, placed him alongside other frontiersmen with more substantial political accomplishments, including not only Crockett, but Andrew Jackson, Abraham Lincoln, and even George Washington—all figures to whom Cody would compare himself late in life.[7]

But as we have seen, Cody had little time for politics. It was the stage that entranced him. Standing before that sea of faces, Cody issued his tongue-tied greeting, bowed, and "beat a hasty retreat into one of the cañons of the stage."[8] Those "cañons of the stage" would become his next frontier, as he ventured onto the boards to play himself before large and mostly enthusiastic audiences.

Resonating with a range of cultural traditions and shifts, the comic story of Cody's dramatic career probably entertained as many people as his plays ever did. The audacious leap to the stage by a man with no theatrical training appealed to a public which still preferred innate talent, or natural genius, to educated skill. Just as they preferred the militiaman to the professional soldier, in the theater they loved watching the amateur dramatist upstage professional actors. At the same time, as we shall see, the spectacle of Buffalo Bill Cody playing himself also attracted audiences fascinated with copies, mimicry, and theatrical self-presentation, as expressions of industrialism and middle-class imitations of elite culture, and of the increasing acceptability of imposture in everyday social relations.

The catalytic intersection of Cody's career with these arteries of popular culture began during his visit to New York, and continued in the months afterward, as Buntline importuned Cody to come back to the East and play the role of Buffalo Bill on the stage. Finally, Cody agreed. In the fall of 1872, he left Fort McPherson for Chicago, in the company of his friend and fellow army scout John Burwell "Texas Jack" Omohundro, a Cody acolyte whose ambitious frontier imposture (he began scouting at Cody's instigation after arriving in Nebraska in 1869) made him even more eager than his mentor to attempt a theatrical career. Buntline was disappointed when the scouts arrived without the genuine Pawnee Indians he had been promoting. For their part, the scouts were horrified to discover that Buntline had not yet written the play in which they were to appear five nights hence. So, too, was the owner of the theater who had agreed to host their show, and after he backed out, Buntline contracted to rent the theater for a week, at a price of $600. As Cody recalled it, Buntline then took them to a hotel, where he sat down to write. Four hours later, he "jumped up from the table, and enthusiastically shouted 'Hurrah for the Scouts of the Plains!' That's the name of the play. The work is done. Hurrah!"[9]

Buntline directed Cody and Omohundro to "do your level best to have this dead-letter perfect for the rehearsal" the next morning. Doubting that they could learn the lines in less than six months, "we studied hard for an hour or two, but finally gave it up as a bad job, although we had succeeded in committing a small portion to memory." When Buntline dropped by to hear Cody's recitation, the scout "began 'spouting' what I had learned, but was interrupted by Buntline: 'Tut! Tut! You're not saying it right. You must stop at the cue.'

" 'Cue! What the mischief do you mean by the cue? I never saw any cue except in a billiard room.' "[10]

When the play opened four days later, General Sheridan and a phalanx of Chicago's upper crust came to see it, along with rows of mechanics and other laboring men. In the drama, Buntline, as Cale Durg, an old trapper, enters the stage accompanied by his friends Buffalo Bill and Texas Jack. In the first act, they face off against Indians, played by forty or fifty "supernumeraries," or "supers," today known as extras. Blasting away with pistols at the supers, they rescue the heroine of the piece, Cale Durg's ward, a virtuous white woman known as Hazel Eye. In act 2, Mormon Ben, a Latter-day Saint with fifty wives, covets Hazel Eye for his fifty-first. To this end, he schemes with his henchmen, Carl Pretzel, a German, Phelim O'Laugherty, an Irishman constantly in need of a drink, and Sly Mike. All of these were standard melodrama types, the ethnic parody a product of the city's ethnic and racial tension. Immigrants Pretzel and O'Laugherty are enemies of the home and domestic order, like polygamous Mormons and the Indians in act 1. When Mormon Ben makes off with Hazel Eye, the Indians attack him and recapture her. Shortly before she is to be burned at the stake, her hands are untied by the good Indian maiden, Dove Eye (played by the famous dancer Giuseppina Morlacchi; one critic described Dove Eye as "the beautiful Indian maiden with an Italian accent and a weakness for scouts"), and she is rescued by Buffalo Bill and Texas Jack, who enter shouting, "Death to the Redskins!" and blast away until all are dead. So the action continues, with evil white men (Sly Mike), derelict immigrants (Pretzel and O'Laugherty), and white men so evil their whiteness is questionable (Mormon Ben), allying with bad Indians to steal the beautiful white woman, only to be laid low by the white, native-born scouts' voluminous gunfire in almost every act. Ultimately, of course, evil is vanquished, Buffalo Bill has Hazel Eye in his arms, and the curtain comes down.[11]

Plays about frontier history were very popular in the 1870s. These included upmarket productions like *Horizon, Across the Continent*, and Frank Mayo's *Davy Crockett*, all of which were hailed as true American art.[12] But in the case of Buntline's bloody, action-packed spectacle, the reviewers were condescending when they were not dismissive. Cody recalled one who remarked that "if Buntline had actually spent four hours in writing that play, it was difficult for any one to see what he had been doing all that time."[13] Others noted the woodenness of the frontiersmen, the mostly working-class audience, and the imponderable plot, all brought together by the appearance of the famous dime novelist and the famous scout. "Such a combination of incongruous drama, execrable acting, renowned performers, mixed audience, intolerable stanch, scalping, blood and thunder, is not likely to be vouchsafed to a city a second time, even Chicago."[14]

The company toured the Midwest and Northeast the rest of the winter, playing to packed houses. The following year, Cody and Omohundro split with Buntline, and launched out on their own. Omohundro and Morlacchi married in the fall of 1873, and by the following year they had broken away from Cody to form their own theatrical company.

Cody persevered without them. His theatrical company, soon called the Buffalo Bill Combination, toured through the next decade. Consistently, he played the role of Buffalo Bill in frontier melodramas where the unifying theme was the liberation of a virtuous woman from savage captivity and her restoration to her home and family. His popularity was gigantic. So was his monetary reward. In 1880, he took home profits of $50,000. More, Buffalo Bill's stage career introduced him to formal show business, and was in turn the stage from which he launched his much larger, more complex outdoor spectacle, Buffalo Bill's Wild West show.[15]

Cody's fun, of course, entailed tremendous labors on his part, and on the part of his family. Within weeks after Cody's departure from North Platte in the fall of 1872, Louisa joined him in St. Louis, where *Scouts of the Prairie* was appearing. She traveled with him throughout the rest of the season, trundling along with their three children: daughter Arta, now six; son Kit Carson, who turned two on the road; and another daughter, Orra Maude, only three months old that fall.[16]

During the following year, the Cody family relocated to be nearer the theater circuit, moving to a new home in West Chester, Pennsylvania, where William Cody had cousins. But Louisa disliked West Chester. During his divorce trial, William Cody explained that his relatives "were on the Quaker order and she didn't like their quiet ways, and she was not friendly with them."[17] So Louisa and the children continued to travel with the show. In the fall of 1873, family and theatrical combination set out on the road again, wife and children traveling along with Cody until March of 1874. That month, when the show reached Rochester, New York, Louisa seemed to like the town. "We decided that there would be the best place to take up our residence, as the town was centrally located and I would be more apt to be at Rochester than I would be in most any other town."[18]

Ultimately, the family home again became tangential to Cody's stage orbit. Tragedy struck in 1876, when five-year-old Kit died of scarlet fever, moments after William Cody arrived home from his show in New York. One wonders if the pain of losing their only boy motivated the Codys to return West. In 1878, Louisa took Arta and Orra back to North Platte, where Will Cody had bought them a house in the now substantial town of stores, churches, farms, and businesses. Stage drama would continue to be Cody's major occupation through 1883, when he initiated the Wild West show, an entertainment self-consciously modeled on the Plains and for which North Platte would be a central base and point of departure. By that time, he was the leading actor of frontier melodramas and a wealthy man.

IN HIS AUTOBIOGRAPHY and in popular memory, the encounter between mime and man, the actor playing Buffalo Bill and the real Buffalo Bill, became the central narrative moment of Cody's first New York tour. His theatrics amused crowds partly by calling attention to the uncanny resemblance between the romantic images of him created by writers and actors (Art) and his real self (Nature) and inviting them to separate the two if they could. In this respect, his stage career was a new departure in his now customary, artful juxtaposition of original and copy, a western scout who looked suspiciously similar to his many representations in the popular press.

Audiences in New York, the capital of American theater, first encountered Cody as the "King of Border Men," in Ned Buntline's serialized story in the *New York Weekly*, in December 1869. Any impulse to dismiss him as a simple fiction was complicated by his appearance in *New York Times* coverage of minor Indian skirmishes in 1870, and then again in reports of the extravagant hunting trips of General Sheridan in 1871, and probably in other news stories which have since been lost.[19]

Cody's press reputation was continuing to grow at the very moment that he stepped into New York society. Sometime in 1872 or 1873, William E. Webb's memoir and western travel guide, *Buffalo Land*, arrived on bookseller shelves (Webb was the division agent for the Kansas Pacific Railroad who had forced Cody's town of Rome into oblivion). Although Buffalo Bill appears only briefly in the book, he ambles across Webb's pages (as across Buntline's) alongside the not-quite-imaginary Wild Bill Hickok, with the author praising Cody as "spare and wiry in figure, admirably versed in plain lore, and altogether the best guide I ever saw."[20]

Cody's rise to fame was partly a function of the changing mass press. He arrived in the popular eye as newspaper editors hit on the technique of manufacturing news rather than merely reporting it. The master of this strategy was James Gordon Bennett, Jr., publisher of the *New York Herald*, who was a member of Sheridan's hunting expedition in 1871, and who that very year sent a former Indian war reporter named Henry Morton Stanley to Africa in search of the "missing" Dr. Livingstone. In the hands of Bennett and his imitators, wilderness scouts, guides, explorers, and explorer-journalists were all manifestations of the white vanguard, conveying civilization to dark and savage places. Readers devoured press accounts in which adventurous journalists themselves increasingly became the subject of "news." Reports of Stanley's adventures in Africa, in fact, covered columns of print right alongside coverage of the Grand Duke Alexis's hunt the following year. For the rest of his life, Buffalo Bill Cody served as a useful story for any writer with a deadline. Not coincidentally, Bennett was one of those who invited Cody to New York and hosted him on his arrival. He had an uncanny nose for a story.[21]

The grand duke's hunt provided New Yorkers with their most vivid version of Cody before he arrived in their town. Although his role in the expedition was minor and he was overshadowed by Custer, he received his best coverage in the *New York Herald*, whose reporter took time out to consider "the genial and daring Buffalo Bill," a "genuine hero of the Plains." Even at this point, much of the fun in watching Cody came from his verve in assuming the costume of romantic hero to please the crowd, and his amusement at his own audacity. When the medical doctor attending the Grand Duke Alexis asked Cody if he always dressed in the "spangled buckskin suit" of that morning, related the correspondent, Cody grinned. "No, sir; Not much." He went on, wrote the reporter: " 'When Sheridan told me the Duke was coming I thought I would throw myself on my clothes. I only put on this rig this morning, and half the people in the settlement have been accusing me of putting on airs,' and then Bill laughed heartily, and so did the Doctor, the Duke, and the whole imperial crowd."[22]

In February, at least two events reminded New Yorkers of the recently completed tour of the grand duke. The first was the debut of a new act, "The Grand Goat Alexis," at a prominent burlesque theater, in which a goat rode a horse around a ring, with a monkey thrown on his back, "and the horse thus bears a couple of stories of animals round and round the ring, amid the wildest shouts of laughter."[23] The second, of course, was the arrival of Buffalo Bill.

Throughout his visit to New York, his representation in the press and on the stage could be measured against his real person, a kind of interplay between dramatic Cody and real Cody, the former on the stage at the Bowery, the latter frequently sighted in downtown New York, at the Union Club, the Leiderkranz masked ball, and at the fashionable racetracks.

New Yorkers could continue this Cody game even after the man left the city. Almost as soon as he went back to Nebraska, Ned Buntline published a new Buffalo Bill novel, *Buffalo Bill's Best Shot*, which continued to work the line between truth and fiction with a romance inspired by the hunt with the Grand Duke Alexis. Even if they passed up the chance to read it, New Yorkers saw announcements of it over three successive days in the *New York Times* and elsewhere.[24]

Once he moved onto the stage, Buffalo Bill Cody would be a news staple for the rest of his life, moving back and forth over the line dividing the real and the fake, Nature and Artifice, his stature as a "real westerner" underscoring the interplay of the two. Synopses of his plays and reviews of the dime novels about him appeared in the same newspapers that reported "real" news about his cattle drives at his Nebraska ranch, his guided hunting expeditions with English aristocrats, and his Indian fights across the Plains. To audiences, then, Buffalo Bill's life was a fascinating mixture of theatrical romance and bloody reality, much like the West itself.[25]

CODY'S OCCUPATIONS on the Plains had all been tied to the expanding railroad, and his stage stardom, too, was partly a product of the railroad and the ways it revolutionized the theater. In earlier days, a theater owner (often a renowned actor) would hire a company of actors to work in residence, performing plays in repertory for a whole season. After the Civil War, the railroad made sedentary companies obsolete. Now, theatrical stars became the center of companies known as "combinations." Opening at a prominent theater in New York, usually in early autumn, the combination then went on tour via the nation's new railroad networks, performing a selection of plays in many different cities and towns. Troupes disbanded at the end of the season, usually in late June. The promoter, or star, could then begin the process of hiring anew and commissioning new plays for the next season. As New York historians have observed, "The city had become a manufacturer of dramatic commodities," and theater was becoming at least as much an industry as an art.[26]

Buffalo Bill's fame grew as he grafted his earlier guiding and scouting persona onto this new form of commodity production. To say the least, the theatrical career was an unlikely turn. "That I, an old scout who had never seen more than twenty or thirty theatrical performances in my life, should think of going upon the stage, was ridiculous in the extreme."[27] But if the frontiersman's metamorphosis into stage star seems counterintuitive, in another respect the stage was a fitting venue. Actors, like spies and scouts, were traditionally a marginal class in America. Professional deceivers, they were reviled by the Puritans as liars and blasphemers, and by subsequent generations of Americans for their suspicious facility with disguise. In the many warnings that moralists and urban reformers issued about the confidence man, the theater figured prominently as one of his preferred venues for the introduction of virtuous youth to urban sin and decadence. After all, the confidence man, the consummate seducer, was himself a skilled actor.[28]

These prejudices against the theater had weakened considerably by the 1870s, by which time successful actors were no more unpopular than successful lawyers (conversely, low-rent thespians were every bit as reviled as hack attorneys). But suspicion of actors as disreputable and their entertainments as immoral remained a backdrop for Cody's entire career.[29] Nate

Salsbury, Cody's managing partner for many years in the Wild West show, began his show business career as an actor after the Civil War, at which time his cousin warned him that "the majority of the American people think that a man who is talented lowers himself by going on to the stage."[30]

Thus, Cody's new appeal was in some ways analogous to his appeal as a scout. Just as surrounding himself with socially dubious mixed-bloods and Indians made him stand out as a white guide and tracker, by entering the arena of actors—professional impostors—he both compounded the layers of skepticism around his own persona and simultaneously enhanced the currency of his authentic hunting, scouting, and Indian fighting. Meeting a genuine frontiersman who seemed to embody the progress of the nation was one thing, but seeing him in a context of outright fakery, supporting a drama in which he banished the savagery of the frontier, upped the value of his real biography.

Just as important, Cody's stage debut was not accidental, but a calculated development of his entertainment product. Out on the Plains, the western show that Hickok, Cody, and others crafted for tourists—tall tales, shooting exhibitions, hunting displays, and the projection of a heroic persona in keeping with popular expectations—begged a central question: if the audience was coming west on the train to see the performance, why not put the show on the train and send it east? Showmen had staged frontier exhibitions before. P. T. Barnum's failed New Jersey buffalo hunt of 1843 was a prime example. The transcontinental railroad made such attempts easier, at least potentially. Thus, in 1872, while Buffalo Bill was visiting New York, museum impresario Sidney Barnett hired Cody's friend and neighbor in Nebraska, Texas Jack Omohundro. The Texan was to accompany a herd of buffalo and a group of Pawnee Indians to upstate New York, where they would perform a mock buffalo hunt for tourists at Barnett's museum. Although Omohundro and several others put in much time and effort capturing buffalo, government agents refused to allow the Pawnees to travel east. Texas Jack backed out, too. Nonetheless, the staged hunt went forward. In August of that year, Wild Bill Hickok served as master of ceremonies for Barnett's show, in which a delegation of cowboys joined a party of Sac and Fox Indians from Oklahoma. The crew performed a mock buffalo pursuit on the grassy foreground of America's most renowned wilderness monument, Niagara Falls. But the event proved difficult and expensive to stage. Barnett lost money and folded the show.[31] Still, few doubted that moving the show of western progress to the East had a future. The question was how to make it happen.

At the time of Hickok's appearance at Niagara Falls, Cody's first theatrical performance in Chicago, with Texas Jack Omohundro, was only three months away. Theatrical drama had the advantage of being far more familiar to audiences than the kind of outdoor arena exhibition that Barnett and Hickok were presenting, and on the stage Cody could incorporate rope tricks, shooting displays, and other aspects of western show spectacle which he would one day display in an arena. Read carefully, Cody's protestations of dramatic ignorance in fact suggest the omnipresence of theater on the frontier, and its familiarity to him. The "old scout" (he was twenty-six) "had never seen more than twenty or thirty theatrical performances."[32] It might seem a sizable total by today's standards, but Cody's estimate was probably low (the better to emphasize the implausibility of his career turn). Frank North, legendary scout and friend of Cody's, lived in Colville, Nebraska, where he kept a journal during 1869. It was a busy year for the young North family. There was not only a new baby at home, but also a lumber business and rental properties to tend, two major expeditions to fight the Cheyenne, and a social calendar packed with reading circles, dances, and concerts. Nonetheless, Frank North saw fourteen plays at Omaha theaters in 1869 alone.[33]

Although its inclusiveness had faded in previous decades, theater was traditionally the nation's foremost democratic entertainment, presenting a large variety of productions for all classes, and in all regions. Even in Iowa, at the time Cody was born, theatrical troupes performed in English and German.[34] On the Great Plains, theaters were among the first buildings erected in new towns. Stage drama, in fact, preceded the stages. In Kansas, as on earlier frontiers, soldiers often entertained each other and surrounding settlers with dramatic companies at their posts. Traveling dancers, singers, magicians, jugglers, and acting troupes made their way along the trail to Denver by 1859, frequently stopping to perform in Leavenworth and other Kansas towns.[35] Major E. W. Wynkoop, who fought in the Plains Indian wars with Cody in the late 1860s, became founding president of the Amateur Dramatic Association of Denver in 1861.[36] Theaters operated in Leavenworth right through the Civil War (the esteemed John Wilkes Booth even appeared there).[37]

By 1867, William Cody had named his favorite buffalo rifle "Lucretia Borgia." Some speculate that he heard of the famous Italian poisoner and erotomaniac from the play of the same name, a popular nineteenth-century offering which was showing in St. Louis when Cody was stationed there with the Union army in 1864. But it is just as likely that he saw the play in Denver, where it was playing when the fourteen-year-old Cody was there in the winter of 1860.[38] In the Kansas cow towns, minstrel shows and burlesque proliferated, along with opera and melodrama.[39] By the time Cody arrived at Fort McPherson, there was a post theater in operation there, too.[40]

Yet, for all Cody's exposure to theater as an observer, for him to become a stage actor was a daring move. It was one thing to have seen some plays, and to tell stories and dress in costume for tourists and soldiers in Kansas or Nebraska. It was quite another to interpret a script and entertain a packed house in Chicago, New York, or Memphis. Equally important, after a short apprenticeship with a professional (Buntline had adapted numerous novels for the stage, and occasionally acted himself), Cody somehow mastered management of a theatrical company, too.

His autobiography suggests that he found his bridge to stage acting in his experience as a hunting guide. In his early days with Buntline, he adapted his renowned storytelling to stage performance, filling in his acting gaps with his own narrative drama. On his opening night, when Buntline stepped forward in his role as "Cale Durg" and gave Cody his cue, he later recalled, "for the life of me I could not remember a single word" of the script. Buntline then prompted Cody with a different line, "Where have you been, Bill? What has kept you so long?"

At that moment, Cody noticed in the audience one of Chicago's renowned wealthy sport hunters who had been on one of the more colorful hunting trips he had guided. "So I said: 'I have been out on a hunt with Milligan.'" Milligan was a leading light of Chicago's social scene, and the audience roared.

Buntline, never one to stick to a script when a better line appeared, went with the drama Cody was creating: "Well, Bill, tell us about the hunt." As Cody recounted: "I succeeded in making it rather funny, and I was frequently interrupted by rounds of applause." Whenever the story wandered off, "Buntline would give me a fresh start, by asking some question." In this way, Cody wrote, "I took up fifteen minutes, without speaking a word of my part; nor did I speak a word of it the whole evening."[41]

ORIGINAL/COPY

Thus Cody extended and recast the drama he staged around the campfires of his guided hunts, finding in the East a vast, lucrative market for his form of entertainment. Only months before, a newspaper correspondent had described Cody's "wonderful" campfire stories, related "in the presence of all the paraphernalia of frontier life upon the Plains." On the stage, Cody appropriated the same "paraphernalia of frontier life"—guns, knives, whips, hats, boots, and ropes—and dressed the part, as he had for his hunting clients, in lavish suits of buckskin and velvet and fur, complemented by a broad hat and his hair falling to his shoulders.[42]

His manipulation of those props was central to his authentic demeanor, and his stage plays called for his character to demonstrate his abilities with gun and whip, with stunts that would one day become part of his Wild West show. "Mr. Cody's shooting was very fine indeed," wrote one reviewer in 1879. "He shot an apple from the head of Miss Denier, and then taking a mirror he turned his back to the young lady and shot it from her head again. He also knocked the fire from a cigar which was held in the mouth of Mr. James. His shooting and use of the 'cow driver' is simply marvellous."[43]

Historians and critics long ago established that Cody's stage success came from the friction between his frontier authenticity and its context of theatrical fakery. His performance simultaneously validated and called into question his own imposture as a "genuine" frontiersman, delighting audiences who could debate and argue over how "real" Buffalo Bill was. Playwrights often adapted cheap novels for the stage, but in the plays of Buffalo Bill, Texas Jack, and the other stars of frontier melodrama, the heroes were "real" people, and whether or not they believed the hyperbolic publicity, the audience loved the novelty.[44] Thus, the packed houses that greeted Cody, Omohundro, and Buntline in New Haven and other places expressed popular desire to see the heroes they knew from "weekly story papers, and the semi-occasional novelettes" about them, according to a contemporary writer.[45] As Roger Hall has observed, "the presence on stage of an actual participant in frontier events reinforced the vicarious and psychological connection of the audience to those events."[46]

But to describe Cody as authentic, a self-evidently "real" man conveying elements of the real frontier, only scratches the surface of his allure. Historians have carefully retraced nearly every Cody performance. They have analyzed his few surviving scripts, and pored over his advertising. But exclusive attention to the real William Cody has blinded us to the faux Codys, the numerous actors who continued to play "Buffalo Bill" at the same time William Cody did, and for many of the same crowds. Moreover, in addition to professional actors who struck their own poses as the stage character "Buffalo Bill," a sizable number of frontier scouts followed Cody to the stage and so closely mimicked Cody's scout persona as to make audiences wonder who really was the authentic frontiersman.

"It is within an exuberant world of copies that we arrive at our experience of originality," writes Hillel Schwartz.[47] And Cody's originality was considerably enhanced by the wide mimicry of his imposture, which placed him less at the center of a theater of the original than in the dance of original *and* copy that defined the essence of frontier melodrama. To be sure, William Cody *was* Buffalo Bill, and this gave the stage character a purchase in off-stage—real—life. But the proliferation of Buffalo Bill impersonators on the stage meant that, in a sense, Buffalo Bill the stage character was both real *and* fake—and William Cody's achievement was to encompass both sides of that coin.

The theater of mimicry and copy in Cody's stage performance might be said to have begun when he confronted Studley playing the Buffalo Bill role. The two together, Studley and Cody, provided poles of fake and real, a simultaneous display of the copy and the original that resonated with popular fascination for such contrasts, notably by providing space to wonder which was which. Was Studley imitating Cody? Or vice versa?

We may speculate that Cody's continuing presence in New York enhanced the appeal of his stage impersonators by prolonging this tension. The standard run for a new melodrama was two weeks. Studley ran his "Buffalo Bill" for a month. Indeed, immediately after the last curtain fell on Studley's faux Buffalo Bill at the Bowery, the play opened again, on March 18, at the Park Theater, with J. W. Carroll as its faux Cody. The same day, in a sign of Buffalo Bill's popularity, a parody—a faux faux Buffalo Bill, called *Bill Buffalo, with His Great Buffalo Bull*—opened at Hooley's Opera House, in Brooklyn.[48]

To audiences, Buffalo Bill balanced somewhere between real man and theatrical representation. By venturing onto the stage himself in the fall of 1872, Cody enhanced the tension that charged the character's appeal. If the move made him more popular, it also lent frisson to the performances of fake Codys, particularly in New York. At the beginning of the theatrical season, the drama *Buffalo Bill* played for a week in mid-November, at Wood's Museum, with James M. Ward in the title role. One month later, New York theatergoers could read news coverage of the real Buffalo Bill's performances in Chicago, and as Buntline, Cody, and Omohundro toured the Midwest—St. Louis, Cincinnati, Indianapolis, Toledo, Cleveland—the actor J. B. Studley began playing Buffalo Bill again in January of 1873, at New York's Bowery Theater, and then again during the last week of March at the Park Theatre.[49] The news of Cody's imminent arrival in New York reinforced the appeal of Studley's Buffalo Bill, making it the advance "bill" for the real Bill.

Studley's performance closed on March 30. The next evening, the real Cody opened with Buntline and Omohundro in *Scouts of the Prairie* at Niblo's Garden, where they played until mid-April.[50] Then, following a brief stint at the Brooklyn Academy of Music, Cody's troupe left New York. A month and a half later, the real Cody was touring the workingmen's theaters of industrial upstate New York, while, back in the city, Studley was in the Cody role again, at the Theatre Comique.[51]

The compelling entertainment in this concoction of reality and representation came at least in part from its resonance with a fad for playful imitation which permeated late Victorian America. As manufacturing and mass production came to define the American economy, copies of things increasingly replaced real things. The basis of middle-class culture was imitation of elites. Machine production of goods, cheap but realistic imitations of furniture, clothing, and architecture, allowed middle-class people to appropriate elite fashions easily. Mimicry and copy thus became central to middle-class life.[52]

In this context, self-styled arbiters of taste like Edith Wharton hewed to the authentic, but to most people, the empowerment of imitation was too great to ignore. If copies of authentic goods allowed middle-class people to express equality with elites on the cheap, why not celebrate imitation? In this spirit, middle-class people intentionally confused the fake and the real as a form of cultural play, turning the imitation into a category of its own. The most daring imitations were those that crossed the line between Nature and Art, mimicking the one with the other. Thus, many middle-class parlors displayed paper flowers mingled with real flowers, wax or marble fruit in bowls of real fruit, real ivy (grown from cuttings in a bottle of water) climbing wallpaper on which were printed realistic ivy patterns, and iron furniture shaped like twigs and branches. This interpolation of fake and real proliferated across American living rooms, a new aesthetic that created enjoyment by fooling the senses, simultaneously celebrating industrial mass production and domesticating it within the parlor, and honoring the skill of the decorator.[53]

In its cultural implications, it went far beyond living room decor, expressing the playful, entertaining mixture of trick and truth behind the period's most popular entertainment, the artful deception. It also resonated with the most successful plays and novels, which explored mimicry, doubles, disguises, and imposture at length. Henry James was fascinated with imitation in middle-class life, and Mark Twain's parade of double identities, fakes, and tall tales wound through every one of his books from *Roughing It* and *Huckleberry Finn* to *Life on the Mississippi* and his own autobiography.[54]

Reviews of Buffalo Bill plays are too sparse and fragmentary to allow us insight into the fascinating give-and-take between the real man and his stage imitators. Were there actors who played Buffalo Bill more convincingly than Cody did? We cannot know, but the bait-and-switch of fake and real in the Cody game amounted to playful deception which mimicked and lampooned the more serious deceptions of commerce. Advertisements for dramas starring Cody and Omohundro appeared in long lists of ads for other commodities—umbrellas, skin cream, hair dye, and hats—with the ubiquitous call to brand loyalty, "Accept No Substitutes." Where New Yorkers had to select the best and most effective products from a host of imitators, the frontier melodrama turned the parade of real and fake into a harmless entertainment. Perhaps there were loyalists who believed Cody was the only acceptable "Buffalo Bill." But the continuing popularity of the faux Codys suggests that for audiences, the real Cody was a kind of substitute after all, a stand-in for the dramatic Cody popularized by J. B. Studley and others. A sip of distilled authenticity was refreshing, but the cocktail of dramatic actor and historical actor was what made the show fun. J. B. Studley played Buffalo Bill again in October of 1876, his performance again the "advance Bill" for the real Bill Cody, who appeared in *Scouts of the Plains* in Brooklyn the following week.[55] Frank Dowd (or Doud) played Buffalo Bill at the Theatre Comique early in the summer of 1877; William Cody played in *May Cody, or Lost and Won*, at the Bowery Theater at summer's end.[56] Stage mimicry of Buffalo Bill continued even after his stage career ended. As late as 1891, during the peak years of his Wild West show fame, vaudeville theaters were performing short comic plays about his life, such as *Buffalo Bill Abroad and at Home*, their outrageous fakery a counterpoint to his avowed authenticity.[57]

But in the late 1870s, professional actors cooled to the role of Buffalo Bill, and by the 1880s, Buffalo Bill stage plays sans the actual William Cody were the exclusive domain of cheap variety theaters. The waning popularity of Cody's professional imitators can be traced in some degree to the emergence of at least a half-dozen other frontiersmen claiming to be "authentic" scouts, each appearing in melodramas with frontier themes, constituting a genre of performance that Cody's publicist, John M. Burke, called "the scout business."[58]

Although punctuated by the rhetoric of reality, and purveyed by scouts who were themselves symbols of authenticity, the scout business provided mimicry more subtle and entrancing than even the alternating appearance of fake and real Codys. So many scouts moved onto the stage, inspiring so many dime novels and ever more stage plays, that professional actors were no longer necessary to carry off the impression that somebody was being imitated, and somebody might be real. In fact, the genre of frontier melodrama that Cody kicked off spawned so many "real" frontier heroes playing themselves, so thoroughly appropriating the props, gestures, scripts, and even the biographies of one another, that the stars of the entertainment could be seen alternately—or simultaneously—as "genuine" heroes *and* as imitations of one another. Thus, in October 1874, Donald McKay, an army scout in California's Modoc War, appeared in a play about the life of Kit Carson, alongside a troupe alleged to consist of real Warm Springs Indians. One month later, McKay himself became the subject of *Donald Mackay*, a play in which actor Oliver Doud Byron played the California scout.[59]

There were others. After Cody and Omohundro split with Buntline, the novelist persuaded another resident of North Platte, by this time a primary staging area for western imposture, to take his show east. Thus, Charles "Dashing Charlie" Emmett, a scout for the Second Cavalry, starred as himself in a Buntline play apparently based on the life of scout Frank North. *Little Rifle, or, The White Spirit of the Pawnees* was successful enough that Emmett took the drama with him when he, too, split with Buntline. Venturing out to impersonate himself (or was it Frank North?) in stage plays, he was buoyed by the company of esteemed actress Alice Placide.[60] Emmett played New York City in the spring of 1874, and assisted Cody with a benefit performance in November. Emmett's *Little Rifle* followed on the heels of Byron's *Donald Mackay* at Wood's Museum the same month.[61]

How much the scout business was predicated on scouts imitating one another, to be imitated in turn by actors who sometimes claimed to be "real" western heroes, can be seen in the twisted tale of representation surrounding Cody's mentor in artful deception, Wild Bill Hickok. As we have seen already, Cody imitated Hickok in his early days, appropriating elements of his biography, such as spying in the Civil War. On the stage, Cody continued to work the Hickok vein. In his first stage appearance, Buffalo Bill fought "Jake McKanlass," loosely based on one of Hickok's real-life victims, Dave McCanles, with a bowie knife. By 1874, he was parroting some of Hickok's other tall tales, claiming to have ridden for the Pony Express. By casting himself and Hickok in *Scouts of the Prairie* in 1873, he upped the ante in the contest between fakery and reality, with two scouts named Bill who looked and dressed very much alike, each an "original" western hero.

According to Cody, the role of Wild Bill Hickok became a prominent one for professional actors, too, sometimes in unconventional ways. Where scouts represented themselves on the stage and off, professional actors—or confidence men—sometimes took to representing themselves as scouts, both on the stage and off. Thus, Cody relates that after Wild Bill Hickok's brief tour with his company in 1873–74, a rival stage company hired an actor to play the role of Hickok onstage, and to impersonate the gunfighter in public venues such as restaurants, saloons, and on the street. In Cody's account, the last stage appearance of the real Wild Bill Hickok was when he leapt onto the boards and thrashed this impostor in front of a packed house, just before returning to the West.[62]

Whether or not Cody's Hickok tale was apocryphal, it captures the heightened tension between fakery and reality that energized frontier melodrama to its core. Before frontier melodrama emerged as its own subgenre, the standard melodrama's devotion to disguises and masks, with villains, heroes, and long-lost children continually donning new faces and new identities, was central to its appeal for audiences consumed with the artistry of imitation. The obvious impostures provided dramatic irony, allowing the audience insight into the action that the characters did not have, resolving it when the masks came off at drama's end.[63]

The story of Hickok in the theater, punching the daylights out of somebody mimicking him, suggests how much the stars of frontier melodrama not only parodied all drama but also performed parodies within parodies. At times, the scouts in the dramas were so similar as to be almost interchangeable, and the genre threatened to swallow the "authentic" men who succeeded in it. There were two Jacks, "Texas Jack" and John "Captain Jack" Crawford (the latter emerged quickly on Omohundro's coattails in the mid-1870s). To the consternation of both men, audiences and seasoned show troupers alike often confused them.[64] Paradoxically, this was an appeal of the frontier or "border" drama. As the number of "real" scouts in "true" border dramas multiplied, myriad variations on the theme of authenticity and fakery permeated the action, making the typical masks and clumsy disguises of ordinary melodrama seem tame by comparison.

Buffalo Bill endured longest in the genre, and came to stand as its most "authentic" product. For this reason, scouts and actors who sought bona fides as frontiersmen attached themselves in one way or another to him. But in fact, he developed his own character by borrowing freely from others, particularly Hickok. For two years, in 1875 and '76, Cody played the lead in a play originally written for the lawman, *Wild Bill, or Life on the Border.* Because so many people confused Cody and Hickok anyway, few members of the audience probably realized that he wasn't the play's title character. But even if they were ignorant of Buffalo Bill's imitation of Wild Bill, the play contains dizzying twists on the theme of reality and fakery that pervaded the frontier melodramatic genre. The action swirls around counterfeiters who disguise themselves as Indians. Thus, the real scout plays a scout, opposite actors who play villains who fake Indians who fake money.[65]

The denouement of the play resolves the many tensions between the fake and the real in favor of the latter. The character of Bill Cody apprehends the malingerers, and rescues George Reynolds—the father of Cody's love interest, Emma Reynolds—who has been kidnapped by the counterfeiters. In the end, the counterfeit ceases: the white men no longer play Indians, and they no longer make false money. The true scout, Buffalo Bill, whose fidelity is reinforced by the fact that he is "playing" himself, finds "true" love with virtuous Emma, the "true woman."

Not all of the mimicry attached to the scout business was playful. On occasion, it veered into fraud, which posed real dangers for the leading lights of the scout business. For the game of authentic-and-copy to work, for audiences to enjoy the artistry of imitation, somebody had to be "the real thing," that standard of reality against which the imitation could be judged. Cody's prospects hinged on retaining his status as the "real" Buffalo Bill. Should he lose his grip on that role, there was no other for him. He was not a professional actor.

In this sense, offstage impersonators posed a threat, something Hickok appears to have understood in his violent reaction to his impostor, and something Cody and Omohundro had to confront as well. After their first season together, Buffalo Bill and Texas Jack began carrying endorsements from military officers and western acquaintances, something that they each continued to do throughout their stage careers, because fraudulent theatrical companies, featuring actors claiming to be them, often traveled ahead of their own troupes.[66]

In other cases, actors who played scouts in productions featuring real scouts like Cody and Omohundro would branch out on their own, trying to sell themselves as authentic frontiersmen. When Texas Jack took a break from the Buffalo Bill Combination in 1874, Cody temporarily replaced him with an actor. His identity remains a mystery, but he appeared as—and claimed to be—Kit Carson, Jr. Mustered out of the company on Omohundro's return in 1875, he formed his own stage company and set out to make a name for himself in the scout business.[67]

The efforts of Kit Carson, Jr., were in vain. His combination failed.[68] But

Cody in the stage outfit of black velvet and silver trim in which he killed Yellow Hair (whose name was mistranslated as Yellow Hand). Cody's theatricalism in Indian war had everything to do with the competitiveness of frontier melodrama. Courtesy Buffalo Bill Historical Center.

he infuriated Cody, a fact that suggests how serious a matter imitation and impersonation could become for the stars of frontier melodrama. The business was fiercely competitive, with so many scouts qua actors and actors qua scouts that enduring as the chief draw required constant attention not only to stage production, but to authentic frontier exploits as well. Cody's entire stage career depended on his remaining the figure that other figures were imitating, even if much of his stage persona was a skillful imitation of other scouts, like Wild Bill Hickok, and, possibly, of other actors as well. We may assume that it was for this reason that Cody, who regularly made more in a week at the theater than he took home in a whole season of scouting, returned to the West to scout for the army in 1874, on the Big Horn expedition, and again in 1876, as the Great Sioux War burst upon the northern Plains.[69]

His careful attention to theatrical trappings in the scalping of Yellow Hair had everything to do with the endless one-upmanship of the scout business. Indeed, Cody's attention to theatrical effect in the killing (his costume, his shout "*First scalp for Custer!*") and his realism in staging it (same costume, same shout—and the real scalp, too) entangled event and performance so thoroughly that historians and Cody partisans would debate for decades whether the killing was real or somehow faked. The movement of the encounter from battlefield to stage was so smooth that at least one man swore the enmity between Cody and Yellow Hair actually began in the theater. In 1936, longtime Rochester resident Robert Hicks told historian A. E. Sheldon that Cody had hired Yellow Hair for his stage combination in 1874, but one night Buffalo Bill flattened him with a roundhouse when the Cheyenne drank too much and began insulting ladies backstage. At that moment, claimed the alleged eyewitness, Yellow Hair swore vengeance, and the feud culminated two years later, at Warbonnet Creek.[70]

In fact, Cody knew the frustrations of Indian fighting well enough to know, the moment he heard that Custer had fallen, that the Indian wars finally had a genuine battlefield martyr, a figure who would stand for the U.S. Army's conquest of the Plains the way Stonewall Jackson had stood for the Confederate cause in the Civil War. By becoming Custer's authentic avenger, shedding symbolic first blood and returning with the scalp to the eastern stage, Cody could claim to be the embodiment of the frontier hero, the white Indian who ventures over the line between civilization and savagery to vanquish evil by adapting savage methods, and then ventures back, without ever compromising his innate nobility.[71]

But timing was as important as symbolism. News of Custer's death hit the nation's newspapers on July 4. The Fifth Cavalry was in the field and did not hear till July 7. On July 18, Cody wrote to Louisa that he had taken Yellow Hair's scalp, and a few days later he sent the scalp, warbonnet, shield,

Yellow Hair's belongings, on display in a Rochester, New York, storefront. Cody displayed them in the lobbies of theaters, too, but many condemned the practice. Courtesy Buffalo Bill Historical Center.

and other trappings to Rochester, where they were displayed in the window of a friend's shop, with a large poster explaining that Buffalo Bill had killed and scalped Yellow Hair in revenge for Custer's death. On July 23, the *New York Herald* ran the story of the Cody–Yellow Hair fight.[72] Buffalo Bill became not only Custer's avenger, but the *first* of those avengers. All others were imitations. Accept No Substitutes.

In 1877, Cody's publicist, John Burke, noted privately, and in his typically cascading prose, that "Bill has had every advantage that could possibly assist a man, from the Sioux stirring up a stink, to poor Custer's misfortune, and Yellow Hand's [*sic*] unfortunate accident, with the hirsute incident, a 'custom more honored in the breach than in the observance' but very efficient in working up the 'bauble reputation.' "[73] Yellow Hair's scalp became Cody's trademark, distinguishing him in the scout business so effectively that other scouts' attempts to mark their own authenticity always seemed to mimic his. The futility of competing with Cody's brand of authenticity was perhaps most apparent to John "Captain Jack" Crawford, the self-styled "Poet Scout," who starred briefly in Cody's combination in 1877–78 before going on to a lifelong rivalry with Buffalo Bill. Crawford was an Irish immigrant and Civil War veteran who emigrated from Pennsylvania to the Black Hills of Dakota Territory in 1874 (a move which may have been inspired by watching Cody's theatrical troupe perform in his hometown of Pottsville, Pennsylvania, in 1873).[74] Crawford became a correspondent for the *Omaha Bee* and an early settler at Custer City, Dakota Territory, where he set himself up as captain of his own company of volunteer scouts at the beginning of the Sioux War of 1876. Cody met up with Crawford during his scout forays that summer, and threw him an assist by recommending him to the military command as his own replacement when he left the Plains in August.[75]

Cody's authenticity as scout and race hero was such that when the war against the Sioux continued in 1877, he did not bother to join. Crawford signed on as scout for the army again, and his military career culminated at the battle of Slim Buttes, where many of the Sioux who vanquished Custer were finally subdued. Crawford was reported to have killed and scalped a Sioux warrior during the battle. But, whether it was because of his own reticence about the deed or his inability to attach a name to his victim, or because it was too much a copy of Cody's "original" act of the year before, as a publicity device the scalp proved of limited use in his subsequent theatrical career.[76]

In the fall of 1877, Crawford joined Cody's stage troupe, playing Yellow Hair in the reenactment of the fight on Warbonnet Creek. Seriously injured in a stage mishap, he soon decided to form his own theatrical company, letting it be known that he felt abandoned and manipulated by Buffalo Bill. Cody was angry and told Crawford that "had the accident not occurred I think you had [already] made up your mind to start out for yourself." Cody's ire suggests how jealously he guarded his own authentic status, but it also hints at how difficult the scout business was. "People have flattered you until you think . . . that you are a great man. Jack, go ahead," Cody urged. "You will find out that all that glitters is not gold."[77] Nonetheless, Cody would not try to stop him. "I wish you success and I will never do a thing to hurt you." The two men remained friends, but Crawford's jealousy at Cody's success made him bitter as old age approached. In bringing Buffalo Bill to stage stardom, he wrote on one occasion, "Ned Buntline created the most selfish and brutal fake hero ever perpetrated on the American people."[78] Crawford's accusations notwithstanding, the fakery of Buffalo Bill paled beside the fakery of his many imitators, like Crawford, whose jealousy and mimicry of Cody only enhanced Buffalo Bill's claim to being "the real thing."

LIVING THE STORY

All stage art is a mimicry of real life, but the scout business so confused the categories of real and fake, action and mimicry, that to one *New York Times* correspondent it seemed to presage a new kind of theater, the "Drama of the Future," which would "illustrate current history through the painting of actual events, by the real actors in them." This new art form would "call upon the conspicuous personages of current history, on getting through each marked phase of their careers, to have dramas written describing the same, and go about playing star engagements in the chief character." Of course, there was a real danger that people would (as Cody did, especially in the case of Yellow Hair) deliberately seek "strange adventures" or even court "deadly perils," all "with the idea of acquiring attractive material for a success on the boards." Nonetheless, "the lives of most people are already more histrionic than they think"—or admit. There were, after all, "infinitely more actors and actresses in real life than there can possibly be on the stage."[79]

If the "Drama of the Future" never materialized, if those occasions of real people playing scenes from their own life remained the exception and not the rule, in truth the stage plays of Buffalo Bill did not much resemble it, anyway. Although the *Scouts of the Prairie*, *Knight of the Plains*, and the other Buffalo Bill dramas pretended to mimic Cody's real life, they were elaborate, expansive fictions. Their story lines featured plenty of references to actual people, including the Grand Duke Alexis, Cody's younger sister May, Texas Jack, Wild Bill Hickok, and, of course, Buffalo Bill himself. But beyond these simple allusions, the plays bore almost no relation to Cody's real life. He never foiled a ring of counterfeiters who were dressing as Indians, he never fought Jake McKanlass, or anybody with a similar name, and he never rescued his sister May from Mormons.

The trick of being the "real" Buffalo Bill was, of course, to tie his biography to his stage performances and lend them authentic resonance, especially when they were untrue, which was almost always. Thus, in *May Cody, or Lost and Won*, his sister is abducted by Mormon patriarch John D. Lee during the historical Mormon attack on an emigrant wagon train at Mountain Meadows. Her brother, Buffalo Bill, disguises himself as an Indian and rescues her. But before they can celebrate, he is arrested at Fort Bridger, and put on trial for being a spy. Ultimately, he is exonerated and the play reaches its happy ending.[80]

The play was written by Major Andrew Burt, an army officer and friend of Cody's. Like other melodramas and like most dime novels, too, it was a response to recent news events, in this case the 1877 execution of Mormon patriarch John D. Lee for his part in the notorious Mountain Meadows massacre twenty years before. William Cody never claimed that his sister had actually been abducted, but it was at this time that he began to claim that as a boy he had been on a wagon train that was raided by Mormons and forced to retreat to Fort Bridger, and this tall tale became a prominent story in his autobiography, which he published two years later.[81] For every real event which Cody acted out on the stage, his plays featured dozens that never happened at all. Rather than a drama in which historical people acted out their real accomplishments, Cody's melodramas were more often fictional tales which he appropriated as "true" after starring in them.

Such revelations raise other questions—notably, if Cody was making dramatic fictions into his autobiography, why didn't anybody call him on it? Why did audiences seem unable, or unwilling, to recognize the deception? The answer hinges on the role of the West in melodramatic imagination. The Far West and its peoples were still remote enough that audiences first encountered them through the press. Correspondents like George Ward Nichols and Ned Buntline interpreted the lives of Hickok, Cody, and Omohundro through the lenses of dime novels and melodramas, and often by resorting to the tropes of the genre. The mythology of progress which western events seemed to validate, the clearly visible ascent of civilization, was easily incorporated into melodramas of frontier heroes restoring virtuous women to domestic bliss—which, in the workings of melodrama, was the heart of civilization itself. Melodrama idealized domesticity. In play after play, the melodrama reinscribed the notion that personal happiness, democracy, the future of the republic, and just about every other desirable condition depended on domestic contentment, which in turn depended on chaste marriage, and of course, the "true" and unstained woman. Just as the triumph of civilization over savagery was understood as the triumph of domestic order, the salvation of the settler's cabin, so the melodrama's core plot was the rescue of the virtuous woman and her restoration to the home.[82]

Thus, audiences projected melodramatic fantasies onto Hickok, Cody, and Omohundro even before they saw their plays, envisioned them saving white women from Indians even before they "saw" them do just that on the stage. The heroes' appearance in these theatrical performances authenticated the fantasy. Just as important, these figures could continue taking part in the real, offstage adventure of western progress, their exploits perpetuating the blend of authentic and fantastic. Thus, throughout their careers in the public eye, stage scouts sought to embody western progress by carrying on high-profile, self-consciously progressive lives in the offstage West. In addition to fighting Indians through 1876, Cody launched into ranching in northern Nebraska. Omohundro, Crawford, and Hickok sought profits in mining companies.[83] In each case, they entered industries which represented progress, the coming of pastoralism or industry to the savage wilderness. Each skillfully avoided, or avoided publicizing, other ventures less materially tied to progressive mythology, such as managing railroad or stage lines, or opening yet another business in one of the many western towns where saloons, barbershops, and dry goods stores proliferated. Cody turned down an officer's commission in the army.[84] Tellingly, none became a farmer in the 1870s, as if the culmination of progress—the redemption of the garden from the wilderness—was too much denouement and insufficiently compelling for the drama they sought to play out. Thus, they inscribed the forward motion of civilization, the advancement of progress, into their life stories. They proved the myth true, thereby heightening the authenticity of the very fictional plays they showed each theatrical season.

Absent the mythology of progress to play out in his offstage life, the stage character of Buffalo Bill might have vanished after brief popularity, or perhaps gone on to become an entirely fictional character, with no appreciable tie to the real William Cody. Such a trajectory obtained in earlier cases of real people represented on the stage. In 1848, New York playwright Benjamin Baker created the character of a heroic fireman named Mose. The character was based on a real person, Mose Humphrey, a typesetter for the *New York Sun* and a volunteer firefighter renowned among the newspaper workers who crowded theater galleries. Represented by a popular actor, Francis "Frank" Chanfrau, who had grown up in the Bowery himself, Mose became a huge draw for theaters. Because he was a "real" person, the character could not be copyrighted. Thus, after 1848, Mose cropped up in numerous novels (at least one of them by Ned Buntline) and plays (at one point, Chanfrau played Mose in two different productions playing simultaneously at rival theaters). Before long, Mose became a kind of folk hero, a Paul Bunyan of Manhattan, who was said to have jumped across the Hudson, to have blown ships back down the East River, and to have carried a streetcar with the horses dangling.[85]

But by that time, he was no longer attached to his inspiration, the real-life fireman. We may speculate that this separation between myth and man would likely have occurred even if Mose Humphrey had stepped into the role to play himself. After all, firemen were heroes, but they did not represent a moment in a larger progress, except in the most abstract sense. Cody, the hunter and Indian fighter, had initiated the rise of civilization in the West. The mythology was so self-evidently "true" that it played on the stage as well as it supposedly "played" in the West. Theoretically, he could spend his remaining years living out the subsequent stages of civilization's ascent as rancher, farmer, patrician, and revered town founder. Indeed, that is precisely what he attempted to do.

He had more options than people like Mose Humphrey. For the machinists, typesetters, artists, firemen, clerks, and doctors who might have played themselves onstage, the real challenge was less that their lives had no drama than that they could not infuse their offstage lives with the narrative that western progress conveyed, and which made the continuing appearances of western scouts, especially William Cody, so interesting for theatrical audiences. Melodramatic fantasy was harder to sustain around "real" figures from other regions because regional history either fit less comfortably into the mythology of ascendant civilization, or because that history was too remote. There were dramas aplenty about southern life, including wave after wave of *Uncle Tom's Cabin* reprises. But southern history, with its descent into slavery, read more like American-history-gone-wrong. White southerners were too associated with slave owning to allow a single progressive hero to champion the region's regressive story. Northern history was easier to narrate as heroic saga, but its moment of redemption from wilderness was far enough back in time that its protagonists were long since dead.

Frontier melodrama had no such constraints. Its core stories were the rise of white civilization and the restoration of domestic bliss. As a narrative it was vague enough not to offend and yet it resonated with a broad range of urban and small-town concerns, including the need for a civil order, for the protection of the family from hostile forces, and for the continuing dominance of white men in a society ever more diversified by waves of immigration. Indians were too alienated from the civil order to object to dramatic misrepresentation. The melodrama's white and immigrant villains, bent on miscegenation and thievery, went far beyond the bounds of defensible behavior. The frontier's centrality to American ideas of history and progress provided not just a theory of American development, but a powerful story about how people behave and how events unfold. The advancement from primitive hunting to modern commerce, from savage disorder to enlightened civilization, provided a ready-made narrative, a backstory, to every drama set there. In other words, audience expectations of frontier stories were so powerful that they could look past the blatant fiction of these dramas and embrace the "real" frontier heroes as proof that their expectations and assumptions about the frontier were mostly true.

In one more sense did the frontier West have an advantage as a setting that combined real people and mock play: the frontier line had long served as a mythical dividing point between fakery and reality. Frontier melodrama's mixture of fakery and real people was so compelling because the West itself was synonymous with that same mixture. The West was, in a word, a humbug, and if the drama that presented it most truthfully was itself an artful deception, the West in the 1870s, with its many boosters making impossible but still alluring claims for its promise, had itself become an apt symbol for the fakery and irresistibility of the theater, the locus of the actor's outrageous claims and seductive power.

MIDDLE-CLASS SYMBOL,
WORKING-CLASS HERO

If the *New York Times* correspondent who predicted the "Drama of the Future" was mostly incorrect about the future shape of American drama, in one respect the prediction expressed a popular, little-appreciated idea which made Cody's stage appearances so satisfying. By asserting that there were "infinitely more actors and actresses in real life than there can possibly be on the stage," the correspondent touched on pervasive concerns about the imposture of modern living in the 1870s. The interchangeability of original and copy was an entertaining parody of mass production and consumer fashion, but the scout business also resonated with even broader cultural trends toward the acceptance of ordinary people as imitators, or actors, in day-to-day living. Superficially, Buffalo Bill, Texas Jack, and the other protagonists of frontier melodrama offered a critique of theater by eschewing the title of actor, as if to reinforce traditional prejudice against actors and theatrical drama. "They do not pretend to be actors, i.e. 'Buffalo Bill' or 'Texas Jack,' " wrote one critic; "they simply present to the view of an audience scenes in actual border life, similar to those which they themselves have passed."[86] The deception that he was an actual man, not an actor, was a consistent feature of Cody's career, and a decade later he continued the pretense. "I'm not an actor—I'm a star," he told an interviewer in 1882. "All actors can become stars," he explained, "but all stars cannot become actors."[87]

The success of the untrained "anti-actor" in a domain of trained professionals was, in a sense, a series of elbow jabs to the ribs, an ongoing inside joke between him and his fans, who adored him less for his acting than for his willingness to send up professional theater itself. Stage drama, after all, depends on a pact between actor and audience: one pretends, the other pretends to believe. By refusing the title of actor, Cody announced his inability to pretend—then went on the stage anyway, as if to say that acting was for professionals, but *imitating* actors was the domain of the natural man. In this sense, his presence on the stage was a parody of the entire theatrical industry.

If the real Cody was no actor, it followed that he was incapable of disguising himself. There was no veil to come off. But once the novelty of seeing Buffalo Bill onstage diminished after the first couple of seasons, Cody began commissioning playwrights to layer more complex impersonations on top of his stage identity, and the character of Buffalo Bill began to take up more complex disguises. In Cody's 1878 production, *The Knight of the Plains*, his character assumed three different identities: an English nobleman, a detective, and a Pony Express rider.[88] The "real" William Cody was now assuming new masks which fooled other characters, but not the audience.

The effect was less to renounce acting than to embrace it. Professional thespians in the drama relied on Cody's presence to make these dramas work. They had to pretend to be tricked by his unlikely disguises. The play within the play reinforced the larger message of Cody's stage career: any man can pretend, act, manipulate the professionals, and succeed. White American manliness and imposture were not antithetical. Manly men took to acting like frontiersmen to the wilderness.

Imitations of the "real" Buffalo Bill were one source of Cody's success; the enthusiastic reception of this message—that all white men can be actors—suggests another. Theater was by no means universally respected in the 1870s, but it was accruing acceptance as Americans came to see it as a reflection of new forms of social interaction. The rapidly accumulating wealth of the middle classes in the second half of the nineteenth century led to new forms of conspicuous display, and the development of industrial production placed ever less emphasis on traditional yeomanry and ever more on sales and marketing as pathways to wealth and respectability. Where they had once aspired to a society in which Christian trust was pervasive and one's intentions were self-evident, increasingly Americans "were learning to place confidence in more elaborate forms of self-presentation," in the words of scholar Karen Halttunen.[89] Americans had begun to see their own dependence on manners and middle-class facades as a kind of theater of everyday life. This was the reason for the rising popularity of "parlor theatricals," elaborate, amateur productions with curtains, painted sets, prompters, dramatic lighting, and a full array of props. Across the country, urban middle-class people staged these shows for friends and neighbors in their living rooms. Such displays expressed middle-class dependence on—and confidence in—complicated manners and social rituals to explain themselves. The message of the parlor theatrical was, essentially, "Life is a charade."[90]

In no small measure, Buffalo Bill embodied and expressed the everyday American's facility for theatrical display and upward mobility. Thus, Buffalo Bill's character was not just the exclusive purview of Cody or his professional imitators. Middle-class men across the country took to playing Cody, just like real actors, in parlor theatricals. In 1874, out at Fort Abraham Lincoln, in Dakota Territory, that icon of middle-class manhood, George Armstrong Custer, played the role of Buffalo Bill in his elaborate living room production of *Buffalo Bill and His Bride*, with Libbie as his leading lady.[91]

Whether or not P. T. Barnum ever saw Buffalo Bill's stage plays, they provided the requisite mix of authenticity and imposture of his own entertainments. Indeed, contemporaries remarked on the similarity between Cody's new art and Barnum's. Back in Nebraska, in her cabin not far from Fort McPherson, Ena Raymonde, a friend of Cody and Omohundro, read reviews of their stage appearances in the fall of 1872. "Verily, life is a humbug," she mused, "and he that is the biggest humbug, has the best chance for humbugging the rest of his fellows."[92]

On the frontier, indeed, Buffalo Bill was an object of fascination and dispute. Locals argued about him and Texas Jack much as they argued over Hickok and other artists of western imposture. But his success at integrating himself into the mythology of the West as an icon of middle-class theatricality made him a favorite symbol for settlers by the early 1870s, in ways that Hickok, teetering between lawman and outlaw, could never be. Locals in the vicinity of Fort McPherson ordered Cody's portrait photo from the photographer in North Platte. Ena Raymonde took the time to hand-tint hers.[93] Participants at an 1872 masquerade ball in Wichita, Kansas, ordered their masks from Kansas City. Among the visages that evening were a Spanish cavalier, the goddess of liberty, Satan, and Buffalo Bill.[94]

It may be, as one scholar has argued, that "personal conduct in societies based on the premise of upward mobility is characterized by a highly theatrical presentation of self."[95] In which case, Cody's appeal as a symbol of theatrical self-presentation, a man who played his "real" self in the theater, was all the more central to his age. So what prompted him to leave the stage after over a decade of astounding success? Why take a risk on a bold new entertainment like the Wild West show, which was so unlike the stage in its size, complexity, and dramatic messages?

In fact, there were reasons aplenty, beginning with the ways the limited appeal of the theater eventually constrained Buffalo Bill's marketability. Antitheatricalism had declined, and the "respectable" middle classes no longer shunned all theaters as disreputable. But theater performances usually appealed to one class or another, and critics encoded the class composition of audiences in their reviews. In general, middle-class, white-collar men would not take their families to productions patronized by working-class men (where prostitutes and lower-class women could also be found). On the other hand, respectable theaters were generally too expensive for middle-class people, and they grew more expensive as the century progressed. "By the mid-1880s," says David Nasaw, "the average theater ticket cost a dollar, two-thirds of what the nonfarm worker earned in a day." Most city residents simply could not afford such prices.[96] Urban nightlife was ever more the domain of wealthy young sports who had enough fiscal and social capital to afford its corruptions, and lower-class workers, many of them immigrants, who guzzled beer in the concert saloons and vaudeville theaters of the day.[97] Museums, which banned drink and prostitution, were more acceptable entertainment venues. But most working- and middle-class people had few or no affordable, reputable nighttime entertainment venues.[98]

Cody had worked hard to restore himself to the middle class after the

The Cody family—Arta, Orra, Louisa, and William Cody—as middle-class bastion, c. 1880. The theatrical melodrama seldom drew the crowd to match Cody's aspirations to respectability. Courtesy Buffalo Bill Historical Center.

Civil War. He kept the middle-class company of officers and entrepreneurs in Kansas and Nebraska, and in Rochester his daughters went to private school, and the Cody family lived in a well-to-do, tree-lined district. As a public figure, he was symbolic of middle-class entertainment with his seamless moves between real guiding, hunting, and Indian fighting and his fictional representations of those same activities.

But in the city, Cody's message seems to have been most empowering, or at least most popular, among working people. They swarmed to the theaters to see Buffalo Bill. His willingness to authenticate the entertainment with his presence invited their own participation, which they proffered in raucous fashion. In Portland, Maine, in 1873, a reviewer related how "an urchin, remembering that one character, at least, in the play yet survived, exclaimed 'Hold on; wait till the show's through—*Dutchy ain't dead yet!*'" In 1875, an audience member shouted as Buffalo Bill wrestled with a stage bear: "Shoot him, Bill! Run in on him and kill him!"[99]

In his early days, critics complained that Cody's lowbrow entertainment was displacing the classical theater of Edwin Booth and the French actor Charles Fechter, and Cody himself reportedly joked that he would run Booth and Fechter into New Jersey by playing Shakespeare right through, from beginning to end, with Ned Buntline and Texas Jack to support me. I shall do Hamlet in a buckskin suit, and when my father's ghost appears "doomed for a certain time," &c., I shall say to Jack, "Rope the cuss in, Jack!" and unless the lasso breaks, the ghost will have to come. As "Richard the Third," I shall fight with pistols and hunting knives. In "Romeo and Juliet" I shall put a half-breed squaw on the balcony and make various other interpretations of Shakespeare's words to suit myself.[100]

Reviews were often scathing, and left no doubt that Cody's appeal was chiefly to the lower class. *Scouts of the Prairie* was "one of the worse specimens of unmitigated trash we have ever seen on any stage . . . belonging to that order of the drama which finds a home at the Bowery or Wood's Museum," wrote a New York correspondent, referring to the preferred theaters of working-class audiences. But, he warned, it "would scarcely be tolerated" even there.[101]

There were members of the elite in the audience at Cody's first performance: ranks of military officers and sports like Milligan, and many others bought tickets on that night and throughout his career. But critics separated such people from true Buffalo Bill fans, implying that elite enjoyment came less from Cody's drama than from the spectacle of lower-class enthusiasm for it. After panning *Scouts of the Prairie*, another critic summarized, "Thus the lower million are delighted and many of the 'upper ten thousand' amused."[102]

From its beginnings, Buffalo Bill's drama inspired considerable social criticism because of its implied messages to these ardent lower-class followers. Reformers disdained dime novels and cheap melodrama because their lurid violence and appeal to base emotions, their sensationalism, threatened to ignite the barely restrained passions of the laboring masses, who were, after all, thinly disguised savages, many of them from alien shores and prone to strikes and violence.[103] "All the small boys (and some of the big ones too) of this city are now practising the Indian war hoop [*sic*] after the style of Buffalo Bill and Texas Jack," wrote one reviewer. "At all hours of the night the unearthly yells can be heard in our streets, to the disgust of all peaceable citizens." As if to imply the burden this imposed on law and order, the critic went on: "It is currently reported that one policeman in Station Four has become totally deaf in consequence of those infernal yells."[104]

Cody made efforts to turn his plays into middle-class family entertainment almost from his earliest days on the stage, and there were hints of their potential to become a unifying national art. Buffalo Bill's early appearances alongside the ex-Confederate Texas Jack Omohundro earned praise as a gesture of national reconciliation. In the words of one critic, "here was the 'blue and the gray' blended together in one harmonious strain of good fellowship . . . a bright example to the rising generation."[105]

Cody's break with Buntline, after his first season on tour, reflected his impulse to steer clear of the writer's well-earned reputation for class antagonism and anti-immigrant violence. In a long and tumultuous literary and political career, Buntline had scaled impressive heights as rabble-rouser and nativist. He was a founder of the anti-immigrant American Party, commonly called the Know-Nothings, in the early 1850s. Prior to that, in 1849, he was a ringleader of the Astor Place Riot, a melee between thousands of working-class New Yorkers and the state militia outside a production of *Macbeth* which starred an English actor. Buntline and the other leaders of the fracas intended to send a political warning about the dangers of Anglophilia and un-American class hierarchies. But the riot grew so violent that the militia fired repeatedly on the crowd, killing thirty-one people and wounding over a hundred.[106]

The Astor Place Riot is the very conflagration which historians credit with driving a wedge between the dramatic tastes of upper-class theatergoers and their lower-class counterparts, thereby dividing the market for theatrical offerings. Buntline's violence, then, helped to create the genus of lower-class entertainment to which Cody was routinely consigned, and from which he fought to escape throughout his stage career. Buntline served a year in prison for his role at Astor Place, but he was hardly finished. In 1852 he fled St. Louis after being indicted for sparking bloody anti-German riots during that year's election. Twenty years later, he was finally arrested for that crime during his sojourn in the city with Buffalo Bill and Texas Jack. This embarrassing moment gave acerbic critics an opening they did not need, but could not forsake: "It is said that Buntline's participation in the little affair here some twenty years ago was merely the advance advertisement of the appearance, this week, with his troupe."[107]

For the first year and a half of her husband's stage career, Louisa Cody sometimes served as troupe seamstress. She accompanied Buffalo Bill on the road, with their three children, Arta, Orra, and Kit.[108] If, as seems likely, the presence of his own middle-class family reinforced Cody's longing to make his entertainment palatable for middle-class family audiences, he was frustrated. He and Buntline tried various methods of luring respectable women to the drama, including the staging of matinees—daytime performances appealed to family audiences—and offering free cabinet photographs of Texas Jack, Morlacchi, Ned Buntline, and Buffalo Bill to every "lady" who attended.[109]

Endeavoring as he was to fashion his melodramas into family entertainment as early as his first year on the stage, we can only wonder what possessed Cody to invite the broody brawler Wild Bill Hickok to join the troupe in the following year. Hickok's reputation for bloodshed was exaggerated, but Cody knew it was not groundless. Out west, Hickok was a gunfighter and a bona fide killer. He fought often with his fists, many times against the odds, and he usually won. In Missouri, Kansas, and Nebraska he had killed several men in gunfights.[110]

In contrast with Hickok's frequent dark moods, Cody was unfailingly cheerful and gregarious. He rarely fought with his fists, and when he did, accounts are in disagreement about how the fights ended. When journalists asked Hickok how many white men he had killed, he gave them vastly inflated totals or demurred, muttering words to the effect that "I never killed a man who didn't need killing." In 1875, a lawyer in Westchester, New York, asked Cody if he had ever shot anyone, by which he meant anyone other than an Indian. Cody grew dark with anger. "No! What do you ask me such a thing for?"[111]

Hickok's addition to the company thus was hardly in keeping with Cody's

From left to right: Wild Bill Hickok, Texas Jack Omohundro, and William F. Cody, 1873. Courtesy Buffalo Bill Historical Center.

goals for respectable entertainment. There are hints that it did not sit well with the Cody family, either. To be sure, how the Prince of Pistoleers and Mrs. Cody fared as melodramatic troupers sharing the same trains, carriages, hotels, and backstages we shall never know. Shortly after William Cody's death, Louisa Cody dictated her own memoirs, in which she recalled the tour as yet another blissful episode in her long (and in reality, troubled) marriage. As she recalled it, Hickok arrived during a performance, and Cody was out on the stage. Hickok, "stumbling about in the darkness, looked out and gasped as he saw Cody. 'For the sake of Jehosaphat!' he exclaimed, 'What's that Bill Cody's got on him out there?' "

Louisa asked if he was referring to Cody's clothes, but "Wild Bill shook his head and waved his arms. 'No,' he was growing more excited every minute, 'that white stuff that's floating all around him.' "

"Why, Mr. Hickok," she explained, "that's limelight."

"Wild Bill turned and grabbed a stage-hand by the arm," she remembered, "then he dragged a gold piece from his pocket. 'Boy,' he commanded, 'run as fast as your legs will carry you and get me five dollars' worth of that stuff. I want it smeared all over me!' "

The account is fictional (Hickok knew what limelight was, and craved it), but it captures the friction Louisa witnessed that year. Indeed, reading between the lines of William Cody's autobiography suggests the Cody-Hickok stage venture was an uneasy arrangement. Hickok, increasingly jealous of Cody's success, got less compliant as the tour continued. He brawled with billiard room toughs even when Cody implored him to avoid public violence for the sake of the troupe—and presumably, for the sake of the Cody family. He tortured the actors who played Indians in the drama, intentionally firing his pistol blanks so close to their bare legs as to burn them. "Bill's conduct made me angry," recalled Cody some years later, "and I told him he must either stop shooting the 'supers' or leave the company."[112]

Hickok left. Cody was genuinely sorry to see Wild Bill go, but Hickok's unwillingness to modify his violence for the sake of the combination's image made him a dubious theatrical partner at best. Cody told the tale as if he gave Hickok the chance to stay, and he may have, but evidence suggests that his departure was only part of a wider shake-up in the company. Hickok departed the company at Rochester, on March 11, 1874—the very day that Louisa and the children separated from the company for a home in that city. Hickok and Louisa, respective embodiments of rough-hewn brawler and middle-class domestic order, likely disembarked at the same platform. One wonders if they were speaking.[113]

But for all his labors, Cody's imposture as the ideal Indian fighter was not easily transported to the stage as respectable entertainment, in part because the American public was itself divided on questions of Indian policy, and in part because literary and artistic notions of Indian fighting were not easily made real without creating controversy. In taking Yellow Hair's scalp, Cody situated himself in a liminal position, as the civilized man *driven* to scalping and savage war by the excesses of the Indians who had "massacred" Custer. As the white Indian, he could ostensibly cross the line into savagery and defeat Indians with their own methods, while retaining civilized virtues so as to avoid becoming savage himself. By and large, as we have seen, the maneuver was successful, with the "first scalp for Custer" reaffirming his status as white Indian and theatrical star.

But his descent into Indian modes of combat came with a cost. To Americans, scalping was generally barbaric, a savage gesture beneath civilized society, and beneath professional soldiers, who mostly abhorred the practice. His display of Yellow Hair's scalp and personal belongings at theaters sometimes brought public condemnation, particularly in the strongholds of reformers in New England. The scalp display was banned in Boston, and even in the heated aftermath of Custer's death, his most ardent press supporters, the editors of the *New York Herald*, condemned it as "a disgrace to civilization."[114] Some fans chided these critics for their sentimentalism, but not all of them were so easily dismissed. Even one Fifth Cavalry trooper, Chris Madsen, a Danish immigrant, was horrified when Cody scalped Yellow Hair, and asked him why he did it. Cody responded that the Cheyenne had a woman's scalp at his waist and an American flag for a loincloth.[115] In other words, the Indian's offenses were so far beyond the pale as to *require* a savage response. The rationale may have let some critics rest easier with Cody's bloody trophy, but the very fact that an explanation was necessary suggests how troubling Buffalo Bill's "real-life" heroism could become for a public continually roiled by arguments over violence and bloodshed in civic life and in war.

By the late 1870s, Cody parried some of his critics' barbs with a gentler drama. Sometimes reviewers even encouraged the "better class" of theatergoers to attend. In *Buffalo Bill at Bay*, a reviewer reported, "The orchestra is excellent. . . . There is no gun firing, except when Bill gives his [shooting] exhibition," at the middle of the drama, and there was "no slaughtering, so that timid women need feel no aversion to attending."[116] His *Knight of the Plains* drew a moderate amount of praise, too, both for the improvement in Cody's acting and the absence of gratuitous violence, so that "this new departure is drawing everywhere large audiences of ladies, and the best show-going people."[117] Wrote another critic, the play was "a vast improvement over all others in which this star has appeared."[118]

By this time, Cody had already outlived his biggest competitors. Wild Bill Hickok had married Agnes Lake, a prominent circus owner, and might have launched an early Wild West show had he not been murdered in 1876.

Texas Jack died of pneumonia in Leadville, Colorado, in 1880. Captain Jack was reading his execrable poetry and had all but abandoned the stage. William Cody was seemingly secure as the supreme frontier melodramatist. He was on the verge of respectability.[119]

And yet Cody's very success at domesticating his drama threatened to undo him. The fun of Buffalo Bill, after all, had been the interplay between the fake and the real, anchored by his authenticity as the original frontier hero. The death of prominent scouts, and the absence of frontier war to produce any more, removed much of the imitation and took away, too, much of the genre's fun. Just as significant, if Cody's plays were coming to resemble the upmarket version of western melodrama, more like *Across the Continent* and *Horizon*, then he was simply becoming more like other actors. The energizing element of his presence, his symbol as a common man who made a stage career out of fooling professional actors, would vanish the minute he gained critical acceptance as an actor. In this sense, for all his success on the boards, there was not much chance that he could ever translate it into solid middle-class family entertainment.

The failure to do so would have dire consequences. Cody's career in the 1870s was a straddling act, in which his theatrical appearances and the dime novels about him appealed to the working classes, but his symbolism as an amateur whose theatrical presentation outstrips the professionals resonated with the middle class. Theatrical tastes had once unified American culture, with classical Shakespeare, turgid melodrama, and popular farces playing at the same theaters—indeed, on the same evening—for audiences made up of every social class. But since Buntline's incitement to violence outside the Astor Place Theater, class tastes had steadily diverged, with the "better class" of theaters becoming so expensive as to be out of range for middle-class families, and lower-class theaters presenting material that would never be translated into more lucrative middle-class fare.[120] Without more purchase on middle-class loyalties, Buffalo Bill faced a working-class future.

Indeed, as social space, the theater was dubious enough that Cody's reputation as a lowbrow draw would be almost impossible to escape there. The critics who praised Cody's late-1870s performances did so with surprise, contrasting this "new" Cody with the one everybody knew—and *that* Buffalo Bill might have been a symbol to the middle class, but he was clearly a hero to the white working class. Cody usually avoided the bald appeals to nativist bigotry with which Buntline was associated. But there can be little doubt that *Scouts of the Prairie*, with its native-born scouts fending off Indians, Mormons, and immigrants—savages all—reinforced the nativism of American laborers, who adored it. Even more, there is plenty of evidence that this segment of his audience saw Buffalo Bill as their hero in the struggle against the privileged classes and foreign immigrants. The 1870s were a decade of economic calamity and labor unrest. The Panic of 1873 and the Great Strike of 1877 set labor and capital at each other's throats, and often pitted laboring American natives against immigrant "scabs." In the economic downturn that followed 1873, renters in the New York region rose up against the impositions of landlords. The Tenants Mutual Society of Montgomery County, which reportedly "countenanced the burning and destruction of the property of exacting landlords," included among its members one Charles Montanye, "familiarly called 'Buffalo Bill.'" Montanye was arrested in a civil suit alleging his participation in numerous fires that had scorched the holdings of prominent landowner and rentier George Clark.[121]

While one faux Cody allegedly burned property in Montgomery County, another was battling German and Irish rivals for domination of a tenement house in the city slums. In a Hell's Kitchen rookery lived "a Yankee calling himself 'the renowned Buffalo Bill'" and "a fellow known as 'Dutch John'" who competed "at times very fiercely for the honor of being known as 'boss' of this place." This faux Cody, a teamster, "affects beneath his dirt the appearance and manner of a frontiersman. Slightly but powerfully built, he is 6 feet 2 inches in height, with flowing hair, and weighs a trifle over 200 pounds." Quarreling over the affections of a woman, Buffalo Bill had stabbed Dutch John several years before, but since the wounded man refused to make a complaint, the police could do nothing.[122]

Like the stage character who was their namesake, both of these faux Codys appeared in the press because of their violence in defense of honor, but unlike him, their victims were not frontier savages, but landlords and immigrants. Where Cody and his professional imitators provided a theater of imitation and an embrace of theatricality in everyday life, these amateur imitators implied an all-too-real connection between Cody's stage theatrics and working-class violence.

They might have been case studies for other critics of Cody's drama, who condemned it for appealing to the passions of working-class natives and rough immigrants whose absence of self-restraint was their primary social failing, and one all too evident in the volcanic labor upheavals of the 1870s. In January 1874, the *Hartford Daily Courant* wrote that Cody's play was "the most extreme kind of dime novel dramatized. It draws for the same reason that a dime novel sells."[123] For newspaper readers, the words "sensation" and "thrilling" were code words for appeals to unthinking emotion, so that superficially positive reviews of Buffalo Bill's drama had, for the discerning reader, a cautionary message. Thus, when a Cincinnati paper reported, "'The Scouts of the Prairie' have become the lions of the stage among that class of people who delight in thrilling romance," readers concerned about the social composition of the audience would note the reference to "that class" and "thrilling romance." The rest of the review would affirm their suspicions: "For a sensation play of blood, scalps, and whooping Indians, 'The Scouts of the Prairie' answers every purpose."[124]

Inability to control one's appetites was a defining condition of barbarism, and a criticism that social observers leveled at Indians and working-class people alike, especially "gallery gods," the laboring men and boys who took their title from the cheap seats in the galleries of the nation's theaters. Journalist DeBenneville Randolph Keim, in his memoir of General Philip Sheridan's 1867–68 winter campaign, indicted the Cheyenne for their "savage natures, incapable of restraint," which "render them by instinct foes to progress and the cause of humanity."[125] Only a few years later, the frontier hero who banished Cheyenne barbarism appealed so to the savagery of his theatrical audiences that, in Indianapolis, "the whoop of despair of the dying Indians is answered back by the yell of triumph of the gods of the gallery, who failry [*sic*] split their shirts by the convulsive beating of excited lungs."[126]

The fact that native-born city toughs and rebellious workingmen appropriated the name of Buffalo Bill suggests how much they claimed him as one of their own in their battles against the impositions of landlords, employers, and immigrant rivals. If Cody did not separate himself from his most voluble partisans, he risked slipping into savagery with them, becoming a class renegade. In the combative urban politics of the 1870s, Buffalo Bill was not necessarily a benign figure. Cody's drama was too subversive ever to be middle-class fun.

His currency as a popular symbol limited by class friction and audience biases, by the late 1870s Cody was looking for ways to enhance his middle-class reputation. He wrote his autobiography with such a subdued tone, in the summer of 1879, that critics marveled at its avoidance of blood-and-thunder braggadocio. He continued to plan a performance tour of Europe, although it did not come off. Finally, he began to envision a different kind of show altogether.[127]

CHAPTER EIGHT

Indians, Horses

B Y THE LATE 1870S, the quest for a middle-class following and the competition of the scout business drove Cody to new heights of theatrical innovation. His shows grew larger and more complex, his plays not only less violent, but more spectacular. He put horses onstage, decreased the amount of gunplay in the performances, and enhanced special effects such as electrical lighting.

Most historians trace the origins of Buffalo Bill's Wild West show to the gathering amplitude of these stage productions. But it was Cody's cultivation of Indian performers in the late 1870s that led most directly to the Wild West arena. This, too, was tied to his search for a better class of customers. For in many ways the boldest and most innovative move he made to capture a middle-class audience was to make Indians more visible, at the same moment that a consciousness of their supposed vanishing—along with all other vestiges of the frontier—became ever more pervasive.

Although Cody claimed to know a great deal about Indians, the truth was that in the 1870s he knew few Indians, and these but superficially. Pawnees and other detachments of Indian auxiliaries had been his subordinates in scouting parties, but there are no hints of any deeper relationship between them than that of friendly acquaintances. In 1872, journalists credited Cody with convincing Spotted Tail and his warriors to join the buffalo hunt with the Grand Duke Alexis, and they assumed (in keeping with the dime novel frame in which they pictured him) that the white Indian must know Indians from personal experience. In fact, he knew only enough about the Sioux to defer to those who knew them better. Thus, he approached Todd Randall, "an old frontiersman . . . who was Spotted Tail's agent" and who had lived among the band for years and who spoke fluent Lakota, to persuade Spotted Tail to come hunting.[1]

On the Plains, then, Cody's bonds with Indians were less significant than his ties to white men who knew Indians. In fact, most of the Indians who made Cody's acquaintance did so after the Indian wars, and they did it through show business. Indians had been part of American entertainments for a very long time, and in Cody's day they frequently appeared as exotic living exhibits or curiosities in circuses and museums. Many of these performers came from the ranks of eastern or midwestern tribes whose autonomy had long since vanished. Thus, a party of Iowa Indians toured with George Catlin in Europe in the 1840s, and midwestern Sac and Fox peoples provided the performers for Barnett and Hickok's mock buffalo hunt at Niagara Falls in 1872. Battered by the loss of their lands and by waves of epidemic disease, and forced into the wage economy with the worst jobs (if they could get anybody to hire them at all), these people learned American notions of Indians through hard experience. We can only wonder how much they shaped their performances to subvert, reinforce, or otherwise influence American ideas of Indianness.[2]

Until 1877, practically all of Cody's stage Indians were played by "supers," or white extras. But from the very beginning, a few Indians found their way into Buffalo Bill stage plays, their presence a hint of future possibilities. In 1872, Carlo Gentile, an Italian photographer touring southern Arizona, ransomed—or bought—a captive Yavapai boy from a band of Pima Indians. Gentile subsequently took the boy to Chicago, gave him the name Carlos Montezuma, and hired him out to play the role of Azteka, an Indian boy who shot arrows at Buffalo Bill and Texas Jack in *Scouts of the Plains*, during its debut performance in Chicago and on tour afterward.[3] Grown to manhood, Montezuma would become a physician, a leading Indian intellectual, and a relentless critic of the Bureau of Indian Affairs and its reservation policy.[4] As a child onstage, Montezuma took his place amid the fake Indians represented by the supers. Thus the scout business, in its dance of real and fake, featured some mix of real Indians and imitation ones, original and copy. But the mimicry of this spectacle was so poor, the supers so obviously fake, that critics complained. Real Indians were hard to find, though, so Cody dismissed Montezuma and resorted again to supers for the first few years.[5]

Cody's inspiration to hire Sioux performers reflected a shift in performance possibilities for Indians only recently subjugated by the U.S. Army. Where earlier Indian performers came from tribes that had been defeated many years before, Indians who came to the stage in the 1870s increasingly had careers that in some ways paralleled Cody's, with gutsy leaps from the Far West, and the frontier of combat, to the theater and the melodrama. Their own frontier imposture, in which they combined elements of Indian life and culture with popular expectations, creating new performances that would appeal to American audiences, was something that many of them learned in the West, where Americans flocked to Indian villages and dances. Soldiers watched as Osage scouts performed hours of scalp dances after returning with Custer from the Washita in 1868. Crowds of soldiers and civilians from Fort Laramie gathered to watch the huge Plains Indian pow-wows during the treaty negotiations of 1867. Residents of Fort McPherson and ranks of itinerant teamsters turned out to watch the Pawnee scouts perform war dances the night before they departed on the Republican River expedition, with the Fifth Cavalry and scout William Cody, in 1869. Watching Sioux dances at Fort Robinson, in Nebraska, was a major social pastime for American soldiers and civilians well into the 1870s.[6]

Among the Lakota, dances could be social affairs or sacred rituals, depending on the dancers and the context. Social dances were jovial and festive, and often accompanied by feasts. It did not take long for some Indians to adapt steps from social dances to entertainment, and the American market for public amusement. In 1874, a group of Lakota performers charged settlers for admission to their dances at the opening of a Nebraska county. Selling their performances and images became standard. By 1877, Lakota fresh from their campaigns against the army were charging white photographers $6 each for photographs.[7]

Like Cody himself, many of the first Indian performers in frontier melodrama had also been scouts for the U.S. Army, an occupation in which they encountered American fascination for Indian performance. As we have seen, Pawnee scouts had been performing mock Indian battles and mock attacks for hunting parties and railroad executives for over a decade by the time Cody hired some of the tribe to join his theatrical combination. By the late 1870s, there was enough of an entertainment industry swirling around Indians that Indian performers moved fluidly between shows. Some of the Indians in Cody's troupe came from other theatrical companies, including Donald McKay's troupe of Warm Springs Indians—who had served as scouts in California's Modoc War.[8]

Cody abandoned the practice of hiring other white scouts after the bitter falling-out with Captain Jack Crawford.[9] Immediately thereafter, he began to search out Indian performers, recognizing that his ability to marshal them east and onto the boards heightened his reputation as a white man who "knew Indians." Of course, the presence of Indians, particularly Lakota Sioux men, so soon after the death of Custer, also charged the rapidly aging scout business with a new bolt of authenticity. Where other combinations required supers to play Indians, real Indians enabled Cody to again assert his prominence as the besieged purveyor of the real, surrounded by faking competitors. Thus, in the fall of 1877, Cody recruited Oglala Sioux Indians from the Red Cloud Agency for his theatrical season.[10] As translator, he commissioned John Y. Nelson, a buffalo hunter and fur trapper who lived near Fort McPherson and was married to a Lakota woman from Whistler's band. The two Sioux men with Cody that year were identified as Man Who Carries the Sword—known as Sword, he was an in-law of Nelson—and Two Bears.[11]

Identified only as "Buffalo Bill and Scouts," this photograph depicts at least two members of the Buffalo Bill Combination of 1877–78: William Cody, center, and George Sword, Lakota warrior and scout-turned-actor, front right. The unidentified Indian man to the left of Sword might be Two Bears. Courtesy Buffalo Bill Historical Center.

Sword and Two Bears hailed, respectively, from the Oglala and the Hunkpapa divisions of the larger Lakota tribe, and in that sense, their people were among the most recent enemies of the U.S. Army. But the Lakota had no tradition of central organization or state hierarchy. Even at the peak of the Sioux War in 1876, some Lakotas urged accommodation with the United States. The very reason that Sheridan had chosen Spotted Tail for the Grand Duke Alexis hunt was that Spotted Tail was a strong advocate for peace between Lakotas and Americans. Similarly, both Sword and Two Bears had been prominent peace advocates. Sword was a nephew of Red Cloud, who had encouraged cooperation with the Indian agent at Red Cloud Agency and offered to guide Professor Othniel C. Marsh on his hunt for fossils in the Sioux badlands in 1874. He later scouted for General George Crook, and in 1876 he helped Colonel Randall Mackenzie attack a Cheyenne village. That same year, he sought out Crazy Horse at the behest of the army command, in a vain attempt to persuade the great warrior to surrender.[12]

The following year, in 1878, Cody ventured to Indian Territory to hire Pawnee actors, whose acquaintance he had made during his days as hunting guide and scout with Frank North. In subsequent years, he alternated between Pawnee and Lakota actors, with Nelson as his go-between for the Lakotas and Gordon "Pawnee Bill" Lillie as his translator and agent with the Pawnees.[13] By this time, numerous Indians who had fought in the Sioux War were performing on eastern stages. Twenty Utes were featured in Barnum's circus in 1881, and Sioux Indians showed up at Bunnell's Museum in Brooklyn that same year.[14] Sitting Bull himself went on the stage with an "authentic" display of Indian life in 1884, playing to packed houses in New York and Philadelphia.[15]

Other than Sitting Bull, we know very little about these Indian performers as individuals, but it seems safe to assume that they came to the stage because it offered a way of earning good money, and making contacts with powerful people to outmaneuver the officials who stifled their autonomy on impoverished reservations. In an interview with a Baltimore newspaper, Sword and Two Bears were pleased to be traveling and seeing the East, "learning the ways of the pale faces" and presumably making a living, too.[16] Accustomed to advocating peace even at times of war, they were Lakota innovators unwilling to accept either armed resistance to the United States or American terms of Lakota defeat. In these ways, Sword and Two Bears were typical of the Indian performers who followed them into Buffalo Bill's amusements, on the stage and in the arena years later.[17]

For many Americans then and now, the idea of Indians reenacting scenes of frontier conquest in these blood-and-thunder, Indian-slaughtering melodramas suggests that impresarios like Cody were exploiting and humiliating them. But Indians were not naive about American desires. Their refusal to assume humiliating roles compelled Cody to commission plots allowing his Indian performers a place of considerable honor, within the constraints of the genre. Thus, Cody pointed out to one interviewer that Sword and Two Bears were his friends in the stage drama of 1877, because "it would hardly be politic to use them" in any other way.[18] In *May Cody, or Lost and Won*, the villains of the piece were Mormons and a band of "bad Indians," or renegades, played by supers. As with most dime novels, Indian savagery in *May Cody* was the product of *white* villainy—the malevolent Mormons, in this case, who entice Indians to attack a wagon train. The noble savages, played by Sword and Two Bears, help Buffalo Bill to recover his sister, vanquish the evil whites, and thereby remove the impulse for any Indians to be bad any longer. A similar plot was to be found in his 1880–81 production, *The Prairie Waif*, in which relatively few Indians died, but "a half dozen Mormons . . . are slain whenever the play threatens to grow monotonous."[19]

Civilization marches on, crushing the threats to domestic order in the woman-stealing Mormons while treating Indians fairly—but ushering their primitive world into the abyss, too, in the end.

So it was in the remainder of Cody's stage melodramas that Indians, if they figure in the action at all, are routinely divided between noble savages (played by real Indians) and savage savages (played by supers), all of whom are vanishing. The drama reprised a classic depiction of Indians that allowed Europeans and Americans to utilize Indians as symbols without understanding them as complex people.[20] This division was integral to the plays even in the early 1870s, but the arrival of real Indians in the roles marked a new departure. Where non-Indians like Morlacchi had represented "good Indians" such as Dove Eye in *Scouts of the Prairie*, now "good Indians" played themselves, just as the white scouts represented their own characters. The imposture suggested that nobility was, after all, the most reliable—"real"— Indian trait.

Cody's intuitive sense of the public longing for noble savages as true, uncorrupted, honest primitives fading before the onslaught of modern, industrial commerce was the source of much of his success in the later years of his stage career and, of course, in the Wild West show. Scholars and Buffalo Bill enthusiasts rightly marvel at his sympathy for Indians, which he began to articulate in the late 1870s, at the very moment he brought real Indians to the stage. "In nine times out of ten," he was fond of saying, "where there is trouble between white men and Indians, it will be found that the white man is responsible." Often, he buttressed this political commentary with references to Indian nobility. "Indians expect a man to keep his word. They can't understand how a man can lie. Most of them would as soon cut off a leg as tell a lie."[21] He routinely criticized the failure of Americans to abide by their treaties, warning that "there is just one thing to be considered" where "the management of Indians" was concerned: "That is, that when you promise him anything you must keep your word; break it, and the trouble commences at once." Urging his compatriots to "take an Indian by the hand and make him a friend," he also defended federal purview over Indian affairs from detractors who thought each state should administer its own Indian policy.[22]

As he developed his contingent of Indian performers, increasingly he made his own violence against Indians look like a last resort. "I never sighted down my rifle or drew my knife on an Indian but I felt almost sorry for it, and I never did it when I could help it," he said in one interview.[23] He blamed the Indian wars on white aggression. Thus, in 1879, he told a local newspaperman, "There are a number of men who make it a profession to steal horses from the Indians. . . . In fact, there is a regular market for them.

Although I have had many a tough fight with the red man my sympathy is with him entirely, because he has been ill-used and trampled on by those whose duty it was to protect him."[24]

Cody's sympathy for Indians might be dismissed as a show business fiction, were it not so consistent in later years. His Wild West show hired so many Indian performers, paying such good wages for enjoyable work, that it earned a lasting place of respect and even admiration among the Lakota. To this day, tales of Cody's friendships with his Indian performers circulate at Pine Ridge.[25] Lakota scholar and activist Vine Deloria, Jr., author of the famed *Custer Died for Your Sins*, concludes that for its time, "Buffalo Bill's relationship with the Indians, absent the aura of show business, seems above average in the positive human qualities of justice and fair play."[26]

That Cody's understanding of Indian peoples developed to the point where it could earn such praise from Indians themselves speaks volumes about how much the performance needs of his entertainment changed his views. For in the beginning, Cody's stance toward Indians was complex and not consistently benign. Until he began hiring Lakota performers in 1877, his sympathy for Indians was sometimes absent from his pronouncements, and even after he hired them, he continued to glory in his role—onstage and off—as the scalper of Yellow Hair. More bloodthirsty still, during California's Modoc War of 1873 he told a reporter for a St. Louis newspaper that when it came to Indians, "I have shot and stabbed'em, cut their bowels out with my knife, harpooned'em, clubbed'em to death, and in fact killed'em in every way you can think of, except talking'em to death." Vowing to "take a run out to the lava beds" and take enough scalps "to stuff a rocking-chair for the old woman," Cody promised that he and Texas Jack "won't leave a pappoose [*sic*] a week old."[27]

Fortunately, Cody did not make good on his offer. Indeed, such Indian-killer rhetoric was confined to the earlier period of Cody's career. As he tailored his persona for middle-class audiences, a more benign Buffalo Bill emerged and the talk of clubs, harpoons, and baby-killing soon vanished.

It may be that his move to distance himself from the Indian-hater image reflected his increasing adherence to his dime novel persona. In the fiction of the 1870s, the character of Buffalo Bill was more benign than vengeful. Indian-hating, bloodthirsty scouts featured in American fiction of an earlier period, such as Robert Bird's 1837 novel *Nick of the Woods*, and in the many cheap novels and stories that circulated about "Old Dan Rackback," the "Great Exterminator," and about Lew Wetzel, the famous Kentucky scout, who "to his dying day, carried out the very letter of the vow he had made" never to let anything "screen an Indian from his vengeance."[28]

But, as one scholar has observed, these virulent Indian haters were "too choleric, too unrestrained and bloodthirsty" to be romantic heroes. By the

1870s, the best-selling dime novels downplayed Indian hating in favor of Indian civilizing, and their romantic protagonist, the noble white scout, reclaimed Eden from the wilderness and ensured the propagation of settler homes and families.[29] Like other fictional heroes in this period, the Buffalo Bill who appears in dime novels is drawn to the West because it is a natural setting. As a natural man, he evokes a Romantic appreciation of wilderness, as paradise waiting to be reclaimed, with himself as the scout who blazes a path for civilization to follow. He may fight Indians, but if so, it is because they represent a direct and immediate threat to white civilization. He is a skillful warrior, but not a vengeful one.

The power of the cultural imperative toward restraint of the bloody passions, even in dime novels, is evident in the literary career of the notoriously choleric and all-too-often unrestrained Ned Buntline. In the writer's first Buffalo Bill novel, the action begins with the shattering of the Cody family and ends with its restoration. Buffalo Bill dispenses violence and claims retribution on the way to the story's end, but they are means to his end: the establishment of settler domestic bliss. The most dangerous enemies are not Indians at all, but evil white men who have turned renegade. Nowhere does Buntline's Buffalo Bill excoriate Indians for being Indians. Nowhere does he vow to obliterate them.

That so much tolerance flowed from the pen of an immigrant-bashing firebrand like Buntline suggests how far middle-class, reformist ideologies of manly moderation had penetrated even dime novels. By the 1870s, American manliness was thoroughly infused with ideals of spiritual and bodily temperance.[30] White men might fight and kill Indians if provoked, but hatred—of Indians or anybody else—was anathema to most Americans, because it was a savage, degenerative condition. It flew in the face of dominant middle-class virtues of self-control and restraint. Monomania for revenge precluded love, procreation, or the advancement of civilization. Like addiction to drink, it could become a monstrous obsession. If Americans became vengeful killers like Indians, then savagery would have won the day. Thus, Henry Morton Stanley would write from the 1867 Hancock expedition against the Cheyenne, "Extermination is a long word, but a longer task, and civilization cannot sanction it."[31] Thus, Buffalo Bill's stage character, like his dime novel character, was a romantic man, whose violence was controlled enough to be regenerative. He was a race hero, not a race avenger; an Indian fighter, even an Indian killer, but not an Indian hater.

Of course, even after the early 1870s, the exigencies of war made Cody's development of his persona as Indian apologist and sympathizer difficult and uneven. Immediately upon hearing of Custer's demise in 1876, he set out to scalp an Indian. He was reenacting the "duel" with Yellow Hair early in 1877, just before he hired Sword and Two Bears—and he performed *The*

Red Right Hand, with the Yellow Hair scalping in it, during the season that Sword and Two Bears were with him. Afterward, in the Wild West show, the scalping of Yellow Hair was a central spectacle for decades. In Cody's day-to-day life, the actual scalp took on great personal importance. He traveled with it, keeping it in a safe in his private railway car during his Wild West show days.[32]

And, at the same time he denounced the breaking of treaties, Cody continued to seek profits from the practice. In 1875, he and Kit Carson, Jr., served as figureheads for the Boston Black Hills Expedition, a group of speculators trying to mount a gold-mining expedition to the Black Hills of Dakota Territory. In the Fort Laramie Treaty of 1868, the U.S. government guaranteed Sioux title to those hills. As reports of gold in the region began to circulate, the Indians made clear they had no intention of relinquishing their claim. Agitation from the Boston Black Hills Association and similar groups convinced federal authorities that the treaty of 1868 was unenforceable, and thereby began the sequence of events which led to the Sioux War of 1876–77, the dispossession of the Lakota from their promised home, and their further impoverishment.[33] In later years, Cody told newspaper interviewers that the Lakota had only been defending what was rightfully theirs. In 1885, when Sitting Bull toured with Buffalo Bill's Wild West, Cody gave one interviewer a thumbnail history of the Sioux War, in which he attributed Sitting Bull's onetime hostility to the United States as a defense of his home. "Their lands were invaded by the gold seekers," he explained, "and when the U.S. Government failed to protect them they thought it was time to do it themselves." In this case, mindful of needing government permission to have Sitting Bull with him, Cody softened his antipathy toward government bureaucrats, who "did all they thought they could do," but to no avail, since "the white men wouldn't be held back."[34] That he had encouraged American seizure of the Black Hills at the time did not trouble him.

Similarly, in the early 1880s, Buffalo Bill supported efforts to "open"—Indians would say "steal"—Indian reservations for white settlers. Indian Territory, today's Oklahoma, had been guaranteed to Indians, including not only Cherokees and others removed from the East, but also the southern Cheyenne and some Arapaho, whom Cody fought in Kansas. By the 1870s, many Indians were leasing parts of their reservations to Texas cattlemen for pasture. Speculators and political opportunists began to excoriate Indian treaties as the tool of rich cattle barons. Foremost among these "boomers" was David "Oklahoma" Payne, who kicked off a populist campaign promising new opportunities for aspiring farmers if they could defeat the "corrupt" politicians who protected the "special interests" of Indians.

In 1882, Cody bought forty shares in Payne's prospective colony, representatives of which soon marched into Indian Territory. U.S. authorities did what the law required. They removed Payne and his followers, and gave Payne a court date. With the would-be settlers perched on the border, Payne was out of money. Cody found him a place in the Wild West show to tide him over, but the "intrepid leader" who defied military orders to stay out of Indian Territory and "defended his cabin" there "against scores of his wily foes . . . until his name has become a terror to the Indians of that region," died suddenly in 1884.[35] His efforts reached fruition posthumously, in 1885, when Congress began "buying" Indian land—whether or not the Indians wanted to sell—and the land rushes of the late 1880s and early 1890s made Oklohoma synonymous with agrarian opportunity—for non-Indians.[36] Cody never made any money on his Oklahoma investment, but nonetheless his support for the abandonment of treaties and the dispossession of Indians contradicted his many public statements about the dishonor of the practice. In deed, if not in word, he kept company with the broad swath of Americans who denounced the breaking of Indian treaties but consciously profited from it.

The real question thus becomes less how Cody derived his sympathies for Indians than how he fashioned a persona of Buffalo Bill that could denounce Indian conquest at one moment and become its most visible advocate in the next. Of all Cody's characteristics, it is this profound ambivalence about Indians that seems most impenetrable.

But in this respect, perhaps more than in any other, Cody's perspective on the Indian question borrowed directly from the politicking of army officers. Buffalo Bill may have turned his back on political office, but in his theatrical depiction of Indians he held a political brief for the army command, something that further encouraged their support of his theatrical and stage career. For the army that fought Indians on the Plains, the administration of Indian affairs was a large prize in an ongoing political fight in the nation's capital. Traditionally, the War Department was responsible for Indian affairs, and for this reason the army secured a great deal of authority and a large budget well before the Civil War. But in the reforms of 1849, the Office of Indian Affairs was moved from the War Department to the Department of the Interior (where it survives to this day, as the Bureau of Indian Affairs).[37]

The change did not sit well with the army, who now saw themselves as enforcing an Indian policy cooked up mostly by distant politicians and Washington bureaucrats. For the rest of the century they angled to regain control of Indian relations. Thus, in the 1860s and '70s, army officers often blamed the federal government—by which they meant the Department of the Interior—for failing in its duties to Indians. Beginning in 1869, President Grant's Peace Policy placed Indian reservations under the supervision of Quakers and other Christian missionaries. The army's responsibilities were restricted to pursuing Indians off the reservations. The Peace Policy was a favorite target of criticism among army commanders, who felt that they understood Indians better than any missionaries.[38]

Much as critics denounced Cody's stage plays for plotless violence, they had a coherent political message in that they propagated the army's position in the struggle for control of Indian affairs. *Scouts of the Plains*, Cody's 1873–74 drama, was highly critical of the Peace Policy, under which churches administered reservations while the army patrolled outside their boundaries. As one critic noted, "All through the play there is a Quaker Peace Commissioner dropping in everywhere most inopportunely, and who gets scalped—as he deserves—before the close."[39] The Peace Policy had collapsed by 1875. But until the twentieth century, army officers continued a drumbeat of criticism of federal bureaucrats and religious reformers for malfeasance, naiveté, or general misconduct in Indian affairs. Throughout the period, Cody underscored his support for the army position in his public statements. Thus, his lament that "the Indian" had been "ill-used and trampled on by those whose duty it was to protect him," a sentiment he repeated in various forms throughout his life, was a thinly veiled criticism of the civilians who ran the Office of Indian Affairs, and who were responsible for administering reservations.[40]

Less pointedly, and in some ways more surprising, his ambivalence toward Indian conquest and his sympathy toward defeated Indians were also products of his long exposure to army officers. To be sure, America's leading Indian fighters were and are rightly notorious for some of their pronouncements about Indians. General Philip Sheridan was said to have remarked that "the only good Indians I ever saw were dead." Paraphrased as "The only good Indian is a dead Indian," Sheridan's remark has been a banner of Indian hating for more than a century.[41] Whether or not Sheridan ever uttered the remark, others said similar things. Upon hearing of the destruction of Captain Fetterman's command at Fort Phil Kearny in 1866, General William T. Sherman had wired the White House: "We must act with vindictive earnestness against the Sioux, even to their extermination, men, women, and children."[42]

But calls for extermination were rare among army commanders. Indeed, officers' views of the Plains Indian wars can best be summarized as ambivalent, and highly contingent upon conditions of war or peace. General George Crook, for whom Cody scouted in the summer of 1876, frequently blamed white settlers for pushing Indians "beyond endurance" until they took up arms, waging wars which the army "had to fight," even though "our sympathies were with the Indians." Treated fairly, he thought, "the American Indian would make a better citizen than many who neglect the duties and abuse the privilege of this proud title."

Crook had as many critics as any other officer in the army, but on the subject of Indians, his views were widely shared. General Oliver Otis Howard, who pursued Chief Joseph in the Nez Perce War of 1877, was of the opinion that Indians, at least, stole only only from enemies. They kept promises, too. When asked if he thought Indians were especially treacherous, he replied, "No, not so much as the Anglo-Saxon." General Nelson Miles, a personal friend of Cody's who commanded troops against the Sioux, Cheyenne, Apache, and Nez Perce, wrote that Indian warriors showed "courage, skill, sagacity, endurance, fortitude, and self-sacrifice of a high order," and they followed distinctive "rules of civility." These magnificent people, he thought, ill deserved America's "haughty contempt." Even Philip Sheridan was not above sympathizing with them. "We took away their country and their means of support, broke up their mode of living, their habits of life, introduced disease and decay among them, and it was for this and against this they made war. Could any one expect less?" To Sheridan's mind, reservation poverty was the major cause of Indian warfare, and entirely the fault of the Office of Indian Affairs and the ignorant reformers who posed as "Friends of the Indian."[43]

Coming from commanders who routinely defended soldiers for killing Indian women and children, such sentiments might seem contradictory. But the ambivalence was genuine, deeply rooted, and widespread. Preparing to kill Indians in combat, soldiers (and their families) denounced Indians as bloodthirsty savages who merited destruction. Removed from imminent battle, soldiers valorized their opponents as noble, stalwart defenders of home and family, more primitive but still honorable versions of themselves.[44]

Of course, such sentiments said more about soldiers than Indians. Only a valiant soldier could defeat a valiant enemy. Venerating their opponents as noble savages allowed officers to claim the status of alienated men of honor in a dishonorable age. To their way of thinking, the Plains Indian wars were mostly the result of greedy frontier settlers, merchants, and their cronies, who manipulated a distant, disengaged Washington bureaucracy into declaring war on victimized, misunderstood Indians, all in an effort to grab Indian land and army supply contracts.[45]

Cody's complaint about white thieves who supplied the "regular market" for stolen Indian horses thus echoed the complaints of many army officers who saw Americans, particularly of the lower-class variety, as the real savages of the frontier. Consistently, his stage plays borrowed from dime novel conventions and military rhetoric that placed Indians at the mercy of evil whites. "General, it is not the Indians who are the first cause of difficulties," Buffalo Bill asserts in *Life on the Border*. "It is the white men who disguise themselves as Indians and commit these depredations, then the Indians are to blame for it. Then away goes the military for them and that brings on an Indian war."[46]

There was truth to the contention. American criminals who disguised murders and thefts by planting Indian clues—moccasin prints, arrows, unshod horse tracks—were common on the frontier. But white settlers who stole from Indians were even more widespread, and officers castigated them. Captain John Bourke, a veteran of the U.S. Army's Apache campaigns, denounced reckless, idle, and "dissolute" settlers for starting Indian wars. In Texas, officer James Parker wrote his mother, "I would like to go on a scouting expedition after renegade Texans and hang up every scoundrel I caught," for the horse thieving, rapine, and murder they visited upon Indians. Major Alfred Lacey Hough denounced Colorado's "wholly unscrupulous" frontier settlers for being "ambitious men who care only for their own interests" and who stirred up trouble with Indians to bring on a federal Indian war and an infusion of federal dollars into the local economy.[47]

As enlightened as such views seem, they were also self-serving. Where the army's war on Indians verged on atrocity, officers (and scouts like Cody) held themselves blameless, and pointed at settlers, bureaucrats, or Indians for starting the conflagration into which duty thrust them.[48] Thus, in the minds of officers, at least, the army did the nation's dirty work. When they were not in combat, the army stood between frontier settlers and Indians, and they understood their role as protectors of each from the other.

If the Indian wars were bereft of honor, why did Cody and so many officers fight them? Why not resign? Simply put, resisting duty would not have improved matters. Popular Darwinian and Anglo-Saxonist ideologies found numerous exponents among the educated and comparatively well-read officer corps. To them, the march of the white race and its higher civilization made the destruction of Indian culture—the Indian "race"—inevitable. For Indians to surrender to the farms and industry of the higher American civilization was the only possible outcome of the race confrontation described by the frontier line. Lieutenant Colonel George Forsyth, in a typical statement of this widespread philosophy, acknowledged that "the Indian has been wronged, and deeply wronged, by bad white men." Nonetheless, "it must always be borne in mind that, cruel as the aphorism is, 'the survival of the fittest' is a truism that cannot be ignored or gainsaid and barbarism must necessarily give way before advancing civilization."[49]

If warfare and skullduggery were the means through which civilization triumphed, as far as the army was concerned, that was the fault of distant bureaucrats or greedy settlers. Officers usually saw themselves as honorable mediators between civilization and savagery, even when they had to fight Indians who had been wrongly provoked. By vanquishing their Indian opponents as quickly as possible, and moving them expeditiously to reservations, they were giving the Indians a peaceful home—in which they could pass quietly into oblivion.

In reality, of course, Indians were not about to vanish. Their survival strategies included performing dances and other cultural practices for cash, something Cody's stage shows and his Wild West show facilitated. But the belief that they were about to disappear, in a development that was as inevitable as it was unfortunate, remained a dominant stream of American thought well into the twentieth century.

Indians, indeed, were only the most prominent of the "vanishing" peoples, landscapes, tools, trades, occupations, and customs that preoccupied nineteenth-century Americans. The rhetoric of vanishment described categories of beings or things that disappeared to make way for more highly developed successors. It was central to the ideology of progress, and woven through contemporary notions of biology, industrial development, and politics. Naturalists, like officers, influenced Cody's views on retreating Indians, buffalo, and the frontier. In the late 1860s Cody hunted buffalo "specimens" for America's leading taxidermist, Professor Henry A. Ward of Rochester (with whom he frequently socialized afterward, as a resident of that city), and in 1871 he guided Professor Othniel C. Marsh, of Yale University (whose continuing search for dinosaur bones was later assisted by another guide, George Sword). Ward, Marsh, and others related the region's ancient past in stories of brutal competition, violent extinction, and the ineluctable ascendance of higher orders. According to Cody, Marsh "entertained me with several scientific yarns, some of which seemed too complicated and too mysterious to be believed by an ordinary man like myself; but it was all clear to him."[50] Whether or not his self-effacing shrug at Marsh's science was false modesty, Cody understood evolutionary thought at least as well as most Americans did. Darwinian evolution, after all, could be read as a variation on the larger narrative of progress and upward development that had preoccupied American thinking since the beginning of the United States.

Buffalo Bill's Wild West show stands in popular memory as a symbol of Gilded Age confidence. But the centrality of Indians to it, as noble savages doomed to vanish, in truth reflected the conflicted views of most Americans on the subject of the frontier, which they loved and destroyed through their own progress. Cody's exposure to Darwinism, the theory of civilization, and the army command provided him with a ready rhetoric of Indian vanishment, a development so preordained and inevitable that it rendered Indian hating not only distasteful, but excessive. In time, he adapted this language to his Wild West show as a whole. The show, like the Indians, was predicted to disappear as time swept away the "originals" who represented life in the show's Far West. In adapting the sentiments of officers and scientists for his own needs, Cody borrowed a language that combined scientific prediction with certainty about the political advent of the United States in the Far West, but which was also shot through with profound uncertainty about the *moral* quality of that succession. Even as Americans swept out across the Plains to force the ineluctable conclusion of progress, Cody remained less convinced of its righteousness than of its inevitability.

Ambivalence: this was the defining characteristic of American sentiment on westward expansion. And ambivalence was where Cody arrived after searching for the right language to tell stories to the public about real Indians, initially Sword and Two Bears, ultimately all the others who followed in the decades after his stage season of 1877.

As Indians became essential to the spectacle of Buffalo Bill, the need to expand the performance space from stage to arena became increasingly evident. For if Indianness were to be put on display, Indians would have to be on horses.

On horseback, Plains Indians were both enemies and inspirations. Cavalrymen, who venerated great horsemanship, were astounded at Cheyenne, Lakota, and other Indians who galloped bareback amid stampeding buffalo, firing continuous streams of arrows without putting hand to reins. In warfare, their horsecraft was awesome. Hooking one heel over a horse's back, they clung to the sides of their mounts and used the animals' bodies as shields from enemy fire, and the showier men even returned fire from under their horse's necks. They could retrieve fallen comrades from teeming battlefields, at top speed and without dismounting. (Alternatively, one shocked officer reported that a Cheyenne brave scooped up a soldier's corpse at full gallop, stripped him naked, dashed out his brains, and discarded the body—without even slowing down.)[51] "Having never seen the riding of Arabs, Turcomans, Cossacks" or other "world renowned riders," wrote one officer, "I cannot say how the Indian compares with them, but I am satisfied that he is too nearly a Centaur to be surpassed by any."[52]

The appellation "centaur" was a popular compliment in the nineteenth century, often used to reflect the manly bearing of a gentleman on horseback. Indian centaurism simultaneously invited and compelled soldiers to master horses in new ways. After fighting a Cheyenne war party in 1868, one troop of soldiers "were seen to mount from the right-hand side, Indian fashion; others to get on their horses' backs by catching hold of the animals' tails and giving a spring—also an Indian fashion. There was not a trooper in camp who had not made an effort to ride beneath his horse instead of above him."[53]

Even before this, at least one officer who found his own green troopers no match for the "centaurs of the desert" took extraordinary measures. Lieutenant George Armes, commander of the Second Cavalry, sought to remove the lopsided Indian advantage on horseback with new training methods at Fort Sedgewick in 1866. By the time he was finished, crowds gathered to watch his men "stand up on their horse's bare back and ride around the ring at a gallop," and "spring on and off their horses" at full speed, while the animals leapt over hurdles.[54]

Armes intended the unorthodox training to enable his men to challenge Indian warriors on open battlefields, but his techniques soon earned the censure of his superiors, who upbraided him for turning his men into "circus riders."[55] The criticism was ironically apt. Training soldiers to victory required, after all, defeating Indians whose thunderous, circling formations resembled nothing so much as "the grand entree of a circus," in the words of Colonel Richard Irving Dodge.[56]

Comparisons of Indians and Indian-style riding to circus tricks reflected the widespread notoriety of circus entertainment in the nineteenth century, and the early devotion of the circus to horseback stunts. Generals ridiculed George Armes for creating a training regiment that looked like a circus, but the modern circus was, in fact, birthed by a cavalryman in 1768. It was the brainchild of Philip Astley, a retired English cavalry officer who hit upon the idea of charging admission to the crowds who came to observe students at his London riding school. The diameter of Astley's performance space, forty-two feet, was an accommodation to the minimum needs of horses turning at a gallop, and it became the standard size for the circus ring.[57]

Circuses had changed considerably by the time Cheyenne and Sioux challenged Americans for control of the Plains. Over the course of the nine-teenth century, European and American circuses gradually combined clowning and horseback stunts with menageries, acrobatics, and trapeze acts. In 1796, the elephant made its first appearance in an American circus, and for the next hundred years American impresarios competed to acquire ever more exotic animal attractions.[58] P. T. Barnum would say that the ele-phant and the clown were the pegs on which the circus was hung.[59]

But cavalry training regiments like the one Armes devised had led Philip Astley to develop the circus in the first place. Now, despite official resis-tance, riding stunts found a new home in the cavalry as soldiers sought to match Indian horsemen. By the 1890s, horseback acrobatics would be installed as official cavalry drill, and detachments from the trick-riding U.S. Sixth Cavalry appeared regularly in circuses and, most famously, in Buffalo Bill's Wild West and Congress of Rough Riders of the World, where their "military exercises" and "exhibition of athletic sports and horsemanship" included standing up on the backs of running horses.[60]

Buffalo Bill's Wild West show took the European cultural form of the circus and naturalized it on American soil, reprising it as a horseback spectacle with Indian riders, indigenous American performers whose genuine skills had begged comparison to the circus long before they ever moved into the show arena. Cody's move from theatrical stage to a show arena crisscrossed by galloping horsemen reflected the fascination with horses that he shared with Indians. On the Plains, his buffalo-hunting prowess was reinforced by his use of Indian-trained buffalo horses, animals specially conditioned and taught to mimic the movements of running buffalo as they carried hunters alongside them. He bought his favorite mount, Brigham— "the best buffalo horse that ever made a track"—from a Ute Indian (who presumably demanded a high price for him).[61] Through the 1860s, he bought and sold horses to compete in the fervid horse-racing scene at army forts. These contests were a theatrical form in their own right, with visiting Indians, settlers, and scouts challenging tourists, soldiers, and one another to paying races. Riders were known to trumpet their invincibility with midrace stunts. After one Comanche horse beat army competitors in two races on the same day, his owner cruised to a third victory while facing backward, taunting the trailing soldier and beckoning him closer.[62]

By the time he was a scout, Cody was not only a racer but a trick rider, too. In the winter of 1869–70, in a race against a soldier at Fort McPherson, Cody "rode the horse bareback; seized his mane with my left hand, rested my right on his withers, and while he was going at full speed, I jumped to the ground, and sprang again upon his back, eight times in succession." He drew inspiration for this stunt, he said, from the circus, "and I had practiced considerably at it."[63]

In 1869, Dan Castello's Circus and Menagerie became the first circus to cross the country on the transcontinental railroad. When it appeared in North Platte, William Cody saw it.[64] (Although Cody did not say so, he may have seen the riding stunt before he visited the circus. His opponent in the trick-riding race was from the Second Cavalry, the regiment of "circus riders" trained by George Armes, and for all we know Cody's opponent matched his performance, leap for leap.) The convergence of the railroad circus with William Cody's Plains career was no accident. Circuses were widespread in American life and culture throughout the nineteenth century, but railroad expansion, the rise of corporate investment, and a revolution in print advertising—especially poster production—made for a renaissance of circuses after the Civil War.[65]

Cody, who rose to fame by engaging the liminal subcultures of scouting and theater, observed another twilight social space beneath the big top. The circus was a morally questionable enterprise, with a long and checkered history. It was indisputably a European cultural form, and its most famous performers were European, or claimed to be.[66] With its bizarre freaks, strange animals, and scantily clad men and women—to say nothing of its androgynes and hermaphrodites—it was a disturbing spectacle of ambiguous races and genders, with a wide reputation for criminality. Early circus impresarios frequently cut deals with gamblers, grifters, and confidence men who followed them from town to town. At times, pickpockets plied the crowds so adeptly that few customers had any money to purchase admission from the shortchange artists working the ticket window.[67] Circus graft, and circus nonconformity, inspired a great deal of anticircus violence, particularly in rural areas where local men and boys regularly battled circus workers in public brawls.[68] An itinerant community that defied conventional social categories, the circus was infused with a carnivalesque spirit, the threat (or promise) of society turned upside down. For these reasons, clergymen often denounced it as the devil's own playhouse, and "respectable" people often avoided it.[69]

But the circus was a paradox, and by the latter 1870s Cody saw in it the glimmer of an opportunity. Where the crudest stage production was inevitably in the shadow of Shakespearean drama—actors who were not great tragedians would never achieve real praise—circuses had fewer respectable conventions to live up to, leaving reviewers and newspaper editors less constrained in their range of circus writing. In general, their coverage of circuses was so "soft," or playful, that press agents from other entertainments were often surprised at how easy the art of circus promotion could be. Small-town and big-city editors alike reprinted circus press releases as news items, without comment.[70] Although many eschewed the circus as overly European, immoral, and decadent, the railroad allowed for much larger, more dazzling circuses which continued to draw viewers from all social classes, who sat together under one canvas tent. In this sense, a glamorous big top represented a better hope of capturing a democratic audience, including the middle classes, who had had steadily deserted the theater since Ned Buntline led the mobs outside the Astor Place Theater at the middle of the century.[71]

In 1869, the appearance of Castello's circus in North Platte was so novel that the many social anxieties stirred up by circuses in general remained in the background. But in the 1870s, William Cody, who discerned divisions in popular culture at least as well as he followed the divide on the Plains, witnessed a burgeoning of circus performance, the public concerns attending it, and the efforts of his contemporaries to overcome them. In 1871, the year before he began his stage career in New York, P. T. Barnum, the artful deceiver, recast the circus as middle-class entertainment. Barnum tied his reputation for "moral" entertainments to the brilliant management of W. C. Coup. Together, the two made bold advances in circus showmanship. They solved the problem of loading circuses on trains quickly (devising ramps to load all circus animals, props, and matériel from one end), and turned the traditional one-ring entertainment into a three-ring extravaganza. In New York, they leased the old New Haven railroad station at Madison Avenue and Twenty-seventh (future site of Madison Square Garden) and built upon it the Great Roman Hippodrome.[72] There, in 1874, they debuted "The Congress of Nations," which Cody undoubtedly saw, and in which a parade of simulated royals and lavishly costumed entourages, including the queen of England, the pope, and the emperor of China, led an American contingent of cowboys and Indians into the big top as the opening act of a huge show of elephants and chariot races.[73] By 1880, Barnum had merged his spectacle with that of James A. Bailey, making it one of the nation's largest entertainment enterprises.[74]

The presence of Indians in Barnum's circus, as elsewhere, signified the passage of history. Circuses had borrowed from history before. In 1856, in Missouri, the Mabie Brothers Circus combined with Den Stone's Menagerie and Tyler's Indian Exhibition to present a historical pageant, with reenactments of a buffalo hunt, Indian dances, Pocahontas saving John Smith's life, and a (thrilling?) demonstration of Indians gathering corn.[75]

Cody's enterprise would work much more directly with historical materials, as we shall see. But in envisioning an entertainment that featured Indians, horses, and himself, it required no great leap to imagine cowboys in the mix. American and Mexican cowboys alike were fond of horseback performance. Americans and Mexicans had herded cattle for centuries by 1860, but it was the post–Civil War American cowboy who became a mythic figure of renown, and the Great Plains was his birthplace. Outfits began driving cattle from Texas to Kansas soon after the Civil War. Relatively few of these cattle made it to Nebraska at first, but the famed rancher J. W. Iliff ranged cattle in the western Platte River valley by the early 1860s, and John Bratt brought Texas cattle to the region in 1869. That same year, Texas Jack Omohundro trailed a herd of cattle from Texas to North Platte, where he sold them all to ranchers, who were now dispersed across western Nebraska. Omohundro took a job tending bar for a local saloonkeeper (Lew Baker, father of Johnny Baker, later the "boy marksman" in the Wild West show) before moving down to Fort McPherson at the urging of his new friend, William Cody, where he became an occasional schoolteacher and a scout.[76] In 1874, the Western Trail, which drew cattle from Texas to its northern terminus at Dodge City, Kansas, was extended farther north, to Ogallala, Nebraska, west of North Platte, which became the major railhead for Nebraska cattle outfits. The town of North Platte now sat firmly in the middle of a thriving cattle region, and acquired a thick layer of cowboy culture atop its military and mercantile origins.[77]

In the late 1870s, Cody became a rancher and saw cowboy horsemanship up close. In partnership with Cody, Frank North and his brother Luther established a large ranch on the Dismal River. The Cody-North Ranch grazed its large herds across the Sand Hills, but lost money due to stock theft and heavy winters. In 1879 Cody and the Norths sold the outfit to John Bratt for $75,000.[78]

Cody plowed his theatrical profits into ranching, but like most ranch owners, he was an absentee owner who was never a cowboy. When he appeared at annual roundups, other ranchers and roundup bosses indulged the stage star and prominent ranch owner by letting him drive a few steers and dry heifers, but they kept him away from cows and calves, because his penchant for horseback drama made him a poor drover. "When I was bossing the round-up and the bunch became excited," wrote John Bratt, "I would call Cody out" to get him away from the cattle. This the thespian "took good naturedly, knowing well that rough handling of stock meant loss of flesh and shrinkage in value."[79]

For his part, although Cody complained that "there is nothing but hard work on these round-ups," and that he "could not possibly find out where the fun came in," he attended because he could make them something of a party.[80] For several years, his celebrity, his flamboyant, gregarious manner, and his alcohol—"brought along as an antidote against snake bites, and other accidents"—energized festivities at the Dismal River roundups. "The cowboys were always glad to see the Colonel and the cattle owners and foremen would vie with each other in showing him a good time," recalled John Bratt, who routinely collected the cowboys' guns in anticipation of the festivities.[81]

These affairs included spectacular competitive displays of cowboy mastery over animals. Bronco riding, roping contests, horse races, and riding wild steers were primary features of roundups across the West, and the Dismal River roundup was no exception.[82] The ethos of competition among cowboys in the United States and Mexico reflected their ongoing effort to turn the drudgery of work into challenging play. Competitions to see who could sit untamed mounts the longest—"bronco busting"—were common wherever cowboys accumulated, and roping contests and horse races were ubiquitous, too.[83] A favorite cowboy pastime was "picking up," originally a Mexican game, in which contestants on running horses picked up coins, handkerchiefs, or virtually any small object placed at a designated spot on the ground.[84] Cowboys at the Dismal River roundups played the pickup game, and not surprisingly, it found its way to the Wild West arena as a display of "cow-boys fun."[85]

He may have been bored by the work, but Cody left the Dismal River roundups impressed with their exhibition of "most magnificent horsemanship" by cowboys who possessed "the greatest dexterity and daring in the saddle."[86] The Sand Hills roundups inspired his organization of the Old Glory Blowout, the Fourth of July celebration which he organized at North Platte in 1882. Because the spring roundup for western Nebraska was occurring at the same time, the widely advertised event drew many cowboys, who were enthusiastic contestants for its cash prizes. After a morning parade, which terminated at a private racetrack, the program went forward with songs and speeches. Once the formal events were over, cowboys took turns roping and riding several buffalo and Texas steers that Cody had procured for the event, in a raucous spectacle that delighted the crowd. There was also a full slate of horse races, including not only cowboy-style free-for-alls but elegant trotting competitions in which horses belonging to Cody and other well-to-do merchants and ranchers faced off. That night, there were fireworks.[87]

Scholars often credit the Old Glory Blowout with inspiring the Wild West show. Others credit Nate Salsbury, who was Cody's partner in the show from 1884 to 1902. Late in life, Salsbury claimed to have envisioned a show of horsemanship as early as 1876. He recounted an 1882 meeting at a Brooklyn restaurant at which he and Cody agreed to join forces. "I invented every feature of the Wild West Show that has had any drawing power," he wrote.[88]

We shall see below what Salsbury's influence on the Wild West show actually was. But he never claimed to have proposed more than a show of cowboys and "Mexican riders." Not even in his defensive, self-aggrandizing memoirs did he remember himself as having brought Indians into the conversation with Cody. There were no Indians in the Old Glory Blowout, either. In reality, since the day he became a scout, Cody had been revising, recasting, and exploring the boundaries of his frontier imposture by following Indians. He posed as the white Indian by getting close to them (but not too close) on the Plains. He shored up his melodrama and his frontier authenticity by bringing Indians to the stage in the East. Now, he imagined them as the center of a new drama that would allow them to perform the horsecraft that awed him and so many of his contemporaries. The resulting entertainment would offer new opportunities to more Indians than Cody or they imagined. And before they were done, over three decades later, it would offer not just Indians and cowboys, and Cody, but many others, too, new ways to imagine themselves and America in the modern world.

CHAPTER NINE

Domesticating the Wild West

T HE FIRST-EVER dress rehearsal of the Wild West show occurred in 1883, at Colville, Nebraska, the home of Frank North and the Pawnees who made up the show's Indian contingent that year. According to eyewitness L. O. Leonard, when the Deadwood stagecoach trundled into the arena, Buffalo Bill invited the town council, including the mayor, a beloved but notorious blusterer named "Pap" Clothier, to ride in the coach. For the first two passes around the showgrounds, the coach rolled merrily along, and its occupants waved to the crowd.

On the third pass, the Pawnees swept into the arena. The coach passengers were expecting it, but "the mules had not been advised of this part of the program, nor had they been trained to Indian massacre." The animals surged forward, the Indians in hot pursuit, the driver barely able to keep the coach's wheels on the ground as it rounded the turn. When Buffalo Bill and his cowboys suddenly went into the action as the rescue party, nobody had told the Indians to break off the attack. Terrified by several dozen howling men on horseback and the thunder of guns, the mules stepped up the pace. "As the coach, Indians, scouts, and Cody swept past the crowd again, the mayor stuck his head out the window, waved his hands frantically, and shouted, "Stop: Hell: stop—let us out."

But the driver had all he could do to keep the stage on its circular course without rolling it over. The mules did not halt until they were thoroughly winded. At that point, the enraged mayor "leaped out of the coach and made for Buffalo Bill, ready for a fight."

Fortunately, before Clothier could reach Cody, a local wit named Frank Evors climbed to the top of the coach. "Look at them, gentlemen." Pointing to the dazed town council and the infuriated mayor, Evors declaimed his pride in these men who "risked their lives . . . for your entertainment." Clothier now turned back to the coach and went after Evors, who escaped. Meanwhile, Frank North rode up to Cody with some advice: "Bill, if you want to make this damned show go, you do not need me or my Indians. . . . You want about twenty old bucks. Fix them up with all the paint and feathers on the market. Use some old hack horses and hack driver. To make it go you want a show of illusion not realism."[1]

In an era riven with concern over the bawdy or otherwise "unsuitable" content of public amusements, the dress rehearsal was an inauspicious beginning for an entertainment Cody hoped would "catch the better class of people."[2] He was hunting for the elusive treasure sought by many other entertainers: middle-class women, and the family audiences their patronage assured. Thus he had a dilemma on his hands.[3] A tamer spectacle was necessary. However, the Wild West show's commitment to borderline violence— gunplay, horse breaking, and other physically dangerous performances—was central to its attraction as a "true" picture of "life in the Far West."

From 1883 until its last days, the authenticity of Wild West performers was a major audience draw. In many ways, the show's high-speed simulacrum of combat, animal mastery, and marksmanship was a spectacle of "real" historical actors whose virility was a bulwark against the artificiality and decadence of modern civilization. Throughout the 1870s, on his forays as hunting guide, Cody had crafted himself as an antidote to the anxieties of city sports seeking manly restoration in wilderness pursuits. In the 1880s, his show addressed an emergent and popular obsession with the supposed decay of American civilization. True, Americans celebrated westward expansion in literature and paintings on the theme "Westward the Course of Empire Takes Its Way" (a line from an eighteenth-century poem by Bishop George Berkeley, on the inevitability of civilization's westward march). Some of these paintings were appropriated and mimicked in the colorful posters of Buffalo Bill's Wild West show. But Americans of the Gilded Age were also highly conscious of what we might call the law of social gravity: a society that traveled up the arc of progress must eventually come down.[4] The popular rationale for Indian wars had been the need to restrain savage passions and advance the cause of progress. But as the Indian wars ended, the very restraining hand of civilization seemed to be "overcivilizing" white American manhood, snuffing it out, burdening masculine energies until they became perverted and feminized.

The most coherent statement of these popular fears came in 1880, when the physician George M. Beard catalogued a host of symptoms for what he identified as a new malady in his book, *American Nervousness*. In company with many other medical professionals of his day, Beard saw an epidemic of strange anxieties gripping American men, including extraordinary "desire for stimulants and narcotics . . . fear of responsibility, of open places or closed places, fear of society, fear of being alone, fear of fears, fear of contamination, fear of everything, deficient mental control, lack of decision in trifling matters, and hopelessness."[5] He gathered these disparate, neurotic symptoms under the rubric of a single illness, which he gave the name "neurasthenia." In his view, neurasthenia afflicted the civilized whose work required "labor of the brain over that of the muscles." Thus its most common victims were white, middle- and upper-class businessmen and professionals. Overtaxed by commercial and managerial demands, their neurasthenic bodies were rendered "small and feeble." An epidemic brought on by the civilizing process run amok, neurasthenia represented something more than a psychological condition. By undermining virility, it endangered the future of the white race and its civilization. In Beard's words, "there is not enough force left" in neurasthenics "to reproduce the species or go through the process of reproducing the species."[6]

The impact of Beard's work was widespread, and the specter of neurasthenia subverting and corrupting white America aggravated other racial fears that became pronounced in the 1880s. Immigration from Germany, Ireland, and other northern European countries had provoked social anxiety and political upheaval for over a generation when the river of immigrants suddenly acquired new tributaries. In the decade following 1880, almost a million, mostly Catholic and Jewish, immigrants from southern and eastern Europe joined the nearly four million from western and northern Europe. Increasingly, the proportion of Slavs, Russian Jews, Italians, Poles, and other eastern and southern Europeans surpassed that of northern Europeans.[7]

Since the days in the 1840s, when Ned Buntline rallied his first anti-immigrant mob, native-born Americans had feared their Anglo-Saxon, Protestant republic was becoming a polyglot nation. The so-called "new immigration" ramped up those fears. To many observers, the new immigrants were base savages, like Indians. Although their large numbers of children proved their biological fertility, they were short on "manly" attributes such as sobriety, thrift, and self-control. The United States was in the process of becoming an urban nation even without the new immigrants. After the Civil War, native-born Americans migrated to the cities in such numbers that by 1920 the farmer's republic was truly a thing of the past. But the cities that were coming to define American life were also immigrant bastions, especially in the tenement districts teeming with crime, squalor, poverty, and vice. If the cities were the future, they were also a savage frontier poised to swallow white America.

At this moment of urban peril, the other frontier, in the Far West, finally closed. With the U.S. Census Bureau's 1890 declaration that the frontier no longer existed, a defining condition of American life blinked out. Cultural and political responses ranged from attempts to preserve wilderness landscapes in national parks to elegiac paintings and novels. The gathering sense that the future would be more urban, less natural, more corporate, and less individualistic pervaded American culture.[8]

In cultural terms, frontier and city had long been mirrors which reflected and sometimes inverted each other. Many saw urban disorder as displaced frontier savagery. As the cities grew larger and more diverse, and as the frontier receded further into memory, Americans adapted the rhetoric of frontier conquest to metropolitan problems. Beginning in 1886, urban reformers, many of them educated women, sought to domesticate what they called the "city wilderness" through the establishment and administration of "settlement houses." These were centers providing immigrants with child care and with education in the rudiments of civility, including the English language, civics, the arts, and personal hygiene. Situated in the most "savage" urban districts, they were in a sense an urban analogue to frontier missions among the Indians.[9]

At the same time, artists and writers increasingly—and paradoxically—presented white virtues as products of frontier struggle and the westward movement of Anglo-Saxondom. The shift ran counter to frontier realities, of course. Throughout the nineteenth century, miscegenated scouts, Mexicans, "half-breed" renegades, Indian captivity, and traditions of intermarriage among settlers and Indians had contributed to an image of the frontier as a place of sexual decadence and racial decay. The Americans who actually conquered the polyglot West, as we have seen, included a multiracial, multiethnic army, Indian and mixed-blood auxiliaries, and a diverse group of settlers, too.

But now, at least in the minds of many thinkers, the relatively empty spaces of the trans-Missouri West became a final, fading crucible of whiteness which stood in gleaming contrast to the mongrel city. Frederic Remington, a Yale dropout who was born and raised in rural New York state, first went west in 1881, when he took a temporary job on a Montana ranch. He became one of the most influential and dyspeptic artists of the era, his oil-painted, vanishing West an antidote to a modern, degenerate America that was overrun with "Jews, Injuns, Chinamen, Italians, Huns—the rubbish of the earth I hate." His fantasies verged on ethnic cleansing. "I've got some Winchesters and when the massacring begins, I can get my share of 'em, and what's more, I will. . . . Our race is full of sentiment. We've got the rinsin's, the scourin's, and the Devil's lavings to come to us and be *men*—something they haven't been, most of them, these hundreds of years."[10]

Whether depicting eastern strike or Indian war, Remington's sketches, paintings, and essays (including images and musings on Buffalo Bill's Wild West show) were suffused with a sense that white American racial strengths were frontier virtues, and that they were about to be lost amid rapidly multiplying and unmanly immigrants.[11] He had much company in these views. While immigrants soared in numbers, the declining fecundity of native-born Americans furrowed the brows of social observers. As early as 1865, the state census chief for New York concluded that there was "no *natural increase* in population among the families descended from the early settlers." In 1869, another observer noted the speed with which Americans and Europeans alike were pouring into the cities. "But the most important change of all," he concluded, "is the increasing proportion of children of a foreign descent, compared with the relative decrease of those of strictly American origin."[12]

By the 1880s, the persistence of these trends and the rising consciousness of neurasthenia culminated in a pervasive fear of the eclipse of the white race. The year after Buffalo Bill's Wild West debuted, Theodore Roosevelt fled his home on Long Island for a ranch in Dakota Territory. When he returned, in 1886, he reentered New York politics and began his six-volume *Winning of the West*, a paean to the racial vigor of western pioneers which foreshadowed his call to "the strenuous life" for white men, and his reservations about birth control as "race suicide" for white people.[13] Although Americans came to admire Remington and Roosevelt as authentic westerners, the two men were decidedly late in exploring the region and its cultural resonances. Their assumption of western identities, as cowboy artist and cowboy president, respectively, followed partly in the tradition of frontier imposture pioneered decades before by William Cody and others.

But the resort to the West as a bastion of white America suggests how the Wild West show (which both Remington and Roosevelt patronized), as it debuted in 1883, anticipated and expressed wider cultural preoccupations with the decay of white manliness. Before long its publicists began to explain it this way, and by 1894 audiences had entered the spirit of the thing. Ogling a show cowboy in Brooklyn, a member of the Women's Professional League of New York exclaimed, "Those are the kind of men that excite my admiration. . . . Big, strong, bronzed fellows! How much superior they are to the spindle-shanked, eye-glassed dudes!"[14]

Frontier originals who had subdued the savage wilderness, the Wild West show's "real" men at once reenacted their exploits and fought a defensive withdrawal before advancing artifice, civilized decadence, and the new immigration. At the very moment when psychologist G. Stanley Hall and others were beginning to suggest innoculating Anglo-Saxons against the epidemic of overcivilization by cultivating the violent tendencies of boys, Cody's show so convincingly enacted "the drama of existence" that, in comparison, wrote one journalist, "all the operas in the world appear like pretty playthings for emasculated children."[15]

The manly hysteria of these reviews, with their ongoing critique of mainstream, middle-class culture as castrated, immature, and sentimental, suggests that as much as the Wild West show expressed anxieties over racial decay and the new immigration, it was also part of gathering cultural reaction against the cult of domesticity. The virtues of home and woman were central themes in American culture, and settlement houses were only a hint of future possibilities for womanly public reform. Many social critics looked to woman suffrage as a means to broaden women's influence. When Buffalo Bill's new show played Chicago in 1883, it overlapped with the annual convention of the National Association for the Advancement of Women, whose president, Julia Ward Howe, gave one of many addresses on the reformist potential of women voters.[16]

To put it mildly, the suffrage movement had critics. Behind the era's many warnings about overcivilization, neurasthenic collapse, and immigrant takeover of American cities, there lurked a barely concealed revulsion at women's gathering influence. The early Wild West show, in its ardent appeal to masculine, undomesticated emotions, expressed a gathering backlash against the influence of women in literature, theater, and public life. Frederic Remington construed his lust for race war as a healthy corrective to the plague of *womanly* sentiment. In literature and ultimately in film, such ideas would culminate in the supremely anti-domestic genre of the Western, beginning with Owen Wister's novel, *The Virginian*, in 1902.[17]

Scholars of western film have penned some of the most trenchant analyses of Buffalo Bill's Wild West show. According to its most influential historian, the appeal of Buffalo Bill's spectacle lay in its antidomestic presentation of race war as a solution to the unruliness of cities and savage labor unrest. With Indians standing in for immigrant strikers, and cowboys and cavalry representing the ruling class, the show was a bloodthirsty, reactionary drama. When the Indians slaughtered Custer's cavalry in the arena, and Buffalo Bill took his revenge on Yellow Hair, the spectacle implied that violence against all savages, be they Indians or immigrants, was not only necessary, but a hallowed American tradition.[18]

Such grim interpretations of the show have some merit, as we shall see. But in 1883, Wister's novel and the birth of "the western" were a full twenty years away. Domesticity yet reigned as a virtue and the bedrock of civilization. Americans of all classes were deeply divided over how best to respond to the era's frequent and sometimes violent confrontations between strikers, factory owners, and the forces of the law. To succeed as middle-class entertainment, Cody's new show would have to appeal across a divided political spectrum. Within a few short years, it did. Wild West show audiences included right-leaning fans like Remington and Roosevelt. But as we shall see, prominent reformers and leftists could also be found there. And, vastly outnumbering all these, there were many middle-class women and families, too.

The key to Cody's achievement in making a mass entertainment out of frontier myth was less in his depiction of racial hostility and free-flowing blood than in the way he framed his spectacle's violence to make it a show that middle-class women could attend. Only through their patronage could he attract their children and their husbands, too. Much as Cody sought a new kind of manly entertainment to escape the bonds of melodrama, the raucous Nebraska dress rehearsal suggested that drawing "the better class of people" might require reassuring the audience of his show's safety and good order. It might require, in other words, a restraining hand.

Cody's previous biographers and Wild West show historians have been loath to trace his tailoring of show attractions to suit his audience, perhaps because so many people claimed to have originated show attractions, and because he left few written clues to his performance ideas. But Cody himself originated most of the show's central features, and he retained creative control over its performances for its entire life. Despite what Frank North is alleged to have said to Cody at the Wild West show's first dress rehearsal—"You want a show of illusion, not realism"—there was less of a barrier between the two categories of experience than we might think. "Realism" has had many meanings, but in terms of visual art, in this period it referred to a mixture of fact and affect in ways that were convincing even if they were not truthful to every detail. In other words, it evoked an emotional response through artful deception. Thus, many "realistic" portrait photographs contained painted backdrops of forests or mountains. Viewers knew that these were studio portraits with landscape paintings in them. Nonetheless, they acclaimed them as realistic because they supposedly conveyed the rugged character of the individual being photographed, whether he was Teddy Roosevelt, William Cody, or an Omaha dentist.[19]

Working from the rough 1883 beginnings, Cody retained the illusion of realism, to such a degree that not only were fans impressed with the show's authenticity, but even the artist Max Bachmann would call William Cody "the pioneer of realism in American Art," an accolade which is as indicative of his show's popular reception as it is overstated. Cody's achievement was to temper the show's warrior ethos, making it acceptable to a broad public riven with doubt and discord over the urban, industrial future.[20] As much as Americans sought refuge in the mythic West as a masculine space, they remained anxious to protect the home—and civilization—as a bulwark against violence and unbridled passion.

How then, could Americans become domestic, leave the frontier in the past, and yet avoid neurasthenia? How could they retain frontier virtues amid civilization, without decaying into effeminacy or savagery? These were questions which preoccupied Americans, and with which Cody and his managers grappled as they embarked on their new enterprise. If the Wild West show began drawing rave reviews for its express virility only three years after its disastrous dress rehearsal, it did so by containing that virility within a framework of historical progress that culminated in household order. During its most successful years, the show's embrace of race war was balanced by its display of national progress through family and hearth. As Cody was to discover, before the Wild West show could succeed, it had to be domesticated.

CODY'S NEW "ENTERTAINMENT," as he described it in early 1883, would not "smack of a show or circus." It would "be on a high toned basis," and would consist of "representations of life in the far west by the originals themselves."[21] Cody had been projecting an artfully deceptive persona and biography for at least fifteen years. Now, with the help of his talented publicist, John Burke, he distilled his bricolage of feat and fiction into show publicity. The primary vehicles of Cody's publicists were colorful posters and show programs, which were pamphlets running into dozens of closely typed pages, with text that explained the "historic reality" of each show scene and introduced the biographies of the principals. According to the small booklet audiences purchased for a dime, Cody was a "genuine specimen of Western manhood." A "celebrated Pony Express rider" who became a Nebraska legislator and defeated scout William Comstock in a legendary buffalo-killing contest, he had guided William Sherman on his expedition to negotiate a treaty with the Comanches and the Kiowas (a mission actually performed by Hickok, not Cody), and in serving with the Fifth Cavalry he achieved "intimate associations and contact with" a slew of army officers, including "the late-lamented Gen. Custer." Buffalo Bill stood before the masses as the embodiment of an idealized life story.[22]

The seam between truth and fiction, fake exploits and real deeds, was so artfully sewn as to be all but invisible. In a sense, Buffalo Bill was an inversion of a Barnum exhibit, the stitching of his deception culminating not in some freakish monkey-fish or ape-man, but a consummate American man who embodied the progressive mythology of the frontier. Audiences could pick and choose what they were willing to believe, and some were never convinced that Cody was everything he claimed to be. The *New York Dramatic News* referred to Cody as "Blufferblo Bull."

Indeed, doubts about Cody's history on the frontier followed him throughout his career with the Wild West show, and rumors circulated that he merely lifted the identity of Buffalo Bill from its rightful owner. Some of Cody's Plains contemporaries even advanced such a case. In 1894, his old rival Captain Jack Crawford introduced a newspaper reporter to "the real Buffalo Bill," one William Mathewson of Wichita, Kansas. A former hide hunter who had become a prominent banker, Mathewson had indeed been one of many to claim the "Buffalo Bill" name before Cody did. Now, he alleged that Cody was nothing but his former employee and grandiose imitator. The subject created a stir in the press. Although Cody's long list of military endorsements and his reputation as a worthy entertainer allowed him to ignore the charges, rumors persisted of some more genuine Buffalo Bill, out there in the West, or perhaps only in memory. But for most, the continuing questions about Cody's history and identity made his convincing imposture all the more remarkable—and amusing. "He is a poseur," wrote one reviewer, "but he poses impeccably."[23]

So with most spectators. Even when they detected the fakery, it was mixed so skillfully with Cody's bona fides as an Indian fighter, buffalo hunter, and scout, so thoroughly obscured by his reputation as an experienced entertainer, and so widely imitated by other impresarios that the emphasis on "originals" took on a double meaning, with Cody once again at the center of a playful interchange of real and fake that quickly outdistanced the tired formulas of the frontier melodrama. Buffalo Bill's performers were the standard from which so many copies were struck that Wild West shows became a subindustry within the larger industry of public amusements, and by 1884 newpapers were already referring to the genre as "Buffalo Bill shows."[24] Cody's many imitators, such as Gordon "Pawnee Bill" Lillie, Nevada Ned, and "Mexican Joe" Shelley, tailored life stories to resemble his, cultivated an appearance like his, assembled similar shows, and in the case of Samuel Franklin Cody (real name: Franklin Samuel Cowdery) even pirated his name, all of which reinforced William Cody's reputation as initiator of frontier simulacrum, the "original" Wild Westerner.[25]

Among the real westerners on display in the show arena, the most original frontiersmen of all were Indians, who, as indigenous primitives, represented the untamed passions which middle-class audiences feared and, increasingly, coveted. In Cody's earliest plans for the show, Indians were its primary attraction. Even before he had hired any cowboys, Cody wrote to the secretary of the interior about recruiting the best-known Indian of the age. "I am going to try hard to get old Sitting Bull," he told his partner. The most famous surviving Sioux chief from the battle of the Little Big Horn was a powerful symbol of Indian resistance and savage passion. Only in 1881 had he returned from Canada, where he took refuge after the death of Custer. "If we can manage to get him our ever lasting fortune is made."[26]

But the Indian office judged Sitting Bull too dangerous to be allowed off the reservation. Cody turned to the Pawnees. They had done fine work for his stage show, and he hired Frank North, the commander of the battalion of Pawnee scouts, to recruit them.[27]

Leadership of the new company was another matter. In the spring of 1882, Cody had discussed the idea of partnership in this new venture with actor-manager Nate Salsbury. But that fall, Cody first approached William

"Doc" Carver about becoming his partner. Carver was a dentist who had left his home in Illinois and moved to North Platte, Nebraska, in 1872. He bought 160 acres of land on the banks of Medicine Creek, but forsook farming for the vigorous industry of frontier imposture. He practiced marksmanship fervently, sported broad-brim hats and beaded buckskins like the most flamboyant scouts. The Sioux became the subject of his most outrageous lie, in which they allegedly abducted him as a child but eventually became so impressed with his marksmanship, and so fearful of his lust for revenge against them, that they nicknamed him "Evil Spirit of the Plains."[28]

Just as Cody entwined his life fictions with Hickok's myth, "Evil Spirit" embroidered his with Cody's. He actually met Cody for the first time in 1874, when Buffalo Bill guided Carver and a party of sports on a hunting trip in Nebraska.[29] Soon after, Carver began claiming that he and Buffalo Bill were old friends who had hunted together for years, with Carver (here turning Cody into his own William Comstock) proving himself the superior marksman and champion buffalo hunter of the world.

Cody also approached Salsbury again, but the latter wanted no part of a show with Carver, whom he considered "a fakir in the show business" and who had a reputation for primping (Cody himself had said that Carver "went West on a piano stool").[30]

Another critic had said that Carver "had sunk a lead mine trying to learn to shoot."[31] But if that was true, Carver learned, indeed. At his 1878 New York debut (where Texas Jack threw targets for him), he demonstrated marvelous accuracy and endurance, using a rifle to shatter 5,500 airborne glass balls in under 500 minutes. Afterward, Carver's shoulder was so sore he could barely move, and his eyes burned for days.[32] Subsequently, he ventured to Europe for several years, where he won shooting titles, awards, and much public acclaim. Upon his return, he billed himself as "Champion Shot of the World."[33]

Carver later claimed that he originated all of the ideas for the Wild West show, but Cody's letters to him indicate otherwise. Cody rejected Carver's proposed names for the show—"Cowboy and Indian Combination" and "Yellowstone Combination"—because, as he warned Carver, "the word combination is so old and so many shows use it." Cody was looking for a "smooth high-toned name" which "will be more apt to catch the better class of people." He suggested "Cody & Carver's Golden West," and ultimately the two settled on a longer name, but one that reflected Cody's vision of this amusement as less a "show" than a place: Buffalo Bill and Doc Carver's Wild West, Rocky Mountain and Prairie Exhibition. Throughout the long life of this entertainment, Cody and his managers refused to call it a show, preferring to emphasize its educational value with the word "exhibition." The word gave it a veneer of middle-class respectability, and offered audiences a

way of attending without fear of being corrupted by the notoriously decadent world of show and theater. From its first year, journalists called it "The
Wild West."[34]

On a range of other issues, Cody issued directives and Carver followed
them, or tried to, including orders to have his picture taken, and then
retaken, with his buckskin suit taken in (Carver liked his suit baggy, and it
made him look shapeless), posters made in a particular way, orders to check
into having an electric generator for night performances ("it will make many
a dollar if it can be worked"), orders to have illustrations made for their
extensive show program, to follow up on Cody's negotiations for use of
showgrounds in Omaha and Chicago and for the show's passage on the railroads.[35]

As the dress rehearsal implied, the all-male cast of the Wild West show,
fronted by two masculine stars, pushed the show's male energies to the limit.
But in this earliest attempt to fulfill popular longings for white heroes, Cody
actually overlooked certain traditional ideals of frontier manliness. In American culture, ideal men such as frontier heroes were supposed to balance a
preponderance of manly strengths with some womanly virtues. The frontier
line, in this sense, was not only an imaginary divide between wilderness and
settlement, the man's space of the outdoors and the woman's space of the
house. It was also the border between male and female characteristics in one
person. Frontier heroes balanced the (manly) fearlessness of the savage with
the (womanly) restraint of the civilized, and in consequence, contemporary
descriptions of them are so gender-bending as to strike modern readers as
twisted, or even queer. Thus, Wild Bill Hickok's admirers noted that he had
"the shoulders of a Hercules with the waist of a girl," that the deadly man's
eyes were "as gentle as a woman's," and that "in truth, the woman nature
seems prominent throughout, and you would not believe that you were
looking into eyes that have pointed the way to death to hundreds of men."[36]

Similarly, an 1872 columnist covering the hunt with the Grand Duke
Alexis described the heroic, virile Buffalo Bill as possessed of "a smile as
honest and sweet as that of a love sick maiden."[37] Melodrama, with its
emphasis on the salvation of true womanhood and the civilizing influence of
domestic harmony, had been an appropriate vehicle for Cody's stardom precisely because it placed his masculine form in a larger context of feminine
virtues. An 1879 interviewer began his description of Cody as flat-out
manly—"Tall, straight as a straight line, with magnificent breadth of
chest"—then introduced female attributes: "small hands evidently of great
power, a remarkably handsome though almost girlish face, hair of which a
woman might be proud, and a soft melodious voice."[38]

Cody's new extravaganza being an effort to escape the confines of melodrama, its first incarnation abandoned any pretense of domesticity or wom-

anly restraint. Neither Cody nor Carver was much of a manager, and both demanded treatment as stars. Their incompatibility was heightened by the fact that both were masculine sharpshooters, symbolically violent figure-heads for a show of race war and high-speed horseback pursuits, the whole infused with copious amounts of gunpowder and testosterone.

The masculine figureheads led a cast that was entirely, raucously male. Like other westerners, North Platte locals bragged about and bet on their shooting, horse breaking, and steer roping. By 1883, the town had been home to most of the nation's frontier melodrama stars and many of the "real" dime novel characters, including not only Cody, but also Charles "The White Chief" Belden (who was stationed at Fort McPherson shortly before he was killed in 1870), Texas Jack Omohundro, "Dashing Charlie" Emmett, John Y. Nelson, and of course Doc Carver. Plenty of other locals wanted their chance at frontier imposture. For the first season, Cody and Carver hired a raft of them. These included William Levi "Buck" Taylor, a six-foot-five Texas cowboy who first rode up the trails to Nebraska with a herd of cattle for the Cody-North Ranch on the Dismal River in 1879. Once he signed on with the Wild West show, he took a starring role in frontier melodrama during the off-season, touring with Buffalo Bill's Dutchman and Prairie Waif Combination in 1885–86, and he ultimately became the subject of several dime novels.[39]

Con Groner, billed in Wild West show publicity as "the Cow-Boy Sher-iff of the Platte," had been county sheriff in North Platte since the early 1870s. He was also a physically large man who was said to have apprehended Jesse James (although he had not).[40] In addition to Frank North, the impre-sarios also brought in cowboys from the ranches of western Nebraska, including Jim "Kid" Willoughby, Jim Mitchell, Tom Webb, and roughly two dozen others.

The show consisted of three categories of acts: races, "historical" scenes, and demonstrations of "real" or "natural" skill, that is, talent derived from workplace necessity, not for entertainment (like the circus). This last cate-gory including bronco riding, rope demonstrations, and shooting acts. After opening with a parade of Indians and cowboys, along with elk and buffalo, the action began. The first act was an Indian horse race, with as many as ten Indian competitors. It was followed by a reenactment of the Pony Express, "in which the riding and changing of saddle covers was done with startling rapidity," according to one reviewer. Next came the attack on the stage-coach, followed by a race between an Indian runner and an Indian horseman (with a turn at fifty yards, it was actually close). Together, these scenes sug-gested the speed of Indians—and the necessary speed of settlers in outracing them.

If any observers had anticipated another circus, by this point, they knew the Wild West show was different. In American culture, the presence of Indians had long implied the presence of history.[41] By featuring them in patently "historical" scenes with actual props from western history—the Pony Express *mochila*, or mail saddle, and the Deadwood coach—the show-men sent a message that this spectacle was neither an "ethnological con-gress"—a display of exotic primitives adjunct to a menagerie—nor a mere circus-style display of peculiar skills and speed.[42] In Cody and Carver's arena, foot- and horse races established the central ethos of the show as competition, and the overtly historical scenes—the Pony Express and the pursuit of the Deadwood stagecoach—emplotted the performance with American history, here depicted as a grand race, or a running battle, between Indians, whites, and Mexicans.

These initial racing and historical acts were followed by shooting demonstrations by Buffalo Bill, Doc Carver, and Adam Bogardus, a former market hunter from Illinois who had set many records for competitive pigeon shooting and who was also the developer of the clay pigeon. Seeking to persuade the audience that shooting competitions were more than frivo-lous or destructive, show publicity transformed guns from implements of destruction to regenerative and constructive tools of frontier development. After all, claimed the program, the bullet was "the pioneer of civilization," which "has gone hand in hand with the axe that cleared the forest, and with the family bible and the school book." Without the gun, warned the pro-gram, "we of America would not be to-day in the possession of a free and united country, and mighty in our strength."[43]

Beyond its relevance to martial exploits and the "clearing" of the fron-tier, the sharpshooting of Cody, Carver, and Bogardus was a feat of indus-trial might that inscribed guns as technological wonders and their operators as almost superhuman masters of machinery. Recounting Carver's first New York shooting exhibition, the program explained that during the 7 hours and 36 minutes in which he performed, "he raised to his shoulder 62,120 pounds, or 31⅛ tons in weight," and while working the lever of his rifle, "he moved 248,480 pounds with the middle finger of his right hand." Through-out, he "withstood from the recoil an aggregate weight of 298,176 pounds," or 149 tons.[44] The machinery of the gun thus empowered the marksman in unprecedented ways, energizing him to move prodigious amounts of matter and allowing him to innoculate the audience against the epidemic of ner-vous exhaustion which plagued American manhood.

Such feats of martial skill and technological mastery were followed by primitive scenes of the white race's skill at domesticating nature, the "Cow-boys Frolic," in which cowboys rode bucking broncos, and then roped, threw, and momentarily rode Texas steers. Later in the season, they added displays of "picking up." The penultimate scene, the "Buffalo Chase," in which cowboys drove buffalo toward the crowd before turning them back to their corral, reinforced the message of the second half of the show: that white male mastery of technology (guns) and of nature (horses, cattle, and buffalo) was self-perpetuating and total. The last act, a furious ride around the arena by the Pawnees, closed the show with a scene of wild nature and real Indians, as if to say that the challenges of conquering the frontier remained, even though Indians were now defeated. The show would go on, redomesticating the wild nature within it in every performance.[45]

Much as this New World historical pageant steered away from the Old World circus, Buffalo Bill's "thoroughbred Nebraska show" deployed a unifying symbolic device that was ancient and European: the centaur. To sit a horse "like a centaur" was a socially respectable aspiration in the nineteenth century, suggesting a command over animals and manly bearing in the saddle, and comparisons of riders to centaurs was a ubiquitous cliché. In the first season, show programs hailed Buck Taylor as "the Centaur Ranchman of the Plains."[46]

But the most famous centaur in the show was, of course, Buffalo Bill himself. He provided the central historical actor—the authentic American—for the show's display of history. Beyond his symbolic role, though, it was not clear what Cody would do in the arena. He soon carved out his performance space. When Doc Carver left the crowd restive one day by missing every one of his targets, Cody brought them to their feet by mounting his horse and galloping around the ring, blasting amber balls thrown into the air by an assistant.[47] On this day and ever after, he—like other sharpshooters in the show—used birdshot in his rifle, because bullets would have traveled beyond the arena and potentially inflicted damage or casualties. But even so, the feat displayed extraordinary marksmanship. The act was quickly installed as a regular attraction, with Cody labeled "America's Practical All-Round-Shot."

Even without a gun, Cody evoked a wondrous commentary with his riding. In the urban centers where the Wild West show found its most enthusiastic audiences, streets were jammed with horse-drawn vehicles, but few people rode horses, and most urban residents probably never learned to ride. By the 1880s, horseback riding was mostly an elite leisure pursuit, and the image of a single man on a horse evoked memories of a noble, rural past.[48]

Partly for this reason, and partly through his mastery of the gun, which infused him with martial power, the sight of Buffalo Bill on a horse left audiences breathless. Buffalo Bill "rides his horse as if he were a part of the animal," wrote an 1885 columnist, and in 1886, New York journalist Nym Crinkle called Cody "the complete restoration of the Centaur." Crinkle's imagery was so potent that in future years it was reprinted or plagiarized by

"The Complete Restoration of the Centaur." Buffalo Bill Cody on horseback, c. 1887. Viewed through a portable "stereoscope," images like these allowed families to view three-dimensional scenes of the Wild West show and savor Cody's centaurism in the comfort of their own living rooms. Courtesy Buffalo Bill Historical Center.

English publishers, American writers, and Wild West show press agents (who may, in fact, have originated the idea and given it to Crinkle).

> No one that I ever saw so adequately fulfils to the eye all the conditions of picturesque beauty, absolute grace and perfect identity with his animal. If an artist or riding master had wanted to mould a living ideal of romantic equestrianship, containing in outline and action, the mien of Harry of Navarre, the Americanism of Custer, the automatic majesty of the Indian and the untutored cussedness of the cowboy, he would have measured Buffalo Bill in the saddle.[49]

London journalists referred to the Wild West show as a gathering of "Transatlantic Centaurs," and even before Cody's arrival in London for the first time, *Punch* magazine hailed him as "the Coming Centaur."[50] The centaur reappeared in E. E. Cummings's 1917 tribute to Buffalo Bill on horseback, shattering

> *onetwothreefourfive pigeonsjustlike that*
>
>   *Jesus*
>
> *he was a handsome man.*[51]

As the mythical creature that marks the ultimate limit between culture and nature, the centaur was in many ways the perfect vehicle for an exposition of frontier life. In the words of one scholar, the centaur represents "the beast within man erupting," or "the division within man between unreasoning, homicidal monster and angel."[52] The creature's hybridity—the upper body of a man with the body of a stallion—highlighted its virility. Centaurs of myth were notoriously unreasonable, their masculine lusts and combative instincts overwhelming their human faculties. They were profoundly undomestic, even antidomestic, preferring open spaces and the forest to the constraints of home. They were creatures uncontained, and notoriously unhoused.[53]

Through inclusion in a spectacle of race war, the centaur symbol acquired additional layers of meaning. Indians, "savage centaurs," most approximated the horse-men of myth. The show's white centaurs, Cody and the cowboys, embodied reasoning attributes of masculinity combined with the stallion's virility and power. Their presence suggested the need for an infusion of natural power—horse power—into white men to ameliorate their loss of nerve force, declining virility, and other symptoms of overcivilization. Just as the Pony Expressman of earlier decades had come to symbolize the monstrous fusion of polyglot frontier and white manhood, Cody's centaur, and the ranks of centaurs in the Wild West show, represented not only the domination of the West's wild nature by Americans, but also the reinvigoration of the white race. Thus, the show's centaurism complemented the efforts of such organizations and developments as the Boy Scouts, the YMCA, the Boone and Crockett Club, collegiate athletics, and much of the broader conservation movement to instill in American manhood some approximation of natural vigor—what Theodore Roosevelt would call the "strenuous life"—to fend off the neurasthenic effects of modern business and the city.[54]

Cody's monstrous fusion of horse and man arrived in the East to announce the triumph of civilization and the regeneration of white men and the white race through frontier conflict and technological progress. Where Carver mastered the machine of the gun, Cody's shattering of amber balls from the air with a rifle as he raced around the arena on horseback naturalized the violent technology of the gun through his mastery of the horse. If the image of Buffalo Bill as Winchester-toting centaur heightened Cody's masculine image in particular—"Jesus he was a handsome man"—it did so in part by connecting that image to a progressive narrative of white Americans as people (Cody himself) who sprang from nature (the horse) to master technology (the repeating rifle). Throughout the performances, wilderness—animals and Indians—continually fell away before the advance of the American centaur, his settlements, and his technological prowess.

The story of technology and progress mediated by the ancient centaur energized one of the most durable of show scenes, the "Attack on the Deadwood Coach." The Indian pursuit of the coach, and its rescue by Buffalo Bill and his cowboys, proved as durable as the Pony Express reenactment, and arguably the most thrilling, "never equalled by an act in hippodrome or theater," in the words of an early reviewer.[55] In this scene, Indian centaurs pursued not just a stagecoach, but an Abbot and Downing Concord coach, a powerful icon of American artisanship.[56]

As early as 1874, a correspondent remarked that "in the far West" the stagecoach "may be called the advance-guard of civilization," but in most of the eastern states the railroad had already made it "a thing of the past."[57] Just as savagery vanished before the wheels of the stagecoach, so those wheels themselves gave way to machine-powered axles. East and West, anticipation of the coaches' final passage became widespread by the early 1880s, symbolic of the passing away of the frontier, of master craftsmanship before mechanization (the Concord coach was so meticulously handcrafted that only three thousand of them were ever made), and of horse-drawn conveyance by steam locomotive and electric trolley, the revolutionary technology which, by 1896, was carrying passengers in ninety-three towns where Buffalo Bill's Wild West appeared.[58]

Cody's show publicists claimed that the coach had begun its career in 1863, journeying from New Hampshire to California by ship, seeing service in California, Oregon, and Utah, before becoming the "original" Deadwood coach, plying the route between the railroad depot at Cheyenne, Wyoming, and the gold-mining town of Deadwood, in Dakota Territory, in 1876. On this final segment of its twenty-five-year odyssey, wrote the publicists, it passed through "Buffalo Gap, Lame Johnny Creek, Red Canyon, and Squaw Gap, all of which were made famous by scenes of slaughter and the deviltry of the banditti." Ultimately, it was "fitted up as a treasure coach," carrying gold bullion from the mines and enduring spectacular robbery attempts, including the notorious Cold Spring holdup and another in which Martha "Calamity Jane" Cannary drove it to safety. Allegedly, Buffalo Bill had ridden in this very stagecoach, with Yellow Hair's scalp and several others in hand, when he returned from his scouting duties in 1876. "When afterwards he learned that it had been attacked and abandoned and was lying neglected on the plains, he organized a party, and starting on the trail, rescued and brought the vehicle into camp."[59] Indians who attacked it in the arena were said to be "the near relations of the Indians" who attacked it on the Plains.[60]

Cody anticipated the consignment of all the West's stagecoaches to history (stagecoaches would not cease the Deadwood run until 1890), then collapsed them and the biographies of show principals all into one coach. In tracing the route of the Deadwood stage through dark places full of evil— Lame Johnny Creek, Squaw Gap—the scene evoked the mythic progress of

America through benighted savagery to civilization. At the same time, the symbol of the "vanishing" coach suggested that the era of frontier conquest itself was closing.

Of course, even beyond Cody's fictionalized biography, the fakery of show programs was considerable, and nowhere more so than in the story of this stagecoach. Cody had not ridden out to save the coach from abandonment, but rather had ordered the vehicle from Luke Voorhees, manager of the Cheyenne and Black Hills Stage line, specifically for the show.[61] He did not leave the Plains via this coach, or any other, the summer he killed Yellow Hair. Instead, he took a steamer to Bismarck and a train to Rochester.[62] This coach had no steel armor, was never a treasure coach, and had not been the target of the Cold Springs holdup.[63]

But through its convergence of historical events and mythic symbolism, the Deadwood stage became an object of near-spiritual veneration for the audience, a select few of whom passed through its doors during each performance. Stagecoach rides for audience members became a premier attraction of the Wild West show in every one of its future years. Pap Clothier's more amenable successors included countless journalists, local councilmen, and, in 1887, the Prince of Wales and other European nobles, aristocrats, and celebrities who lined up to ride in the vehicle at Earl's Court, London. In 1890, one of them, Lord Ronald Sutherland Gower, was astonished to come upon Buffalo Bill's Wild West show in Italy. "I made again the circuit of the ring in the Deadwood coach." Although he "had so often been inside" the vehicle at Earl's Court, he had not dreamed "that I should repeat the drive under the shadow of Vesuvius."[64]

By entering the coach, audience members became protagonists in the show's historical narrative, and heirs to its myth. In its confines, they reenacted America's passage through savage darkness and emerged victorious, like the Americans who had civilized the frontier. And as Americans watched European royals, urban elites, and elected leaders climb eagerly into the coach, they saw their history and a favorite show validated as high culture.

Thus, the Wild West show scene was simultaneously nostalgic, for a racial frontier that was passing, and forward-looking, with the wheels conveying the spectators-turned-passengers away from the primitive past and toward the technological future of wheels and guns that echoed from its driver's seat. It was both a symbol of progress, looking forward to the passenger trains and the mechanical future that awaited the audience, America, and the world, and an anachronism, a handcrafted marvel in an age of mass production, a historical artifact conveying the lived experience of the frontier for the amusement of the modern city.

DERIVING CULTURAL MESSAGES like these from show scenes helps explain why the Wild West show became such a powerful factory of images and mythology, but it also makes it too easy to overlook Cody's fundamental audacity, his reach for mythic trajectory in a show based substantially on circus entertainments, which remained far from respectable in middle-class parlors. The circus was "the devil's playhouse," wallowing in fraud, graft, and freaks who violated boundaries of all kinds. In their long quest for middle-class acceptance, circus impresarios often used biblical tropes to sell their attractions as moral education. One 1835 showman even staged "A Grand Moral Representation of the Deluge with Appropriate Sacred Music."[65] P. T. Barnum, the sage of Bridgeport whose avoidance of outright fraud earned him a reputation as a "moral" entertainer, made a systematic effort to equate his circus with biblical spectacle. He billed his hippopotamus as the "Behemoth of Holy Writ, spoken of by the Book of Job." His African warthog became "the Prodigal's swine," and his camel "the ship of the desert." Pastors and reverends trooped to his show for the free passes he distributed to the clergy. The efforts paid off. "The Greatest Show on Earth" was a rollicking success.[66]

By 1882, Cody had watched Barnum play his hand at the circus game for a decade. No doubt drawn by the comparative softness of press reviews, and by the large and heterogeneous audience, he followed the New Englander's example. Cody and his partners imitated Barnum's manner of loading trains. Like Barnum, Cody hired private detectives to patrol the grounds and travel with the show, running off known con men.[67]

But Cody went Barnum one better, creating a circus that was a distinctively American spectacle. Where clowns and elephants defined the circus, Cody had none. Where the circus was synonymous with the big top, Cody's Wild West show had an open arena. In later years, he commissioned canvas awnings for the grandstands, but the performance space remained uncovered. The ostensible rationale for the lack of a roof was that shooting acts would quickly destroy a tent. But the view of the sky over the arena also created a symbolic connection to the wide frontier of memory and to nature, which publicists cannily exploited. Rain or shine, Wild Westerners worked beneath an open sky.[68]

Cody's masterstroke was to avoid overt religious references in favor of a secular frontier myth with himself—or an artfully constructed version of himself—at the center. Barnum and other impresarios could grasp at the sacred. But overt religiosity was on the decline in the late nineteenth century, as religion permeated secular life and lost much of its power as a separate realm of authority.[69] Besides, even for the most devout Christians, the Bible was an Old World text, with no material connection to the New World (a matter which evinced no little spiritual anxiety in America). Even if audiences could have participated in it, the Pentateuch and the Gospels were not easily dramatized by clowns, high-wire walkers, and bearded ladies. For many, Barnum's piety smacked of a cynical ploy.

Cody's show forsook conventional religion for nondenominational faith in progress—" 'Buffalo Bill's Wild West' is not a show in the theatric sense of the term, but an exposition of the progress of civilization."[70] The effect was to give the circus a makeover so compelling and comprehensive as to make it unrecognizable.[71] In its glory years, Buffalo Bill's Wild West would generate gigantic poster art, including some of the largest show posters ever created. In 1898, one poster depicted the show's main acts, including the "Attack on the Settler's Cabin" and the "Charge up San Juan Hill." It consisted of 108 sheets of poster paper, running 9 feet high and 91 feet long. A few circus competitors produced even bigger advertisements, and Ringling Brothers commissioned a poster more than twice as large. But the Ringlings' depiction of separate attractions told no story. Impressive as it was, it looked like a big collection of smaller posters.[72]

The effect of the advertising was analogous to that of the entertainments. Cody's attractions included many that could be found in the circus: Indians and cowboys and Texas steers were featured in Barnum's "Congress of Monarchs" as early as 1874. Not long after 1894, a sideshow of circus freaks was attached to the Wild West show. But in popular memory, even the most discordant Wild West acts could be subsumed into, or obscured by, the narrative arc of progress and frontier development. In contrast, the circuses of Ringling Brothers, Barnum and Bailey, and others remained a pastiche of the weird and the fabulous.

Presenting a national origin myth (one that conveniently elided the origins of slavery and the Civil War of recent memory) and allowing the audience limited participation in it, the Wild West show succeeded in convincing many that it was not a circus at all. Commentators and promoters intuitively grasped the distinctions. "There is as wide a gulf between the 'Wild West' and the Circus as there is between a historic poem and the advertisement of quack medicine," wrote Steele Mackaye.[73] The distinction made sense to the public. " 'Isn't this better than the circus, now?' was the delighted expression heard on every hand," recounted an 1885 reviewer. So with the critics, who raved. They extolled. They waxed. But their very reluctance to describe the vivid presentation of frontier mythology as a circus in fact proved how successful Cody was at naturalizing the circus on American soil, turning it from a European import to a domestic entertainment.[74]

From its opening night in Omaha, Cody and Carver's Wild West moved on to Council Bluffs, Iowa; Springfield, Massachusetts; then on to Boston; Newport, Rhode Island; and Brighton Beach, New York, before closing out the season at Chicago. Throughout, the success of Cody's new concoction of frontier, circus, and artful deception could be seen in reviewers' frequent comparison to the greatest showman of all. "The papers say I am the coming Barnum," wrote Cody to his sister.[75] The *Hartford Courant* went further, proclaiming that Buffalo Bill had, "in this exhibition, out-Barnumed Barnum."[76]

And yet, for all its successes, the Wild West show was a volatile combination of personalities and performance whose future was by no means secure. Carver, the self-styled "Evil Spirit of the Plains," could be a fine marksman, but he was a third-rate performer. His shooting was uneven, his temper bad. After missing a series of targets one afternoon, he broke his rifle across his horse's ears and struck an assistant.[77] Such open demonstrations of violence and cruelty were never going to be acceptable in any public entertainment, let alone the family attraction that Cody was trying to build.

On top of the threat of violence, Cody, Carver, and their cowboys drank hard all summer. Many performed badly or missed shows altogether. Later accounts claimed that an entire car of the show train was reserved for liquor. "It was an eternal gamble, as to whether the show would exist from one day to the next, not because of a lack of money but simply through the absence of human endurance necessary to stay awake twenty hours out of twenty-four, that the birth of a new amusement enterprise might be properly celebrated."[78]

What accounts for the management failures of Cody, a stage veteran who over the course of a decade in show business had mastered theatrical presentation and the demands of running his own stage company? Although he admitted to heavy drinking at times, he could be tediously pious on the subject of alcohol and performance. "In this business a man must be perfectly reliable and sober," he lectured a wayward associate in 1879.[79] Why did he fail to follow his own advice at the outset of his new venture?

Partly, his missteps in the summer of 1883 reflected his limitations as a manager. He always had been more performer than manager, but the distinction between these talents became more visible as the size of his cast grew. Where he had directed and organized groups of up to two dozen stage players in the 1870s, now he was responsible for dozens of people, props, animals, and all of their transportation arrangements.

In facing this daunting task, he cannot have been helped by the prospective unraveling of his family. In 1882, he filed suit against a cousin for appropriating and selling a Cody family property that had belonged to his grandfather, the father of Isaac Cody. Since the parcel was in downtown Cleveland, it was worth a great deal of money, and for a time Cody and his sisters anticipated a windfall of fifteen million dollars. They endured legal setbacks throughout 1883, finally losing the case—and all the money William Cody had invested in it—in 1884.[80]

As his new show wobbled and his lawsuit waned, William Cody's marriage spiraled downward. Louisa Cody resented his show career almost from the beginning. According to William Cody's later testimony, she objected to actresses and the mores of the stage. He claimed that she witnessed him kissing his troupe's actresses goodbye at the end of a season, and her subsequent jealousy throughout his stage career kept him "very much riled up . . . In fact it was a kind of a cat and dog's life all along the whole trail."[81]

The marital tensions, and the death of little Kit Carson Cody in 1876, may have contributed to her decision, in 1878, to move back to North Platte, away from his stage circuits, which took him through Rochester. He gave her $3,500 to move there, and sent money to support her thereafter.[82] In 1882, as he prepared for his new show of western pioneering, he also publicly reinscribed the show's myth of advancing civilization back into his own life. Out in Nebraska, he built up his North Platte ranch, "Scout's Rest," for public admiration as much as private enjoyment. He expanded his holdings to four thousand acres. The estate supported hundreds of cattle and horses, and an elegant Victorian home, with irrigation ditches, tree plantings, and alfalfa fields. The Cody home in town had been a local tourist attraction before. Now, at the newly expanded holding by the tracks of the Union Pacific railroad, Cody ordered "SCOUT'S REST" painted across the roof of his barn in letters large enough that railroad passengers could read it and recognize the home of the famous Buffalo Bill. The beautiful house and verdant fields proved his powers as domesticator of the savage frontier.[83] People who sat in his show audience might find themselves on the train, there witnessing the "real-life" frontier progress of the scout-turned-rancher-and-family-man as they crossed the Nebraska prairie.

In truth, Scout's Rest was less evidence of Cody's home life than it was artful deception. Louisa refused to live there, preferring the family home in the center of town. Even though another daughter, Irma, was born to the couple early in 1883, their mutual suspicions increased. Cody raised money for his new show and his ranch by mortgaging properties, and he was furious when Louisa refused to sign mortgage papers for the home in North Platte. He demanded the money he had sent her, and was astonished to learn she had invested in other properties, which she put in her own name. "Well, I have got out my petition for a divorce with that woman," he told his sister Julia in September of 1883, in the middle of his first Wild West show tour. "She has tried to ruin me financially this summer," he went on. "I could tell you lots of funny things how she has tried to put up the horse ranch and buy more property & get the deeds in her name."[84]

The divorce was halted by tragedy. In October, daughter Orra suddenly died. Cody left the show and accompanied Louisa, Arta, and Irma to Rochester, where they buried Orra next to her brother, Kit. "If it was not for the hope of heaven and again meeting there," wrote Louisa, "my affliction would be more than I could bear."[85] Her husband dropped his suit for divorce.

Meanwhile, between the imminent violence, the extravagant debauchery, and the seething jealousy of its principals, the Wild West show threatened to come apart. The combativeness of its stars could only weaken an entertainment based so heavily on a presentation of men from the "half-civilized" West. Popular culture had a long tradition of venerating noble savages, and in this respect there was a script for presenting Indians in ways that could appeal to audiences. But by no means were cowboys universally regarded as heroic. With wide newspaper coverage of fights between farmers and cattle ranches in Kansas, and fierce range wars across much of the Far West, the public knew "cow-boys" as rough men who seldom distinguished between herding and rustling.

Such characteristics, it seemed, were only fitting for a group that drew its members from so many races. Most cowboy gear and methods originated among Mexican herders, and what became known as "cowboy culture" emerged from a vigorous interracial exchange of droving skills, terminology, and equipment on the southern Plains. The post–Civil War cattle industry employed many black, Mexican, Mexican American, and mixed-race cowboys alongside the white and tenuously white, particularly the Irish. In 1874, Joseph McCoy, the founder of Abilene, published the first history of the cattle trade, in which he denounced cowboys for their "shiftlessness" and "lack of energy." He held Mexican cowboys to be cruel, mean, and murderous. But even white cowboys were prime examples of frontier degeneracy, plagued by laziness and an unwillingness to leave the open spaces or even feed themselves properly (McCoy thought the absence of vegetables from their diet problematic). "No wonder the cowboy gets sallow and unhealthy, and deteriorates in manhood until often he becomes capable of any contemptible thing; no wonder he should become half civilized only, and take to whiskey with a love excelled scarcely by the barbarous Indian." Prone to "crazy freaks, and freaks more villainous than crazy," these "semi-civilized" brutes rendered it "not safe to be on the streets, or for that matter within a house, for the drunk cowboy would as soon shoot into a house as at anything else."[86]

Not surprisingly, the term "cow-boy" was often one of reproach, signifying someone who belonged to a lawless, itinerant, working class that, with its sensual appetites, obvious villainy, and continual threats of violence against civil order and the settler's home, too much resembled the laboring mobs of the East. In 1883, as if anticipating the great railroad strike that would grip Texas and much of the Southwest a few years later, cowboys in West Texas went on strike in the hopes of securing wages of $50 per month. This and similar efforts later in the decade all failed. But to the managerial classes, the cowboys' very act of striking seemed to justify the darker warnings about them.[87]

The Wild West show made cowboys into symbols of whiteness only through a balancing act, combating their border image on the one hand and portraying them as aggressively physical and autonomous on the other. Programs distinguished Wild West show cowboys, "genuine cattle-herders of the reputable trade" from "the cow-boys' greatest foe, the thieving criminal 'rustler.' " At the same time, publicity separated "American cowboys" from "Mexican and mixed race" vaqueros—and left black cowboys out of the picture entirely. Earlier cowboy performers had begun the process of whitening to better market themselves as middle-class attractions, and Wild West show publicists made use of these efforts, notably in an 1877 article by Cody's erstwhile stage partner, Texas Jack Omohundro. The educated scion of a wealthy Virginia planter, Omohundro had been a Texas cowboy in the 1860s, and later a scout with Cody at Fort McPherson. As he broke away from Cody's stage combination in the mid-1870s, he shored up his public persona by burnishing the cowboy image in a series of articles he penned for the periodical *Spirit of the Times*.

Omohundro died in 1880, but with a show full of cowboys to promote, Cody's publicist, John Burke, republished Omohundro's cowboy defense in his Wild West show programs. There audiences could read the lament of Cody's deceased friend about how "sneeringly referred to" and "little understood" cowboys were. Omohundro claimed that cowboys were "recruited largely from Eastern young men," including "many 'to the manner born.' " Thus the mongrel, violent, degenerate range riders of many accounts became, in Omohundro's hands, adventurous, entrepreneurial, white youths who succeeded through patience, persistence, and expert horsemanship. Cowboy experience cultivated the "noblest qualities" of the "plainsman and the scout. What a school it has been for the latter!" As white men infused with rugged nature, these protoscouts were on the way to being like Buffalo Bill himself. And like him, they would soon disappear before "modern improvements" encroaching upon the "ranch itself and the cattle trade" that employed them.[88] They were the embodiment of American manhood: cultured, vigorous, natural—and vanishing.

But for all Omohundro's attempts to elevate the social stature of cowboys, their image as frontier degenerates endured. In 1883, the American public was fully saturated with the recent, real-life bloodshed of western range wars. The Tombstone troubles launched that southwestern town's "cowboy faction" and their opponents, the Earp brothers, to national notoriety, and New Mexico's Lincoln County War saw the declaration of martial law in southern New Mexico in 1878, and the rise, demise, and apotheosis of William "Billy the Kid" Bonney by 1881.[89] The Wild West show would have to improve the cowboy's public image if it was to draw respectable audiences. Unless the chaotic energies of the Wild West cast were contained and directed, the show's short, disastrous career would become a spectacle of frontier savagery triumphant, in which drinking and carousing (followed by bankruptcy) would make it a monument only to the failures of America's most famous living frontiersman.

HOMEWARD BOUND: SALSBURY, OAKLEY, AND THE RESPECTABLE WILD WEST

Unable to resolve his many differences with his new partner, Cody was barely breaking even by the end of the summer.[90] The show's tempestuous, overly masculine cast attracted a crowd that resembled it. In late October 1883, the *Chicago Tribune* reported that five thousand people turned out to see the Wild West show, and dropped hints aplenty that the audience was not quite respectable. Although all entertainers hoped to attract as big an audience as possible, "decent" people were likely to avoid a crowd that was racially mixed. And so it was at Buffalo Bill's show, where "the crowd was a mixed one, and the newsboys and bootblacks formed a large and important element of it." In the Wild West camp, "ferocious-looking prairie-terrors" lassoed "the ubiquitous gamin."[91] The reviewer, in fact, seemed as preoccupied with the show's youthful, impoverished enthusiasts as with the entertainers.

> They had seen the parade of the buckskin-clad heroes and painted savages, and their thoughts turned toward the interior of the yellow-covered novels and five-cent libraries through which they had waded in company with daring scouts. Their energy in selling papers and giving shines was redoubled, and one would have thought to see them all over the track that there was not a gamin in the city.[92]

The reference to dime novels was a coded warning, much like the hidden clues to the disreputable crowd at Cody's theatrical performances. Newspapers and other organs of culture regularly condemned dime novels as lurid, violent inducements to crime. In the same column as the above review, the *Chicago Tribune* reported on two teenage thugs who beat and robbed two men on a streetcar, under the headline "The Dime Novel. Two of Its Heroes on Trial for Highway Robbery."[93] The reviewer's description of a destitute army of youthful crime enthusiasts swarming to a show of prairie bad men can hardly have been reassuring for prospective middle-class customers.

Nate Salsbury saw the show in Chicago and predicted it would fail. Within days, Cody gave him the opportunity to prevent it. According to Salsbury, "Cody came to see me, and said that if I did not take hold of the show he was going to quit the whole thing. He said he was through with Carver, and that he would not go through such another summer for a hundred thousand dollars."[94]

In Salsbury, Cody sought out one of the most experienced and successful theatrical managers in the country. Born in 1845, Nathan Salsbury was an orphan by the time he was fifteen, when he joined the Union army. He fought at Chickamauga and Nashville, among other battles, and was eventually taken prisoner. After the war, he entered the stage, playing with various minstrel companies before forming his own Salsbury's Troubadors in 1874.

Beginning with this small-scale variety show of songs, dances, and comedy routines, Salsbury became a primary developer of what became known as musical comedy. Where variety performers presented unrelated routines of singing, dancing, and comedy on the same stage, Salsbury placed them together in a unified narrative, a simple play about a picnic, entitled *The Brook*. In the course of an afternoon outing, a cast of characters ventured out on a picnic, where each character performed her or his routines, then returned home again. As one theater historian has observed, this was "hardly an earth-shaking plot," but it nonetheless "revealed the possibility of stringing an entire evening of variety upon a thread of narrative continuity instead of presenting heterogenous acts."[95] It was extremely popular. For twelve years, Salsbury's Troubadors toured the United States, Australia, and Great Britain, to considerable fame and a not inconsequential fortune. They earned something approaching middle-class respectability. The same newspaper that warned readers about the Wild West show also condemned the clumsy play that Salsbury's Troubadors performed in Chicago (*My Chum*, by Fred Ward), but the reviewer's complaint was that the drama was beneath the talents of these "genial people" whose successes with *The Brook* and other comedies had fulfilled their mission of "amusing the public."[96]

Many modern readers, understandably ignorant of how Cody was inspired by his experiences on the Plains, have accepted Nate Salsbury's self-aggrandizing claim to have created all of the major attractions of the Wild West show. Salsbury's overstatement is so crude it barely requires refuting. Most of the show's enduring scenes, including the "Pony Express" and "Deadwood Stagecoach Attack," appeared in the first season, as did various versions of the Buffalo Hunt. So, too, did demonstrations of cowboy skill, and Cody's own display of horseback shooting, not to mention the exhibition of Indian dances and combat between Indians and cowboys: all were part of the 1883 season, before Salsbury joined. Cody had been developing an entertainment based on Indians and real frontiersmen—especially himself—for over a decade. Before Salsbury came along, most of the elements for a successful show were on hand.

Still, Salsbury's contribution was significant. His earlier success flowed from his ability to make narrative drama from distinct entertainments. In his hands, skits of dancing, singing, and juggling became related "acts" of a larger story, such as *The Brook*. In contrast, Cody's experience was in melodrama, a genre which came with one-size-fits-all narrative about restoration of the true woman to home and domestic bliss. His new arena presentation being in part an effort to escape the constraints of melodrama for frontier history, but it left him flailing for a new narrative structure. The Wild West was already exciting and dramatic, but its lack of clear direction was apparent in its narrative confusion, notably the absence of a suitable ending. As spectacular as the buffalo hunt was, it failed to resolve the combative drama of the earlier white-versus-Indian scenes, and therefore proved anticlimactic. Cody's efforts to rectify the situation resulted in some bloody spectacles indeed. Perhaps in an artistic expression of what it felt like to run the Wild West show during its first season, the final act of the Chicago show program for 1883 was "a grand realistic battle scene depicting the capture, torture, and death of a Scout by the savages." This was followed by a vengeful conclusion, which veered close to the degenerative Indian hating Cody had scrupulously avoided: "The revenge, recapture of the dead body, and victory of the Cowboys and Government Scouts."[97]

Cody and Carver had an acrimonious falling-out at the end of the 1883 season, and in 1885 Cody finally won a subsequent lawsuit over who was entitled to use the name "Wild West." Meanwhile, Salsbury had joined the Wild West show, catching up with the encampment in the spring of 1884 at St. Louis. He later recalled that he found Cody leaning against a fence in plug hat, "boiling drunk," surrounded by "a lot of harpies called 'Old Timers' who were getting as drunk as he at his expense." According to Salsbury, Cody's spree "lasted for about four weeks," when he became so ill "he was knocked out and had to go to bed."[98]

Salsbury's first demand was sobriety. Cody agreed. "I solemnly promise you that after this you will never see me under the influence of liquor. . . . [T]his drinking surely ends today and your pard will be himself. [A]nd be on deck all the time." The partners demanded temperance among their employees, too, and devoted much of their publicity to the "orderliness" and sobriety of the camp.[99] Although he occasionally strayed, in future years Cody generally was sober during the show season.[100]

Salsbury next applied his sharp sense of drama to Cody's alluring but incoherent assemblage. Although it is not clear when the Cowboy Band came on board, Salsbury's career had been in musical theater, and it seems likely he exerted his influence in this respect. By 1885 the show had an orchestra consisting of several dozen professional musicians dressed as cowboys. Like the bands that accompanied circuses, the Cowboy Band provided musical pacing for show acts. Beginning each show with "The Star-Spangled Banner" as an overture (although the song would not become the national anthem until 1931), their music set the mood during each act and then provided bridges between them.[101]

Salsbury's arrival also coincided with the addition of one new "tableau," which would play a major role in the show's success. Beginning in 1884, and continuing almost every year through 1907, the climactic scene of Cody's show was the spectacle of a house in which a white family, sometimes a white woman and children, took refuge from mounted Indians who rode down on the building. The attackers were in turn driven off by the heroic Buffalo Bill and a cowboy entourage.[102]

The "Attack on the Settler's Cabin" tapped into a set of profound cultural anxieties. For nineteenth-century audiences a home, particularly a rural "settler's" home, was imbued with much symbolic meaning.[103] The home itself presupposed the presence of a woman, particularly a wife. The home conveyed notions of womanhood, domesticity, and family. When the Indians rode down on the settler's cabin at the end of the Wild West show, they were attacking more than a building with some white people in it. To many in the audience, the piece conveyed an attack on whiteness, on family, and on domesticity itself. With its new ending, the Wild West show adapted the melodramatic rescue of the home for arena performance, allowing the cowboys and their leader, the scout (a famous melodrama star, after all) to rescue the nation's domestic unity from the threat of Indian captivity, and thereby bring the furious mobility of the show—the constant racing of its races—to a rest.

Middle-class people distinguished themselves from other classes partly by their emphasis on private, quiet home life, on what the historian Mary Ryan has called "entrenched domesticity."[104] By putting home salvation and family defense at the center of the show's climax, Cody and Salsbury made their performance resonate with widespread middle-class concerns, and began the work of coaxing middle-class urbanites away from their homes long enough to see the show.

The guiding hand of Salsbury thus steadied the show combination in the 1884–85 season. Salsbury continued to appear with his Troubadors, leaving Cody to manage the show from day to day, until he and Cody could be certain the new venture would succeed. After opening in New York to great fanfare late in the summer of 1884, the Wild West show floated on steam-

ATTACK ON THE BURNING CABIN.   GRAND FINALE OF "THE WILD WEST."

"Attack on the Settler's Cabin." The finale of the Wild West show for most of its years, a symbol of white family defense against threats to domestic order and femininity. Buffalo Bill's Wild West 1885 Program, author's collection.

boat down the Mississippi, playing small towns along the way. The venues were hardly suitable for so large and expensive a show, and the audiences could not cover expenses. Calamity struck when the show's boat collided with another craft. The cast and crew escaped unhurt, and they saved the Deadwood stage and the bandwagon. But the rest of the equipment was lost, along with most of the animals. In Denver, Nate Salsbury was about to appear onstage to sing a comic opera when he received a telegram: OUTFIT AT THE BOTTOM OF THE RIVER WHAT SHALL I DO. CODY. Salsbury replied: GO TO NEW ORLEANS AND OPEN ON YOUR DATE. HAVE WIRED YOU FUNDS. SALSBURY.[105]

It is testament to Cody's abilities as manager that he was able to do so. Within two weeks, he had bought new livestock, including buffalo, and was showing in New Orleans. Indeed, he saw the show through its worst-ever season: forty-four days of straight rain. "The camel's back is broken," he wailed. "We would surely have played to $2000 had it not been so ordaned [*sic*] that we should not," he told Salsbury. "I am thoroughly discouraged. I am a damn condemned Joner,"—and, like Jonah, a curse to his partner— "and the sooner you get clear of me the better."[106] But managing to retain twenty-five Indians, eight cowboys, and seven Mexicans, he saw the show through the New Orleans season.[107]

Bolstered by Cody's die-hard persistence, he and Salsbury continued their effort to balance the Wild West's centaurism with domestic themes. That year, Salsbury honored a request for an audition by a lissome, diminutive woman. In no small measure, her addition to the Wild West show would contain its heaving masculinity and establish it as an enduring success. Her name was Annie Oakley.

Born Phoebe Ann Moses in Darke County, Ohio, in 1860, she was the fifth child of a twice-widowed mother. She was also a natural with guns who excelled at the common childhood practice of hunting for the family table. Indeed, the girl produced extra meat for sale to hotelkeepers. When she was fifteen, during a visit to a sister in Cincinnati, one of her customers arranged a shooting match with a traveling trick shooter named Frank Butler. The event left Butler beaten—and smitten. He and the four-foot-eleven-inch huntress married a year later. Having abandoned the surname of Moses, which she had never liked, she took the stage name Oakley. Butler became her manager, and they were practically inseparable until their deaths within three weeks of each other in 1926.[108]

In the era of the artful deception, many shooting acts were stage trickery, with candles snuffed out, matches lit, and apples split by hidden devices rather than closely aimed bullets. In this sense, all shooting acts walked a line between trickery and authentic skill, and audiences wondered at them just as at magic shows and card tricks.[109]

In contrast, Oakley's shooting was genuine, and remarkable. In April 1884, at Tiffin, Ohio, she wielded a .22-caliber rifle against 1,000 glass balls thrown in the air—and broke 943 of them. In February 1885, she loaded her own shotguns in a nine-hour marksmanship marathon that saw her shatter 4,772 glass balls, out of 5,000 thrown. Three years later, at Gloucester, New Jersey, she took a $5,000 bet that she could not shoot 40 of 50 pigeons released from 30 yards away. She downed 49.[110]

Although she took much satisfaction in her new life in public entertainment, her performance venues usually failed to please her. Shooting acts were often staged in theaters, where they served as filler, appearing between the farce and the main feature, for example. But the 1870s, the very moment when Oakley began appearing on stages, witnessed a kind of sexual insurrection with the advent of burlesque. Although later audiences would equate burlesque with strip shows, the earlier form of burlesque was distinctive for its all-female companies (indeed, the most famous burlesque companies were owned by women). Burlesque troupes normally staged parodies, and their stars played roles formerly reserved for men, often addressing the audience with witty political puns and risqué dialogue. All of these innovations shocked conventional morality.[111] By 1875, burlesque performance and shooting acts alike were moving to variety and vaudeville theaters, where a series of separate routines—a boys' choir, snake charming, a juggler, a one-act comedy, a shooting demonstration, a magic show—followed one upon the other. Many of these theaters played to working-class male audiences, especially immigrants. They sold alcohol on the premises, and shows were even more risqué than the original burlesque.

Oakley had a profound aversion to burlesque, lowbrow variety theaters, and their "blue" shows. With Butler, she sought out vaudeville theaters that courted "respectable" women for their audiences with "ladies' nights" and free sewing kits, dresses, or other "domestic" prizes, and with "clean" shows—no liquor on the premises, no dirty jokes, and a reticence about bare flesh on the stage.[112] Vaudeville impresario Tony Pastor was one of the first to attempt this strategy. Oakley preferred his theaters over most others, but her opportunities there were limited. In 1884, when she and Butler went to see Cody's show in New Orleans, her act was a feature of the Sells Brothers Circus, an amusement about which she was less than enthusiastic.[113]

In the beginning, Annie Oakley was drawn to the Wild West show for many of the same reasons that other Americans bought tickets to see it: it was wholesome entertainment. Unlike the circus, the Wild West show featured a romantic frontier hero as its star attraction, and for all its dubious male swagger, it was missing much of the liminal sexual content of circuses, burlesque, and other traveling amusements. Salsbury's reputation for "clean" shows, and the progressive narrative and open-air setting of the performances, reinforced these characteristics. By 1884, the show was already advertising itself as "America's National Entertainment," and billing its attractions as educational and suitable for children.[114] The "Attack on the Settler's Cabin," after all, carried a clear message that Buffalo Bill stood for family preservation, making the Wild West show an outpost of family entertainment in a wilderness of decadent urban amusements.

It was in early 1885, during the awful New Orleans stint, that Salsbury watched Oakley run through her routine. Adam Bogardus—sick, soaked, and depressed—had just quit the show. In discussions with Cody, Salsbury recommended trying Oakley as a replacement for Bogardus, for three days at Nashville. Her ascent to a stardom that rivaled Cody's began when, at the end of her trial period, Salsbury and Cody hired her and then ordered $7,000 worth of poster, billboard, and herald art touting her act.[115]

Buffalo Bill's Wild West show rarely advertised individuals, and the heavy commitment to publicizing Oakley's presence suggests that the owners understood she was more than a novelty. For an entertainment chockfull of shooting acts, the twenty-five-year-old woman provided gallons of symbolic glue that both contained the show's violence and bonded its gunplay to family. Buffalo Bill's gun-toting centaur combined with Adam Bogardus's stalwart blasting of clay pigeons were impressive, but even with show programs touting "The Rifle as an Aid to Civilization," men with guns were borderline figures. Shooting, after all, was destructive, not productive. Gunmen suggested war, and in a show that staged race war as amusement, the predominance of shooting stars pushed the envelope of acceptable chaos to its limit.

As we have seen, marksmanship implied industrial efficiency and technological reinvigoration, but it had wider resonances, too. Crowds were drawn to shooting acts by the almost magnetic tension between the explosive destruction of the gun and the controlling hand of the shooter. In eschewing waste—of bullets, or energy—the symbol of the marksman resonated with the rhetoric of capitalism and civilization. Corporate moguls of the late nineteenth century trumpeted new efficiencies as they consolidated and monopolized whole industries in the 1880s and '90s. The ability of American settlers to support more people on less land was a primary rationale for the conquest of the West which the show depicted. Mastery of guns suggested the precise deliverance of death; it implied flawless justice, and the ultimate harnessing of nature to human ends.

But it also had obvious, though unspoken, sexual connotations. Indeed, marksmanship was a coded display for an entire ideology of sex and race. Victorians understood men and women as fundamentally sexual beings. To many, the success of individuals and nations was contingent on the control of male sexuality. Some saw semen, the "male essence," as the source of manly ambition and energy. Too-liberal dispersion of it led to the loss of both. Others were convinced that each organ had only so much "nerve energy," and that overutilizing one organ drained all the others. Wholesome marital sex made men temporarily limp. Illicit, excessive sex made them perpetually languid, indolent, and passive—neurasthenic. Men who restrained their lust, on the other hand, were more likely to be physically and mentally "hardened," primed to exploit opportunity where it opened.[116] White men triumphed over dark men, and American civilization advanced at the expense of savagery, precisely because of the alleged superiority of white men at controlling their sexuality.

Of course, the perceived threat of overcivilization had led to refinements in this thinking. Some, notably the psychologist G. Stanley Hall, had suggested less emphasis on the restraint of male passion and more on the channeling of it, the better to avoid nervous exhaustion.

But whether one believed in old-fashioned restraint of male passions or the newer gospel of channeling them, the marksman was a near-perfect symbol, his ability to control the direction and delivery of his bullets a metaphor for his ability to contain and channel his desires. The death-dealing machine of the gun was symbolic of life-planting male organs, its lethal bullets an inversion of the "male essence" that planted the seeds of life. The sharpshooter stood for sexual restraint, the conscious redirection of masculine energy, individual success, and national power.

The allure of this symbolism was heightened by its relevance to the increasing racial and class violence of American cities after the Civil War. In the pervasive labor upheaval of the 1870s and '80s, working-class men and many immigrants from Ireland, Italy, Poland, and elsewhere rebelled against frequent, industry-wide wage reductions. In the subsequent violence, strikers wielded clubs, rocks, torches, and sometimes guns. In 1877, beginning with railroad workers in Maryland and West Virginia, what came to be known as the Great Strike burned along the railroad lines to Chicago, Kansas City, and other cities. A crowd of 20,000 demonstrated in Chicago. The railroad station in Pittsburgh burned to the ground. Dozens died in confrontations between strikers, police, militia, and federal troops.[117]

In response, terrified authorities and legislatures created new institutions to restrain "savage" labor, including urban armories and, in 1877, they reformed National Guard units. National Guardsmen were successors to the old militias, which in a few notorious cases had been composed of workingmen reluctant to fire on strikers. The new National Guard formalized command hierarchies and provided greater militarization. Above all, it promised to put guns in the hands of men who would use them against rebellious workers. Businessmen created volunteer guard units during the strike. Afterward, they helped support the National Guard with voluntary donations, and filled its ranks enthusiastically.[118]

Thus, proficiency with firearms came to be seen as practical, even vital for the defense of middle-class interests in the 1880s and '90s. The National Guard, its business supporters, and the nascent National Rifle Association (formed in 1871) opened dozens of shooting ranges for National Guard regiments. They also sponsored regional and national shooting competitions to encourage "the steady advance in marksmanship" of this new institution, "on whom we largely depend in the last resort for the preservation of public order."[119]

While the marksman embodied an answer to deep-set anxieties about the need to strengthen masculinity and class power among white men, he also contained a message about restricting access to guns. For, without exception, the shooters in Buffalo Bill's Wild West show, as in the many other shooting acts of the Gilded Age, were white. Just as the destructiveness of the gun was restrained by the marksman who kept his bullets within a minimal "spread" on the target, his performance implied that the gun's power would not undo him, that he could contain it, and keep it from spreading into the hands of racial others.

In this way, as in many others, the Wild West show rewrote western history to correspond with the mythic needs of its middle-class, white audience. Outside the show arena, throughout American history, hands of all colors had gripped the shooting iron. Although bullets and firearms were expensive

on the Plains, Cheyenne and Sioux snipers targeted American officers to terrible effect. In 1868, the first moments of the battle of Beecher's Island in
Nebraska saw the surgeon mortally shot, the commanding general severely
wounded, and his subordinate officer, Lieutenant Beecher, killed (and his
name given to the battle).[120]

Of course, there were Mexican and African American marksmen, too,
but significantly, no Indian, Mexican, or other nonwhite sharpshooters
emerged in the genre of performance shooting after the Civil War. Hostility
to minority displays of gun prowess complemented a gathering political
movement to keep guns from minority hands. At the dawn of the twentieth
century, African Americans saw their gun-toting privileges curtailed in the
South, and gun-ownership rights of noncitizen immigrants vanished altogether in Pennsylvania and New York. In the West, once the Indian wars
ceased, state legislators increasingly demanded that Indians be banned from
hunting or carrying firearms off the reservation.[121]

In contrast to its reflection of gun rights as a white privilege, or talent,
the show's horse and footraces soon became multiracial. In 1884, the first act
of the show, after the "Grand Entree," was a "Grand Quarter Mile Race,
among four Mexicans, four Cowboys, and four Indians."[122] Interracial races
kicked off the show's action in most years thereafter, introducing the show's
drama as a display of American history told in social Darwinist terms, or a
"race of races." This contest was not fixed. Any racer—of any race—might
triumph. White victory could be construed as proof of white superiority. An
Indian or Mexican winner suggested that racial competition was ongoing
and potentially tragic for a white race that allowed itself to flag. Against the
possibility that white failure in the opening races might signify a larger
racial degeneration, the show retained its comic ending partly by rendering
the power of the gun a uniquely white province.[123]

After Salsbury came on board, he and Cody adapted the all-white shooting display to make it still more acceptable. Having banished Doc Carver's
"Evil Spirit," they enhanced the family context for the show's most famous
shooter, Adam Bogardus, by placing him in performance with his four
sons.[124] Featuring white families in shooting acts was a standard way of making destructive gunplay appeal to family audiences, embedding it in a regenerative context of kin. Show publicists referred to the Bogardus "shooting
quintette," suggesting a performance similar to the popular family singing
acts of the period.[125] But it also communicated the essence of controlled,
directed masculine desire common to all shooting acts: the faithful marksman who was a faithful and potent husband, producing four strapping
marksman sons. With the Bogardus family, shooting became a demonstration of filial piety and inherited—therefore racial—virtue.

But Bogardus had just quit the show, and now Oakley's image as a virtuous white girl, or a girl-bride, provided a regenerative female context for the show's exhibition of lethal weapons, her femininity a stunningly ironic paradox for a display of gun proficiency. The symbolic meanings of the act reinforced the larger ideology of middle-class domesticity and restraint. Superficially, her performance was simple, spectacular marksmanship. But it was her inspired imposture as a middle-class farm girl and housewife that made her shooting skill so entrancing.

Indeed, her embodiment of a feminine domestic ideal suggests her acting skills were every bit as remarkable as her shooting. The Moses family had been hardscrabble farmers in rural Ohio. Annie Moses was six when her father died, nine when her stepfather passed away. Her mother, unable or unwilling to care for her children, dispersed them. Brothers and sisters went to neighbors. Annie spent a year in the county home, then another two years with a cruel farm family. "The man was a brute," she later recalled, "and his wife a virago."[126]

She returned home only by running away, to discover her mother remarried to one Joseph Shaw. He was kind enough to take her in but he, too,

By 1902, Annie Oakley's sixteen years with the Wild West show had come to an end. Her hair dyed, she was still youthful, even virginal, an icon of middle-class femininity. Courtesy Buffalo Bill Historical Center.

soon died. This time, Annie kept her place at home by making enough cash to be invaluable, as the proficient market hunter she had become. Within four years, she figuratively left the house forever as Frank Butler's wife. Only then did she learn to read.

In her publicity, Oakley made much of her devotion to her mother and siblings. "I know this much," she told a London interviewer in 1887, "if I had my mother living with me here I should be in no hurry to get back to the States."[127]

But in more private ways, she could not get far enough away from her origins. It is said that she took the name Oakley because children at the county home taunted her with a singsong refrain, "Moses poses." This could be true. But her eagerness to seize a new identity, and her thoroughness in burying the old, suggest a deep anger. Annie Moses went after her old surname like a fury. Before she became Oakley she tried out the name "Mozee." Her experiment extended to changing family records, rechiseling "Mozee" on Moses family tombstones, and waging a consequent feud with her brother, who retained the Moses name.[128] When she failed to expunge that name from history, she abandoned Mozee for still another.

Perhaps her new and most famous identity was preferable because it severed all connection to the Moses name. Whatever her reasons, there is no indication that Annie Oakley's affection for Frank Butler was anything but deep and constant. But if Annie Mozee began her path to stardom with her marriage, her refusal to take her husband's name to the stage with her— even he called her "Miss Oakley" in newspaper interviews—suggests she might have been dubious about its value.[129] Indeed, marrying a divorced trick-shooting Irish immigrant from the vaudeville circuit was no sure ticket to better fortunes. Butler made his way to the stage after arriving from Ireland in 1863. When the couple went out on the stage together, they entered the same world of widespread disrepute that Cody occupied in the 1870s. On its face, the idea of her becoming a middle-class attraction by this route seemed absurd.[130]

But Annie Oakley was never one to take no for an answer. She insisted on star billing, and she got it. Her act featured a woman pushing—or bursting— a whole series of cultural constraints. She earned a livelihood by drawing a gun on her husband, shooting a dime from between his thumb and forefinger, the ember off a cigarette between his lips, a playing card in his hand held edgewise toward her, so that the bullet sliced the card in two. She could do all of these stunts with her rifle held backward over her shoulder as she sighted in a mirror. When Butler released two clay pigeons, Oakley would leap over a table, pick up her gun, and shatter them both before they hit the ground. In another event, he held small cards in his hand. She fired at them, then he threw them into the stands. Spectators beheld these souvenirs in awe: two-inch by five-inch cards with her picture at one end and a one-inch-wide, heart-shaped bull's-eye at the other—with a bullet hole through it.[131]

Oakley's spectacle entranced middle-class audiences partly because she appeared as a respectable, domestic figure. Her entrance in the arena "was always a very pretty one," wrote Dexter Fellows, longtime press agent for the Wild West show. "She never walked. She tripped in, bowing, waving, and wafting kisses." She was less than five feet tall, and with her delicate, youthful features, and a dress that reflected the latest middle-class fashions, her large rifle or shotgun looked oddly out of place. "Her first few shots brought forth a few screams of fright from the women, but they were soon lost in round after round of applause." If the pretty, diminutive, respectable woman could handle the guns so masterfully, then surely the display was safe to watch. "It was she who set the audience at ease," recalled Fellows, "and prepared it for the continuous crack of firearms which followed."[132]

Annie Oakley's act made powerful use of her symbolic femininity. Where Victorians believed that men were bedeviled by surging passions that they struggled to restrain, the better class of women were "naturally good," more able to restrain their passions unless somehow corrupted. Thus, the best way of containing the surging desires of manhood was a faithful marriage. A good wife was the sole recipient of a good husband's physical affections, and in this connection, she was vital to the restraint and direction of his passions.

At first glance, a performance in which a small, girlish—even virginal— woman raised a gun to her husband might seem to subvert these principles. Indeed, cultural anxieties about the place of women in public and private life were pronounced in the 1870s. As much as they were symbols of domestic order, as Carroll Smith-Rosenberg writes, "from the mid-nineteenth century on woman had become the quintessential symbol of social danger and disorder."[133] The power of the home as symbol depended on a connection with woman. And the possibility that women might wish to sever or reshape that bond generated a large amount of cultural anxiety. Indeed, American society was as transfixed by the problem of shoring up womanly domesticity as it was by the presumed failure of manly virility, for the Industrial Revolution both called women to work for wages and created a new bourgeoisie for whom a principal symbol of status was a stay-at-home wife. The dangers of the new cities were legion, from crime and prostitution to alcoholism and many, many threats of nervous disorder. But none was more confounding than the danger of women *choosing* to leave the dwelling place of men, either to work or in more symbolic ways, by availing themselves of birth control or abortion.[134] The willingness of white women to combat established notions of home and domesticity in this way left them open to accusations of weakening the culture or, in the parlance of the time, the white race.

Conceivably, Oakley might have been seen as a revolutionary who challenged and resisted the burdens of her sex, earning a salary by mastering the quintessential male technology of her day while her husband-manager took a subordinate role. But the combination of her targets—the cigarettes, money, and cards in his hands—created a symbolic male profligacy which she restrained with her firearm. Where Oakley's alchemy of blushing femininity with astonishing marksmanship signified the restraining power of woman over the gun, it also suggested the power of women—especially white, middle-class women—to restrain and direct the gun's inversion, male desire. Annie Oakley did not subvert middle-class ideals of marriage. She reinforced them. The woman who raised a rifle to her husband paradoxically embodied the perfect wife. Where white marksmen stood for racial strength against the surging, savage hordes of immigrant labor, Annie Oakley holding a gun was the perfect symbol of the racial strength to be had in domestic union of wifely virtue and male passion, which was, after all, the hearth of the race itself.[135]

Oakley balanced her arena inversion of gender roles with a strong social conservatism in day-to-day life. As a female sharpshooter *and* a symbol of domesticity, she stood in opposition to Calamity Jane—a genuine cross-dressing frontier woman who was named as a driver of the Deadwood coach in show programs. John Burke and other publicists made a great deal out of the fact that Oakley designed her own costumes and did her own needlepoint on her dresses. In her tent at the showgrounds, journalists to whom she served tea praised the "quiet and ladylike manner in which she acts the part of hostess."[136] While she was an avid bicyclist, she had little time for suffragists and other "New Women" who seized on the bicycle as a vehicle of female liberation. To Oakley, cycle sports were properly feminine, but "many women abuse the glorious sport by making such a feature of century runs, riding until worn out, and wearing bloomers."[137]

For whatever reason, she never had children of her own. Throughout her career with the Wild West show, she remained in the role of virgin and surrogate mother, to Indians, cowboys, or the assortment of schoolchildren and orphans in the crowd.[138]

Her interior life remains so remote that it is hard to say what private concessions she made to fulfill public demands, but there are hints they were considerable. In Dexter Fellows's estimation, "she was a consummate actress," her public gaiety and womanly graciousness a self-conscious projection. Her trademark of shooting holes through playing cards made "Annie Oakley" a synonym for a free ticket, which was identified by a punched hole. "The further connotation of getting something for nothing also applied to Annie's code of living." She never hired taxis to the showgrounds, but rode on wagons transporting show equipment instead. The show did not play on Sundays, when most performers took rooms in hotels for their stopovers. Annie and Frank always stayed in their Pullman car. On the showgrounds, she never bought her own soft drinks, but walked next door to Cody's tent and filled her pitcher from whatever he had bought.

She was the Wild West show's most powerful symbol of domesticity, her combination of marksmanship, femininity, temperance, and frugality a huge marketing asset for a show of border life. As Fellows recalled, "the sight of this frail girl among the rough plainsmen seldom failed to inspire enthusiastic plaudits." But in the show community's everyday life, her fierce attention to some virtues excluded others, such as generosity, or genuine hospitality, once the journalists left her tent. "During the nine years that I was with the Buffalo Bill show," wrote Fellows, "I never saw her take a drink of anything stronger than beer, which she would imbibe only when someone else paid the bill."[139]

But Oakley's attractions were not lost on Cody and Salsbury. Learning from their success with her, they hired other women performers, including Lillian Smith, "the California Girl." Although Smith's sharpshooting rivaled Oakley's, the latter's display of petite domesticity outshone Smith, who was heavy and single. The California Girl soon married one of the show's cowboys, Jim "Kid" Willoughby. But in 1889 she ran away with another man. (If that did not terminate any chance she had of replacing Oakley as the public's favorite sharpshooting lady, she later exploited her dark skin to take up a new role as an "Indian princess" named Winona, and appeared in competing Wild West shows.)[140] Other white women with the show included Georgia Duffy, wife of cowboy Tom Duffy; Della and Bessie Ferrell, who were hired to represent "frontier girls," later cowgirls; and Emma Lake Hickok, whose "Exhibition of Fancy Riding" was naturalized to western soil by her surname, which she took from her deceased stepfather, Wild Bill.[141]

Despite Oakley's many claims that the Wild West company was one big family, she appears to have resented the presence of Lillian Smith and other white women performers who came on board in her wake.[142] For a time, tensions between Oakley and the show owners sent her packing. In November 1887, when Buffalo Bill's Wild West left London for Manchester, Annie Oakley and Frank Butler left the Wild West for their own tour of Europe. During 1888, publicist John Burke recorded the success of the Wild West show in London in a book, fondly recalling Lillian Smith's introduction to Queen Victoria—"Young California spoke up gracefully and like a little woman"—but failing even to mention Annie Oakley.[143] She and Butler did not return to Buffalo Bill's Wild West until the 1889 season, after which she remained a major attraction with the show until her final departure, in 1901.[144]

Fitting Oakley into the show's mythological canvas ultimately opened up whole new vistas for Cody and Salsbury. Where the number and exuberance of Cody's roving, energetic, raucous, and warlike horse-men had threatened to overwhelm the homey virtues of his Wild West show, the presence of white women allowed Cody to selectively domesticate the entertainment. Even before he began to exploit the centaur imagery, Cody deployed white women performers in one of the most enduring acts—in which he often featured himself—near the center of the program: the "Virginia Reel on Horseback," sometimes called the "Quadrille on Horseback." Usually this scene depicted a community in transition, either on their way across the prairie by wagon train or in the midst of building a ranch or town. A celebration would be called for, the music struck up, and because no dance floor could be found, the young men and women would square off and begin a Virginia reel—on horseback.[145]

This might seem a silly novelty, and it might have been intended as a parody of high society. In New York's most elegant ballrooms, quadrilles and other fancy dances were such standards that, in 1883, guests at one elite Manhattan ball performed a quadrille on the backs of hobbyhorses—which were covered with real horsehide—as a joke.[146]

However Cody visualized it at first, the Virginia reel on horseback became one of the most enduring and consistent of show scenes. In 1887, an English critic, one of the few observers who took the time to write about it, described the spectacle of Buffalo Bill and three cowboys dancing with four young women on horseback, as "a grateful relief" from the "bloodcurdling" attack on the emigrant train which preceded it, "a performance at once pretty, graceful, and pleasing."[147] The dance scene first appeared in 1886, and appears to have been a feature of the show in every year thereafter.[148]

In its importance, it was not unlike later dance scenes in western movies, from Edwin Porter's *The Great Train Robbery* in 1903 to John Ford's *Fort Apache* in 1948. In these films, the good guys—white guys—are recognizable as harbingers of civilization in part because they dance with women, particularly white women. Their opponents do not. The forces of Progress in these films often do a Virginia reel or a quadrille, which is an exuberant, community-oriented dance with measured cadence and somewhat specific steps.

Similarly, the Wild West show required the equestrian Virginia reel to remind (and reassure) audiences of the superiority of white people in the making of domestic space, in settling. There were Indian women in the show (and a well-developed Indian domestic order backstage, too). Indians had shaped land to their own uses for millennia. Now, out on their reservations, Indians were busily building new wood-frame houses and cabins. But in the terms of performance, in the story the Wild West show told, Indians were unable to make homes, to settle, to domesticate the land. They represented a kind of *ur*-mobility, the embodiment of nomadism, the opposite of settlement.

In the equestrian dance scene, cowboys (centaurs) were allowed by cowgirls (female centaurs) to ritually enter domesticity and community by dancing in an organized if energetic fashion, on horseback. The scene distinguished for audiences the white centaurs—who were capable of making homes, of settling—from their Indian opponents, as well as from Mexican, Cossack, or gaucho riders, whose shortcomings flowed from the classic centaur condition, hypermasculinity leading to savage behavior, all constantly aggravated by the absence of home and family. Indian dances were also featured in the program. Many of these were social dances, such as the Omaha, grass, and corn dances, which Indians traditionally performed for visitors.[149] But show publicity emphasized the "war and scalp dances," whose rhythms marked them as antithetical to the domestic dance that the whites performed. Simply put, the presence of white women allowed white men to "tame" their savage natures, an option Indians, Mexicans, and others ostensibly did not have. Doing it on horseback provided levity for what was no doubt a comical scene, but it also suggested that the male-female bonding which created domestic union, the keystone of settlement, would take place amidst the mastery of nature, represented by the horses beneath the riders.

The presence of white women in the cast thus enabled a range of adjustments to the entertainment which helped to make it a more domesticated, respectable show. It is not too much to say that the prominence of Oakley's sharpshooting act heightened other show attractions. Notably, it charged the "Attack on the Settler's Cabin" with powerful new meanings. The scene of Indian men attacking a cabin was preeminently a display of a vulnerable white woman, usually played in these early days by the show's camp matron, Margaret "Ma" Whittaker. The dramatic tableau enacted the beginning of the recurring American nightmare of Indian captivity, and it resonated with the show's appeal to manly virtues.[150]

But by ending the show with a depiction of woman powerless and dependent on man, Cody and Salsbury also eased anxieties created by Oakley and other women sharpshooters. By sketching a dangerous landscape of savagery in which the only safe place for a woman was the house and the only safe social condition was dependence on mounted white men, the show cast what one scholar has called a "narrative of sexual danger," wherein the wider cultural anxieties about women leaving the home were expressed in melodramatic display of female vulnerability.[151] In that sense, the "Attack on the Settler's Cabin" made Oakley's act all the more acceptable, and popular. As much as her display reinforced the importance of the marital covenant, we might see the "Settler's Cabin" scene as a symbolic constraining of women for any spectators who still had doubts about the "proper" place of women after watching Oakley raise a gun to her husband. Any anxiety about masculine power remaining from the spectacle of the virginal, girlish, dead-shot Oakley could be put to rest after seeing the savage men driven off by the white men, who arrived just in time to prevent the victimization of the helpless white woman in the show's final scene.[152]

The scene also appealed to Wild West show audiences for other reasons. Americans may have been enamored of settled homes, but they were also painfully aware of the mobility required for the social and economic advancement that allowed the purchase of homes in the first place. Across all social classes, geographical transience was one of the most salient characteristics of American life.[153] By exploiting tensions between mobility and homemaking, and placing those tensions at the center of a progressive myth of American conquest, the show spoke to some of the most prevalent cultural tensions of the age. In essence, by bringing the heroes home at the end of the show, Buffalo Bill's Wild West suggested that the proper return of the conquering hero was to the hearth, and to the settled domestic order.[154]

The appeal of such a message drew strength from its flexibility. It could be conservative or progressive. Throughout this period, progressive women seized on the icon of the home as their "proper" place, from which they would work to reform society. Women reformers called for "domestication" of urban society, and it was not coincidental that Jane Addams and Florence Kelly sought to transform urban America through the "settlement house" movement. Thus, the connection between women, home, and settlement could be a powerful tool for reformers.[155]

Just as important, the "Attack on the Settler's Cabin" allowed urban men to think of themselves in new ways, to re-create urban manhood by looking to this simulacrum of the frontier West. As suburban neighborhoods began to draw residents away from the cities in the late nineteenth century, many men were attracted to them because they separated women from the dangers—and diversions—of the city.[156] The move to the suburbs, in other words, was a way of keeping women at home, of keeping them literally "domesticated." According to historian Margaret Marsh, in the suburbs men and women together formed a sort of compromise. Women gave up the city, in return for a kind of "masculine domesticity," in which men took more of a hand in the running of the home, and in raising children, in part so that their boys would have "manly" role models close by.[157] Moreover, just as the Wild West show was conceived as a family entertainment, so too suburban homes were designed to assure, even compel, family togetherness, as an antidote to the ostensibly antifamily city. In this context, Buffalo Bill's Wild West show purveyed family togetherness and wholesome education, and Cody's symbolic act of riding to the home at the end was entirely suitable for middle-class men of the Gilded Age and, later, of the Progressive Era.

Through the "Virginia Reel" and the "Settler's Cabin," Cody and Salsbury symbolically reminded their audience that the centaur was only the vehicle of progress, not its culmination. The social Darwinism of show teachings, the emphasis on race *progress* through racial *collision*, was underscored by the constant motion, the racing of its many races, including white people. The constant speed of the white cast throughout the show required the show's creators to self-consciously remind audiences that whites, unlike their racial competitors, were bound to become domesticated and settled. Thus, the "Virginia Reel on Horseback" almost always occurred somewhere around the middle of the program and the "Attack on the Settler's Cabin" at the end.[158] The show thus reinforced that the story of the West was not just one of Civilization trumping Savagery, and Culture springing from Nature, but Fixity and Settlement triumphing over Mobility and Nomadism, or, better yet, (white) Domesticity as the culmination of American history. For most of its years, the story of the Wild West show ended with a homecoming, a return to the scene of a white family domicile, settled, rural, and virtuous. This, the show seemed to be saying, was where (and how) the Pony Express trail and the Deadwood stage line and, indeed, the history of the West should—would—end.

IN SURPRISING WAYS, Oakley also provided a personal and performance bridge to the show's presentation of Indians. Cody intuited that the more "wild" the Indians in Buffalo Bill's Wild West, the more alluring the show would be. His efforts to recruit Sitting Bull failed in 1883, but in 1885, having acquired the endorsement of General Sherman, he succeeded in gaining the permission of the Indian office to take Sitting Bull on tour.[159]

Government permission was one thing. Sitting Bull's agreement was another. According to Salsbury, it was only after seeing a postcard of Annie Oakley that Sitting Bull warmed up to the Wild West proposition, because he already knew her. The chief of the Hunkpapa Sioux had seen her perform in 1884, while he was touring with the Sitting Bull Combination in St. Paul. According to Oakley, he nicknamed her "Tatanya Cincila," or "Little Sure Shot," and it was in many ways the most important title she earned in all her long years of show business. She claimed Sitting Bull had adopted her as his daughter, a story the Wild West publicity crew trumpeted far and wide.[160] The title and the story of Indian adoption suggested that she was an American native, tied to the soil and the continent's first peoples without any sexual implications of captivity or blood mixing.

Whatever Sitting Bull's estimation of Oakley—and we have only Oakley's word for it—her symbolic importance and the implication that she was adopted family of the show's most famous Indian both suggest the importance of family as container for the show's most violent energies. When Sitting Bull joined the show for the 1885–86 season, show publicists used his relationship with Oakley to present him as a suitable family attraction. Similarly, his official adoption of Nate Salsbury extended his kinship to the show's proprietor who most resembled the middle-class, managerial white men in the show's target audience.

Such gestures seem to have been effective. Sitting Bull was still reviled by some as the killer of Custer, but when he first joined the show, at Buffalo, he was "loudly and repeatedly cheered," according to one eyewitness.[161] During that year, he took no part in the reenactments or in any show scenes. He merely rode his horse around the arena in the opening presentation. His own family proved a vital component of his presentation. He sold autographed photos of himself to fans, and cabinet photos of him with wives and children circulated widely. Journalists who interviewed the legendary Sioux warrior saw him alongside his wives and children in the show's tipi village. "Sitting Bull is much better *en famille*," wrote one critic, "and showing himself just as he is for the benefit of Eastern sight-seers than promoting scalping expeditions in the far west."[162] For the audience, this transition from fearsome enemy to family man and show attraction marked the potential beginning of Sitting Bull's (and other Indians') passage from savagery to civilization. In an age when entertainments were often considered a threat to civil society, Buffalo Bill's Wild West could claim to be doing the work of civilization, bringing primitive Indians into a modern, and domestic, order.

Civilian authorities barred Sitting Bull from returning to the show after 1886, and the public never completely abandoned their perception of him as a savage.[163] But the partial and temporary transformation of Sitting Bull's image foreshadowed how Cody and his managers would present the Wild West show as a tool for domesticating the savage nature that appeared there, the wild animals, Indians, Mexicans, and border whites whose frontier energies so often verged on chaos in the show's first season. Annie Oakley functioned as a symbolic restraint on those same energies until she left the show in 1901, after which bronco-busting women like Annie Sheaffer served the same purpose.

By 1886, the show's central pieces were assembled—the frontier scenes of mobility and the domestic scenes of fixity, with Annie Oakley and Frank Butler as the married couple at the center, and Cody as the paterfamilias of the organization. The Wild West was approaching respectability, as Salsbury arranged for a summer-long appearance at Erastina, the newly created amusement grounds on Staten Island. Within access of the crowds and the media markets of New York City, the show became more than a spectacle in the arena. The public read of Indians attending a neighborhood church, and

Sitting Bull enjoyed his year with the Wild West show in 1885, and journalists were intrigued to encounter the most famous living Lakota as a family man. Courtesy Buffalo Bill Historical Center.

singing "Nearer My God to Thee"—in Lakota. Cody and Salsbury began keeping the camp open on Sundays, and many residents of the greater New York area sought relief from summer heat there. Cowboys, vaqueros, and Indians chatted amiably with families from Manhattan and Queens. Con Groner told tales of prairie fires and outlaws. The Indians acquired hammocks and strung them between trees in the Erastina woods, and had a dog roast while sightseers wandered through the "romantic camp of the Indians and cowboys."[164] By the end of the summer, writes Annie Oakley biographer Walter Havighurst, "newspapers were reporting details of the Wild West as though it were a vital and eventful province of America."[165]

CHAPTER TEN

The Drama of Civilization:
Visual Play and Moral Ambiguity

THE SHOW FINALLY CLOSED at Erastina in late September. Normally, the properties would then have gone into winter storage, and the cast would have gone home. But Salsbury had made other arrangements, renting Madison Square Garden for a winter performance season. Because the venue was indoors, and because New York audiences had already seen Buffalo Bill's Wild West during its months at Erastina, Cody and Salsbury commissioned a new artistic director, noted New York dramatist Steele Mackaye, to develop a new attraction. Mackaye adapted and reshuffled the usual acts of the show, telling the entire story of American pioneering and settlement from the beginning of the American colonies to the mining towns of the Far West, calling the production *The Drama of Civilization*.

Mackaye also hired British artist Matt Morgan to paint scenery for the Madison Square Garden shows. Morgan had just completed a series of twelve Civil War battle paintings. They were on display in St. Louis, and they were huge: 27 feet high and 45 feet long. Mackaye specified that each painting for *The Drama of Civilization* was to be even larger—40 feet high and 150 feet in length—and curved. With the show's action encompassed by these gigantic, vivid renderings of forest, prairie, and mountain scenes, the blurring of history, nature, and action would convey an unprecedented sense of realism.

More than any event prior to the show's journey to the United Kingdom, the spectacle of *The Drama of Civilization* at Madison Square Garden marked the ascension of Buffalo Bill's Wild West to middle-class entertainment and respected cultural institution, its newfound esteem capped by the warm critical reception of "Custer's Last Rally," which was added to the show in January 1887. In adding a historical battle to his more generic representations of "frontier life," Cody to some degree mimicked other entertainers, who had been reprising historical battles for popular amusement at least since Astley's circus presented "The Battle of Waterloo" and "The Taking of Seringapatam" in London early in the nineteenth century. In the summer of 1886, audiences flocked to the "The Burning of Moscow" at a New York auditorium.[1]

Of course, Cody had inscribed his own name in the drama of Custer's death ever since the scalping of Yellow Hair, and his reenactment of this battle therefore had a high degree of authentic resonance. But the Custer segment could easily have been construed as a tasteless attempt to capitalize on a dead hero's reputation. Instead, it achieved the near-sanctity of ritual, partly through the visual elements Morgan and Mackaye developed. Under Mackaye's stage direction, with its huge artistic backdrops, *The Drama of Civilization*, and especially "Custer's Last Rally," became practically an animated version of a gigantic panorama painting like "The Battle of Gettysburg" and "The Battle of the *Monitor* and the *Merrimac*," contemporary works that awed audiences with their overwhelming size and visual effects, and their hushed veneration for the fallen.

Indeed, even before the Madison Square Garden performances, the Wild West show might have been described as a confluence of panorama and live performance. Panoramas had first appeared in the late eighteenth century in Europe, and Americans had been animating them in various ways for decades. In 1846, John Banvard debuted his giant mobile panorama of the Mississippi River. Advertised to be "three miles long" (it was probably no longer than 1,500 feet), this painting unscrolled across a stage before crowds who loved the scale representation of the entire Mississippi River Valley. To watch it was to take a virtual tour of the river. Others soon copied Banvard's method, and audiences flocked to these moving, "educational," thoroughly entertaining representations of entire rivers or overland trails.[2] Three themes emerged most often in moving panoramas: travel on the Mississippi, travel overland for exploration and migration, and the growth of San Francisco and the California goldfields.[3] Panoramas often highlighted Indians, and some featured displays of Indian artifacts as an adjunct to the main show.[4] The shift from geographic journey to historical event was an easy one. "The Mexican War" and a "Mechanical Panorama of Bunker Hill" both proved popular. "Part entertainment and part education, part hyperbolic bluff, and part high-minded instruction, the panoramas engaged topical events as well as escapist fantasies," writes Martha Sandweiss. They were precursors, she notes, to "public pageants, newsreels, and grade B westerns." And, we might add, to the Wild West show.[5]

Indeed, the close approximation of Buffalo Bill's Wild West to moving panoramas cannot have been an accident. Like moving panorama paintings, the Wild West show advertised its attractions as a virtual journey to the frontier, "Eclipsing in Animated Scenes a Year's Visit to the Yellowstone Park."[6] Panoramas were visual products of the artist's long journey along the frontier, just as the Wild West show was the product of Cody's frontier life, and both forms of amusement recounted their founders' adventures and achievements in thick, detailed show programs, which broke the amusement into separate "acts" or "scenes" and explained the historical import of each.[7] Both were acclaimed for their "realism," with the Wild West show endorsed for showing the West "as it was," and some moving panoramas allegedly were endorsed by riverside inhabitants who recognized their houses, barns, oak trees, and even their individual horses: "[I]f there ain't old Bally and the white mare, well, it *is* surprising how the mischief he come to get it so natural I don't know, *stop the boat and let me get out*."[8]

As popular entertainment, moving panoramas were at their apogee in the mid-1840s, when Cody was born. By the 1860s, they had all but vanished from city venues, in part because the expansion of railroads made it possible to encounter a "real" panorama out the window of a train. But their acres of unscrolling canvas continued a lively trade in small towns and at county fairs, where some of their subjects were even closer to Cody's heart. A "Panorama of the Sioux War" appeared in Minnesota as late as 1870, and "Sioux Outbreak," presumably depicting the recent Ghost Dance and the Wounded Knee massacre, made its debut in 1892.[9] But for the most part, the genre was dead.

Whether or not Cody ever saw moving panoramas—and it is difficult to see how he could have avoided them—their influence on his show is unmistakable. Buffalo Bill's Wild West, "Artistically Blending Life-Like, Vivid, and Thrilling Pictures of Western Life," combined circus-style horse stunts with a living reprise of the moving panorama, adhering so closely to the latter genre that spectators were reassured by its familiarity as they were thrilled by its real action.[10]

Indeed, the Wild West show was only one of several entertainments to experiment with visual artistry as a means of recapturing the thrills of moving panoramas. In the early 1880s, at the very moment that Buffalo Bill's Wild West debuted, new joint stock companies began producing "cycloramas" in the United States. These were static, but gigantic, circular paintings, which spectators entered through a tunnel and stairs to view from an elevated platform in the center of the circle, where the huge richly colored canvas wrapped completely around them. The artists incorporated trompe l'oeil techniques, and extended them by situating earthen landscapes and wooden figures in front of the canvas to merge with the painting; sometimes they provided scented air and "authentic" sounds to blur the boundary between representation and reality. The cycloramas were a new form of visual experience, and observers gasped to find they had "become of a sudden a part of a picture."[11]

Trompe l'oeil seized the imagination in smaller formats, too. At the very moment that Cody launched his new show, crowds flocked to see the work of William Harnett and other artists whose invisible brushstrokes and attention to shading and texture fooled many observers into thinking that the subjects of their paintings—crumpled letters and tattered banknotes, old books, bleached buffalo skulls, dilapidated hunting gear—were not paintings at all, but cleverly lit arrangements of real objects hanging on a wall.[12]

The public's interest in trompe l'oeil and their vigorous debates over what the paintings represented reflected a combination of nostalgia for a rustic past evoked by the "historical" subjects of these works, and the same eagerness to debate and resolve tricks and hoaxes that P. T. Barnum exploited with his humbug. As historian James W. Cook has written: "For both Barnum and Harnett, the ultimate goal was to produce a highly unstable, perpetually contested brand of verisimilitude," one that resonated with the visual trickery and confusion of advertising and the modern city.[13] Trompe l'oeil was in keeping, then, with the same tradition of artful deception that ran from western tall tale through Barnum's FeeJee Mermaid and into the ongoing life and show of William F. Cody.[14]

Publicists and reviewers already referred to the Wild West show's "Pictures of Western Life." Now the show flowed into the era's confluence of history, entertainment, and eye-tricking spectacle.[15] The show had carried a plywood set of mountains at least since 1885, but they paled before *The Drama of Civilization*, with its panoramic paintings of forest, plain, and valley of the Little Big Horn as backdrops to its live reenactments. All of the elements used to heighten perceptual confusion in the period's panoramas and cycloramas were deployed at Madison Square Garden: landscaping in front of the painting to extend its visual deceptions; battered props such as the Deadwood coach, saddles, guns, whips, and other items that seemingly tumbled out of the canvas. To this were added real horses, longhorn cattle, buffalo, and moose, careful lighting to enhance effects such as the prairie fire, real wind to blow real leaves across the stage in the scene of the cyclone. Real shouts and cattle calls and moos and whinnies and bellows echoed from the roof. Authentic smells wafted. On top of all this, the people who acted out the history evoked by the giant painting behind them were "frontier originals," genuine Indian veterans of the Custer fight and real cowboys, too, and of course, William Cody himself.

Critics spoke of *The Drama of Civilization* as a "great living picture," but they were almost at a loss for words to describe it. Over the next decade, whenever the Wild West show appeared for long stands at suitable venues, Cody continued to utilize panorama backdrops, landscaping, ventilators, lights, smoke, and other special effects in ways that made his show almost as much a visual wonder as a performance.[16] The huge painted backdrop and a large forested hill landscaped into the arena inspired London reviewers in

1887 to speak of the show's *"coup d'oeil"*—overthrowing of the eye.[17] Reviewers at the 1888 winter shows in Manchester, England, were ecstatic over the show's action "on a huge plain level with the stage and drifting into a perspective upon it." Indeed,

> the distance from the extreme end of the auditorium to the back of the stage is so great that a horseman galloping across the whole area diminishes by natural perspective until the spectator is fairly cheated into the idea that the journey is to be prolonged until the rider vanished in the pictured horizon. The illusion, indeed, is so well managed and complete, the boundless plains and swelling prairies are so vividly counterfeited, that it is difficult to resist the belief that we are really gazing over an immense expanse of country from some hillside in the far West.[18]

Show reviews and old photographs from the 1890s reveal entryways through the paintings, sometimes at the tops of the hills built up against them. Cowboys, soldiers, Indians, and others burst from the paintings and galloped down the hills, or scaled them at high speed and vanished into them.[19]

A rare photograph of the Little Big Horn reenactment from Ambrose Park shows the cavalry charging into Indians who look too few in number to resist them. Off to the right, barely visible, mounted Indians retreat. But we know that crowds of Indians to ensure the Boy General's defeat must be about to burst forth from the entryway in the middle of the canvas. What stands out, though, is the painting itself. On a canvas 440 feet long and 49 feet high, the Montana prairie sweeps down to a bend in the Little Big Horn River, bringing the water to the rim of the arena. The river bends at the turn in history; the water laps at performance edge. The painted sky reaches up from river and plain to join with the real sky above; only the protrusion of one tall chimney and the upper story of a distant building above the canvas hinder the effect. The soldiers in the foreground of the photograph charge toward the Indians in the middle ground. Mounted Sioux ride eerily out of the painting, sweeping toward the soldiers whom they will usher into history. The smoke from army guns rises into the Little Big Horn's cloudless sky. The Indians and soldiers seem almost to have become part of the painting—or to have stepped out of it, into life.[20]

Of course, the blue-painted skies of the Wild West contrasted sharply with the roof of Madison Square Garden, and sometimes even with the real sky, which clouded up, and was often dark with soot, especially in industrial London and Brooklyn. But the smudge of gray or black hanging over the giant canvas in a sense heightened the authenticity of the painting and the performance. After all, industrial smoke (like a roof) was another element of

Artifice, and if it marred the city sky above the canvas with proof of civilization's progress, it both validated the show's teaching—civilization was inevitable—and made the painted frontier Nature on the giant canvas all the more realistic for being pristine and unmarked.

In reprising Custer's defeat against this background, Cody rode the wave of "Custer's Last Stand" paintings, cycloramas, lithographs, drawings, and other reenactments which soon made the battle of the Little Big Horn the single most depicted moment in American history. More, he shaped popular expectations of the scene. Earlier illustrations picture the battlefield as a barren prairie or rocky hilltop. But in 1896, the same bend in the river was incorporated into a lithograph of "Custer's Last Stand" which, as an advertisement for Budweiser, went into at least 150,000 prints and hung in practically every bar in America.[21]

In most years, when Custer's death was not reenacted, the panorama featured not the Little Big Horn, but towering western mountains. A grainy 1892 photo suggests that the backdrop of that year was a pastiche of fictional and real mountain peaks, which corresponded closely with the way actual mountains were depicted in popular paintings. Thus, the tallest peak soars

"Trick of the Eye." The Seventh Cavalry charges into the Lakota, who beckon the soldiers into a giant painting of the Little Big Horn battlefield— and into history. Courtesy Denver Public Library.

up to the left, a cross of snow on its granite crown. The image came from Thomas Moran's 1875 painting, *Mountain of the Holy Cross*. The actual mountain was so difficult to locate among the many peaks of the Colorado Rockies that for years commentators were not certain whether it was real or not. Moran pictured it soaring above surrounding summits, its white cross a sign of the providential blessings of American expansion, and the image was soon reproduced as a lithograph for middle-class living rooms.[22] In Cody's arena, it was a recognizably authentic frontier image, the cross hanging like God's own star over the American conquest on the plains below.[23] In other words, the wilderness of the Wild West was realistic in part because it seemed to merge into the space of the arena, and in part because it so closely approximated the visual West already familiar to audiences who had never been west of the Hudson, or the Atlantic.

Buffalo Bill and his Wild West were astonishing to watch not only as frontier people fading before advancing civilization, but as authentic, historical people in a complex dance with copies of western landscapes so artfully contrived as to confuse the senses. They were thus a commentary on mass production, on manufacturing, on mechanical reproduction of art at every level and of every kind. By dashing in and out of giant paintings, inscribing real deeds and fake ones alike in show programs, and traveling back and forth between "real" West and "show" East, Buffalo Bill's Wild West invited audiences to draw a line between real and fake, historical and representation. But on another level, they provided a thrilling display of courageous, authentic people who would not quail before a blizzard of representations that threatened to overwhelm them. Photographs, press reviews, colorful posters, panorama paintings, pen-and-ink drawings, show programs, lithographs, history books, and many other media provided "true life" illustrations of western settings and show principals. Much of the fun of the show was seeing the "real" people and measuring how they stacked up against their own images.

The copies were not always benign, and paradoxically, Cody used copies of himself to wage an ongoing battle against his imitators. By offering an entertainment that resembled Buffalo Bill's Wild West show, performance rivals such as Doc Carver, Adam Forepaugh, Pawnee Bill, and a host of others simultaneously underscored Cody's status as the "original" and threatened to overwhelm the unique appeal of his entertainment. Cody fought them furiously, plastering his posters over theirs and hauling them to court for trademark infringement when he could.[24]

But in many ways, Cody's artistry was to juxtapose the copy and the original, and then stitch them together with his own person. In later years, movies projected action onto the screen. But they could not replicate the experience of watching the seemingly genuine frontier conquerors move back and forth through painting and landscape, connecting history and the present. As historical people, they came toward the audience through time, out of history and into the modern world of electric trolleys, telegraphs, telephones, and mechanical stuff which sometimes poked out from behind the canvas.

Just as they darted back and forth between painting and life, so they flickered through the life stories inscribed in show programs. The biographical and historical "articles" in these dime pamphlets were studded with authentic detail and fictional narrative elements, as illuminating and as deceptive as any brushstroke. They provided a curtain from which the cast advanced and into which they might return, over and over again, in city after city, decade after decade. Was Cody the real Buffalo Bill? Was he really in the Pony Express? Was the Deadwood coach the real Deadwood coach, and had it done all that he said it had? Was Red Shirt really a chief? Were those real cowboys? Had any of these people been at the Little Big Horn, and if so, which ones? Show programs and press agentry, like the visual deceptions of the arena, blurred the line between what really happened on the Great Plains and what the audience wanted to believe had happened. The result was a gigantic show of alternating real and fictional elements with reverberations far beyond the circus or the panorama, encompassing a powerful mythology of national greatness, but one whose meaning was constantly up for grabs.

IN IMPORTANT WAYS, the show's visual messages had a political counterpart, providing a space in which to consider and even debate the era's many political arguments, without necessarily acceding to any single point of view.

With its narrative of American expansion and Indian war, and its endorsements by military men who were also political figures, Buffalo Bill's Wild West had a sharper political edge than most other entertainments. The Gilded Age is recalled today as an era of glamour and excess. But it was also a time of fierce partisanship, when the nation was evenly divided between two parties who fought bitterly over every presidential contest, and whose leaders struggled to stem or co-opt popular discontent brought on by rapid industrialization. Disputes between labor and capital, strikes and their armed suppression, riots, and the near shutdown of whole cities followed one after another in the last twenty-five years of the nineteenth century. Between 1881 and 1905, the United States saw nearly 37,000 strikes, involving 7 million workers. In 1893 a fierce depression struck, and by 1894 the Pullman strike paralyzed the railroads. President Cleveland called out the army, placing Chicago under martial law and giving armed escort to the scabs who ran the trains. At the same time, the expansion of farms and mines in the West, "the progress of civilization," glutted producer markets, forcing crop and mineral prices sharply downward. Western farmers, miners, and laborers united to demand government regulation of market and railroad.

Given the show's middle-class popularity through cycles of labor uprising and suppression, most historians follow the lead of Richard Slotkin, who sees in the harsh rhetoric of fans like Frederic Remington and Theodore Roosevelt proof that Buffalo Bill's Wild West taught its public "that violence and savage war were the necessary instruments of American progress." Whether the enemy were Lakota Sioux or determined strikers, bloodshed was the path to peace.[25]

These arguments are not without some truth. Remington himself wrote articles describing the putative heroics of frontier cavalrymen, like the captain of the Seventh Cavalry in Chicago who looked "as natural as when I had last seen him at Pine Ridge, just after Wounded Knee" as he faced down the "anarchistic foreign trash" who manned the barricades of the Pullman strike in Chicago, making the city "much like Hays City, Kansas, in early days." During the same period, he wrote glowing reviews of Buffalo Bill's Wild West, "an evolution of a great idea," whose arena he visited to "renew my first love."[26] A contingent of U.S. cavalry joined the Wild West in 1893, and veterans of Indian war and urban uprising rode side by side in the arena. In 1897, the Wild West camp included a cavalry sergeant—"a slim, quiet young fellow [who] has the bronze medal for bravery at the battle of Wounded Knee"—and an artillery sergeant who "was out at Chicago during the riots."[27] Modern readers, remote from the Indian wars and the political arguments they ignited, are easily convinced that reenacting them was a right-wing celebration of imperialism and bloodshed.

But right-wing appeal offers at best a partial explanation for the success of Buffalo Bill's Wild West. The show was a mass entertainment. Americans were no more in agreement about the rights of workers than they were on Indian policy. To draw millions of Americans to its bleachers over so long a career, and to achieve consistently glowing reviews from critics and newspapers on different sides of so many political questions, the Wild West show had to reach across deeply etched partisan and ideological lines. How did the show rise above these national divisions?

Part of the show's appeal lay in its projected amnesia about the nation's most recent wounds. "America's National Entertainment" contained almost no references, visual or literary, to the Civil War. In a period when each party sought traction by blaming the other for that conflict, the war's absence almost allowed audiences to forget it ever happened.

Cody preferred that approach himself, and in other ways, too, he avoided party battles. His own commitments to party were highly changeable. A pro-Union Democrat in the Civil War, he ran for office in Nebraska as a Democrat in 1872. He joined a march for Democratic President Grover Cleveland in 1888. Cleveland won the popular vote but lost the electoral college in his reelection bid that year, in one of the hardest-fought contests in memory. Despite the partisan hostility that pervaded the country, in March 1889 Cody was an honored guest—and Louisa a member of the reception committee—at the inauguration of Cleveland's Republican successor, Benjamin Harrison.[28] In 1897, Cody attended the inaugural of Republican William McKinley. That same year, he was trying to organize the Democratic Party in his newly founded town in Wyoming.[29]

Cody's nonpartisanship, so atypical for men of his era, was also reflected in his entertainment. Even its ownership was bipartisan, with Cody the Democrat teamed up with Nate Salsbury, an ardent Republican. On a cultural level, Cody appealed across party lines with an amusement that told two layers of stories. The most persistent narrative, what we might call the foundation, was present in every historical scene, and it depicted the progress of civilization. This was a story that was widely accepted to be as true as gravity. Whether one liked it or not, commerce would triumph over savagery.

Layered on top of that story were many others—about Buffalo Bill, Indians, cowboys, soldiers, cowgirls, animals, hunters, and many other figures and characters—which could be interpreted in many distinct and contradictory ways. Indian conquest could be read as good or bad, or both, and the disappearance of the buffalo could be an occasion for happy reflection on the expansion of pastoralism and commerce or as a sad commentary on the wasteful corruption of modern society—or both. Cody's press agents, and Cody himself, steered a middle course between narrating civilization's advancement as inevitable and allowing audiences to make up their own minds about what it meant. The solution, as we shall see, lay less in didactic teachings about the need to shoot leftists than in the appealing to the audience's own ambivalence about race war, the closure of the frontier, and all the other events that followed in the wake of progress.

That ambivalence was sorely tested by the events of 1886 as *The Drama of Civilization* took place. In the first six months of the year, there was a dramatic strike in the coalfields of Pennsylvania, another against McCormick's reaper works in Chicago, and a streetcar strike in New York that culminated in riots between strikers and police. Beginning in March, the Great Southwestern Strike paralyzed railroads in Texas, Missouri, Arkansas, and Kansas, and eleven people died in violence between strikers and armed marshals in East St. Louis.[30]

The Southwestern Strike failed in early May, but by then, another episode of political violence riveted the public like none in the nation's history. On May Day, in cities across the country, about 200,000 unskilled laborers, skilled craftsmen, socialists, and anarchists went on strike in support of the eight-hour workday. Violence was minor or nonexistent in most places. But in Chicago, 40,000 strikers paraded the streets before joining the ongoing strike at the McCormick reaper factory. Chicago police opened fire on the crowd, killing four. In response, the International Working People's Association, a small, mostly German-speaking anarchist group with only a hundred members in the city, called a mass meeting to protest police brutality. Between 2,000 and 3,000 demonstrators turned out to hear speeches the next day, at Haymarket Square.

The meeting was uneventful till the end, when the remaining three hundred people in the crowd began to disperse as two hundred police suddenly arrived. Then somebody in the crowd threw a bomb into police ranks. The blast was huge. It threw fifty policemen to the ground; eight of them died. The remaining police opened fire on demonstrators, who tried to flee, and in the confusion and panic the police wounded sixty of their own number. How many demonstrators died is unknown, but estimates place the number at seven or eight, with three dozen wounded.

What inspired the activists upon whom the wrath of the state now descended? Anarchism was often incoherent as a political philosophy, but by 1886 the term generally implied revolutionary socialism. To some degree, the anarchist movement was born of striker frustration at their powerlessness before armed police and soldiers in the upheaval of 1877, and by authorities' attempts at denying leftists the handful of election victories which they rightly won thereafter. In 1881, a convention of anarchists in Paris praised the recent assassination of Tsar Alexander II and endorsed the principle of armed insurrection to secure a socialist future.[31]

With the Haymarket bombing, anarchists became terrorists in the public mind. Although the identity of the perpetrator was unknown (and strike supporters claimed it was an agent provocateur acting on behalf of factory owners), the immediate consequence of the tragedy was America's first red scare. The nation's newspapers published chilling rumors: there was a transatlantic anarchist conspiracy ready to flatten Chicago with thousands of bombs hidden beneath the streets; the Haymarket bomb was the signal for a general uprising; the anarchists would seize control of the country. In the panic, Chicago authorities, industrialists, middle-class residents, and many laborers turned against anyone or anything that suggested immigrants, labor organizers, or radicalism. Police conducted dozens of raids, incarcerating and beating hundreds of unionists, socialists, anarchists, and others.[32]

Ultimately, eight defendants went on trial for the Haymarket violence. Testimony placed six of them elsewhere at the time of the bombing. The remaining two were on the speakers' platform and could not have thrown the bomb. Despite their clear innocence, the jury convicted all eight, sentencing seven to hang. (Four were actually hanged, one died in jail, and the last three were pardoned in 1893.) The verdict was popular during 1886, while the nation's newspapers were consumed with visions of bearded, bomb-throwing immigrants, and while workers, businessmen, and factory owners closed ranks against leftists of any stripe.

Comparisons between strike violence and frontier savagery were already a tradition, a way of indicting strikers as "barbarous" aliens. In fact, native-born Americans were among the activists. (One of the Haymarket convicts, Albert Parsons, was practically an alternative William Cody. Born in Texas, as a young teenager Parsons was a scout for the Confederate Army.)[33] But ever since the Great Railroad Strike of 1877, and probably before, Americans had blamed labor unrest on "foreign" ideas rather than workplace conditions, and on inferior immigrant "races"—Irish, Germans, Bohemians, Poles, and others among the working masses. The rhetoric reduced class strife to a racial issue, so that to most of the middle and upper classes, labor trouble meant immigrant trouble, or race trouble, which threatened American civilization as much as Indian resistance did, and which could theoretically be dealt with in the same way. The redeployment of frontier army troops to the nation's cities in 1877 and to Chicago in 1894, and at other times of labor unrest, and the formation of newly professionalized National Guard units to put down labor rebellions, made comparisons to Indian war easy for journalists, whose coverage of strikers was infused with the rhetoric of "savage" labor.[34] Calls for violence against radicals mounted. "There are no good anarchists except dead anarchists," howled the *St. Louis Globe-Democrat.*[35]

The Drama of Civilization debuted at this moment, and in its presentation of a "natural" history of American expansion, it was indeed a soothing and reassuring spectacle for audiences mostly united in their fear of anarchy and seditious foreigners. The newly designed show featured four "epochs" of American history, the progress of which was narrated and explained by an orator (a feature Mackaye borrowed from moving panoramas and which proved so successful that Cody retained it for the rest of his show's long career), and which we can follow through the eyes of a reviewer.[36] The first scene was the epoch of the Primeval Forest, before the arrival of Columbus. Bear, deer, and elk wandered across the moonlit stage, anticipating the arrival of two Indian tribes—Sioux and Pawnee—who clashed in combat, "and a rough-and-tumble massacre" closed the scene.

The Prairie epoch followed, in which Buffalo Bill hunted a herd of buffalo while guiding a wagon train of emigrants. A display of camp life was followed by a simulated prairie fire, "the fighting of fire with fire—the stampede—deer, buffalo, mustangs, Indians, and emigrants—all fleeing together."

The Cattle Ranch was the next installment, "illustrating the cowboy in his glory, riding the bucking mustang and lassoing the bounding and bumptious steer." Indians made a surprise attack, but were soon dispatched by Buffalo Bill and a troupe of cowboy reinforcements. The final "epoch," the Mining Camp, included a duel, the arrival and departure of the Pony Express, and the Deadwood stage (robbed by a party of "road agents" rather than Indians this time). Finally, the giant ventilators roared to life. Dummies soared to the rafters, the mining town of tents collapsed before the cyclone, as the curtain dropped.[37]

The Drama of Civilization featured no overt references to strikes, labor unrest, or police brutality. This was part of its appeal, as an escapist departure for an imagined frontier. But, given the pervasive rhetoric equating strikers and savages, and the hysteria over the anarchist specter in 1886, we can be sure that many saw in *The Drama of Civilization* a parable of antiradicalism.

In January, Cody, Salsbury, and Mackaye debuted the last addition to *The Drama of Civilization*, "Custer's Last Rally." The army had been in the background of the show from its beginning. Publicists inscribed Cody's Union army and cavalry scout service record in show programs, and a Union veteran, Sergeant Frederick Bates, presented the American flag during each performance. But "Custer's Last Rally" represented the first time Buffalo Bill's Wild West included a scene of the U.S. Army in frontier combat. To a degree, it appealed to the public's increasing fascination with the professional military. Although the U.S. Army was traditionally shunned in peacetime, American men, as we have seen, were fearful that their neurasthenic bodies would fail before the bristling, uncontained savagery of immigrant workers and increasingly looked to uniforms and military drill—including shooting at targets—to restore their manhood. Amid the widespread fakery of manufactured, middle-class comfort, military combat seemed to offer authentic, "real" experience that modern men lacked.[38]

In one sense, "Custer's Last Rally" seemed even more real than other acts in the Wild West repertoire, representing as it did a specific historical battle, the nation's most famous Indian encounter, with which Cody had a long and personal affiliation. Where the Deadwood coach and the Pony Express attractions collapsed many events into one simulacrum, this was a purportedly faithful depiction of a single, profound event, the death of America's foremost martyr to Indian conquest, staged by the man who avenged him.

The scene opened with a camp of General Custer's troops, who began the action by marching out of the camp in pursuit of Indians. A scout discovers a Sioux village, where "Sitting Bull and his warriors are apparently engaged in the innocent pastimes of prairie life." After the scout returns and informs Custer of the Indians' location, "The sound of a bugle is heard. The Indians instantly prepare an ambush." Custer's troops then rush onto the open stage. "The bugler sounds the charge. Custer waves his sword, puts spurs to his charger, and, followed by his men, rides down upon the Indian village like a cyclone." There surrounded, the Indians overwhelm the troops in hand-to-hand combat. "Custer is the last man killed, and he dies after performing prodigies of valor."[39]

In reality (as we have seen), Custer had presided over a regiment that resembled the industrial workforce from which they were drawn: Irish, German, Italian, and other immigrants, as well as poor American-born natives. They were restive, prone to desertion and even mutiny. His actual experience as their commander was closer to that of factory owners who faced the constant threat of worker revolt than to the unbesmirched hero of "Custer's Last Rally."

But Cody's cowboys assumed the role of loyal soldiers and thereby whitened the Seventh Cavalry in memory. In contrast to the ominous "racial" divisions between immigrants and middle-class America which culminated with the Haymarket bombing, "Custer's Last Rally" emerged as a mythic moment of American unity and self-sacrifice. Conservatives appreciated the scene. Soon after Buffalo Bill's Wild West closed at Madison Square Garden, New York's Eden Musee invited patrons to compare two new, side-by-side waxwork dioramas: one was *Custer's Last Battle;* the other, *The Chicago Anarchists.*[40] At least one moral message seemed clear. As Theodore Roosevelt told a gathering of New York Republicans that year, "There is but one answer to be made to the dynamite bomb, and that can best be made by the Winchester Rifle."[41]

But Roosevelt was a politician, and reducing the meaning of Cody's spectacle to a single teaching, especially one so pointed and political, fails to account for the political variability of Cody's audience. Popular enthusiasm for hanging the Haymarket suspects continued through the winter. But thereafter, passions cooled. Opinions diverged. Influential critics, including the editor of the prestigious *Atlantic Monthly*, William Dean Howells, began questioning the fairness of the court proceedings and the government's case. Many labor organizations began demanding a new trial. Most people probably remained in favor of the death sentences, but a vocal and respected portion of the middle class joined working-class activists in opposing them. By December of 1887 the argument about justice and the Haymarket affair had polarized the country.[42]

The continued popularity of Buffalo Bill's Wild West amid this changing political context, long after the Haymarket hysteria had subsided, suggests that its appeal went beyond any single didactic message. To conclude that its central teaching was that strikes should be met with military response over-simplifies its complex spectacle. Rather, the show sent many different messages simultaneously, and audiences interpreted them in different ways to suit a very wide spectrum of political leanings that developed and changed over time.

To grasp the complexity of the show's teachings, we should keep in mind that most people who saw Buffalo Bill's Wild West did not see the Custer reenactment. Scholars have long assumed that Custer's death was Cody's most durable attraction, but it was in fact only a temporary addition, and Cody reprised it infrequently. After showing the scene for two months at Madison Square Garden, the Custer battle was not seen in the United States again until 1893, for the second half of the show season in Chicago. It appeared regularly in 1894, but disappeared again the next year. It featured in some shows, but not others, in 1896 and sporadically again in 1898. After 1898, it was never shown in the United States again.[43]

Its placement within the show also reduced its significance. Custer's death was the climax only in parts of two show seasons: first, in early 1887, and second, from August to October of 1893.[44] On the other occasions when it appeared, it was one of the acts in the middle of the show lineup. The show's regular and most popular climax remained the more domestically oriented "Attack on the Settler's Cabin."

To be sure, audiences may have connected the show's generic imagery of Indian war with the challenge of labor unrest even without the Custer sequence. Cody's target audience was middle class, not working class. Perhaps he synchronized performance of this most military "tableau" with shorter moments of public outrage against strikers, as in early 1887, when anti-anarchist sentiment was at its peak, and in late 1893 and in 1894, when most middle-class voters seem to have supported the use of federal troops, including the Seventh Cavalry, to break the Pullman Strike (and when genuine Seventh Cavalry veterans—and Sitting Bull's horse—were included in the battle of the Little Big Horn sequence).[45]

But neither Cody nor his managers left any trace of the motivations and considerations that went into the making of show acts. The timing of the Custer reenactment probably reflects Cody's intuition more than any conscious strategy.

Moreover, the story of how the Custer segment came to be staged at Madison Square Garden in 1886 highlights the mythic domesticity that tempered its more reactionary messages. For all the scene's masculine heroics, the development of "Custer's Last Rally" hinged on the intercession of another woman. Cody had many endorsements from army officers. But none had quite the elevating power of the one he secured from the widow of the Little Big Horn herself, Elizabeth Bacon Custer.

SHE WAS CALLED LIBBIE, and by 1886, she was America's most famous widow, a national icon of bereaved devotion. She was not only a woman. She was a lady. The daughter of a well-to-do Michigan lawyer, she struggled financially after the death of her husband. Publicly, her elegance, and her careful balance of veneration for her husband's memory with charitable public service, made her a well-respected figure in New York society. She was trustee of a women's hospital, a board member of the Bellevue Training School of Nurses, and secretary for the New York Society of Decorative Arts.[46]

Since 1876, Libbie Custer had crusaded to elevate George Custer's image out of the morass of controversy which threatened to engulf his battle standard. She lent private papers to hagiographic writers, lobbied behind the scenes to ostracize surviving junior officers whom she blamed for her husband's destruction, and asserted a near-proprietary interest in Custer memorials. When wealthy backers erected a statue of Custer at West Point without consulting her, she led the successful campaign for its removal. Afterward, no one contemplating a public tribute to George Custer could ignore her.[47]

Early in 1885, she published the first of three memoirs about her married life, *Boots and Saddles: Life in Dakota with General Custer.* The book obscured the couple's often troubled marriage with a portrayal of their household as a bulwark of domestic unity and peace on a frightening frontier. It sold 15,000 copies in the next nine months, inspiring Libbie Custer to write "a boy's book that I may implant my husband in the minds of the coming generation."[48]

That book was slow to be written, perhaps because she began to suspect it was unnecessary. She watched Buffalo Bill's Wild West at Erastina the following July, announcing "she was much pleased" with the exhibition.[49] In August, she received a letter from William Cody requesting her permission to stage the reenactment of her husband's death, promising to "spare no expense to do credit to our exhibition and deepen the lustre of your glorious husband's reputation as a soldier and a man." The educational scene, he wrote, would acquaint the audience with "the valor and heroism of the men who have made civilization possible on this continent."[50]

Convinced that Cody's reenactment would raise the general's reputation, she endorsed it, and frequented Madison Square Garden during rehearsals for the January debut of the Custer sequence. Show producers made skillful use of her presence to sanctify their popular entertainment as respectful history. Libbie Custer had never seen the Little Big Horn battlefield.

Nonetheless, "she will be announced as superintending the picture of the spot where her husband was killed," wrote Steele Mackaye.[51] She was often sighted at rehearsals. She befriended and socialized with Annie Oakley. On opening night, she observed "Custer's Last Rally" from a private box.[52]

The presence of Custer's widow at the premiere ensured its acceptance as both an accurate representation and a respectful gesture to a fallen hero, but it contained other messages, too. Most obviously, Libbie Custer's very public involvement reinforced the show's family appeal.

In a sense, even while he lived, Custer's Indian war was a family show. The general had a huge public reputation and a well-crafted public persona, and his marriage was a prominent feature of both. Libbie followed him to the Plains. Their nieces often camped and hunted with the glamorous couple, along with an ever-present entourage of young officers, tourists, and well-connected reporters. Tom Custer, George Custer's brother, was a decorated army captain serving on George Custer's staff. Still more Custers joined the Indian fighting forays of the Seventh Cavalry as civilians on a lark, binding command and kin in the popular imagination. At the Little Big Horn, fallen clan members included not only George Custer, but also his brothers Tom and Boston Custer, Autie Reed, his nephew, and his brother-in-law Lieutenant James Calhoun, the husband of his sister, Margaret. For the public, his defeat was not just a military debacle. It was the fall of the House of Custer. Cartoons depicted Indians holding scalps of "the Custer Family." If Crazy Horse and Sitting Bull did not complete the drama by capturing Libbie and the other Custer women, the public nonetheless saw Custer's collapse as conjoined family and national disasters, a material realization of the abstract cultural links between frontier war and the threat to the family.

Custer's family image grew in the decades after his death in large part through Libbie Custer's exertions, especially her elegiac memoirs and lectures which memorialized him through his marriage to her. In her hands, the violent, mercurial, and libidinous officer became an icon of fidelity and chivalric manliness, a man who paced the floor for hours with a sick puppy in his arms and changed the route of his march to protect the nest of a prairie hen and her brood.[53] Buffalo Bill's Wild West show ascended to the pinnacle of American show business as the Custer memoirs flew out of bookstores, in the 1880s and '90s. By including the Custer reenactment along with the "Attack on the Settler's Cabin" (and in some cases substituting one for the other), Cody tied frontier race war firmly to white family protection, and both of them to his own persona.

The resonance of "Custer's Last Rally" with urban race war and industrial violence no doubt explains some of its popularity. But Libbie Custer's embrace of this spectacle also sent a powerful, countervailing message about

the limitations of vengeance for civilized people. Urban, middle-class families, who saw the home as a bulwark against the violence and alienation of
the city, sat awed before the spectacle of the Custer family sacrificing themselves for the containment of savagery, reenacted under the guiding hand
and imprimatur of Mrs. Custer. At least as much as "Custer's Last Rally"
linked cavalry and public order, the centrality of family in this epic of the
civilizing process validated spectators' own domestic longings.

We can only wonder—as New Yorkers must have—how Libbie Custer
brought herself to view the reenactment of her husband's death, starring
some of the Sioux men who exchanged fire with Custer's men that day. Years
later, when Buffalo Bill's Wild West visited Custer's hometown of Monroe,
Michigan, the show's Indians received a visit from Nevin Custer, the only
Custer brother who was not at the Little Big Horn. "When Cody explained
to them through an interpreter that the man with him was General Custer's
brother," recalled press agent Dexter Fellows, "the older of the red men
stepped a pace backwards. Mr. Custer looked at them for a few seconds and
walked away." Men "such as these" had killed his brothers, Nevin Custer
told Cody, with tears in his eyes, "but I suppose they thought they were
right."[54]

Lakotas showed extraordinary courage in their show travels, but rarely
did it take anything like emotional courage for a spectator to attend. Nevin
Custer's effort to meet the Sioux men who fought the war and to see the war
from their point of view was in keeping with his bereaved sister-in-law's
stance in 1886, and it underscores what many Americans intuited upon taking a seat in the Wild West show audience. To watch "Custer's Last Rally"
was in some way to join Libbie Custer in grief, and to assert willingness to
sacrifice for civilization. But just as important, it was also a gesture of reconciliation, and forgiveness.

Securing Libbie's endorsement provided Cody a success that was
astounding on several levels. He had had nothing to do with Custer on the
Plains. The martinet of a general who had refused the society of the scout
was now memorialized by him. For her part, Libbie Custer knew of Cody's
differences with her husband. She could be militant in continuing George
Custer's many grudges long after he was in the grave. But when Cody asked
her permission to reenact the battle, if the memory of George Custer's cool-
ness to Cody gave her any pause, she gave in to the man most ideally situated to sanctify her husband's memory.

Cody took the step of impersonating Custer himself, donning a wig and
taking up the sword (although Custer had cut his hair short before the 1876
campaign, and he did not carry a sword that year). In future years he
assigned the Custer role to Buck Taylor and other cast members, freeing
himself to stage a highly fictitious, futile dash to Custer's rescue by Buffalo

Bill, followed by his signature "First Scalp for Custer" reenactment. But that January of 1887, there was no revenge scalping. Instead, the show allowed space for Indian valor, as it heightened Custer's heroic image. Cody's assumption of the Custer role for the opening weeks of "Custer's Last Rally" meant the blond, balding, angular general suddenly appeared taller, broader, darker, and far more handsome than the real Custer had ever been. The widow certainly appreciated the display. In the second volume of her memoirs, *Tenting on the Plains*, she praised Cody's performance, although she camouflaged her own thoughts by putting them in the mouth of her black servant, Eliza. "Well, Miss Libbie, when Mr. Cody come up, I see at once his back and hips was built precisely like the Ginnel, and when I come on to his tent, I jest said to him: 'Mr. Buffalo Bill, when you cum up to the stand and wheeled round, I said to myself, "*Well*, if he ain't the 'spress image of Ginnel Custer in battle, I never seed any one that was." ' "[55]

Libbie Custer expressed her ambitions for the performance, and her gratitude to Cody, in a subsequent letter commending him for "teaching the youth the history of our country, where the noble officers, soldiers, and scouts sacrificed so much for the sake of our native land." Just as she linked scouts to officers, and thereby assisted Cody's ongoing effort to raise the reputation of frontier guides, she thanked him "from my heart for all that you have done to keep my husband's memory green. You have done so much to make him an idol among the children and young people."[56]

As much as *The Drama of Civilization* resonated with middle-class fears of labor violence, it could only do so by symbolically resolving industrial discontent, making strikes vanish through Progress. If the vanquishing—and, ultimately, vanishing—of Indians was inevitable, so, too, was the disappearance of troublesome labor.

Just as Henry Morton Stanley and dozens of army officers eschewed the extermination of Indians as beneath American civilization, so the Custer reenactment, in featuring genuine Indian opponents of the fallen general, suggested that Indians—and by extension—immigrants, could be included in popular education and entertainment, turned into cooperative wage laborers, and thereby incorporated into the nation. Self-restraint was the essence of civilized manliness. If civilized people demonstrated firmness (military force) combined with mercy and justice, even the bitterest enemies of Progress, men such as Sitting Bull (who had been with Buffalo Bill just eighteen months before, and whose role as the mastermind of Custer's defeat was played by another Oglala man in 1886) and Gall (who had ridden down on Custer's command in 1876, and was now appearing at Madison Square Garden) could be persuaded to submit, and to become loyal employees in the grand pageant of American history.[57]

By January of 1887, there could be no doubt that the Indian presence in

Madison Square Garden contained a liberal message as much as a reactionary one, a prescription for national self-restraint in the ongoing confrontation with savages, be they immigrants or Indians. In *The Drama of Civilization*, wrote journalist Brick Pomeroy, "we see the entire West with its great dramatic history that pioneers, indians, cow boys, home builders and *all* are making, and see it as a wonderful picture, backed by the grandest and most extensive and expensive scenery and stage appliances ever witnessed in this country."[58]

Libbie Custer's poignant, devoted forgiveness warns us against seeing the fight against Indians as a validation of anti-labor violence, since Americans were so divided on the morality of Indian conquest in the first place. As we have seen, army officers and Cody himself frequently denounced the nation's treatment of Indians as unfair and unbefitting a great nation. Brick Pomeroy, whose enthusiasm for the show's masculinity reached a fever pitch in 1887, wrote that spectators at *The Drama of Civilization* would see not only heroic "pioneers" in the "primeval wilderness," but Indians, those "wily savages whom the whites with their lies, tricks, and avarice have made alert even to cruelty."[59]

Wild West show publicists quoted or reprinted Henry Wadsworth Longfellow's poem about the battle of the Little Big Horn, "The Revenge of Rain-in-the-Face." Although in reality it was Custer who attacked a peaceful Sioux village, Longfellow's verse contains many allusions to Indian savages who ambush the heroic General Custer (as they did in Buffalo Bill's Wild West); Rain-in-the-Face himself cuts out Custer's heart, and

> *As a ghastly trophy, bore*
> *The brave heart, that beat no more*

For spectators seeking to blame Indians (and strikers) for their own destruction, the poem had much to offer.

But there was a profound ambivalence even here. Longfellow's poem was partly a meditation on the timing of Custer's thunderous defeat, which came during 1876, the centennial of the Declaration of Independence, the "Year of a Hundred Years." The poem's last verse contained a stark message about where the moral blame for Custer's demise must fall:

> *Whose was the right and the wrong?*
> *Sing it, O funeral song,*
> > *With a voice that is full of tears,*
> *And say that our broken faith*
> *Wrought all this ruin and scathe*
> *In the Year of a Hundred Years.*[60]

For those who saw Indian anger and Custer's death as the result of America's dishonorable breaking of treaties, Longfellow's poem was an affirmation. It turned "Custer's Last Rally" into a thrilling (and entertaining) demonstration of the tragedy that ensues from "broken faith."

The poem complemented the rhetoric of ambivalence Cody had developed since the 1870s to explain the presence of Indians in his entertainments—and perhaps to articulate his own beliefs. In 1885, he explained Sioux war aims to a newspaper correspondent. "Their lands were invaded by the gold seekers, and when the U.S. Government failed to protect them they thought it was time to do it themselves. The Government did all they thought they could do, but the white men wouldn't be held back. No one can blame the Indians for defending their homes. But that is all passed."[61]

Superficially, Cody's account reads like an endorsement of Indian resistance. But on closer reading, it is arresting how many different moral directions Cody maps out in four sentences: the Sioux faced a hostile invasion; the government failed in its obligations; the Sioux stood up for themselves; the government did all it could do; the invading white men were too energetic and determined to be stopped; the Indians should not be blamed for defending their homes (the attack on the settler's home began with an attack on the Indian's home); but it is all in the past, there is nothing to be done (so come in, enjoy the show).

Cody's ambiguity condenses the Wild West show's version of history into a list of wide-ranging possible readings which, taken together, made it possible for audiences to differ on the morality of Indian conquest without having to cease their enjoyment of the performance. Whether you wanted strikers shot or appeased, there was a seat for you at the Wild West show.

For all the scholarly emphasis on the conservatism of Cody's show, ambiguity was central to its presentation of the march of progress and key to its success in its most popular and profitable years. Divided public opinion on labor strife and political violence made more prescriptive approaches impossible for a mass entertainment. Steele Mackaye himself joined his friend William Dean Howells in condemning the government's handling of the Haymarket trials as "a national folly and a national disgrace."[62] In 1897, when the show's celebration of militarism was at its peak, critics still saw it as a show that allowed audiences to make up their own minds about the morality of Indian conquest. "The admirers of Daniel Boone, the pioneer, and Kit Carson, the scout, readily recognize in the show how courage, determination, keenness of sight, accurateness of aim and unswerving perseverance won for them the names which are idolized," wrote one reviewer. "Those who have sympathy for the Indian, feeling that the red man has been mistreated by the settlers and the Government," the same writer continued, "have their hearts warmed at the sight of such a fine collection of them, and rejoice in their feats of horsemanship."[63]

It was beloved by conservatives and liberals alike, but perhaps the ultimate proof of the Wild West show's flexible meaning was its appeal to leftists, the most famous of whom was Edward Aveling. An Englishman who was husband to Karl Marx's daughter, Eleanor, Aveling was the kind of revolutionary who made Remington's trigger finger itch. The "riddle of modern society," wrote Aveling, would only be solved "by the abolition of private property in the means of production and distribution, leading to a communistic society."[64] This same man, socialist and revolutionary, saw Buffalo Bill's Wild West as "the most interesting show in a most interesting country."[65]

His admiration for the Wild West show is striking in part because Aveling skewered romantic facades in a way few other writers did. During his 1886 tour to investigate the prospects of socialism in America, he never traveled to the West. But his encounters with cowhands in eastern exhibitions led him to become the first writer to describe them as proletarians: "In a word, out in the fabled West, the life of the 'free' cowboy is as much that of a slave as is the life of his Eastern brother, the Massachusetts mill-hand. And the slave-owner is in both cases the same—the capitalist."[66] He joined many others in demanding a new trial for the Haymarket suspects.[67] His many interviews of American workers were grist for his subsequent study, *The Working-Class Movement in America*, which he coauthored with his wife in 1891.[68]

Aveling's encounter with the Wild West show began in 1886, at Erastina, after an acquaintance insisted he see it. To the son-in-law of Karl Marx, the show told the story of "life and death in the Rocky Mountains, where the wave of savage life is beating itself out against the rock of an implacably advancing civilization."[69] Cody's portrayal of social evolution appealed to leftist notions of dialectic and revolution as much as to the social Darwinism of reactionary conservatives. The fascination of it, Aveling wrote, "is in part due to the coming face to face with conditions that in some sense represent our own ancestral ones." Like pioneers of modern anthropology such as Lewis Henry Morgan (and Karl Marx, too), Aveling looked at primitive peoples and said, "They are what we once were." Indians embodied the universal primitive. "These dusky Indians . . . yet remind us of the earlier forms of savage man whence we have evolved, not by any manner of means always in the right direction."[70]

Buffalo Bill's Wild West, with its triumph of cowboys over Indians, pastoralism over hunting, evoked the development of ever more complex civilizations, a process that was, to the minds of all Cody's contemporaries, of every political stripe, as unstoppable as evolution itself. Capitalists, conservatives, liberals, socialists, and communists fought one another bitterly, but all saw the triumph of commerce over savage chaos as ineluctable. Notions of cultural relativism, which allow Americans to think of other cultures as distinctive, but not inferior, were decades away. Belief in the necessary departure of "primitives" from the face of the earth was practically universal. Capitalists believed the dispossession of Indians paved the way for farming, commerce, and private property. Socialists and communists saw Indian defeat, and the advancement of modern wage work and private property, as inevitable steps in the destruction of feudalism and the emergence of class divisions (which would result, inevitably, in revolution, the abolition of private property, and the advent of proletarian utopia). Where these camps differed was on the question of how civilization should progress once savagery was conquered. But Edward Aveling and Frederic Remington shared a strong enthusiasm for Buffalo Bill's Wild West because they also shared a deep faith in the defeat of primitives as the necessary price of better worlds to come.

Cody's patrician kindness and artful pose as a frontiersman allowed Aveling to believe that his consummately modern show—a legal corporation which relied on industrial transport, a wage-earning cast, and steam-powered presses for its colorful posters, newspaper notices, and tickets—was fundamentally premodern, lying outside the contemporary world of wage reductions, workplace mechanization, and surplus labor.[71] To Aveling, Cody represented an earlier race of white men fundamentally different from the modern white race of corporate bosses. Cody's race was "*vanishing* as the Red Indian, its foe, vanishes."[72] In other words, Cody looked forward to the modern capitalist order, without actually being part of it.

So it was that Aveling, the socialist, practically moved into the Wild West show camp, first at Erastina in 1886, and then in London the following year. He mused on the experience almost as enthusiastically as any Frederic Remington. "Have I not spent days and nights in camp with them; been present at 'Saddle-Up!' time, and behind the scenes at the performances; ridden outside the Deadwood coach; slept in Buffalo Bill's tent?" His list of show acquaintances included many show cowboys, including Jim Mitchell, Buck Taylor, "Bronco Bill" Irving, and "Tony Esquivel, the most handsome, the most charming, the most daring of them all—are not these my friends?"[73] The most astonishing of these, to his mind, was William Cody himself: "Very tall, very straight, very strong; the immense frame so perfectly balanced, so cleanly built, knit together so firmly and symmetrically, that until you stood by it and felt it towering over you and, as it were, absorbing your own lesser individuality, you hardly recognized what giant was here." But no matter the physical description, wrote Aveling, "nothing of this—and, indeed, nothing—can give any idea of the immense personality" of this "extraordinary man."[74]

Cody's energetic charisma flickers through account after account over a century later. Between comparisons to the centaur of old, and testaments to his physical beauty and his "immense personality," we may yet discern a presence which awed the most jaded reviewers. Advising Mackaye about how to work with Cody, his partner Nate Salsbury—who had a testy relationship with Buffalo Bill even in these most rewarding years—took it upon himself to explain Cody's genius. "You will find him petulant and impulsive," wrote Salsbury to Mackaye, "but with good, crude ideas as to what can be evolved from your material."[75] Salsbury resented Cody's intuitive command of their joint enterprise, and he was both bemused and intimidated by how completely Cody's presence could control not only a performance but also backstage machinations. "Cody, in many respects, is a man of steam-engine power," explained Salsbury, in a more thoughtful, private moment. But just as important as his energy, Cody's physicality seemed to contain the conflicting elements of the show—cowboys and Indians, progress and chaos—within his own body. "In his tremendous physical power, he is the only man who can control, and keep in subjection, the various antagonistic elements of such a show," wrote the managing partner.[76]

Steele Mackaye's son later called *The Drama of Civilization* "a new form of folk-temple for the worship of a new heroic age," and there can be little question that the Madison Square Garden season of 1886–87 placed the Wild West show on the horizon of New York audiences as a cultural attraction.[77] As with other appearances of Buffalo Bill's Wild West, reviewers had their share of complaints and fun with the Madison Square Garden season, describing the orator's descriptions as "insufferably long," denouncing the "lame conclusion" of the prairie fire scene, and providing colorful, and condescending, names for the show Indians.[78] But in terms of the show's acceptance as a historically educational and socially redeeming entertainment, the winter at Madison Square Garden was an overwhelming success, dispelling any lingering doubts about its attractions for "respectable" people. Where *The Drama of Civilization* looked enough like the Erastina performances to inspire playful or disparaging reviews, the aura of sanctity surrounding the reenactment of "Custer's Last Rally," with its visual imagery that seemingly carried the audience right into the painting and into history, upped the show's cultural capital.

The Wild West show's acceptance as a suitably domestic exposition of life in the Far West owed much to the incorporation of Annie Oakley, Emma Lake Hickok, and other women into its mythology. In New York, other factors behind the newfound respectability of Buffalo Bill's Wild West included Steele Mackaye's direction, Matt Morgan's paintings, and Nate Salsbury's business sense. Without the intercession of Libbie Custer, the Wild West show's signature educational scene, "Custer's Last Rally," could not have been staged at all.

But Cody himself remained its central feature. His authenticity relied on many things, especially the participation of Indians in his drama, and we shall explore their motivations in another chapter. But the idea of such a "drama of civilization" without him is unthinkable. New York audiences knew Buffalo Bill from over a decade on the stage. One measure of his new venture's success was that in contrast to the mostly working-class fans of his frontier melodramas and his first Wild West show season, audiences at Madison Square Garden in January 1887 included a broad cross-section of New Yorkers. According to one journalist, "statesmen, artists, military men, teachers, writers, musicians, business men, politicians, artizans, mechanics, and others who desire to know as much as possible about the history of their country" flocked to the show, "interested as we never saw an audience before."[79] The patronage of veterans and military officers validated the show as both historically authentic and socially acceptable. Cody's press agents distributed lists of officers in attendance. General Sherman saw it twenty times.[80] It was so popular that branch ticket offices were opened in Brooklyn, Jersey City, and Newark.[81] Show management arranged discount ticket prices for members of the Grand Army of the Republic, and schools sent crowds of students to afternoon matinees.[82] A colorful children's book titled *A Peep at Buffalo Bill's Wild West* soon appeared, with the principal lessons of the show explained in simple, awful rhymes.[83] Buffalo Bill was, at long last, respectable family entertainment.

Hints in show reviews suggest that the spectacle of Custer's demise, with Custer "represented by Buffalo Bill, who wore a wig to represent Custer's auburn locks," met with near-sacred veneration. Reviews describe audience behavior with numerous references to order and respectfulness, suggesting that during this winter season, the Wild West show left far behind the raucous audiences of Cody's melodrama days, and approached a kind of incipient high-culture appreciation normally displayed in opera houses and the upmarket theaters that produced Shakespeare.[84]

Ordinarily, the Wild West show was an outdoor entertainment. But in a sense, its highly successful appearance in Madison Square Garden in the winter of 1886–87 suggests how much its rampant, raucous centaurs had been domesticated for popular entertainment, and how much that domestication allowed its harsher themes of race war to be reconciled with liberal ideals of race reconciliation and the rule of law. Just as the show featured "the pioneers with families at work in sun and shade to open and cultivate the soil, to build and beautify homes," so too the theater itself was as comfortable as "a cheery parlor."[85] Divided as they were over the question of anarchy and whether it should be met with force or forgiveness, middle-class audiences who were traditionally loath to venture downtown for enter-tainment could feel safe in venturing into the heart of New York for this nighttime show, where comfort, amusement, and the sacralization of Amer-ican history flowed together under the guiding hand of America's most famous westerner.

As the show wound down in February, a new rumor began to circulate through the press. Nate Salsbury had received an inquiry from the organiz-ers of the American Exhibition in London. After a series of telegrams and messages, he and Cody made it official. Buffalo Bill's Wild West was going to Europe.

CHAPTER ELEVEN

Wild West London

O N MARCH 31, 1887, Buffalo Bill's Wild West show sailed out of New York Harbor, bound for Great Britain. "There was a dense crowd on the dock, shouting and whooping and gesticulating for dear life," wrote one observer. The celebrated Cowboy Band played "The Girl I Left Behind Me," a U.S. Army standard (and the same tune that accompanied Cody and the Fifth Cavalry as they set out to fight the Dog Men in 1869), as the ship *State of Nebraska* headed out to sea with 209 Wild West show passengers, including more than ninety Lakota Sioux men, women, and children. Below deck were almost two hundred horses, eighteen buffalo, and assorted mules, elk, Texas steers, donkeys, and even deer.[1]

The crossing was rough, with giant waves, rolling decks, and seasickness. The horses suffered from poor ventilation, and the ship's captain ordered holes cut in the deck to provide them air. Several buffalo and elk died en route. Show workers threw them into the sea.[2]

After docking at Gravesend, the Wild West show began rehearsals at the newly constructed showground adjacent to the American Exhibition, in West London, at Earl's Court. Cody, Burke, and Salsbury had seen to it that the show had some of the best advance press in England's history, and its arrival was widely anticipated. It did not hurt that Salsbury had arranged for the show to be attached to the American Exhibition, a display of American paintings and manufactured products, and a diorama of New York City— with a scale model of the newly completed Statue of Liberty in the miniature harbor—meant to attract British investment and consumers for American products. It did not hurt, either, that the exhibition itself was timed to coincide with Queen Victoria's Golden Jubilee, the national celebration of her fiftieth year on the throne. William Gladstone, already a three-time prime minister, visited the show a week before the opening.[3] In May, the Prince of Wales attended an advance performance of Buffalo Bill's Wild West. On his recommendation, Queen Victoria commanded a private showing for herself.[4]

Buffalo Bill's Wild West cast, 1887, in London. Courtesy Buffalo Bill Historical Center.

Her visit inspired one of the show's most enduring legends, inscribed in a new edition of Cody's autobiography the following year by press agent John Burke. According to Burke, the queen's visit was an honor of "unique and unexampled character." Not only was she sovereign of the United Kingdom and Europe's longest-reigning monarch, but "ever since the death of her husband, nearly thirty years ago," she had "cherished an invincible objection to appearing before great assemblages of her subjects."[5] Her stalwart grief proved no match for the glittering allure of the Wild West. On the afternoon of May 11, Queen Victoria arrived at Earl's Court with a large entourage of "uniformed celebrities and brilliantly attired fair ladies who formed a veritable parterre of living flowers around the temporary throne."

Victoria's arrival would have been memorable all by itself, but in Burke's telling, it was immediately followed by "a very notable incident, sufficient to send the blood surging through every American's veins at Niagara speed." Opening the performance, the Wild West show's standard-bearer presented the American flag, with the orator explaining that it was "an emblem of peace and friendship to the world."

As the standard bearer waved the proud emblem above his head, Her Majesty rose from her seat and bowed deeply and impressively toward the banner. The whole court party rose, the ladies bowed, the generals present saluted, and the English noblemen took off their hats. Then—we couldn't help it—but there arose such a genuine heart-stirring American yell from our company as seemed to shake the sky. It was a great event.

For the first time in history, since the Declaration of Independence, a sovereign of Great Britain had saluted the star spangled banner, and that banner was carried by a member of Buffalo Bill's Wild West.[6]

London was awash in Europe's royals, all of them paying their respects to Victoria. Her endorsement assured their attendance in the coming months. On June 20, the Prince of Wales arrived at the showgrounds, trailing an entourage which included the king of Denmark, the king of Saxony, the king and queen of the Belgians, the king of Greece, and a slew of lesser titles, too. So it was, wrote Burke, that the Deadwood coach "had the honor of carrying on its time-honored timbers four kings and the Prince of Wales that day, during the attack of the redskins."[7] After the show was over, the Prince of Wales joked with the showman, "Colonel, you never held four kings like these before."

"I've held four kings," replied Cody, "but four kings and the Prince of Wales makes a royal flush, such as no man ever held before."[8]

Buffalo Bill's Wild West was a hit in England in 1887, and these stories of Cody's success have entertained the American public ever since. Much of their appeal, then and now, is in the validation they convey. The queen bows to the American flag, acknowledging the ascent of the former colonies to modern power. The heir to her throne, a nobleman from a great house, takes his seat atop the frontier coach, makes a pun about poker (an American game), and finds himself both entertained and outwitted by Nature's Nobleman. Queen and prince pay homage to America's frontier history *and* American entertainment, to America's triumph over the wilderness and to American culture. If there were any doubts that Buffalo Bill's Wild West was something more than just another cheap show, the imprimatur of Queen Victoria and her family dispelled them.

The royal endorsement of Buffalo Bill's show proved a marketing bonanza. Cody told the story of four kings riding in the Deadwood coach for years afterward, and so did other members of the show, in Great Britain and elsewhere.[9] The Prince of Wales was allegedly so fond of the Deadwood coach joke that he told it on himself, and if he did not, other Londoners soon did.[10]

For the larger British public, Cody would have been hard to miss even before the queen expressed her pleasure with his show. British readers, like their American counterparts, had been devouring fictional romances about Buffalo Bill since the 1870s, and now he materialized before their eyes.[11] He did not disappoint. "The representative frontiersman of his day" and his touring "exposition" of real Indian warriors, genuine Anglo cowboys, Mexican vaqueros, and women sharpshooters became enormously popular.[12] Society columns dubbed him "the lion of the season." The frontier hero became perhaps the most sought-after party guest among the United Kingdom's upper classes.

Catapulted to these heights, Buffalo Bill's Wild West would be a major attraction in Britain for many years, the lights dimming over its last appearance in the United Kingdom only in 1904. By then, the show had become the best-known representation of America. And Cody, the warrior from the frontier West, had become the world's most famous American.

Particularly in the show's early years, the American press had a giant appetite for stories of Cody's European triumphs. Newspapers began publishing them even before Burke ghostwrote them into Cody's new autobiography in 1888.[13] Some Americans sneered that British respect for Cody, a simple showman, reflected their decadence.[14] Others were more amused at British credulity in accepting Cody's show as elite entertainment, like the anonymous poet who composed the following tongue-in-cheek ditty about American entertainers in Britain:

> *Our plays put the Londoners all in a rage,*
> *They howled our comedians off of the stage;*
> *Our daintiest actresses met with a groan;*
> *They let our tragedians severely alone,*
> *But Art is triumphant. The city so vast*
> *Bows down to American genius at last!*[15]

Still others were genuinely thrilled by the queen's bow to the American banner, and the excitement endures. Buffalo Bill's importance as a vehicle for American renown across the Atlantic has long outlived him. Most Cody biographers and many historians of the show down to the present day relate the four kings joke with the Prince of Wales, and the story of how Buffalo Bill was the first showman in over a quarter century to lure the prince's grieving mother out of her sad palace and into the bright light of the arena, where she bowed to the Stars and Stripes and enjoyed an afternoon of rollicking entertainment.[16]

Heady stuff. Had the events not been real, wrote John Burke, wise men might have "bet that it was a Yankee hoax."[17]

Burke's choice of terms was practically an elbow to the ribs. The master of the Yankee hoax was P. T. Barnum, and as with his attractions, there is both truth and fiction in these Wild West tales. To be sure, eyewitness accounts confirm that the prince rode on the Deadwood coach that June, and Cody may have been the driver (as he was when the prince's wife returned the following day with most of their children).[18]

But witnesses also agree that the Prince of Wales clambered onto the coach with only one reigning monarch, the king of Denmark. His other companions on the ride were his wife, the Princess Alexandra (who was also the king of Denmark's daughter), and three princes (two of them his own sons, the other the crown prince of Sweden and Norway). The joke about the four kings may be real—there were four kings watching the show, and perhaps the Prince of Wales was referring to Cody having "held" four kings in his audience, rather than in the coach. But there is a lilt to the language, a flowery turn of phrase—"such as no man ever held before"—which hints that Cody's exchange with the Prince of Wales was the product of press agent Burke's fertile imagination.[19]

For her part, the queen did command a performance of the Wild West show on May 11. She commanded personal meetings with Annie Oakley and Lillian Smith, and with Red Shirt, who was advertised as "chief" of the show Indians, too. She burbled over two Lakota babies. Her mere presence was the highest honor a show could receive in Britain, and she really did command a repeat performance shortly afterward, when the prince and his family rode in the coach (although she did not attend). Her enthusiasm for Cody's entertainment played a huge part in its success that season, and in all the years to come.

And yet Burke's puffery twisted some facts and invented others to embellish even this remarkable endorsement. True, Victoria refused to visit the theater until the 1890s, as she mourned the death of her beloved Prince Albert for over three decades. But her Wild West afternoon was not her first venture to a public entertainment, even in 1887. Victoria was an ardent circus fan, and an earlier sign of her emergence from mourning was her attendance at a circus from the Paris Hippodrome, in March 1887, when Cody and Salsbury were still in New York. Just as she would do with the Wild West show at Earl's Court, she attended a private performance of the French circus at the newly constructed Olympia theater, then ordered a repeat performance (perhaps because she had not seen enough of the see-sawing elephants Jock and Jenny).[20] For all the red, white, and blue bunting in which Americans draped the Wild West show, for Victoria it was another circus outing. Back at Windsor, she recorded the afternoon in her journal: "An attack on a coach & on a ranch, with an immense deal of firing, was most exciting, so was the buffalo hunt, & the bucking ponies, that were almost impossible to sit."[21]

And what of her bow to the American flag? Cody's publicist painted a solemn scene: a "standard bearer" who rode out "during our introduction," and "waved the proud emblem above his head," before a monarch who bowed low. The English press who witnessed the scene told a very different story. The American flag did not appear until the middle of the show, between the Indian dances and Emma Lake Hickok's fancy riding, when it was presented to the accompaniment of "Yankee Doodle." One suspects that protocol dictated that foreign flags should dip before the throne, and that the monarch would acknowledge the gesture with a nod, whereupon the flag could be raised. In any case, this was precisely what happened; according to *The World* newspaper: "When, in the course of the performance, Serjeant [*sic*] Bates brought down the 'star-spangled banner' . . . and lowered it before the Queen, she inclined her head twice in recognition of the courtesy."[22] Another newspaper featured pen-and-ink drawings of the encounter: Old Glory lowered almost to the ground, Cody and the flag-bearer bowing their heads, before an all-but-impassive queen.[23] The musical accompaniment to the gesture suggests a very different story from the legend. "Yankee Doodle" was originally a British song deriding rebel foolishness at the outset of the American Revolution. In the course of the American victory, colonists themselves took up the song as an expression of their courage. When we realize that the banner of the United States was unfurled to the American Revolution's most patriotic tune, and then was lowered in honor of the queen, the scene suggests the *reverse* of the famous legend: not the queen honoring the American flag, but the American showmen symbolically recognizing their debt to Her Majesty for attending.

The artful deceptions of the Wild West show's not-quite-true royal stories, and their enduring uncritical acceptance even by the sharpest American historians, suggests the potency and sophistication of the multilayered entertainment that Buffalo Bill's Wild West provided by the time of its European debut. The show had thrilled audiences with a story in the arena for some years already. With its European tours, Buffalo Bill's Wild West garnered press and a new following at home through stories about encounters between Cody, his cast, and their far-flung audiences. For the rest of its days, much of its fascination for the public lay in the ocean of newspaper accounts that explored less the drama of arena performance than the show community's passage through the world. Americans read about Buffalo Bill's Wild West in Europe in newspapers, in the two books which John Burke produced to memorialize the tours, and in show programs which breathlessly recounted European adventures.

Cody never allowed his American audiences (or his European ones, for that matter) to forget his royal successes, which were emblazoned across show posters, some of them gigantic. One 1895 poster, plastered across fences and walls from Waterville, Maine, to Montgomery, Alabama, featured a blue map of the North Atlantic world, with ships and a red line demarcating the show's progress through western Europe, the "World's Wondrous Voyages" of the Wild West show. "From Prairie to Palace Camping on Two Continents Distance Travelled, 63,000 Miles, or nearly three times around the globe." In the margins were inset images of Earl's Court, "Buffalo Bill and the First American Indians That Have Visited the

Adriatic," as well as common postcard images of Glasgow, London, Hamburg, and other cities. The poster was part advertisement, part scrapbook, allowing viewers to savor the travels of the Wild West show as they might imagine the Grand Tour of a relative or neighbor, and to see them as the embrace of America's story—and her culture—by an enthralled Old World. Other posters were even more direct in turning royal and official show visits into endorsements. Two more posters depicted "Distinguished Visitors to the Wild West," with portraits and titles of each royal or official visitor—"King of Sweden," "W. E. Gladstone," "Duchess of Leinster," and "H.M. the Queen" (Victoria, of course), arrayed around the portrait of Buffalo Bill. Still another depicted the 1903 visit of King Edward VII (who, as the Prince of Wales, had ridden on the Deadwood coach in 1887) to the Wild West camp in London. At least one 230-square-foot billboard depicted Cody doffing his hat in gratitude for the adulation of European "Presidents, Pope and Potentates, Statesmen and Warriors."[24]

The presence of "primitive" Wild Westerners, especially the show's Indians, invited press agents and other correspondents to invert standard American travel writing. Usually, American traveler-authors like Theodore Roosevelt, Richard Harding Davis, and Mark Twain recounted the adventures of civilized, democratic white Americans in backward, colonial regions, or in the aristocratic halls of Europe. Such accounts showcased white American courage and energy and proved America's parity with the great European powers and her progress over savagery. American fascination with travel writing, as with the Wild West's tours of Europe, came amid an aggressive American push for overseas markets. In this connection, published accounts of European adventures of the Wild West cast poked fun at Europeans for being so impressed with barbarism, while they established

"The Queen's Visit to the Wild West Show." Old Glory lowered almost to the ground, before an all-but-impassive Queen Victoria, from The Graphic, *May 21, 1887.*

Americans, especially Cody, as past masters at the ultimate containment of savagery: its scripting into a public amusement, its packaging as a safe, respectable entertainment, and its marketing as a commodity.[25] Thus the Wild West show was both an entertainment export and an ongoing American tour which fans could follow through numerous press accounts and show publicity. In encounters between Cody and the queen, and between Wild Westerners and the Old World in general, loomed tales full of meaning about America's place in the world.

In this respect, as his career in show business continued, Cody's emphasis on his string of "real" frontier exploits was an ever bolder sleight of hand. Like a magician who distracts with the left while he acts with the right, Cody in his frontier biography kept his contemporaries and his historians focused on history and the Far West, while he enhanced his reputation by playing fast and loose with the facts of his show career across the Atlantic, enhancing his reputation in ways that have fooled the most serious historians and writers for over a century. People searching to debunk Cody have assumed that his most outlandish fabrications concerned the fights with Tall Bull or Yellow Hair. Perhaps they did. But the fact remains that while reams have been written reinforcing or discounting Cody's Indian war record, few have examined the powerful legends of his show career.[26]

And yet, this careful perusal of Wild West lore is vital to understanding how and why William Cody assumed the stature he did as an American entertainer *and* an "authentic" hero. We might dismiss the "inaccurate" stories about Cody and the queen as typical show business excess. In some measure, every traveling entertainment blew its own trumpet with fabrications. But the power of these carefully contrived stories to entrance the American public then and now speaks to the symbolic facility of Buffalo Bill's Wild West at representing the United States overseas in ways that no circus or theatrical company could.

Indeed, Cody was hardly the first American to entertain the English royal family. American artists from Joaquin Miller to Mark Twain had traveled to Europe before. George Catlin presented his "Indian Gallery"—a show of paintings, artifacts, and Ojibway Indians in live reenactments of frontier scenes—to Queen Victoria at Windsor Palace in 1843. P. T. Barnum brought Tom Thumb to her in 1844.[27]

These predecessors were not Cody's most immediate concern. The Wild West show's quick, astonishing success, avidly reported in the United States, drew a host of imitators across the Atlantic in his wake. In late 1887, a showman named Joe Shelley brought "Mexican Joe's Wild West" to the United Kingdom, where it toured the provinces. Doc Carver, who had toured Europe as a sharpshooter in the 1870s, teamed up with a new partner in 1889 to star in a show called "Wild America," with which he toured Berlin,

Vienna, Budapest, Warsaw, and parts of Russia and Sweden before venturing to Australia in 1890. In 1889, P. T. Barnum would bring his "Greatest Show on Earth" to London.[28]

But none of the Americans who preceded or followed Cody could match the Wild West company when it came to generating stories merely by their presence. There were several reasons for this. Most immediately, in Britain, as in America, all the shows that followed him moved in his shadow. "The programme" of Mexican Joe's Wild West, wrote one reviewer, "contains many of the features already made familiar to our readers by a long course of 'Buffalo Bill.' "[29] As in the United States, Cody's show of "frontier originals" proved alluring not only because of their authenticity as Indians, cowboys, and scouts, but because they were members of the acclaimed first, or "original," show to bring the frontier to Europe.

But just as important, the quality of arena performance and public deportment by Buffalo Bill's Wild West was very high. Cody was not only a terrific sharpshooter from the back of his horse, not only a superb presence during the show's introduction and other points when he appeared. He was also a savvy, demanding, hands-on director. Cast members recall him as mostly friendly, genial, even kind. But they also remember him keeping a close eye on every performance, frequently "raking up" any performer who failed to please him.[30] He was equally demanding of his staff, too, ensuring that they furnished timely, adequate salaries, comfortable housing, and abundant food in the cook tent.[31]

Cody's energetic attentions helped distinguish his show as more thrilling, its performers more polished, and better motivated. Cody, not Salsbury, chose the show's cowboys, Indians, and other performers. He was careful to have experienced stage drivers at the reins and seasoned cowboys in the arena, and he put a premium on hiring performers who were not only skilled but easygoing. That Mexican Joe was less attentive on this last score would help to explain the very public brawl in his dining tent in September 1887, during which cowboys and cooks brandished knives, revolvers, and a meat cleaver.[32] Cody's close management was a major factor in the show's avoidance of the disasters visited upon Shelley and other reckless impresarios. During Mexican Joe's appearance at the Liverpool Exhibition in October, their "Tombstone Coach" was racing "full speed" through the city when it overturned. The spectacular crash threw two women passengers and a good portion of the band into the street, smashing all their instruments. Four people were rushed to the hospital with severe injuries.[33]

Over more than three decades on the road, Buffalo Bill's Wild West had its share of arena accidents, train wrecks, severe injuries, and even deaths in the ring. But the fact remains that in thirty-three years of performance, no public calamity of this order befell the show's signature Deadwood coach. Cody's careful attention to hiring only skilled drivers (and driving himself when the most prestigious passengers were aboard) ensured a spectacle that was as remarkably smooth and safe as it was thrilling.

Barnum was every bit the professional Cody was, and his show, too, had a certain resonance as an American symbol. Its size—three rings to the traditional one of the European circus—and its frenetic activity called to mind an American factory in the mind of at least one critic.[34] But Cody presented a show not of circus weirdness, but of history in which he had been more or less a participant. He was therefore more authentic, his show more real. Even among the crowd of aspiring Wild West show directors, he had the most extensive frontier biography, in addition to a decade and a half of press notices for his performances. He had been featured in dime novels for almost twenty years. Finally, no other impresario had his military accolades. An 1887 poster which Cody and Burke designed for their London publicity campaign depicted Cody's face surrounded by images of American army officers over the title "Some of the Famous Generals of the U.S. Army Under Whom Buffalo Bill Has Served." Each officer (they were not all generals, in fact) appeared above his testimonial to Cody's courage and daring, and each testimonial bore its author's signature. Pedestrians who paused to admire its fine detail could savor the face of Cody and each man who praised him:

> *"A cool, brave man of unimpeachable integrity."*
>
> —P. H. Sheridan, Lieutenant General

> *"As an Indian scout, he is king of them all."*
>
> —Eugene A. Carr, General, U.S.A.

> *"Your Services on the frontier were invaluable."*
>
> —Nelson A. Miles, Brigadier General, U.S. Army

Cody's usefulness to the American army was perhaps at its peak, and the officers on the poster did not hesitate to attach their name to his standard. (Or at least the living ones did not; Custer was also featured, but with no endorsement.) Given the high social position of officers in the British army, the popular assumption in Britain was that Cody was a high-ranking officer, or at least upper class. This highbrow validation was plastered all over London and surrounding towns. In subsequent years it was reprinted in show programs and pasted to billboards and walls across the United States and Europe.[35]

But of all the reasons for Cody's success at instilling his European tour in

American memory, none is so important as his extraordinary ability to tap American longings for cultural and political validation. The patronage of the Wild West by European elites provided that validation, and it was one of the primary reasons for taking Buffalo Bill's Wild West to Europe in the first place. In traveling the Old World with his entertainment, Cody sought not only to make money, but to acquire a new layer of elite approbation which would protect him and his show from the stigma of circus and carnival back in the United States. Success in Europe would compound the middle-class appeal he had gained with *The Drama of Civilization*.

This ambition in particular reflected his intuitive grasp of America's ongoing cultural inferiority complex, and his sharp artistic sensibilities about how he could address it. To be sure, Americans prided themselves on many things in 1887. American engineers had distinguished themselves technologically, with rates of shipbuilding, railroad production, and mechanization that placed them on par with transatlantic rivals.[36] The rise of the United States from humble frontier origins to modern industrial nation was a powerful story, and Americans were ever pleased to tell it (as they did in the show of canned goods, false teeth, and other American manufactures on display in the American Exhibition, across the "Washington Bridge" which connected Buffalo Bill's showgrounds to the exhibition hall).

But if America's success marked the path of westward-marching civilization, there was no question that civilization itself hailed from the Old World. In this connection, Americans—who were fascinated by the proliferation of artifice and copy in their Industrial Revolution—were profoundly conscious of their culture as an imitation of Europe's original. America might have taller mountains, wider plains, steel production as great as Britain's or Germany's, and hog-slaughter works that exceeded both. But in music, literature, and drama, she remained indebted to Europe.

On this score, American writers and performers were perennially anxious about their originality. If the real proof of a nation's greatness lay in its art, then critics generally concurred that Americans had precious little to offer.[37] "In the four quarters of the globe, who reads an American book, or goes to an American play, or looks at an American picture or statue?" taunted Englishman Sidney Smith in 1820. The question riled Americans for most of the century. Someday, wrote Walt Whitman, "a great and original literature is sure to become the justification and reliance of American democracy."[38] Despite the novels of Melville, the paintings of Thomas Cole and the Hudson River School, and the poetry of Whitman, a sense that America was the cultural poor relative of Europe long persisted on both sides of the Atlantic.[39]

Having endured this inadequacy at least since the Revolution, Americans often answered by pointing to the uniqueness of their natural assets, particularly in the West, where natural wonders balanced Europe's cultural treasures. In the aftermath of the Civil War, the monumental landscapes of Yellowstone, the Grand Canyon, and Yosemite, among others, became widely known for the first time. "Nature's Nation" claimed these landscapes as repositories of natural virtue.[40]

Buffalo Bill's biography and publicity placed his origins firmly in this natural context. His show programs routinely employed a melodramatic cliché in their accounts of Cody, calling him "Nature's Nobleman," to suggest that he was a natural-born aristocrat, the quintessential American whose virtues stemmed from regenerative nature rather than from decadent culture. Moreover, the show deployed a full range of natural props to suggest the "natural nobility" of its western cast, including buffalo, elk, deer, and longhorn steers, and the mountain of dirt (planted with trees) abutting the painted mountain landscape of the backdrop. By creating a show about the white race's encounter with nature, Buffalo Bill's Wild West turned America's most risible shortcoming—its predominance of nature and its absence of culture—into a primary show business asset.

As we have seen, the frontier line was symbolically a divide between wilderness Nature and civilized Artifice, the real and the fake. As a show, Buffalo Bill's Wild West came to stand for the world of the natural and the real, a position it constantly reinforced with its heaping portions of authenticity in Buffalo Bill, the show's Indians, and all its western animals and paraphernalia. In this sense, the meeting of Buffalo Bill with European royals symbolized opposing poles of natural man and cultural man. Where Europe was the font of real culture, the frontier was the retreating space of real nature. Buffalo Bill's eastward journey, from America's regenerative and retreating Nature, to Europe, the source of westward-marching culture, reversed the course of conquest and connected the poles of historical reality.

The result was a current of validation unlike anything Americans had experienced. Journeying from lowly frontier origins to European adulation, Buffalo Bill's Wild West symbolized the advent of the United States as a cultural force, not merely a military or economic one. In Buffalo Bill's success, America herself had finally arrived on the world stage. The fact that the stories were partly fiction made no difference. The very fact that the elusive queen had come to his show and liked it was enough to validate it as something more than cheap entertainment, as something at once cultural and natural.

The usefulness of Buffalo Bill's Wild West to Americans anxious to announce their cultural maturity was no accident. Cody designed the show to travel to Europe. In 1879, he ended his autobiography with an announcement that he would take his theatrical combination to Europe. He did not go, perhaps because he recognized that frontier melodrama was not original enough to satisfy his and his country's ambitions for European sanction. In 1882, before he even began to pull the Wild West show together, he was requesting new testimonials to prove his authenticity for European audiences. "I have long had a desire to visit England but have [been] deterred from doing so by the thought that I might be classed among the many impostors who have gone before me claiming to be Scouts and frontiersmen," he wrote General Miles. "I want to be treated like a gentleman by those I may meet over there and as it is possible that I may make the trip in the near future, I would like to add your testimony to the credentials I am securing from other distinguished officials that I am the veritable W. F. Cody known as Buffalo Bill and have acted as scout and guide for you."[41]

Cody and Salsbury, seasoned showmen with over a quarter century of theatrical experience between them, were intimately familiar with their compatriots' anxieties where culture was concerned. Their chief associations were among American actors, singers, dancers, and musicians, and especially reviewers and critics. They crafted Buffalo Bill's Wild West as an answer to the endless lament for an original American performance. As a "historical exhibition" it propagated the American story through dramatic reenactment, and the title they attached to it—"America's National Entertainment"—was an answer to the call of Whitman and others for an art that would express American greatness.

Even prior to its ascent to widespread respectability, Buffalo Bill's Wild West show gained an eminent fan who recognized its potential for overseas validation. In September of 1884, Cody received a letter out of the blue.

Dear Mr. Cody:

I have seen your Wild West show two days in succession, and have enjoyed it thoroughly. It brought vividly back the breezy wild life of the Great Plains and the Rocky Mountains, and stirred me like a war-song. Down to its smallest details, the show is genuine—cowboys, vaqueros, Indians, stage coach, costumes and all; it is wholly free from sham and insincerity, and the effects produced upon me by its spectacles were identical with those wrought upon me long ago by the same spectacles on the frontier. Your pony expressman was as tremendous an interest to me yesterday as he was twenty-three years ago, when he used to come whizzing by from over the desert with the war news: and your bucking horses even painfully real to me, as I rode one of those outrages once for nearly a quarter of a minute. It is often said on the other side of the water that none of the exhibitions which we send to England are purely and distinctively American. If you will take the Wild West show over there, you can remove that reproach.

Truly Yours,
Mark Twain

The endorsement was a rarity, and high praise indeed. P. T. Barnum was a close friend of Twain's, but try as he might, he could never persuade the author to endorse his circus.[42] Cody, on the other hand, received Twain's letter unsolicited. Not surprisingly, show publicists reprinted it in newspapers and show programs, for many years.[43]

How much Twain recognized the artful deceptions of the show is hard to say. But coming from the author who did more than any other to present American identity as an imposture, the letter is as telling for scholars as it was confirming for audiences. Mark Twain himself presented the West as a grand series of adventures, double meanings, and charades in his 1872 *Roughing It.* Passing the scene of an 1856 stagecoach massacre, in which all hands but one were killed, Twain noted there must have been some mistake, "for at different times afterward on the Pacific coast I was personally acquainted with a hundred and thirty-three or four people who were wounded during that massacre, and barely escaped with their lives. There was no doubt of the truth of it—I had it from their own lips."[44] *Roughing It* was devoted in large part to these stories about stories, enhanced by Twain's own talent for the tall tale, which renders the book one giant puzzle, or wonder, through which readers join Twain in the most essential and entertaining of all frontier experiences, trying to separate truth from fiction.

Thus, where many have read his endorsement as proof of the Wild West show's unswerving devotion to an unexpurgated West, Twain's praise reflected his subtle appreciation of the artifice and imposture that went hand in hand with the display of real western figures and all those buffalo, elk, mules, and "painfully real" bucking horses. Like all "realistic" art, it was less devoted to copying every detail of western experience than to producing the same emotions the frontier once did. Thus "the effects produced upon me by its spectacles" were "identical with those wrought upon me long ago by the same spectacles on the frontier." In other words, Cody's show was a remarkable demonstration of verisimilitude, a displacement of the West via the railroad and the arena that came off as remarkably convincing, "free of sham and insincerity."

Once we acknowledge the centrality of artful deception to Twain's sense of the "real" frontier, his endorsement of Buffalo Bill's Wild West makes a great deal of sense. In his eyes (one of which was ever winking), the show was a spectacle of real cowboys and real Indians and the nation's most famous scout, all assuming the same poses which one would expect on the real frontier. Like the westerners he had encountered in the West, Cody and his cast claimed to have survived stagecoach attacks, fought Indians (or cowboys, if they were Indians), and tamed bucking broncos. Some of them even had done such things, and replicated it in the arena. They were utterly convincing, whether they were truthful or not. Twain had watched in wry amusement as actual westerners played at being westerners in the West (and as scribe and miner, he joined them). What pleased him was how remarkably well these westerners did it in the East, too.

To Twain, the show of western reality was an imposture of frontier imposture. In recommending that it venture across the water as an "original" entertainment to confront Europe's "real" culture, he was suggesting a benign but elaborate masquerade. America's foremost connoisseur of literary imposture could only find such an idea hilariously appealing.

Americans' profound sense of cultural inferiority was reinforced by a vigorous transatlantic exchange of artists and art. British performers found new audiences for their work among Americans hungry for Europe's "real" cultural products, and the rewards could be lucrative. In 1811, the English actor George Frederick Cooke visited the United States, and for the rest of the century English performers, writers, and painters followed his example. In 1885, Oscar Wilde toured America, to widespread acclaim. As Cody well knew from all his years on the stage, in the United States, English actors routinely drew larger crowds, and earned bigger receipts, than their American counterparts.[45]

American performers who traveled the opposite direction met with some success—an actor named Joseph Jefferson was a big hit as Rip Van Winkle in London in 1875—but generally the praise and renown they earned was qualified by critics who saw Americans as, at best, imitators of English and Continental art.[46] After reviewing the display of American paintings at the American Exhibition that adjoined the Wild West show, one London critic described U.S. painters as having ceased their devotion to English painters only to become followers of the French, so that "nothing very original, nothing pointedly national, has come of it."[47]

To be sure, the critics were often wrong. The exhibit which featured "nothing pointedly national" included paintings by Albert Bierstadt and Thomas Moran, whose work has since been venerated as American classic, but which the reviewer discounted for its "false mechanical colour and photographic dulness of *mise-en-scene.*"[48]

Snobbery and overstatement aside, America's performance arts were, by and large, still recognizably European in origin. American theater, circus, and even nascent vaudeville too closely resembled European art forms to be distinguished as uniquely American. Minstrelsy was an important exception.

Derived from traditions of music and dance among slaves, American minstrels were a popular entertainment in Britain, to which the British had no indigenous counterpart. But by the 1880s, most minstrel acts were comprised of black people, singing tunes made popular by white singers in blackface a generation before. The very fact that it was *black* music and dance meant that white Americans could not easily claim it as their culture. For a white public that saw America as a white nation, the success of minstrelsy overseas was more embarrassment than honor.[49]

No, in American minds, Europe was the source of real culture. From its capitals in Paris, London, and Rome, art of all kinds flowed westward. The process involved a whole range of cultural products, from plays and operas to frock coats and couches. In all these things, European aristocrats set the standards of fashion, and American elites spent much money copying them. The American middle class, in turn, mimicked elite fashions with cheap imitations, readily available through mail-order houses such as Sears & Roebuck and Montgomery Ward. (And lower-class people, of course, able only to get the cheapest imitations or used goods, were characteristically "out of fashion.") Americans could tell a great story about their civilization's triumph over savage wilderness, but they were inevitably conscious that the apparel they wore, the shows they watched, the books they read, and the music that inspired them were either European or copies of European originals. As far as culture was concerned, America herself was a copy. Europe was the anvil of the real.[50]

The importance of the Wild West show as a natural, or real, symbol of real American culture helps explain why Europe's embrace of it became so important, and why Cody and his partners worked so hard to repeat the patronage of the British crown—and the fanciful tales they spun about it—for years afterward. The 1887 season in Britain was only the beginning of a long European connection. In total, Buffalo Bill's Wild West show spent nine of its thirty-three years, almost a third of its life, in Europe. After a year in the United Kingdom, Buffalo Bill's Wild West toured the United States again in 1888, before venturing to Paris in 1889 for six months at the Exposition Universelle. There followed an exclusive tour of France, Spain, Italy, Austria-Hungary, and Germany, which lasted from late 1889 until 1892. After that, the show finally returned to the United States again for its legendary six-month stand outside the 1893 World's Columbian Exposition in Chicago. For the rest of the 1890s, Buffalo Bill's Wild West toured the United States and enjoyed dramatic fame and praise for its "conquest" of the Old World. But even then, its European days were not done. The show returned to Europe again late in 1902, and remained there, touring as far east as Ukraine, through 1906.

The Wild West show's tenure in Europe had a gigantic influence on

European perceptions of America. But just as important, its European successes changed the way Americans perceived the Wild West show, the meaning of frontier mythology, and their own history. Cody's reception before "the crowned heads of Europe" gave him cachet as the impresario of a show that was real culture, but it also reinforced the narrative of Cody's life as an ongoing tale of political and social progress. The "representative man" of the American frontier had ventured "from Prairie to Palace." At a time when American tourism to Europe was surging, encounters of New World travelers and Old World hosts became the subject of numerous novels and nonfiction accounts, including Mark Twain's *The Innocents Abroad* and *Tom Sawyer Abroad*. After all, it was an American, George Francis Train, who had wagered back in 1870 that he could travel around the world in less than eighty days, and thereby inspired Jules Verne's *Around the World in Eighty Days*.[51] The travels of Buffalo Bill's Wild West in Europe, and the numerous published accounts of them, provided a vehicle for reflecting on the passage of Americans through Europe as a millennial moment, the meeting of past and future, old civilization and new.

"What, then, is the American, this new man?" asked Hector St. John de Crèvecoeur in 1782. The question has been repeated by every generation since, on both sides of the Atlantic.[52] Now Cody tendered his answer: "I am." The white Indian from the Great Plains was the representative American, and his show was America itself. At its most superficial level, Buffalo Bill's Wild West encouraged Americans to face Europe's history, culture, and monuments with the courage of their origin as frontier people, honest men and women who came by their gentility "naturally," who need not hide their true natures under the mask of artifice. In the London press, Cody was acclaimed a modest, sincere, authentic hero, whose gracious manners were "natural" products of the frontier, and whose show business success was attributed over and over again to his spectacular "realism."

Meetings with royalty and other notable Europeans, and also visits to European landmarks, were staged and recounted in ways to enhance these effects, perhaps most famously (after the meeting with Victoria) in Rome. The passage of the Wild West show to Rome, the foundation of Western civilization, "famed of the famous cities," was anticipated from the time of the show's first success in London. In 1887, a British journalist penned a poem, "Buffalo Bill and the Romans," that humorously reflected on the rise of Cody's English stardom, the expansion of American power it symbolized, and his destiny in Rome.

> *I'll take my stalwart Indian braves*
> *Down to the Coliseum*

> *And the old Romans from their graves*
> *Will arise to see'em;*
> *Pretors and censors will return*
> *And hasten through the Forum,*
> *The ghostly Senate will adjourn*
> *Because it lacks a quorum.*
>
> *And up the ancient Appian way*
> *Will flock the ghostly legions,*
> *From Gaul unto Calabria,*
> *And from remoter regions;*
> *From British bog and wild lagoon,*
> *And Libyan desert sandy,*
> *They'll all come, marching to the tune*
> *Of "Yankee Doodle Dandy."*
>
> *Prepare the triumph car for me*
> *And purple throne to sit on,*
> *For I've done more than Julius C.——*
> *He could not down the Briton!*
> *Caesar and Cicero shall bow,*
> *And ancient warriors famous,*
> *Before the myrtle-bandaged brow*
> *Of Buffalo Williamus*

In the final verse, the great civilization of President Grover Cleveland led the triumphant Americans as heirs to the Roman Empire:

> *We march, unwhipped, through history—*
> *No bulwark can detain us—*
> *And link the age of Grover C.*
> *And Scipio Africanus.*
> *I'll take my stalwart Indian braves*
> *Down to the Coliseum,*
> *And the old Romans from their graves*
> *Will all arise to see'em.*[53]

The Italian tour, especially its Roman debut, was carefully scripted, and Burke's history of it carefully contrived, to meet these expectations. The same newspaper editor who had been Cody's champion since Sheridan's lavish hunting expedition of 1871, James Gordon Bennett, Jr., now dispatched at least one correspondent to cover Buffalo Bill's Italian adventure. Thus the *New York Herald* apprised American readers of the show's Italian triumphs in 1890. Three years later, when Burke published the company's memoir of the tour in yet another Cody biography, *"Buffalo Bill" from Prairie to Palace*, he interspersed his own commentary among reprints of the *Herald* articles. The show did not appear at the Colosseum ("too small for this modern exhibition," said John Burke), but it did perform before an audience of 65,000 in the amphitheater in Verona ("a rival of the Coliseum itself," wrote the ecstatic journalist). According to the *Herald* writer, the amphitheater was in fact the largest building in the world, "although the Wild West Show quite filled it." The account included elements of the arena's venerable history, so American readers could savor the performance of frontier heroism and American progress in a building erected by command of Emperor Diocletian in A.D. 290 and restored at the behest of Napoleon in 1805.

Americans dreamed of visiting the Vatican, and some even did so. But they could only fantasize about meeting Pope Leo XIII as the Wild West company did. Burke related how Cody, with a delegation of cowboys and Indians, attended "a dazzling fete given in the Vatican by his holiness Pope Leo XIII." Burke made it sound as if the Vatican threw a reception for the Wild West show, and that the crowds who attended, from "the gorgeous Diplomatic Corps" to the ranks of dukes and princes, turned out to see Buffalo Bill. In reality, the crowds and Cody's cast gathered for an anniversary celebration of the pope's coronation.[54]

With cowboys and Indians, the latter "painted in every color that Indian imagination could devise," the American press depicted the encounter with the pope as a meeting between Christian pontiff and heathen barbarians. Symbolically, Rome's civilizing project now became America's mission. "The cowboys bowed," wrote the *New York Herald* correspondent, "and so did the Indians. Rocky Bear knelt and made the sign of the cross. The pontiff leaned affectionately toward the rude groups and blessed them."[55]

For Cody himself, the triumph of the show's Roman passage was doubly sweet. Over twenty years before, he had given the name of Rome to his nascent Kansas town, expressing his ambitions as founder of empire and civilization. Even now Cody told the story of how William Webb "made Rome howl" like some savage chieftain when he founded neighboring Hays and withered Cody's dream.

But the Wild West show provided him a theater of civilization and progress like no prairie town could have. On the one hand, cowboys and Indians, whether they appeared before the queen or the pope or simply in the streets of European villages and towns, offered a portable story of progress equally useful, for different reasons, on both sides of the Atlantic. Every American could revel in the ascent of these rustic frontiersmen to the theaters of power and the halls of civilization. Was this not the American story? On the other hand, every European who met the cowboys and Indians could presume to offer lessons in civility and advancement. Was this not Europe's legacy? In an age of colonial expansion, with Britain, France, and Germany appropriating large parts of Africa, Asia, and the Pacific, the spectacle of these "rude" and "primitive" peoples venturing to Europe for money and cultural patronage seemed to confirm Europe's civilizing mission. The sight of Cody's troupe among Europe's ancient ruins and monuments suggested stories so powerful and relevant that their mere appearance in the streets could become newsworthy. As both the impresario of the traveling show and the star of the story it told, Cody was a living conduit of history, embodying a merger of action and representation, Nature and Artifice, so electrifying it was almost impossible not to watch.

Other shows had famous audiences and fabulous endorsements, and at times they perhaps made advertising out of the day a famous person visited or how an endorsement was proffered. But none could make such a potent myth of progress out of those stories as Buffalo Bill's Wild West. Only a show that approximated a popular historical narrative, a "historical exhibition," could have an accompanying "historical text." When these newspaper stories of papal benediction and Roman conquest were reprinted in show programs alongside Cody's alleged biography as Pony Express rider, buffalo hunter, and Indian fighter, they seemed to prove America's progress like no other popular entertainment. Small wonder that few questioned the stories of royal bows to the American flag, kings in the Deadwood coach, papal fetes for the Wild West company, or anything else from Burke's purported histories of Wild West conquests. If audiences suspected they might not be completely factual, these meetings with the queen and the pope had been reported in the press when it happened. If the details were not correct, the stories were true enough. None doubted that Europeans saw Americans as possessed of real art, real culture. Buffalo Bill, the self-made man from the frontier, the realm of Nature, had proved it.

As an American impresario who received unprecedented endorsement from European elites, Cody did much to reassure Americans about the distinctiveness and the appeal of American culture in general and his show in particular. Just as Buffalo Bill "naturalized" theatrical entertainment by presenting a real frontiersman in the footlights, just as he made the circus into a domestic entertainment by presenting it as American frontier history, here his European successes validated him, American history, and U.S. entertainments, as bona fide culture. Small wonder that Americans have been grateful to him ever since.

FOR CODY, of course, these were years of personal success and fun. He was not a little impressed with himself. "We leave for Rome on Monday," he wrote a friend as the crew packed up in Naples. "This has been the trip of my life & I tell you a big undertakeing to take such a big outfit into strange countries. I know of no other managers who dare risk so much." The show's European triumphs put his rivals to shame. "I guess Barnum is sorry he followed the Wild West across the Atlantic. I see he closes in London today. Well three months was a long stay for a circus. I guess he wishes he had closed two months ago."[56]

Cody's victories in the fierce competition of show business proved his supreme abilities as a capitalist and a purveyor of an entertainment product. But more than P. T. Barnum or any other show impresario, he seemed to represent America to the world. If Rome failed him in Kansas, this show of the Kansas plains in Rome gave him the mantle of conqueror and civilizer. That day at the Vatican, the papal blessing was not restricted to his cowboys and Indians. "The Pope looked at Colonel Cody intently as he passed, and the great scout and Indian fighter bent low as he received the pontifical benediction."[57] No showman had ever been so blessed.

WHILE CODY'S success in Europe had many uses for Americans, Europeans did not admire the show simply because they liked Americans. Buffalo Bill's Wild West drew huge crowds in the United Kingdom and on the Continent because of the ways it spoke to European desires and anxieties. A full accounting of the show's meaning for its diverse European audiences would require a book in itself. But Buffalo Bill's debut in London in 1887 opened the doors to its success on the Continent. The story of how Cody's message was received in England reveals the allure of American frontier myth in Britain and Europe, but also the full range of cultural statements the show inspired in its turn. The golden myth of the Wild West offered promise and peril to Victoria's Britain, and how British people responded to its fun and their own forebodings about it can instruct us in the real power and meaning of frontier mythology in Europe as well as in the United States.

IN JUNE, almost two months after the Wild West show docked at Gravesend, Cody took a coach trip in Oatlands Park, London. For all the celebrity sojourns in the Deadwood coach that summer, this little-noticed outing offers clues to the deeper fascination of the Wild West show for English audiences. On this day, Cody was the guest of Henry Irving, England's greatest living actor, as was John Lawrence Toole, a friendly theatrical rival of Irving's. The two renowned actors and the season's social lion, whose posters had made his long black hair and Vandyke beard easily recognizable throughout London, sat together on the box. The three drew gasps and, occasionally, shouts of approval from onlookers.

But some of the most important, and least noticed, influences of the Wild West show involved a fourth passenger, one who was probably unknown to most observers that day. Large and red-haired, engaging and solicitous, Bram Stoker, the future author of *Dracula*, was also aboard with Cody, Toole, and Irving.[58]

This probably was not Stoker's first meeting with Cody. The two had likely met in the United States at least a year before. Stoker corresponded with Cody and with the showman's staff. He most likely attended the Wild West show in London. Henry Irving was Cody's most renowned social patron that summer, and Bram Stoker, who followed Irving's every move, had a front-row seat at the American's conquest of London society.

In 1897, ten years after Buffalo Bill's London premiere and at the height of his fame, Bram Stoker introduced another frontier figure to the English capital. Commander of the Christian forces against the Ottoman Turks hundreds of years before, the "bravest and most cunning of Transylvania's sons" on the Turkish frontier, his purpose in London was very different from Buffalo Bill's. So was his reception. After turning one wealthy young woman into a vampire and nearly snagging another, he was chased out of the capital by an international posse of English, Dutch, and American men, who tracked this nemesis to Transylvania, vanquished his Gypsy bodyguards, and killed him within sight of his castle.

Unlike William Cody, Count Dracula was, of course, an entirely fictional creation. This did not prevent his becoming an object of immense fascination. Among the reading public, the count would become almost as popular as Buffalo Bill. Appearing for the first time in 1897, the novel *Dracula* was in paperback by 1900. It has never been out of print since, and the count's many film incarnations have made him the preeminent nineteenth-century monster.[59]

Superficially, the contrast between Cody and the count could not be greater. Benign hero and malign villain, one is the center of a progressive myth of regeneration and renewal; the other embodies the decadence and the terrifying power of the gothic imagination. It is well established that Stoker's monster had many inspirations and literary precursors, including a century of bloodsucking forebears.[60] Less recognized is how much Stoker's masterpiece turns on the frontier mythology of Buffalo Bill.

Weird as it may seem, Buffalo Bill and his Wild West show were important inspirations for Bram Stoker's *Dracula*. In Cody's drama, as in *Dracula*,
the frontiers of racial encounter were invested with the possibility of degeneration and the necessity of race war. Tracing Stoker's famous novel to its
roots in Cody's spectacle illustrates how late-nineteenth-century progressive frontier myth and the literature of gothic horror represented fictional
worlds that were homologous—that is, divergent but sprung from common
origins, on mythic race frontiers. Cody himself saw his creation as historical
epic, which joined the white race to the spilling of blood across the frontier.
We shall see that *Dracula*, although a novel set in the world's largest city, is
also, crucially, a frontier tale. For showman and author both, continual westward expansion and continual race war secured the racial destiny of white
people. But they differed, ultimately, on the promise of frontier warfare.
Cody believed in it as the salvation of the white race; Bram Stoker's view,
shared by many compatriots, was much gloomier. In his most famous novel,
frontiers became almost as dangerous to the race as vampires.

The connections between Buffalo Bill and Count Dracula take us well
beyond the popularity of American frontier myth in late Victorian England.
Dracula, as literary scholar Steven Arata has written, is a novel of reverse
colonization, in which "the colonizer finds himself in the position of the col-
onized, the exploiter is exploited, the victimizer victimized." In this analysis,
the powerful Count Dracula invades imperial England and comes very close
to reducing it to his "imperial" domain. By removing the race essence of his
victims, their blood, he turns them into vampires and extends, in the words
of the novel's chief monster hunter, his "vampire kind." In a fundamental
way, he underscores the racial weakness of his victims and the transformative racial power of his own monstrosity.[61]

The appeal of Cody's Wild West show for English audiences flowed in
part from their own obsession with racial decay, which was at least as great as
that of the Americans. The late nineteenth century saw widespread concern
in Britain about slowing birth rates, the steady loss of international competitiveness, the growing ranks of the city poor and of a combative, strike-
prone industrial working class, the continued shrinking of rural villages, and
a general decline of English political and industrial power, all accented by
the diminishing fortunes of the nation's aristocracy and upper classes. To
many observers, progress seemed in danger of stopping and reversing itself.

The most popular explanation for these complicated developments was
the weakening of the Anglo-Saxon race. In September, as Cody prepared to
take his show north to Manchester for a winter of indoor performances, one
Dr. Joseph Milner gave a lecture on the condition of the English people at
the Islington Agricultural Hall. Warning that Britain's increasingly urban
people were ill-nourished and smaller than their rural ancestors, Milner

postulated that they were degenerating, moving backward down the evolutionary ladder, in "a reversion towards an earlier and lowlier ethnic form. While the residents in the country remained Anglo-Danes, town dwellers approached the smaller, darker Celto-Iberian race." To see the frightening truth, one need only compare the scurrying little workers in London's East End with "the massive folk seen in country towns on market day," or visit the wax museum of Madame Tussaud and compare "the crowd of small dark living beings with the substantial fair personages sitting there in effigy."[62]

Milner echoed widely held views, which were pervasive in the literature of the period, notably Robert Louis Stevenson's *The Strange Case of Dr. Jekyll and Mr. Hyde* (1886), H. Rider Haggard's *She* (1887), and the fiction of Rudyard Kipling, all of which explored the implications of diminishing white manhood, adrift in a world of rough, industrial cities and dark, menacing colonies.[63]

To be sure, Britain and other nations of western Europe in general saw themselves as exemplars of progress and apogees of civilization, just as the United States did. Belief in the redemptive value of civilization for the poor benighted savages of the world energized their imperial expansions and their nationalism, both of which grew dramatically in these years.

But the dramatic demographic changes and political strife that came with industrialization made Europeans, like Americans, highly sensitive to the darker aspects of Progress. Since civilization itself was racial (the gift of white people to the world), it was almost impossible to understand the decay of civilization as anything but the decay of the race (although French, English, Germans, and others differed on exactly who was "white"). Just as Americans began romanticizing the "barbarian virtues" of dark people, and trying to find ways to infuse white manhood with them, Europeans contemplated the decay of civilization and the corruption of the modern with meditations on barbarism and the nobility of the primitive.

This gigantic project encompassed many aspects of European art and culture, and Buffalo Bill's Wild West resonated with them in dramatic, even inspirational ways. London commentators were bedazzled by the many rhetorical tropes and images which flowed from the Wild West show's vibrant tension between primitive and progressive energies, but no theme was so pronounced in the show's reception as the fear of racial decay. For this reason, most commentators were lavish in their praise of Cody and his show in 1887. Its drama was overtly optimistic, depicting white Americans—Anglo-Americans—invigorated and racially empowered by the experience of conquering the frontier. And yet, between the lines of adulatory show reviews lurked an abiding ambivalence, even a fear, of the powerful American virility on display in Buffalo Bill's arena. Amid all the English enthusiasm for the Wild West show's regenerative promise of frontier warfare glimmered a specter of reverse colonization by racially powerful frontier warriors, the Americans, which observers seemed unable to escape completely.

For all the differences between the Wild West show and *Dracula*, there can be little question that Stoker had the American West on his mind as he composed the novel, in which his representative American was an almost-cowboy from the far western frontier named Quincey Morris. A Texan, he joins the tale's European protagonists. Stoker had traveled in America, and seems to have admired the place.[64] But reading between the lines of the novel, one has to wonder how deep his admiration ran. Of the three young male protagonists who chase Dracula down and dispose of him, Morris is disturbingly incompetent. His trigger-happiness and poor aim endanger his friends, he fails in simple assignments to follow the vampire, and in the attempted capture of Dracula in London, the count escapes when Morris bungles. So consistently does he parade his ineptitude that other questions arise. Why did Stoker make his representative American, his westerner, such a fool? For that matter, is Morris just a buffoon? Or are his numerous blunders a mask for a deeper malevolence? He is presented as a racial relative of the book's English protagonists, and in a crucial scene his blood is transfused into one of the count's English victims—who then becomes a vampire. Whose side is the American on?[65]

The answers to these enduring riddles of Stoker's plot and intent are connected to the novel's racial implications, which become salient when read against the backdrop of Buffalo Bill's Wild West show. Its drama, in which the American Anglo-Saxons are hardened in the crucible of frontier race war, had a distorted reflection in *Dracula*, a dark parable about urban Anglo-Saxons threatened by a frontier hero gone bad. In the twentieth century, scholars have often examined the racial and cultural anxieties that underlie horror and western film genres.[66] Tracing the shadowy connections between Bram Stoker and William Cody provides some startling clues not only about the meaning of the novel *Dracula*, but also about William Cody's signal, and probably unwitting, contribution to the development of frontier and gothic traditions as racial myths in the transatlantic fin de siècle.

To look at Cody's glorious legend in the shadowy twilight of Stoker's art is to discover new meanings within it. While scholars of Cody and of the frontier routinely evaluate Wild West show nostalgia and frontier triumphalism, they have been less willing to acknowledge its darker twin, the contemporary fear of the frontier as a place of racial monstrosity. This anxiety had stalked Cody's career ever since he consorted with mixed-blood scouts on the Great Plains, and Cody himself had played on it, by situating himself as the unquestionably white man who yet mastered the miscegenated—degenerated—world of frontier and wilderness. The conjoined study of Buffalo Bill and Count Dracula suggests such fears informed a gothic frontier myth, featuring not a clear-cut conquest of the wilderness by white settlers, but the transformation of the pioneer into something more racially powerful—and infinitely twisted—that threatens the decadent metropolis.[67] The points of contact between the creators of these tales, Stoker and Cody, combined with the many significant correspondences between novel and show, command our attention. From the relative superficialities of plot and character to the deeper issues of the book's perspectives on race—blood—the ghost of Buffalo Bill's Wild West haunts this greatest work of vampire fiction.

THE PERSONAL HISTORIES that connect William Cody and Bram Stoker reveal how entangled the social and literary worlds of frontier myth and gothic terror actually were. *Dracula* is, in the words of Richard Davenport-Hines, "an intensely personal book," through which Stoker responded to developments in his private life.[68] Figures in *Dracula* were often warped reflections of friends and colleagues in the London theater world. Cody's arrival among that circle constituted Stoker's most immediate and significant exposure to the American West prior to his visit to California in the 1890s.

William Cody and Bram Stoker were almost exact contemporaries. Stoker was born in Dublin, in 1847, the son of an Anglo-Irish civil servant, and educated at Trinity College. His early writings consisted of theater reviews for Dublin newspapers and horror stories, which made him a favorite of Dublin's literary elite, including Lord William and Lady Jane Francesca Wilde, parents of Stoker's college acquaintance, Oscar Wilde. In the late 1860s, Stoker was much taken with the stage performances of a young English actor named Henry Irving, the leading light of the new Romantic school of acting. In 1876, the same year Cody took the "first scalp for Custer," Stoker met the thirty-eight-year-old Irving at a private gathering where Irving recited a poem in his honor, which sent Stoker into what he called "something like hysterics."[69] Irving was well on his way to becoming the Victorian era's most famous actor, and by 1878 Stoker had signed on as manager for his London theater, the Lyceum. Stoker worked for Irving for the next twenty-eight years, until the actor's death, and the relationship profoundly affected his life and his literary work.[70]

That Irving provided an uncertain bridge to a life of culture and wealth helps to explain Stoker's obsessive interest in the actor's affairs. Stoker was not only adulatory of Irving, but captivated by his presence and devoted to following his every move. As one contemporary remarked, "To Bram, Irving is as a god, and can do no wrong." Stoker's wife, Florence Balcombe Stoker, was a legendary beauty. She rejected Oscar Wilde's proposal of marriage to accept Stoker's, and George du Maurier, the author of *Trilby*, acclaimed her one of the three most beautiful women he had ever seen. But the marriage was cold, and Stoker's devotion to Irving subsumed his personal affections. In the considered judgment of one biographer, Stoker's friendship with Irving was "the most important love relationship of his adult life."[71]

For all this, Stoker seems to have been largely unappreciated by his employer and idol. Henry Irving was a self-absorbed and profoundly manipulative man. He enjoyed cultivating rivalries between his followers, and to remain in his circle required constant, careful courting of his notoriously fickle affections. Understandably, Stoker felt most secure when Irving took an interest in him personally, as he did in the early 1880s, and he became anxious and jealous when Irving turned his gaze to other men, as he did by 1885.[72]

Scholars have long agreed that the keys to the Dracula tale's origin and meaning lie in the manager's relationship with Irving in the 1880s. The later years of that decade and the early 1890s—the period of Stoker's first work on *Dracula*—were years of crisis for the manager, as he fought with others in Irving's company to defend the position he had worked so hard to attain. The friction provided the basis for new literary directions. He began to write his rivals for Irving's attention into his morbid fiction, such as his depiction of the Austin brothers, employees of Irving's whom Stoker envied and despised, as bloodthirsty twins in his horrifying tale "The Dualitists," which he published in 1887.[73]

There is virtual unanimity on the point that the figure of Dracula, which Stoker began to make notes for in 1890, was inspired by Henry Irving himself. Stoker originally intended the work as a play, with the tragedian in the leading role (Irving derided the novel—"Dreadful!"—and would have nothing to do with it).[74] Stoker's numerous descriptions of Irving correspond so closely to his rendering of the fictional count that contemporaries commented on the resemblance. He would remain devoted to Irving, producing a gushing two-volume memoir after his employer's death. But Bram Stoker also internalized the fear and animosity Irving inspired in him, making them the foundations of his gothic fiction.[75]

As significant as Stoker's experience in Irving's circle was in these years, it is surprising that no scholar has noticed how deeply Buffalo Bill Cody ingratiated himself with that circle in the same period. When Cody and Irving first met is not clear. Cody read of Irving's 1883 arrival in New York in the Chicago newspapers, which ran banner headlines announcing the event, just as he was appealing to Salsbury to manage the Wild West show at the close of its first season. Of course, Cody's theatrical reputation was in lowbrow melodrama, and any chance for an introduction to highbrow Irving was remote. Most likely, England's leading actor met Cody for the first time in 1886, when the Englishman saw the Wild West show at Erastina. Irving gave the show a rave review in advance of its 1887 London debut, predicting it would "take the town by storm." Even before the show embarked for London in 1887, people were introduced to Buffalo Bill as "friends of our mutual friend, Henry Irving."[76]

Irving and Cody found each other useful. By befriending Irving, an actor who had received unprecedented elite and royal patronage (William Gladstone offered to make Irving the first actor to receive a knighthood in 1883), Cody found entree to English society and validation for the cultural message of his educational exposition, culminating a strategy for enhancing his own myth which he had been developing for at least a decade.[77] For his part, Irving was a slender, pale man, his appearance ill-suited to the commanding stage roles he so enjoyed.[78] Consorting with Cody reinforced his position as a masculine and authoritative figure. Their companionship in certain ways embodied and expressed the busy exchange of cultural statements across the Atlantic that typified this and later periods. Americans sought out actors like Irving to provide elements of high culture that seemed weak or absent in much of the United States, and to reassure themselves by appreciating "highbrow" theater that they possessed at least as much potential for cultural development as Europeans. English people drew on frontier spectacles and myth for their own complicated reasons, not least of which was a need for reassurance about their own racial and political destinies.

In April 1887, shortly after the arrival of the Wild West show in London, Cody took his cowboys and Indians to see Henry Irving in a play at the Lyceum. As stunning as the stage performance was, the real show was this Wild West appearance in the audience.

This was a vintage Buffalo Bill moment, when an ordinary activity became a performance imbued with mythic significance for cast members and for the public on both sides of the Atlantic. The Wild Westerners' costumed visit to the Lyceum highlighted the achievements of American civilization in making the progress from rude and savage origins to this apex of Western culture, the premier theater in London. Seating Red Shirt, "chief" of the show Indians, and Buck Taylor, "King of the Cowboys," in the royal box suggested the "natural nobility" of the cowboys and Indians, and simultaneously validated the royal traditions of England as springing from a warlike and "natural" past. Irving exploited the event to full effect, inviting cowboys, Indians, and Cody onstage after the show, thereby becoming one of their manly company for a moment. On their departure, crowds jammed the streets to watch.[79]

Through the early summer of 1887, even a cursory reader of society columns could track their movements together. At Cody's invitation, the actor attended a special showing of the Wild West show before its public opening. He returned for opening day, too, and thereafter he had a private box at the Wild West arena. He hosted Cody at dinner parties at his own Lyceum's Beefsteak Room and escorted him to numerous dinners at the most fashionable London clubs. As in New York, invitations to Buffalo Bill frequently mentioned Irving as a mutual acquaintance, and an autographed photo of the American would remain in Irving's possession until the day he died.[80]

The London theatrical world—Stoker's world, and the cultural milieu in which *Dracula* was conceived and written—received Buffalo Bill's Wild West with what can only be described as near hysteria. The Wild West show inspired theatrical comedies, burlesques, and even a melodrama, entitled *Buffalo Bill.* Gilbert and Sullivan, fresh from their success with *The Mikado,* were rumored to be contemplating a musical comedy about the Wild West.[81] Cody inspired new fashion: men and boys began to appear with red sashes tied around their waists, and some even sported large "Buffalo Bill" hats.[82]

Stoker could not have helped but notice Cody's influence in any case, but the American's connection with his employer put him at the center of Stoker's attention. Irving did more than socialize with Cody. He spent so much time promoting the Wild West show that newspapers attributed its commercial success to him, the actor serving as a kind of highbrow analogue to the mass advertising of the show's colorful, ubiquitous posters. "Mr. Irving, the tragedian, and Mr. Partington, the bill-poster, have each contributed to make Mr. Cody, alias 'Buffalo Bill,' the most talked about man in London."[83] Cartoons in the penny press depicted them together, with Irving as Cody's patron, or advance agent.[84] Inseparable but distinct as they seemed to be in the public eye, humorists exploited the paradoxical friendship by making them interchangeable. Comics referred to Irving as a "great western showman" who would soon transform himself into a "Texan cow-boy" in order to attract Queen Victoria to one of his performances the way she had been lured out to see the Wild West show. Stoker himself saved a clipping from *Punch* magazine alleging that Cody would shortly take over the part of Mephistopheles in *Faust* (which Cody and his Indians and cowboys had watched at the Lyceum).[85]

In May, after watching the official opening of the Wild West show, Irving congratulated Cody on his London debut. "No one rejoices more than I do at your business success which may ever continue." Apologizing for being "tied to the stake here day and night," Irving offered to "drive you into the country in the company of a few good friends, of which I am, I shall be proud to call myself one."[86]

During all this time, Stoker watched the actor's relationship with the

*Henry Irving, England's great trage-
dian, the first actor to be offered a
knighthood—and Cody's social patron in
1887 London. Courtesy Shakespeare
Birthplace Trust, United Kingdom.*

frontiersman closely. He treated all of Irving's friendships with a mixture of
suspicion, envy, and resignation, and since he was as much Irving's social
secretary as his theater manager, he perhaps knew more about his
employer's affection for Cody than anybody but Irving himself. Twenty
years later, the manager looked back on the season that Buffalo Bill "struck
London . . . like a planet," and recalled how he and Irving together drove
the American to Oatlands Park, where the roads were thronged with a for-
tuitous, ready-made audience of people. The grouping of Cody, Irving, and
Toole "took the public taste," wrote Stoker, "and we swept along always to
an accompaniment of admiring wonder, sometimes to an accompaniment of
cheers."[87]

For the next few years, Cody and Irving were found together at surprising times, and in such degree that they seemed to shadow each other. The
English actor made a special trip to Bristol in 1891 to meet Cody—with his
usual retinue of Sioux Indians—at the Bristol train station.[88] That same year,
Buffalo Bill's Wild West and Irving's *Macbeth* overlapped in Glasgow. When
Irving was feted at Glasgow's Pen and Pencil Club, who should appear for
the dinner but William Cody, who himself became the subject of a drunken,
patriotic homage by an expatriate American with the temerity to toast the
frontiersman during Irving's party.[89]

Stoker had his own relationship with Cody, although like all of the manager's social bonds that were mediated through Irving, it paled in contrast to his employer's high-profile companionship with the American. Stoker requested, and received, souvenir photographs of Cody in 1887, as well as a complimentary season ticket to the Wild West show when it returned to London in 1892. He received Cody's requests for theater tickets on the American's business card, and from his business partner Nate Salsbury he received gifts, "beautiful Indian arrows which I shall always value," in 1893.[90]

What did Stoker think of Cody? Hints survive in long-unnoticed places. In the early 1890s, as *Dracula* progressed, Stoker wrote other gothic stories, including one about an American frontiersman (like Cody, from Nebraska) who is crushed in an iron maiden by a vengeful black cat at a castle in Germany. The frontier figure was so useful to the author that he resurrected him as the Texan vampire hunter Quincey Morris, in *Dracula*.[91]

The author explored themes of the American West further with a west-

THE TWO GREAT WESTERN SHOWMEN.

Henry: "Yes, Bill, nobody knows better than I the value of the 'puff preliminary.'"

Bill: "Henry, you've made business boom for me over here, and I guess I'll do you the same good turn when I get back among the boys."

Cartoonists lampooned "The Two Great Western Showmen," Buffalo Bill Cody and England's leading stage actor, Henry Irving. From Illustrated Bits, May 21, 1887.

ern novel, his only work set on the American frontier. Published in 1895, *The Shoulder of Shasta* features an Englishwoman, Esse, who takes a tour of California. There she falls in love with an American frontiersman bearing the memorable if unfortunate name of Grizzly Dick. But what stands out, for anyone who knows Stoker's social context in the 1890s, is how very familiar Grizzly Dick is. His hair flows down over his shoulders, he wears embroidered buckskins, and in a singular oddity, this hunter's daily wardrobe includes high black boots with Mexican spurs. At one point, a man in the novel compares him to Buffalo Bill Cody, a rather unsubtle hint of the character's inspiration, for Dick's outfit is almost a point-for-point description of Cody's costume in his most famous photographs from the 1887 London season.[92]

It is a singular story in other ways. In a genre characterized by frontier heroes who save white womanhood from the clutches of wilderness savagery—wild animals, Indians, and bandits—Esse falls in love with Grizzly Dick after *she* saves *him* from a bear. He is oblivious to her affections, and she pines away for him, growing weak and deathly pale after her return to San Francisco. Her salvation arrives in the form of a strapping English artist named Reginald (he might as well have been called Bram; Stoker was proud of his physique, and his athleticism) who becomes her new love interest and her fiancé. Her health returns as she forgets all about Dick.

The climax comes when Dick, through a miscommunication, receives an invitation to Esse's party in San Francisco. Dick abandons his buckskin for silk. He arrives a fop, his hair professionally curled beyond recognition, desperately trying to fit himself into urban society. He makes the transition from frontier to high society, like Cody did, but does what Cody would not: adopt the dress of his social betters. He has become a fool. Insulted by snobby guests, he pulls his bowie knife. Then, humiliated at his loss of control and horrified that he has drawn a weapon in the company of ladies, he hurls the knife to the ground, where the blade plunges into the floorboards. None of the men present is strong enough to remove it—except for Reginald, who presents it to Grizzly Dick as a gesture of friendship. In the ambivalent ending, Dick is persuaded to put his old clothes on, and he returns to the wilderness, while Esse and Reginald are left happily to marry.

If the novel is a flirtation with the American frontier, it also suggests the frontier is best left alone, and frontiersmen best left out there. In this light romance, it is the English artist-gentleman, Reginald, who embodies the right balance of manly power and gentility. The frontiersman is comical when he is not dangerous, and perhaps his greatest threat is the unreasoning, extreme infatuation he inspires in English womanhood, which causes Esse to wane before she is rescued by the cultured, manly, and very English hero. In fact, Esse's malady—her pallor, her listlessness, her loss of weight,

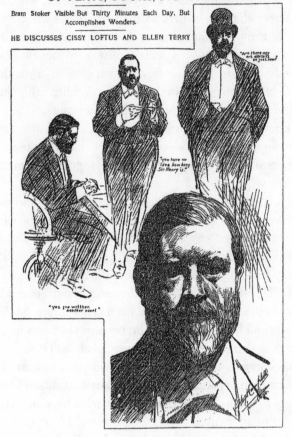

SIR HENRY IRVING'S MANAGER TALKS
OF PLAYS, BOOKS, PICTURES AND WAR

Bram Stoker Visible But Thirty Minutes Each Day, But
Accomplishes Wonders.

HE DISCUSSES CISSY LOFTUS AND ELLEN TERRY

Bram Stoker, 1901. The North American (Philadelphia), November 21, 1901.

her increasing detachment, and her inability to think about anything other than the mountain man—mimics the one that strikes the doomed Lucy Westenra after her visit from a frontier hunter who provokes an all-consuming passion in Stoker's next, and most famous, novel.[93]

The Shoulder of Shasta appeared in October of 1895. Less than two years later, the same publisher issued *Dracula*, the novel Stoker had been crafting for seven years.[94] It was by far his most ambitious work. In his fiction, Stoker had been exploring questions about frontiers and borders for the previous four years. But, speculating on the origins of *Dracula*, we could do worse than to revisit that coaching party in 1887. It was summer, the coach path winding through the trees. The spontaneous cheers for the men on the box must have seemed as natural as the setting, and perhaps made Stoker pon-

Stoker's description of "Grizzly Dick" matched this famous photograph of Buffalo Bill in London, 1887. Courtesy Buffalo Bill Historical Center.

der—as he often did—the sources of celebrity and its dark power. Perhaps the impromptu performance of these divergent geniuses side by side—Cody in all his unassuming genuineness and Irving in all his imperious assumptions—germinated in Stoker the seed of his Dracula tale. To be sure, the powerful tension between the virtuous frontier hero and the decadent life-draining monster would occupy center stage in his novel.

Of course, the ease with which the Wild West show appealed to English racial fears owes something to the way Cody conceived it as a response to analogous American anxieties.[95] As we have seen, in Cody's hands, the frontier became the setting for a constant race contest, a crucible of American whiteness, where the destiny of Anglo-Saxon America was shored up against the implicit decay of the cities, the Industrial Revolution, new immigration from southern and eastern Europe, and a host of other ill-defined threats and pervasive cultural fears.[96]

In making the social Darwinist contest between races the center of American and world history, Buffalo Bill's Wild West discounted and elided issues of class conflict. "Custer's Last Rally" was not performed in London in 1887. Instead, audiences saw the usual climactic scene, the "Attack on the Settler's Cabin."[97] By making the salvation of the home its paramount message, the show implied that racial propagation—itself the sign of racial vigor—would go to those who secured the frontier for their families. Burgeoning class tensions in industrial cities, such as London, could be glossed over by an appeal to a mythic natural past of racial conflict in which class simply did not figure.

Cody's centaur and indeed his company of "Transatlantic Centaurs" were but the latest of many monsters, real and imagined, and mostly malevolent, to invade London in the 1880s. In 1885, two years before the Wild West show made its debut, William Stead caused a major political and social scandal by publishing his *Maiden Tribute of Modern Babylon*, an exposé of child prostitution in London in which he depicted the bestial sexuality of the professional class as a minotaur. In 1886, Robert Louis Stevenson electrified the literary world with his portrayal of a doctor caught between his longing for knowledge and his bodily lust in *The Strange Case of Dr. Jekyll and Mr. Hyde*. In 1888, the year after Cody's departure, mutilated bodies of prostitutes marked the trail of Jack the Ripper, and newspaper coverage of the murders served as a powerful reminder to London women of the dangers of public life, and the supposed safety of the home. Indeed, coverage of the Ripper murders resonated with the imagery of Cody's own "Attack on the Settler's Cabin," wherein a woman is saved from certain debasement only by the shelter of her home and the courage of armed white men.[98]

Cody's centaur was a harbinger of epochal shifts, paralleling his millennial messages in the United States with promises of the triumph of Anglo-American culture, the glories of Western imperial power, and the rebirth of the race in a tide of frontier bloodshed. English enthusiasm for the Wild West show stemmed in no small measure from its depiction of an English diaspora racially resurrected by the frontier. In this sense, the show's success expressed a gathering transatlantic conviction that the English and the Americans were part of a shared "race empire" of Anglo-Saxon expansion. Historians have explored connections between the Wild West show and the frontier thesis of Frederick Jackson Turner, but Turner's essay would not even be published for six more years. Cody's extravaganza is more obviously connected to Anglo-Saxonism, which was the most popular historical explanation for America's frontier success in the 1880s. Anglo-Saxonists conflated race and culture, so that the origins of liberal democracy, constitutional monarchy, representative government, and most other venerable English and American traditions were derived from racial characteristics of ancient tribes—Angles, Saxons, Jutes, and Vikings—formed under oak trees in the German forests. According to the theory, these racial attributes hardened in battle with racial inferiors—Romans, Picts, and Celts—during a long process of westward expansion, and were cultivated and preserved from continental decadence in the western bastion of the British Isles and, later, in the United States. By 1887, enthusiasm for such notions had reached near-hysterical proportions. Theories about the common Germanic origins of British and Anglo-American culture and institutions dominated historical writing and reverberated in packed lecture halls on both sides of the Atlantic. At the opening of the American Exhibition, just before Buffalo Bill's Wild West kicked off its first London performance, Archbishop Farrar prayed "fervently" for the "further development of the two Leviathans of the English-speaking race."[99] To most observers in Britain, the Wild West show was a dramatic reenactment of Anglo-Saxon triumph.[100]

Anglo-Saxonism was, of course, a variant of Aryanism, which was itself a theory of westering race history, in which Germanic peoples, Teutons, themselves originated on the high plateaus of Asia, as Aryans, who migrated west over millennia. The variations and contradictions of Aryanism did not preclude its appeal, also on both sides of the Atlantic. Americans, from Walt Whitman to General Arthur McArthur, endorsed it as history.[101] In Britain, in the very summer that Buffalo Bill's show received rave reviews in London newspapers, the Aryan myth was still proving useful as a rationale for empire in India, with columnists reinscribing the now-hoary notion that the Raj constituted England's return to the land of her Asian origins, "charged with conveying Western ideas to the race from whom our civilization came."[102]

Bram Stoker turned to Aryanists for crucial background details of Count Dracula's origins. And *Dracula*, like many of his other novels, was informed by a popular Anglo-Saxonist tradition that British and Americans were descended from ancient Viking raiders, the berserkers.[103] These invocations of mythic race history suggested connections to the American frontier myth; Aryanism and Anglo-Saxonism were coeval with the development of American frontier mythology, and in many respects they were its relatives. In all these myths, the racial energies of white people aged in the East and were renewed through bloody encounters with barbarians in the West.[104] The tale of Aryans passing from Asia to Europe and in the process becoming Britons was as analogous as it was prefatory to the story of Britons migrating west and becoming Americans.

In this sense, Indians in the Wild West show could be seen as at least symbolic stand-ins for Britain's own "savage" opponents, particularly the

Irish. In 1887, the United Kingdom was beset by political controversy over the question of Irish home rule—Gladstone's signature political issue—and the threat of Irish revolutionaries. Two days after her introduction to Red Shirt and the Lakota babies at Earl's Court, Queen Victoria traveled to London's East End for another official function. Large cheering crowds lined the route, but "what rather damped the effect," the queen wrote that night in her journal, were the small number of people "booing and hooting . . . all along the route . . . probably Socialists and the worst Irish." But "considering the masses of Socialists of all nationalities, and low bad Irish, who abound in London," she judged the outing a success.[105]

Visitors to the Wild West camp invoked comparisons between the most primitive westerners and Britons. One London cartoonist imagined an Irish woman, a "Hibernian matron," latching on to an Indian in the Wild West camp as she mistakes him for her runaway husband. "I found ye out at last, Tim, ye blagyard, after lavin' me an' yer five childher to the waves iv the worruld. Little I thought iv findin' ye here—goin' about like an ould turkey-cock wid yer tail an' feathers."[106]

But as much as Buffalo Bill's Wild West show seemed to resonate with British myths of race origin and race strength, as much as it could be a symbolic crutch for British imperialism, it was simultaneously troubling for audiences concerned about racial decay. On the one hand, the show enhanced the sense of racial kinship between the United States and Great Britain, so that *The Times*, for example, could intone on the day of its departure, "The Americans and the English are of one stock." In this vein, columnists suggested that English manhood could take lessons from Cody's cowboys.[107]

On the other hand, such musings often called into question the racial viability of the English. Race, in the nineteenth century, was thought to be inherited through blood, but also subject to change by new environments.[108] "Of one stock" they may once have been, but were the two nations yet of the same race? Or had the frontier experience so altered the Americans that they had become something different? To see cowboys like Buck Taylor and Dick Johnson "amongst a group of self-complacent little City clerks it might be imagined that the individuals belonged to separate species."[109] In 1888, the Metropolitan Police began their search for suspects in the Jack the Ripper murders by interrogating political radicals and racial minorities whose barbarous instincts might have incited the crimes. The Wild West company sailed for New York from Hull on May 11, 1888, inadvertently leaving behind at least four Lakota men who were lost in the city.[110] In their search for a way home, they went to London, where they were quickly picked up by the police. "The police questioned us and let us go," Nick

Black Elk recalled many years later. "They had probably blamed us with something that had happened."[111]

In addition to American Indians, police in pursuit of the Ripper interrogated socialists, "Asiatics," and Greek Gypsies, before moving on to three more of Cody's own, "persons calling themselves Cowboys who belonged to the American Exhibition," who had stayed behind in London, and whose racial identity was questionable enough to earn them a place on this list of potential savages.[112]

After somebody claiming to be the murderer used what might have been American slang in several letters sent to the police and the press, some speculated that the butcher of Whitechapel might be a "Texas rough." Such images of rough-hewn western violence, of course, resonated to some degree with the recently departed Wild West show and the many references to Texas that it called to mind. Although Cody attempted to fashion an image of his cowboys as "real" frontiersmen and safe, respectable entertainers, the facade was hard to maintain. Cowboys in the camp were on display for hours at a time, and they were often taunted or treated as museum exhibits. Indians and other performers suffered just as much, but white cowboys appear to have been less patient with objectification by fans. Late in 1887, Dick Johnson, the "giant cowboy," got into a fistfight with another patron at a London pub. When the police arrived, Johnson tried to flee before engaging two constables in a bruising brawl. Although Cody and the Prince of Wales intervened in an attempt to lessen his punishment, Johnson did six months' hard labor at Pentonville Prison before rejoining the show in Manchester. The event was widely covered, in both the regular and the comic press, as if it confirmed the burgeoning savagery of American white men.[113]

The conspicuous growth of American cultural and economic power conjured notions of British decline which only enhanced such anxieties about the ascendant "American race." Even before Buffalo Bill's Wild West announced it was coming to London, such a flood of American investors, tourists, and entertainers had inundated Britain that critics began to fulminate about the "American Invasion." Cody's popularity brought such concerns to a head. In the show business world, theater owners and managers, among them Bram Stoker, read commentary about the threat of competition from American shows.[114] Beyond entertainments and popular amusements, the proliferation of Cody's image and the symbols of his show announced the penetration of British industry and consumer markets by American capital, goods, and advertising. As one newspaper wit described it,

> *I may walk it, or 'bus it, or hansom it: still*
> *I am faced by the features of Buffalo Bill.*

Every hoarding is plastered, from East-end to West,
With his hat, coat, and countenance, lovelocks and vest.[115]

One cartoonist drew a montage of cartoons over the caption "The Worship of Yankeedom." At the top left was Cody, portrayed as a sharp Yankee-gone-West, a spindle-shanked New Englander in a swallowtail coat and cowboy hat, his pockets bulging with coin. "Now I've landed the brass I guess I'll leave you Britishers and skeedaddle across the Herring Pond," he announces.

Others images evoked the American commercial challenge even more directly. One portrayed a bowler-hatted Londoner confronting a whole series of buildings labeled "stores" and complaining, "Call us a nation of shopkeepers Bah! Why there is not a shop left in the place—they are all Americanised and made into stores." Another showed a collection of canned goods whose labels identified them as "Preserved Peaches," "Oysters," "Prawns," "Asparagus," and "Tinned Tomatoes," with this last can wearing a cowboy hat and announcing to the others, "Well Boys, I think we've done the trick anyhow!"[116]

Such images were adaptations of an older European critique of America's hard-driving commercialism, a Yankee characteristic which alienated Old World cultural commentators for decades. Charles Dickens had announced years before that Americans were crass, finagling operators and cultural tyrants, and many other Europeans criticized Americans' relentless pursuit of manufacturing and the dollar to the exclusion of art, poetry, and humanity. America represented a gigantic paradox. Many continued to think of her as a primeval wilderness, where there was no culture, where Indians roamed a vast hinterland and Yankee settlers scrabbled in the forests. At the same time, her manufacturing, fierce market expansion, and corporate capitalism made the United States a metaphor for modernity.[117] The American Exhibition of 1887 captured both these facets, with an exhibit of American products joined by a bridge to the Wild West camp. But Cody's giant commercial success in London, the ubiquity of his advertising and the crowds of paying customers, in a sense made the manufactured exhibits redundant. Buffalo Bill's commercialism embodied the paradox of America, and captured every single anxiety about a foreign power that seemed both wilderness and commodity, culturally impoverished and perpetually for sale.

Cody's sexual appeal made the leap from these economic and cultural concerns to issues of biology, or race, that much easier, for the spectacle of an "invader" who was irresistible to English womanhood easily reinforced fears of English racial decline. At least one columnist compared him to Jung Bahadur, a Nepalese warrior prince whose visit to London in the 1850s included an affair with an Englishwoman, a scandalous event long remem-

"The Worship of Yankeedom" criticizes American commercialism. Note the parody of Cody, top left, in which the frontiersman is a money-grubbing Yankee in disguise. Moonshine, *October 22, 1887.*

bered in bawdy songs at late-night supper clubs.[118] Although journalists fixated on Cody's tent in the show camp, he spent most evenings in a rented London apartment, where another journalist recalled that he was "embarrassed by an overwhelming mass of flowers which come hourly from hosts of female admirers."[119] Cody, as we shall see, enjoyed the company of women in London. When Bram Stoker received a note from Cody via a young woman, written on the American's calling card, requesting two seats at the Lyceum for one "lovely little actress," the manager did not have to wonder who would be sitting in the second seat.[120]

Cody's performance for Queen Victoria was charged with many different layers of irony and tension. Not the least of them centered on his appeal as a manly foreigner amusing the British monarch. His "conquest" of the notoriously reclusive queen sat uneasily with her public, and her patronage of the Paris Hippodrome and the American Wild West embittered British performers who waited in vain for her command. Vesta Tilley, a popular music hall singer, roused her audiences with comical but pointed verse:

> She's seen the Yankee Buffaloes,
> The circus, too, from France,
> And may she reign until she gives
> The English show a chance.

The queen's long absence from London's greatest cultural attraction, its theaters, particularly chagrined Londoners. "Her Majesty has honoured the French circus at Olympia and the American boom at the Buffalo Billeries with her presence, but never since the death of her beloved consort has she set foot, even as an august audience of one, in an English show place."[121] Even performers in working-class music halls, like Vesta Tilley, took this as a slap.

> May Queen Victoria Reign
> May she with us long remain,
> 'Til Irving takes rank
> With a war-painted Yank,
> May good Queen Victoria Reign.[122]

There was something more than envy in these demonstrations. Unrest in the London theatrical world echoed a wider public dissatisfaction with the queen's continuing insistence on private showings of the few entertainments she did attend, and exclusive, private viewings of public exhibits, including the American Exhibition, which was closed to the public during her visit. "It would not have done any harm had her Majesty, just for once, tolerated the presence of her subjects in the same public building as herself" when she attended the American Exhibition, wrote one columnist.[123] Wrote another, "It is evident by her recent actions that her Majesty is not altogether disinclined to be amused, provided, of course, that her subjects do not witness her enjoyment."[124]

The queen's unwillingness to be seen was a constant theme among penny papers and highbrow society journals because it was no trivial matter. Like the inhabitants of many nations, Britons were riven by distinct regional identities, class tensions, and fierce party differences, all of which were apparent in 1887 as they rarely had been before. Against the surge of Irish nationalism, workingmen's strife, and other disputes that tore at the fabric of the United Kingdom, "the Queen is the symbol of the unity of the nation; she represents the integrity of the Empire," wrote the editor of *The World*. It was, after all, to see the queen that "her children, from every quarter of the world, flock to this island, recognising in it . . . their real home and Mother Country."[125]

With a monarchy that was long on tradition and short on ceremony, the foremost ritual of the British nation was the viewing of the queen.[126] She was the head both of the church and of the state. Royal representatives, symbols, and images of Queen Victoria were legion, but only the presence of this most hereditary monarch could provide her disparate peoples an authentic bond with the nation and its storied history. Only the proximity of her person allowed the ritual of nationhood to commence. For the great pageant that was the Jubilee, the celebration at a half-century's reign, to function as it should, for the nation to be united, the queen had to make an appearance, or, rather, many appearances. Her passage through a street or a hall allowed bystanders to unite in adoration, whether that meant cheering her coach or simply gathering to watch respectfully while she performed official duties. No other institution provided the cohesive power of the British monarchy—but that power could only be exercised if she made herself visible to her subjects.

And this was the essence of her failing in 1887, a reclusiveness so complete that it bordered on a crisis of state. Controversy swirled around her unwillingness to be seen on the way to the Jubilee service at Westminster Abbey, with editorialists lamenting that "the reasonable wishes of hundreds of thousands of people to see the Queen on her way to the Abbey, and to witness some kind of State, have been yielded to with extreme reluctance."[127] Observed another, "The Monarchy is in part a pageant and a symbol, and a pageant which is not displayed, a symbol which is not shown, cease to be a pageant and a symbol."[128]

At a moment when socialists advanced the cause of abolishing the monarchy, these critics implicitly made the point that Victoria's ongoing seclusion was doing the job for them. Describing her tour of the working-class districts of the East End, one journalist was troubled by the pointed reproofs to the crown in the banners draped across the street: "God bless our Queen. May she come more frequently to the East End" and "We love our Queen, but we don't often see her." Such informal, and reproachful, messages gave the impression that "long disuse and hard times have both helped to make street adornment a lost art in London."[129] If only Victoria would be seen more often, "street adornment" and its corollary, class deference, could perhaps be reestablished.

This was the political context of the Wild West show's audience with

Queen Victoria. In a limited sense, Cody's attraction was analogous to the queen's. The "representative man" of the American frontier was a living bond between spectators and the frontier history of Britain's former colonies, just as the queen connected her audience to mythic national unity. But where Cody's show was an amusement that allowed spectators to decide what was real man and what was representation, where authentic frontier stopped and fake began, Victoria's authentic presence among her subjects was the central pillar of the British state. Commentators insisted on it because, for all the superficial similarities between royal appearances and show business, the queen's progress was not just another "show." In this sense, Cody—showman, businessman, and American—was an unsuitable attraction to place before her hallowed British self. For many Britons, her eagerness to be seen by his large assemblage of primitives, but not by her own subjects, was insulting and worrisome.

Cody aggravated these anxieties by bragging about his triumphs to a Texas friend in a letter which American and British newspapers soon reprinted, and which Stoker no doubt saw. "I have captured this country from the Queen down, and am doing them to the tune of 10,000 dollars a day." Cody made it abundantly clear that to him the patronage of Britain's hallowed monarchy was a crass commercial triumph:

> Talk about show business, there was never anything like it ever known, and never will be again, and with my European reputation, you can easily guess the business I will do when I get back to my own country. It's pretty hard work with two and three performances a day, and the society racket, receptions, dinners etc. No man . . . was received better than your humble servant. I have dined with every one of the royalty, from Albert, Prince of Wales, down.[130]

Queen Victoria's enthusiasm for Cody's Wild West show—the fact that he had "captured this country from the Queen down"—underscored his sensual appeal, to common women as well as the elites listed in *Debrett's* social register, according to one humorist.

> All the women in London are what is metaphorically and obscurely known as "dead nuts" on Buffalo Bill. I don't know if there be a Mrs. Buffalo Bill. If there is, she must at this moment be tearing her own or (more likely) her husband's lovely black hair out by the yard with jealousy. One female possessor of the Blood Royal, three Duchesses, seven Countesses in their own right, and eighty-six dittoes with no rights excepting wrongs, have each and every Debretted one of 'em offered up

their richly jewelled hands and highly chaste hearts to beauteous Buffalo Bill.[131]

Cody had at least two affairs during the late 1880s, although both of these were with American women, as we shall see in another chapter. But Cody's appeal to British women was a constant subject in the London press. The attraction of numerous women to Buffalo Bill's show, to his table, and, it was widely presumed, to his bed, was threatening to English people concerned that racially degenerate Englishmen no longer captured the fancies of Englishwomen.[132] In a humorous penny press verse in 1887, an anonymous woman admirer celebrates Cody as "Nature's perfected touch in form and grace." Lamenting that her male compatriots do not wear clothes like Cody's, she pulls back from this last appreciation as she realizes:

> *But, 'tis the MAN we lack—not costume. Place*
> *Yours on the usual product of the race*
> *And see how soon 'twould look absurd and vain,*
> *And tailors' art be welcomed back again.*

As if to emphasize the point, the verses were followed by a brief essay on the great opportunity awaiting "the genius who invents a male bathing dress that will not give away the fact that the wearer is bow-legged, cross-eyed, knock-kneed, flat-footed, and hump-backed."[133]

Degeneration theory was always a province of the "respectable classes," a way of ascribing biological causes to subversive social change.[134] That Cody should become an icon for those classes is perhaps not surprising, and in the first few months of his English fame, they made an almost exclusive claim to Cody's associations.[135] As one writer commented on the show's opening: "Such a vast concourse of the cream—or it may be as well to say the *creme de la creme*—of society is seldom seen at any function."[136] For an aristocracy spiraling downward in power, wealth, and influence, beset by demands for power sharing from their social inferiors, the show's implicit teaching that history's most important contests were between races, not classes, must have seemed reassuring.[137]

Aristocratic enthusiasm was tempered, though, by the nagging anxiety behind the fanfare, a warning refrain about the American expansion and eagerness for combat that were so much on display in "Wild" West London. "The Buffalo Bill *furore* is becoming ridiculous," wrote one editorialist. Granting that Cody was a better showman than even P. T. Barnum, the writer asked, "But are these credentials sufficient to justify an outburst of fashionable fetish worship?" Lord Charles Beresford came in for particular criticism, for having "given the Yankee showman a mount on the box-seat of his drag at the Coaching Club meet. *Noblesse oblige;* there is a want of congruity in the companionship of an illustrious British officer who fills an important position in the Government with a gentleman chiefly famed as an adroit scalper of Red Indians."

This critique might be read as a reminder to the upper classes not to go slumming with American arrivistes, but it contained more than a hint of fear about American—and particularly Cody's—intentions and even racial identity, and it resonated with cultural concerns about the "American invasion." Earl's Court earned various nicknames in the press that season, including the "Yankeries" and the "Buffalo Billeries." Cody displayed Yellow Hair's scalp so prominently in his tent it earned some public condemnation; he put it away, but it persisted in another nickname for the showground, the "Scalperies."[138] Some saw Cody as a bloodthirsty con man, a covert savage. One artist lampooned London elites and their Buffalo Bill fixation with a racially charged cartoon, "Our Drawing Room Pets," in which beautiful Englishwomen at a fashionable ball dote on a bearded, suit-wearing Australian aborigine. Identified as "Kangaroo Jim, the Champion Australian Boomerang-Thrower," whose "adventurous youth" was spent "in the Cookaboo Islands" where he has "frequently partaken of roast missionary . . . in banquets he describes with inimitable gusto," he is really nothing more than a "professional street acrobat" in his native Melbourne.[139] Indeed, although Cody advertised himself as a white man, the British press tarred him with the brush of frontier savagery and mixed-blood deceptiveness on more than one occasion. "A fine looking fellow," concluded one journalist, "his face bearing evidence of the presence of Indian blood."[140]

Since 1868, Cody had constructed his white Indian imposture and much of his career by standing as near the race boundary as possible without crossing over, by posing beside Indians without actually being *of* them. Not surprisingly, European critics who were less familiar with all his military patrons and his frontier biography were sometimes uncertain whether and how much his whiteness was colored by this high-wire act on the color line. These critics issued dark warnings, with veiled allusions and comparisons to confidence men who were not quite (or not even) white. In addition to the comparisons to the legendary Nepalese seducer of Englishwomen, Jung Bahadur, the public adoration of Buffalo Bill recalled events seven years earlier, when the Zulu king Cetshwayo was feted by the upper classes in London shortly after leading his armies to stunning victories over British forces in South Africa, and after being defeated and exiled to London. The glittering public image of the Yankee frontiersman was shadowed by the disgraceful memory. Before worshipping at the "shrine" of Buffalo Bill, "London

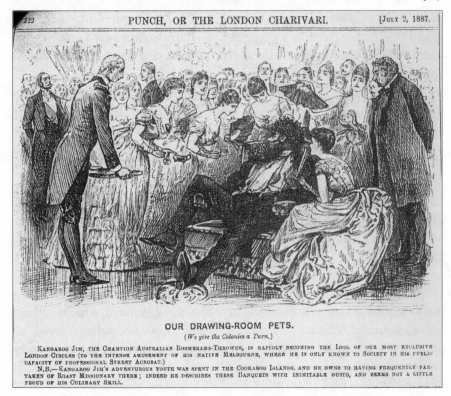

OUR DRAWING-ROOM PETS.

(We give the Colonies a Turn.)

KANGAROO JIM, THE CHAMPION AUSTRALIAN BOOMERANG-THROWER, IS RAPIDLY BECOMING THE IDOL OF OUR MOST EXCLUSIVE LONDON CIRCLES (TO THE INTENSE AMUSEMENT OF HIS NATIVE MELBOURNE, WHERE HE IS ONLY KNOWN TO SOCIETY IN HIS PUBLIC CAPACITY OF PROFESSIONAL STREET ACROBAT.)

N.B.—KANGAROO JIM'S ADVENTUROUS YOUTH WAS SPENT IN THE COOKABOO ISLANDS, AND HE OWNS TO HAVING FREQUENTLY PAR-TAKEN OF ROAST MISSIONARY THERE; INDEED HE DESCRIBES THESE BANQUETS WITH INIMITABLE GUSTO, AND SEEMS NOT A LITTLE PROUD OF HIS CULINARY SKILL.

"Our Drawing Room Pets." Punch *magazine satirizes Buffalo Bill as a cannibalistic Australian Aborigine, "Kangaroo Jim."* Punch, *July 2, 1887.*

society should remember the shame which subsequently fell upon it for its adoration of the black miscreant."[141]

The comparison to Cetshwayo points out the ways that the Wild West show sharpened older concerns about the danger of a war with Americans, a preoccupation of English politicians for much of the nineteenth century, when the British and Americans clashed over the Oregon question, the Southern secession, fishing rights, and a host of other issues.[142] Anxieties about war found official acknowledgment in the proposal to create a permanent court of arbitration to resolve future differences between the United States and the United Kingdom. The first meeting to discuss the idea took place at the American Exhibition of 1887. Indeed, it was timed to coincide with the closing of the Wild West show in November, so that *The Times* could observe, "Civilization itself consents to march onward in the train of Buffalo Bill." In endorsing the court of arbitration proposal, *The Times* summed up the simultaneous adoration and fear that the Wild West show inspired. Crediting Cody for "bringing America and England nearer together," the newspaper also warned that "a serious quarrel between England and the United States would be almost worse than a civil war," a judgment likely shared by the audiences who witnessed the American love of gunplay and combat in Cody's arena.[143]

London audiences of the Wild West show were thus caught in an ongoing double take. The "creme de la creme" cheered for the regeneration of the Anglo-Saxon race on the American frontier. But the shouts were punctuated with furtive glances at these armed, aggressive, and racially vigorous visitors to—or invaders of—an England on a downhill slide. Thus a cloud of anxiety hovered, the bright spectacle of frontier energy and victory dimming now and again amid a drifting fog of worries about expanding slums, the restless colonies, the declining industrial position of the country, themselves all symptomatic of England's precipitous racial degeneration.

GIVEN THE MANY LAYERS of anxiety his show generated, what is perhaps most surprising is how Cody overcame these obstacles and continued not only to profit from his English and European appearances, but to go down in European history as one of the most beloved of American entertainers. To this day, stories of Buffalo Bill's English tours are told and celebrated in pubs, on BBC radio, and in the British press. In extraordinary numbers, European tourists make pilgrimages to the town of Cody, Wyoming, and its state-of-the-art Buffalo Bill Historical Center (where, in the summer of 2004, I saw two teenagers listen in almost sacred devotion as their mother earnestly translated museum exhibit placards into French). Suffice it to say that Cody's showmanship, his attention to entertainment and amusement, his close (but not too close) relationship with European royals and, later on, with European working people, his presentation of Indians in ways that Indians enjoyed and profited from—all these contributed to a show career that was mostly successful in Europe and generally remembered with great fondness. Add to this the history of the twentieth century, the rise of an Atlantic alliance that saw the defeat of Nazism and the Soviet Union, the growth of stable European democracies and social welfare programs that have taken much of the edge off Victorian-era class strife, and the ambiguity of European response to Cody is easily forgotten.

Nonetheless, the dark fears of American power were real in 1887 (and have reemerged today in England and Western Europe), and they point us toward Cody's influence on gothic fiction. The froth of fear on Cody's sunny wake caught Stoker's eye, as he imagined the fictional world of *Dracula* and began inventing a savage race monster from a distant frontier, as well as the Teutonic and Anglo-Saxon posse—and the dubious American ally—that chased him down. As distinct as Cody's show and Stoker's classic might seem at first, even a cursory reading of the novel suggests the many ways in which the American frontier is bound up in it. Stoker's gothic world expressed much of the admiration and fear that English audiences felt for Buffalo Bill, and for Americans generally, through a conflation of frontiers east and west, European and American, like the Wild West arena, a vast borderland of race origin and race war which is the story's true context.

On the surface, *Dracula* is a conventional tale of female vulnerability and male gallantry. The action begins with a young Englishman, Jonathan Harker, traveling to Transylvania to meet the count after Harker's law firm has been commissioned to buy property for the aristocrat in London. The count is a vampire, although his guest does not realize this. He traps Harker in the castle and turns him over to his three minions, female vampires who live in the castle's recesses. Harker escapes and returns home, but Dracula has already left for London, where he plans to use his newly purchased properties as bases for his forays into England. There he will suck the blood of Englishwomen and reduce the country to his domain.

He prevails first upon Lucy Westenra, a wealthy young woman who is a friend of Mina Harker, Jonathan's wife. But Jonathan has glimpsed the count in London, and together he and Mina join forces with Abraham Van Helsing, an elderly "Dutch," or German doctor; Dr. John Seward, who runs a mental asylum; his friend Lord Godalming, who is also Lucy's fiancé; and Quincey Morris, the colorful Texan.

After turning Lucy into a vampire—whom the protagonists skewer with a huge wooden stake—Dracula bites Mina and forces her to suck his blood while she is in bed with her unconscious husband. Desperate to save Mina from becoming a vampire, Harker and his friends pursue the count back to Transylvania, where they arrest and reverse Mina's transformation by killing Dracula just before he reaches his castle.

It is not difficult to imagine how Stoker might have drawn on Cody's popularity to enhance his fictional drama. The bite of Count Dracula constitutes a kind of "abduction" and rape of white women. Since much of Buffalo Bill's heroic persona was connected to redeeming women captured by savages, and given the fabulous plots into which fiction writers inserted him, it is not too outlandish to imagine Nature's Nobleman arriving to do battle with the Lord of the Undead in an effort to rescue the virtuous Mina from impending "vampirehood." We can easily picture what Cody's role in such an adventure might be. Joining the novel's small party of protagonists, Buffalo Bill would race across Europe to intercept the count, "to cut him off at the pass" before he reached his stronghold. He would ensure the party was stocked up on rifles, and lead scouting expeditions to reconnoiter the territory. Dashing to the final confrontation in the Transylvanian twilight, he would dispatch the count's Gypsy troops and deal the death blow to the vampire, plunging his knife—not a wooden stake or a European dagger, but a frontiersman's bowie knife—into Dracula's dark heart.

The irony of my imagined plot is obvious for anyone who has read *Dracula:* change the name of Buffalo Bill to Quincey Morris, and you have the novel's climax. As the experienced hunting guide, it is the American, Morris, who deploys the posse's forces at critical moments. As they prepare to chase the count across Europe, Morris is the one who advises them to stock up on rifles, Winchesters in fact, the very brand that had Cody's exclusive endorsement (the only advertisement in his 1887 London show program was for Winchester rifles).[144] He arrives with the others just in time to battle Dracula at the Borgo Pass, with the dire castle in sight. When Dracula dies in the novel, it is not with a stake through his heart, but Morris's bowie knife. Critics have long pondered Stoker's purpose in creating Morris, the weakest and most peripheral of the three youthful male characters who battle Count Dracula. Equally puzzling is his death. Morris is the only one to die in the struggle with the vampire, and it is his death, not Dracula's, which closes the novel's action.[145]

All this is still more intriguing when we revisit Morris's odd, recurring lapses, or duplicities. Indeed, although it goes unnoticed by the others in the novel, right up until the moment he stabs the villainous Dracula, Quincey Morris is practically malevolent. In shooting at a bat he takes to be the count, he nearly kills others in the party. Instead of pursuing the count forcefully at one critical juncture, he hides among the trees and loses him. When the count is surrounded in his house in Piccadilly, Morris is to guard the window to prevent his escape, but the count escapes anyway—through the window. Were they in league together? Lucy dies and turns into a vampire immediately after receiving a transfusion from Morris. He is the first character in the book to utter the word "vampire"—indeed he diagnoses Lucy—and he is the only one to have had exposure to vampire bats, in Argentina, where they killed his horse. Might he himself have been infected? In the original draft of his novel, Stoker had Morris traveling to Transylvania alone, and at another point he was to enter Dr. Seward's office in the company of the count.[146] What was his role meant to be in the original draft? And what are we to make of his numerous missteps in pursuit of the vampire?

One of the more provocative and thoughtful arguments of recent years, and now a consensus among critics, posits that Morris is a secret vampire. In this reading, his character expresses Stoker's ambivalence about the American ascent to world power in the 1890s. Some see Morris as a dark allusion to the parasitic threat of American capital; others point out that if the novel *Dracula* is concerned with the displacement of racially decaying people by the racially vigorous, then the real danger to England in 1897 comes not from Eastern Europe but from the Americans, represented by Morris.[147] In a sense, Stoker is caught in the ongoing double take of British audiences at the Wild West show, expressing adulation for Americans on the one hand ("If America can go on breeding men like that, she will be a power in the world indeed," says one character about Quincey Morris) and the fear of their regenerative and military power on the other, a fear which finds some resolution in Morris's death at novel's end.[148]

Clearly, William Cody was the inspiration for Quincey Morris. The similarities between the fictional character and the historical Cody are extensive, and go far beyond their predilection for Winchesters. Both are hunters (something they share with Dracula himself), and both have been hunting guides to the aristocracy. Cody's guided hunts with the Grand Duke Alexis, as well as with British aristocrats such as Sir George Gore and the Earl of Dunraven, formed a large part of his biographical publicity in England, where he was far and away the most famous hunting guide of the period.[149]

Morris's origins as a Texan are likely an attempt to locate him "out West" more than anything specific. But they call to mind the 1887 joke about Irving becoming a "Texan cow-boy" to gain an audience with the queen, as well as the speculation that Jack the Ripper was a "Texas rough." As we have already seen, the earlier version of the character in the short story "The Squaw" hailed from Cody's home state of Nebraska.[150] Finally and most important, by the time Stoker began to write *Dracula* in the 1890s, the ubiquity of Buffalo Bill's Wild West show would have made it practically impossible for Stoker to conjure up a western character without thinking of Buffalo Bill.

But if Morris is drawn from Cody, Count Dracula has a good deal in common with him, too. For starters, he is not just a frontiersman, but a frontier hero. As Van Helsing informs the vampire hunters, Dracula "won his name against the Turk," across the Danube "on the very frontier of Turkey-land," where he consistently showed himself to be "the cleverest and the most cunning, as well as the bravest" of Transylvania's sons.[151]

After generations of studying American frontier ideology, historians would do well to move beyond Frederick Jackson Turner's lumping of European frontier concepts into a single notion of "a fortified boundary line running through dense populations." In the 1890s, complex European ideas connected race, culture, and national borders. Nations were thought to be roughly contiguous with patterns of racial settlement, and their frontiers were profoundly racial boundaries.[152] In this connection, the Wild West show served as a kind of allegory for European politics. Articles about "frontier tensions," between, for example, Germany and France, appeared alongside reviews of the show.[153]

Indeed, Stoker's use of frontier rhetoric to describe Transylvania was not new. In Britain, southeastern Europe was the locus of the "Eastern Question," the debate over how best to secure a region crisscrossed by racial frontiers, bordering Turkey's Ottoman Empire, constantly threatening war and the empire's hold on India. Transylvania was a linchpin of the Balkans, and in the travel books Stoker researched it had many similarities to Cody's version of the American West. Its racially segmented, mutually hostile Gypsies, Magyars, and Saxons were analogous to Cody's Indians, Mexicans, and white cowboys. Like the peoples of the American West, they ranged between primitivism and civilization, struggling to carve life from the wilderness amidst continuous race war.[154]

In Europe, Cody and probably Salsbury, too, had become aware of the mutual ideological resonance of American and Eurasian frontiers by 1891. The following year they added mounted contingents from "world frontiers" beyond North America. In 1893 they formally reconstituted the show, expanding its narrative from western history to world history, under the new name "Buffalo Bill's Wild West and Congress of Rough Riders of the World." The new spectacle featured horsemen from the globe's far-flung racial frontiers, including contingents of European cavalry, gauchos, Cossacks, and Arabs. They continued to add and subtract these "frontier" contingents according to their availability. In 1897, the same year that *Dracula* was published, the show featured "Czikos," or "Magyar-gypsy horsemen" who hailed "from that part of Hungary that borders on Turkey."[155] Who the actual performers were remains a mystery, but they represented the same "race" of people from whom Stoker drew Dracula, the horsemen of the Transylvanian frontier who marked the line between Europe and Asia.

Stoker himself compared popular renderings of the American West and southeastern Europe, liberally interchanging eastern and western clichés in his notes and in the final draft of his vampire novel. Originally, the tale included chapters titled "On the Track, Texan in Transylvania," in which Quincey Morris scouted out enemy territory (much like Cody in Indian country) and "Vigilante Committee, Necktie Party," to describe the moment in which the posse plots the count's demise. Tellingly, in his notes Stoker frequently pairs the word "Transylvania" with "Texas" or "the Texan," as if the two frontiers of East and West were somehow inseparable, or interchangeable.[156] Ultimately, his Transylvania, his eastern frontier, could almost *be* the American West in the novel, with Gypsies as its Indians, treacherous and "almost outside all law," Slovaks dressed in "high boots" and "big cowboy hats," and the Western European posse heading off the frontier villain at the eastern European pass.

And the closer we look, the more familiar its principal frontier figure becomes. Like the Americans and the British, Dracula's kin, the Szekelys, are descended from Vikings, who in Dracula's words, "bore down from Iceland the fighting spirit which Thor and Wodin gave them," to stand guard for centuries along "the frontier of Turkey-land."[157] As he recounts their seemingly endless wars, Dracula invokes the heroism of his ancestors. Only later do we discover that he is in fact talking about his own centuries-old exploits in the third person. Dracula "again and again brought his forces over the great river into Turkeyland; . . . when he was beaten back, [he] came again, and again, and again, though he had to come alone from the bloody field where his troops were being slaughtered, since he knew that he alone could ultimately triumph."[158]

Stoker's fictional eastern frontiersman stands in almost perfect counterpoint to the most famous frontiersman of the 1890s, Buffalo Bill. Dracula is the centuries-old warrior hero in the East, defending western civilization's first frontier with non-Christian peoples in Transylvania, "the land beyond the forest." Cody is the hero of the Indian wars in the West, those epic conflicts between Christian America and savage paganism that so darkened America's "land beyond the forests," the Great Plains.

More than this, each of these figures embodies the entire frontier history of his people: Dracula as the eternal warrior from a frontier of ceaseless war (his insatiable appetite for blood mimicking the bloodthirst and stagnation of the Balkan frontier), Cody "the representative man of the frontiersman of the past," hunter, rancher, and, most important, warrior (his having "passed through every stage of border life" embodying the regenerative and progressive powers of the American frontier).[159] Stoker's monster is not just *from* the frontier. Like Buffalo Bill, he *is* the frontier. He retains the powers of a badly twisted nature, so that where Mary Shelley's creature in *Frankenstein* threatened to reproduce himself and destroy humanity, Dracula, like the frontier itself, threatens to *transform* humanity into a different set of beings altogether.[160]

As much as these old soldiers share a frontier history, each also faces a profoundly uneasy future, in which the racial coherence they represent threatens to evaporate. Both arrive in London to announce that the frontier wars are over, the great racial conflicts gone, and with them have gone not only the struggles that generated them but also the Darwinian contests that made their races great. Programs for the Wild West show invoke simultaneously the frontier world that birthed the Americans and its imminent vanishment. The racial conflicts of the ancient and frontier past are now giving way to a white-dominated nation-state.

Count Dracula too longs for a golden age of racial conflict. After regaling Jonathan Harker with his family's martial heritage, the count waxes nostalgic. "Those warlike days are over. Blood is too precious a thing in these days of dishonourable peace; and the glories of the great races are as a tale that is told."[161] Not surprisingly, perhaps, as the great European empires quash the old ethnic wars on the frontier, Dracula, the eternal frontier warrior, seeks to quench his bloodthirst on the weak, effeminate capital of Western Europe, London.

Here the dread lord of Transylvania is a through-the-looking-glass version of Buffalo Bill. Like the American, Dracula comes to London announcing the closure of a racial frontier, and he, too, is possessed of a racial supremacy hardened in frontier battle with racial others. But he is a frontier warrior gone horribly wrong, the vanguard of Western culture turned against the home civilization and in full regression. Count Dracula *is* Buffalo Bill Cody, inverted.

The depth, range, and consistency of these inversions is striking, and we have room to consider only a few. "Nature's Nobleman" was youthful, from common origins but rendered supreme through his encounters with nature. Dracula is ancient, aristocratic, and decidedly "not of nature."[162] Cody the centaur embodied a narrative of progress from nature to technology. Dracula the vampire embodies a narrative without regeneration or progress, and in fact his recurrent morphing into wolves, bats, or clouds of dust suggests his devolutionary nature. Unlike the sharpshooting Americans of the Wild West show who avail themselves of the most modern weaponry, Dracula never resorts to machine supremacy for racial renewal. His is a constant atavism, a return to the most basic and crude of beings, substances, and appetites that mocks the advances of modern civilization.

But Dracula is no mere villain to Cody's hero. It is rather as if his evil powers represent Cody's strengths and virtues carried to unprecedented extremes. Cody's martial abilities, his long military career, his facility with manipulating nature and particularly animals, all have their dark counterpart in Dracula, the ages-old frontier hero who can become an animal at will.

Even Dracula's inability to die, his undeadness, seems to be a distorted echo of Buffalo Bill's frontier life, particularly his exploits in the Indian wars. In the accounts of his military commanders—liberally excerpted in show programs and on posters—Cody's remarkable talents as tracker, fighter, and strategist were charged with a legendary, practically superhuman endurance. In the esteem of General Carr, "Mr. Cody seemed never to tire and was always ready to go, in the darkest night, or the worst weather, and usually volunteered."[163] The sleeplessness of Buffalo Bill and the restlessness of westerners, so prevalent in the enormous energy on display in the Wild West show, rendered the frontier a place of eternal watchfulness, where, in the words of one London columnist, "constant vigilance is the price of existence."[164]

And "constant vigilance" is the essence of Dracula's curse, for as the centuries-old border guardian, Dracula himself has become an eternal sentry, unable to sleep, to rest, to die. As he puts it, his has been the "endless duty of the frontier guard, for, as the Turks say, 'water sleeps, and enemy is sleepless.' "[165] Dracula was created by unceasing war, by a frontier that went one step further than Cody's in refusing to close. So long as it remains open, so too must the eyes of its heroic border guardian. As we learn in the novel, Dracula was once a man. But his passion for victory over the hated Other, itself a characteristic of the racial frontier, led him to a Faustian bargain. In exchange for learning the dark arts which allow him finally to vanquish the Turk, he became the deathless vampire, the eternal warrior.[166] Seen in this light, the career of the young American begins to look like a pale version of Dracula's early days. We might say that to be Buffalo Bill in the war against the Turks is to become Dracula.

Like his application of frontier tropes to Transylvania, Stoker's many inversions of the frontier myth were in keeping with older gothic traditions. In the words of one scholar, "the mingled apprehension and aspiration" of the New England Puritans became the starting point for both the progressive frontier myth of later generations and its gothic horrors.[167] Put another way, regressive gothic literature inverts progressive New World expectations: the Christian errand into the wilderness becomes the traveler's ordeal, the city on a hill becomes the castle ruin (also on a hill) into which the traveler stumbles in the hour of dark need, and the climactic moment of the frontier saga, the removal of wilderness savages by the bearers of light, becomes in its gothic counterpart the transformation of the pilgrim into a monster.[168] In the end, Stoker conceived a vampire world which drew comprehensively on contemporary frontier myth to create a fully realized inversion, a gothic nightmare that stands in close counterpoint to Cody's frontier dream.

It would have been difficult for Stoker to restrain himself from the racial implications of that inversion. Cody himself had stood against the degenerative power of the frontier since his early days as a scout, as a white man in an occupation dominated by Indians and mixed-blood men, on a frontier that had, in the parlance of the day, "corrupted" Spanish conquistadors into conquered Mexicans, and which threatened to work its dark magic on Americans, too. As we have seen, his abilities as a scout were considerable, but officers praised him as much as they did partly because he so closely approximated their fantasies of a white man who mastered the frontier but avoided its interracial temptations. Implicitly, Cody continued to remind his audience of his strengths in this regard, by surrounding himself with white frontiersmen, Indians, *and* mixed-blood families, such as John Y. Nelson, his Lakota wife, and their children, and the Lakota and mixed-blood family of "Bronco Bill" Irving. To see Cody amidst the sexy, polyglot crowd of the Wild West camp was to recognize how "superior" his will must be in rising above frontier sensuality.

Regardless of how much attention Stoker paid to Cody's Great Plains mythology, he would have been familiar with the idea of a racially degenerate frontier. An Anglo-Irish writer who favored home rule, he knew the rhetoric of colonial and frontier degeneracy from a lifetime of "bog trotter" epithets and arguments over British power. America was a hopeful destination for the multitudes of Irish who fled the famine and for many who stayed at home, too. But at the same time, since the beginning of the American experiment, various writers had speculated that Americans were racially degraded by historic and often familial ties to Indians and Africans, relations which were themselves symptomatic of licentious backcountry freedom and America's remoteness from European sources of whiteness.[169] Mexicans, a constant reminder of the frontier's potential for "unfit amalgamation" of Europeans and Indians, were the largest minority presence in the U.S. Southwest in the 1870s (and a major component of Cody's show, too). In the 1890s, the threat of frontier miscegenation yet preoccupied apologists for the American conquest of the Southwest and California, and ultimately it played a large part in restraining U.S. expansion across the Pacific, particularly in the Philippines.[170]

Thus, it is not surprising to find that racial ambiguities swirl around both the novel's frontiersmen. The doomed Lucy compares Quincey Morris to Othello, a curious reference for an infatuated white girl to apply to her ostensibly white suitor.[171] And where Morris suggests Stoker's suspicions about New World frontiersmen, it is Count Dracula who embodies his deepest fears about Americans and the fate of the Anglo-Saxon race. Just as Cody resembled Cetshwayo and Jung Bahadur in the barbs of his critics, just as his face suggested "traces of Indian blood" to some observers, so Dracula is revealed as the embodiment of racial ambivalence, the descendant not only of Vikings, but of their enemies, the Huns of Attila, "whose blood is in these veins," as the count tells Jonathan Harker.[172] Scion of Asiatic *and* Teutonic lineages, not just berserker but Hun-berserker, Count Dracula is a racial hybrid, defying the categories that the frontier line itself purports to demarcate, subverting the civilization which is maintained by blood purity and in defense of which the frontier line is drawn.

Like those who worried that Americans might be too close to nonwhite peoples, to the frontier, to remain white, the novel *Dracula* depicts the frontier as the near edge of a racial transformation which threatens British civilization. In Stoker's vision, miscegenation leads to the replacement of weaker races by the stronger, to the triumph of the frontiersman over the city dweller.[173] The racial frontier is thus key to understanding the real danger of the count, to *seeing* the monster who is in fact either absent or invisible for much of the book. What makes him so very dangerous is that he has a lust for blood befitting a frontier warrior, and that good people cannot tell he is a monster. The source of these talents is the too-permeable frontier line, that too-fragile division between light-skinned civilizers and dark-skinned savages, whose congenital race hatreds can give way without notice to interracial sex. Thus he is a savage, a dark-hearted villain, and yet he is wrapped in skin so white that he seems to be "without a speck of color about him anywhere." Neither red, nor brown, nor yellow, he is "of extraordinary pallor."[174] The most deadly monster to emerge from the frontier is neither an Indian nor a Turk. He appears as a very white man, but is in fact a frontier miscegenate from the ancient past, able to extend his "vampire kind" through his own desire. Unless the novel's protagonists stop this embodiment of the frontier, he is the vision of their racial future.

Westering race myth is in this sense the deeper context of the novel, its genetic bed, just as it was for the Wild West show, with its relentless westward march of Progress and Civilization.[175] Derived from Europe's mythic race frontiers, the war between westering Vikings and Asiatic Huns, Dracula is not just some relic of another country's barbaric heritage, but an inverted race hero who comes straight out of the Anglo-Saxon past. Far to the east, Dracula's kin began the westward progression of Teutonic civilization which Morris is completing. Thus, the centaur and the vampire are not mere symbolic opposites. Rather, Dracula and Quincey Morris, or Dracula and Buffalo Bill, mark the beginning and ending of a mythic drama: the epic birth of Western civilization.

This interpretation explains the curious ending in which the American's death, not Dracula's, signals the novel's climax. The killing of the two race frontiersmen, one from the East—the land of the past—and the other from the West—the land of the future—terminates the thirst for blood and the threat of race mixture that the ancient race wars bequeathed to the English, the virtuous sons of the berserkers. In the capable and dispassionate hands of the bourgeois and racially pure Englishmen who return Mina to England, the nation can become modern, and yet remain progressive and free. Away from the racial frontier, there is still hope for blood purity, restrained passion, and enduring civilization.

The novel thus mimics social evolutionary scholarship of the period in utilizing the frontier as both a historical and a predictive tool. To social evolutionists, the frontier line was, among other things, a purported division between primitive and modern. By looking from metropolis to frontier, cosmopolitans could locate "primitives" and say, "They are what we once were."[176] Stoker suggests that Morris is what Dracula once was; and Dracula is what Morris will become. The relief at the novel's conclusion, where Dracula turns to dust and Morris lies buried, flows in part from this final resolution of the vampire's curse, which itself stems from a frontier that remains open for too long, warping the race that wins it.

While Cody trafficked in nostalgia for frontiers and race wars well into the twentieth century, the novel *Dracula* burst forth at the end of the nineteenth century to issue a warning about them. Perhaps the frontier wars were glorious, Stoker says, but the closure of the frontier is not all for the worse. The frontier is where Dracula comes from, where the dark desires of his eternal longings were cloaked in a white skin. It whetted his bloodthirst, fired his blood passion, and, before that, begat the blood mixing that in turn begat him. Frontiers that do not close bring consummate bloodletting. Frontier wars that do not end require Faustian bargains. They nurture vampires.

Given that the novel *Dracula* plays on pervasive fears of race weakness, Stoker's reliance on myths of race origin for his tale's deep historical context is understandable. Since those myths were characterized by the centrality of frontier warfare, his resort to frontier settings, frontier tropes, and frontier warriors to carry the tale makes a great deal of sense. That he drew on the most famous Anglo-Saxon frontier hero of his day, Buffalo Bill Cody, as an inspiration for his fictional frontiersmen, Count Dracula and Quincey Morris, is hardly surprising, particularly given his obsession with his benefactor's social life and Irving's close attachment to Cody during the years Stoker was working on the novel. Popular doubts about Cody's racial identity, combined with his physical beauty, his "irresistibility," his military prowess, and his ability to master savages and savage nature, all suggest that the novel *Dracula* is a fantasy of the ambivalences that made Buffalo Bill such a figure of power and fascination in late-nineteenth-century London, played out on the dark side.

As an artistic statement, the novel exceeds its origins to become much more than the sum of its parts. Until Stoker's time, most literary vampires were women. For most of the nineteenth century, from Polidori's *The Vampyre* to Le Fanu's *Carmilla* they were eastern, sexy, and very thirsty.[177] In making his vampire a masculine figure, a frontier warrior spawned from a mythic collision of races in the ancient past and out to conquer London, Stoker both inverted Buffalo Bill and imitated his method. As Buffalo Bill had done with the Wild West, he connected his "show," his monster, to the origins of Europe, and his mission to a widely perceived crisis, racial degeneration. The result was to suggest that the ancient vampire is profoundly entangled in the modern English world.

As much as Cody embodied a frontier myth of individual achievement and redemption, the noisy triumphalism of that myth was a counterpoint to its own dark baggage: the lurking fear of the frontier as a place of racial monstrosity and moral decay. Cody's frontier centaur symbolized the transformative power of the frontier, the way that going west and conquering could potentially make of Americans something new, something more free and powerful. The vampire was Bram Stoker's dark vision of the same frontier transformation, the shifting of Self into Other, the loss of will and restraint before a new self that was soulless, consuming, and irresistible.

The connections between Cody and the count suggest how very plastic the frontier mythology of the Wild West show could be for cultural commentators and artists in the countries it visited. The myth of the American frontier became a touchstone for understanding other national histories and contemporary crises. But they also suggest how much the Wild West show itself borrowed from European traditions of race, empire, and warfare to weave its New World spectacle into Old World epic. The progressive dream of Cody's show in fact provided fertile ground for cultural consideration of its darker counterpart, the fear of frontier monstrosity and decay that had long preoccupied Europeans and Americans alike. Thus Cody's appeal to myths of centaurs and race wars as the birthing process of nations found resonance in European concerns with racial degeneration and cultural decline, nowhere better evidenced than in the use of the frontier myth by Bram Stoker, England's greatest gothic novelist.

Broncho Charlie Miller

I T WAS 1887 when the London reporter met the slight young cowboy in the camp of the Wild West show. His name, he said, was Charlie Miller, and his was a simple story of emigrants and settlers. His father was a Scotsman who emigrated to New York, where he married Charlie's mother, herself an immigrant from England. They followed the gold rush west in 1849, and built a home at Hat Creek, in northern California. Their son Charlie was born eleven years later. Charlie was seven years old when local Indians, tired of being dispossessed and killed with impunity, rose up. The Miller home was among their targets. Charlie escaped, and his mother and his brother "only got away almost by a miracle." His father was not so fortunate, and his killing left Charlie's mother without support.

So the family moved to San Francisco, where Charlie attended school for a couple of years. By 1870, the problem of money must have troubled Mrs. Miller, for she sent him to work. He was only nine. But like thousands of other frontier children, including William Cody in Kansas, Charlie herded livestock. His employer, a rancher named Thompson, kept him on for four years, "doing anything and everything about the ranch that a boy could." In 1874, he helped drive two thousand cattle to market in Sacramento, where he met a man named Summercamp. By this time, Miller was "a pretty smart boy on a horse." Just as a Kansas teamster had hired ten-year-old Will Cody to drive horses from Leavenworth to Laramie, so Summercamp hired this thirteen-year-old boy to join him and two other men driving a herd of horses seven hundred miles to Idaho. There were sporadic Indian attacks on other parties along the route, and progress was slow. "At one place, Camp Watson, on Big Meadow Creek, we had to lay up three weeks before we could get along." But in the end, "we never came to close quarters with them," and the party arrived at the ranch in safety. Charlie was soon known as "Broncho Charlie," and he broke horses for Summercamp for the next four years.

The horses Charlie handled, along with other settler livestock in southern Idaho, devastated the camas plants on which the Bannock Indians at Fort Hall depended. Facing starvation, the Bannock and their Paiute allies went to war in 1878. There was panic in Idaho and Oregon, and many settlers joined volunteer militias. But soon the combined Bannock and Pauite forces all but collapsed.

Even by his own account, Charlie Miller's involvement in the fighting was small. He was a civilian dispatch carrier on a few occasions for the army, he said, but he admitted he saw no action until near the war's end. Then, at Blue River, with a party of ranch hand volunteers and professional soldiers, Charlie found himself in an Indian battle. Historians, when they recalled the fight at all, described it as a skirmish. But like so many men who sweat through fights their people soon forget, Charlie Miller remembered it all too well. "This was the first big Indian fight I had been in, and you bet I was pretty well scared to death." He fired his gun a great deal, as did everyone else, but when dusk came, "the Indians went, and we didn't follow them." Their casualties were too high. "We had twenty-one killed and wounded," he recalled, and the Indians took theirs away, "so it is impossible to say what they numbered." The ranch hands and soldiers claimed victory. Charlie thought it a draw.

The Bannocks returned to Fort Hall. Charlie broke horses in Idaho until 1884, when he moved to Colorado to work for a horse dealer named John Witter. Two years later, in September of 1886, a horse "bit me clean through the hand, tearing the sinews and muscles to ribbons." Unable to work, he turned to his remaining family. By this time, his mother had moved back to New York, where Charlie found her. He stayed with her until February 1887, when he visited the Wild West show at Madison Square Garden. He was soon working for Buffalo Bill's show as a bronco rider and, sometimes, in the reenactment of the Pony Express. That spring, he set sail for London with the rest of the cast.

For a ranch hand and horse breaker, the show was more than a paycheck. Charlie's western work was often dreary, usually exhausting, and always underpaid, but he enjoyed the sense of building up a country that it gave him. As he told the reporter, when he first went to Idaho, "it was was a wild, barren desert country." But he and other cowboys who worked there spread word of its minerals, "with the result that to-day the echoes of the hills are awakened," with sound of steam-driven stamp mills, "crushing ore of all kinds." Charlie helped bring the pastoral wave that replaced the primitive hunters; industry and commerce followed. Now, Idaho was "covered with towns and schools; colleges and churches are to be found all over the place." Civilization had come to Idaho, and the fatherless boy who made his way breaking horses had helped to bring it. Charlie Miller was a protagonist of Progress.

It was a simple, gritty story the London reporter heard. How much of it was true is open to question. Charlie Miller's real name was Julius Mortimer Miller, and his descendants believe that he was born in New York and sailed to California as a boy deckhand.

But whatever his origins, and whatever the quantum of truth in his first published stab at an autobiography, Charlie Miller honed the skills of a tall-tale narrator over the course of a very long life. Some of his later stories were true. He and fellow Wild West cowboy Marve Beardsley really did ride in a six-day endurance race against two bicyclists at the Agricultural Hall in Islington. But Miller soon polished old rumors into gleaming facts, then spun them into glittering stories. In the summer of 1887, London gossip had it that Red Shirt, the "chief" of the show Indians, and the Sioux translator, William "Bronco Bill" Irving, were to be invited on a weekend fox hunt at an estate in Hertfordshire. The hunt never came off, but a cartoonist published a humorous series of sketches depicting the imaginary outing, and they made a hit among the show's cowboys. Broncho Charlie made them real in his reminiscences, substituting himself, Broncho Charlie, for Bronco Bill. He told a naive New York journalist about how he barely stopped his good friend Red Shirt from roping a fox during a hunt with some nobility on a huge Leicestershire estate, after which they went to dinner at the Dean of Windsor's house.

By the 1940s, he had convinced many an author that he was the youngest, last, and (by that time) sole surviving rider on the legendary Pony Express (which terminated the year after he was born). In others' tales, some more true than others, Miller joined the Wild West show in 1885 (and knew Sitting Bull); was the pet of Oscar Wilde's cousin, Alice Hayes; met Teddy Roosevelt at his ranch in Dakota Territory and barely missed being in the Rough Riders; became an evangelist on horseback, known as the Converted Cowboy, for the Salvation Army in New York; and fought in the Canadian army in World War I (at the age of fifty-four).

He made remarkable wood carvings, and as an old man in the 1930s, he entertained crowds of Boy Scouts with his mastery of a twenty-foot-long bullwhip, with which he could light matches clenched in the teeth of quivering twelve-year-olds. "He seemed older than god," recalled one awed scout. "I was sitting in the first row on the ground with carrot-colored hair and freckles and he was drawn to me like a magnet. Though petrified, I was too shy to say no when he lifted me to my feet. I became even more petrified when he explained what he was about to do." When Miller lit the match with the whip, "I was so glad to feel the flame under my nose I almost forgot to spit out the match. I asked him if he would a hold a match for me so I could light it with my .22 caliber rifle, which I had done, though not under someone's nose. He declined, saying he had lived so long by not being stupid, and that I didn't look like Annie Oakley to him."

Of course, Miller's language turned into a highly colored vernacular, full of ki-yi-yi's and whoopie-ti-yo's. He was the subject of articles, interviews, even a children's book celebrating his alleged Pony Express career, and was a featured guest in community parades. When he died, in 1955, he was wheelchair-bound at Bellevue Hospital, where he received up to fifty letters a day, many addressed only to "Broncho Charlie."

Where some wrote breathless summaries of Miller's true-to-life adventures, other less credulous observers marveled at the art of his deception. It might even have been Miller's wide New York press coverage that inspired—or appalled—New York novelist Thomas Berger to conjure a suspiciously similar, albeit fictional character, a man of almost-impossible vintage named Jack Crabb. In two novels and one movie (starring Dustin Hoffman), protagonist Crabb, better known as Little Big Man, danced across an imaginary stage as Cheyenne renegade, gunfighter, sole white survivor of the battle of the Little Big Horn . . . and veteran of Buffalo Bill's Wild West show.

Miller's audacity of later years drew inspiration from many sources, but there can be no doubt his apprenticeship with the West's most artful deceiver was his mainspring. His mastery of the whip and wood-carving was the real foundation on which he built the fantasies his audiences so enjoyed. But compared to the yarns of his later years, the life story he told that London reporter in 1887 was a mild-mannered synopsis. With Cody's exhibition, Miller found both validation for his life and instruction in entertainment. On the one hand, Buffalo Bill's Wild West gave him the chance to perform his horse breaking as a moment in the march of Progress, making it an important piece of American history. Miller was inspired and grateful. On the other hand, the Wild West show taught Charlie Miller that when it came to the West, people want to hear tales that are nearly unbelievable, but not quite. William Cody's show, after all, was the story of a western life—or so the showman said. So why not make your own show, with an all-but-unbelievable version of your life as the central attraction? In 1887, he was a little abashed to be so bold, but he was learning a lot from Buffalo Bill. "I think it is the only show on earth," he told the London correspondent. "I dare say you will laugh at this, but I think so, nevertheless." Being at the camp, he once remarked, was "was just like gettin' home." In fact or in spirit, for the rest of his extraordinary days, Charlie Miller was never far from that Wild West community of Indians, cowboys, and consummate showmen.[1]

CHAPTER TWELVE

Wild West Europe

T HE SUCCESSFUL British year closed in May 1888, when the Wild West show sailed directly to Staten Island and opened a two-month stand at Erastina soon thereafter. Salsbury had already arranged for a return to Europe. In 1889, Buffalo Bill's Wild West opened at the Exposition Universelle in Paris, where the new Eiffel Tower provided a startling view of Paris and an ironic backdrop for photographs of Indians and cowboys. The Paris season was almost as successful as the London debut year. Sadi Carnot, the president of France, attended the show, as did the shah of Persia.

For more than a year, Cody and the Wild West show remained on the Continent. After closing in Paris in November, the show headed south, to Lyon and Marseilles. By New Year's Day, they were performing in Barcelona, Spain. Gate receipts were not good in Spain, where epidemics of Spanish influenza and typhoid kept crowds light. Frank Richmond, the show's noted orator, died in Barcelona, as did at least four Indians. Cutting the Spanish tour short, Cody and Salsbury ushered the Wild West show to Naples, Italy, for three weeks. There followed three weeks more in Rome, and two-week stands in Florence, Bologna, Milan, and Venice. In late April 1890, the show ventured into Germany and Austria, with two-week stays in Munich and Vienna. Through late October, they played Dresden, Leipzig, Magdeburg, Hanover, Braunschweig, Berlin, Hamburg, Bremen, Cologne, Düsseldorf, Frankfurt, and Stuttgart, where the 1890 season finally came to a close.[1]

FOR ALL THE GLAMOUR of the European tour, and for all the sensual mystique of his public image, Cody's private life was lonely and troubled. His settler's cabin had long since expanded to a house of many rooms, but the strife between him and Louisa threatened to blow it apart. He had forsaken divorce when Orra died, but he kept it in mind. In 1885, and for most of 1886, he and Louisa kept separate homes in North Platte, with him out at

Scout's Rest Ranch and her at the older home in town known as the Welcome Wigwam.[2] Their daughter Arta tried to heal the breach between them in long letters to her father, sent from the finishing school she was attending in Chicago. "I would give anything if our home was bright and cheerful," she wrote. "Do not blame or feel angry toward dear mamma. . . . Do not say, dear papa, that you will go to Europe, and never return, for that is not right. You know you love your native land and will be glad to return to it, when you come back, covered with victory."[3]

In 1885, during an appearance with the show in Illinois, Cody met a Kentucky widow named Mollie Moses. She was an artist, and presented him a picture of him she had drawn. They struck up a correspondence. In the beginning, he told Moses he was a bachelor. "My wife and I have separated but no divorce yet," he explained, after she confronted him. "Thats what I meant by saying as yet I am a single man." Writing from Scout's Rest in 1886, he invited Moses to a rendezvous at the St. James Hotel, in St. Louis. "I have got you the white horse and a fine saddle. Suppose you have your habit." They exchanged letters and small gifts, but their separations were long. Moses pined. She asked to join the show. He was indulgent on many scores—"Yes, little girl, just as soon as I can I will send you the locket with the picture"—but on this, he turned her down. The letters ceased.[4]

Cody's disputes with Louisa continued. In 1886, he went directly from Erastina to Madison Square Garden, until late February 1887. Then he departed for England at the end of March. In London and Manchester, William Cody wrote many letters to his sister Julia and to her husband, Al Goodman, who managed his ranch. But there were none to Louisa, and the family was roiled by the continuing threat of divorce.[5]

Perhaps because his real family relations were so tenuous, he shored up his family image with public displays of sincere paternal devotion. He took twenty-one-year-old Arta with him to London, where she kept house for him and accompanied him on many public outings. He sent her on a tour of the Continent with Ed Goodman, Julia and Al's son, and at the end of 1887 Arta and William Cody took a two-week tour of Italy together.[6]

In Britain, Cody's real social life revolved less around royalty than around the theater, which was after all the world he knew best, and where he could be found most evenings. Irving and lesser dramatists were his most constant companions. While Arta enjoyed the Continent, Cody consorted with an American actress named Katherine Clemmons. He may have met her as early as 1886, in New York. Cody allegedly called her "the finest looking woman in the world," but she had little talent. She posed for pictures with the Wild West camp in London, and traveled with them off and on during their European tours.[7] She soon had a financial stake in her relationship with Cody. In the fall of 1891, she persuaded him to lend her the services of the Wild West managerial staff, some of the trained horses, and a dozen Indians for a melodrama called *White Lily*. He saw the play on his return to Britain, and he paid for the company's tour of the English provinces. Reviews were mediocre. The drama closed without ever playing London. But Cody and Clemmons remained lovers and business partners for two more years.[8]

Although Louisa Cody knew about her husband's affairs, money had been at the center of the Codys' disputes from their earliest days together. And, for all the barbs of London critics about the sharp Yankee who was flush with British gold, money remained their prime point of contention. Many newspapers reported exorbitant show profits. Some claimed it made one million dollars in London. "If you see any place where I can invest some money, I can send it—for we have a few scads now," Cody wrote to his brother-in-law in July 1887. "There is lots of money to be had in this country for 3 percent—and if you hear of a big syndicate that has got a good thing that requires a lot of money, I believe I could float it over here."[9]

However much Cody made—and he made a lot—the wealth never lasted. His inability to save for the future contributed to his legend as a show business tragedy, a frontier ingenue with childish enthusiasms, who could never quite grow up and sit on his bankbook. Where did the money go? He invested much of it in Scout's Rest and his other properties. The rest seemed to vanish. He had a taste for fine belongings, like the extravagant four-in-hand coach which he ordered and which he drove around North Platte with crowds of elegant guests.[10] In addition to maintaining two homes in the town, investing much money in his ranch, and supporting his sister Julia and her husband, he also gave money to his other siblings, and to his friends. His generosity with business partners, family, and employees played a large role in draining his accounts by the end of his life.

But there is more to the story than Cody's profligacy, for Wild West profits were stunningly uneven. One month Cody could be swimming in cash. The next, he could be seeking lenders in desperation, trying to buy replacement animals, transportation, or lodging for the cast and crew. Canvas rotted, trains crashed. The constant drain of salaries, food for cast and feed for livestock, could bankrupt the show if unforeseen expenses emptied the cash box. His most recurrent emergency was competition from rival circuses and shows. Publicity costs spiked whenever other shows competed for audiences in the same markets, a situation which required heavy poster production, extra bill posters, and more advance men—all of which came at a high price. Thus, even as crowds flocked to Erastina, in the summer of 1888, Cody was scrambling for cash to pay off loans in North Platte. "This big fight against opposition has taken all our ready cash for a while," he complained to his brother-in-law. "Business is not good." He had borrowed $5,500 from a banker in North Platte, and the note was due in a week. "I don't know how I will come out." He longed to mortgage his property to raise twenty thousand dollars for a two-year term, but he was constrained by Louisa, whose signature was required because her name was on the real estate deeds. "If Lulu would only help me a little I could tide over like a flirt, but she won't sign her name to anything."[11]

Publicly, this most wealthy of North Platte couples seemed happy. Whenever he returned, he was well received among the merchants, lawyers, and doctors of the town. Together, he and Louisa made the rounds of dinner parties and receptions in his honor, as well as operas, dances, and socials. They even attended the Omaha inaugural ball of the Republican governor, John Thayer, in 1886.[12]

But his extended absences must have galled Louisa. With the show in Paris, he missed Arta's wedding to Horton Boal, a young Englishman who had recently relocated from Chicago to North Platte, where he opened an insurance business.[13]

Cody's visits to North Platte were tense. One winter night in late 1889, he appeared in the ranch manager's house, where sister Julia lived with her husband.

"Al, Julia, are you awake?" he asked.

"What do you want, Willie?"

"Get up, come out here, and talk."

The Goodmans rose, and sat with him in the dining room.

"How can I stand it?" he asked. "I can't stay over there in peace with her. I want you to tell me what to do. It is more than I can stand. I don't want to leave my children." He was crying.

"Willie, it will soon blow over, never mind," Julia comforted. Al Goodman took Cody out for a carriage ride in the cold night. When they returned, an hour later, Cody slept at the ranch house. The next day, his sister and brother-in-law urged him not to separate from Louisa. By the end of the day, he had gone back home to his wife and daughters.[14]

His stay was fleeting. He departed for Europe again in early 1890.

———————

WE HAVE SEEN how uneasy the London public could be with the juxtaposition of Cody, the ever-so-visible American, and Queen Victoria, the monarch whose reclusivity betokened British decline. In Paris, in 1889, Buffalo Bill was almost as popular as he was in Britain. Although there was no French counterpart to Anglo-Saxonism that allowed Parisian fans to claim a racial bond with Americans, France, too, was captivated by progress, civilization, and the banishment of savagery from the globe. Buffalo Bill's Wild West also narrated the progress of Western civilization in general, and the romantic trappings of Cody's white Indian, especially his long hair and goatee, invited comparisons to d'Artagnan, the heroic musketeer of Alexandre Dumas.

But even here, there were surprising applications of his image to contemporary politics, as Buffalo Bill became a parody of a political figure who had recently been undone by his self-promotion as centaur-hero. The politics of Paris were superheated for three full years before Cody's arrival. In 1886, the nation's minister of war, General Georges Boulanger, exploited his position to create a gigantic cavalry review on Bastille Day. He was handsome, charming, and he rode a stunning black stallion named Tunis. The public—or part of the public—was entranced.

Subsequently, Boulanger manipulated public longing for national greatness by maneuvering his country to the brink of war with Germany, from which France pulled back only after President Jules Grévy pushed Boulanger from office. A crowd of twenty thousand rallied on Boulanger's behalf, singing songs about his virtues and cheering his name. As an active military officer he could not hold elective office, so throughout 1887 he kept his face before the public with a modern publicity campaign, emblazoning his image across posters, clothing, candy, and even imitation coins. In 1888, he was discharged from the army for his intrigues. He turned the tables on his opponents by winning election to the Chamber of Deputies, with a two-to-one majority in Paris. A hundred thousand people gathered to cheer him. His allies urged him to seize the moment, and stage a coup d'état.

But Boulanger dithered. His enemies mobilized. He soon fell from favor as he was pursued to Brussels and then London on charges of plotting to overthrow the government. As his face disappeared from billboards, Buffalo Bill's face went up.

Quickly, commentators began comparing the two men. Both were handsome and charming. Both looked good on a horse—so good, in fact, they evoked the tradition of the "man on a horse," the empire builder Napoleon, whose militarism and grand ambitions were disgraced in terrible defeat. One humorist wrote an exposé in which he revealed that Buffalo Bill *was* Boulanger in disguise, with a horse that mysteriously changed colors (Cody's horse was white, of course). In lyrics sung to the tune of a song that was originally composed as a tribute to Boulanger, satirists suggested the French officer was only a showman, whose place in the hearts of his countrymen had been taken by a more benign amusement:

> *Brave General, farewell.*
> *Your prestige is no longer,*

Our delight, we hasten to tell,
is the hero of the Wild West.
All here is decadence,
military and civil—
Hurrah for our France
And long live Buffalo Bill.[15]

Cody's usefulness as a parody of Boulanger only begins to suggest the wide resonances the Wild West show had for fin de siècle Parisians. At the Exposition Universelle in 1889, its fans included at least two painters who would soon ascend to world renown. "I have been to Buffalo's," wrote Paul Gauguin to his friend Emil Bernard. "You must make all efforts to come to see it. It is of enormous interest." Another, very different painter, Edvard Munch, was also drawn to the show of the man he called "Bilbao Bill," whom he recorded as "the most renowned trapper in America." As Munch told his father, "He has come here with a large number of Indians and trappers and has set up an entire Indian village outside Paris."[16]

For Gauguin, the symbolist, and Munch, the expressionist, the show meant very different things. Gauguin fancied himself a primitive in the skin of a modern. He spoke of himself as a renegade, an outlaw, and a half-cast (his mother was half Peruvian, and he hinted at a Martinique slave in his ancestry). He blamed the modern world for crushing the creative and benevolent savage who yet coursed in his veins. His longing to escape the stultifying conformity of urban civilization would drive him to Tahiti in 1891.

He was working toward that departure by 1889, and the exposition of 1889 is said to have been his greatest inspiration, particularly the "native villages" from Morocco and Tahiti. If Gauguin walked through Cody's Wild West camp—and it is hard to see how he could have resisted—the celebrated mixed-bloods and "squaw men" such as John Y. Nelson, Bronco Bill Irving, and Billy Bullock, as well as Antonio (Tony) Esquivel and Vincente Oropeza, represented the very men-between-races that Gauguin saw in himself. He adored allegory, and his paintings—one of which was entitled *Where Do We Come From? What Are We? Where Are We Going?*—were intended to be moral and historical fables, and in this limited sense his aims resembled Cody's.[17]

Munch was a very different painter from Gauguin, and the Wild West show entranced him in different ways. Robert Hughes observes that Munch shared a key insight with his contemporary Sigmund Freud "that the self is a battleground where the irresistible force of desire meets the immovable object of social constraint."[18] This was indeed the paradox at the heart of the mythical white Indian, the figure who synthesized the Indian's wild, anarchic freedom with the constraints of white civilization. The white Indian had been an American icon in Europe at least since the novels of James Fenimore Cooper, and Cody himself represented the figure for French audiences as he did for Americans.

In a sense, Munch's paintings explored the failure of modern people to approximate the white Indian. His stark images presented people tormented, alienated from nature and from communal identity in the modern city. If he did not draw specific inspirations from the Wild West show, we can see why he was impressed enough to mention it in letters to his father. With its holistic, natural world of primitive villages and socially integrated people, on the verge of being swept aside by market and machine, it corresponded with his view of modernism's terrible ascent.[19]

Compared to the longer, more direct relationship that Bram Stoker had with the Wild West show, the encounters between Gauguin, Munch, and Cody's amusement were brief and fleeting. Cody himself had little patience with symbolists or expressionists. He took a strong interest in representational art. As he told painter Charles Stobie, he liked paintings to be "as near true to nature as possible."[20]

This explains his preference for the work of another French painter, Rosa Bonheur, and it suggests why his visual presentation of the vanishing frontier appealed to her. By 1889 Bonheur was a legendary painter of the rustic. She was sixty-seven years old, and something of a recluse at her estate in Fontainebleau. Her favorite subjects were poignant farm scenes and heroic, noble beasts of the field, especially cattle and horses. Her most famous painting, *The Horse Fair*, depicted an auction of Percheron horses, the animals' bobbed tails and gigantic muscles bathed in sunlight. Shortly after the painting's spectacular debut in 1853, Bonheur's fame spread across the Atlantic. By 1859, the *United States Journal*, an American magazine devoted to middle-class readers, was offering a free lithograph of the work with every new subscription. Eventually, Cornelius Vanderbilt acquired the eight- by sixteen-foot canvas, which he donated to the New York Metropolitan Museum of Art in 1887. Cody, who was breeding horses at North Platte and who had a lifelong fascination with the animals, probably knew the painting long before he knew its artist. In 1896, for a brief time, he put two hundred Percheron and Norman horses into his arena as a "living tableau" of *The Horse Fair*.[21] Her interests and her technique placed her alongside Cody, firmly in the nineteenth century, as a nostalgist for the organic world of field and farm, which was vanishing before the advent of machine and city.

Bonheur arrived at the Wild West show late in its Paris tenure, in October 1889, and Cody allowed her to paint anywhere she wanted on the showgrounds. She produced at least seventeen paintings from this visit, depicting buffalo, Indians, and—in what became her most famous painting in the United States after *The Horse Fair*—Cody on horseback, a large painting that hung in one of his houses at North Platte for many years. Although Bonheur's reputation has faded since, her fame in 1889 was considerable. Wild West show photographers posed her with Cody, Red Shirt, and Rocky Bear outside Cody's tent, and took other photographs of her as she painted camp scenes. Almost a decade later, Cody incorporated some of these photographs in a show poster that depicted Rosa Bonheur painting him, as if to remind his audience he was not just a showman, but a historical subject in his own right.[22]

As we have seen, Cody crafted Buffalo Bill's Wild West to be "true to nature," or realistic, by reworking real elements into an organic simulacrum which evoked the emotional experience of the authentic. In this, he kept company with Bonheur, and differed mightily with Gauguin and Munch, who exaggerated or manipulated the human form to make larger poetic and philosophical statements. But the interest and enthusiasm the Wild West show evoked even from the youthful avant garde imply that its themes and symbols resonated with the most profound cultural questions of the day. Just as Edward Aveling saw in the show a display of social evolution, in Europe its vivid portrayal of primitivism and progress colliding in mythic combat was a living, breathing reprise of the dialectic that created, in Freud's words, "civilization and its discontents." Buffalo Bill's Wild West simultaneously affirmed the rise of the modern world and entertained some of its most potent critics.[23]

The political resonances of the show's primitive valor were more far-reaching even than its uses as parody. Buffalo Bill's Wild West returned to Europe early in the twentieth century. In the south of France, in 1905, the show became a fascination for the Marquis Folco de Baroncelli-Javon, who for years afterward corresponded with Lakota performers Jacob White Eyes and Sam Lone Bear, and the vaquero Pedro Esquivel (who answered all Baroncelli's letters in flawless French).[24] Baroncelli was a personal friend of the great Provençal poet Frédéric Mistral, with whom he shared a belief that the south of France, and especially his home region of the marshy, sun-splashed Camargue, was a realm of ancient myth and folk traditions which had been all but obliterated by an occupying French government and the Catholic Church. He called the people of the region his "race," and conjured for them an ancestry that extended to ancient times. Baroncelli referred often to the Albigensian Crusade of the thirteenth century, when the pope unleashed a crusade against the Cathars, a primitivist sect denounced as heretics. The center of the Cathar movement was in the south of France, which became the site of terrible bloodletting and persecution. Baroncelli saw this both as exemplary of his homeland's colonization by

Paris, and as a precursor to Sioux experience in the United States. Locating his "noble brothers" among the show's Indians, he took a number of them out for lunch in Marseilles. Subsequently, he dressed in Sioux headdresses and moccasins (which he bought from Indians in the Wild West camp), wrote letters to "my Indian brothers" (sending along an "English translation of the work, in Provençal, of our great national poet, Mistral, to whom we all sent from Marseilles a card which we all signed if you remember"), and pined for an imagined—and lost—regional autonomy (which we may presume in part expressed his aristocratic alienation from democratic Paris).[25]

Baroncelli and Frédéric Mistral together met Cody, who was described in the local press as having "the build of d'Artagnan and the hat of Mistral," in 1905, when the show wintered for five months near Marseilles, and Baroncelli continued to visit Indians and cowboys in the camp for months afterward.[26] The show's devotion to the mythic centaur found an acolyte in Baroncelli. The marquis was an advocate for the mounted, trident-bearing cattle drovers of the Camargue, the so-called *gardians*, who were celebrated by Mistral and Baroncelli himself as symbols of racial purity and throwbacks to rustic, premodern regionalism, much like the cowboys of Wyoming and Texas. Baroncelli also wrote poems, one of them to the native bull of the Camargue, which he believed was descended—like Aryan people—from forebears who swept westward out of Asia, and which he presented as the source of Europe's ancient bull-monsters, the Minotaur and the god Mithra. (The heroic bull spirit of his poem "Le Taureau" explains his past, *"I have known the centaurs."*)[27]

In fact, under Baroncelli's guidance and the patronage of Mistral, the code of the stalwart, masculine, mounted *gardian* developed contemporaneously with that of the taciturn Anglo cowboy, who was enshrined as America's hero with Owen Wister's *The Virginian* in 1902. As inspiration for the valorizing of a "folk" type, Mistral's poetry was like Wister's work. Just as the American novel helped lure Thomas Edison and others to capture the romance of the Wild West's "vanishing cowboy" on film, so a Paris crew arrived at Baroncelli's estate only shortly after the Wild West company left Marseilles on its 1906 tour. The marquis wrote to his Sioux friends that the firm sought "to cinematograph all the scenes described in this poem and it is I, my guardians, my oxen, and my horses who represented those scenes."[28]

The uses of film in extolling revamped folk myths of this sort expanded to western movies, and some of the first films created in France were westerns. One of these was directed by Jean Hamman, who claimed inspiration from Buffalo Bill's Wild West, which he saw in Paris as a child, in 1889. Hamman, also a friend of Baroncelli, began calling himself "Joe" in deference to his cowboy fantasies, and in furtherance of which, in 1904, he went to Montana, where he worked as a cowboy on the Ranch 44. There he met a

Cody nephew, Henry Goodman. He returned to France by 1905, where he reunited with Goodman and met Cody when the Wild West show's French tour of that year got under way. Hamman was a painter and a poet, and he soon became a filmmaker, directing one of the first westerns in any country, *Cowboy*, in 1907, in which he featured real *gardians* and which he set in the Camargue. He also produced one of the earliest Buffalo Bill movies, in 1909—while Cody was still performing in the Wild West show—called *Les Aventures de Buffalo Bill*.[29]

Baroncelli and others denied that Cody shaped the development of *gardian* traditions, and even suggested that Cody borrowed ideas from them.[30] But the question of who influenced whom only distracts from the larger truth: the Wild West's "living pictures" of heroic primitives, fighting a losing battle against the higher civilization and the advent of the modern, exemplified a much larger, transnational search for premodern traditions on which modern national identities paradoxically depended. In this sense, Buffalo Bill's Wild West was one of a large number of thoroughly modern enterprises engaged in what Eric Hobsbawm calls the "mass production of traditions." By reshaping folk and regional traditions into national myths, Cody joined historians, filmmakers, dramatists, novelists, and poets in providing identities for the citizens of the new constitutional monarchies and nation-states that were so quickly replacing the monarchies and empires of the past.[31] But, while his picturesque evocation of the frontier myth provided a unifying story and identity for Americans, its central narrative of beleaguered primitives provided grist, however unintentionally, for a diverse range of people across Europe whose relationships to the modern state ranged from chauvinism to alienation.

In this connection, the show's lasting influence in Germany, as in France, was most directly through its Indians. The nation of Germany was only twenty years old when Buffalo Bill's Wild West debuted there in 1890, and mythic images of the American frontier and its noble savages—and savage savages—had been standards of German art and fiction for most of the nineteenth century.[32] George Catlin's Indian Gallery had been popular in Germany four decades before, as were the Missouri River watercolors of the German Swiss artist Karl Bodmer. Long before Cody arrived, a string of German novelists and adventurers produced lurid western tales through which their readers fantasized about America's economic opportunity and freedom from lingering feudalism, and the mythic racial unity of her primitive tribesmen. Of course, large numbers of Germans had emigrated to the United States, and their accounts of the country and its frontier fueled enthusiasm for things western.

Not surprisingly, Indians had become a feature of German amusements well before Cody arrived in 1890. Zoos often incorporated ethnological exhibits, and there was an Indian village at the Dresden Zoo by 1879.[33] Buffalo Bill's Wild West so enhanced enthusiasm for the primitive spectacle in Germany that by 1906, when Cody's show made its second tour of Germany, cowboy and Indian performance was a standard offering in circuses. Beginning in 1912, the famed Circus Sarrasani of Dresden began a permanent cowboy-and-Indian feature, "Sarrasanis-Wild-West-Schau." American Indians found steady employment in Germany, moving through Buffalo Bill's Wild West on a round that took them from show, to circus, to ethnological exhibit, and back again, often selling "authentic" crafts to make extra pay. Edward Two-Two, a Lakota from Pine Ridge, worked this circuit for many years. When he died, in 1914, he was buried in Dresden at his own request (and where his grave is reportedly still tended by hobbyists and descendants of his German friends).[34] In 1929, Marquis de Baroncelli received a postcard from his old friend Sam Lone Bear, who was again in Dresden, working for the Circus Sarrasani.[35]

German fascination with Plains Indians as romantic symbols of a preindustrial age, bound together through the blood of a united race, spurred a range of other German developments and practices. Most prominent among these was the work of Karl May, a prolific German novelist whose most famous literary characters were a heroic German, Old Shatterhand, and his Indian sidekick, an Apache chief named Winnetou. Winnetou debuted in May's fiction in 1875, and his most popular novel was the three-volume *Winnetou*, which he published in 1893, capitalizing on the western enthusiasms stirred by the Wild West show's 1890 German tour. May wrote eighty novels, about a third of them westerns, which resembled American dime novels but with a twist. Throughout, Old Shatterhand and his "good Indian" friend, Winnetou, battle "bad Indians," including many Oglala Sioux. As in the United States, the "bad Indians" of the plot are driven to their evil deeds by bad white people. But in May's West, the bad whites are, of course, Americans. In the course of the novel, they are made to suffer the wrath of the righteous German avenger, Old Shatterhand.

Like other Europeans, including Baroncelli, Karl May routinely denounced American treatment of Indians. "The Indian is also a human being and possesses human rights; it is a heavy sin to deny his right to exist and, bit by bit, remove his means of existence."[36]

But to read May's fiction is to realize that he desired less the autonomy of Indians than the hegemony of Germans, who in May's fictional world master the frontier far better than Americans, and subjugate its Indians in proper German fashion. The popularity of his German hero who brought justice and removed savagery from the dark frontier in part expressed German longings for empire, for the exclusive right to usher primitives into modernity. May's imagined world would differ from his own modern world

in that its Germany would be far more influential than her corrupt and decadent rival, the United States. May's covert nationalism, cloaked in Romantic
idealism and fronted by the noble savage Winnetou, helps to explain the
broad appeal of his novels. In an era of growing nationalist fervor, May's
westerns were gigantic best sellers among Romantics, expansionists, imperi-
alists, and pacifists alike.

May's lurking German chauvinism also explains why he was not friendly
toward Buffalo Bill or his Indians, whom he accused of betraying their
race.[37] Although he posed for photographs in western gear that looked
much like Cody's, his name is absent from the list of people who visited
Cody during his years in Europe. May never met Cody, and he never saw
the real West. Perhaps there was no need. His fictionalized landscapes met
the desires of his reading audience. Indians came to Germany with Buffalo
Bill's Wild West and other shows. When necessary, May posed as their protector from the Americans, a real-life Shatterhand.[38]

Not long after May died, his widow opened the "Villa Bärenfett," or
Villa Bear's Grease, to house the combined artifact collections of May and a
friend, Patty Frank, who had been inspired to collect Indian handcrafts after
serving as a stable hand for Buffalo Bill's Wild West in Frankfurt am Main in
1890. The Villa Bear's Grease became a center for the burgeoning crowds of
German enthusiasts, or "hobbyists," who, beginning around 1900, dressed
up as Indians, cowboys, and trappers. Eventually, hobbyists dressed in
"authentic" Indian and cowboy clothing, learned Indian languages, and
hosted real Indians and cowboys from visiting Wild West shows to teach
Plains Indian lore and history, and even to hold memorial talks on Karl
May's grave. The first known "Cowboy Club" in Germany was founded in
Munich in 1913. (It was preceded by the first French hobbyist organization,
the Club Blue Star, founded by Joe Hamman in Paris in 1908.) As in France,
some of the first films produced in Germany were westerns, featuring cowboys and Indians.[39]

Hobbyists had counterparts in America. The Boy Scouts and a predecessor organization, the naturalist (and Boy Scout cofounder) Ernest Thompson Seton's "Woodcraft Indians," encouraged children to learn Indian lore
as a means of connecting with nature, and later enthusiasts elevated the
practice to a full-fledged avocation. American hobbyists saw Indian lore as
the pathway to native identity and an authentic bond with American wilderness. German hobbyists had some of the same motives. They saw themselves as "like Indians" in their racial unity and their reverence for nature.[40]

But the similarity between Indian hobbyists in the two countries masked
distinctive nationalist impulses underlying their respective devotions. On
the one hand, Americans seized on Indian lore to become white Indians,
empowering them in cultural and military struggles with decadent Euro-

peans. On the other hand, German enthusiasm for Indian play implied their potential "hostility" to the Americans who so oppressed their "Indian brothers."

THE COLLISION of primitive and progress was the ineluctable truth of world history, and Europeans saw it happening not only in the United States, but around the globe. Anglo-Saxonism and Aryanism, with their histories of races advancing from east to west, provided a narrative history of race advancement for Europeans like Bram Stoker and Folco de Baroncelli. For its believers, to look across geographical space into alien country was to look backward in time. As we have seen, remote regions of profound ethnic conflict provided a tableau of the march of social evolution, which could be read in the racial "types" that represented each of its stages.[41] Thus, in Buffalo Bill's Wild West, the progress of civilization went from savage Indian through Mexican and "half-civilized" cowboy to the "representative man" William Cody, who had been through "every stage" of frontier development.

British travel writers, among others, saw eastern Europe's Gypsies, Saxons, and Magyars in a roughly similar sequence. Savage Gypsies eternally pursued stagecoaches (although on foot, not on horseback), and Saxon herders were either indolent and vicious, or stalwart and brave, or some combination of all these (like cowboys), as the needs of the writer dictated.

For this reason, the "Attack on the Deadwood Coach" resonated with European notions of progress as much as with American. In depictions of remote regions of Europe, as in America, wheels were the exclusive technology of civilized people, who alone harnessed the driving energies of the universe. Savages—Indians, Gypsies, and Asiatic bandits—attacked stages and other wheeled vehicles almost as a genetic trait, as if they were unable to resist the moving target of the higher races whom they could not destroy.[42] On both sides of the Atlantic, stagecoach attacks represented obstacles on the road to civilization, the savagery of the assailants both fearsome and doomed before the wheels of progress turning rapidly beneath the coach. Baroncelli was not only a patron of Indians, but of Gypsies, too. To him, they were mystical descendants of Europe's original peoples. He honored them as "the Indians of Europe."[43] (Of course, such ideas were not Baroncelli's alone, and Buffalo Bill's Wild West and Congress of Rough Riders of the World obliquely incorporated them with the addition of the mysterious "Magyar Gypsy Czikos" in 1897.) When Marquis Folco de Baroncelli entertained Indians and some cowboys from the Wild West show, his beloved *gardians* rode alongside them in a street parade, the better to situate the mythic horse-men of the Camargue in their proper moment in the march of civilization.[44]

Frontiers, then, were not just an American place or process. They were Eurasian, too. And the presence of Americans allowed Europeans to reimagine their relation to the march of progress in new terms, to see themselves as Indians or cowboys, or both.

The notion of global racial frontiers partly inspired Cody and his staff to reformulate the Wild West show as an exhibition of worldwide combat between primitive and civilized. Of course, they took only the most "manly" racial types they could find, which meant that they took only those "primitive" or "semi-civilized" men who rode horses into war. The Congress of Rough Riders of the World reinscribed America's frontier history not just as racial conflict, but as the *last* of the many conflicts in the east-to-west march of white civilization. Eurasian borders became clearly racial boundaries, "frontiers" of combat in which progressive races extinguished savage races, and Progress marched on.

CHAPTER THIRTEEN

Ghost Dance

THE VERY FEATURE of Cody's entertainment which drew millions over its long life—the enthusiastic participation of Indians—has done the most to discomfit many Americans who remember it. Were the Indian performers extorted, duped, or both? Robert Altman's 1976 film *Buffalo Bill and the Indians* presented Buffalo Bill's Wild West as the fulfillment of America's darkest expectations about the frontiersman. Paul Newman's Cody appears as a self-promoting drunk who exploits Indians, especially Sitting Bull, to enhance his own reputation and make money. Altman, like many others, presumes that Indians were simple, naive victims of Cody's chicanery.

So, when the Brooklyn Museum opened a large exhibit on Buffalo Bill's Wild West in 1984, many were surprised to see an essay in the exhibit catalogue by Vine Deloria, Jr. The famed Lakota scholar, activist, and author might have been expected to denounce the Wild West show. (Among his many books is a scathing and best-selling indictment of federal Indian policy called *Custer Died for Your Sins*.) But Deloria painted Wild West performers like Sitting Bull, Young-Man-Afraid-of-His-Horses, and Gall as nobody's fools, men who joined the show for very good reasons. As he pointed out, Buffalo Bill's Wild West show offered them a chance to escape reservation travel restrictions, see the larger world, and make decent money. If the show presented Indians as primitives, they were nevertheless noble equals of their "civilized" opponents, such as cowboys, the U.S. Army, and later on, the many contingents from European armies. Furthermore, in working for Cody, Indians learned a great deal they could not have learned otherwise. "As a transitional educational device wherein Indians were able to observe American society and draw their own conclusions, the Wild West was worth more than every school built by the government on any of the reservations." The knowledge Indians gained from their tenure with the show offered them at least some hope of protecting themselves from the worst excesses of the government. And if they acted out highly fictionalized battles, well, that was "preferable to a complete surrender to the homogenization that was overtaking American society."[1]

Surprising as the essay was for many readers, Deloria echoed teachings of Lakota elders passed down since the earliest days of Buffalo Bill's Wild West. Indians discovered a realm of opportunity in the Wild West show that they had almost nowhere else. In a time of crushing poverty and fierce cultural suppression, the show in some cases made possible the survival of family and culture.

For the Lakota, then, the stakes in Wild West show performance were huge, as they were for Cody, too. William Cody was well aware that without Indians, there would be no unblemished primitives, no noble savages, for civilization to overcome in his entertainment. Without the Lakota, there was no show.

Indians flocked to the Wild West show because they were innovative, courageous men and women searching for a means of economic and cultural survival, and the show offered better hope for that than just about any other paying job. But their enthusiasm for it would be sorely tested, as a new ordeal descended on the Lakota in 1890. That year saw a crisis that nearly flared into civil war across the Great Sioux Reserve and that culminated in an army massacre of the poorest, most defenseless Indians. In the process, it nearly destroyed Buffalo Bill's Wild West. Cody persisted, to reemerge the following year with a newly invigorated show. The 1890s would be his most successful decade of all. Over three million people would see Buffalo Bill's Wild West in 1893 alone.

Among the many factors that allowed it to emerge from this period unscathed, Cody's own sagacity for show business cannot be discounted. But by far the greatest factors in the show's survival were its Indian performers, men such as Black Heart, No Neck, and others who had come to rely on popular entertainment for their survival. Americans today are rightly suspicious of show business and self-promoters, and their skepticism about Cody's employment of Indians is understandable. But the fact remains that Sioux men who fought at the Little Big Horn and never quailed before an enemy, and who energetically volunteered to work and travel in the show industry, were on a fearsome road. They were desperate to save their people from the calamity of 1890, and their efforts to do so likely preserved at least some Lakota lives. In so doing, they saved Buffalo Bill's Wild West show, and Cody's career, too.

OVER THE ENTIRE thirty-three years of Cody's Wild West performances, more than a thousand Indians chose to perform with his company. Why?

Black Elk, who fought at the Little Big Horn as a young teenager, and who went on to become a holy man (his autobiography is a classic of Amer-

ican Indian literature and theology), recalled his reasons for joining the
Wild West show in 1886: "I wanted to see the great water, the great world
and the ways of the white men; this is why I wanted to go. . . . I made up my
mind I was going away . . . to see the white man's ways. If the white man's
ways were better, why I would like to see my people live that way."[2]

Black Elk was disappointed in the ways of white people, but he stayed
with the show through its English tour the following year. He was pleased to
dance for Queen Victoria, and to see her pass in a parade some days later.
"As the Queen passed us, she stopped and stood up back to where the Indians were sitting. All her people bowed to her, but she bowed to us Indians."
Like the popular memory of Victoria's (fictional) bow to the flag, Black Elk
recalled her homage to the Lakota with exhilaration. "We sent out the
women's and men's tremolo then. . . . Then we all sang her a song. This was
the most happy time!"[3]

Subsequently, Black Elk and several others were accidentally left behind
when the Wild West show left for the United States (the occasion of their
interview by London police looking for the Ripper). He spent the rest of
1888 and part of 1889 traveling through France, Italy, and Germany with
Mexican Joe's Wild West show, trying to earn enough money to buy a ticket
home. For a time, he lived with an English "girl friend" and her family,
becoming so ill at one point that he nearly died. But finally, he learned that
Buffalo Bill's Wild West had returned to Europe and was showing in Paris.
Black Elk took the next steamer across the English Channel. "When I got
there Buffalo Bill had gathered all the people together there and they gave
me four big cheers. Buffalo Bill asked me if I was going to stay or go home.
I told him that I was going home. He bought me a ticket and gave me ninety
dollars. We then had a big dinner on my account."[4]

Cody's good humor, kindness, and generosity with money and time
became legends among the Sioux and Cheyenne who worked with him.
George Dull Knife, a northern Cheyenne who lived at Pine Ridge, rode
with Buffalo Bill's Wild West for most of the 1890s. He told stories of Cody
abandoning his hotel room to sleep in Sioux tipis in the Wild West camp.
Late in life, his son, Guy Dull Knife, recalled a day when his father returned
to the reservation with Buffalo Bill. There was a party that night, and the
next day Cody introduced the Dull Knife children to a trick pony he had
brought with him. "Whenever there was a loud noise, the horse fell down
and played like he was dead. Pretty soon, all of the kids started standing next
to the horse and clapping their hands as loud as they could. The horse would
fall down and then everyone would really laugh and so we did this for a long
time. It was about the best time we ever had."[5]

In part, these happy memories suggest how the Wild West show provided Lakota with space in which to explore ways of transforming Indian-

ness rather than seeing it destroyed. By the 1880s, the Plains Indian wars were over. Attention now turned to "civilizing" the reservations, a process that entailed the complete destruction of Indian cultures and the assimilation of Indians into white society, "to kill the Indian and save the man," in the words of educator Richard Henry Pratt.

Assimilation was the cause of self-styled "friends of the Indian," mostly eastern reformers who saw it as the logical culmination to the march of progress. If Indians were defeated, what happened next? Since civilization was carried by race, and races were distinguished partly by their peculiar practices—language, religion, clothing, methods of child rearing—then to eliminate savage culture would secure civilization. The two basic assumptions of assimilationists, then, were that only one standard of civilization existed, and Indians should be forced to conform to it. Fixity had to trump mobility. Each Indian should be compelled to stay in one place, in a house (a settler's cabin), outside which they cultivated farms and built schools and churches, and inside which they created domestic order through monogamous marriage. By forcing Indians to assimilate the values of middle-class Protestant culture, reformers hoped to make a first step toward unifying the diverse, even polyglot country, whose immigrants and freed blacks needed as much "Americanizing" as Indians did.[6]

Reservations became laboratories for assimilation in the 1880s, but much earlier, authorities had conceived them as educational zones where Indians would learn farming and Christianity. By 1883, the year the Wild West show debuted, reservation superintendents, or Indian agents, justified expenditures by documenting the number of acres plowed, schools built, and wages dispensed for "honest labor." Bureaucrats like these had little interest in seeing their charges leave the reservation with private employers, unless the work was in "civilized" pursuits.

Indians were not allowed to leave the reservation without a pass from the agent. Hunting for deer, picking chokecherries, or visiting relatives on another reservation required a personal appeal at agency headquarters, which was often miles from the homesite, and in the opposite direction of the intended trip. The agent, for his part, could be counted on to exploit every angle to see that "his" Indians stayed put. Along the passage between savagery and civilization, conditions of itinerancy or even migrant labor were trapdoors to barbarism. For civilization to triumph once and for all, the fixity which Americans idealized (and which the Wild West show portrayed at its climactic settler's cabin defense) must be imposed on Indians.

So it was that Buffalo Bill's Wild West, the entertainment which climaxed with a show of settlers securing their stationary cabin against mounted, mobile Indians, paradoxically offered Indians an otherwise unthinkable mobility. In practically no other way than with a Wild West show could Lakota hope to travel overseas, or through eastern cities, especially with dozens of other Lakota for company. Although Cody claimed that the Indians were carefully supervised, in day-to-day show life they frequently ventured out from the camp on walking tours or even jaunts of several days' duration. As the years wore on, such outings were less and less supervised, and Indian freedom within the bounds of the show increased.[7]

Travel away from the reservation allowed Lakotas to better retain proscribed spiritual and cultural traditions. By 1883, U.S. authorities had banned all Lakota religious ceremonies, except for overtly Christian ones. But Lakotas in the Wild West show, charged with reenacting Sioux defeat in the arena, found ample means of resisting spiritual alienation in the show camp. Wherever Buffalo Bill's Wild West made an appearance, a cluster of Sioux tipis soon rose on the horizon. Although most of the performers were men, women and children also accompanied the show. There were lots of experiments with new technologies and amusements. Accordions appeared in the show camp in Germany, and Lakota men could be found shouting and betting over games of dominoes. But all this innovation came amid a little Sioux village that provided a comforting simulacrum of a real village for the performers, with meals cooking over camp fires and the familiar rhythms of Lakota language on every side.[8]

Cody made no effort to constrain religion in the camp. Show Indians had learned to be circumspect about their religion where whites were concerned, but on the road, they disguised some of their rituals, like Poe's purloined letter, in plain sight. Visitors to the show camp often commented on "Indian steam baths." These small, canvas-covered domes were actually sweat lodges, sacred structures, in which Lakotas made offerings and prayers before any new endeavor.[9] They popped up wherever the show went in Europe, from London to Hamburg, so that Wild West Lakotas engaged the many challenges before them with the help of all the spirits they could implore—and without a prying agent around to order their sweat lodge dismantled.

The help of spirits was welcome, because traveling great distances, sometimes across the Atlantic, was terrifying and often dangerous. North Atlantic storms and European illness took a heavy toll, and there were injuries and even deaths in the show. All circus-style entertainments were physically perilous workplaces, and the Wild West show was no exception. Cody himself was hurt on occasion. "There is hardly a day that some on[e] isn't hurt," wrote Ed Goodman, Cody's nephew, who took a job selling programs in 1886. "The day Uncle Will got hurt there were 3 Indians, 2 mexicans, 1 cowboy, 1 hostler, and 1 canvas man got hurt. It was a general day for to get hurt. . . . Dick Johnson got two ribs broken this morning."[10] The peril that performers faced made the show all the more relevant to their audiences, many of whose members endured almost incomprehensibly hostile workplaces. Between 1890 and 1917, some 72,000 railroad workers died in workplace accidents; two million were injured.[11] Dangerous amusements were fitting for people with dangerous jobs.

Camp injuries were endured with few complaints, but every death was doubly unfortunate for Indians, whose numbers had been declining for decades in the face of starvation, epidemic disease, and American expansion. The prospect of dying far from home, with no hope of burial there, was a lonely one indeed. The term *oskate wicasa*, "show man," was a badge of honor, and Lakotas honored their courage with songs, such as this one composed for Sam Stabber, otherwise known as White Buffalo Man.

> *There's going to be a Wild West show*
> *Someone asks you to go*
> *White Buffalo Man*
> *Be of courage*
> *Whenever that steamboat whistle toots*
> *Your heart will begin to pound.*[12]

By moving away from the reservation, Lakotas not only learned of the world; they were able to represent at least some familiar aspects of Sioux culture to the larger world, and to preserve and develop those aspects for themselves. The 1883 ban on Lakota religious ceremonies extended to dances. But, beginning that same year, and continuing for the rest of the Wild West show's life, some of the forbidden dances appeared in the show arena. A banned dance is more imperiled than a forbidden book, because if it is not performed, it will quickly fade from collective memory. Although Wild West Indians did not perform the most sacred dances for crowds, it is not too much to say that social dances like the Omaha Dance and the Grass Dance were preserved partly through the Wild West show.

In fact, down to the present day, Lakota dancers credit Wild West show performers with taking dangerous journeys to protect vital traditions of music and dance that had been driven underground on the reservation. Through Buffalo Bill's Wild West, Indian performers blazed a path out of the Indian agent's domain for their forbidden dances and songs, carrying them into the show arena and ultimately into the performing arts such as Indian dance theater (which remains a popular spectacle in the United States and especially in Europe), and high-stakes Indian dance competitions such as those at the Frontier Days celebrations in Cheyenne, Wyoming. In the twentieth century, Indian powwows became central to song and dance

Lakota women and children were central to arena scenes of village life, and even more important as the center of Lakota community behind the scenes. Courtesy Buffalo Bill Historical Center.

traditions for many Indian peoples. The modern powwow, with its dances, craft exhibitions, and Indian food, open to all, in a sense began with the Wild West show. This legacy helps to explain why the late Calvin Jumping Bull, a descendant of Sitting Bull and Black Elk whose prowess as dancer and singer earned him a place in the Cheyenne Frontier Days Hall of Fame in 2004, credits Buffalo Bill with helping to preserve freedom of expression for Lakota people.[13]

In addition to its cultural rewards, the most immediate attraction for Lakota joining the Wild West show was money. Even small amounts of cash were a boon to Lakota families struggling in the harsh new world of federal wardship. In 1883, the primary source of subsistence on the Sioux Reserve was rations, payments of food from the government in return for land ceded by the Lakota in the Fort Laramie Treaty of 1868. The treaty stipulated the government could reduce rations when Indians became self-supporting. By the 1880s, agents labeled individual Indians "self-supporting" and slashed their rations, in an effort to force them into wage labor and farming. Famine crept across the reservation.[14]

Lakota in Buffalo Bill's Wild West were thus driven to perform in order to keep their kin and themselves from desperation. As attractive as the money was the work itself. On the reservation, employment at digging ditches or grading roads was poorly paid, stultifying, and scarce. Riding a horse and performing dances and mock attacks in Buffalo Bill's Wild West was scarce work, too, but for Indians raised to Plains war, it had the virtues of being familiar and relatively lucrative. On the reservation, a man who secured one of the scarce positions as agency policeman could expect $8 per month, a figure which inched up to $10 by 1890. Other work, such driving a freight wagon, chopping wood, or making butter, was sporadic and paid even less.[15]

In contrast, the standard wage for Indians in the Wild West show was $25 per month, with translators and prestigious men designated as "chief" of the show contingent earning monthly salaries of $75 or even $125. With the show's abundant food and the suit of clothes given to all departing Indian men (always useful for formal occasions, and for appearing before authorities back home), show Indianship paid well. Cody committed himself to hiring whole families (to retain the camp's "moral" atmosphere), and in time wives earned $10 per month, with extra cash allowances for children.[16]

To secure Indian women's participation, Cody and Salsbury paid them their salaries directly; the usual amount was $10 per month.[17] Some earned more, depending on who their husbands were. Ella Bissonett, who was married to the translator, Bronco Bill Irving, made $25 a month.[18] The presence of children sometimes resulted in an increase in wages by another $5 or $10 per month for child support.[19]

Indians committed their funds to farming and livestock raising. But those who did soon discovered that vigilance and continuing contact with home were required to keep property from being stolen, a cause in which they secured the assistance of William Cody. In 1891, writing from Germany, the showman requested that the agent at Pine Ridge investigate the complaints of his Indian contingent, who told him "that the lands formerly occupied by some of them were taken up by other Indians" while the show was out of the country.[20] That same year, Indian women prevailed on Cody to take their part in other disputes over property back home. Relatives at Pine Ridge wrote letters to Calls the Name, a Lakota woman traveling with the show. Letters informed her that the reservation's model farmer, a white man named Davidson, had absconded with a horse and colt belonging to her. Davidson told her family that since Calls the Name was off the reservation, she had sacrificed her property. At the request of Calls the Name,

Cody wrote to the agent repeatedly, reminding him that the woman was "absent with consent of the Government" and therefore "entitled to all benefits same as if present."[21] He wrote also to General Nelson Miles, imploring him to intervene and give Calls the Name "her rights and justice."[22] Whatever the outcome of these petitions, Indians made Buffalo Bill—the champion of white expansion which had cost Indians almost all their property—into an important ally for Indian entrepreneurs.

Wild West show managers calculated that they paid $74,300 in wages alone to Pine Ridge Indians between 1885 and 1891. Moreover, the amount increased rapidly over time, so that where Sioux employees received $11,500 in the 1886–87 season, by 1889 there were far more Indians in the show, and in total they received $28,800. In the same year, freighting paid an unknown number of Indians at Pine Ridge a total of $9,051. Other jobs paid less. The show was the reservation's most lucrative employer, and one of its biggest.[23] True, other performers received better pay than the Indians did. Cowboys made between $50 and $120 per month. But for Indians, the relative superiority of show wages over other options meant that auditions for Buffalo Bill's Wild West show and similar enterprises drew large, enthusiastic crowds at Pine Ridge.[24]

But if Indians seized on the Wild West show as a path into a wage economy, it was, paradoxically, a source of great discontent for American reformers. The entertainment industry was the antithesis of civilized pursuits to Indian agents, who could be as antitheatrical as Puritans where Indians were concerned. In part, this reflected popular sentiment. The nascent industry of traveling outdoor amusements gave rise to a new term, "the show business," beginning in the 1880s, and like its predecessors, this form of public entertainment was morally dubious.[25] As we have seen, circus entertainers were an itinerant, racially ambiguous crowd in an industry renowned for graft and corruption. More, the mobility of show troupers gave them a suspicious resemblance to nomads. This, compounded with the thievery and confidence games that flowed in the circus's wake, led Americans to label show workers as "gypsies." The emergence of Indians as show performers thus compounded their essential savagery with a veneer of "gypsy-ness."[26]

Missionary zeal amplified the antitheatricalism of the U.S. Indian Service. To officials, Wild West shows were too much like the theater and the circus to escape their corruptions and deceptions. They brought venereal disease, debauchery, drunkenness, and laziness. Besides, such displays too often emphasized Indian *differences* from whites—their dances, warfare, horsemanship, and other relics of savagery—which agents were trying to extinguish. They were exactly the opposite of the assimilation that reservation agents sought.[27]

This ideology was a major obstacle to Cody's success and to his Indian employees, too. Working together, often intuitively, the white showman and the show Indians devised strategies to overcome it. They crafted a new rhetoric of Indian presentation, which led Cody to some of his earliest breakthroughs in the domestication of his show for the middle-class public. As we have seen, Cody followed in the tradition of circuses and museums, which touted their "educational value" to reassure an anxious public, and seized on "historical exhibition" and "education" in his advertising, offering a show that was not only amusing, but enlightening.[28] But, just as he promised to educate the audience, he also turned the educational rhetoric inward, onto the show cast. As early as the late 1870s, in order to counter the objections of Indian reformers to having Indians work on the stage, Cody presented his amusements as a vehicle for the education of Indians in the rudiments of civilization. It may have been Indians who gave him the idea. In 1877, a journalist reported that Sword told him how much he enjoyed traveling with Cody's stage combination, learning "the ways of the pale faces for his own good," and Two Bears announced that he would raise his five children "like white people."[29]

Intuitively, Cody understood that the middle-class public needed to perceive the show as beneficial to Indians before they could let themselves enjoy it. To this end, John Burke and other publicists constantly emphasized the various ways that Buffalo Bill's Wild West show introduced Indians to civilization while protecting them from its blandishments. "Among the changes of [Indian] habit and ideas which have been effected" by Cody's "intelligent and kindly discipline," wrote one 1885 reviewer, were "the adoption of Christian and civilized attire and even manners, and some progress in the acquisition and use of our language." At the same time, "it was quite noticeable that they had escaped, as aboriginal visitors rarely do, the corruption of some of the vicious and demoralizing habits of our civilization."[30] Ideally, Cody's show community was a kind of schoolhouse or home for Indians abroad in civilization, a place in which they learned about the modern world but were also protected from it.

Such images not only reinforced the show's benefits to Indian performers, but enhanced its appeal as a safe place for the entertainment of white families. After all, that which enlightened Indians could not be bad for civilized people. Buffalo Bill's Wild West invited crowds to believe that in being amused, they civilized Indians. This was no small consideration. In the mid-1880s, the average nonfarm worker made about $1.50 per day.[31] Admission to the Wild West show was fifty cents for adults, twenty-five cents for children. A family of four spent a day's wages, $1.50, on admission, 10 cents for a program, more for food and drinks, and for traveling to and from the showgrounds. So, on the way home from the show, a middle-class town dweller could weigh the expense. Was Buffalo Bill's show worth all that money and time? Year after year, they concurred it was, in part because the show entertained them, and in part because of the great ends their entertainment served. Their day with Buffalo Bill helped educate all those Indians. This was a marvelous age, indeed, when a person could strike a blow for progress and civilization merely by being amused.

Successful as this strategy was for Cody, it also meant that any hint of Indian degradation in the show could wreck its middle-class appeal. Thus, Cody's management tended carefully to popular images and official perceptions of Wild West show Indians. When a complaint about Indian drunkenness and immorality in the Wild West show reached federal authorities in 1886, Cody's able publicist, John Burke, reassured authorities such transgressions were impossible: no drinking was allowed by Indians, the only Indian women with the show were married (Burke ignored the issue of interracial sex, as if daring federal authorities to suggest that white women could be so debauched), and the work was too arduous to leave them enough vigor for immorality. To assuage the doubters, Cody and Salsbury promised to pay $100 a month plus expenses "to any philanthropic society agent, any secret service agent, or any person designated by appointment or intimation, to accompany and supervise the personal conduct" of Indians.[32] Such provisions quickly found their way into the show's standard contract with Indian performers.[33]

Still, the show's rising profile meant that any misstep with Indians might easily play into the hands of assimilationists. Indeed, this soon happened. In January of 1887, as critics raved about Buffalo Bill's Wild West and *The Drama of Civilization* at Madison Square Garden, a New York congressman called for an investigation of this entertainment which, in his mind, had de facto government sponsorship to exploit Indians.

In response, George Bates, who was responsible for Indian supervision within the show, indignantly referred authorities to the Reverend C. H. Maul, pastor of the Baptist church at Mariner's Harbor on Staten Island, "whose church was attended [by Indians] twice each Sabbath for three months"; the Reverend Henry Ward Beecher, Plymouth Church, Brooklyn; the Reverend T. DeWitt Talmadge, of Brooklyn Tabernacle, "where our Indians attended [a] divine service and where they are to attend again next Sunday"; and the Reverend Mr. Hughes, of Trinity Baptist Church in New York, "where they attend Service every Sunday evening."

If a schedule of religious observance befitting the most zealous Christian was not enough to convince the doubters, Bates supervised an ongoing Indian tour of the institutions of civilization, including New York's City Hall, "where the Indians were taken, introduced, and instructed in the working of the city government"; the offices of the *New York World*, where they were "instructed in newspaper making"; as well as Central Park, Belle-vue Hospital, Blackwell's Island, the post office, and a public school.[34]

Despite these assurances, and despite the complaints of Cody and his managers that Indians had long been part of medicine shows and other unsavory entertainments without federal authorities paying the least atten-tion, the Indian office put the Wild West under intense scrutiny. Other shows may have hired Indians, but by 1886, the Wild West show hired by far the most. To the Indian office, the Wild West show was most of all a new genre of Indian performance, wherein dozens of Indians, some of them renowned war leaders, simulated life before conquest. Officials needed a new policy to go with it. So authorities sent letters of inquiry to every reser-vation agent, requesting their report on which Indians had been out with Wild West shows or other entertainments, what impact the experience had on them, and what influence such figures retained among their tribe after their return.

Although no evidence emerged to support critics' charges of moral debasement in Buffalo Bill's Wild West show, the case against it developed as Indian agents performed a two-part harmony of antitheatricalism and assimilation. Their reports condemned shows for encouraging "idleness and dissipation," and making Indians reluctant to wear Euroamerican clothing, farm, and attend church or school. They encouraged disregard of "proper authority."[35] Like reenacting train wrecks and robberies for young boys, let-ting Indians perform in Wild West shows did not "encourage the Indians in legitimate or honorable habits of industry," wrote one agent.[36] "The only show that an Indian should be connected with or take an interest in," wrote another, "is the State or County Fair where he can exhibit his farm produce and well kept stock on the same footing as the white man, where the show-ing would be creditable to the Indian and to the Department."[37] No agent spoke in favor of Wild West shows, and the litany of evil attributed to them—syphilis, drunkenness, debauchery, rebelliousness, laziness, and just plain sin—suggests how much the convergence of Indians and show busi-ness brought America's latent antitheatricalism to the surface. "I do not think the Government should permit Indians to connect themselves with shows," wrote a Kansas agent. The Indian having been educated to the "romantic barbarism" of "stage robbery, daring feats of horsemanship, and fantastic dressing" for centuries, "he should now be taught useful practical lessons of real life; such as will secure him a sound body, comfortable cloth-ing, a permanent home, and the knowledge, that by honest toil alone, men become happy, successful, and even great." Show business could only be a "material and moral injury to the Indian who engages in it."[38]

The powerful hold of antitheatrical prejudices on the Indian office only echoed broader middle-class sentiment. The vehemence of these opinions meant that Cody could never allow his show to be presented merely as a show, a series of acts in an arena, if it was to survive. To succeed, Cody—and the show's Indians—had to convince detractors that under the frontiersman's guiding hand, Indians were not just playing in a drama of civilization; they were passing from savagery into civilization. The public had to be persuaded that Indian performers—who appealed to white, middle-class audiences because of their racial distinctiveness—were becoming more like middle-class white people in the audience (a sequence which could only result, ultimately, in the "vanishing" of Indians, and of the show itself). Buffalo Bill's Wild West became not just a show, but a community balanced on a razor's edge between the savagery of entertainment and the enlightenment of civilization.

Cody intended his imposture as a great scout to be the opposite of the frontier confidence man on the Plains, but here the rhetoric of Cody's opponents situated him as a confidence man. (The charge has proved durable: it is, in essence, the same complaint that director Robert Altman made about Cody in 1976, in *Buffalo Bill and the Indians*.) Many believed Cody was corrupting the innocence of his charges, the naive and honest Indians, by shepherding them into an industry of decadence, a realm of savagery that compounded the flaws and lapses of civilized man. The "moral and spiritual degradation" of show Indians was "fearful to say the least," wrote an agent. "A bright young man goes to one of these shows for a few months and when he returns he has lost all the bright manly looks indicative of purity and all respect for himself and for the white man's instruction." Indeed he had become one of "a worthless and criminal class bringing back all the vices" of those he had associated with, including gambling, venereal disease, and addiction to "intoxicants."[39]

Cody continued to fend off these complaints as they poured into the offices of Indian Service bureaucrats in Washingon, but in the end their sheer persistence finally provoked a crisis in 1890, after a particularly hard year for Indians in Buffalo Bill's Wild West. Injuries were common enough, but it was illness that carried away at least four of the Lakotas with the show during the European tour that year. Two of these, Featherman and Swift Hawk, became ill and were left in the care of doctors in a Marseilles hospital. Show managers arranged a private room and personal care for them, and left money for them to return to the show when they were well. But they died soon after. Another man, Goes Flying, died of smallpox in Naples. Still another, Little Ring, died in his sleep from heart disease.[40]

Coming on the heels of the investigation into the effect of show business on Indians, these Indian deaths seemed to validate antitheatrical prejudices, and assimilationists were not long in saying so. Their opportunity came when five Indians departed the show early and arrived in New York, bound for home. Cody's managers had paid their passage through to the reservation. They were accompanied by Fred Mathews, stage driver for the Wild West show and a former officer in the Pawnee scouts. But one of the Indians in this group, Kills Plenty, was taken ill and had to be hospitalized in New York. His companions—Eagle Horn, White Horse, Bear Pipe, and Kills White Weasel—waited for him to recuperate. He, too, soon died.

With few exceptions, Indians were not citizens in 1890, nor would they be until the Indian Citizenship Act of 1924. They could not vote, and when they returned from overseas, these indigenous Americans had to pass through immigration control. On their way through the port of New York, Kills Plenty and his companions met retired General James O'Beirne, the assistant superintendent of immigration in New York. According to O'Beirne, the men complained that they received poor treatment and poor food in Buffalo Bill's show, and that they had secured permission to return home only after great suffering on their part. Later, after Kills Plenty died, newspapers reported that they fell to weeping when O'Beirne showed them a photograph of their dead comrade. Such open displays of sorrow conflicted with ideals of white manliness and noble savagery alike. "The fact that these Indians were able to cry is an evidence that they have been weakened by contact with civilization and the show business," reported a columnist.[41]

O'Beirne's allegations may have been imaginary, and his paternalism, while typical of officials who dealt with Indians, was certainly misplaced. "The Indians with Eagle Horn," he wrote, "came here without an interpreter, or anyone to conduct them, or to supply their wants, excepting a boy from an immigrant boarding house who fortunately came to me."[42] In fact, Fred Mathews had accompanied them. Besides, Indians routinely set out on excursions of a day or longer while in Europe. Some of the Indians in this party could speak English. The idea of Indians traveling alone shocked Americans, but being able to do so was one of the reasons why Indians worked with Buffalo Bill in the first place.

Whether or not the Indians had actually made any complaint, O'Beirne forwarded his version of the encounter to authorities and the press. Suddenly, the Wild West show was at the center of a major scandal over the treatment of Indians. Charges of mistreatment, all of them relayed by O'Beirne or other officials, splashed across the front pages of major dailies, along with cartoons of Uncle Sam taking disaffected Indians under his wing after they fled Europe and the Wild West show.[43]

By the time the 1890 season ended, then, the assimilationists were on the verge of victory. Cody and Salsbury faced the very real prospect that they would not be allowed to hire Indians again. Caught by surprise, Cody dispatched John Burke to rebut the allegations. But by this time, even Cody's sympathizers in the government had to agree to an investigation of those

Indians still with the show. When they returned to the United States in the early fall, No Neck, Black Heart, and others testified before an inquiry in the Office of Indian Affairs, which weighed the morality of show business as much as Indian employment in it. "You are engaged in the exhibition or show business," observed the acting commissioner of Indian Affairs, A. C. Belt. "It is not considered among white people a very helpful or elevating business. I believe that that which is not good for the white people is not good for the Indians, and what is bad for the white people is bad for the Indians."

The Indians, however, defended their work as adamantly as any white performer, and they turned the inquiry into a pointed denunciation of Indian policy by comparing conditions in the show with those at Pine Ridge. The contrast reflected poorly on the Indian Service. Rocky Bear began by pointing out that he had long served the interests of the federal government, or "the Great Father," by encouraging the development of reservation agencies. He worked in a show that fed him well, "that is why I am getting so fat," he said, stroking his cheeks. It was only in returning to the reservation that "I am getting poor." If the Great Father wanted him to stop appearing in the show, he would stop. But until then, "that is the way I get money." When he showed his inquisitors a purse filled with $300 in gold coins—"I saved this money for to buy some clothes for my children"—they were silenced.

Black Heart, too, denounced the allegations of mistreatment. "We were raised on horseback; that is the way we had to work." Cody and Salsbury "furnished us the same work we were raised to; that is the reason we want to work for these kind of men."[44]

The inquiry concluded in Cody's favor. But if the charges were overblown, there is a possibility that frictions within the Indian contingent contributed to them. According to press correspondents, the five Indians who passed through immigration and triggered the investigation had complained not only that food and clothing in the show were scarce (charges which proved incorrect), but that "Rocky Bear, the chief, and Broncho Bill, the interpreter, are cruel in their treatment of the Indians." Allegedly, when White Horse reached home he planned to tell his cousin Red Cloud about the matter, "and the probable result will be that Buffalo Bill will be compelled to hire a new lot of Indians."[45] At the inquiry, the other Oglalas vigorously denied the shortage of food and clothing. But curiously, none of them denied that there had been disputes over Rocky Bear's leadership.

Indeed, it would have been unusual had there not been some tension over it. Oglalas were not a modern state, but a decentralized people, a network of kin with chiefs who led by persuasion and example. Their transformation to wage-earning employees required considerable adjustments on their part, most of which remain hidden from us. Within the show, Indians vied with one another for the privileges Cody dispensed, particularly the office of "chief" of the Indian contingent, since it paid $125 per month, considerably more than standard performance roles. Jealousies and rivalries among Indians sometimes affected their performance. Rocky Bear would quit the show and go home after being refused the position of contingent chief in 1892, and Luther Standing Bear would blame his lackluster early performance as chief of show Indians in 1903 on subversive advice he received from a jealous Oglala underling, Sam Lone Bear.[46]

These rivalries help explain why some of the most vehement critics of Indian employment in Wild West shows were actually other Indians. On the reservations, questions of who went to the show, and how they were paid, inspired some controversy, and rivals of the Indians who were fortunate enough to be selected sometimes attempted to influence the show—or terminate it—by importuning each other and the government. Red Cloud's interference kept some Oglalas from joining in 1887, making it necessary for Cody to request that fifteen more men be sent to him just before the show left for Europe. Two years later, the aging chief sought payment of twenty-five cents per month from each Indian who went with Buffalo Bill's Wild West.[47] In 1897, he and several other Lakota demanded that the government force Cody and Salsbury to break off their agreement with James F. Asay, a trader in Rushville, Nebraska, who allowed Indians to swap a month's wages for store merchandise in advance of their show contracts, but who levied "the most outrageous charges" for his goods.[48]

In later years, on the reservation, Indians sometimes borrowed the rhetoric of white critics to combat the influence of show Indians. In 1901, the Oglala Tribal Council petitioned the government to "grant no more permits or contracts to any white man to take out any Indians for exhibition purposes" because "it is a well known fact that these Indians have visited houses of ill fame while with the show and have brought home disease," and they "neglected their cattle and property and are worthless after they have returned."[49] Chauncey Yellow Robe, a graduate of Carlisle Indian school who translated for Rocky Bear and Black Heart at the inquiry of 1890, would call for the termination of Wild West shows in 1914. "The Indians should be protected from the curse of the wild-west show schemes, where the Indians have been led to the white man's poison cup and have become drunkards."[50]

Perhaps some of the Indians in the returning party sought to utilize the press against Rocky Bear and Bronco Bill Irving as a way of forcing Cody to remove them from their show positions. When Rocky Bear left the show early in the 1892 season, Cody related how "all save *one* Indian were unanimous in saying *they were glad*," an anecdote which reflects less on Rocky Bear's leadership qualities (he was contingent chief again in future years) than on the continuing rivalry over leadership positions within the show.[51]

Such disputes may have come to the surface in conversations with O'Beirne, who did not speak Lakota well enough to do without a translator, and who appears to have relied on George Crager, a plainsman of dubious talents and even more dubious motivations. Crager, in fact, exploited the controversy to wangle a position as translator for the next season in Buffalo Bill's Wild West show, and his own relations with Indians were stormy, as we shall see in another chapter. The entire 1890 controversy may have erupted out of a potent mixture of minor Indian allegations of poor leadership, the grasping ambitions of George Crager, and the overweening piety of James O'Beirne.[52]

The most unusual aspect—perhaps the only unusual aspect—about the dispute within the Lakota contingent in 1890 was its elevation to a public spectacle. When one weighs the care that show Indians took to defend their jobs year after year against intra-Lakota rivalries and white critics, one cannot escape a nagging sense that a special bitterness or, perhaps, a higher degree of anxiety aggravated the show's Indian camp that year.

This was, indeed, quite likely. For, just as the Wild West show's Indians were experiencing new levels of dissension, the community of the Great Sioux Reservation was roiled by a gathering storm. Rocky Bear, Black Heart, White Horse, and other show Indians could hear thunder over the horizon as early as 1889, while they were traveling in Europe. On March 4, 1890, Rocky Bear bowed low and made the sign of the cross before Pope Leo XIII. We cannot know what he was thinking, but whatever prayers he offered were fervent. The struggle at Pine Ridge to survive a capricious government and a dolorous conquest threatened to unhinge the fragile social order. Before another year was out, many Lakota lives would be lost, and Buffalo Bill's Wild West, too, would nearly find a grave in the prairie. The story of the Ghost Dance troubles, how the show became part of them, and they part of the show, tells us a great deal about how much Lakota men and women valued the Wild West show. Buffalo Bill Cody was a legend for saving white women and families from Indian attack. Now, the Indians of Buffalo Bill's Wild West sallied home, desperate to save their families and friends from a final catastrophe. They were not always successful. But in the process, they rescued Buffalo Bill from the clutches of sentimental reformers and saved for themselves some small opportunity in the atrocious world of U.S. Indian policy.

———

JUST AS THEY SOUGHT to end the Wild West show as a pornography of savagery, Indian reformers sought to eradicate what made Indians distinctive from whites by breaking up Indian reservations and forcing the narrative of progress to its agrarian conclusion. As early as the Treaty of 1868, the Sioux had been encouraged to take up individual parcels for farming.[53] In the 1880s, Congress began the process of "allotment," or tearing Indian reservations to pieces, assigning individual parcels of 160 acres to Indian heads of household, and handing over the remainder to white and immigrant settlers.[54]

In the Treaty of 1868, Americans promised the Sioux all of the future state of South Dakota that lay west of the Missouri River. None of this land could be ceded without signatures from three-quarters of all Lakota men— or so the treaty guaranteed. In the subsequent agreement of 1876, the Lakota were forced to give up the Black Hills in a cession of lands along their westernmost boundary. In the Dawes General Act of 1887, the government attempted to force allotment on the Lakota, but the men refused to sign. So, under the terms of a special allotment bill in 1889, Congress mandated that they split their reservation into six separate reservations, with each Indian head of household now taking 320 acres, surrendering the better land between them to white settlers for $1.25 per acre.[55]

Allotment, the pet project of idealists who genuinely believed themselves to be pursuing the Indians' own best interests, did much to make Indians the poorest minority group in America, costing them about a hundred million acres by 1928.[56] Allotment was one prong of a multipronged assimilation effort, and on top of forced education, suppressed religion, and the circling monster of starvation, it brought bitter divisions as Indians grappled with the question of how to respond. Lakota anxiety over the new land cession soon spread to the Wild West show. In an attempt to secure the support of leading Sioux men, in late 1889 federal negotiators approached Indians in Buffalo Bill's Wild West show in Europe, asking them to sign the 1889 agreement. To a man, they refused.[57]

But on the reservation, a heavy-handed campaign to force the Lakota to sign the agreement finally achieved success after General Crook took charge of negotiations. By early 1890, the twenty-two-million-acre Great Sioux Reserve had been broken into six reservations totaling just under thirteen million acres. Oglalas and some northern Cheyenne now lived on the much-reduced Pine Ridge Reservation. Brulés lived at Rosebud; Hunkpapas at Standing Rock. The government then opened the ceded land to settlement by non-Indians, with none of the safeguards for Indian property that Crook had promised.[58]

This treachery was followed by a severe reduction in rations, after Congress, searching for ways to cut the budget, ordered a 10 percent reduction in funds for Sioux "subsistence and civilization." Beef rations plummeted by one million pounds at Pine Ridge, two million at Rosebud. On top of these miseries, epidemics of measles, influenza, and whooping cough ravaged the reservations. There were only 5,500 people at Pine Ridge, and by early 1890, 45 of them were dying every month.[59] Forced education of Indian children in government schools split families apart at this time of trouble, and even seeking comfort or assistance in the spirit world was forbidden.

Then came the Ghost Dance. Originating in the vision of a Paiute man in Nevada named Wovoka, the Ghost Dance was a mixture of traditional and Christian belief which took different forms on different reservations. Its most remarkable and uniform characteristic was its announcement of an Indian messiah. To investigate rumors of this savior, several Lakota men, including Kicking Bear, Short Bull, and others, ventured to Nevada by train in 1889. They met with other Indians during their travels, and returned home to spread Ghost Dance teachings at Pine Ridge. In Lakota hands, particularly those of Kicking Bear, the dance became considerably more militant than it had originally been. In Wovoka's revelations, Ghost Dancing was supposed to bring on a new world in which all of the dead Indians would rise and the natural world would be restored. White people would return to Europe.[60] At Pine Ridge, Kicking Bear taught that whites would be eradicated beneath a layer of earth, from which would spring grass, buffalo, and resurrected Indians, too. Variations on the Ghost Dance appeared at reservations across the United States, but only in Kicking Bear's teachings did it include the preparation of so-called "Ghost Shirts," which he claimed would repel bullets.[61]

For all the militant trappings, the Ghost Dance expressed Lakota fear, not aggression. Having endured relentless persecution for dancing and prayer throughout the 1880s, Ghost Dancers knew they courted censure and worse. Oglalas followed the dictates of conscience. Some danced. Most refused.[62] Increasingly, doubters feared that the Ghost Dance would bring no new millennium, only more unwelcome attention from authorities. At times, shooting nearly erupted between Ghost Dancers and their Lakota opponents.[63]

But even the most ardent Ghost Dancers knew that there was little likelihood they could mount any kind of armed resistance to the U.S. Army. As fears of a "Sioux outbreak" grew among area whites, authorities debated how to respond. When Indian agents asked Ghost Dancers to stop dancing and report to agency headquarters in the fall of 1890, the vast majority of dancers stopped, and began their trek to the agency.[64]

The many broken promises of the 1880s perhaps made some confrontation likely, but one last factor made it all but inevitable at Pine Ridge: the arrival of a new and tremendously incompetent Indian agent, Daniel F. Royer. An ignorant and contemptible bureaucrat who achieved his office through a return of political favors by the new administration, he was so fearful that he rarely ventured out of sight of his headquarters. "Young-

Man-Afraid-of-His-Lakotas," as the Sioux called him, wrote breathless warnings that half of the reservation was under the spell of the Ghost Dance and refused to obey orders by Indian police to stop.[65] In the months ahead, he repeatedly requested army occupation, triggering not only a confrontation between Ghost Dancers and soldiers, but a showdown between officials in the Indian Service and the War Department, whose traditional enmity over the administration of Indian reservations and Indian policy flared anew over who was to blame for the Ghost Dance troubles.

In keeping with the stance of most army officers, General Nelson Miles saw the Ghost Dance tensions as the fault of civilians in the Indian office and in Congress who insisted on cutting rations to the Sioux until they starved. In his estimation, the trouble would likely disappear if it could only be contained while the Indians were properly provisioned. When the Department of the Interior finally requested the help of the army late in 1890, Miles's response was to surround areas where the Ghost Dance had a large following, and request that all Indians come into the agencies, where they would receive all of the rations promised them under the agreement of 1876.

The strategy was not without risks. Miles knew that the Lakota could not win a military conflict, but bloodshed was a serious possibility. In the fourteen years since the battle of the Little Big Horn, Lakotas had acquired an unknown number of twelve-shot Remingtons for hunting. Any serious conflict would destroy the Indians in the end, but they could kill more than a few settlers in the meantime, and probably some soldiers, too. Miles believed that if they were given food to take the edge off their desperation, and confronted with strong troop presence to dissuade potential warriors, the Indians would stop the Ghost Dance soon enough.[66]

His sense of urgency may have been partly humanitarian, but this crisis also presented him with a grand opportunity to achieve a major goal of army commanders for the previous forty years. If he moved forcefully, he might be able to establish the dominance of the War Department over the Department of the Interior and their underlings in the Indian Service. The Sioux and other "large powerful warlike tribes, that have been for years a terror to the north-west States and Territories," he wrote, should be placed "entirely under military control, and at once."[67] His first step toward this goal became to arrest Sitting Bull, who was showing signs of joining the Ghost Dance.

At this point, he requested the assistance of the West's most famous scout, Buffalo Bill Cody. In fact, Cody had been unable to attend the inquiry into his treatment of Indians in Washington, because he had gone to Chicago for a banquet. There he met General Nelson Miles, who gave him orders to "secure the person of Sitting Bull and and [*sic*] deliver him to the nearest com'g officer of U.S. troops, taking a receipt and reporting your action."[68]

For almost twenty years, Buffalo Bill had burnished the army's public image. He had consistently taken its side in fights with the Indian Service, whose functionaries were targets of his barbs in the press and, earlier, of Indian retribution in his stage plays. Officers had returned the favor by providing him with a litany of testimonials and endorsements. Miles's decision to send Cody after Sitting Bull thus served two functions. First, it was a continuing gesture in the army's reciprocal relationship with the showman, an effort to lend celebrity stature to the army as they grasped for control over Indian affairs. Second, it was an attempt to bring in Sitting Bull without killing him.

The tale of Cody's attempt to arrest Sitting Bull is shrouded in legend and the mists of antitheatricalism. Cody's aims remain unclear, but his choice of companions has not raised the opinion of most historians. Still in Chicago, not yet bound for the reservation, he teamed up with two old friends. One of these was Frank "White Beaver" Powell, who had known Cody since the late 1860s, when Powell, then an army contract surgeon at Fort McPherson, ushered Cody into the Platte Valley Masonic Lodge. Powell was a Gilded Age pitch man, hawking everything from Mexican colonization schemes to "White Beaver's Cough Cream—the Great Lung Healer." He was several times elected mayor of La Crosse, Wisconsin, and he sometimes toured with the Wild West show as an exhibition shooter. Patients who climbed the stairs to his medical office passed shelves lined with the organs he had removed in his surgery, preserved in bottles of alcohol.[69] Cody's other companion was Robert "Pony Bob" Haslam, a former Pony Express rider who was occasionally a booking agent for the Wild West show, and who would end his days as a down-and-out celebrity steward at the Hotel Auditorium in Chicago.[70]

While in Chicago, at meals with this dubious cohort and an audience of a journalist or two, Cody began to play up the threat of the Ghost Dance, or the "Messiah Craze," simultaneously hiding his own thoughts in his now-customary ambivalence about Indian fighting. According to one correspondent, he warned that "of all the bad Indians, Sitting Bull is the worst. . . . He can always be found with the disturbing element, and if there is no disturbance he will foment one. He is a dangerous Indian and his conduct now portends trouble." But not to worry. Cody's own show troupe, especially Rocky Bear and Bloody Shirt, had returned to the reservation and "will do what is necessary to defeat Sitting Bull."[71]

To another, he reportedly mused about the Sioux: "I don't know yet whether I shall fight them or not. It might not look exactly right for me to do so, for I have made a fortune out of them, but if they get to shedding innocent blood I may, if I can be of any service, go up there." Most of all, he wanted Americans to know the seriousness of the threat. "A religious Indian is the most disastrous kind," he explained to a newspaper correspondent.

"This is very likely to be the most gigantic uprising of Indians ever known," with 10,000 warriors facing off against only 4,000 soldiers. Frank Powell reinforced the message: "It may be the greatest uprising the Indians have ever undertaken."[72]

Without ever promising to fight the Indians or even announcing that he was out to arrest Sitting Bull, he headed west with Powell and Haslam. When he arrived in Bismarck, North Dakota, a newspaper correspondent wrote that he was on the way to Sitting Bull's camp with a commission "the details of which cannot be made public at this present."

At this point, the story grows murky. Reportedly, Cody filled two wagons with gifts for Sitting Bull, "a hundred dollars' worth for every pound the Old Bull weighs," and set out from Fort Yates dressed in his showman's best: patent leather shoes, silk stockings, and a dress suit.[73]

Cody's plan to apprehend Sitting Bull, if that is what it was, was foiled by the Indian Service, specifically by Indian agent James McLaughlin, who wanted to arrest Sitting Bull himself. Popular accounts have it that McLaughlin conspired with Lieutenant Colonel William F. Drum, the commander of neighboring Fort Yates, to waylay Cody with a drinking fest while he telegraphed Washington with a request that Miles's order to Cody be withdrawn, on the grounds that the arrest of Sitting Bull would inflame the reservation. According to lore, Drum did his duty but Cody's capacity for drink surpassed that of the most hardened veterans. Officers took the assignment in shifts, and most of them had passed out by morning. Not Cody. By 11 a.m., he had left Fort Yates and was on his way.[74]

But McLaughlin had one last card to play. He instructed two scouts to lie in wait for Cody up the road. When they met up with him, they told him that they had just come from Sitting Bull's camp, and that the old chief had left it by another route. He was now on his way to the agency. The ruse worked. Cody turned back.

By that time, McLaughlin's telegram had reached Washington. President Benjamin Harrison wired to rescind Cody's order to arrest Sitting Bull. Cody left the reservation, and Sitting Bull, to the authorities.[75]

The more colorful aspects of this story are the most suspicious. If it matters, Cody vigorously denied that he was wearing his fine street clothing on this expedition, and he published these denials in the press and in show programs.[76] As for the whiskey ambush at Fort Yates, evidence suggests that Cody drank the afternoon he arrived, but not that evening. The only accounts of the all-night bacchanal are from officers who claimed to have heard about it, not to have participated, and whose memories were published long after the events in question. "Bill was induced by the hospitality of the officers to stay at Fort Yates all that day; but great was everybody's surprise to see him emerge from his host's quarters next morning smiling and happy, asking for his transportation, all ready for the start to Sitting Bull's camp." The best surmise is that Cody spent the night sleeping, not drinking.[77]

Other aspects of the story, whether they are true or not, do not reflect so badly on Cody. If indeed he brought wagons laden with gifts, this would have appealed to Sitting Bull, who saw himself as the leading chief of the Lakotas (although most Lakotas disagreed). Gifts were a gesture of respect, and just as important, they helped maintain his own prestige as he redistributed them to his circle. Whatever Cody had in mind, whether it was an actual arrest or some scheme which would result in Sitting Bull returning to the Wild West show, gifts would have smoothed the way for the conversation that followed. Cody and Sitting Bull had parted friends in 1885, and Cody had given the chief a favorite gray horse and a western-style hat. Reportedly, a relative jokingly tried the hat on one day, angering the chief. "My friend Long Hair gave me this hat. I value it very highly, for the hand that placed it upon my head had a friendly feeling for me."[78]

Hints that he still felt warmly to Cody emerged even in 1890. John Carignan, a teacher on the reservation near Sitting Bull's camp, was approached by Sitting Bull several days after Cody's failed mission. The chief "wanted to know if it was true that Buffalo Bill was at the agency." Carignan told him that Cody was there, "and that he wanted to see him." The teacher hoped Sitting Bull would go to the agency, "but he said he could not get away just then, as he had to instruct his young people in their new Religion."[79]

McLaughlin sent the Indian police to arrest Sitting Bull two weeks later, with predictable, tragic results. Because they answered solely to the white Indian agent, not tribal elders or the people, the very existence of the Indian police violated the democratic norms of Lakota society. This particular detachment of Indian police consisted of young men who despised Sitting Bull for old insults and because he represented an old order which threatened the advancement of the new. Allowing these internecine rivalries to find expression by sending young Lakotas to apprehend a venerated chief in his own camp broke the code of peace that governed relations between Lakotas. Shooting erupted, and Sitting Bull was killed instantly. Soon the Indian police were trapped in Sitting Bull's cabin, exchanging gunfire with warriors from among Sitting Bull's 150 followers. Sitting Bull's son and six other Hunkpapas died, as did six policemen. It is said the horse Sitting Bull received from Buffalo Bill in 1885 danced to the sound of gunfire, sitting on his haunches, raising his front hooves to the sky. Some said it was just an act. Some said it was a prayer.[80]

The shoot-out at Sitting Bull's camp was followed by two weeks of occasionally tense negotiations, as Ghost Dancers increasingly gave up dancing to come to the agencies for the food the army was delivering. But on December 30, disaster struck, when shooting erupted at Wounded Knee Creek between the band of Minneconjou Lakota chief Big Foot, who was now allied to a remnant band of Sitting Bull's followers, and the Seventh Cavalry, which had been sent to apprehend them. Big Foot and his people had agreed to go to the agency, and army commanders on the scene appear not to have anticipated trouble. But violence broke out during attempts to disarm the Indians, whose weapons included an unknown number of the twelve-shot repeaters Miles had been so concerned about. As two soldiers grappled with a young man who refused to hand over his gun, a gun went off, followed by a general eruption of gunfire from the army. Lakota men scrambled for their weapons, but the melee quickly turned into a massacre. The Seventh, Custer's old regiment, opened up on crowds of fleeing women and children with rapid-fire Hotchkiss guns that delivered exploding shells. There were only 120 Sioux men on the scene, facing more than 450 well-armed soldiers. Somewhere between 170 and 190 Indians were killed, few of them men, and even fewer with guns. Big Foot, too, was killed. The Seventh did not escape unscathed, either. Twenty-five soldiers were dead and 37 wounded.[81]

By this time, Cody was back at North Platte. In early January, he received a message from Nebraska's governor, John Thayer, and subsequently met with him. Back in 1889, at Cody's request, Thayer had appointed him a brigadier general as aide-de-camp in the Nebraska militia, just prior to Buffalo Bill's second European tour. The rank was supposed to be a show business prop, but now Thayer gave him a real mission. Like General Miles and most observers, Thayer appreciated that panicky settlers threatened to unleash more bloodshed. After talking the matter over with Cody, the governor commissioned him to "proceed to the scene of the Indian troubles and communicate with General Miles," and also to travel the border between Nebraska and the reservation, where he should "use your influence to quiet excitement and remove apprehensions upon the part of the people." Finally, he should "call upon General Colby," the commander of Nebraska's National Guard, and apprise him of his own "views as to the probability of the Indians breaking through the cordon of regular troops."[82]

For all the excitement over this "Sioux war," Cody's mission was symbolic, and pacific, and his real challenge was not to face down the Indians but to calm the fears of Nebraskans. Before the Ghost Dance began to trouble them, a fierce drought reduced many farmers to desperation. They pleaded for food and support. Then, in November of 1890, as rumors of the Ghost Dance proliferated, they began to imagine an Indian uprising, and demanded bayonets and bullets to put a stop to the Sioux. Nobody was more aware of the edgy, homicidal fears gripping western Nebraska than Governor Thayer, whose office was swamped by the settlers' demands, and who knew that if there were any further violence, it was likely to come from the zealous and ill-disciplined Nebraska militia.[83]

Thayer also knew that the likelihood of any Indians breaking through a cordon of thousands of troops to reach the militia was practically nil. We may speculate that what he feared most was that with tensions so high, nervous Nebraska guardsmen might slaughter any Indians they came upon. The publicity would do no good for Nebraska. Cody knew this, too, and by telling it to General Colby, it was hoped that he could begin to persuade Colby and his National Guard troops, who were positioned along the border of the reservation, to lower their guns and prepare to leave.

This was a real challenge. The public was not yet convinced that hostilities were over, primarily because over two dozen journalists from local and national papers, more than in any other Indian conflict, had congregated at the agency trading post at Pine Ridge and at the store of James F. Asay, an old Cody friend, in Rushville, Nebraska. From the back offices, they churned out phony accounts of impending Indian violence. Many of the stories were completely fabricated, anticipating the "yellow journalism" which fomented the war with Spain eight years later.[84] The volume of press scrutiny made it a media event, perfect for the symbolic appearance of Buffalo Bill. John Burke went to Rushville and Pine Ridge, where he hobnobbed with newspapermen throughout the trouble, assiduously promoting the importance of Cody's mission, and telegraphing newspaper reports under Cody's name. Buffalo Bill, whose very presence had been generating news stories for more than two decades, was a great attraction among journalists who needed sensational stories for their readers. His appointment as aide to the governor of Nebraska and his army endorsement not only as a scout but as a potential diplomat to hostile Indians made him into the living embodiment of the fantasy frontiersman at a moment of maximum media exposure.

In the aftermath of the dreadful winter's events, which killed Sitting Bull and hundreds of Lakota men, women, and children, the army imprisoned the primary evangelists of the "Messiah Craze" at Fort Sheridan (the post had been erected near Chicago after the Haymarket bombing, at the request of city industrialists, to ensure a quick army response to any future labor uprising).[85] General Miles suggested to Cody that he take the Fort Sheridan prisoners to Europe with him, on the grounds that removing them from the country would allow the situation to cool, and that the exposure to Europe would impress them with "the extent, power and numbers of the white race." The commissioner of Indian affairs had already announced that no more Indians would be allowed to participate in show business, but Cody recruited the Nebraska congressional delegation—and the influence of General Miles—to overwhelm his opposition. For their part, many of the imprisoned Lakota were only too happy to join the Wild West show. According to one correspondent, Kicking Bear greeted Cody after a month and a half in the stockade with "For six weeks I have been a dead man. Now that I see you, I am alive again." Kicking Bear and twenty-two of the prisoners joined seventy-five other Sioux in the Wild West show camp, sailing for Antwerp on April 1, 1891.[86]

Controversy over Cody's profits from exhibiting these prisoners of war dogged him only briefly.[87] In the years since, his willingness to publicize his own involvement in putting down the Ghost Dance has come to seem distasteful, especially since the complicated series of events that the Ghost Dance represented has been reduced in popular memory to the killing of Sitting Bull and the massacre at Wounded Knee.

But on close inspection, Cody's conduct at the time of Wounded Knee is difficult to condemn. Historians have paid much attention to the ways Buffalo Bill crafted the battle of the Little Big Horn into a popular attraction. In Europe the captive Ghost Dancers joined the reenactment of Lakota victory over Custer. But Cody staged no "Battle of Wounded Knee."

Perhaps because of his refusal to reenact it, Cody's impact on public perceptions of Wounded Knee has been all but ignored. His aversion to staging a Wounded Knee simulacrum probably came from several sources. In all probability, his Indian performers would not have tolerated it. But also, the American public and press were split on the causes and meaning of the event. Many of the same newspapers that had bayed for blood in the weeks leading up to the massacre now turned around and denounced it. Others hailed the heroism of troops under savage fire. The army, too, was riven. No fewer than eighteen veterans of Wounded Knee received Congressional Medals of Honor. But General Miles himself called it "a general melee and massacre," and ordered a court of inquiry into the conduct of the Seventh Cavalry's commanding officer, James Forsyth. (When the court of inquiry exonerated him, Miles ordered another, with the same result.) Until the end of his days, the general would lobby in vain for congressional compensation for Wounded Knee survivors, victims of an event he considered "most unjustifiable and worthy of the severest condemnation."[88]

This was the cultural divide that Cody's entertainment followed, like a watershed on the Plains, allowing audiences to stake out their own opinions on the recent bloodshed without detracting from the spectacle of Ghost Dancers in the arena. Insofar as his position influenced popular memory of Wounded Knee, it was to establish the killings as a "massacre" of Indians rather than a "battle" of heroes. The show gained new authenticity by featuring Ghost Dance evangelists, but Cody, Burke, and others worked hard to create a middle ground where audiences could enjoy watching the Ghost Dance prisoners without necessarily embracing the violence perpetrated against them at Wounded Knee. Cody had, in fact, been careful to stake out an ambiguous space on the conflict since before his attempt to bring in Sitting Bull, as he warned about the "serious threat" of a Sioux uprising, but refused to commit to fighting the Indians himself.

Cody maintained his ambiguity throughout the conflict. When he returned to the reservation at Governor Thayer's request in early 1891, the massacre at Wounded Knee had already happened. In articles that went out under Cody's name to the *New York Sun* and the *New York Herald*, and which subsequently reappeared in Wild West show programs, Cody and Burke celebrated the army command, but they also broke with the most egregious, bloodthirsty propaganda. Cody's articles provided both grist for popular fantasies about dangerous Indians and an oddly politic suggestion that further violence was unlikely, so long as the government abided by its agreements with the Indians.[89] According to Cody, there were 3,000 well-armed Indians in the vicinity—but 2,500 of them were friendly to the government. "It is like cooling and calming a volcano. Ordinary warfare knows no parallel." The army had handled the situation masterfully. "The situation to-day, *so far as military strategy goes*, is one of the best-marked triumphs known in the history of Indian campaigns." Indian raids on settlers had been prevented. The "dangerous game" had been caught in a "trap," the Ghost Dancers held inside a "military wall" so that they could be calmed by the assurances of "progressive Indians" among them. He lauded all the officers in the conflict, who not only endured "much privation" themselves but "have expressed great sympathy for their unhappy foe and regrets for his impoverished and desperate condition." Warning that "the Government and nation are confronted by a problem of great importance" in "remedying the existing evils," Cody concluded that "intelligence and quick legislation can now do more than the bullet." The articles, in other words, claimed no heroics for Cody, but continued Buffalo Bill's career-long endorsement of army strategy over regrettable Indian Service policy and the fickle, ration-slashing Congress.[90]

At the same time, Cody refused to endorse the violence of Wounded Knee. In the midst of praising the "presiding genius" of General Miles, Cody qualified his remarks: "I speak, of course, of the campaign as originally intended to overawe and pacify the disaffected portion" of the Indians. After all, "the Big Foot affair at Wounded Knee Creek was an unlooked for accident."[91]

Accident or not, back on the road, Wild West show programs incorporated Cody and Burke's articles in a Barnumesque presentation of history, which allowed audiences to debate the meaning of the Ghost Dance and make up their own minds. Just as Barnum had presented his most curious exhibits, his FeeJee Mermaid and the What Is It?, alongside rival expert opinions so the audience could feel safe believing in the exhibits or in criticizing them, Buffalo Bill's Wild West programs offered different perspectives on the Ghost Dance and its climax at Wounded Knee, from which the audience could take their pick. Cody's newspaper articles from Pine Ridge were reprinted, along with a January 1891 telegram from General Miles to Cody in which the officer announced the situation was well in hand and that Nebraska state troops could withdraw. Readers who skimmed the programs might focus on Cody's warnings about the "savage foe," overlook his imprecations against the failure to attend to the needs of the Sioux, and decide the Wounded Knee outrage was justified, or unavoidable.

But for spectators sympathetic to the Ghost Dancers, the programs included alternative viewpoints. Cody's careful distancing of himself from Wounded Knee—the "unlooked for accident"—was complemented by a lengthy, anonymous essay on "Ghost Dances in the West," reprinted from the magazine *Illustrated America*. The piece concluded that the Ghost Dance was an honest expression of Christian faith by a people who had been cheated of their land. "As they brooded over their wrongs, the scarcity of rations, and miserable treatment, imagine with what joy they hailed the coming of Him who was to save and rescue them." But it was not to be. "Even this last boon and comfort was refused by their conquerors," who suppressed "the worship of any Indian who should dare to pray to his God after the dictates of his own conscience."

Recognizing the contentiousness of the issue, Burke inserted a parenthesis after the essay, advising of its source, commending it for being "in many respects very accurate," but warning that "the compiler gives it without comment, as the whole matter has yet to be investigated to get at bottom facts." (In fact, the essay to some degree anticipated Dr. James Mooney's federally commissioned inquiry, in which the Ghost Dance was described as the millennial dream of an oppressed people, in 1896.)[92]

Bridging these conflicting viewpoints, and offering a middle ground for any who were uncomfortable choosing one or the other, was an essay on the Ghost Dance by Burke himself. The press agent suggested the tragedy was coda to a conquest that was less than moral, but certainly inevitable. The Indians' "grand and once happy empire" had now been "brought thoroughly and efficiently under the control of our civilization, or (possibly more candidly confessed) under the Anglo-Saxon's commercial necessities." After all, Burke reminded his readers, if "civilization" was the fate of the world, its progress was suspiciously fast where profit margins were greatest. The savagery of Indian warfare, he mused, was of course the fault of Indians. But their fading resistance, "in another cause," might represent "courage and tenacity as bright as that recorded in the pages dedicated to the heroes of Thermo[p]ylae."

The essay appeared with a drawing titled "After the Battle—Field of Wounded Knee—Campaign 1890–91." Drawn from photographs taken right after the massacre, it depicted dozens of dead Indians and empty, sagging tipis beneath a background of brooding hills. In the distance two soldiers and a scout with a wide hat survey the carnage. Snow lies thick on the fallen.

Whatever position one took on the event, Burke concluded, "the inevitable law of *the survival of the fittest*, must 'bring the flattering unction to the soul' " of the Indians who were conquered, and who would eventually "march cheerily to the tune of honest toil, industrious peace, and fireside prosperity."[93] In the end, civilization would embrace Indians, too. However it came, come it must. The show program's presentation of Wounded Knee reflected all the humanity—and all the self-acquittal—of America's traditional ambivalence toward Indian conquest. Buffalo Bill was many things, but by the time of Wounded Knee, he scouted mostly the terrain of ambiguity and ambivalence, the only place where mass entertainment could engage the injustice of massacre.

For Cody himself, the Wounded Knee imbroglio and the haste with which the Indian Service backed away from responsibility for the massacre allowed him to regain official trust in his treatment of Indians. This was a remarkable turnaround from the events of only two months before, when his show was held hostage to Indian Service inquiry. Authorities did not forget about the controversy, however, and they continued to keep close tabs on Indian education in the Wild West show.

For its part, the army did not manage to wrest authority over Indians away from the Department of the Interior. But they did succeed in placing a military officer in charge of Pine Ridge for at least the next few years. During that time, Cody had no trouble acquiring permission for Indians to leave the reservation with Buffalo Bill's Wild West. The acting Indian agent, Captain George LeRoy Brown of the U.S. Eleventh Infantry, was a friend of Cody's, with views on Indian performers that were close to the showman's:

Of course you understand that I share the feelings of all Army Officers in [regard] to your show and am very thoroughly convinced of its advantages as an educator for the Indians. It is conceded on all hands that traveling is a good civiliser and educator for white men. After a good many years of experience I fail to see any difference in the fundamental traits of character between an Indian and a white man, and the same causes, seem to me, to produce the same results, without regard to color, and differ only in degree.

Brown facilitated Cody's requests and made suggestions about how to circumvent antitheatrical Indian reformers and bureaucrats.[94]

Although he did no scouting in 1890, Buffalo Bill provided a symbol of Indian expertise and frontier savvy for an army hoping to recover Indian governance for themselves as the twentieth century approached. In the aftermath of Wounded Knee, the army continued these efforts. Troops marched through the reservations in a show of force, then returned to their posts, armed and waiting. Regular combat forces were stationed at Fort Robinson, on the southern edge of the Pine Ridge reservation, until 1919.[95] They had put down the revolt that happened on the Interior Department's watch, a fact that gave them much credibility on Indian affairs. Cody's status as their most eminent civilian ally, and as employer of the Ghost Dance evangelists the Indian Service could not contain, would make it extremely difficult for the Indian office to challenge him, for a few years at least.

Cody owed his comeback to various people and influences: to his connections to the military and his friendship with General Miles, to his ability to maintain his pose as frontier scout without actually shooting at anybody, and to his extremely able publicist, John Burke. But his success in turning the dispute to his favor must be attributed above all to choices that Oglala performers made during the Ghost Dance troubles. The Wild West show's Indian performers would have suffered most from an official ban on Indian travel with Cody's show. In this sense, the victory over the Indian Service was at least as much theirs as it was Cody's. Although they remained silent on their motivations, it is not hard to see how they reinforced their image as "progressive" Indians. Back in Washington, in late 1890, as they rose to leave the inquiry into their treatment in the Wild West show, acting commissioner Belt warned the show Indians that "some little excitement" was "growing out of the religion of your people, who believe in the coming of a new Messiah." He implored them to "use your influence and your exertions on the side of the Government."[96] Rocky Bear, Black Heart, and the others may have taken Belt's request as an order. If they feared that joining the Ghost Dance might impede future work with the Wild West show, they were probably correct.

Back at Pine Ridge, they certainly behaved as if such matters were on their minds. The Lakotas in the Wild West show refused to endorse allotment while they were traveling in 1889, but upon their return in 1890, they overwhelmingly supported the government in its fight against the Ghost Dance. U.S. agents hired dozens of Oglalas to scout for the army and serve as tribal policemen. So many of the show's Indians were among these that agent Royer, who had been a strong critic of the Wild West show before the troubles, now commended it. The Indians who returned from Buffalo Bill's Wild West show "stood by the government to a man," wrote Royer. "The great number of them belong to the police and scout force." John Burke telegraphed news of the alliance between the show's Indians and government forces during the troubles. Show publicity later extolled it.[97]

In fact, not all the men who had been with the Wild West show became government supporters, and at least one fought the army. But even his story suggests how the men and women who survived that killing winter decided to turn away from the Ghost Dance promise and toward the the limited cultural continuity and economic opportunity of the Wild West show.

Black Elk, who had caught up with Buffalo Bill in Paris after his two-year odyssey in Europe, returned home in 1889 to find his people starving. He became a leading Ghost Dancer. This was a decision he came to regret. When Big Foot and his people fell at Wounded Knee, Black Elk heard the shooting and rode to help the survivors. He had no gun, but charged the scattered troops again and again, driving them before him. He wore his Ghost Dance shirt. No bullets harmed him. With other refugees, he gathered at the stronghold between Manderson and Oglala, until he heard there was peace. Returning to his home at Pine Ridge, he found the people had fled in terror after the massacre, and were now in a fierce skirmish with more U.S. soldiers at nearby Drexel Mission. Black Elk rode into this battle, too, and was shot in the side. An older warrior, Protector, ran up to him and steadied him on his horse. "Let me go, I'll go over there," said Black Elk, gesturing toward the troops. "It is a good day to die so I'll go over there."

"No, Nephew," said Protector, tearing up his blanket and wrapping it around Black Elk's middle to keep his guts from falling out. Then he told Black Elk to go home. "You must not die today, you must live, for the people depend upon you."[98]

On the other side of this conflict, Rocky Bear, No Neck, Black Heart, and the others did not embrace the government because they thought its Indian policy was fair. To them, there was simply no other choice if the Lakotas were to survive another day. Young-Man-Afraid-of-His-Horses, a great warrior who had been in the Wild West show, and emerged a government supporter and a critic of the Ghost Dance, told Black Elk, "If this were summer I would have joined you and had it to a finish. But this is winter and it is hard on our children especially, so let us go back and make peace."[99] If most of the men who performed with Buffalo Bill came down on the side of the army, it was because it was a lesser evil in a most evil time.

When the shooting was over, and the dead were buried, and the spring came again, Buffalo Bill's Wild West offered hope of a better day. "Better" was not saying much. The glamorous horizons of Buffalo Bill's Wild West had their limitations, too. Cody provided seasonal work, not permanent employment. At \$25 per month, the show paid far more than reservation jobs. But even with food, lodging, and a new suit of clothes thrown in, Indians received less than cowboys, and less than the regular wage of white men who worked in everyday jobs like bricklayers or plasterers.[100] The show employed dozens of Indians. But it could not employ more than a fraction of the reservation. In a time of wage deflation and pronounced labor unrest, Indians with no experience of the modern workplace, and who faced fierce racial discrimination and were not allowed to leave the reservation to find work, had little hope of other employment. The truth is that Indians performed in the Wild West show because in its day it was a fine place to work. But that truth underscores an inescapable fact: there were so few other places for Indians to work, and congressmen and bureaucrats were so penny-pinching, and the public was so apathetic, that Indians starved to death in spite of the Wild West show.

For the Lakotas who encountered it, Buffalo Bill's Wild West was a small creaky bridge to an uncertain future—but a bridge it was. For its Indian showmen, and their families, the show was not only a nostalgic glimpse of a vanishing West. As the events of the Ghost Dance suggest, it was a barely visible pathway, bending through a dark and frightening place, perhaps to a better tomorrow.

Standing Bear

H E WAS BORN a Minneconju Sioux, in 1859, by the cold, clear waters of the Tongue River, where his people sheltered from the winter blasts. He came of age hunting buffalo, fighting the Crows, and the Americans. He was a veteran of the battle of the Little Big Horn, where he fought when he was seventeen. As he later put it, he feared "the white men would just simply wipe us out and there would be no Indian nation."[1]

He was called Standing Bear. The name was not uncommon among the Lakota, and other men who shared it found their way to the Wild West show over the decades. (Luther Standing Bear, a Brule Sioux who joined the show in 1903 and who went on to become a movie actor, an author, and an activist, was no relation to this Standing Bear.)

In 1887, Standing Bear joined Buffalo Bill's Wild West for its debut European season. He was with the show again in 1889 and 1890, during the Paris exposition and the tour of the Continent. In Vienna, he was injured in the show arena. Neither documents nor family tradition indicate what the injury was, but it required hospitalization. With several other Indians in the 1890 season, Standing Bear was left behind to recover. When the show departed Europe, Cody and Salsbury left a ticket for him at the American consulate, and instructions with the hospital on how to retrieve the ticket.[2]

Like many other Austrians, the nurse who tended Standing Bear, Louise Rieneck, was fascinated with Indians. She had seen the Wild West show in Vienna. As a Lutheran in Catholic Austria, she was already a social outsider. She was something of a linguist as well. Other than German, she read Latin and spoke French and English. From her patient, she began to learn Lakota.

Standing Bear was hardly alone in becoming the focus of a European woman's attention. He was a cousin of Black Elk, who had an English girlfriend, and of Red Shirt, who was admired by many women in Europe. Standing Bear was in the Paris camp in 1889 the day the prodigal Black Elk caught up with Cody's show, and probably sat with him that night at the cel-

Standing Bear, c. 1892. Courtesy Arthur Amiotte.

ebratory dinner. Many years later, Black Elk recalled the English woman he had just left. "I told my girl that I would go first and she would come afterward." He was unable to keep that promise.[3]

Family tradition suggests Standing Bear had a wife at home. If so, they may have been in contact while he was in Europe. Many show Indians dictated letters to European and American friends, and sent them through the Indian agent on the reservation.[4]

Sometime in early 1891, while he was convalescing in Austria, Standing Bear received word of the calamity at Wounded Knee Creek. His wife was dead. Not long after, he realized he could not leave Louise. Early in 1891, Standing Bear and Louise Rieneck were married. Then the couple was bound for the United States. On February 16, their ship, the *Standia*, docked in New York. Standing Bear arrived with Louise, her parents, Ernst and Hedwig Rieneck, and two young girls, Maria, age two, and Martha, age three, whose relationship to Louise has never been established. The entire family moved to Pine Ridge, but after a few years, Louise's parents missed certain amenities (among them, says family tradition, the beer and wine which were illegal on the reservation). With Martha and Maria, they moved to Chicago, where they prospered in dry goods.[5]

Standing Bear never joined the Wild West show again. His wife, who was soon known as Across-the-Eastern-Water-Woman, gave him much comfort and a reason not to stray too far. From the time he and Louise moved onto the reservation, they formed a powerful partnership that joined their shared energy and innovative spirit. His extensive female kin taught Louise about making a Lakota household. She brought them her knowledge of European medicine, horticulture, and animal husbandry.

The couple provided services others could not. Poverty and disease took a heavy toll on neighbors and family. Traditionally, the Sioux placed their dead on scaffolds. Now, officials dictated that all bodies must be interred in the earth, in caskets. The caskets were simple wooden boxes, but they were expensive, and they were only available at the government commissary at Pine Ridge, a full day away by wagon. The time it took to travel there was almost as great an expense as the money.[6]

Louise knew basic carpentry, which she taught Standing Bear after they bought some hammers, saws, and a plane. She ordered velvet, linen, and silk from her parents' store in Chicago. Before long, neighbors drove from miles away for the simple, lined caskets, which they paid for in cash or in kind at

Louise Rieneck, age sixteen, in Dresden, Germany. Courtesy Arthur Amiotte.

Standing Bear's home. Louise also made silk and paper flowers, and taught the skill to local Lakota women.

After 1900, Standing Bear and Louise moved to a new location on Whitehorse Creek, west of Manderson, where many of his extended family (including Black Elk) were settling. There, he plowed verdant meadows for a large garden. They continued to make caskets, and Louise's knowledge of European medicine proved a boon, too. She ordered basic medicinal supplies through her parents in Chicago, and for decades, she was something of an unofficial country doctor who delivered babies, tended the ill, and dispensed medicines and advice.

Three daughters, Hattie, Lillian, and Christina, were born to Standing Bear and Louise. In the reservation era, Pine Ridge society was increasingly divided between "mixed-bloods" and "full-bloods." Mixed-bloods generally affected western clothing, were bilingual in Lakota and English, and had many contacts among white businessmen and more access to cash. Full-bloods spoke mostly Lakota, and their associations were more restricted to Lakota-speakers. They were generally poorer than mixed-bloods. Although the labels were racial, in reality such identities had as much to do with cultural choices as with ancestry. There were many children of mixed unions who did not identify with mixed-blood culture, and many full-bloods who assumed certain attributes of mixed-blood identity, too.

For their part, Hattie, Lillian and Christina moved gracefully on the mixed-blood/full-blood divide, attending the mixed-bloods' "white man dances" in beautiful European-style dresses they made with their mother on her sewing machine, and their father's traditional Lakota dances and ceremonies in Lakota-style dresses embroidered with beads and elk teeth. In fact, mother and daughters turned the cabin into a veritable factory of clothing: western- and Lakota-style dresses, as well as shirts, pants, and quilts, rolled off their sewing tables. At the same time, they continued to make moccasins of hand-tanned deer and cow hide, using traditional awls.[7]

So the family prospered. Seasonally, Standing Bear and his relatives drove their cattle between pastures at Whitehorse Creek and the high meadows of Red Shirt Table, where their cousins, the families of Red Shirt and High Eagle, helped tend their herds. Back at Whitehorse Creek, they cut hay for the winter, and before the fall frost, they slaughtered cattle and dried beef for winter storage and for gifts to neighboring families that were an obligation of their comparative wealth. The women of Standing Bear's family taught Louise to gather and preserve chokecherries, buffalo berries, wild currants, and plums; she taught them to make savory German preserves, like sauerkraut, and pickles in brine. With plentiful cattle, and with the men bringing in deer occasionally, there was always a pile of hides that needed tanning, or gardening to do. Relatives and friends in need could drop by, offer their work, and take home food, clothing, and moccasins. Standing Bear's influence grew. He became a chief of his local community, renowned for his generosity.

Although he resisted allotment, like many Lakotas, Standing Bear eventually reconciled himself to it. By 1911, he and Louise had a large, hand-hewn log cabin, painted white, with a shingled, pitched roof, wooden floors, and frame windows. Two years later, visiting officials reported they also had a cabin and a barn and 640 acres of land, with 80 acres under plow. They owned one hundred cattle and thirty horses. At a time when the average U.S. worker made just $621 per year, they had $1,000 in savings.[8]

In Wild West show drama, Standing Bear and other Indians were powerful symbols of the theory of history embedded in the concept of race. They embodied pure, unalloyed primitivism and savagery. Through conflict with another pure race—of white, civilized people—they were subdued. Buffalo Bill's cowboys guaranteed that the Indian race would be contained within its original borders—Indian bodies—by enforcing a perimeter around the body of the vulnerable white woman in the settler's cabin, away from which they drove the Indians.

But through performing in the same Wild West show that expressed white supremacy, Standing Bear and a few other Lakota men found wives across the racial divide at the turn of the century. For the Lakotas, the only thing that made marrying white women a strange concept was white hostility. Race was less a factor in Lakota identity than residence and behavior. By living among Lakota and acting Lakota, one became Lakota. In some ways, Standing Bear's marriage to Louise was traditional. Lakota culture allowed for marriage of alien women through capture in war or through friendly alliance. Any Cheyenne, Pawnee, or American woman who married a Lakota man, learned to speak Lakota, and made a home with him among Lakota, became Lakota.[9] Perhaps because intermarriage was a traditional means of creating alliances with powerful families and peoples, Sioux men who won the hands of white women were often ambitious and forward-looking. In 1890, while Standing Bear was convalescing in Vienna, a Santee Sioux man named Winner—who had taken the name Charles Eastman—became the first Indian to receive a medical degree, from Boston University. In the same year that Standing Bear married Louise Rieneck, Dr. Charles Eastman married Elaine Goodale in New York.[10]

For all its exclusionary racial teachings, Buffalo Bill's Wild West show was a vehicle for at least a few, and probably a great many, Indian men to meet and love white women, and in at least a few cases the lovers married. Although the vast majority of its cast did not have the experience of Standing Bear and Louise, for some, Buffalo Bill's Wild West show, spectacle of

Standing Bear and Louise (Across-the-Eastern-Water-Woman), at their cabin, with granddaughters Rose Two Bonnets and Lula Two Bonnets, c. 1915. Courtesy Arthur Amiotte.

race enmity, became a path to a future that reconciled blood and culture. The future lay in mixing peoples together.

This was Standing Bear's strategy. He refused to learn English himself, but insisted that his children and grandchildren learn it. He refused baptism, too, until his daughters prevailed on him late in life. But at the same time, he and Louise grafted European and Indian business and craft techniques onto one another to make a new living, to carve out a new kind of story about the Lakotas and Europeans, which they would live. The contours of that story floated beneath the surface of frontier ideologies like Buffalo Bill's. But still, they hearkened to a real frontier history of mixed blood, which, as we have seen, typified relations on the northern Plains for many people throughout the nineteenth century. Standing Bear and Louise simply dismissed all the stigma of "miscegenation" among Europeans and Americans, and embraced that venerable legacy of mixed marriage as the path to a bright future.

Standing Bear devoted himself to history and art. While his daughters were growing up, he spent most evenings, after his work was done, painting scenes of the Lakota past, especially of his own generation, in traditional style, on large pieces of white muslin. He consulted with neighbors, his age-mates, on details of the images, and the deeds and events they recorded. In 1930, the poet John Niehardt arrived on White Horse Creek, asking to interview Black Elk. Standing Bear joined the discussions. Two years later, when Niehardt published *Black Elk Speaks*, Standing Bear's testimony appeared with Black Elk's, and his illustrations appeared throughout the book. To this day, his art is among the most evocative, and coveted, of the period.

Louise and Standing Bear lived at White Horse Creek until 1933, when she died soon after being in a car accident. The reservation reeled from depression and drought. Standing Bear grew tired, depressed. He passed later that year.

Arthur Amiotte is one of Standing Bear's great-grandsons, and like Standing Bear, he is an artist. Amiotte works from his studio in Custer, South Dakota, and his renowned collages explore his family history, min-gling painted images of Indians—including Standing Bear—with early auto-mobiles, frame houses, and photographs of Indians at church, on the road, and in Europe.

Much of Amiotte's early inspiration came from stories he heard from his grandmother Christina, a daughter of Standing Bear and Louise who lived in the home her parents built until 1985, and continued their tradition of generosity all her days. As Amiotte grew up, she related stories of the many relatives who would travel to White Horse Creek, to pitch their tents out-side the Standing Bear home in warm weather. There were people garden-ing, tanning hides, plowing, and butchering cattle, and children playing ball with inflated cow bladders. In the evenings, after they turned the lamps out, Standing Bear and Louise lay in their bed, with family and sometimes guests sleeping on the floor in bedrolls. In the darkness, they told stories. Some were ancient tales. Some told of Standing Bear and his age-mates, and their adventures in Europe. Sometimes, Standing Bear and Louise performed the dialogue of the characters in the stories, and their ability to mimic voices enthralled the children, and kept them in stitches. This tradition, too, con-tinued after they were gone. Christina and her husband, Joseph Mesteth, a mixed-blood of Lakota and Mexican descent, told their stories to their chil-dren and grandchildren.

This was more than entertainment. In the darkness, the children drifted off, to sagas of hero-creators, warrior ancestors, and long, strange trips with Buffalo Bill all weaving the space between waking world and sleep, where the consciousness of a people resides.[11]

CHAPTER FOURTEEN

Cowboys, Indians, and
the Artful Deceptions of Race

T HERE WERE MANY OTHERS in Cody's cast alongside the Indians. In the Wild West camp, Indian and non-Indian motivations became profoundly entangled, and white cowboys, Mexicans, and others worked with Indians in a kind of integrated traveling town or community. No contingent existed on its own; all depended to some degree on the cooperation of others. In this sense, the story of the camp is less in the experience of any one contingent than in the relations among them. Unfortunately, while thousands of people worked in Buffalo Bill's Wild West, only a handful left any record of the experience. Paradoxically, we know most about the show's most impoverished and least politically powerful performers, the Lakotas, because federal authorities took such an interest in them. For the rest, the cowboys, cowgirls, vaqueros, Cossacks, Japanese, Hawaiians, and European soldiers, we know very little. But even these fragments of evidence can be revealing. Why cast members joined the show, and how they made it function, speak volumes about the limits of its racial ideologies in day-to-day life, and it tells us much, too, about William Cody's legacy in the larger West.

For all its devotion to "authentic" racial types and historic blood feud, to look beneath the surface of show publicity is to realize the depths of Cody's artful deception of race. The arena performance of race distinction and white supremacy hinged on a sizable amount of race mixing, cultural borrowing, and even crossing of the color line. The dramatic presentation of white supremacy only became possible through the cast's enthusiasm for beguiling the Wild West's racial frontiers.

Given the real racial tensions in the American West and elsewhere, racial strife between contingents was perhaps inevitable. The center of camp social life was the dining tent. Luther Standing Bear (no relation to the Standing Bear who married Louise Rieneck) joined the show in 1903. He recalled, "The Indian village would always be located not far from the dining tent."[1] Other groups flocked to the tent, too, and it was a kind of social center, but contingents ate at separate tables, with Indians at one table, the cowboy band at another, Mexicans at still another.[2] Segmented seating allowed for fast meals and suitable quantities of food at each table, but it reinforced social constraints on mixing. In 1890, Warren H. Vincent, a Wild West show cowboy, reassured his parents that he was in no danger from smallpox, which killed a number of Indians during that year's European tour. "We cow punchers was exposed this much," he wrote. "We ride among them during the performance."[3]

Performers' segmentation derived partly from their disparate origins and languages. The cowboys' reasons for working in the show were not dissimilar to those of the Indians. Out on the range, cowboy work was dull when it was not dangerous. The hours were interminable and the pay was low, all conditions which led to the cowboy strike of 1883, which broke under pressure from ranch owners who easily exploited cowboys' transience as well as the cowboys' own sense that their work was a temporary occupation which would lead to better things.[4] The Wild West show presented cowboys as upwardly mobile white men rather than exploited manual laborers, and its performance held some advantages over regular range work. The advancement of barbed wire turned the open range into a series of pastures, and autonomous long-distance riders and ropers into poorly paid "Ph.Ds"— posthole diggers—who suffered the same long hours and the same low pay the industry had always offered. Harsh weather was the norm, too. On the northern Plains, late blizzards struck even in May. As Wild West show cowboy Harry Webb put it, "Frost-bitten noses and feet and fighting cattle in blizzards and belly deep snow talked loud on the side of Buffalo Bill."[5]

With wages as high as $120 per month, the show paid better than many ranches, in addition to offering a chance for travel, and new circles of friendship and romance. Many of the show cowboys were married, and wives often accompanied the troupe on tour. Because the Wild West show toured only during the warm months, all employees had to find other work during the winter. Many went back to ranch work, mining, or even other shows. Most cowboys appear to have anticipated moving up from the ranks of cowpunchers to other businesses, perhaps to being ranch owners, or cattlemen, whose income and social standing far exceeded those of cowboys.

Of course, the show was no refuge from hard work. "By the end of three weeks several riders decided there were easier ways of living than bronc riding and had gone home and a couple of others had been fired because they were trouble makers," recalled Harry Webb.[6]

Trouble came in many guises, and the rough life of the show camp became rougher with personal rivalries. On the road, as on the range, the culture of cowboys was imbued with practical jokes and one-upmanship. When his close friend and fellow show cowboy George "Gaspipe" Mullison began seeing a married woman during their tour, Webb frightened her away with tall tales about Mullison's long career in crime out west. After the fist-fight that followed, Mullison and Webb did not speak for six weeks. Mulli-son renewed their friendship by one day secretly switching the bridle of Webb's bronco with a shorter mule bridle. As Webb's bronco began to buck in front of the crowd, "I was flung to right and left like a straw dummy in a cyclone." Moments later, he picked himself up from the ground "with chaps around my ankles," two sprained wrists, and a "mouth full of tanbark and horse manure." Mullison helped him to the sidelines, with some advice: "Now you smart son of a bitch, I reckon you'll think twice before you scare another girl away from me."[7]

Circling around these encounters was Cody, who often excoriated cow-boys and other performers for misbehaving or for what he perceived as uninspired performance. The showman's temper was hot, although his lan-guage was almost always folksy and clean. "Dog-gone your pictures, cow-boy, if you expect to be with this trick very long you better get the lead out of your britches! You move like a man seventy five years old!"[8]

Aggravating relations between contingents was a pervasive sense that Cody favored the Indians. "Mr. Cody sometimes gets on a tantrum and rakes up the first person he meets whether they are to blame or not," wrote C. L. Daily, a sharpshooter in the 1889 shows in Paris. "The reason he went for me was because in the act before some of the Indians did not do quite right and of course he couldn't scold them as they couldn't understand him." Daily being "next at hand," Cody "poured his wrath on me."[9]

This perception that Indians benefited from favoritism was not restricted to cowboys. Indians were pleased to recount similar episodes, such as the day that Buffalo Bill stormed into the camp cookhouse and berated the staff for giving the Indians inferior food. "My Indians are the principal feature of this show, and they are the one people I will not allow to be misused or neglected," Cody warned the cook. "After that we had no more trouble about our meals," recalled Luther Standing Bear.[10]

At first glance, the experiences of show performance might be said to approximate show community. In the arena, cowboys represented white men, people with the most political power. Indians were ostensibly noble, but as primitives they were doomed. That their pay was lower than cowboys' was in keeping with the show's overall racial hierarchy and ideology.

But insofar as certain conditions had to be met to retain Indian perform-ers, Cody and his managers went out of their way to placate the least socially privileged people in the Wild West show. C. L. Daily was probably correct that Cody was reluctant to criticize his Indian performers publicly, but it was not merely because he did not speak Lakota. He dared not risk embarrassing them in front of the other performers, lest they complain to federal authorities or, even more perilous to him, refuse to return. Without the vanishing primitives, the spectacle of progress lost all meaning.

Professional pride (and fear of Cody's wrath) motivated performers to excel in the arena, and each contingent's efforts to polish its own appearance at the expense of others also enhanced racial tensions. Cowboys sometimes exploited their position as the most autonomous performers to secure special benefits. Thus, Luther Standing Bear recalled that the chief of the show cowboys "had general supervision over both horses and men," giving him more authority than any other contingent chief in the show. In the 1903–4 season, "when an unbroken horse would be brought in, this cowboy chief would give it to an Indian to ride bareback." Once the animal was "broken," the horse "would be taken away from the Indian and given to a cowboy to ride." After enduring this for some weeks, "it began to be just a little too much to stand." When an Indian performer finally refused to ride the unbroken horse assigned to him, Standing Bear confronted the cowboy chief, who tried to dismiss him by suggesting, "You will have to see Buffalo Bill about the horses."

Standing Bear retorted, "You know very well that Buffalo Bill does not know what you do with the horses," and warned that the Indian performer in question would not ride unless his old horse was given back to him. "That was all," Standing Bear remembered, "but the boy got his horse back in time to enter the arena with the others."[11]

Such accounts suggest that racial tension backstage was as important as it was in the show's version of history, where race was the means of knowing whether a performer stood for savagery or civilization. Since the show's earliest days, publicists had drawn a blood line of demarcation between the cowboy, "usually American," and the vaquero, who "represents in his blood the stock of the Mexican, or it may be of the half-breed." Even from the cheapest seats, audiences could distinguish between these frontier rivals. In contrast to cowboys, who wore angora chaps and six-guns, Mexicans wore sombreros with huge crowns, satin jackets, and pants. As show programs explained, the degenerate vaquero was "more of a dandy" than the cowboy, so "fond of gaudy clothes" and gigantic spurs that upon seeing him ride into a frontier town "the first thought of an eastern man, is that a circus has broken loose in the neighborhood."[12]

But for all these distinctions, the show's racial boundaries were not as impermeable as they looked. For one thing, cowboys were not always white. Oklahoma produced large numbers of mixed-blood cowboys, and some of these joined Buffalo Bill's Wild West as white men. Thus Tom Isbell, a veteran of the Cuban campaign's Rough Rider regiment whom Theodore Roosevelt described as a "half-breed Cherokee," joined the show in 1899 to reenact the attack on San Juan Hill, and returned to perform as a cowboy during the 1903 tour of Europe.[13] Jim Cook, a cowboy in the 1888 show, was also alleged to be of mixed parentage.[14]

We might call these men "secret mixed-bloods," because they passed as white. But other performers straddled several different racial lines, or frontiers, at the same time, and in ways the audience could not help but notice. In 1896, the contingent of American cowboys included Pedro Esquivel. Even if audiences did not know that he had been a "Mexican vaquero" in earlier seasons, they could not have avoided noticing his name, which would have labeled him Mexican anywhere in the West. Such blurring of racial lines often occurred, with show performers crossing first one racial divide, then another, to appear in various contingents in a single season, or even in a single show.

Gauchos were supposedly even more decadent than Mexicans, and the new gaucho contingent recruited in 1892 further emphasized the racial subversions of frontier life. "The civilization that the Spanish colonists took with them to the Llanos gradually became subdued by the savagery of the new situation," until their gauchos, with their "fiery" Spanish temperament aggravated by an "infusion of native Indian blood," were acknowledged to be even more degenerate than other show riders, a fact reflected in their gear. A gaucho in need of footwear simply slaughtered a young horse, stripped its leg from the knee down, then sewed up the end and put his own foot inside, shaping it "to the leg and foot while still warm" to form "a leather stocking without heel or toe." These men literally wore the legs of their horses, as if they had become hybrid horse-men, their mixed race underscored by mixed species.[15]

But all this racial degeneracy was an act. Sometime vaquero and American cowboy Pedro Esquivel was also chief of the show's gaucho contingent in 1896. One of his fellow gaucho performers that year was Ben Galindo, whose name also appears on the list of cowboys. Thus, racial degeneracy and whiteness were performed, or embodied, by the same men, on the same afternoon.

In fact, although genuine gauchos joined the show in 1893, none of them remained by 1896, and the projection of the gaucho "race" required the imposture of skilled imitators. Fortunately for Buffalo Bill, he had the Esquivels. Brothers Joe and Tony Esquivel were cowboys from San Antonio. They met Cody in the early 1880s when they arrived in North Platte with a herd of cattle from Texas, and either or both of them could be found in Buffalo Bill's Wild West for decades thereafter.[16]

Pedro Esquivel may have been a cousin, or no relation at all, to Joe and Tony. But whatever his origins, in 1896, both he and Ben Galindo, the cowboy-gaucho-Mexicans, were joined among the gauchos by Joe Esquivel. Similarly, Tony Esquivel was billed as the "champion Rough Rider of Mexico" in London during the 1887 season, although he often rode with the cowboys.[17] By 1898, Joe Esquivel had represented everything from savage, miscegenated gaucho in 1896 to chief of white cowboys, a status he achieved again in 1902, 1903, and 1905.[18]

There were real Mexican nationals in the show, about whom very little information survives. The vaquero contingent included Vincente Oropeza, a legendary roper whose performance inspired the young Will Rogers. Oropeza worked bullfights in Mexico when he was not with the Wild West show, and we may assume that other Mexicans also worked internationally, appearing in bullfights or other entertainments in Mexico, and in Wild West shows and circuses north of the border at different times of year.[19]

Cody left no clues to his reasons for simultaneously casting the Esquivels as Mexicans, white cowboys, and gauchos, but we can guess that their facility with animals and men was a factor. They could perform the rope tricks and horseback feats required of both cowboys and vaqueros, and if Joe Esquivel played a gaucho in the arena, then he likely learned their signature skill of throwing the *bola*, a leather thong with iron balls at each end, from the genuine gauchos who were with the show in 1893.

But at least as important as the Esquivels' arena talent must have been their powers of persuasion over people, especially the show's cowboys. Cy Compton, Ed Richards, and other cowboys included renowned rodeo performers and horse breakers. Generally, the contingent was hardworking and well behaved. But like cowboys on the Plains, they gambled and drank in the off-hours. As Harry Webb suggests, fists were as legitimate a means of resolving disputes as practical jokes—and almost as entertaining.

As we have seen, the show's viability as a respectable family entertainment required sublimation of cowboy aggression. In this connection, motivating cowboys and keeping them in line required formidable diplomatic and managerial talents. Clues suggest the Esquivel brothers had these in abundance. Recall that Pedro Esquivel was fluent enough in French to correspond with the Marquis Folco de Baroncelli. Tony Esquivel's daughter recalled that her father grew up speaking Spanish, English, and Polish (having learned the last language from his mother, a Polish immigrant to Texas). After several years in the Wild West show, he had mastered Lakota, perhaps the better to defuse the tensions that sometimes arose between show Indians and cowboys.[20] Tony Esquivel commanded respect simply through his horsemanship. "The best rider in the show got thrown yesterday," wrote cowboy George Johnson from London in 1892. "He is a Mexican and he has been with the Show for eight years."[21] Recalling his confrontation with the show's chief of cowboys, Luther Standing Bear credited Cody with intervening on behalf of the young Indian who had been given one of the cowboys' sour mounts. But smoothing over such disputes was part of the cowboy chief's job. That year the cowboy chief was Joe Esquivel, who may have acted without Cody's direction.[22]

Similarly, cowboys and Indians played antagonists, but behind the scenes relations were more complex because at least some of the white cowboys had Sioux families. By the early 1880s, William "Bronco Bill" Irving, a white cowboy, had earned a reputation as a top hand and a superb bronc rider in South Dakota's Black Hills. He also spoke fluent Lakota, a considerable asset in his marriage to Ella Bissonett, a Lakota woman. He joined the Wild West show at its beginning, and remained with Cody and Salsbury for many years. Cabinet photos of the Irving family, with Ella in traditional Lakota finery, her husband in cowboy hat, chaps, and moccasins, and their five-year-old son, Bennie, wearing a similar Indian-cowboy costume, were popular in London and elsewhere.[23]

Similarly, William "Billy" Bullock joined the show's cowboys in 1883. His father, William G. Bullock, had been a merchant in the Lakota country since the early 1860s, when he took a Lakota wife. His marriage cemented a political alliance with the Oglalas, whose leaders, particularly Red Cloud, regarded him as a trusted ally and a go-between in negotiations with the U.S. government. By the late 1870s, William G. Bullock was ranching in the Black Hills. Billy, his mixed-blood son, became a skilled roper and bronc rider, and hired on as a Wild West show cowboy for the first five years of the show.[24]

In 1883, Irving and Bullock traveled together from Pine Ridge to Colville, Nebraska, for the show's first dress rehearsal, the occasion of Pap Clothier's ordeal. On that journey, they were accompanied by John Y. Nelson, the white man whose marriage into Red Cloud's family had been an asset to Cody ever since 1877, when Nelson traveled with Cody's stage troupe as a translator for Sword and Two Bears. In the Wild West show, Nelson sometimes drove the Deadwood stage. On other occasions, he was the hunter who was just returning to the settler's cabin as it was attacked. On still other occasions, he appeared as a cowboy. But always, his skills as an interpreter, and as a venerated senior member of a Lakota family who was also a white man, made him an essential go-between for Cody and his Indian performers.[25]

Cody shifted from Pawnees to Lakotas in 1886, and the move was eased by the show's prior acquisition of Irving, Bullock, and Nelson, three show cowboys who were fluent in Lakota, and married to or descended from Lakota women. Irving and Bullock in particular were widely noticed for their cowboy skills, while Irving's son Bennie often could be found among the Indian contingent. In cabinet photographs, he wears beaded moccasins and a cowboy hat, and is billed as "The Smallest Cowboy in the World."[26]

According to legend, in 1885 John Y. Nelson's children—who venerated Red Cloud as an ancestor—appeared in the "Attack on the Settler's Cabin," as white children facing imminent abduction by Indians.[27]

To understand how the show community cohered, then, we must see its peoples as possessing not only cultural differences but also conjoined histories which had long required at least some of them to innovate in living arrangements and to mediate deep differences. Mixed-blood familial relations were no interracial utopia. John Y. Nelson claimed that whenever his wife's people went to war against the American army, he left his tipi to scout for the troops, while his wife, and presumably his children, stayed with the Sioux.[28]

During the late 1870s, a Sioux horse raid swept up a number of horses from William G. Bullock's ranch in the Black Hills. His partner, Jim Hunton, took Billy Bullock and other cowboys to retrieve the horses. They succeeded, but during a gunfight with the Sioux raiders, Hunton was killed. "Some of the Indians we have in this show were in that horse-stealing expedition," Billy Bullock explained to a London correspondent in 1887. The chief of the show's Indians in 1887 was Red Shirt, "and I won't swear that Mr. Red Shirt didn't have a hand in it," remarked the cowboy. "They are all very close, however, as to which of them shot Jim."

But Billy Bullock did not carry grudges. He might have warred against some of the Indian contingent in the past, but some of them were kin. "Mr. Red Shirt is my uncle," he explained, perhaps with some exaggeration (or perhaps not). "He is a very good sort of fellow. . . . He and I are very excellent friends. You see I speak his language, and whenever he wants anything fixed up he usually comes to me. I also do his correspondence, especially the private part of it."[29] So, too, with "Bronco Bill" Irving. Rocky Bear, head of the show's Indian contingent in the late 1880s and at various times in the 1890s, was Bronco Bill's father-in-law. (The close ties between them may have aggravated complaints about Rocky Bear and Irving among those Indians on whose behalf O'Beirne complained in 1890.)[30]

How do we reconcile the show's displays of mixed-blood men and their Indian families with its message of white racial triumph? Cody's publicists struggled with this very question, and they came up with some powerful answers. One strategy was to raise the class status of mixed-blood men. John Y. Nelson became one of "the most honored and reliable" men who "by general honesty of character and energy, has gained fame and respect among whites and Indians." Billy Bullock was identified in show programs as "a half-breed Sioux, and a good combination of the best blood of that justly-famed fighting nation, allied, through Indian rites and ceremonies, with the blue blood of the East."[31] Elevating the class status of Nelson, and of Bullock's white ancestors, made their interracial unions seem less socially subversive, because upper-class status made them remote from the middle-class audiences who flocked to the show.

In other ways, mixed-blood families were less frightening than we might suppose, not unlike Annie Oakley's display of feminine sharpshooting. In this sense, the families of Nelson and Irving were more like freaks in the circus, their weirdness underscoring the "normality" of whiteness among the cowboy contingent. They were miscegenated exceptions that proved the rule of white racial purity. For the most part, cowboys looked white. Indians were convincingly "Indian." The presence of a few mixed-blood families suggested the possibility of race mixing, and the temptation of interracial sex. But in doing so, it simultaneously underscored the virtues of the majority of white cowboys, and of Cody himself—and, by extension, of American white men—in resisting frontier temptations, especially Indian and Mexican women.

But for us, performers' transgression of the show's race lines suggests the illusory nature of race itself. Show publicity notwithstanding, skills like bronco busting and rope throwing were not biologically transmitted. They were cultural attributes which were learned and practiced. Just as the first U.S. cowboys acquired their skills because they were willing to mimic Mexican vaqueros, Cody's Wild West show could not have existed without the crossing of racial boundaries that gave rise to cowboys who spoke Spanish, French, and Lakota.

Racial identities are cultural artifacts which masquerade as "natural" categories. In this sense, they are an ongoing deception which the public practices every day. The ability of some people to "pass," to deceive the public into believing they are of one race when their ancestry supposedly consigns them to another, subverted the supposedly "natural" boundaries that defined America's racial hierarchies. The slipperiness of racial characteristics in this regard, and the confusion that ensued as Americans tried to sort individuals into ever more complicated "racial" groups on the basis of supposedly self-evident features—skin color, head shape, nose size, and so forth—combined with their centrality to social order, made them a fit subject for popular amusement. They were at the heart of artful deceptions like Barnum's What Is It? and the minstrel show, in which white performers so convincingly donned blackface and assumed "Negro" song and dance traditions that many audiences ceased to see them as white men. Conversely, when African Americans began performing minstrel shows after the Civil War, they were often suspected of being white men in disguise.[32]

The Wild West show, and its Congress of Rough Riders, was a kind of reverse minstrel show, with its nonwhite members occasionally masquerading as white men to better persuade a largely white audience of their own superiority. Buffalo Bill cast racially Mexican wranglers and mixed-blood men as cowboys, appropriating their skills as white. Sustaining a narrative of white racial destiny paradoxically required racially subversive casting of nonwhite performers in white roles.

As STANDING BEAR and Louise Rieneck have shown us, Wild Westerners crossed racial frontiers not only semisecretly within the show but also in day-to-day life. Newspapers had a field day when a Pawnee man they called "Push-a-Luck" eloped with a white woman from Newark in 1886, and reports of other Indians in romantic relations with whites occupied press columns, too.[33] John Shangrau, Lakota interpreter for the show and a mixed-blood of French and Sioux ancestry, married a Liverpool woman in 1892.[34] During the Wild West show's second tour of Europe, Nate Salsbury hired a governess for his children, an Englishwoman named Clara Richards. In 1893, she married Tony Esquivel—he who embodied "the stock of the Mexican or the half-breed." They had five daughters before his death in 1914.[35] Collectively, the cast of the Wild West show was like one of the era's popular magicians, their racial imposture a giant sleight of hand; with one hand they encouraged audiences to believe in immutable barriers and interminable competition between races as historical fact while with the other, in private, they befuddled, contradicted, and dissolved those same racial lines.

Indeed, Indian men were practically overwhelmed with offers of white women's companionship. Billy Bullock translated Red Shirt's correspondence in London. "You would be surprised at the number of letters he receives, and from ladies, too. I guess your English ladies are original," said the bemused Bullock to a reporter.[36] Jacob White Eyes, who toured with the Wild West show through southern France in 1905–6, carried on a relationship with a Frenchwoman.[37] After he returned to Pine Ridge, White Eyes fondly recalled the comparative sexual openness of Europe. "I would like to have some Bull-fight postal card and some Ladies photograph without clothing," he wrote to Marquis Folco de Baroncelli. "[I]t is pretty scarce in America."[38]

For all the transgression of racial frontiers by the Wild West cast, and for all the shifting back and forth between white, Mexican, and gaucho identities in the show, Indians were one touchstone of authenticity which remained constant in the arena. Buffalo Bill's theatrical melodramas had presented dozens of non-Indian "supers" as Indians, and competing circuses and Wild West shows passed off peoples of all races as Indians at one time or another. But non-Indian performers were not allowed to pose as Indians in Buffalo Bill's Wild West. Just as Cody did not allow others to pass themselves off as him (although many claimed he did), he protected the authenticity of the show's Indians, recognizing them and himself as essential to the umbrella of authenticity which allowed the show's larger fictions to remain credible.[39]

But even if all the show's Indians were "genuine Indians," the many questions circulating about what constituted Indian identity enabled its Indian contingent, and the show's impresarios, to play vigorously with Indian authenticity. Show programs portrayed them as—and audiences believed them to be—members of separate tribes: Arapaho, Cheyenne, Pawnee, Shoshone, Crow, and Sioux. The reality was far simpler. After early experiments with Pawnees and Wichitas, Cody turned almost exclusively to Oglalas. Thus, each of the show's "tribes" was a group of Lakotas, mostly Oglalas, mounted on horses of a distinct color.[40]

We may speculate that Indians used the show for their own ruses, jokes, and impostures. The numerous "chiefs" who appeared with the show were rarely real chiefs, and playing to audience desires for an encounter with the primitive, noble savage must have been as humorous and sometimes perhaps even as rewarding as it could be tiresome.

But in becoming a forum for the creation of Indian identities, the show not only intensified emphasis on certain cultural attributes such as tipis, warbonnets, war-painted horses, and specific dances, but also facilitated acquisition of new skills which became an essential part of modern Indian practice.

In this sense, the ethnic and racial deceptions of the Wild West show were more than an amusement. Although cowboys, Cossacks, Mexicans, and German cuirassiers were not allowed to pass over the race line and assume Indian identities in the performance, Indian performers were allowed and even encouraged to travel in the opposite direction. Luther Standing Bear recalled that his fine regalia took a beating from London fog and soot in 1903. Finally, Johnny Baker, by this time arena director for the show, told him that he should save his best gear for the days when attendance was high, and that on other days "I might take the part of a cowboy if I chose." "This was a change for me," recalled Standing Bear, "and I enjoyed it very much."[41]

To judge from extant photographs of the "backstage" showgrounds, Indians frequently put on cowboy gear, particularly hats and the long-haired angora chaps which Buffalo Bill's Wild West made synonymous with "cowboy" prior to 1900. Some were accustomed to these trappings before they joined the show. The advent of the livestock industry on the northern Great Plains led reservation Indians to acquire cattle, and the Oglala and Brulé Lakota owned thousands of animals beginning in the early 1880s. In tending those herds, they enthusiastically borrowed and syncretized cowboy equipment and techniques from Americans the same way Americans had appropriated them from Mexicans. In the last years of the decade, Lakota artist

Amos Bad Heart Bull sketched scenes of Indian cowboys at Indian roundups, working in boots, spurs, hats, and even dusters, tending herds that numbered 10,000 in 1885 and 40,000 in 1902.[42]

Outside of the Wild West show, Indians' development of an indigenous cowboyhood met with resistance from the same Indian Service officials who championed allotment and railed against Wild West shows. In the popular ideology of progress, after all, cattle herding was a successor to hunting, but it was only a precursor to farming, the foundation on which civilization rested. Thus, one official in Montana warned, "herding leads to a nomadic life," and "a nomadic life tends to barbarism."[43]

Nevertheless, Sioux cowboys and cattle owners helped generate an Indian cattle industry which lasted almost two generations. Many of the Indians who moved into the show arena after 1900 were experienced cowhands. Indian cowboys worked for ranches off the reservation, too, and many of them moved into rodeo. By 1920, Lakotas such as George Defender and David Blue Thunder were taking first place in competitions against white cowboys, and performing feats of horsemanship from Miles City to Madison Square Garden. As rodeo itself developed partly from Wild West show precedent, so, too, did its parallel, Indian rodeo. At the Rosebud Reservation (formerly the Spotted Tail Agency), home to most of the nation's Brulé Sioux, the earliest Indian rodeos closely resembled Wild West shows; a six-day affair in 1897 included races, bronco riding, steer riding, and a reenactment of Custer's Last Stand, "Mixed Bloods Against Full Bloods."[44]

Thus, Indians appropriated the racial symbolism of the Wild West show for their own purposes, and—in ways that remind us again of Vine Deloria, Jr.'s contention about the show as educational space for Indians—Buffalo Bill provided a kind of undercover arena in which Indians could acquire and demonstrate cowboy skills, even "out-cowboying" the show's cowboys by dressing in cowboy clothes and performing their stunts as well as they did.

At Pine Ridge, the reservation livestock industry finally fell victim to government hostility, the leasing of Indian lands to non-Indian cattlemen, and allotment, which broke up many of the finest range lands. Lakota cattlemen sold their last large herd in 1917.[45] As a major employer at Pine Ridge from 1886 until 1916, Buffalo Bill's Wild West show overlapped almost perfectly with the reservation's cattle industry. Until its very end, cattle raising seemed one of the best hopes for a prosperous Lakota future. The Wild West show offered a means of integrating cowboy culture and Lakota culture.

Back at the reservation, show wages paid for cattle and horses, as well as wagons, farm tools, and other necessities. As early as 1892, agents at Pine Ridge were complaining about small amounts of money from Buffalo Bill's

Indians—$5 and $10 sums in greenbacks—which arrived at the Indian office with letters "in Indian" informing the agency which friends or relatives should receive the money, and in what denominations. Fast Thunder, one of the Wild West show's Indian contingent, was said to have acquired four thousand cattle by 1896, and a comfortable cabin with "splendid" farm fields.[46] Less wealthy Indians in the show routinely sent money home, too.[47]

Indians in the show augmented their wages by selling Indian crafts, especially " 'bead work' made into moccasins, purses, etc.," for which they received "very large prices," according to Nate Salsbury. There was a market for Indian crafts on the reservation, but it appears to have flourished in the Indian camp at the Wild West show, because of the connections Indians built with non-Indian suppliers and customers. Cody and Salsbury bought materials such as brass beads at wholesale prices, and sold them at cost to show Indians, who made them into souvenirs for sale to tourists and kept the profits for themselves.[48]

Men profited handsomely from this trade.[49] But beadwork and moccasin manufacture were traditionally women's occupations, and it appears that Indian women in the show exploited the market for Sioux crafts assiduously. This might explain why Calls the Name, the sister of No Neck (chief of the show contingent in the 1891–92 season), had $260 in cash and goods during that year, after receiving only $112 in salary from Cody and Salsbury.[50]

If Calls the Name's experience is any guide, Indians manufactured and sold Indian crafts to museums and collectors across Europe. Calls the Name sold some of her goods to the show's translator, George Crager, and perhaps used him as an intermediary with outside purchasers. Early in 1892, Crager approached the Kelvin Grove Museum in Glasgow about selling his "collection of Indian Relics." Among the goods he sold were a pair of buckskin leggings embroidered with beads, which he claimed had been worn by Calls the Name in 1876, the year of the Little Big Horn fight. In reality, they were probably of recent vintage. Some of the other materials Crager peddled, including a pair of moccasins embroidered with brass beads and a shield that is of minimal craftsmanship, are on display today in the Kelvin Grove Museum, and they appear to have been products of the show's Indian craft industry.[51]

In all likelihood, Indians commissioned Crager as their sales agent, to sell the goods to the museum and return at least some of the cash to their Indian manufacturers. But Crager was a publicity hound. (He finagled his way into the show by translating for the show's detractors, including James O'Beirne, in the controversy that engulfed the show in 1890.) When he discovered that his name would not be preserved as a museum "donor" unless he gave at least some of the goods away, he quickly did so.

Wild West Indians/cowboys, 1909. Indians sometimes disguised themselves as white cowboys in the show, allowing white spectators to claim Indian riding skills as a white racial characteristic, and giving Indian performers a chance to display cowboy techniques they used to tend growing cattle herds at home. Courtesy Buffalo Bill Historical Center.

Such maneuvering likely helped Crager earn a poor reputation among the Lakota. In late December 1892, Charging Thunder, a Lakota man in the show's Indian contingent, clubbed George Crager over the head backstage, knocking the translator out cold. Charging Thunder apologized, blaming the fight on whiskey which some publican allegedly slipped into the lemonade he ordered. But given the variety of goods Crager hawked to the museum, and his dubious reputation, it appears likely that tensions over Crager's sale of goods contributed to Charging Thunder's ire. In any case, Charging Thunder spent thirty days in a Scottish jail as a result.[52] Crager left the show after one season, and returned to Pine Ridge, where he joined the staff of the Indian agency.[53]

AT THE END of each show season, Buffalo Bill's Wild West provided a letter of recommendation for every performer. Cowboys who learned performance arts in Buffalo Bill's Wild West show frequently went into western films, other Wild West shows, and rodeo. As we have seen, here was always a wide streak of performance art in cowboys, who strove to approximate their romantic fictional counterparts even in the days of the Long Drive from Texas to Kansas. But over time cowboy skills became so oriented to entertainment that by the Wild West show's final years, around World War I, at least some riders came to Cody's show having learned their skills not on the range but in circuses and other entertainments. Those who wanted to remain cowboys found that the best living was to be had in performing the identity for somebody else, rather than living it on the range.

Meanwhile, show wages grew in importance for Indians, who had less room than cowboys to maneuver into other occupations. For a brief time after the disaster at Wounded Knee, the army ensured the Lakota their full rations, but discounting and punitive withholding soon began anew. By 1900, rations were only about 70 percent of their stipulated treaty levels, amounting to one pound of beef and 5.75 ounces of flour per person, per day. In 1902, the government announced a plan to eliminate rations for all "able-bodied men," the better to force them to work for $1.25 per day, usually at hard manual labor, such as fence building, road grading, or dam construction.[54] By the end of the summer, wrote Luther Standing Bear, "The Indians were all heavily in debt to the storekeeper."[55]

These conditions drove Luther Standing Bear to join the Wild West show that very year. Others who joined the show in this period were similarly motivated, and some of them used the show to advance their ongoing political battle with the Office of Indian Affairs. In 1908, three Lakota men with Buffalo Bill's Wild West—Bad Cob, Edward Brown, and William Brown—took time between shows in New York for an angry meeting with the commissioner of Indian affairs. Bad Cob complained that the agency interpreter, a Lakota, was holding two salaried jobs which could better be given to two different men. The Browns were particularly confrontational, and their grievances reflected the frustration of educated Lakota men. William Brown was a graduate of Carlisle, and Edward, too, was a school graduate. Edward "said that he is anxious for any kind of job whereby he can earn a living, and that he believes that there are enough returned students on the Pine Ridge Reservation to do a good deal of the work which is now done for the Government by white persons, and wanted to know why the returned students are not given this chance to get ahead." William Brown pointed out that even the lowest-paid work was unavailable to him. Why couldn't he get road work on the reservation? Why couldn't he be an assistant farmer? The Browns and Bad Cob, reported the commissioner, "were very insistent on these matters."[56]

Such complaints were not new, but Indian office functionaries customarily read them in letters or heard them from third parties, not from the Indians themselves, and certainly not in New York, hundreds of miles from Pine Ridge. However startling it was for the commissioner of Indian affairs in 1908, Indian use of the show as a means to confront policymakers was not new. Show performers' geographic and social mobility had been influencing Sioux politics for a generation. In 1885, Sitting Bull had used his tenure with the Wild West show to cultivate relationships with whites he would not meet otherwise. In 1887, Lakota performers discoursed late into the night on the significance of their meeting with Queen Victoria. After this all-night discussion, "every one of his young men resolved that she should be their great white mother."

The sentimentalism of press accounts obscures the significance of such meetings. Throughout the eighteenth and for most of the nineteenth century, Lakota leaders cultivated alliances with European monarchs in hopes of restraining or influencing American policy. In the aftermath of the Plains Indian wars, the development of a new peacetime strategy for building relationships with foreign leaders—a kind of Sioux foreign policy—was now under way. As recently as 1881, Sitting Bull and his followers had been living in Canada, where they fled after the battle of the Little Big Horn to secure the protection of "the Grandmother Country" and of Queen Victoria from the vengeful Americans.[57] Red Cloud requested that Nate Salsbury bring him an English flag in 1887, and Black Elk recalled that the queen bowed to them that year. In a sense, Red Shirt and his successors in the show were trying to open diplomatic channels.[58]

For William Brown, the chance to meet officials face-to-face no doubt had a special resonance. The new century was not kind to the Lakota, and as their complaints in 1908 suggested, it was especially frustrating for those who were educated. They had completed compulsory education at government boarding schools. Their skills and training should have qualified them for clerkship or even managerial positions. But they usually met with the same racial prejudice which stymied the ambitions of black, immigrant, and other nonwhite men and women: white employers would not hire them except in the most menial jobs.

Meanwhile, government agents tried to compel self-sufficiency. In 1902, Brown was dropped from ration rolls after authorities decided he was capable of fending for himself. When he tried to acquire work on road-building crews, he was turned away, because government-funded labor was reserved for those "unable to exist without assistance." In the eyes of officials, Brown's herd of three or four dozen cattle and his ownership of an allotment disqualified him.[59]

Reductions in agency rations compelled families, including William Brown's, to combine scarce wages with the few traditional resources remaining, including wild foods. The challenges of gathering were greater than ever, because many of the best root and berry grounds were now beyond the bounds of the reservation. In October and November many Indians ventured off the reservation to unclaimed public lands where they hunted deer and small game and gathered chokecherries, other fruit, roots, and herbs to stock their larders for the winter. In the fall of 1903, Brown led his wife, children, and two other families into the Black Hills in northeast Wyoming. It was late summer, and the weather was good. The agent had given them a pass to be off the reservation. Berries were plentiful. The party traded moccasins to local ranchers for mutton. By all accounts, their tour of the backcountry was peaceful.

Like white men traveling in turn-of-the-century (or present-day) Wyoming, some of Brown's party had guns. But they hunted no large game. On their return, Brown's group joined up with Charlie Smith, also known as Runs-to-It, another Carlisle-educated Lakota who was on a similar expedition with his own extended family. The two groups joined for the trip back to the reservation. Together, they made up a train of fifteen wagons, full of Indian men, women, and children, making their way deliberately back to Pine Ridge.

On the evening of October 30, Sheriff Bill Miller, of Newcastle, Wyoming, arrived at the Indians' campsite with a posse. After Brown's wife fed them dinner, the posse attempted to arrest the Indians for hunting deer without licenses. Smith refused to submit to arrest, contesting the right of a sheriff from neighboring Weston County to make an arrest in Converse County, where the meeting took place. Brown struck a more diplomatic pose. At first, he offered to accompany the sheriff to Newcastle. But, as the other Indians were intent on leaving with Smith, he decided to remain with them. The lawmen left without making any arrests.

The Indians hastened to the reservation. They traveled all night, covering fifty miles in the next twelve hours. Sheriff Miller, meanwhile, deputized more locals. With his reinforced posse, he lay in wait for the Indians where the road crossed Lightning Creek. Consisting of mostly "cow-boys and bartenders," the posse was, in the words of the official who investigated what happened next, "no Sunday-school class."[60]

Afterward, surviving members of the posse claimed that they had ordered the Indian wagon train to halt, and the Indians had opened fire.

Surviving Lakota said they never saw the lawmen until they stood up from hiding and began shooting, without so much as announcing who they were. The Indians turned their wagons and tried to escape, but almost immediately twelve-year-old Peter White Elk was killed when a bullet took the top of his head off. Charlie Smith, who flew to the boy's aid, was soon mortally wounded. Loudly singing his death song, he kept up a vigorous return fire, accompanied by William Brown and several other men, who took up positions around him. The shooting lasted only a few minutes. The posse killed four Indians that day, including Charlie Smith and his wife. Two white men, including Sheriff Miller, also lay dead.

Outside their hometown of Newcastle, the sheriff and his posse were roundly condemned. The event was a regional scandal. But none of the surviving white men was ever tried or punished.

Surviving Indians, on the other hand, were tried for murder, and their acquittal came about because, as one local white man put it, "the worst of the party are dead."[61] A series of hearings, trials, and investigations of *Indian* behavior followed. The homicidal white hostility toward poor people on a berry-picking expedition grieved and rankled the Lakotas. "We think the sheriff and his posse are guilty of murder," explained Oglala council members George Sword and Jack Red Cloud in an open letter to the public, "but because they are white men we believe they will not be tried." If any Indian had done such a thing, on the other hand, "he would undoubtedly get the full extent of the law." Back at Pine Ridge, Lakotas preserved Charlie Smith's death song. Across the reservation, in painting, song, and story, they memorialized the savage white attack on a peaceful wagon train of Indian families.[62]

Brown's participation in the Wild West show was motivated by many of the same desires and responsibilities that took him on gathering expeditions into the Black Hills: the need for food and medicine, the chance to sell crafts, the freedom of travel, the requirements of his family. Five years later, authorities still regarded William Brown with suspicion, because of Sheriff Miller's attempt on his life. They dismissed his 1908 appearance in the Office of Indian Affairs as the agitations of one "chroni[c] fault-finder and trouble breeded," who was, after all, "in that unfortunate row in Wyoming between the state officers and a party of Pine Ridge Indians."[63] Combined with his show business career, this history gave Brown a dire reputation, indeed.

The many ironies of his predicament suggest the complexity of Wild West show performance for Indians in general at the turn of the twentieth century. William Brown was a man of skill and economic savvy, as the size of his cattle herd suggested. In 1889, not long after he returned from Carlisle, he was married and had a daughter, and the Indian agent described him as "a good young man." Yet he had almost no prospects for employment despite having followed the "the white man's road" to Carlisle and beyond.[64] Like many others, his growing frustration with the lack of opportunities for educated Indians made him more contentious in the years after his return from Carlisle. As Brown was all too aware, depictions of Indian savagery in the Wild West show informed the continuing prejudices of white Americans against Indians. In 1903, Wild West show audiences watched Indians leave their tipis and raid the settler's cabin, and it was possible to believe that they had not changed in the many years since the Plains Indian wars.

And yet Brown's opportunities for countering the brutality of bigots who attacked an Indian wagon train extended to performance of this "historical" reenactment in which Indians attacked a white wagon train. From that curious platform, he retained a limited mobility, earned a livelihood, and even challenged Indian office bureaucrats and their racist policies. By being in the Wild West show and conforming to an old stereotype of Indian savagery, he became in some small way a partisan of Lakota progress.

Brown and other Lakota saw how education, the ability to read and write and argue the law, and mobility beyond the reservation allowed them at least to demand justice (without necessarily getting it) in the most egregious insults like the killings at Lightning Creek. These tools helped in the fight against the downward revision of rations and against the continuing racism of Great Plains society. In this sense, Buffalo Bill's Wild West was not just an economic portal, or a vessel for cultural and racial mixing; it was an arena for pushing the limits of Indianness itself.

This may indeed be its greatest contribution, and Buffalo Bill's most enduring legacy. In the grand scheme of progress, Indians were to disappear into history, followed shortly after by the cowboys who succeeded them, who would in turn vanish before farmers and commerce. The Wild West show drew vast crowds on the strength of its principals as vanishing attractions.

But paradoxically, the performance wonders in the Wild West show made audiences and performers alike wonder if they would ever vanish, or even if they should. In 1890, cowboy Warren G. Vincent, from Wyoming, wrote to his father from the show camp in Rome. He had been unable to see his father before he left the United States, and he wanted the older man to know why his son, a hardworking cowboy who loved the range, had done something so odd as to join a traveling show. The first time he saw the show, explained Vincent, he was drawn to its realistic combat, the high drama of horsemen unhorsed, then rising to fight again. "It was the best thing I ever saw in my life to see horses, men, and Indians falling."

But it was the show's suggestion of a potential for change and transformation that captivated Vincent. In the Wild West show's potent mythology, the frontier turned men into horse-men, and lowly country folk like Cody himself into rich showmen. It was a heady vision for a young cowboy, who scraped, scrambled, hustled, and prayed to get enough money for horses, cattle, and some land of his own. And although he had no obvious love for Indians, he well understood how much they sought a new West through this show of the Old West. His reasons for joining the show were in this sense the same as theirs. "I cannot explain the diferant acts," he told his father, "but if you could see this show it would make you think that cowboys and indians amounted to something."[65]

CHAPTER FIFTEEN

Buffalo Bill's America

A FTER WOUNDED KNEE, Cody did not learn he would be allowed to hire Indians again until March of 1891. Salsbury sought out new contingents of racial primitives—other Others—who could replace Indians. By the time the show regrouped in Strasbourg, in the spring of 1891, Salsbury and Cody had incorporated twelve Cossacks and six Argentine gauchos, as well as two detachments of regular European cavalry—twenty Germans, and twenty English—to join twenty Mexican vaqueros, two dozen cowboys, six cowgirls, a hundred Sioux Indians, and a cowboy band of thirty-seven.[1]

The additions were the culmination of Salsbury's earlier ideas for a show of world horsemen, paralleling developments in European circuses, which were employing Cossacks, Arabs, and other exotic trick riders and horsemen in Europe in the 1890s.[2]

This new Wild West show now toured parts of Western Europe. In Germany, Kaiser Wilhelm II was a fan. Annie Oakley recalled "at least forty officers of the Prussian Guard standing all about with notebooks" to record the show's rapid deployment of railroad, horses, and ranks of men in arms. German military interest was echoed across the Atlantic, where the American army was studying circuses for similar reasons.[3]

After Germany came Belgium and the Netherlands, then a tour of the British provinces. Late in the fall, there was a reprise of *The Drama of Civilization* at the East End Exhibition Hall in Glasgow.[4]

Despite the size and military presence of the new Wild West show, Cody found himself ever more besieged behind the lines. Louisa insisted that the newly married Arta and her husband, Horton Boal, assume management of Scout's Rest Ranch. Cody resisted, for it would mean evicting his sister Julia and her husband, Al Goodman. "I want you to live there just as long as you are contented there," Cody wrote his brother-in-law. Louisa made life difficult for the Goodmans, and Cody lamented it. "I often feel sorry for her. She is a strange woman but don't mind her—remember she is my wife—and let it go at that. If she gets cranky just laugh at it, she can't help it."[5]

But after a bitter squabble the Goodmans abandoned the fight and moved back to Kansas. Louisa, whose relations with Julia had always been cool, now had an ally at Scout's Rest in her daughter Arta. Her victory was short-lived. Arta and Horton abandoned the job within three years. Al Goodman returned to manage the ranch again. But this time, mindful of Louisa's hostility, Julia stayed away.[6]

In the spring of 1892, the Wild West show returned to Earl's Court, London. There was another command performance at Windsor Castle for Queen Victoria, who was enamored of the Cossacks.[7] The tour was a success, but the novelty of the Wild West had faded considerably since 1887. To repeat the great fanfare of their London debut five years before, Cody and the company had to wait till the following spring, when the newly christened "Buffalo Bill's Wild West and Congress of Rough Riders of the World" opened outside the gates of the World's Columbian Exposition in Chicago.

Extensive newspaper coverage of Cody's European successes heightened popular interest in the show, which had not toured the United States since 1888. In Chicago the new format recharged the show's authenticity and its frontier myth. Cody's connection to Sitting Bull and the Ghost Dance troubles, and the continuing presence of Ghost Dancers like Kicking Bear and Short Bull, provided a red-hot connection to the Far West and the American frontier, which in turn facilitated a depiction of the new acts—Cossacks, gauchos, and European cavalrymen—as relics of ancient racial frontiers.

To a degree, the circus roots of the new racial segments suggested the continuing dance of the Wild West show with the big top. Railroad circuses proliferated in the 1890s, until over a hundred of the giant amusements toured the United States after 1900. As modern corporations that displayed exotic peoples for popular amusement, the Wild West show and its circus competitors constituted "a powerful cultural icon of a new, modern nation-state," in the words of historian Janet Davis.[8]

But the Congress of Rough Riders also hints at how the show's extended European sojourns had taught Cody and his publicists to speak of Eurasian and American frontiers in the same breath. When the Wild West cast visited the field of Waterloo in 1891, Cody told a journalist about the "striking resemblance" of this battlefield to the Little Big Horn. (Of course, the comparison allowed readers to make up their own minds about whether Custer was "the Napoleon or the Wellington of the conflict. He looked out for the arrival of Major Reno, who was destined either to be the Blucher or the Grouchy of the close of the fight.")[9]

Back in Chicago, the opening at the world's fair reflected the development of the show's marketing strategy. By this time, Buffalo Bill's Wild West practically orbited the world's fairs and exhibitions which proliferated in the United States and Europe, from the New Orleans Cotton Exposition of

1885 to the Exposition Universelle in Paris in 1889. As popular celebrations of progress which explored the meaning of national expansion and new-found prosperity, world's fairs were ideal places for traveling entertainments to pitch their tents, especially a show of the "progress of civilization" like the Wild West show.[10]

The center of the World's Columbian Exposition of 1893 was the White City, a group of huge, neoclassical buildings, constructed of wood and plaster on reclaimed marshland along Lake Michigan, symbolizing the glories of America and containing exhibit space for every state and many nations, too. The architectural heart of the fair was the Court of Honor, a grand plaza with a huge pond and a fountain in the middle. Soaring over the watery mirror of the pond was the Statue of the Republic, a sixty-five-foot-tall, gold-plated Lady Liberty. The statue, the gleaming white buildings, the arcing fountains could move visitors to tears with their "inexhaustible dream of beauty," in the words of poet Edgar Lee Masters. They could also be subjects of ridicule: the statue was widely known as "Big Mary."[11]

The Wild West show was not in the White City, but outside the fair proper, along the route to the entrance, on what became known as the Midway Plaisance. Fair organizers reserved this space for exhibits that were too commercial, or too similar to circus or carnival attractions, for inclusion in the edifying White City. But Cody's success in this location was a finger in the eye of fair officials, who came to regret their decision to exclude him. Because of the joint attractions of the White City, the Wild West show, and the Midway, Cody and Salsbury sold well over three million tickets in 1893, making profits of over a million dollars. It is said that spectators sometimes mistook the Wild West show for the World's Fair, and went home satisfied.[12]

In recent years, scholars have followed the crowds to Buffalo Bill's 1893 season, taking imagined walks up the Midway for lessons in the rise of mass culture and Gilded Age notions of race, conquest, and progress. The kaleidoscopic attractions of the World's Columbian Exposition in many ways reflected or amplified aspects of Wild West teachings. Exhibits and displays on the Midway were situated so that those featuring the most "primitive" peoples—South Sea islanders and mock Ethiopian villages—were farthest from the White City. As one approached the gates of the exhibition proper, one encountered ever whiter, more "advanced" peoples. The Wild West show was right outside the White City gates. The social evolution of the Midway and the world's fair echoed the social evolution of Cody's arena (while inside the fair, one hot July night, historian Frederick Jackson Turner expounded on the role of "free land" in stimulating social evolution along the American frontier). Tickets to the Wild West show announced it as the "Key to All," as if its story of relentless progress organized the fair's mysteries and unlocked the narrative which explained them all.[13]

But for modern readers who want to know how Gilded Age Americans thought about Buffalo Bill's Wild West, the 1893 season is at best a slippery key to a hall of mirrors. The world's fair, the Midway, and the Wild West show were infused with so much exhibitionism, outlandish display, performance, exotica, hoax, fraud, artful deception, and amusement as to turn an imaginary trip to Cody's show into a fun-house tour. The swirling cultural disjunctures of the world's fair left many observers disoriented even at the time. There were swimming races and boat races in the newly dredged lagoon in Lake Michigan, between Zulus and Turks. Visitors floated by in mock Venetian gondolas, poled by real gondoliers (imported from Venice) in ancient costume. Fair exhibits included a chocolate Venus de Milo, a giant horse and rider made of prunes, and, over in the Wisconsin Pavilion, a 22,000-pound cheese.[14] In August, there was a Midway ball—one paper called it the "Ball of the Midway Freaks"—at which a white-clad, fez-wearing George Francis Train (said to have been the inspiration for Phileas Fogg, hero of Jules Verne's *Around the World in Eighty Days*) led a procession of exotic women onto the dance floor at the fair's natatorium. In short skirts made of tiny American flags, they waltzed and quadrilled with eminent Chicago gentlemen in black dress suits until four-thirty in the morning.[15]

The image of Cody's show as a bastion of Americanism and originality in a world of effete culture was already traditional. In 1893, Chicago critics welcomed Buffalo Bill's Wild West as a natural, American counterpart to all the mock Greek and Roman statues, bone-white neoclassicism, and flat-out weirdness of the White City. "There," wrote Amy Leslie, pointing to the Wild West, "is the American Exposition." At Buffalo Bill's Wild West and Congress of Rough Riders of the World, visitors could "find Americans, real Americans . . . if not in the audience in the performance."[16]

The bizarre distractions of the world's fair context make it harder to deduce what visitors saw in the Wild West itself, and besides, the show's whopping 3.8 million admissions were perhaps less significant than they seem. Unknown numbers of those millions were return customers. The show sold 2 million tickets during the 1886–87 appearances at Erastina and Madison Square Garden, when the number of return visitors (who had no Midway Ball, gondolas, or giant cheese to attract them) was probably much lower.[17] In the end, most Americans who saw the show saw it not in Chicago but much closer to home, and the constant cross-references between White City and Wild West in 1893 tell us more about the meaning of the world's fair than they do about how most Americans understood the Wild West show in its most successful decade.

The Chicago season of 1893, where the Rough Rider spectacle unfolded amidst a global extravaganza, underlies the common historical argument that Cody's new format infused America's newfound overseas ambitions with frontier mythology and expressed public sentiment for empire. To be sure, Cody's show did resonate with U.S. foreign affairs, in complex ways, as we shall see in the next chapter. But public commentary about the show suggests the Rough Rider drama engaged the public on more familiar ground: the challenges of urban living, industrialization, and immigration, all of which touched and shaped daily life for the millions who attended the show in 1893 and after.

In this regard a more revealing season than that of 1893 is the following year's six-month stand in Brooklyn, which was in many ways the apogee of its long stands. The show's open-air ambience was in keeping with the way most spectators saw it, whether it was appearing in Elkhart, Indiana, or Stockton, California. Moreover, the venue was an independent, fully industrialized city, allowing us to see how the nostalgic spectacle of the vanishing (or vanished) frontier appealed to the increasingly urban populace. The completion of the Brooklyn Bridge in 1883 had initiated a furious expansion. By 1894, Brooklyn's overall population approached 900,000, and was growing by 25,000 people per year. It was already half the size of New York, which was the nation's largest city and the destination of most Brooklyn commuters who, six days a week, crossed the new bridge to work. Most of Brooklyn's buildings were homes, but it was also America's fourth-largest industrial metropolis. Half the sugar in the United States was refined there. The city's giant grain elevators had four times the capacity of New York City's, and its piers unloaded the cargo of four thousand ships a year.[18]

For our task, the city provides a better indication than a world's fair of how the show was received. In contrast to the phantasmagoria of the World's Fair, there were no competing attractions for the Wild West in 1894. Construction of Brooklyn's legendary amusement parks at Coney Island would not begin for another year.[19] The Wild West show's Brooklyn summer was the culmination of over a decade of show appearances, and it was also the last of the show's long stands in the United States. Beginning in 1895, a new partnership with James A. Bailey, of Barnum & Bailey, would put the show on the road for one- and two-night stands.[20]

Historians have often summarized the show's new format—Wild West and Congress of Rough Riders of the World—as merely an expanded version of the original entertainment. But it was more than that. Judging by the growth in clippings pasted into surviving scrapbooks, the appeal of the Congress of Rough Riders was deeper and broader than the original Wild West show. The crowds who came to see it were distinct from the crowds of the mid-1880s, and they saw it in different ways. Although nostalgia for the frontier was as great as ever, the show was now much more than a spectacle of a vanished world. In surprising ways, audiences drew lessons in the challenges of urban life, and their possible solutions, from this show of frontier drama.

One key to relevance for Cody's Rough Riders in this urban setting was its gathering of frontier rhetoric and Indian war into a discussion that incorporated many of the immigrants and new Americans who constituted the modern city. As Matthew Frye Jacobson has observed, in the closing years of the nineteenth century, America was preoccupied in part with the necessary import of labor to produce the profusion of goods and services that defined the industrial economy.[21] America's encounter with the world was occurring not only overseas but also within American borders. Cities teemed with strange, sometimes mysterious, and often frightening immigrants and alien neighborhoods. The urban middle classes—white, English-speaking, and educated—felt ever more besieged. The Congress of Rough Riders, combining Eurasian and American riders, whirling with color and martial ardor, and arrayed in a grand historic narrative, provided a story and a means of understanding America's place in a world that often seemed to be overrunning the United States.

In doing so, the Rough Rider additions layered new meanings onto Cody's entertainment which few could have foreseen at the debut of the Wild West show a decade earlier. Part of the Rough Riders' appeal was the way they allowed Americans to experiment with an older tradition of ethnic comparison. As we have seen, Americans compared their frontier horsemen, especially Indians and cowboys, to a host of legendary, exotic riding contingents, including Cossacks, Gypsies, and Turkmen. In the same breath, they compared them to riders in the circus, an amusement which after all was founded by Philip Astley, a cavalry officer from foreign shores, and which often featured exotic (or exotic-looking) trick riders. William Cody ventured a sort of comparison between Cossack riders and American cowboys in an interview with a Philadelphia journalist in 1888: "I don't know anything about cossack riding, because I never saw any of it, but I will guarantee that our men can do anything that cossacks can do and more, too."[22]

Allowing Americans to witness the real riders of legend, and to make their own decisions about which peoples produced the best horsemen, was no small thing. As we have seen, the lone horseman was a fading figure in the modern urban world, but his command of the animal reflected his control of nature and signified the strength or weakness of racial energies. As Frederic Remington observed about the show's Rough Riders, "The great interest which attaches to the whole show is that it enables the audience to take sides on the question of which people ride best and have the best saddle. The whole thing is put in such tangible shape as to be a regular challenge to debate to lookers on."[23]

At another level, Cossack, German, English, and, later, Arab and other Eurasian horsemen provided the show a historical rationale for its journeys in the Old World, at once explaining Cody's long absence in Europe (the American frontiersman had gone to Europe to see old frontiers) and fending off any suggestion that he or his cast of Nature's Noblemen had been corrupted by their long sojourn in the halls of Culture. In promoting the Rough Riders, Cody's publicists played up the imminent danger of war along Europe's convoluted racial frontiers, and held up the Wild West show as a force for peace. Buffalo Bill maintained amity between his company's "half-savage" cowboys and Mexicans and its warring Indian tribes (all those "Pawnees," "Arapahoes," "Crow," and "Cheyenne," who were actually Lakota Sioux). He advanced international arbitration as a means to keep the peace between Britain and the United States in 1887. Now, he presented the Wild West show as a calming influence in Europe's simmering border contests. In 1890–91, some of the cast had wintered over with the show's livestock "at the foot of the Vosges Mountains in disputed Alsace-Lorraine," wrote John Burke. Even in 1890, competing French and German claims to the region (which would contribute to the First World War in 1914) menaced "the peace not only of the two countries interested but of the civilized world. . . . What a field for the vaunted champions of humanity, the leaders of civilization! What a neighborhood wherein to sow the seeds of 'peace on earth and good-will to men.' What a crucible for the universal panacea, arbitration!"[24]

Back in the United States, the constant reference to armed European frontiers assisted Cody's imposture as world peacemaker, a pose which balanced the show's increasing militarization. The Congress of Rough Riders of the World offered a synthesis of world history, in which mounted race warriors clashed in grand Darwinian combat from the Old World to the New. Its Cossacks, gauchos, and European military riders appeared alongside its premier attraction, the New World cowboys and Indians, reinforcing the show's traditional emphasis on the East-to-West course of American history by suggesting a historical movement of an ancient, ongoing race war from Eurasia to North America, echoing the stories of Anglo-Saxonists and Aryanists alike.

At the most superficial level, the champions of this unending race war were cowboys, the show's version of distilled whiteness, despite all the non-white men who actually road as cowboys in the show.[25]

Whatever the racial composition of the participants, the horseback stunts of the new contingents were so striking that the word "centaur" sprang from publicity even more often than before. The galloping gaucho was "a near approach to the mythical centaur," like "the North American Indian, the Cowboy, the Vaquero, the Cossack, and the Prairie Scout." Gauchos wrapped their bolas—leather thongs with iron balls at each end—around posts from sixty feet away, and subdued fierce broncos by riding them in pairs. Cossacks stood on their heads in the saddle, hung off the sides of their horses until their heads brushed the ground, and stood on the backs of galloping horses, slicing the air with powerful sweeps of their swords.

Hailing from the Old World, the show's new racial segments were practically living ancestors of the American cowboys, but they were degraded by miscegenation that blurred the ancient race frontiers they supposedly guarded. Cossacks were widely known in the United States as semi-civilized (or semi-savage) warriors from the Russian Empire. In reality, they were often as racially ambiguous as American range cowhands. But in Cody's show Cossacks were "of the Caucasian line." They were "the flower of that vast horde of irregular cavalry" that the czar had "planted along the southern frontier of the Russian Empire" to contain Asiatic enemies. But programs also said they miscegenated with Muslim Circassians, until they were "as much Circassian as Cossack." Exactly how white they remained was left for the audience to decide. One London writer saw through the Cossack disguise, reporting (truthfully), that they were trick riders from the province of Georgia, and not actually "Cossacks" at all. Another, who had substantial experience with Russian Cossacks, surmised, "Their peculiar accent and unmistakeable gestures, as well as certain movements in their dance, created a strong suspicion in me that they are Caucasian Jews."[26]

Of the frontier originals on display, the only racially "pure" contingents were cowboys and Indians. The racially degenerate Cossacks, gauchos, and Mexicans suggested the constant threat of race decay that awaited racial enemies who forsook combat long enough to embrace.

The white American cowboy, a master of the frontier whose blood remained unmixed, would conquer the world, ushering in the new millennium of white civilization, itself signified in Buffalo Bill's "conquest" of Rome and the Old World, now recounted in show brochures and memoirs. Cowboy horses were as racially pristine as the cowboys themselves, and publicists went to great lengths developing a theory of equine evolution that paralleled the show's history of frontier whiteness. Each year, Cody replenished the show's stable through off-season purchases of horses that would look right in the ring. But in the Rough Riders' debut season, their horses were said to be a "race" descended from the horses of Cortés, on the backs of which the first conquistador appeared as a "four-legged warrior." Dissatisfied even with this pedigree, John Burke reached into dim mists of the primeval, to the ancestor of all horses, an animal that was polydactilic, that is, multitoed. "Some instances have been known in modern times, and ancient records give stories, of horses presenting more than one toe. Julius Caesar's horse," he wrote, "is said to have had this peculiarity." Caesar's horse inspired ancient Roman soothsayers to predict "that its owner would be lord of the world." Horses of the Wild West show (newly returned from the conquest of Rome) were mustangs of the Southwest, whose peculiarities similarly portended American power. "Most of the polydactyl horses found in the present day have been raised in the southwest of America, or from that ancestry bred."[27]

As racially distilled men, hardened in frontier combat, astride animals in whose veins pulsed the blood of ancient, world-conquering horses, cowboys were bulwarks against the modern age and all its miscegenated, manufactured, and artificial blandishments. They and their nation were bound for glory.

Buffalo Bill's entertainment was only one of many to valorize frontier race heroes as repositories of national virtue in the age of the mongrel city. Novelist Owen Wister contrasted cowboys, "Saxon boys of picked courage," with immigrants, those "hordes of encroaching alien vermin, that turn our cities to Babels and our citizenship to hybrid farce."[28] The Congress of Rough Riders reinforced white supremacy as the culmination of world history, and thereby affirmed the subordination of immigrant ghettoes, as well as the segregation of races, Jim Crow laws, and the tidal wave of lynchings which swept the nation in the 1890s.

ALL OF WHICH makes surprising how much the show now appealed to immigrants, too. As immigrants and their American-born children increased in numbers, they confronted Anglo-Saxonism and American racism not by demanding separation or cultural exclusiveness, but through rituals of assimilation. One of the most popular ways of asserting American identity was by going to public amusements, where immigrants were so numerous that they were now an economic force.[29] A glance at Brooklyn makes this point. In 1890, the U.S. census enumerated 806,343 Brooklyn residents. Over 260,000 of these—one-third of the populace—were foreign-born. One-third of these, the largest immigrant group, were Germans, who numbered 94,000. Another 90,000 were Irish.[30] Some saw the show, or heard about it, during its European tours. Even before the show debuted, many were drawn to America partly by fantasies of lawless frontiers (where there were no punitive elites to demand taxes or labor), abundant buffalo (free meat), and easily dispatched Indians (people even lower down the social ladder than European peasants). In the 1880s, the show's best seats cost fifty cents, too much for most immigrants. But the cheap seats, at twenty-five cents, were within reach, if barely.[31]

Ethnic affinity with Rough Rider contingents increased the show's appeal for Germans, and other immigrants, too. We may speculate that during the show's six-month stay in Brooklyn, German Rough Riders, the cuirassiers, relaxed in Brooklyn's many German beer gardens, and found a semblance of the homeland in the "Klein Deutschland" of the Williamsburgh neighborhood. In Milwaukee, home to a large German population, immigrants jammed the stands and cheered the cuirassiers in 1896. Perhaps there were Arabs, such as the Syrians who moved into lower New York in the 1880s, who forged American identities through the debut appearance of Arabs in the show in 1894. At least one of these performers saw his Wild West tenure as a ritual of Americanization. George Hamid was a Lebanese immigrant and acrobat who became owner of the Hamid Morton Circus, as well as of the Steel Pier in New Jersey and the New Jersey State Fair, on his way to becoming "the king of the carnival bookers" by the 1940s. He traced his success to his first job in American entertainment, in 1906, when he began his stint as a "Riffian Arabian Horseman" in the Congress of Rough Riders (he also told a tall tale about learning to read from Annie Oakley—who had left the show in 1901, and probably never had anything to do with George Hamid).[32]

The stories of Germans and of Hamid are compelling, but whatever the strength of ethnic bonds between immigrant audiences and their Wild West counterparts, some immigrants—especially the Irish and Germans—were drawn also to American performers as naturalizing symbols. Where Remington and Wister saw cowboys and soldiers as a last bastion of Anglo-America in an immigrant world, the cowboy and army contingents fairly bristled with Irish and German names like McCormack, Gallagher, Ryan, McPhee, Shanton, Schenck, Franz, and Kanstein.[33] Irish and non-Irish readers alike could imagine themselves as frontier Indian fighters, when "Trumpeter Connolly, of the Seventh Cavalry," recounted his sanguine experience at Wounded Knee for a newspaper reporter. These ethnic names reflected the presence of Irish and German immigrants in the actual West, and the maturation of their descendants as Americans.[34]

The challenges of becoming native to a new country seem to have been on the minds of Germans in another way. A few surviving reviews from the German American press suggest that the presence of German soldiers, who are barely mentioned, was less important to German immigrants than the show's tour of Germany, which was recounted in detail. In a sense, the show's tenure in Germany gave the Wild West a cachet with German immigrants through a naturalizing process that mirrored what German immigrants hoped to experience in the United States. One reviewer explained, with some enthusiasm, that the show had recently wintered over in Bennefeldt, in Alsace Lorraine. The following spring, "when Col. Cody returned to Bennefeldt, his cowboys had almost become German." At the same time, Cody's press agents reached out to Germans by speaking of German American cities as worthy counterparts to citadels of German culture in

Europe. "Milwaukee is the only city in the United States that can be compared to a German city," John Burke flattered the reporter from Milwaukee's *Deutsche Eindrucke*, "and rightly deserves to be called the Munich of America. In no other city do you find the age old German charm that dominates here."[35]

Indeed, Cody himself might have been as appealing to immigrants as to native-born whites. His ancestors were English and Breton French, but in 1899, his younger sister Helen Cody Wetmore wrote a new biography of him in which she traced the family lineage to ancient Irish kings. How she came upon this story is not clear, and perhaps most immigrants never heard about it.

But even if they were unaware of Cody's putative Irish roots, Cody's white Indian imposture was a powerful symbol among the Irish. London audiences equated Indian and Irish savageries to deride the Irish. But in the United States, the Irish were so thoroughly urbanized that competition with real Indians was not a factor in day-to-day life. Comparisons of Irishmen and Indians were less insulting to immigrants, and even had some romantic potential. Irish ward politicians dominated New York politics for decades after taking over Tammany Hall, the New York gentleman's society named for a seventeenth-century Delaware chieftain. Through the 1890s, every May 12, or "Tammany Day," the increasingly Irish membership of Tammany Hall—who called themselves "braves"—paraded the streets with painted faces, carrying bows, arrows, and tomahawks. Newspaper correspondents joked about meetings between Buffalo Bill's Indians and the "great chief" Dick Croker, the Irish-born boss of New York's Tammany machine.

Among Irish Americans, then, symbols of Indianness and white Indianness were easily adopted, and adapted, to signify (in no particular order) political power, American identity, ethnic unity, a "noble" past, and Irish oppression at the hands of British and Americans alike. When Buffalo Bill's Wild West and Congress of Rough Riders opened in Brooklyn, notables in the boxes included not only the mayor of the city, but A. W. Peters, "chairman of the General Committee of the Tammany Society, and Patrick O'Donahue, another magnate in the New York Democracy."[36]

In a sense, the potential for inclusiveness in the Rough Riders was greater than in the old Wild West show, as Cody and Salsbury constantly adopted new Rough Rider contingents to resonate with current events, especially wars. Cody recruited Japanese soldiers during the Russo-Japanese War of 1905, and Cuban insurgents and Filipinos as conflicts in their homelands began. But as savvy as the technique was for recharging the show's authenticity, it paradoxically created frictions and imposed new limits on the show's appeal for old fans. In 1901, the Congress of Rough Riders incorporated a regiment of Boer veterans from Britain's ongoing war against the Republic of the Transvaal, in southern Africa. In New York, sympathy with the Boers ran high, especially among Irish ward politicians and city officials. But that same year, Cody also signed a detachment of Canadian Mounties, who were allied to the British in the war against the Boers. Show managers hired these mutual enemies as a means of refreshing Cody's peacemaker image, extending his old claims to having brought warring tribes into amity in the interests of educating the public.

But just as hiring real Indians continued to place Cody's amusement in the midst of political battles between the army and the Indian Service, the practice of hiring imperial troops and colonial rebels entangled the show in bitter politics. In the afternoons before opening in a new town, the show cast often paraded through city streets to drum up public enthusiasm for the show. Irish officials in the police commissioner's office denied Cody a permit for the cast parade, on the grounds that a "strong sentiment against the presence of British soldiers in the Street[s] of New York" made his Canadian Mounties a threat to public order. Salsbury was livid. He and Cody managed to have the decision overturned, but the incident suggests how tapping into the drama of ongoing wars around the globe both provided a range of identities and attractions for an ethnically diverse audience (Boers as anti-British heroes to the Irish) but also threatened to trap the Wild West show in complex webs of ethnic and imperial contention.[37]

Moreover, for all the ways the Rough Rider spectacle spoke to immigrants, it probably appealed even more to the American-born children of immigrants, a new population that was gaining in political and cultural influence. By 1890, there were over 300,000 American-born children of immigrants in Brooklyn.[38] By the time Cody's show camp pitched its tents in south Brooklyn, they were asserting themselves in the workplace and in urban neighborhoods. As citizens and speakers of English with as much education as most native-born whites, many of them took up clerical positions in factories and warehouses or sales positions in stores. These were white-collar workers, increasingly anxious to separate themselves from common laborers (among whom numbered many of their parents). But exactly where these new Americans stood in the class hierarchy was not clear. The office work they performed had been extremely limited or even nonexistent prior to the massive explosion in industry and the wave of corporate consolidation that swept the country in the last decades of the century. According to Eric Hobsbawm, in the United States this new "petty bourgeoisie of office, shop and subaltern administration" actually outnumbered the working class by 1900.[39]

Whether they were middle class or working class, white collar or blue collar, the rising prominence and disposable income of the new Americans ensured that by the 1890s, they were taking an ever larger role in Brooklyn elections through the influence of the German-American Association, the German Democratic Union, the Swedish Association, and other civic groups.[40]

To this point, few of these people could feel they were part of American history. Native-born Brooklyn elites construed American history, and the history of their city, as a story of New England settlers and their descendants. In 1880, some of Brooklyn's self-identified New Englander upper crust founded the New England Society in the City of Brooklyn. Taking Plymouth Rock as their symbol, this frankly nativist organization vowed to "commemorate the landing of the pilgrims" and "encourage the study of New England history." Rather than public-spirited festivals which invited mass participation, they celebrated "Forefather's Day," which defined historical connection as family descent.[41]

The New England Society's story of America was narrow and exclusive, but it was merely an expression of the dominant narrative of American history in 1894. Anglo-Saxonism reigned, and American history remained mostly a tale of Britons moving west. Irish, Germans, Italians, Poles, Slavs, and others found virtually nothing in this narrative to confirm their sense of national identity in either the Old World or the New.

In contrast, the Congress of Rough Riders appealed to the burgeoning ranks of adult children of immigrants by gathering symbols of Old World nations into its New World frontier spectacle. Caught between classes and between nationalities, these spectators sought escape from ethnic labels and confusing class hierarchies by immersing themselves in a broad "American" public, especially in crowds at the era's popular amusements, from baseball to vaudeville.[42] Ethnic types, or stereotypes, paraded on the vaudeville stage. The clueless German in peaked cap and wooden shoes, the belligerent Irishman, and the carefree Italian were all standards of variety performance by the 1890s. But, as David Nasaw points out, the potential ire of the multiethnic audience prohibited the grossest ethnic slurs, and many ethnic German, Irish, and Italian spectators enjoyed these performances because in lampooning the rustics just off the boat, the comedy honored immigrants and first-generation Americans as seasoned residents. The ethnic parody was ultimately unifying, with the diverse ethnics united in bonhomie and camaraderie by the end of the sketch, so that divided urban immigrants could imagine themselves to be part not merely of an ethnic group, but also of a city, or a public.[43]

Cody's show of the 1890s encouraged similar sentiments. The Rough Rider display parodied none of its members, but the Wild West show gestured to vaudeville in ways that suggest its ethnic and "racial" teachings should be understood in a spirit of vaudeville unification. Jule Keen, the

Wild West show treasurer, was a vaudeville veteran who played a comic German on the stage, and he sometimes inserted the act into the Wild West show (where his rustic German brought laughs to the mining camp just before it was destroyed by cyclone in *The Drama of Civilization*).[44]

Thus, direct ethnic connections to Rough Riders were important, but specific cultural bonds were likely less significant than the wide range of possibilities for affinity and identity created by the show's ethnic and racial variety. In 1893, the show's opening number, a "Grand Review of Rough Riders of the World," consisted of a high-speed, choreographed equestrian display in which "Fully Equipped Regular Soldiers of the Armies of America, England, France, Germany, and Russia" galloped through the arena. By 1894, that opening was itemized more variously. The "Grand Review" now introduced "Indians, Cowboys, Mexicans, Cossacks, Gauchos, Arabs, Scouts, Guides, American Negroes, and detachments of the fully equipped Regular Soldiers of the Armies of America, England, France, Germany, and Russia."[45]

Even where they had no direct linguistic or other cultural tie to these Rough Rider contingents, the kaleidoscopic, multiracial Rough Rider spectacle provided an increasingly diverse public with a visual frontier myth extending beyond the Anglo-Saxon-versus-Dark-Savage narratives of earlier writers and artists, and far beyond the Plymouth Rock fetish of New Englanders. To be sure, the show walked a fine line, confirming for white Americans that their cowboys reigned supreme, but presenting European contingents as progressive, noble warriors and descendants of historic frontiersmen. Whether one had been born in Europe or in America, to see the Congress of Rough Riders was to imagine one's people as hardy, powerful, armed horsemen.

In 1894, the show still included many of its Wild West acts, such as the "Attack on the Deadwood Coach," "Cowboy Fun," shooting by Annie Oakley, the "Battle of the Little Big Horn," the "Attack on the Settler's Cabin." But it also incorporated a military musical drill, featuring the Seventh U.S. Cavalry (Custer's regiment, which also appeared in the "Battle of the Little Big Horn"), and the British, French, and German contingents. The "Riffian Arabian Horsemen" performed high-speed riding and juggling of rifles and swords, along with tumbling displays. The old horse races between cowboys, Mexicans, and Indians now featured "a Cowboy, a Cossack, a Mexican, an Arab, a Gaucho, and an Indian."

The effect was not only to Americanize the global frontier, justifying American empire, but also to internationalize the American frontier, inviting once-excluded peoples into the American myth. With the cowboy reigning supreme, the Indian the lowest on the ladder, and everybody else somewhere in between, the Congress of Rough Riders expressed the white supremacy and national chauvinism of most Americans.[46] Just as the cowboy conquered Indians, so he had conquered the world. And yet, by bringing more people under its awnings and into its mythological canvas, the show provided the diverse residents of the divided city of Brooklyn, and other cities where it played, a powerful sense of belonging, or at least the potential for belonging, to their new nation, its history, and its public.

In this sense, Cody's development of the Congress of Rough Riders paralleled the work of scholars and writers who were broadening American history to incorporate generations of immigrants traditionally excluded from Anglo-Saxonist narratives. Inoculating himself against the sting of Anglo-Americanism in his six-volume *Winning of the West*, Theodore Roosevelt wrote his forebears from the Netherlands into the ancient tribes of Anglo-Saxons whose descendants settled the United States.[47]

More significant for the development of American history as a discipline was the work of Frederick Jackson Turner, who delivered his classic essay, "The Significance of the Frontier in American History," at the same Chicago World's Columbian Exposition where the Congress of Rough Riders debuted in 1893. In an exploration of the frontier and its recent closure, Turner argued that "free land" was the defining condition of American history, and that along its westward-moving edge American society went through a continual process of social evolution, from hunter to industrialist. The essay caught the era's intellectual anguish over the rapid modernization of America, but it also shaped a generation of historical scholarship, making the history of the American West into a major academic field.[48]

In the decades since, critics have rightly taken Turner to task for his overemphasis on manly white actors and for his vague and contradictory use of terms. But none of that detracts from how adventurous he was in opening his historical frontier to people who were not Anglo-Saxon. His mentor, Herbert Baxter Adams, had extolled, in essays like "Saxon Tithingmen in America" and "The Germanic Origin of New England Towns," the wonders of Saxon institutions as they were transported to the United States. Adams was, in a sense, writing from the same script as the New England Society of the City of Brooklyn, making the Puritans into hardy Anglo-Saxons, both fulcrum and lever of American history.[49]

Turner turned the story of American history around, arguing that Norwegians, Swedes, Germans, English, and others had been transformed into Americans by the process of "winning a wilderness." Among its inspirations were Turner's vivid memories of his hometown of Portage, Wisconsin, which was surrounded by Norwegian, Scottish, Welsh, and German settlements, and whose townspeople, as he knew them in the 1870s and '80s, were a "real collection of types from all the world, Yankees from Maine & Vermont, New York Yankees, Dutchmen from the Mohawk, braw curlers from the Highlands, Southerners—all kinds."[50] Turner's "types from all the world" look substantially white to modern readers, but they were only tenuously white in the days their ships were docking at Ellis Island, and they had little or no claim to Anglo-Saxon traditions. True, Turner removed Indians from his story except as an obstacle to be overcome, and his frontier thesis had no place for Mexicans, nor for the mostly urban "new immigrants" from southern and eastern Europe, nor for the Chinese or other Asians. But even so, "The Significance of the Frontier," like Cody's Congress of Rough Riders, was a myth-busting punch at the Anglo-Saxonist orthodoxy, an attempt to broaden American history beyond its narrow racial tie to Britain, and to incorporate at least some American-born children of immigrants into national history and myth.

The revamping of historical myth in Cody's arena suggests how much the quest for larger audiences has shaped portrayals of the American past. The discipline of American history emerged in American universities only in the last few decades of the nineteenth century, at the same moment that the term "show business" was invented to describe the emergent industry of entertainment.[51] Turner and Cody were on opposite sides of the same historical coin.

On the facts, the Congress of Rough Riders was no more persuasive than Turner's thesis. The notion that all peoples were "warriors" embroiled in ceaseless race conflict was a social Darwinist conceit with little connection to the lives of real, mostly urban immigrants and their children. Cody's new story had no place for any ethnic group that had no horseback tradition. Except for the brief exceptions like the inclusion of the "Magyar Gypsy Cizkos" in 1897, which may have beckoned to eastern Europeans, the show was far more inviting to northern and western European immigrants, like the Irish and Germans, than it was to the "new immigrants" from southern and eastern Europe. (Cossacks, after all, were shock troops of the czar and persecuted many Russian Jews who emigrated to America.) But none of this detracted from its appeal as a somewhat more inclusive visual myth of global frontiersmen, so varied and diverse that one could see the show as a template or reflection of polyglot America, the enactment of a more democratic myth for a more diverse nation.

And yet, there were limits to the show's ability to influence popular historical narratives. Sitting a horse in the Rough Rider show proved no guarantee of a place in popular western myth. The absence of historical consciousness about one Rough Rider contingent remains striking. Show programs note the appearance of "American Negroes" in 1894 and 1895. In

1899, black veterans of the Cuba campaign reenacted their exploits in the "Battle of San Juan Hill." Show programs mention "American Negroes" through the early 1900s, suggesting that African Americans have a history in the show that awaits further research. In 1900, two white soldiers from the show's U.S. Artillery detachment were shot and wounded in a brawl with town police in Prairie du Chien, Wisconsin.[52] Dexter Fellows, a Wild West show press agent, recalled that the fight erupted when a white U.S. cavalry-man, a German cuiriassier, and "a burly black in charge of a detachment of Negroes from the Ninth Cavalry" were challenged by a drunken deputy constable "who could barely speak English." Fights between circus perform-ers and local police were hardly news, but since barely restrained violence and gunplay were more central to Wild West appeal than to other traveling amusements, this explosion of public violence threatened to frighten crowds away. Fellows worked overtime to soothe excited correspondents after the episode.[53]

The mix of immigrant, native white, and native black figures in this inci-dent (and the absence of Indians from it) suggests a complex mixing of mes-sages about possibilities for American identity within the show. The immigrant deputy constable hints at that rising generation of immigrant children who were increasingly in evidence among the audience.

But what did the presence of black U.S. soldiers among the Rough Rid-ers say to the audience about African Americans in American history? Show publicity barely mentions them. Newspaper correspondents spoke of them almost not at all, and scholars of the show seem to have overlooked them entirely. There are many photographs of cowboys, Indians, Cossacks, and a few of Mexicans in the show. Images of cowgirls are not rare. But a paltry handful record the presence of the buffalo soldiers. Did African Americans attend the show? If so, we may assume they were segregated, as they were at circuses and other traveling amusements. But why did so few notice their presence in the arena? Why have these Wild Westerners been largely for-gotten?

The most likely answer is that African Americans had no story of their own in the Wild West myth, which was essentially made of three strands. Indians were the dispossessed noble savages who once roamed the prairies. Mexicans were the descendants of the first people to encounter Indians, the Spanish who fell into decadent race mixing and failed to properly conquer them. Cowboys were the vanguard of the white race who succeeded Mexi-cans, and finally brought progress and civilization west.

There was no black component to that tripartite narrative, and Cody's modification of his message in the 1890s did not address that shortcoming. The Congress of Rough Riders gave every detachment a genealogy that originated among ancient horsemen—gauchos from Spanish conquistadors, Cossacks from "the Caucasian line," Arabs from the horsemen of the desert who appeared even in the Old Testament. But not black soldiers. They merely appeared in the show lineup, with little or no explanation.

In real life, blacks had fought Indians, trapped beaver, hunted buffalo, cowboyed cattle, built homesteads, and run almost every form of commercial outpost in the U.S. West. They had also joined Indian tribes, married Indians, and fought American expansion. They had, in other words, done everything that whites and Mexicans had done (there were black Mexicans, too) and sometimes more. Their absence from narratives of western history would become a standard failing in academic halls and popular culture alike. With the Old West as the crucible of white American virtues, and with western mythology an escape hatch from the contemporary political impasse of Reconstruction and the segregation of Jim Crow, blackness was not something easily incorporated into the western story.

All of which makes it even more interesting that Cody tried to put blacks into the show at all. He seldom spoke of black people. He scouted for black cavalry detachments in the West, and he knew their virtues. But his autobiography derided black soldiers as cowardly and childlike. Neither Cody nor Salsbury ever explained why they incorporated buffalo soldiers into the Wild West show in 1894 and after.

But if the Congress of Rough Riders represented a savvy attempt to keep pace with an ethnically expanding public, there are some pretty good clues that the proprietors foresaw black spectators as potentially a large part of that public, too. Like the Rough Rider appeal to immigrants and first-generation Americans, such a gesture would need to be shrouded in white supremacy. But if blacks could be included in a way that did not offend whites, there was a possibility of drawing even bigger crowds.

These may have been the considerations that motivated Cody and Salsbury to plan a new show of African American history in 1894, hoping it would appeal to black audiences and the public at large. *Black America* opened at Ambrose Park in 1895. The attraction was billed as a "Gigantic Exhibition of Negro Life and Character," showing "the Negro as he really is . . . placed in the amusement world as an educator with natural surroundings." With a display of black people moving from "savage, to slave, to soldier, to citizen," the show rationalized slavery as the necessary passage for savage people (featuring "reproductions of life in Africa," complete with "native African dances") but also valorized black fighters for the Union during the Civil War. Urged the poster, "Come and see the best drilled cavalry company in the United States."[54]

Cody himself was excited by the new enterprise, which he described in terms suggesting that it would combine minstrelsy and history. "Negro

Unidentified Wild West show buffalo soldier, c. 1900. Cody and Salsbury introduced African American cavalry veterans, "buffalo soldiers," to Buffalo Bill's Wild West and Congress of Rough Riders of the World in 1894. Because they didn't have a thread of their own in the mythic tapestry, the press seldom recognized them, and their contributions to western settlement and the Wild West show both have been largely forgotten. Courtesy Buffalo Bill Historical Center.

humor and melody will in this show reach the acme of perfection," he told a newspaper reporter. The spectacle would feature "phases of plantation life." Presumably, some of these were happy enough to allow audiences to enjoy the singing. Others would show "the auction block and the whipping post."[55]

Black America failed, and it is not hard to see why. The humor and condescension of minstrelsy allowed little pathos on the issue of slavery. The show's comic elements sat uneasily alongside representations of black misery (and white savagery) at the whipping post and auction block, and of black valor and heroism in the fight for the Union and emancipation. In the Wild West show, Indians were easily admired. White homeowners and job seekers in Brooklyn and elsewhere did not compete against Indians. Moreover, since Indians were vanishing, they would not need to compete against them in the future, either.

But black people coming into their own in *Black America* were another matter. African Americans competed with immigrants and whites for jobs in urban New York. There were just over 11,000 black people in Brooklyn, and

24,000 in Manhattan. Resisting black advancement was a primary criterion of whiteness. An amusement depicting black people making progress, showing their advance, hinted that they might have an equal right to some share of wealth in greater New York. Even if African Americans found some attraction in it, it was likely too expensive for most, and in any case its cast of six hundred was too expensive to support on a relatively small segment of the mass public. (There were only 70,000 African Americans in all of New York state.) For true believers in white racial identity, a show of black progress made no sense. Blacks had no history. Whiteness claims history for its own.

Black America lost money. Cody urged Salsbury to give it more time. "I am putting every dollar I make" with the Wild West show "into Black America," he wrote.[56] But within weeks, the show closed. A newspaper correspondent later reported that Nate Salsbury "spent enough money to free Ireland in organizing 'Black America,' with which he thought to charm the people of the North." Instead, "the venture . . . cost him $110,000 and convinced him that the white man has no use for his colored brother except for

Unidentified buffalo soldier and cowboys emerging from Wild West show tent, c. 1900. Courtesy Buffalo Bill Historical Center.

the twelve hours immediately preceding the closing of the polls on election day."[57]

FOR ALL ITS APPEAL to immigrants and first-generation Americans, Buffalo Bill's Wild West targeted the urban middle class who were, to say the least, extremely enthusiastic about the addition of the Congress of Rough Riders. The long stand of 1894 provided the public with opportunities for return visits, and more newspaper commentary than when the show was traveling. Cody and Salsbury chose the Ambrose Park showground for its accessibility to large audiences and the press. Seeking to replicate the success of the 1893 summer in Chicago, Salisbury cut a deal with the Thirty-ninth Street Ferry company to lease a twenty-four-acre parcel next to the ferry docks in south Brooklyn. For six months, spectators steamed from Manhattan or any of the other New York communities directly to Ambrose Park, or they crossed the Brooklyn Bridge and made their way south to the showground on the trolley line. The result was an outpouring of journalist commentary on Buffalo Bill, his Wild West show, and his colorful, heroic cast and their camp, which was dutifully preserved by show personalities who jammed their scrapbooks full to bursting with newspaper clippings. In earlier years, reviews focused on the arena performance and on the adventures of cast members, especially Cody, in the cities the show visited. But by this time, the Wild West camp itself had become a *place*, a space understood through stories told about it. In 1894, with six months of exposure to the camp, journalists delved deep into the show's symbols and meaning.[58]

We must be wary of reading too much into those stories. Many of them were planted by John Burke, Cody's longtime press agent and every journalist's best friend, who sat with press delegations telling stories and amusing anecdotes and the history of the show for hours on end, day after day. Sometimes Burke concocted new stories; other times he encouraged journalists to recycle other writers' material. Sometimes correspondents came up with original stories (which Burke then read and, if he liked, trumpeted as his own). His blustery, jovial narratives inspired miles of newspaper columns, which transmitted the show's messages to the hinterlands. These accounts were the dominant mode of understanding Buffalo Bill's Wild West even for people who only got to spend one afternoon with Cody and his massive entourage, and for those who never saw it at all.

Much press commentary focused, as it always had, on the savage and semisavage Wild Westerners and their encounters with the city. Indians, gauchos, "Riffian Moors," and cowboys ventured to schools, newspaper offices, and other modern venues, always in awe, in recurring expression of the civilizing virtues of the city, and the wide-eyed wonder of rustics at the fast pace of urban progress.[59]

But by 1894, more than in previous years, the show camp itself was the main attraction. Show tickets and other publicity encouraged spectators to arrive up to two hours early and tour the bizarrely placid settlement which was no mere agglomeration of people, but a living representation of progress, against which audiences could measure the historical, social, and political advancement and meaning of their own communities.[60] Here they could see buffalo, Indians, cowboys, and perhaps meet Annie Oakley or any of the other leading lights of the show.

In 1894, Buffalo Bill's Wild West had (or claimed to have) a population of 680 people, including performers and support staff. Journalists called it "a little tented city."[61] Some called it "the White City," as if the World's Columbian Exposition's moral messages about the supremacy of American civilization and its greater destiny were now conveyed by the Wild West show.[62]

Indeed, Buffalo Bill's frontier simulacrum seemed to anticipate the modern city at least as much it recalled the vanished frontier. In London, in 1892, Frederic Remington mused on the meaning of the Wild West camp for modern urbanites. "As you walk through the camp you see a Mexican, an Ogallala, and a 'gaucho' swapping lies and cigarettes while you reflect on the size of the earth."[63] The catalogue of disparate races, thrown together in one place, implied violence and primitivism—but it also echoed a standard device of writers seeking to convey the racial anarchy of the modern city. The reformer Jacob Riis published his photographic exposé of immigrant ghettoes, *How the Other Half Lives*, in 1890, the very year the U.S. Census Bureau declared the frontier closed. He spoke of the tenements—"where all influences make for evil"—as a kind of replacement frontier.[64] (Indeed, Riis himself was an immigrant from Denmark, and such a fan of James Fenimore Cooper that when he arrived in America in 1870, he strapped a giant navy revolver to the outside of his coat—à la Hickok—and sauntered up Broadway, expecting to find "buffaloes and red Indians charging up and down.")[65] In lower Manhattan, he wrote, one could find "an Italian, a German, a French, African, Spanish, Bohemian, Russian, Scandinavian, Jewish, and Chinese colony . . . The only thing you shall vainly ask for in the chief city of America is a distinctively American community."[66]

When Riis searched for a "distinctively American community," he meant a neighborhood of English-speaking, native-born Americans. Cody's "little, tented city" was not that. But, as Amy Leslie and other critics had observed at the World's Columbian Exposition, it represented, for all its racial primitivism, a kind of ideal American community: a spectacle of racial anarchy wrought into progressive order by American frontier genius.

"The Little Tented City." The Wild West camp became the premier attraction of the show, tantalizing visitors with a view of America, its frontier past, and its technological, professionally managed future. Note the electric generator in the foreground, not far from the buffalo pen, suggesting the fusion of nature and technology in Cody's entertainment. Buffalo Bill's Wild West 1898 Courier, author's collection.

The Wild West camp consisted of rows of tents along paved streets and cinder walkways between and among flower beds and small gardens, and to tour it was to contemplate both the frontier past and the urban future.[67] The disparities between Indian tipis and the modern amenities of Cody's tent—"the size of a small farm house," and divided into rooms, according to one reviewer—were themselves a lesson in the material advantages of civilization and progress. In Cody's tent, "we see a telephone, curtains, bric-a-brac, carpets, pictures, desks, lounges, easy chairs, an ornate buffet, refrigerator, and all the furnishings of a cozy home." By contrast, in a tipi standing nearby "we see a circular board floor (it should be dirt) within a ring of canvas. On a sheet of metal are the smouldering embers of a fire that makes a tepee at once a home and a chimney." To visit first one and then the other "is to be able to compare the quarters of a modern general with the refuge of a Celtic outlaw in the seventeenth century. By just so much have we advanced; by just so much has the Indian stood still."[68]

But there was more than frontier history on display. The construction work required by the show was touted as an achievement and spectacle in its own right, a display of the show's ability to transform the city.

In 1894, the camp's transformation of south Brooklyn also conveyed important messages about the show camp's civilizing mission. "The interior of the grounds was a surprise," wrote one visitor, "for on the large plot of waste land there has been laid out a beautiful summer park, with trees, shrubbery, flowers, and beautiful paths."[69] At various times, the Wild West appeared not only near but *in* gardens, as in its appearance at London's International Horticultural Exhibition in 1892. Although modern readers might find the pairing of broncos and buttercups an odd contrast, in the late nineteenth century they were bookends for the story of civilization, which began in savage nature and culminated in the garden. Proximity of show to gardens echoed its domestic culmination, the salvation of the settler's cabin and the replacement of the wilderness with the pastoral, and for this reason, landscape gardening was a major activity amid show tents and tipis.

The mix of urban and pastoral at Ambrose Park resembled what many urbanites desired for their own exploding industrial cities. New York's reformers often pointed to the city's lack of parks and greenery as a source of social degeneracy. According to Jacob Riis, the common street urchin, that "rough young savage" who so terrified civil society, became a sweet-natured child in the presence of flowers. "I have seen an armful of daisies keep the peace of a block better than the policeman and his club, seen instincts awaken under their gentle appeal, whose very existence the soil in which they grew made seem a mockery."[70] Park landscapes and urban gardens, like New York's Central Park, helped soothe the city's rough modernity. So journalists exulted that "Buffalo Bill's Wild West Company has made a garden spot where a few months ago was the dumping ground of South Brooklyn."[71] Where the Wild West show portrayed the settling of the hostile western frontier, the camp's balance of Artifice and Nature symbolically "settled" the darker edges of the city.

The bucolic landscaping was a powerful contrast to the supposedly simmering violence of Wild Westerners, which press agents constantly highlighted. Managing Buffalo Bill's Wild West was nothing like "the management of a light-opera company on the road," for "the people of the Wild West show . . . are all schooled in the theory that it is the proper thing to run a ten-inch knife into the anatomy of anyone who does not agree with 'their particular whim,' " wrote Frederic Remington.[72]

Given these popular fixations, we might expect that the show's large, multiracial cast would foment anxieties about social disorder. But for the most part, the show's violence did not concern social critics except for its alleged effects on small boys. The boy who sees the show "wakes up the family by uttering weird coyote yells in his sleep. He lassoes a bedpost and the family cat, and fires a toy pistol at imaginary objects while riding the back fence at full speed."[73] The Gilded Age middle class saw rough outdoor

play as contributing to the development of manly, entrepreneurial characteristics like social aggression and risk taking, and as protection against
"overcivilization." In any case, the violence of middle-class boys was constrained by the watchful authority of parents and family, so such influences
were largely construed as positive.[74]

Indeed, in the minds of many, the ways that Buffalo Bill's Wild West
incited such childhood play helped to naturalize urban neighborhoods
through an old American ritual: playing Indian. Many reporters echoed the
one who described numerous "Indian tribes" of seven-year-old boys along
Brooklyn's upper Seventh Avenue. Here, clotheslines had disappeared as
boys made them into lassoes for roping little girls, the trolley became "the
Deadwood Stage," and Tiger Claws, Bounding Elks, Scar-on-Necks, Black
Bears, Howling Antelopes, Bounding Eagles, "and other Lilliputian savages"
rampaged mischievously through the streets.[75] By inspiring such frolicsome
"Indianness," Buffalo Bill's Wild West show assisted in the transformation of
city children into adults who retained frontier virtues.[76]

Beyond its impact on boys, the show's seamless performance and generally law-abiding cast provided a spectacle of urban order to audiences concerned about the social chaos of their own city. The contradictions between
the primitivism on display and the modern science and technology which
made it safe and accessible for audiences created a tension that was dramatic
and fascinating in its own right, and a constant feature of press coverage. For
most of its life, the Wild West show, like circuses and other large traveling
amusements, moved about by rail. During the 1890s, Buffalo Bill's Wild
West required three trains to move cast, animals, support staff, and props. In
addition to its hundreds of Indians, cowboys, gauchos, Cossacks, vaqueros,
European cavalrymen, and other performers, the show employed ranks of
skilled and unskilled laborers. Everywhere the Wild West and Congress of
Rough Riders went, they brought along wheelwrights, harnessmakers,
blacksmiths, ticket sellers, watchmen, butchers, cooks, pastry cooks, wood
choppers, porters (to tend employees on the trains), drivers (to transport
cast members and other workers from train to showgrounds and back
again), canvasmen, and stake drivers, among others. All told, the Wild West
show required almost 23,000 yards of canvas and twenty miles of rope.[77]

Correspondents at home and abroad seemed never to tire of watching
crews load and unload the cars, which was a popular diversion and a means
of thinking about the show as a modern organization, as hundreds of men
raced back and forth unloading materials and animals, erecting tents, sta-
bling horses, and installing the traveling kitchen in a whir of precision that
evoked nothing so much as a factory.[78] Newspapers extolled the wonders
of Wild West show mobility during the 1880s, and after 1894, as the show
went on the road for one- and two-night stands in towns across the coun-

try, its spectacle of a community-on-the-move became a major attraction again.

Meanwhile, in Brooklyn and at other long stands, public attention to the camp's technology, social engineering, and scientific management underscored the modern relevance of a show featuring pre-modern conflict. A few examples make the point. Hoping to avert the harrowing losses from disease which plagued the camp during the European tours, Cody and Salsbury ordered vaccinations of the show cast in Brooklyn, making the Wild West camp a model of modern public health for some observers. "Cleanliness and perfect order are two cast-iron rules in Buffalo Bill's Wild West camp," wrote a reporter on the visit by doctors from the Brooklyn Health Department to administer the "cosmopolitan vaccinating bee."

Columnists lionized Buffalo Bill Cody and Nate Salsbury for this scientific attention to public and employee welfare. But just as significant, the response of the show's cast to the vaccinations provided lessons for the larger city. Although the Indians were "so full-blooded that the least scratch will cause a profuse flow," they submitted willingly. Cossacks, gauchos, cowboys, and "half a dozen Arabs, and as many beautiful Arabian women, negro cooks, and helpers" also went calmly to the needle. The bravado, or at least acquiescence, of the Rough Rider camp stood in sharp contrast to the response of Brooklyn's immigrant neighborhoods in recent vaccination campaigns. During various public health alerts, authorities in greater New York attempted to vaccinate whole neighborhoods. Immigrants distrusted both vaccination and city authorities, and their response was not always cooperative. In Williamsburgh, Brooklyn's large German neighborhood, immigrants hurled "hot water and 'cuss' words" at doctors who tried to vaccinate them.

The cooperation of the Wild West camp suggested that the most primitive and potentially violent of peoples could be brought to the benefits of public health through the governance of white men like Cody and Salsbury.[79] Most of all, the complacent acceptance of the needle among the show's Germans, Indians, and other "savage" or "half-civilized" peoples implied messages for the white-collar enterpreneurs and managers who were the show's primary audience. Brooklyn's troublesome immigrants might yet be brought into the new medical and scientific order which the city's English-speaking professional bureaucracy were applying to the cities. For the reading public, the multiracial and potentially violent city teeming at the show gates could also be tamed by the proper application of authority, managerial skill, and frontier spirit.

The popular interest in public health was accompanied by professional interest in the show's infrastructure. In the historical narrative of the show's arena, old technologies like the Deadwood Stage rumbled their last before

Buffalo soldiers, vaqueros, Indians, and the rest of the cast in 1896. The dining tent was the center of the show community and a frequent subject of commentary, as a place where the heterogeneous community of the Wild West show was welded into social order. Courtesy Buffalo Bill Historical Center.

crowds anticipating new technologies. But that story came to the public through application of those new technologies, and fascination with them made Cody's camp seem both an exhibit of the primitive and a cutting-edge outfit, particularly in its use of the revolutionary technology of electricity.

Edison, Westinghouse, and others began to light up the cities during the early years of Cody's show. Urban dwellers had once feared nighttime in the city as frightening, dangerous, and potentially lewd. Then, in 1886, the Statue of Liberty lit up with electric light (as did the stage lighting in Cody's *Drama of Civilization*, at Madison Square Garden), and in 1893 the electrical lighting and electrical amusement rides of Chicago's White City startled and impressed millions of visitors, and thousands of columnists.[80]

Electrification of the city engendered a new order of night life and public entertainments. Not only did lights make the city safer, but they created a new landscape of visual wonder, brilliant electric advertisements and white illumination which simultaneously brought new attractions into being and seemingly cleansed the city of grit and dirt which so alarmed reformers during daylight hours. In important ways, urbanites knew the working hours were over, and the time for entertainment and leisure had arrived, when the city's new electric lamps blinked on, creating the nighttime, illuminated world of "the Great White Way."[81]

In Brooklyn, electric lighting had begun to alter the city's nightscape by the early 1880s, and shortly before the Wild West show came to Ambrose Park, in the early 1890s, electric trolleys began to run on Brooklyn's busy streets.[82] The trolley was the vehicle of the modern era (the name "trolley" came from the device that conveyed the electric current from wires overhead to the car), and it soon became a ubiquitous feature of the urban landscape in Brooklyn as elsewhere. New York City had 776 miles of trolley track by 1890, and even St. Louis had 169. By 1902, Americans took 4.8 billion rides on the trolley.[83]

The transformation was not easy. Because trolleys were both faster and quieter than stage coaches, wagons, and the old horse cars, pedestrians often misjudged them and paid with their lives. In 1893–94, seventeen people were killed by Brooklyn's Atlantic Avenue Rapid Transit Railroad alone, and public anxieties about the new technology ran high. Ultimately, it gave rise to the nickname "trolley dodgers" for Brooklynites (later inscribed into the city's public amusements when it was applied to their baseball team, the Brooklyn Dodgers). Nonetheless, electrification continued, and Brooklynites could take the Third and Fifth Avenue trolley lines to the Wild West show's front gates.[84]

In fact, a not insubstantial crowd of observers made this trip to see the show's electrical works. The Wild West show, exhibition of vanishing skills and organic technique, was literally, and paradoxically, a beacon for electrical engineers. More than two hundred members of the New York Electrical Society accepted invitations to tour the camp's electrical works and watch the show under its new floodlights, installed and maintained by the Edison Electrical Illuminating Company. Popular newspapers and journals of electrical associations alike recounted these visits and explored the electrical circuitry of the show—"The grounds are lighted by seventy seven 2,000-c.p. [candle power] incandescent arcs, while the buildings and tents require over 800 16-c.p. incandescent lamps."[85] As newspaper writers were fond of reporting, the "Texas," the electrical generating plant at Ambrose Park, was "said to be the largest for the purpose in the world." Given the size of the area to be illuminated (the arena comprised two acres), the challenge of providing illumination had been especially great, and the generators reportedly cost $30,000.[86]

The skillful attentions to the show's electrical apparatus were the culmination of efforts made by Cody and Salsbury at least since the 1880s. Circuses attempted the use of electrical generators as early as 1879, but they soon abandoned them because they were too difficult to transport. In his earliest letters to Doc Carver, Cody had broached the subject of electrical lighting for the show as a way of making more money, and their performance at Coney Island in 1883 included "Grand Pyrotechnic and Electric Illuminations."[87] The show incorporated electric lights at long stands in Europe, in London and in Glasgow, but the 1894 season marked the beginning of the show's almost consistent electrification. By 1896, Cody and Salsbury acquired electric generators to travel with the show, and the Wild West "Electrical Department" employed eleven people. In cast parades through the streets, the mobile, gleaming, steam-powered electrical generating plants, called the "Buffalo Bill" and the "Nate Salsbury," rolled along between contingents of frontiersmen. "The enormous double electric dynamos used to illuminate the Wild West performances are well worth inspecting, as a scientific and mechanical triumph," trumpeted the 1898 show program. "They are the largest portable ones ever made."[88] Even on the road, managers arranged tours of the electrical equipment, followed by performances, for visiting groups of electrical engineers and utility company officers.[89]

Nighttime illumination meant the possibility of two shows a day, one in

Barbershop, Buffalo Bill's Wild West, c. 1890. A widely diverse, orderly company town, the Wild West camp came to represent America itself. Courtesy Buffalo Bill Historical Center.

the afternoon and one in the evening, doubling gate receipts without increasing salary outlays. But it had a larger cultural meaning, too. When the show acquired the sanction of leading "scientists" (as electrical engineers were called at the time), it enhanced its mythic relevance for its audiences as both spectacle of the past and harbinger of the future, a complete reenactment of civilization's rise from nature to technology, the maturation of her people from buffalo hunters to electrical engineers.

The electrification of the Wild West show thus implied a symbolic parallel between show and nation, each of which originated on the frontier and advanced to modernity. The machinery that made the show possible was itself a popular wonder, calling forth a collective emotional and unifying response from observers that approached what the historian David Nye and others call the "technological sublime."[90]

In some ways, the Wild West show's stature was similar to that of the railroad circus. During the 1890s, railroad circuses both imitated and symbolized modern business. They were corporate, technological, hierarchical organizations in which white male owners and operators managed the diverse and the freakish and waged near-constant advertising "wars" in which they plastered entire regions with their posters and handbills, consolidating smaller entertainments beneath ever larger tents and undercutting one another in relentless pursuit of profits. William Cody's show business career, with its beginnings in a small independent theater company and its culmination in a huge, corporate entertainment, paralleled those of the Ringling brothers, P. T. Barnum, James A. Bailey, W. T. McCaddon, and other circus impresarios who bought, sold, and consolidated traveling road shows in efforts to monopolize the industry. The circus and Wild West show business paralleled still larger developments in the American economy, where smaller concerns and entrepreneurs—shopkeepers and artisans—were shunted aside by the behemoth corporations of Vanderbilt, Morgan, and McCormick in the process that historian Alan Trachtenberg calls "the incorporation of America."[91]

Like these monopoly capitalists, Cody was, in the eyes of newspaper correspondents, a captain of industry, a modern business colossus. Nate Salsbury, the managing partner, was responsible for the tedious but essential tasks of routing the show through North America and Europe and tending to its external business matters, such as provisioning and transport. But correspondents preferred Buffalo Bill's pose as owner, director, and manager of the Wild West show, "the guiding hand of the entire enterprise," whose "orders were obeyed" with alacrity. His creative vision and control wrought "realism, naturalism, and precision of detail" from a "heterogenous mass of human beings, representing nearly all the nations on the earth."[92] As the 1890s progressed, Cody's publicists made ever more of his supposed managerial acumen as a "Great Manager," "the organizer of the great exhibition which bears his name."[93]

Other circus owners received similar approbation, and thereby benefited from the era's fascination with corporate directors, but Cody had a special place. He was a frontiersman, a rustic who through his own efforts rose from common men and frontier nature to command what was at once a nostalgic show of the past and a large, modern business with a sharp technological edge. Electricity at the Wild West show underscored this managerial prowess. Unlike the few surviving scouts and old-time westerners, he was not just an aging frontiersman. He was the boss of his own industrial concern. His employees were at least as alien, recalcitrant, and potentially violent as the slew of immigrants who worked for the industrial barons of the age. And in some ways he was better at managing his crew than they were. In a nation roiled by strikes—the Pullman strike occurred that very summer—Wild West show employees continued to perform. Strikers in Chicago faced off against the U.S. Army. At a camp party to celebrate the elevation of Cody and Salsbury to thirty-second-degree masons in Brooklyn, John Burke joked about a strike at the Wild West show. Salsbury, with the Pullman Strikers in mind, took the opportunity to warn the show's workers against any similar "disloyalty" to the nation's armed forces. "He makes the best citizen," he told the assembled cast, "who is most loyal to his Government. So long as you claim a Government as yours, obey its laws implicitly; be loyal to that Government."[94]

The fact that Cody had no formal training as a manager, that his attributes were natural genius that came to him through experience with the show, made him all the more alluring for the new generation of white-collar managers who had little in the way of formal business training themselves, whose multiracial subordinates must have seemed at least as unruly, and potentially as violent and dangerous, as Cody's, and whose jobs were so cerebral and new that many wondered if managing was real work at all. In implying and embodying the modern corporation, Buffalo Bill's Wild West lent the corporation—this most modern and undemocratic of business organizations—both a profoundly American, frontier past and a glorious future as the culmination of progress.[95]

The appeal of this gesture to the public helps to explain Cody's consistent self-promotion as a businessman. For all his buckskin image, during his Wild West show days Cody usually dressed in fine suits, with pointed-toe boots and a cowboy hat, a western version of the modern man of commerce. Throughout the 1890s, he persistently billed himself not just as a frontiersman, but also as an entrepreneur—which puzzled his handlers. "Cody always deluded himself with the thought that he was a good business man," recalled press agent Dexter Fellows. "He was as vain as a popinjay over those things about which he had no right to be vain, and modest to the point of absolute silence regarding the things which, by common consent, entitled him to be proud."[96]

Such critics failed to grasp the centrality of the businessman imposture to Cody's middle-class appeal. Far more than during his early careers as scout or stage star, as an impresario he was a modern and modernizing symbol for engineers, managers, and corporate owners, and for all the middle managers and low managers who aspired to join their ranks, including those white-collar new Americans, too. Managers and owners could look to Cody and see managing and owning and directing not as artificial, effeminate, and alien but as natural, manly, and American.

So, too, he naturalized the modern technology that managers relied upon, from the train that delivered the show and the electricity that lit it to that refrigerator and telephone in his tent. A visit to the Wild West show reassured the visitor that all those alienating, often scary, modern urban developments had a frontier origin. Conversely, Cody inscribed a technological modernism into his frontier myth, as if to suggest that the technology which seemingly spelled the end of the frontier paradoxically might also keep its spirit alive to instruct, inform, and invigorate urban audiences. The show drama portrayed a progressive history in which Americans discovered, traveled across, and finally settled the frontier. The electrical illumination of that drama, and of the camp pathways as well, under the guiding hand of America's preeminent frontier hero, suggested an accompanying natural progression from an open and rustic frontier to an electrically wired world, a profound historical connection between the quintessentially *rural* history presented in the arena and the undeniably *urban* context of the arena and the Wild West camp.

FAMILY REMAINED CENTRAL to the image of the heterogeneous Wild West camp as a progressive settlement. At least as much as it was a model city, the show represented a domestic haven, "a big family" or "Col. Cody's Wild West family," consisting of "cousins from many lands."[97] In fact, as the number of "races" in the show increased, they relied ever more on symbols of family to soothe popular anxieties about violence, the shared living and working spaces of divergent races, and to advertise the show's suitability for family viewing. As husbands and fathers, both Cody and Salsbury were profoundly paternal figures. Cody himself was occasionally joined in the camp by at least part of his family. In 1887, Arta had accompanied him to London, kept house for him, and made the rounds of the social circuit with him, too. In 1893, his young daughter Irma and Mrs. Cody had visited him in

Chicago. And in the summer of 1894, both Louisa and Irma were with him in Brooklyn. Although the family stayed at the St. George Hotel, they could often be seen in his tent on the grounds.[98]

But Cody's family relations were troubled at the best of times, and neither he nor Salsbury could realistically remove their wives and children from their respective homes to be with the show for extended periods. They needed other familial images to anchor the show's domestication. As in earlier seasons, they found these among the show's women, including Indian wives and families, and Annie Oakley.[99]

Further, by 1894, another domesticating female presence had emerged in the camp: Margaret Whittaker, known as "Mrs. Whittaker," or most tellingly as "Mamma" or "Ma," the "official matron of the camp." Her tent was prominently situated, with a white signboard over the doorway proclaiming "Mrs. Whittaker, Matron."[100] Although she was not nearly as famous as Oakley, journalists spent considerable time and print introducing her to the public. Brooklyn newspaper readers learned that the entire camp staff, "whether it is the old scout Nelson or a nursing papoose," depended on Ma Whittaker for care and comfort in the event of injury or illness. She sewed curtains for the Irish lancers and bandaged the fingers of Arabs who tried to do their own sewing. Her tent was a haven of domesticity, carpeted and hung with the fashionable portieres and curtains, full of "herbs and bottles of ointment, thread and needles, Bibles, buttons, goodies for the children, and, when she is there, an abundance of good advice."[101]

In a show where "real" frontier experience was the defining characteristic of the cast, Ma Whittaker gained her authenticity not from being a genuine frontierswoman but from her real role as nurturer and caregiver to the camp's many-hued cast, for whom it was said she "comes as near to filling the position of mother" as "any one but their own mothers."[102] Her encounters with journalists were likely scripted; the show publicity department steered columnists to her and likely helped develop her self-presentation. In any case, Margaret Whittaker claimed to be a former physician and druggist from Philadelphia. Her late husband, "Pop" Whittaker, had been manager to P. T. Barnum and an old hand in show business. She had joined the Wild West show in 1883. Like all of the cast, she told stories about her adventures with the show, and hers were particularly important to reinforcing her image as a maternal figure. Journalists frequently portrayed her as ministering to the needs of the show's young cast, particularly the "girl" sharpshooter Annie Oakley and her "boy" counterpart Johnny Baker (both of whom were, by 1894, married and headed for middle age).[103] When Cody's daughter Irma visited the camp, newspapers depicted "Buffalo Bill's Sweet 'Prairie Flower' Daughter" in front of the tent of "Mrs. Whittaker, Matron."[104]

But, the press also maintained that Whittaker's strongest maternal bonds were with the camp's Indians. Repeatedly, journalists described her ministering to their medical needs, providing their costumes (in a sense, dressing them), and in return, "the Indians will do anything in their power to serve her."[105]

In fact, the adoration of Mrs. Whittaker among the show Indians is perhaps the most consistent observation about her. One of Whittaker's favorite stories encouraged the idea. According to this yarn, in 1885 she had been aboard the steamboat which was rammed by an iron steamer and sunk on the Mississippi River while it was conveying the show to New Orleans. Nearly drowned, "the only white woman on board" was rescued by the show's Indians, who carried her on their backs to shore.[106] Her rescue by Indians, the very people who acted out attacks on white families and white women in the show arena, suggested that camp life, and particularly the domesticating influence of Ma Whittaker, made Indians loyal to and loving of their white "parents," herself and Cody and the white nation as a whole.[107]

By turning white women into "mothers" of Indians in the show camp, publicists obscured the mutual sexual attraction of white women spectators and show Indian men, who often jostled against one another in the arena in ways that would not have been tolerated outside it. White women volunteers from the audience who raced around the arena in the Deadwood stage often thrilled at their pursuit by Indians. In 1893, an Indian rider thrust his arm through the window of the speeding coach and ripped a silver braid from the jacket of Amy Leslie, the prominent woman columnist who was riding inside. According to Leslie, a man in the coach shrieked, and another woman clutched the reporter to her "as if my will had been made in another's favor," but both of them were overwrought, for the Indians "were in fun."[108] When two hundred members of the Women's Professional League of New York visited the Brooklyn showgrounds at Burke's invitation in 1894, the members who rode in the Deadwood coach were playfully captivated. One correspondent reported that "Kate Bostwick was frightened almost out of her wits by an Indian who wore a shirt of yellow paint" and shook a feather-covered spear in her face. " 'Oh,' she screamed, 'you brute; take that nasty thing away!' "[109]

The popularity of Buffalo Bill's Wild West with professional women was a partial reflection of Cody's support for women reformers. During the Ambrose Park season, he declared himself a supporter of woman suffrage, and of women in the workplace and women's associations. Such issues often riled middle-class audiences, but when a woman reporter from the *New York Recorder* asked if he supported woman suffrage, he professed not to have thought much about it, then ventured, "Why not?" The majority of women were "quite as capable as the majority of men" when it came to voting, and for that matter, able to work in traditionally male domains like business offices, "so long as she does her work well and is womanly."

"Hurrah! Colonel, you're on our side!"

"Of course, I am."

"Then you don't condemn women's clubs?"

"Far from it. I'd a good deal rather feel that my daughter was at a club with intellectual ladies than out with some men. I think it's a capital idea."[110]

Balancing these endorsements with more conservative views such as enthusiasm for corsets ("They brace a woman up and give her form") and a denunciation of bloomers ("A woman ought to be shot who wears . . . those bloomer things. I think skirts are modest and pretty. I prefer something left to the imagination"), Cody's views on women complemented his persona as patron of professional women performers like Annie Oakley, and it also kept his show on the horizon of middle-class women whose patronage ensured ticket sales to their children and husbands.

In deploying Ma Whittaker as the "mother" of show Indians, Cody and his managers obscured the real Indian family bonds behind the scenes and the important place of Indian women in supporting the show cast on the road. They also reassured visitors that there really was nothing to fear in the arena or in the camp. The reference to Indians as "children" was already an old standby at this time. Because Indians were under the ostensibly benevolent protection of the "Great Father" in Washington, their presence easily suggested a sort of national family structure in which white people were parental figures, who governed peoples of color, the nation's unruly but well-intended children. Infantilizing show Indians was simultaneously a means of discounting their sensual appeal and suggesting their potential for assimilation.

In this connection, Cody's paternalism toward Indians provided new ways for show visitors to think about reform projects. One of the most prominent examples of this was in the ways that show proscriptions against alcohol were seen as potential public policy. The sorry role of alcohol in U.S.-Indian relations had long ago given rise to a myth of Indian inability to imbibe without becoming immediately savage. Cody's show had forbidden alcohol among the Indian contingent (and drunkenness among all contingents) from its very beginning. After some alleged violations in 1894, Salsbury appealed to Brooklyn authorities to enforce laws proscribing the sale of alcohol to Indians. Journalists went on at length about the travails of "Lo, the Dry Indian," but more serious minds used it to advance prohibition for all peoples.[111] "I have my doubts," wrote George R. Scott, "if a drunken Indian is more dangerous than a drunken Englishman, Irishman, German, or American; and I wish that the law was so constructed that it could be applied to the protection of every man, woman, and child in the city, no matter what their color or nationality." Scott maintained that "what is good law for the Indians ought to be good law for the Whites," and that "the Red Men are the only ones treated with proper respect and up-to-date civilization."

Drunkenness and racial violence had a long conjoined history, and reformers saw alcohol as a corrosive that would dissolve the boundary between arena and city, allowing race combat to migrate to the public, where it would begin the race war that always simmered beneath the surface of Brooklyn. Reporter George Scott claimed to have seen three fights "in the neighborhood of the Wild West Show, among Whites and Blacks, that for brutality beat anything that the Indians have as yet exhibited. And drink," he concluded "was at the bottom of all three of the fights."[112] The logic was inescapable: There are no race fights in the Wild West camp, because there is no alcohol there. Just as banning drink has produced peace in the Wild West show, so can it stem the race war that threatens to erupt in the cities of the Gilded Age.

In various ways, themes of management, technology, urbanism, wage labor, and family domesticity all wove through the Wild West show to make it into an analogy for modern America. Rarely were these themes presented separately. Rather, they tended to reinforce one another in critical ways, perhaps most visibly in the public fascination with the provisioning of the show. Journalists who visited the camp kitchen described the enormous appetites of the show cast and how show management satisfied them in part through capital outlay and technological wizardry. The traveling cook wagon, with its five ovens and zinc-lined refrigerator, produced "800 to 1,000 individual steaks every morning," which were "of the highest grade that we can get in the market." As well as steaks, chef W. G. Hatch and his staff of three cooks and thirty-eight waiters produced 140 pounds of mutton, pork, or sausage, 60 pounds of "breaded tenderloins," and 700 to 800 orders of pancakes, along with many gallons of coffee—and that was just for breakfast.

The emphasis on abundant meals—everyone was entitled to all they could eat—reflected the show's management ethos. "Feed a man well and you keep him good natured and willing to work—that's the plan upon which this commissary is run." Unionism was the bugbear of corporate owners, and those managers who could retain managerial control *and* a happy workforce were highly prized. In this respect, Cody's commissary seemed a model for labor relations. At mealtime, hundreds of "happy participants" dined together under one tent, which had "the atmosphere of a perpetual and mammoth pure-food show combined with a protracted Labor Day picnic"—absent the union. The results were noticeable. "They all work hard and this kind of life seems to be good for the appetite." Or, to employ another metaphor which both discounted a class reading of the show's cast and reemphasized Cody's managerial and paternal prowess, "if 'table manners' are a true indication of good breeding, Colonel Cody certainly knows how to bring up a family—and a large one, too!"[113]

HISTORIANS HAVE WRITTEN of the Wild West show as a nostalgic spectacle of a vanished frontier and an icon of Gilded Age imperialism. It was these things. But it was much more. There in Ambrose Park, on the southern tip of Brooklyn, in a lot next to the Thirty-ninth Street ferry dock, sprouted not just a show about race wars past and present. The almost seamless "moving pictures" of the inexorable passage from savagery to civilization suggested that all of these harsh conflicts between white and red, present and past, modern and primitive, could be, and would be, reconciled in the unfurling of the national pageant, as naturally as the flag fluttering from the top of the arena's Rocky Mountains. The show's tenure in Brooklyn, as in other American cities, suggested that America, a new nation sprung from wild nature, would dominate the coming urban and technological age. Her frightening and exploding polyglot cities, clanking, grinding, and spewing the goods and detritus of industry, would be tamed and settled by the same domineering spirit that conquered the frontier, and the same white families who accomplished that tremendous feat would achieve it in America's dark urban spaces.

To be sure, the show's refrain of white mastery can only seem backward today. But, in the end, what is so startling about the Wild West show is how forward-looking a show it was, and how much Buffalo Bill himself represented a harbinger of future events as much as the embodiment of historical development. Many of the more visionary camp observers would see the camp's organization projected into real politics shortly after 1900. As recent historians of the Progressive era have observed, reformers cloaked American problems and potential solutions in the rhetoric of family, much as the Wild West show had done in the early 1890s.[114] From public health to prohibition, electrification to professional social management, a great deal of modern America seemed to swirl out of this spectacle of American history. There was something more than the past circulating around the timeless race wars between cowboys, Indians, Cossacks, and Mexicans. Between the garden plots and the electrical generating plants that lit the grounds, in the spaces between Cody's modern tent with its telephone and office furniture and the smoky Indian tipis, something else flitted about. There, in sparkling and alluring fragments, at the corner of our vision, the future glimmered.

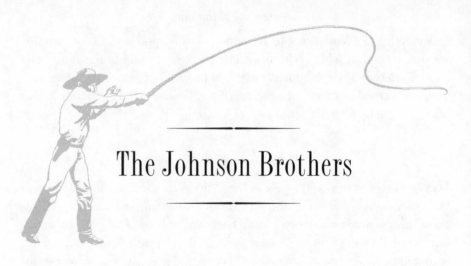

The Johnson Brothers

B ETWEEN 1852 AND 1854, 10,000 Swedes emigrated to the United States. They came for land. Among them were John Johnson and his wife, Karen Svenson Johnson. John worked years in Chicago as a hack driver before he could take up a farm. His son, Rolf, was born in 1856. In 1868, George was born. By this time, their family farm was in the Swedish settlement surrounding Altona, in northwest Illinois. But the droughts of 1874 nearly wiped them out. When two agents from the Union Pacific arrived, touting the benefits of relocating to thinly populated Phelps County, Nebraska (population 110), the Johnsons listened carefully. The family moved to Nebraska with dozens of other Swedes, most of whom took up residence along "the Divide," a high plateau of rich farmland running diagonally across Phelps County. Ultimately, there were seven children, five sons and two daughters. The Johnsons spoke Swedish at home, and like many of their fellow Swedes in Nebraska, they were strong Lutherans. Of an evening, they took turns reciting Bible verses in Swedish around the kitchen table. In some ways, it was an insular life. The Swedes of Phelps marshaled their own political party, taking over the county government from native-born English-speakers in a thunderous victory in 1879.

Nebraska's Swedes were legendary farmers. Through drought, prairie fires, and plagues of locusts, they persevered. Someday, their devotion to farming would become a symbol of Americanness itself. But at the time commentators saw Swedes as weaker immigrant stock. They were unadventurous, cautious, and without the risk-taking attributes of genuine, hard-driving white folks who became cowboys. "Even in the cattle country the respectible Swedes settle chiefly to farming, and are seldom horsemen," sighed novelist and nativist Owen Wister.[1]

Perhaps partly for this reason, each of the Johnson boys grew dissatisfied with farming. By 1890, almost one in five Nebraskans was an immigrant, and if the American-born children of immigrants were added to the mix, the immigrants made up almost half the state's population.[2] Like many of these, the Johnsons each hungered for a ritual to identify himself as American. Each "went west" in symbolic, spectacular ways. In 1877 and again in 1879, young Rolf, then in his early twenties, left home to travel through Nebraska, New Mexico, and Colorado. He tried his hand at trapping beaver. His camp was overrun by stampeding cattle. He hunted buffalo—and just about everything else. Rolf Johnson was an avid reader, and in diaries and letters, he noted his meetings with famous westerners in terms that suggest his own mythic quest for an encounter with nature that would make him into the quintessential American. Thus he recorded his encounters with Bill Doyle, the "noted plainsman," Pony Rogers, a "famous frontiersman," and Ash-Hollow Jack, "the famous scout, hunter, guide, and champion pistol shot of the plains."[3]

But his most famous acquaintances needed no introduction. In passing Red Willow Creek, he described it as "a place where 'Buffalo Bill' and 'Texas Jack' distinguished themselves in battle with Indians about eight years ago." Later, he stopped in North Platte to see Buffalo Bill's house, met Captain Jack Crawford in the Black Hills and on the streets in Denver, and saw Texas Jack at a Denver theater in *The Trapper's Daughter.*

Having soaked up a good deal of the West, both real and imagined, Rolf had his picture taken in a Denver studio. He dressed "in true western fashion": his long golden hair down to his shoulders, a wide-brimmed hat with the brim peeled back in the front, a kerchief around his neck and a sporty jacket with a handkerchief in the pocket. The glowing innocence of that photograph shines through today, as does its uncanny resemblance to the many photos of scout dramatists like Texas Jack, Captain Jack, and the inevitable Buffalo Bill. Rolf settled down to marriage in 1882 and traveled no more.[4]

Young George, twelve years his junior, was fascinated with horses. He was raised on a farm north of Holdredge; his mother recalled that by the age of seven he would be found standing too close to the unbroken ponies his father had bought, no matter how many times she warned him to stay away.

He grew up in the saddle, and like Rolf, he went "West." By this time, the country where Rolf had hunted buffalo was ranch country, whose cowboys had moved from outcasts to heroes. In 1890, George Johnson was cowboying on a spread belonging to Francis Warren, Wyoming's governor. When an uncle advised him that Buffalo Bill Cody was at his North Platte ranch, hiring new cowboys for a revamped Wild West show, Johnson took a trip down to North Platte and tried out. Cody was impressed with Johnson's riding, and with his personable demeanor. He invited the young man to stay at his house in North Platte, which he did for four days. By the summer of 1893, Johnson was part of the dazzling Rough Rider crew that entranced the million-plus visitors to the showgrounds at the World's Columbian Exposition in Chicago. The show may have belonged to Buffalo Bill, but Johnson used it to stage his own frontier imposture. George Johnson, son of immigrants, traveled to the city of immigrants, where as show cowboy and Rough Rider, he was America's native son and natural man.

The American Rough Rider received letters from his mother in Swedish. Indeed, though he was often far from home, the strength of his family bonds was almost otherworldly. When a sister-in-law back in Nebraska unwrapped the newsprint from an item she had bought at the store, she was surprised to find herself holding a page from a New York newspaper. Smoothing it out to read it, her eye was attracted to a brief item relating how a cowboy in Buffalo Bill's show, one George Johnson, had hurt his finger during a roping act but kept right on with the performance. The show was dangerous work, but Johnson was lucky. In eight years as a leading Rough Rider, he sustained only that one injury.

In 1896, Buffalo Bill's Wild West show came to North Platte, Nebraska. The town's population was 3,500. The stands had a capacity of 10,000. The countryside emptied out on the day of the show, as the people of the hinterlands poured into North Platte, eager for Nebraska's own Buffalo Bill, and for the local boys in his entourage. The Johnson family arrived in force, elated at seeing George, who "came riding out and did all his performing right in front of us." To his family, and to George, too, the imposture of Rough Riding was no fraud. That George could take part in Cody's show was proof of the larger opportunity of America. After all, had not the Johnsons, the poor immigrants, become established, all through their own hard work? Was not Buffalo Bill's show, with its optimistic story of American greatness, based on truths like this?

During one of the show's long stands at Madison Square Garden, George met a young woman named Mary A. Moore. She gave him a small Bible. He promised to read it every night. When he returned home to Nebraska, he told his mother about Mary Moore, and soon the two women were regular correspondents. George Johnson and Moore had plans.

The young man, now thirty years old, resigned from the show soon after. Cody and Salsbury were reluctant to lose him. Always an operator, Salsbury had the idea to hire Johnson as a cowboy on his gigantic Square Butte ranch in Montana. Perhaps he could be persuaded to return to the show later.

Johnson went back to Nebraska, and invited his little brother, Robert, to join him in "a trip to the West." So Robert Johnson followed his brother, the local hero who rode with Buffalo Bill, to Montana. They worked on different ranches, George on the Square Butte, Robert with a neighboring outfit. In the ranch bunkhouse, George Johnson was a friendly, mentoring presence. Long after, cowboys remembered him as the smiling, genial top hand who every evening read a chapter of the small Bible he kept by his bed. He didn't care if everybody saw him.

In the fall of 1899, George and Robert rode in the seasonal roundup together. On the morning of November 12, George rode past his brother, smiled, and remarked, "Red brought me a letter from Mother, but I have not had time to read it." Moments later, he roped a steer. Just as the rope tightened, his horse stepped into a gopher hole. Robert recalled, "At the speed he was going it jerked the horse high in the air and he hit the ground with his feet in the air and George tight in the saddle."

They carried George Johnson to the camp on a piece of canvas. Within hours, he was dead.

If a man can be judged by how warmly and richly remembered he is, George Johnson must have been a good man indeed. Nate Salsbury and the other owners of the Square Butte ranch paid for a copper and brass casket, and a gigantic gravestone made of Vermont granite. Cowboys sent along the pair of antelope legs that hung over the bunkhouse door where Johnson

Buffalo Bill's Wild West cowboys, Chicago, 1893. Note the racial mixture of the cowboy cast. George Johnson, son of Swedish immigrants, is in the back row, fourth from the left (under the X and the arrow drawn by a proud relative). Note the Mexican cowboys, too. Courtesy Phelps County Historical Society/Nebraska Prairie Museum, Holdredge, Nebraska.

slept. Mary Moore sent a fan of palm leaves, which would hang on the wall in the Johnson family home for decades. Back in Nebraska, his was the first funeral held in the new church. The congregation sang "Hah Skall Oppna Parleporten"—He Will Open the Pearly Gates. Over a hundred teams of horses escorted his body from the church to Moses Hill Cemetery, where they laid his body in the ground.

***

SIXTY YEARS AFTER George died, an elderly Robert Johnson recalled his journey west with his brother in a letter to his extended family. It was not as fresh or as wide-eyed as Rolf's western diaries, but it marked the story of his own western migration, his rite of passage into the heart of America. Robert Johnson explained again how George had died, how he, Robert, had taken his body fifty miles, to Fort Benton, Montana, and then traveled with it on the train to Holdredge. He recalled how devastated he was to meet his mother and sisters on the platform, their faces wet with tears.

> *Now across the great divide*
> *and at the home ranch door*
> *I know he will meet and warmly greet*
> *the Boys who have gone before.*

But as if to capture some glimmer of the optimism that was in George, the still-grieving brother retrieved some of the Rough Rider's old stationery, which he had saved all those years. The relatives who received his Christmas letter in the age of *Sputnik* and Elvis Presley were surprised to see the bold, elegant letterhead—"Buffalo Bill's Wild West"—with the preprinted date line, "Chicago, 1893," and over it, in Robert's emphatic block numbers, "1959." Robert Johnson remembered his brother, the son of Swedish immigrants and farmers, through the Wild West show, its cowboys, and its glorious Chicago season. He inscribed across its page his own memory of his brother and their trip to the mythic outpost of the vestigial West. Over four decades after the show had closed for good, family memories of George Johnson yet traveled through the medium of Buffalo Bill's Wild West show, which would be a part of the Johnson family saga as long as there was a Johnson family.

Robert Johnson's resort to Wild West show stationery was a nostalgic gesture of hope in a hard season. Remembering George still made him tearful. "My heart is heavy to night," he wrote to his relatives. Maybe he was just depressed, an old man, his farm parched in what seemed to be an emerging drought. Only a quarter inch of moisture had fallen so far that year. His letter complete, he went to bed. When he awoke, he found the day unexpectedly bright. He scribbled one last note in the margin beneath that flamboyant letterhead: "I have two inches water in my rain gauge. Wonderful."[5] Then he mailed the letter.

PART THREE

CHAPTER SIXTEEN

Empire of the Home

T OURING ACROSS the United States, the Rough Rider spectacle expressed gathering public sentiment for an American empire during this decade of unprecedented overseas expansion that saw U.S. military engagements from Cuba to the Philippines. The American thrust for empire began in domestic strife, a decade of which shaped William Cody's show and his offstage life in profound ways. In 1893, as the world's fair wowed the public, the nation was gradually overwhelmed by the worst economic depression in memory. Before it was over, some 8,000 businesses and 360 banks failed. Crop prices were already down, and farmers anguished as they fell even further. Wages plummeted. Jobs disappeared. In the winter of 1893–94, one in five American workers, perhaps as many as three million people (100,000 in Chicago alone) had no work. In the spring of 1894, Ohioan Jacob Coxey led the nation's first march on Washington, a group of about 100 jobless men demanding unemployment relief. "Coxey's Army" inspired many followers. In the Far West, large gangs of unemployed men organized themselves into "industrial armies" which intimidated or overpowered guards and rode the rails for free.[1]

Manufacturers and others blamed the crisis on "overproduction" of goods, on the absence of markets for the abundant sewing machines, bicycles, soap, clothing, and other products pouring from American factories and fields (and so abundantly on display at the Chicago world's fair). As Americans staggered through the downturn, the clamor for overseas markets began to grow. The frontier was closed. New horizons beckoned, if only America could be strong enough to stave off European empires that threatened to close her out of lucrative commerce in Asia, Africa, and the Pacific. This expansionist surge peaked in 1898, when the United States won a lightning victory in the Spanish-American War, seizing the remnants of the Spanish empire in Cuba and Puerto Rico in the Caribbean, the Philippines in the Pacific, and annexing Guam, Samoa, and Hawaii in the process.

The spectacle of the Congress of Rough Riders of the World kept America's increasingly imperial stance in the minds of Americans throughout the decade and after. At no point was the flow between entertainment and expansionist politics more obvious than in 1898. Many assume Cody's Rough Riders took their name from Roosevelt's. The reverse is true. Theodore Roosevelt's First Volunteers adopted the Rough Rider name from Cody's show and took it to the top of San Juan Hill and into American history. Some of Cody's troupers joined Roosevelt's troops, and after the war, in 1899, a genuine detachment of Roosevelt's Rough Riders appeared in the Congress of Rough Riders to reenact their famous charge into the Spanish guns.[2]

Although Cody and Roosevelt became passing friends, in the beginning the gauzy overlap between real history and public entertainment masked tensions between them. The aspiring politician staked a claim not only to the charge up San Juan Hill, which practically guaranteed his election to the governorship of New York, but also to the history of the campaign, which he published in The Rough Riders, a lively, self-aggrandizing account that appeared in 1899. In the book, Roosevelt distanced himself from Cody's show, insisting the Rough Rider name was bestowed by the public "for some reason or other." He claimed to have resisted it, "but to no purpose," and when commanding generals began to refer to them by that name "we adopted the term ourselves."[3]

These disingenuous denials reflect the antitheatrical leanings of the era's most theatrical politician (dubbed Theater Roosevelt by some wags). Whether or not he saw Buffalo Bill's Wild West and Congress of Rough Riders of the World, he imbibed freely of its manly regionalism. His regiment's ideological premise was that a volunteer force of western cowboys, sheriffs, outlaws, Indians, and even some "half-breeds," combined with a smattering of easterners who were "western" in spirit (including Roosevelt himself), could, through their hardy warrior virtues and their natural self-reliance, perform at least as well as a regular army regiment. Roosevelt's Rough Riders were as heavy on "real western men" as Cody's Wild West show, and included their share of frontier army veterans, too (including the aging Chris Madsen, who had been at Warbonnet Creek when Cody scalped Yellow Hair).[4]

In reenacting the history of a regiment that drew its name from the show itself, the "Battle of San Juan Hill" to a degree reprised Cody's fusion of historical action and representation in the scalping of Yellow Hair over two decades before. But the gesture to Roosevelt, in deflecting attention onto the blustering politician and away from Buffalo Bill, came with a risk. Roosevelt's refusal to acknowledge the show as an inspiration was itself a challenge to Cody's authenticity. Cody's press agents fired back at TR's demurrals. If the "manner in which Colonel Roosevelt" introduced the

Rough Rider name to the Spanish had "made it historically immortal," Buffalo Bill's Wild West had been the first to introduce it to the world. Through Cody's labors, not Roosevelt's, audiences had "grown to understand, fully appreciate, and unboundedly admire" the Rough Rider title.[5]

The spat with Roosevelt may have originated in Cody's earlier ambivalence about the man, which TR could have read as hostility. When and where they first met is not clear, but the two men circled each other warily after Roosevelt returned from Dakota Territory and ascended to New York political command in the mid-1880s. In 1887, Chauncey Depew told a raucous, pro-Roosevelt meeting of the New York Republican Club, "Buffalo Bill said to me in the utmost confidence, 'Theodore Roosevelt is the only New York dude that has got the making of a man in him.' "[6] If Cody actually said such a thing, the compliment was decidedly double-edged. TR might possess the "making of a man," but if so, it was only "the making." He was still a New York dude.

There was a greater danger, too, in making the celebration of Roosevelt's victory so central to the show. The charge up San Juan Hill marked the high-water mark of America's overseas enthusiasm. Roosevelt's victory was popular. But unlike George Custer, the only other military leader to become the subject of a Buffalo Bill's Wild West scene, Roosevelt returned from his battles a living hero. He was also a political figure; he became governor of New York in 1898, then vice president to William McKinley in 1900, then president of the United States after McKinley's assassination in 1901.

The Congress of Rough Riders threatened to become a political advertisement for the Rough Rider Republican. Cody had reasons for preferring Roosevelt to his Democratic rivals, as we shall see. Even so, many in his audience did not. Populists and many Democrats also favored American expansion, but they reviled the professional army and saw McKinley's acquisition of the Philippines as a disaster. In 1900, Democrat William Jennings Bryan vigorously denounced McKinley's imperialism for placing white American men in the steamy, sensual tropics, on a mudslide to miscegenation and the decline of the white race. He lost the election, but he still won over 45 percent of the popular vote.[7] Bryan had his supporters even then, and he remained a powerhouse in the Democratic Party for many years. For Cody, there was a very real possibility that the mythologizing of Roosevelt would disenchant a large part of the mass audience he needed to fill the bleachers.

The political limitations of the San Juan Hill reenactment help to explain why Cody shelved it about the time McKinley was killed and Roosevelt began swinging his big stick around the White House. In 1901, Cody replaced Roosevelt's legendary charge with the "Battle of Tsien-Tsin," a scene from China's Boxer Rebellion in which "the allied armies of the world" rescued the besieged foreign legations and raised the triumphant "Banners of Civilization" in the place of the "Royal Standard of Paganism."[8]

Various historians have argued that Cody's freewheeling incorporation of recent events into his frontier narrative allowed him to tap popular sentiment for expansion. As the new century began, his show included "Strange People from Our New Possessions," a group of "families" representing "the strange and interesting aboriginals"—Hawaiians, Filipinos, and Guamanians—from places "now grouped by the fate of war, the hand of progress and the conquering march of civilization under Old Glory's protecting folds." The new members of the show "keep step with the marvelous, potential and gigantic expansion of the nation."[9] Some of these, notably the Hawaiian cowboys, or "paniolos," even qualified as Rough Riders. By placing America's expansion into its spectacle, Cody's show implied a direct connection between frontier history and American victory on the world stage. By mingling cowboys and Indians with his professional military detachments, he incorporated symbols of amateur soldiers and volunteers, the kinds of military organization still preferred by a large segment of the populace.[10]

But close inspection of the show and its critics suggests these vague, ambiguous gestures to overseas expansion were politically risky for Cody. Westward expansion itself had been divisive, haunted by fears of racial decay, political disunion, and moral (and financial) bankruptcy. Ultimately, the economic success and overwhelming military victories of western annexation pushed those arguments into the mists of history, where they were easily forgotten. The Wild West show, for all its authentic western Indians, scouts, and cowboys, was by and large devoted to showing the settlement of the Far West that had already happened. The likelihood of any further military action against Indians was small when the show began in 1883, and grew smaller with each passing year. The Ghost Dance troubles erupted so suddenly, then receded into history so quickly, that Cody merely had to strike his usual ambivalent pose, urge the Nebraska state militia to remain calm, and wait for it to end. A popular sense that conquest of the Indians was inevitable limited other questions about the morality of that conquest.

The new expansion (as Roosevelt and his Republicans preferred to call it) or empire (as Bryan and the Democrats termed it) was either a glorious ascendance of democracy and capitalism or a turn from America's virtuous, agrarian past into the halls of imperial corruption. This argument was rarely settled by a sense of inevitability. There were American victories in overseas battles. But underlying factors that facilitated American success in the Far West were largely absent outside North America. The demographic collapse of indigenous peoples through disease had been pivotal to American success in Kansas, Nebraska, and the entire continent, as it was in Hawaii. But disease would play much less of a role in subjugating indigenous people in the Philippines, where enduring connections to Asia ensured long exposure to Eurasian maladies and higher rates of native survival from epidemics.

Also, Europeans contested American power in Asia, Africa, and the Pacific in ways they seldom had in the post-1848 Far West. Isolationists and anti-imperialists could point over and over again to the cost of overseas deployments and the absence of compelling victories to urge the end to overseas adventures. American expansionists would have to articulate and rearticulate a convincing case for sacrificing lives and resources, because in no other way would American power be secured on distant shores.[11]

In some ways, the fear of racial degeneration and undemocratic consequences that flowed from governing imperial subjects loomed largest of all. A primary threat of continuing the Philippines occupation, according to many of its opponents, was the dissolution of soldiers' marriages as they were tempted by polygamous native life. White women sickened in the Philippines, said press accounts. American men, debilitated by the malarial tropics and the temptations of naked primitives, were losing their manhood. Prone to violent excess, horrendous atrocities, and indolence, they were becoming more like the "weak and impotent" British who struggled against the Boers in South Africa, and more like the corrupted Spanish whom they had so recently expelled.[12]

Buffalo Bill's Wild West had always presented Indian conquest in an ambivalent light. Perhaps having Indians play Spanish soldiers in the San Juan Hill reenactment, and Chinese soldiers in the "Battle of Tsien-Tsin" in 1901, was meant to complicate these historical moments, by infusing recent U.S. enemies with the honor of the noble savage.

If so, the gesture failed. The politics of empire were harder to contain in the past. The Indians masquerading as foreigners potentially rewrote the conquest of the American West as an imperial maneuver, upending the older narrative of inevitable, sometimes unfortunate progress across a unified continent. To many, the Chinese who fought the combined American, European, and Japanese forces in the Boxer Rebellion were not rebels, but brave patriots defending their native land. For these observers, Cody's celebration of the Chinese defeat was more propaganda than entertainment. Mark Twain, the great fan of the original Wild West show, had become a major critic of America's overseas engagements. The author who urged Cody to take the Wild West show to Europe in 1884 was less pleased when the show imported foreign entanglements into its drama. Twain was in the audience at Madison Square Garden on opening night, 1901. But he stormed out of the stands in protest at the jingoistic "Battle of Tsien-Tsin."[13]

Cody himself had doubts about American expansion, especially the

Spanish-American War. At the onset of hostilities, he offered to take up arms for the United States and to lend four hundred horses to the army for the campaign. Nelson Miles, now general of the army, appointed Cody to his staff. In April 1898, as the Wild West show began touring, Cody announced he would stay with the show until he was called to service. The 1898 show included a detachment of Cuban insurgents, the fighters for freedom on whose behalf the United States was ostensibly entering the conflict.

But Cody delayed joining. In his private correspondence, he suggested his doubts. "George, America is in for it," he wrote an old friend, "and although my heart is not in this war—I must stand by America."[14]

Miles sent for Cody in late July. By that time, the Cuban campaign was already over, and the general was shipping out for what was to be a series of small, soon-forgotten battles in Puerto Rico. Still Cody could not bring himself to join. His business partners, especially Salsbury, were livid at the prospect of financial losses that would follow on the star's departure and the early closing of the show. "Your bluff about going to Cuba was a brutal violation of your contract," Salsbury later huffed, "and a moral wrong to the people who would have been thrown out of employment if you had been compelled to make your bluff *good*."[15] Cody wrote to his old friend Moses Kerngood, the man to whom he had sent Yellow Hair's scalp in Rochester all those years ago, "I am all broke up because I can't start tonight [for Puerto Rico]." It was impossible for him to leave without "some preparation, and it will entail a big loss and my partners naturally object. But go I must. I have been in every war our country has had since Bleeding Kansas war in which my father was killed. And I must be in this fight if I get in at the tail end!"[16]

But he did not. When Cody lamented that leaving the show would cost him $100,000, Miles advised him to stay.[17]

His reservations about the war stemmed more from his financial liability than from concerns about moral culpability. In that sense, his personal anxieties anticipated national sentiment after 1900. The American army in the Philippines turned from expelling the Spanish to fighting an indigenous rebellion. Combat and slaughter dragged on for years, costing the lives of 250,000 Filipinos and over 4,000 Americans. Even Roosevelt had turned against overseas acquisitions by 1901.[18]

Cody's interest in reenacting overseas engagements waned almost at the same time. He ceased to present them after 1904, when he staged the Battle of San Juan Hill in Britain. The show retained generic displays of global warrior prowess with the Congress of Rough Riders and other exotic peoples, but connections to specific, foreign wars or battles disappeared. The colorful whirl of foreign and primitive peoples continued to reinforce the messages crafted in the early 1890s, about the capacity of white men to manage racially diverse primitives and modern technology sprung from frontier origins. "In its transportation, commissary, arenic, camp, and executive departments . . . the Wild West is at once a model and a wonder."[19]

But even in its glamorous new format, for all its appeal to the press and the public, Buffalo Bill's Wild West show was anything but a guaranteed income. Cody was forty-eight years old in 1894, and the show's Brooklyn summer at Ambrose Park cost him a fortune. "I am too worried just now to think of anything," he wrote to his sister Julia. "This is the worst deal I ever had in my life—for my expenses are $4,000 a day, [a]nd I can't reduce them, without closeing entirely. You can't possibly appreciate my situation—this is the tightest squeeze of my life."[20]

Cody's struggle to shore up the political relevance and profitability of the show accompanied his fading personal interest in performing it. Retirement was a form of vanishing, of fulfilling the frontiersman's destiny, and hints of his permanent departure from the arena began to recur almost as often as the "Attack on the Settler's Cabin." He first hinted at retirement as early as 1877, when he announced he would leave the stage and spend the rest of his days on his ranch.[21] Throughout the 1890s, he mused in public about leaving the Wild West show. For all the difficulties with Louisa, he still returned to Nebraska during every break from the road. He took long hunting and camping trips. As he aged, he seems to have been drawn ever more to home in the West.

The problem was how to find his rightful place there, as the old century gave way to the new. For a man who lived his life as a performance of the story of progress, the real challenge was in the denouement. He was acutely aware that how his life story ended would determine its meaning for the public. Commenting on how stories work, the philosopher David Carr observes that "only from the perspective of the end do the beginning and middle make sense."[22] If Cody's life ended in the poorhouse, his biography would assume the dimensions of tragedy. If he ended it as a weary old showman, much of the authenticity of his early life, and of the frontier story, would be sacrificed. If he capped off his lifelong tale of frontier development with a triumphant culmination of real-life progress, he could validate the frontier myth he claimed as his own. From the mid-1890s on, William Cody dedicated himself to the search for an ending.

His efforts were of two kinds. On the one hand, Cody knew the manifold importance of entrepreneurialism as a real generator of wealth, as the commerce that expressed the maturity of civilization and its final stage of development, as evidence of the vitality and energy that characterized Anglo-Saxondom, and as proof of another great myth of America, the self-made man. To make a living in commerce required an entrepreneurial spirit and a willingness to tolerate setbacks. An estimated 95 percent of American businesses failed between 1873 and 1893.[23] A wise man with money invested in a lot of different places.

Or so Cody seemed to think. His phenomenal energy spun off into dozens of different businesses after 1890. He invested heavily in theatrical productions, particularly in backing his lover, Katherine Clemmons. He bought bonds in a British short-line railroad in 1892. In 1893, he partnered with Frank "White Beaver" Powell to found the Cody-Powell Coffee Company, manufacturer and distributor of Panmalt Coffee. "Three pounds of Panmalt Coffee can be bought for the price of one pound of Java, and one pound of Panmalt is equal in strength and will go as far as a pound of Java, Mocha, or Rio." He offered guiding services for tourist hunters out of Sheridan, Wyoming. For his sister Helen and her husband, Hugh Wetmore, and partly to advertise his other businesses, he bought a newspaper, the *Duluth Press*, and an office building in which to house it.[24]

The survival of American capitalism depended ever more on sales of consumer goods, and that entailed the expansion of sales, the sales pitch. Cody opened his show programs to advertisers. After 1893, audiences could read not only about Buffalo Bill's lifelong adventures and the history of the show, but also pitches for Mennen's Borated Talcum Powder, Sweet Orr & Co. Overalls Pants & Shirts, "The Best Union Made," and Quaker Oats, "the Sunshine of the Breakfast Table—Accept No Substitutes." There were ads for toys, for tools, for guns, for suspenders, and for bicycles. Cody himself endorsed more products personally: "I always use Winchester rifles and Winchester ammunition." The John B. Stetson Company depicted "Buffalo Bill and his Stetson Hat." Another enticed customers with the effectiveness of B. T. Babbitt's Soap, "Used by this Show."[25] In their ongoing quest for markets to stave off overproduction and renew the economy, advertisers found in Buffalo Bill and his frontier originals at least a sheen of authenticity for manufactured goods, and Cody discovered a supplemental, if small, stream of cash.

But as he approached the end of his life, most of William Cody's energy, and most of his cash, too, went into colonizing the great West. In a sense, creating community was a consistent project of his life. He was the son of a town founder, with an attempt at town founding in his own past, and the founder of the exemplary "little tented city" that sprang up in showgrounds on both sides of the Atlantic. The theory of civilization, with its advance from savagery to settlement, practically dictated that the culmination of his lifelong efforts should be a lasting town, with homes and families. With his large, but fluctuating, show profits he tried to make North Platte his own. He founded the town's Buffalo Bill Hook and Ladder Company in 1889. In

1894, he bought expensive uniforms for the town band. (Each member's flashy getup included a huge rosette, worn on the left breast, with Buffalo Bill's face on it.)[26] In partnership with his neighbor, Isaac Dillon, Cody ordered a ditch excavated from the North Platte River to his four-thousand-acre spread, then announced he would divide the property and colonize it with five hundred land-hungry Quakers from Philadelphia.[27]

Most of these projects, including the coffee company and the colonization plan, collapsed in the depression of 1893. Even if they had not, all the civic gifts in the world could not change the fact that North Platte would never bear his image the way he wanted. A patrician, even a philanthropist, he might be. But town founder, never. For the old scout to secure his legacy, and establish civilization in his wake, he would need to make a bolder move.

ACCORDING TO GEORGE BECK, who became Cody's partner in the new town-founding project, Buffalo Bill came late to the game. Beck first scouted a new town site at the foot of Cedar Mountain, in Wyoming's Big Horn Basin, sometime in the early 1890s. From the beginning, he planned to irrigate the land with water from the Stinking Water River, which flowed through it. Among those who accompanied him on his early expeditions was Elwood Mead, state engineer of Wyoming and a prominent irrigation expert, whom Beck had retained as a private consultant. It was an eventful trip. Beck and several of the party got lost and spent the night in the cabin of a lone settler. Mead and Beck surveyed the land and "ran a line of levels" at various places to determine the feasibility of irrigation. Soon after, Mead officially changed the river's name from the Stinking Water to the Shoshone, to make the project more appealing to settlers.[28]

Accompanying Beck and Mead was Horton Boal, friend of Beck and husband of Arta Cody. As Beck remembered it, William Cody heard about the trip from Boal, and "came to me very anxious to get in" on the town-site plan. Beck and his partner, a Sheridan banker named H. C. Alger, "concluded to let Cody in for the reason that at the time he was probably the best advertised man in the world, and we thought that might be of some advantage." They organized the Shoshone Irrigation Company, with Beck serving as secretary and manager, Alger as treasurer, and the world's most famous frontiersman, Buffalo Bill himself, as its president.[29]

Beck chose "Shoshone" as the name of their first town, but the U.S. postmaster rejected it for being too similar to the existing address of Shoshone Agency, on the Shoshone Reservation, in the nearby Wind River Mountains. The partners submitted a new name, "Cody," at William Cody's

insistence, and with Beck and the others persuaded that it could help advertise the settlement. (Had the postmaster rejected that name, they had designated another choice: Chicago.)[30]

Happy to be founding a town that bore his name, William Cody soon
recruited more partners, especially showmen and magnates of print advertising. Nate Salsbury became a partner. At his suggestion, Cody approached
George Bleistein, a Buffalo, New York, businessman who had made a fortune as a printer, particularly of posters for circuses and Buffalo Bill's Wild
West show. Along with two other entrepreneurs from New York, Bleistein
contributed tens of thousands of dollars to the enterprise.

For all that, as far as we can tell Cody himself put the most cash into this
effort. For the better part of a decade, a river of money ran from Buffalo
Bill's Wild West to the Big Horn Basin, scraping canals between river and
settlers, building dams and headgates, erecting pumps, office buildings,
stores, and liveries.

From the helm of a show about imperial glory, "The World's Largest
Arenic Exhibition," Cody was thrilled with the imperial prospect of his
town-building venture. The Big Horn Basin was "an empire of itself," he
wrote. Where Beck planned to found one town, Cody's ambitions were
much larger.[31] He envisioned vast networks of irrigation ditches filled with
sparkling water, lined with eager settlers who would spread it on verdant
fields, and pump it into their thirsty towns, paying the Shoshone Irrigation
Company for every drop. The West's most famous irrigated town, Greeley,
Colorado, "ain't a potato patch" to the acres that Cody and his partners
would make their own. "When one stops to think that all of Utah cultivates
only 240,000 acres and the cities and towns there is in Utah—how many
towns can we lay off and own on our 300,000 acres?" he asked a friend.

In 1897, Cody persuaded Salsbury to partner with him in an additional
concern, claiming a vast 60,000-acre swath on the north side of the
Shoshone River, opposite the Cody town site and extending many miles to
the east. Across this entire area the two showmen hoped to establish farms
and towns which would be served by a different canal, running along the
north side, and which William Cody intended to build just as soon as the
town of Cody was well under way.

For now, "the key note to all" was the roughly 28,000-acre spread on
which the Shoshone Irrigation Company was building Cody town "at the
forks of the Shoshone River," where "the great sulphur springs which we
own" would be a health resort and prime tourist attraction. It was "the
greatest land deal ever," and a fitting retirement, too. "We will all have a big
farm of our own that will . . . support us in our old age and we can lay under
the trees and swap lies."[32] Culmination to Buffalo Bill's long career as the
great domesticator, the town would be a permanent tribute to the man

whose show finished with a brief, climactic act of settlement. He would be wealthy, retired, and the revered founder of real civilization.

As Beck and the other partners had anticipated, Buffalo Bill's Wild West proved a great advertisement. The securing of the settler's cabin, which had long been the show climax, was now recapitulated with real-life domesticity for sale in the town of Cody, where audiences could find not only land, ranches, and farms, but also *homes*. "Irrigated Homes in the Big Horn Basin," the "Greatest Agricultural Valley in the West, NOW OPEN to the Settler and Home-Seeker," blared a full-page ad in the 1896 Wild West show program. "Homes in the Big Horn Basin" became the advertising refrain, and the following year, the pitch assured the crowds that these homes sat in bountiful fields. An arrangement of pumpkins, corn, and sheaves of wheat bore the label "Specimen of Products of Irrigated Lands— Cody Canal," and another featured a wagon train trundling along a fulsome riverbank, with the caption "Cody Irrigation Canal, Big Horn Basin, Wy., 1897."[33]

A program article explained that this was where Buffalo Bill himself recreated in the off-season, in a land that fended off the debilitating anxieties and neurasthenia of the cities. "The settler's cabin and the stockman's ranch houses and corrals" had replaced "the cone-shaped tepees" of an earlier time. "But the air that fills men's lungs with health, their brains with noble thoughts, and their veins with new life, still remains." The air was "so pure, so sweet and so bracing, that it intoxicates when poor, weak, cramped, damp, decayed, smoke-shrivelled lungs are distended by it."[34]

Audiences in 1901 could find the same promises on the back cover of their show programs, as if Buffalo Bill's settlement were where the show actually ended. "Shoshone Irrigation Company Owners of the Cody Canal Has Water Ready for Thousands of Acres of Good Lands." Show spectators could read the official-looking endorsement letter from Elwood Mead, identified as the state engineer of Wyoming (and carefully not identified as paid consultant to the company): "I know of no place in this country which offers to prudent and industrious farmers greater assurances of material prosperity and physical comfort than the Big Horn Basin." The country was "equally well adapted to the purposes of the stock raiser, grain grower, fruit raiser, or market gardener." Mead told the crowds from Bay City, Michigan, to Opelika, Alabama, that "the Cody Canal takes its water supply from one of the largest rivers in the West, and reclaims some of the best land in the State. The completed portion is well and substantially built with an ample capacity to water all the land below it."[35]

Of course, advertising went beyond show programs. Even before any settlers arrived, Cody himself had established the town's first newspaper, the *Shoshone News* (with John Burke as temporary editor), to advertise the basin's potential. By 1899 he had imported a new editor, J. H. Peake, to run the new paper, the *Cody Enterprise*. In the *Enterprise*, and in his Minnesota paper, the *Duluth Press*, he took out large ads, promising land and water, with a drawing of Buffalo Bill welcoming readers to a verdant mountain valley, where they could find "Titles to Homes Perfect."[36] Cody spoke often of the town in interviews with overseas newspapers. "I am making canals for irrigation purposes, opening mines, and acting as agent for the Government in granting concessions to prospective settlers," he told an English reporter in 1903.[37]

Indeed, the town became the new center of William Cody's continuing, almost manic entrepreneurialism. In addition to newspapers, he founded a livery stable, began gold mines and coal mines, and drilled oil wells. In 1902, he opened the elegant Irma Hotel, named for his youngest daughter, with a remarkable collection of western paintings and fine furnishings in a granite building whose design and construction (at a reputed cost of $80,000) he supervised closely. "I am very anxious of getting the concession of putting on an automobile and horse stage line from Cody into the Yellowstone Park," he wrote the state's governor in 1903.[38] Not satisfied with a stage line, he built two hotels along the route.[39]

Many of his efforts failed. Gold, coal, and oil deposits were rapidly exhausted or proved so minute as to be not worth extracting. Nevertheless, as these businesses and the settlement progressed, they, and especially the town itself, increasingly became subjects of the Wild West show. The Burlington & Missouri River Railroad reached the town in 1901. Beginning about this time, a coterie of Cody residents (or people who claimed to be Cody residents) carried a banner, "Cody Delegation of Boosters from Buffalo Bill's Home Town," in the show parade and in the grand entrance into the arena. When the emigrant wagon train trundled before the stands, their canvases read "Take the Burlington Route to the Big Horn Basin," as if to suggest that spectators did not need to endure an Indian attack to participate in the continuing settlement and domestication of the frontier.[40] The ads for the irrigated tracts awaiting the "homeseeker" pointed the way out of the arena and the city. Spectators longing to escape urban threats or their declining prospects in eastern and midwestern farms heard a consistent message: take the train to Cody town, and home.

As the nineteenth century gave way to the twentieth, shifting cultural currents made the "Attack on the Settler's Cabin" and these promises of real western homes ever more resonant for show audiences, and the role of real-life "home builder" even more attractive to William Cody. Public anxieties about the survival of the home and family, and public veneration of home builders, today's "developers," grew more pronounced as the frontier closed, as urbanization maintained its rapid pace, and as depression made Americans painfully aware of the uncertainties of the new industrial economy. The home continued to be the bedrock of American civilization, and those who built them were great citizens indeed. As one commentator put it, "Home building is the best business in the world. The home is the seat of the happiness and the sheet anchor of free government. In the family fireside is planted deep the flag of this republic. Those who broaden the domain of homes are the true patriots and our greatest men."[41]

With their bucolic advertisements and their remote western location, the homes for sale in the Big Horn Basin were decidedly "country homes," the most desirable of all homes. In the popular imagination, country homes included the more elegant city suburbs. They were not necessarily farms. Rather, they were situated somewhat ambiguously in what scholar Leo Marx has called a "middle landscape" between remote hinterland and decadent city. They fused modern technology of the city—ready water, electricity, and telephones—with rural virtue. The country home was, in the words of one anxious proponent, "the safe anchored foundation of the Republic," the "fountain-head of purity and strength," which "will nourish and sustain this nation forever."[42] As the cities erupted in polyglot confusion, the destiny of the white middle class could be secured in these rustic dwellings, nestled in an agrarian empire surrounding the cities, at once supporting them with their produce, and containing them with their virtue.[43]

Advertising for Cody's country home empire masked the hard road ahead for the Shoshone Irrigation Company and the town's early settlers. By 1895, when the company began work in earnest, the West's most arable and desirable land had long since been taken. The swath of Big Horn Basin claimed by the partners was not a blank slate or a showgrounds on which settlement could be projected. It was a real place, with real nature, and that nature did not go easy on pastoral dreams.

Travelers to the company's town site, especially before the railroad reached the town in 1901, had to struggle first with its remoteness. The Big Horn Basin lay behind the formidable Wind River Mountains to the south and the Big Horn range to the east, with the high country of the Continental Divide to the west. Red Lodge, the nearest settlement where supplies could be had, was an arduous two-day wagon ride north, in Montana. (Early surveyors recommended that the region be attached to the state of Montana rather than Wyoming.)[44] Even after the Burlington & Missouri completed its 120-mile spur line from Toluca, Montana, to Cody, the ride from Chicago or other points east was long and tiresome.[45]

Reaching the area was nowhere near as difficult as farming it, however. The Big Horn Basin was a sandy sagebrush flat. The center of it was the driest area in Wyoming, garnering less than six inches of rain per year. An early government surveyor, who saw the basin fifteen years before Beck did, concluded that it appeared "very desolate, except along the valleys" of the Big Horn River tributaries. From the basin's western side, where the company laid out its town site, these tributaries, including the Shoshone River, flowed east into the Big Horn River. The larger river flowed north out of the basin's belly, joined by the Little Big Horn River in Montana and finally pouring into the Missouri River over a hundred miles away.[46]

The Shoshone River was sizable, and like other streams and rivers noted by that early surveyor it was fringed "with cotton-woods and narrow, grassy bottoms." But the water was sulfurous (thus its early name, the Stinking Water), and even this rather pungent riparian oasis was eroded deep into the valley floor. The unwillingness of water to run uphill made simple irrigation ditches inadequate for watering the sagebrush-covered benches that jutted up hundreds of feet from the riverbanks and made up most of the basin's real estate. To bring water to the town site, partners had to contract for a canal that began miles upriver and tracked around a mountain to the lower flats where the town was located.

Finally, even if a steady supply of water could be secured, the climate provided other obstacles. The altitude, four thousand feet, meant early frosts and late snows. Basin winters were not the coldest in Wyoming, but with extremes of thirty degrees below zero, they were cold enough to dissuade most farmers. In the summer, on the other hand, the Big Horn Basin was often the hottest place in all of Wyoming. Winter and summer alike, as the sun warmed the basin floor, heated air rose upward, drawing cold air out of the highlands to the west. A cooling draft can lighten the burden of summer heat, but emigrants were rocked by these unpredictable gusts, which reached sixty miles per hour. Most early visitors found the basin bleak. An early encampment of miners had ventured to the Big Horn Basin in 1870, but they soon departed. In 1895, other than a few cowboys and ranchers on open-range cattle outfits, almost nobody resided in the basin permanently.

The challenges to settling this place with middle-class homeowners were huge. In 1895, George Beck drew up a map to aid him in the work of laying out the first town site. One day, he put the map down, weighted it with a rock, and walked over to talk with his engineer, C. E. Hayden, who was working a few hundred yards away. While they spoke, "a summer whirl wind came along and picked the map up and started it heavenward," Beck later recalled. "Hayden and I followed it as far as we could but it kept going and we concluded our map was recorded in Abraham's bosom."[47]

So the environment of the Big Horn Basin threatened to carry away the tidy visions of town planners. Cody himself would expend vast effort, and a vast fortune, to hold the ordered grids of his towns against the basin's uncooperative nature. As much as it fired him in its early days, and as often as he touted its glories in show programs and press interviews, the project posed a fierce challenge to his business acumen, testing his sense of personal and national destiny. Indeed, only a major shift in government policy toward the arid West would guarantee the settlement's success. In doing so, it relieved William Cody of his town site's burdens. But it also stripped his dreams away.

THE TOWN BUSINESS required extensive advertising, and not a little deception. Thus, in 1896, Cody and Beck fought hard to make their new town, which was little more than a land office, the county seat of the new Big Horn County. Success would guarantee the town a county courthouse and the aura of permanence. After that, both investor capital and settlers would be easier to recruit.

But the designation of county seat was made in an election by county voters, most of whom lived nearer to existing settlements which they favored for the seat. The company's only hope of winning the election was to continue paying work crews who were digging the irrigation ditches and hope this persuaded voters that Cody was a real town, and not another booster fantasy. If the excavation stopped, word would spread quickly that the town was failing and the election would be lost. The problem was, the partners were out of cash to pay the workers, who numbered over a hundred, or to feed the teams of horses that drew the scrapers.[48] So they launched an effort to sell corporate bonds, guaranteed with their personal property, to raise the money they needed.[49]

The bond sales failed, however, because eastern investors were suddenly leery of western investments. Their nervousness grew with the expanding popularity of William Jennings Bryan, the Democratic candidate for the presidency, and his Populist allies, who had threatened to repudiate bonds and mortgages if they were elected. Until financiers were certain he would not be president, no eastern money could be had. Meanwhile, the Shoshone Irrigation Company remained thirsty for cash, for laborers, and for equipment. "I have had the worst time in my life standing off people as I have been told to go slow and I have written letters of excuse for not paying accounts till I do not know what to say to them any longer," wrote George Beck. "Any man we owe a penny to has written in all kinds of English and they all seem to want payment."[50]

The sober solution would have been to shut down operations in the Big Horn Basin until money could be raised. But doing so would have signified the town's prospects were illusory, thereby conceding the county seat fight, and passing up a potential boost to confidence in the town's future among investors, settlers, and the public generally.

The county seat fight was only one of many similar episodes in the early life of the town of Cody. Successful town founding required promoters to deceive much of the public much of the time. The similarities between show business and town business were not lost on the principals. As Beck told Cody, "If we can keep up a show for thirty days now we have a fine chance to make a very good thing."[51] Ultimately, Cody and Salsbury managed to sell an indemnity bond to Phoebe Hearst, wife of California senator and Comstock Lode magnate George Hearst, who advanced them $30,000 on terms of repayment in five years at 7.5 percent.[52] But even so, the county seat fight was lost to nearby Basin.[53] Town founding was an ongoing gamble, in which Cody, Beck, Salsbury, and the other partners wagered heavy sums and much effort on a town that might in the end prove to be more show than substance.

The baleful influence of the Populists on western capital influenced other aspects of Cody's personal finances. In most years, he borrowed money for his show and other businesses, securing loans with mortgages on his Nebraska property. He then paid the mortgages off with show receipts. By 1896, this was proving more difficult, he explained to a friend, because "the damn populists have repudiated so many loans that eastern capital fight shy of Nebraska and Kansas particularly." (Thus, when Beck finally acquired the bond money from Phoebe Hearst, he promptly lent Cody and Salsbury $5,000 of it to open the Wild West show that year.)[54]

William Cody's struggle to raise bond money for his ditches amid the Populist insurgency suggests how much western environment and economics had combined to make the New West something less than the pastoral paradise of agrarian myth or of Wild West show programs. The need for irrigation itself reflected the absence of rain, the single most unifying environmental characteristic of the Great Plains and the interior of the West. Plains farmers had responded to aridity by planting dryland crops, especially wheat and corn, across millions of acres churned up by their plows. The result was a glut of wheat and corn, and steadily declining produce prices. At the same time, farmers bought new technology, on credit, seeding more acres against their declining incomes. Land under the plow more than doubled, and farmers cultivated more land in the last third of the nineteenth century than they had in all the prior history of the republic.[55]

The result was even more overproduction, still lower farm profits, and more unpaid debts. By the early 1890s, wheat was more expensive to raise than it was to buy. Almost half of Kansas farmers were in default on their mortgages. In Nebraska, the brutal droughts of 1893 and '94 drove already reeling settlers to despair.[56]

Just as the European encounter with the wilderness inspired both the frontier dream and the gothic nightmare, so the American encounter with the arid Far West inspired both Buffalo Bill's Wild West, a dramatic depiction of westward expansion as the route to hardy independence, and Populism, a radical politics to recapture independence lost to the very railroads and markets which had made westward expansion (and the Wild West show) possible. The ironies and contradictions of these competing western myths and realities were exemplified in the history of Nebraska, the state that produced both William Cody and William Jennings Bryan. The "Boy Orator of the Platte," Bryan was elected to Congress for the first time in November of 1890 (just as Cody was about to attempt Sitting Bull's arrest). The congressman soon became the leading exponent of "free silver," a catchphrase for abandoning the gold standard in order to increase money in circulation and thus to inflate those depressed crop prices which so plagued western farmers.

Corporate interests saw Bryan as a western radical, almost a trans-Mississippi monster, who threatened the very integrity of the financial system.[57] Nate Salsbury, creditor and part owner of a corporate, railroad-dependent amusement and now busily hawking bonds against a real estate speculation, shared that opinion. "The money market is closed to all kinds of investments and will stay so as long as that blatherskite Bryan is rampaging around the country," he fumed.[58] At times, he considered Bryan a rival western showman who threatened ruin. "I am happy to say," he reported after Bryan's 1896 campaign swing through New York, "that he made the most distinguished failure at Madison Square Garden the other night. . . . He came to paralyze New York and got a body blow that took the wind out of him and [his] ass-*toot* managers, and they have retired to the boundless prairies to rub themselves down with buffalo chip and get some more wind."[59]

Cody remained more ambivalent than Salsbury in his politics. He was not without sympathy for the Populists, and for Bryan in particular. In 1896, the town of North Platte hosted a state irrigation fair, and the organizing committee cast about for an eminent speaker to open the event. Cody recommended Bryan. He had reservations about the free silver campaign—"I don't like some of the party's moves," he told one correspondent—but Bryan was still his candidate, and he was certain he would one day be president. Had Bryan become president, Cody would likely have been at his inauguration. As it turned out, Bryan lost—and Buffalo Bill attended McKinley's inauguration instead.[60]

Cody town's appeal lay in its possibilities for escape not merely from the city, but also from the crisis of the farm. The irrigated fields of Cody town ideally would grow specialty crops, fruit and nuts in particular, and allow residents to escape the price deflation and drought that plagued dryland farmers of wheat and corn.

Indeed, William Cody's effort to found irrigated towns was only one of many similar efforts across the West, where an emerging movement saw in irrigation the chance to redeem the West not from savage Indians, who were no longer a threat, but from increasingly dangerous political trends. For all Nate Salsbury's pique, Populism and free silver were politically moderate compared to other forms of radicalism that swept the West after 1890. Western economics were notoriously unstable. With only a tiny manufacturing sector, the region's jobs were mostly in extractive industries, and wage workers like miners, lumberjacks, farmhands, and ranch cowboys were even more vulnerable than eastern workers to commodity price deflation (a condition which stoked their enthusiasm for the potentially insurrectionist industrial armies in 1894).

Thus, a new union, the Western Federation of Miners, was born in the depression of 1893. Over the next fifteen years, miners and mine owners were locked in bitter, sometimes violent strikes. In 1905, federation members led the charge to create a new, even more radical union, the Industrial Workers of the World. The IWW was a nationwide organization, but its socialist appeal for "One Big Union" was strongest in the West.

Other examples of the furious radicalism of the postfrontier West abound. Socialists grew stronger in many states as Democrats and Republicans failed to ameliorate industrial working conditions, and the state with the largest proportion of Socialist voters was Oklahoma. After the Russian Revolution of 1917, the most hallowed tomb of Communists was the Kremlin wall, which holds the remains of only two Americans. One of them, journalist John Reed, was from Oregon. The other, unionist Bill Haywood, was from Utah.[61] For many thinkers and policymakers, the West's tumultuous, chaotic politics made the country homes of Cody town and other irrigation projects ever more appealing, even necessary, as warm hearths of middle-class sensibility and democracy in a wilderness of political unrest.

But the key to those homes was irrigation. Frontier myth had always promised a path between ideologies of left and right, between wealth redistribution and aristocratic hierarchy. But in the postfrontier West, the old narrative of progress and civilization sprung from the frontier seemed more and more like a poetic fiction which offered no real alternatives. Ranching was supposed to be a precursor to farming, but farms failed in the cold, dry climate of the high Plains, making the region resistant to settlement. In 1900, Wyoming's population had yet to reach 93,000. A state for eleven years, it had attracted slightly more than a tenth of one percent of the seventy-five million people who inhabited the United States. Only Nevada had fewer residents.[62] Indeed, ranching was not only durable but, organized along new corporate lines, it became a barrier to the advance of the domesticity and civilization of the farm. In the 1880s and 1890s, meatpackers from Chicago and other large investors consolidated control of the western range, squeezing out smallholders and homesteaders, who depended on public lands to graze their animals, by enclosing streams and rivers with barbed wire.

The resultant range wars resulted in bloodshed and a great deal of rustling; the most spectacular episode occurred in Wyoming in 1892. East of the Big Horns, in Johnson County, large ranchers with ties to railroad corporations hired a gang of Texas gunmen to assassinate smallholders, many of them homesteaders or small, independent cattle outfits, near the town of Buffalo. The mercenaries descended first on the cabin of Nate Champion, a cowboy who sided with the smallholders. But Champion fought them off all day before perishing in a hail of bullets. Johnson County's sheriff and his posse soon cornered the invading Texans, but large ranchers prevailed on the governor to request federal troops. The army escorted the hired guns to jail. Through intimidation of witnesses and judicial corruption, all of the accused killers and the ranchers who hired them were released.

Each side in Johnson County told a story, and insofar as those stories revealed much larger political and social perspectives, to choose sides was to select one narrative over another. To large ranchers and their allies, smallholders were rustlers, criminals, and vagrants who had to be stopped. To smallholders, large ranchers were greedy corporate monopolists who quashed the common man's dream.

But whatever story one believed, Johnson County's bloodshed underscored the continuing predominance of undomesticated ranching over family farming.[63] Despite modern nostalgia for family-centered ranches, nineteenth-century Americans were suspicious of ranching. Unlike farming, which was bound firmly to family in the popular mind, ranching was renowned for being excessively male, and for not constituting families.[64] Ranching required extensive resource use—dispersed grazing—rather than intensive cultivation. Ranching did not turn the wilderness to garden; it did not complete the ascent of civilization. Many ranchers did not even build permanent homes. In Johnson County and across Wyoming, even large ranch owners with families tended to live in cities. They sought control of the range as a pasture, but not as a home for themselves.[65] So the range was populated mostly by ranch hands, or cowboys. Even in 1900, the 93,000 residents of Wyoming included fewer than 35,000 females.[66]

Among locals, the absence of women signified the absence of families, and of domestic order. Family was the key to social regeneration, the purpose of settlement, and still the most durable rural institution.[67] Rather than the settler's cabin, with its wife and children, Johnson County called to mind an army of gunmen (or deputies) arrayed around a cowboys' (or rustlers') cabin, with bullets flying thick between the principals. Whatever else it was,

the Johnson County war resonated with hypermasculine frenzy. Domesticity was nowhere on the horizon. Progress had stopped. If the story of the
Far West was supposed to be one of progress from ranch and range to farm
and civilization, then Wyoming was in the grip of plot failure.

Ideally, the founding of Cody offered a means out of the narrative
impasse by providing an improved nature for family farms. Indeed, Johnson
County was on the mind of at least one town founder. In 1892, George Beck
himself owned a ranch not far from Buffalo, as well as business interests in
the town, including a flour mill, an electric light plant, and a waterworks.
He later claimed that ranchers invited him to join their invasion, but that he
refused and warned them it would "end in disaster."[68] At the same time, he
had little time for smallholders either, most of whom he considered thieves.
Like most Americans, Beck became convinced that partisans in the class
wars of the Gilded Age were zealots, be they ranchers and homesteaders in
Wyoming or workers and owners in Chicago. What the nation needed was
for both sides to show restraint (or be restrained) until the failing abundance
of the frontier could be refreshed through an application of science, technology, and capital—of the kind Beck and Cody brought to the Big Horn
Basin.

In this sense, William Cody and his partners in the Shoshone Irrigation
Company were part of a much broader movement of professional engineers,
capitalists, and reformers who saw in irrigation a trail that wound safely past
savage ranchers, Populist demagogues, and menacing leftists to the bucolic
country home. Visions of profuse fields along the Cody Canal hearkened to
some of the oldest reform traditions in America. Since the beginning of the
republic, writers and politicians from Thomas Jefferson to Horace Greeley
had lobbied the federal government to remove Indians, build roads and railroads, and restrain land speculators, all to open a "safety valve" on the frontier for American workers trapped in decadent cities.

The term "safety valve" was adopted from a feature of industrial boilers,
a fact which suggests how much the theory reflected urban ideas rather than
western reality. In fact, the West was never a safety valve. Farm making was
too expensive for most urban workers, and few in the cities had any knowledge of farming. But the idea that the West had served as an escape hatch for
the downwardly mobile, a bulwark against class conflict, remained conventional wisdom throughout the nineteenth century. Around 1890, as the
frontier closed, reformers began looking for ways to expand the supply of
arable land to keep open, or reopen, the safety valve. The day of the irriga-
tor had arrived.[69]

Irrigation promised an end to western aridity and its attendant savagery,
and a new start on homemaking along the remnant frontier. Irrigation engineers, water lawyers, utopian idealists, and others banded together in

national associations, created national magazines, such as *The Irrigation Age*, and held national conventions. They designed legislation to irrigate the vast western desert. Their most famous advocate was William Ellsworth Smythe (who—like Cody and Bryan—was from Nebraska). Smythe's 1899 book, *The Conquest of Arid America*, promoted irrigation of the arid West as a means of securing a millennial future: farms and work for the teeming unemployed masses; better health in the dry air; more wholesome, demo-cratic communities (a result of having to work together to dig and maintain canals); national greatness (all the great civilizations of the ancient world had been irrigated desert kingdoms). If these were not reasons enough, Smythe and his allies spoke fervently of "reclaiming the desert," infusing their campaigns with biblical language and the aura of the sacred. Irrigation became, in Smythe's prediction, the culmination of world history, the rise of the American people to a new level of wealth and power which would col-lapse age-old distinctions—between city and country, East and West, pro-ducer and worker, rich and poor—which threatened to tear the country apart as the new century dawned. His was a peaceful answer to Populists, anarchists, socialists, monopolist ranchers, rustlers, and all the other radicals who threatened the progressive march of civilization.[70]

Few could argue with these green dreams. The problem was how to make them come true. Digging ditches was so backbreaking and tedious that few could afford to pay the laborers. The cost of irrigation canals was far more than any smallholder could afford. To provide incentives for capi-talists, in 1894 Wyoming politicians secured passage of a landmark irriga-tion bill, the Carey Act (named for Wyoming senator Joseph Carey).

The Carey Act provided the legal framework for the development of the Cody Canal and the town of Cody. The law stipulated that any private developer who showed he had means and a plan to provide a water supply for an unclaimed desert acreage could file for the right to develop it. Because unclaimed lands in the West remained in federal hands until they passed into private ownership, federal officials had to review the plan. Once they were satisfied of its soundness, they would separate or, in the parlance of the law, "segregate" the acreage from federal holdings. The segregation was then handed over to the state. When settlers arrived, they paid the state fifty cents an acre for up to 160 acres of land.

For his part, the private developer made money by investing in an irriga-tion system and selling permanent water rights to the same settlers for up to $15 per acre. Once the water rights were sold, the settlers assumed owner-ship of the ditch and the irrigation system, which they maintained. The cap-italist who financed the development could then retire, rich and happy.[71] At least, that was the idea.

As much as it appealed to William Cody, to his partners, and to

Wyoming's political leadership, the law proved such a poor vehicle for settling the Big Horn Basin and other places that Congress drafted succeeding
legislation within a decade. The overwhelming fact which the Shoshone
partners could never overcome was the expense of irrigation works. The
Cody Canal was no small ditch. Four feet deep, twenty-one feet wide at the
bottom, and broadening to thirty feet at the top, the completed canal would
run over twelve miles from headgate to townsite. There, it would branch
into more than fifty miles of lateral channels (which the company also had to
excavate), spreading water over almost 20,000 acres. Early estimates of construction costs ran to $200,000.[72] In the end, the Cody Canal cost much
more, and it took years to finish (even after Elwood Mead and others pronounced it "substantially complete"). Workers were hard to find, and excavation ceased completely when the ground froze in the long, often subzero
winters. In 1897, water trickled into the canal from the Shoshone River and
began rushing toward the settlement, a promising moment indeed. But
when the water was within a mile and a half of the townsite, the bank blew
out, and the water poured into the breach, forcing closure of the canal until
the leak was fixed. Cold weather prevented repairs until the following year.
Even then, engineers were flummoxed by the high gypsum content of the
soil, which made it especially porous, leading to more washouts which they
tried to rectify by working straw and hay into the ground. For years afterward, the washout would plague canal operators.[73]

Even when the canal operated, the water froze in winter, and settlers
went back to hauling water from the river again. Delays like this were mor-
tal to the interests of investors, who were hoping for a return on their outlays
within a few years but who watched as years passed and ditch construction
took ever more of their capital.

Settlers were the key to profits, of course. But obstacles prevented the
town from becoming a popular emigrant destination. The remoteness of the
Big Horn Basin, especially before the railroad was complete, meant that
farmers in the basin had no ready market for crops. Water rights were
expensive. In the beginning, the company sold them for $10 per acre. Even
a forty-acre farm would cost $400 for water rights, plus $20 for the land—a
year's wages for the average American laborer.[74] Although the price was
payable over five years, the costs of farm making in Cody remained substantial. A 160-acre farm cost nearly $2,000 before interest. And, for those who
dared to stake their farm on the Cody Canal, an entire year would pass
before a crop matured. Ideally the town could provide a business nexus for
service industries. But few craftsmen could support themselves without the
elusive settlers. Because it required heavy cash investment up front, Cody
town was no safety valve.

In 1896, the Shoshone Irrigation Company contracted with emigration agents (businessmen who took a commission from town builders for recruiting emigrants to settle on their lands). They succeeded in bringing a group of seven families from Illinois to begin the new town. By the end of the summer, only one of these families remained, the rest having been intimidated by the bleak setting, the poor prospects for the canal's completion, and local ranchers whose cattle ravaged their gardens and whose cowboys maligned and frightened them.[75]

The Shoshone Irrigation Company hired a staff member of their own, D. H. Elliott, to recruit more emigrants. He spent months corresponding with the Swedish Association and other emigrant mutual aid societies, trying to entice immigrants to the town site. Touting the advantages of reclaimed desert as a tonic for the ailments of industrialism, he even approached the famous socialist, Eugene Debs. The leader of the Social Democratic Party had announced a "Social Democracy Colonization scheme," a model community where the unemployed could work the land while they waited for jobs. Elliott depicted Big Horn County as the socialists' promised land. "The Big Horn is a new county, very evenly divided, as is also the State of Wyoming, politically, hence, with a very few colonists they could have the balance of power, politically, if they so desired." Cody approved the idea. Shoshone Irrigation Company partners were so desperate to settle the town that even the virulently antiradical Salsbury endorsed it.[76]

But the Social Democrats decided a socialist Wyoming was not in the cards, and ignored the invitation. The company went back to recruiting more conventional settlers. By the end of 1897, the partners had fired Elliott to cut expenses.[77]

To say settlers were slow in coming is not to say there was no interest. Buffalo Bill's Wild West broadcast the opportunities of Cody far and wide. Out in Wyoming, George Beck was inundated with letters from prospective settlers. Howard Martin of Monmouth, Illinois, wrote as "a prospective homeseaker of the far wist," requesting information about "inducements that your Co. has to offer or any and all information pertaining to the country its people climate and if the well water is any part of it alcoli [*sic*]." C. M. Stewart of Brattleboro, Vermont, wanted to know "if we can take homesteds now," under the Carey Act, "that will be watered by your canal." C. L. Goodwin of Sutton Creek, Pennsylvania, requested "all the information a homeseeker would wish to know," regarding "lands you have for sale . . . water rights, least number of acres you sell . . . What is the least number of acres a man can farm of irrigated canal in Wyoming and make a living."[78] If the stacks of letters that arrived in the Big Horn Basin are any indication, would-be settlers seemed to come mostly from other rural areas and small towns. Few wrote from cities. Most knew a thing or two about farming. They asked how soon the frost came, how long the snow lasted, how high the elevation was. Many who were not farmers asked if they could find work making bricks, operating a creamery, or practicing law. Hundreds wrote. Few came.

The town site's remoteness and the reluctance of settlers made company partners as vulnerable to the whims of railroad bosses as any other town founders in the West. Not long before his death, William Cody alleged that he had persuaded the Burlington & Missouri River Railroad to build a line south from Montana, and "if it had not been for me there would not be a mile of railroad in the Big Horn Basin today."[79] In fact, the Burlington & Missouri began planning a transcontinental route past Yellowstone National Park early in the 1890s. The eastern approach to the park, along the Shoshone River, was a likely route. Company representatives toured with Beck and Cody along the river as early as 1895, and there were rumors in the press that the B&M—not Buffalo Bill—would build the town that year.[80]

But, in typical railway fashion, the railroad let others bear the expense of building the town, then extorted their cut. Once the town site was under way, B&M officials announced they would build a spur line to Cody from Toluca, Montana. Cody knew railroads, and the approach of the B&M was both a heartening sign and an uncomfortable reminder of his losses to the Kansas Pacific at his town of Rome in 1867. He wrote to Beck: "Did it ever strike you that we have got to keep our eyes peeled or the B&M might make Cody howl like the K & P made my town of Rome howl?" During a trip to Omaha, the general manager of the railroad, George Holdredge, "said he wanted to talk with me when I got their this fall, but he did not say what about." Cody was certain they wanted town land. "RR are out for the stuff— and I know from experience what they can do. Are we going to be prepared to act liberally with them? For it's going to come to a showdown pretty soon."[81]

He was right. Soon after their tracks began extending up the Shoshone River, the B&M let it be known that the line would stop miles short of Cody town—unless the Shoshone Irrigation Company handed over half the town lots. William Cody and his partners obliged.[82] That November, the railroad arrived—although there was no railroad bridge across the river, and travelers had to walk or find other transport the last mile and a half of the journey.

The completion of the rail line consummated the town founding. Shortly before the first train steamed into Cody, the town incorporated, with a population of 550 (the count was probably inflated).[83] Six years after he began his efforts, Cody's namesake town remained smaller than Buffalo Bill's Wild West traveling camp. Even with the railroad, it was still less well developed than the Wild West show, too. The Shoshone Irrigation Company had promised a town waterworks. But two years after the railroad spur opened, residents were still paying a door-to-door delivery service twenty-five cents a barrel for their water.[84] By 1905, of the 25,000 acres segregated for settlement along the Cody Canal, only 6,500 acres were actually irrigated. In 1907, officials finally judged the Cody Canal satisfactory, allowing the Shoshone Irrigation Company to cede responsibility for the canal to the community. But the list of unhappy settlers was long. By 1910, the litany of canal washouts, flooded fields, and other broken promises left the Shoshone Irrigation Company with a checkered past. Cody and his partners had been sued at least twenty-six times.[85]

The settlers of Cody were overwhelmingly middle class, and they expressed their aspirations to gentility with literary societies, church socials, and, beginning in 1901, meetings of the Cody Club, a gentleman's organization that served as the de facto chamber of commerce.[86] William Cody himself wore a white coat and tails to the grand opening of the Irma Hotel in 1902. "Most of the gentlemen were in evening dress, and a great many handsome and costly toilets were worn by the ladies present," wrote a local journalist.[87]

But a glimpse of the town even years later suggests that for many, such gestures only padded the settlement's rough edges. Nana Haight, a New Yorker and the wife of a pastor, arrived in Cody in 1910. She grew to like many things about her neighbors and the community, but on her arrival she could not hide her disappointment.

> It has only 1000 inhabitants and is fully two miles away from the railroad station; hardly a tree and mostly one story buildings, wooden sidewalks, and a few lights at night. My heart sank when the bus brought us down across a swiftly running river, up a steep hill to the town. . . . Such winds as we have. The children pass our house going to school and go along backing up slowly against the wind. However, they blow home quickly. . . . There is one block with shops on one side and ten saloons on the other. Only two stores that seem to keep everything: paint, drygoods, groceries, and all kinds of goods for hunting. Two butcher shops with terrible meat, tough as shoe leather. Also, a drugstore and two banks, and a few odd stationery, candy, and cigar stores. The tailor is on the other side of the street amidst the saloons, so I have to brave it if I go there. No one ever knows when some man will be suddenly thrown out on the street from one of the saloons.[88]

The spare, undomesticated appearance of the settlement notwithstanding, William Cody's venture in the Big Horn Basin became the focus of his efforts like nothing else since the creation of the Wild West show. To say Cody himself took a strong personal interest in the affairs of the town is a considerable understatement. He became its primary advocate and patrician. After 1901, he began spending each winter at his new ranch, the TE (a brand he bought from friend Mike Russell), on the remote reaches of the South Fork of the Shoshone River, where he built a small house with a white picket fence. From there he soldiered through snow to reassure settlers. Residents remembered that he would "call on families who had established homes along the canal. He always had words of encouragement and complimented them on the splendid homes they had started and improvements they had made." Other times, residents met him driving his buggy along the road. He "would stop to visit with all whom he met, asking how they were getting along and the type of ranching or farming they were doing." Some recalled that his free-spending visits provided the settlement's major source of cash.[89]

He spent most of each year on the road with Buffalo Bill's Wild West. But to judge by his behavior, he saw the town as another show in need of his hands-on direction. Unable to distinguish tasks he should delegate from duties he could not, he wrote hundreds of letters criticizing almost everything about Beck's operation in the town. He complained about heavy expenses and the lack of news from Beck. He insisted on knowing how much money was paid to the company and how it was spent. "This is discouraging," he wrote upon hearing that a new mail route would bypass the town. "Had I been informed of a proposal of this kind I think I could have brought influence to bear." He was full of suggestions—and demands—about the kinds of buildings in the town. "Of course we must have an office building. And while about it, it ought to be big enough to serve as a hotel this winter."[90] And he was especially bitter over the many ditch failures. "It was

Cody, Wyoming, c. 1905. Courtesy Buffalo Bill Historical Center.

neglect and carelessness that the water should be allowed to wash out the new canal," he lectured Beck in 1898.[91]

Such close attention was typical of Cody's business manner. But if it brought him success in show business, it did him little good in the town business. His show made profits, albeit unevenly. The town did not. "I am doing my best to raise money," he wrote Beck. "I tell you it keeps me sweating blood but no use getting discouraged. [I]f you can only protect our name and credit, I will say thank God."[92] Failure to complete the canal in a timely fashion could be disastrous. Officials "will make an unfavorable report of our canal if something substancial is not done," he warned Beck.[93] The result of cumulative poor assessments would be the loss of their segregation, and their investment.

Despite the town's halting development, Cody hoped it would yet provide him means to retire from show business. In 1903, he journeyed with the Wild West show to England again. Ticket sales were nowhere near what they had been on earlier European tours, and Cody spent long days sitting in his private railroad car. "I am going to get out of this business that is just wearing the life out of me," he wrote his sisters. "[T]here is such a nervous strain continualy. And the thing has got on to my nerves. And this must be my last summer."[94] He was too tired much of the time even to be convivial. "I do not go to hotels any more for I haven't the strength to be even talked to. The only ray of pleasure I have is when I get to thinking of dear old TE [Ranch] and the rest I am going to get there."[95]

By this time, it was becoming abundantly clear that Cody and his various partners in the Big Horn Basin had vastly underestimated the cost of irrigation. The Cody-Salsbury plan to irrigate 60,000 acres north of the Shoshone River proved much too expensive even for the most successful of showmen. When Cody and Salsbury commissioned an engineer's estimate of the costs, which included irrigating lands north of the town and providing the town waterworks, even the cheapest alternatives were estimated at a staggering $742,000.[96] Even if they sold water rights to every acre at the highest price the law allowed, their profits would amount to only $158,000, and that only if there were no other expenses along the way: no lawsuits for flooded fields or washed-out headgates, no recruitment of settlers or advertising. By 1901, it should have been clear: irrigation did not pay.

And yet Cody continued to pour money and effort into developing the Cody-Salsbury segregation. Part of the reason was that he had an eye on the Mormons, who had developed irrigation systems not only in Utah but downstream on the Shoshone River, at the town of Lovell. Since arriving in 1900, a small Mormon colony had succeeded in building a town and began eyeing nearby parcels for an expansion. First in their sights was the Cody-

Salsbury segregation across the Shoshone River, which they claimed should be returned to the public domain because Cody and Salsbury had yet to deliver the water they promised. Cody, who had faced off against imaginary Mormons in his stage plays, now spent considerable effort keeping his segregation from falling into their hands.[97]

But if their expanding horizons made him suspect there was potential for more cash in irrigating the desert, he drew the wrong conclusions. Mormon irrigators had a critical resource—communal labor—which Cody town did not. Farmers in Cody wanted the ditch dug for them; Mormons dug their own, collectively, as part of a greater spiritual effort to reclaim the wilderness. They were not fixated on how much money the ditches could make. They were, rather, bound by a spirit of collective religion.

Distracted by the Mormons, Cody appears not to have realized that his own frustrations in the irrigation business mirrored those of other capitalists. From 1894 to 1923, only one in twenty Carey Act projects made a profit. Ditch investments across the arid West paid so poorly that few investors could be found. Private funding of western settlement all but evaporated.

In 1902, Congress sought to remedy the shortcomings of the Carey Act with the Newlands Reclamation Act, a law that dramatically remade the landscape of western irrigation. Overnight, digging and financing large-scale irrigation works became a federal responsibility, administered through a new agency, the U.S. Reclamation Service.[98]

The Cody-Salsbury segregation was ideal for a large-scale irrigation project, and officials from the new agency were after it almost as soon as they had offices to work from. A dam across the Shoshone River would allow them to build a canal across the high northern bench and water a huge tract of land for settlers. Cody himself had made the same assessment, but he was unable to find the funding he needed, and the financial resources of the Reclamation Service far outstripped his. Where he scrambled to raise money in the tens of thousands of dollars, the government planned a network of dams, tunnels, canals, and laterals, and within months had appropriated $2.25 million for the project.[99]

Giving up the segregation was not easy. But as William Cody saw it, if the cards fell right, the government takeover would not hurt his interests. The irrigation works were a very expensive means to an end: making desert into arable, valuable land. He had other prospects on the north side of the Shoshone, including another townsite. As things stood, it was worthless. If the government brought water, though, he could make a tidy sum selling lots. He would not have water rights to sell, but having all those rights to sell along the Cody Canal had not made him a dime. The trick was to get somebody else to pay the high overhead of building and maintaining the canals.

The water, when it came, would turn his desert land to gold. Salsbury and Cody ceded their segregation.

But William Cody, ever the show director, was still convinced he could hurry matters along. He inserted a condition in the documents, stipulating that the federal government had to begin construction of the canals on the north side of the river by January 1, 1904. Should they fail, he would reclaim the segregation and move ahead with private capital—or so he thought.

The government failed to begin construction in time. Cody reneged on the cession and tried to take the segregation back. He had powerful allies in Wyoming, including the governor, Fenimore Chatterton, who saw the showman as a source of cash for a tax-starved state. As the governor told officials, "It has been our experience that Wyomingites through practical business methods rapidly push things to completion, and it is the intention of the land board to stand by Col. Cody, one of our citizens who has demonstrated his ability to do things."[100]

Allegedly, that "ability to do things" included the recruitment of new investors, and it was the prospect of new money that made Cody anxious to keep his options open on the northern bank of the Shoshone River. While touring Britain with the Wild West show in 1903, Cody persuaded a group of wealthy Englishmen to examine the Big Horn Basin. Whether they saw this trip as merely a vacation or an investment tour is not clear, but according to Cody, they struck an agreement. If the canal venture looked profitable, he explained a few years later, "they were to finance and build the North Side canal, for which I was to receive $75,000 in cash, besides a portion of the stock of said company." In late 1903, Cody announced that he had secured $3.5 million in new investment.[101]

But back in the United States, various old allies became alarmed that Cody, by reneging on his agreement to give up the segregation, was going to delay the federal government's development of the north side. The Burlington & Missouri River Railroad had built its spur line to Cody town directly through the Cody-Salsbury segregation. Irrigation would mean a vast increase in the area's appeal for settlers and a dramatic increase in traffic along the rails. Buffalo Bill and his English party had barely reached the West before they were waylaid by representatives from the railroad. "On my arrival at Chicago with these gentlemen I met some of the Burlington railroad officials who were very anxious for me to turnover the North Side proposition to the Reclamation Service." Further down the line, the encounter was repeated. "At Omaha I met other Burlington officials who were very anxious for me to do the same." Cody assured railroad officials these new investors had the money to see the job to completion, and insisted that he and his guests at least continue the tour of the Big Horn Basin.

Cody knew well that the railroad companies would not look after his interests, and he could hardly have been surprised that Burlington officials wanted him to drop the segregation so the government could build waterworks all along their railroad line.

But there was another surprise, and a greater disappointment, waiting for him at the town that bore his name. Cody settlers, still struggling with the inadequate, privately funded Cody Canal, and chagrined at the failure of the Shoshone Irrigation Company to provide a modern waterworks for the town, now bridled at William Cody's meddling in the government project across the river.[102] "On our arrival at Cody the citizens of this place called a mass meeting for the purpose of getting me to consent to letting the Government, as they called it, have the North Side segregated lands for which I held a concession."[103]

As the Republican Club of Northern Big Horn County put it, only government money could guarantee "the construction of this giant system" of ditches which would "bring to our community thousands of energetic citizens, and will add millions of dollars to our property valuations" through "the development and creation of fine ranches and homes."[104] The message to the showman could not have been clearer: get out of the way.

As Cody recalled it, "the Burlington officials and the citizens of Cody and Garland [another town to the east] were so anxious to have the Reclamation Service handle this proposition that I finally consented to their wishes. I gave my English friends a hunt in the Rockies and they returned to England. Seeing how I was pressed to give up the enterprise they did not blame me for asking them to abandon the proposition."[105]

The English hunting party likely had no strong interest in the investment. Cody may have floated news of the $3.5 million investment as a bluff, hoping to force the Reclamation Service to begin construction of the north side canal. If so, in the end, the ruse worked best on the railroad officials, who gave Cody a half interest in their town site of Ralston, thirty miles east of Cody town and on the north side of the Shoshone River, to persuade the showman to give up his segregation.[106] If it was a bluff, then it was about all he had left. By late 1903, Cody and his partners had lost a lot of money. Unless the Englishmen believed that water would somehow grow their investments the way it grew alfalfa, the ditch investment could hardly have been appealing. Even with the Cody Canal mostly complete, William Cody swore under oath in 1904, "We are behind on the canal, as our books will show, to the tune of about $180,000.00"[107] He never made that money back.

In February 1904, Cody released the segregation for good.[108] Thus far, the irrigation business had not broken him, but neither had it provided the retirement, farm, and home he had imagined it would. He now at least had a claim to another town site on the north side. When the government water came through government ditches, he would sell the land. He was not yet done with the Reclamation Service.

In the decade he had been active in the Big Horn Basin, his aspirations for retired domestic bliss had suffered bruising setbacks. He was about to inflict another. In January 1904, as he grappled with abandoning his segregation, he filed another set of legal papers in Cheyenne, making him plaintiff in his own lawsuit against his wife. Buffalo Bill Cody, defender of the settler's cabin, had filed for divorce.

CHAPTER SEVENTEEN

Showdown in Cheyenne

Had Cody's divorce petition succeeded, it would have marked his second dissolution of a long-term partnership in recent years. When Nate Salsbury died after a prolonged illness late in 1903, William Cody found himself unhindered by the man's professional demands for the first time in eighteen years.

Cody still had a managing partner in James A. Bailey, of Barnum & Bailey, who arranged the show's travel schedule and transportation. Salsbury himself had brokered the agreement with Bailey in 1894, when he realized that failing health would keep him from traveling extensively. But Bailey was a behind-the-scenes operator, with no desire for the limelight. His extensive inventory of railroad cars made him a worthwhile partner. He managed the transportation for the show, and he was essentially the local manager in every town where the show appeared.[1]

But Bailey was never a friend. He did not link his name to the show, was less invested in it, and had no personal influence over the star. In this sense, Salsbury's absence left Cody shorthanded, and it may have been responsible for some of his poor decisions. The relationship between Cody and Salsbury was often strained. Their partnership in this respect was akin to that of Rodgers and Hart or Lennon and McCartney, that is, famously creative and notoriously difficult. As co-owners of the show, Salsbury and Cody made decisions about it together. The managing partner was sometimes more careful than Cody in watching the show's bottom line. But even if the Big Horn Basin was a bad investment, Salsbury had not only joined the Shoshone Irrigation Company but encouraged Cody to find other investors, too. Salsbury himself made some disastrous choices for the show, dreaming up the money-losing Ambrose Park appearance of 1894. The next year he created *Black America*, which proved an expensive failure. Both of these drove Cody to invest even more time and effort in the Big Horn Basin in hope of making up show losses.

Tensions between the partners grew. Salsbury knew he was dying. His illness made him less temperate. Perhaps Cody showed signs of impatience.

The managing partner anticipated a split with Cody, or a posthumous legal assault on the Salsbury heirs. Sometime after 1901, Salsbury sat down at his home in Long Branch, New Jersey, to dictate (or possibly type himself) a scathing history of his career with William Cody and the Wild West show. [2]

What he wrote was not for publication, he said, but if it were, he would call it "Sixteen Years in Hell with Buffalo Bill." His grievances were many, starting with Cody's hedonism. "Cody makes a virtue of keeping sober most of the time during the Summer Season, and when he does so for the entire season, he looks on himself as a paragon of virtue and self-abnegation." But when he drank, "he forgets honor, reputation, friend, and obligation, in his mad eagerness to fill his hide with rot gut of any kind." As a rule, said Salsbury, "he would keep at it until he fell so sick that he could not move, or as he used to put it, 'His liver flopped,' and then would co[m]e the strain of getting his head reduced."

Cody's indulgence was nowhere near as irritating as his permanent sense of entitlement. "When he sobers up a little, he is so conceited as to imagine he has had a perfect right to get drunk, no matter at what cost to his associates in business, and takes it for granted that he is so great a man that all the world excuses him because he is a hero and an 'Old Timer' who saved America from going back to the wilderness [as] Columbus found it."

Combined with his womanizing, these habits endangered the reputation of everybody in his orbit. In Rome, Cody visited the homes of dignitaries when he was so drunk "that he could hardly get into his carriage," and, worse, with a woman in tow. Ushered into the drawing room of the British minister, "he remarked to his concubine that 'We can beat this in Nebrasky at a fifty-cent admission shakedown.'"

Salsbury grimaces through his typescript memoir with his head in his hands. "And this is the gentleman that ladies and gentlemen have delighted to honor. Bah."[3]

This "Tin Jesus on horseback" demanded continual attention and adulation. He had "abused every man in our employ who ever showed that he did not regard the Hero as the head and front of the Showman's Universe."[4] Salsbury remarked on the new biography of Cody written by his sister, Helen Cody Wetmore. She called it *Last of the Great Scouts,* "and if she will only insure the verity of her title page," wrote Salsbury, "she will be doing humanity a service. A man may be a 'Great Scout' and a d——d rascal at the same time." Salsbury had had a bellyful of Cody's frontier heroics. After all, "as a private soldier during the Civil War, I smelled more powder in one afternoon at Chickamauga, than all the 'Great Scouts' that America has ever produced ever did in a lifetime."[5]

Cody's misbehavior and ungratefulness were all the more insulting, in Salsbury's eyes, because Buffalo Bill was his creation, "a commercial proposition that I discovered when I invented the Wild West, and picked him out for the Figure Head." He boldly (and incorrectly) proclaimed, "I invented every feature of the Wild West Show that has had any drawing power." To hear the managing partner tell it, he could have been just as successful with any number of other men as his star. "There were others, and there will be others," he wrote, pointing to Cody's many imitators. If any of them "had had the good fortune to be good looking, tall, dashing, and the subject of romantic tale telling for a decade, there would have been some other commercial propositions that could have been developed."[6] More than anything else, Nate Salsbury wanted the world to know that he, the manager, was the reason for Buffalo Bill's worldwide fame. In 1885, on the train from Montreal to Toronto, Salsbury promised Cody "that I would land him at 'the foot of the throne of England.'" Two years later, Cody performed before Queen Victoria. As we have seen, Cody had that ambition in mind before he ever met Nate Salsbury. But the managing partner recalled the idea as his alone. "Of course, he forgot the promise and took the kudos."[7]

Salsbury's rant, though wounded and defensive, still contains some suggestions about the sources of Cody's enduring appeal and creativity, particularly his childlike enthusiasms which sometimes veered into childish impulsiveness. "It would not be so bad," wrote the partner in one of his more reflective moments, "if he had the common intelligence of a child, or if he could remember from one day to another the experience he has already passed through." At least then the show's star would not need to spend large amounts of time "apologising for his BLUNT WESTERN WAYS. . . . I have heard so much of the manly behavior of the WESTERN man since I have been mixed up with him, that I might believe in it, if I did not have Cody for a partner."[8]

The managing partner's account is so wry and vivid that Cody biographers may be forgiven for finding it irresistible. Watching the downward trajectory of the Wild West show after 1900, it is easy to believe much of what rolled off that typewriter in Long Branch. In one of his last acts on this earth, the old comic Salsbury entered the debate that swirled around Cody—Is he a hero, or is he a charlatan?—and came down firmly on the side of the latter.

But for today's readers, perhaps the most fascinating aspect of Salsbury's story is how familiar it is. The drama of the sensible, businesslike manager struggling to contain the unappreciative star is a central narrative of modern culture. In the century since Salsbury's death, his bitter memoir has been echoed by the laments of managers for movie icons, athletes, and rock stars, including Fatty Arbuckle, Babe Ruth, and the Beatles. These stories resonate for audiences in part because of their grand psychological drama, in which the manager plays superego, the containing force, to the id of the star, thereby playing out internal tensions of the consumer era as effectively as a Greek tragedy.

More directly, the recurrent complaint of the manager about the star reflects tensions within modern entertainment itself, whose stars must appeal to mass audiences, a task which requires them to be in part products of professional booking, travel, and publicity staffs, and partly the projection of less quantifiable forces such as charisma and talent.

The tensions between manager and star that pervade Salsbury's account emerged in the era's popular literature at the very moment that Buffalo Bill reached his apogee. They were reflected in George Du Maurier's 1890 novel *Trilby*, which was the source of the Svengali legend. As we have seen, they were also at the heart of Bram Stoker's relationship with Henry Irving, and were central to the novel *Dracula*, which appeared only a few years before Salsbury wrote his account. Salsbury probably never read Stoker's novel. But by the end of his life, he likely would have sympathized with Stoker's fear that the man whose career he managed had drained him of all vitality.

Indeed, the comparison of Salsbury and Stoker suggests the sense of awe and wonder, fear and admiration, that Cody's celebrity inspired in his closest partners. Even dripped in Salsbury's vitriol, we see Cody's irrepressible charisma. He is innocent, needy, and playful. His energy and his appetites are both boundless. Most of all, he exerts a curious power over his audience, which Salsbury exploits but which he only half understands. Recalling the meeting with Pope Leo XIII in Rome, Salsbury wrote that the Sistine Chapel was packed with worshippers that day. The pope, however, was drawn to Buffalo Bill. "As he passed the spot where Cody and myself were standing he looked intently at Cody," recalled the manager, "who looked a picture in his dress coat and long hair." The costume would have been ridiculous on anybody else. Cody was "the only man that I have ever known that could wear it without exciting laughter." Cody bowed his head as the pope passed. "His Holiness spread his hands in token of his blessing, and the good Catholics around us looked with envy at Cody during the balance of the ceremonies."

But in contrast to this sense of wonder, what haunts every word of Salsbury's memoir, are his half-articulated fears. He was terrified of a Cody legal assault, which might deprive him and his family of their share of the Wild West show, which he had worked so hard to sustain. "I have always realized the slender hold I have had on a man that would not scruple to throw me out at a moment's notice if he dared."[9]

For all Salsbury's complaints, he remained with Cody to the end of his life. Despite his intimate knowledge of Cody's many foibles, he too found the star irresistible. This fact seems to have puzzled Salsbury. His hastily composed memoir offers plenty of ammunition for any future showdown with Cody in court. But it also hints at Salsbury's unease with his own vulnerability to Cody's spell. The manager's vehemence could not disguise his own uncertainty. He wanted to believe he created Cody. But in the end, he feared he merely orbited him like all those ignorant fans, suffering the star to abuse him like some lackey. In Salsbury's hands, Cody emerges as beautiful and horrifying, magnificent and monstrous. In Salsbury's deathbed gaze, Buffalo Bill flickers between real and fake, hero and showman, demigod and demon.

———————

SALSBURY'S MEMOIR remained private until years after Cody died. But in a curious way, many of his complaints about the man were echoed in public soon after, when Louisa Cody refused to grant her husband of almost four decades a divorce, and went to court to contest his petition. The trial that followed became a press scandal and the greatest public relations disaster of Buffalo Bill's long career. When William and Louisa Cody faced off in a courtroom, with their lawyers and witnesses, they scripted their marriage into dueling narratives, each battling for the sympathy of the judge. This was a contest in which the old storyteller and showman should have been an easy victor. But as the trial rapidly became a scandal in the mass press, it became a show of its own. Louisa Cody retreated to the settler's cabin, announced her loving devotion to a befuddled old husband, and pleaded with the court to make him desist from his scabrous attacks on her dignity, and especially on her marriage. Meanwhile, William Cody found himself cast as the circling antagonist, the savage bent on destruction of his own home. He was not to have the ending he wanted.

To understand why his suit for divorce went so wrong, we have to understand how central his image as a family man had remained to the Wild West show. To complete the narrative of frontier settlement, show programs emphasized not just his abilities as Indian fighter and hunter, but his accomplishments as a progressive pioneer, who not only conquered the West but domesticated it. His earliest show programs had featured pictures of his comfortable home in North Platte, where he had settled "to enjoy its fruits and minister to the wants and advancements of the domestic circle with which he is blessed."[10] Cody expanded on this image in the 1893 program, by compressing a pair of images on one page, with a poem sandwiched between them. At the top of the page was an image of a savage frontier, a pen-and-ink sketch of Buffalo Bill "Lassoing Wild Horses on the Platte in the Old Days." Below was a photograph of cattle grazing peacefully in front of the Victorian home and a barn clearly labeled "Scout's Rest Ranch," with the caption " 'Buffalo Bill's' Home and Horse Ranch on the Old Fighting Ground of the Pawnee and Sioux."

The narrative sequence was clear, from top to bottom: the progress from frontier to pastoral countryside, from war to peace, and even from open space to domestic space, had been made possible by Buffalo Bill.

The march of civilization is made all the more apparent in the movement from pen-and-ink illustration at the top to photograph at the bottom, and in the transformed nature in the two scenes. The animals in the bottom image do not need lassoing: they graze peacefully, and they even face the same direction, right, like words on the page. Perhaps the most salient component of the bottom image is Buffalo Bill's house, slightly to the left. It is a remarkable Gilded Age middle-class home, planted in the Nebraska prairie in front of a row of trees. Audiences would not need any prompting to associate this elegant home with a wife. The message was clear: by subduing the frontier, Buffalo Bill made homes possible. And he made it possible to keep women—or better, wives—inside them.

Midpage, between the two images, is a telling poem, "Lines Inspired on Witnessing the Prairie Chief Caressing His Baby Daughter, Little Irma Cody":

> *Only a baby's fingers patting a brawny cheek,*
> *Only a laughing dimple in the chin so soft and sleek,*
> *Only a cooing babble, only a frightened tear,*
> *But it makes a man both brave and kind*
>   *To have them ever near.*
> *The hand that seemed so harsh and cruel,*
>   *Nerved by a righteous hate*
> *As it cleft the heart of Yellow Hand,*
>   *In revenge of Custer's fate,*
> *Has the tender touch of a woman,*
>   *As rifle and knife laid by,*
> *He coos and tosses the baby,*
>   *Darling "apple of his eye."*

Thus the prairie centaur featured in the top illustration, the vengeful slayer of "Yellow Hand," has been domesticated by the daughter—and the wife who provided her—in the bottom image. In a limited way, the frontier hero has become a paragon of the new, suburban "masculine domesticity," which situated men in closer proximity to family and home than in previous generations.[11]

So audiences were astonished to read in major newspapers, in the early

LASSOING WILD HORSES ON THE PLATTE IN OLD DAYS.

LINES INSPIRED ON WITNESSING THE PRAIRIE CHIEF CARESSING HIS BABY DAUGHTER
LITTLE IRMA CODY.

Only a baby's fingers patting a brawny cheek,
Only a laughing dimple in the chin so soft and sleek,
 Only a cooing babble, only a frightened tear,
But it makes a man both brave and kind
 To have them ever near.
The hand that seemed harsh and cruel,
 Nerved by a righteous hate

As it cleft the heart of the Yellow Hand,
 In revenge of Custer's fate,
Has the tender touch of a woman,
 As, rifle and knife laid by,
He coos and tosses the baby,
 Darling "apple of his eye."

—*Richmond.*

"BUFFALO BILL'S" HOME AND HORSE RANCH ON THE OLD FIGHTING GROUND OF THE PAWNEE AND SIOUX.

*Cody's image hinged on his being a domesticator of the frontier (top) through
the establishment of the family home (bottom), particularly at the Scout's Rest
Ranch—where Louisa refused to live. Buffalo Bill's Wild West 1893 Program,
author's collection.*

months of 1904, that after thirty-eight years of marriage, Buffalo Bill Cody was suing his wife for divorce. The family, however, was not surprised. The 1890s had been no kinder to the Cody marriage than any of the previous decades. In 1893, while he was showing in Chicago, Louisa made a surprise visit to the house where she had heard that he was living with Katherine Clemmons. She did not find Clemmons. Louisa tore the place to pieces. Upon her return to North Platte, she told her staff, "I cleaned out the house."[12]

In 1898, she went to New York and took a room at the Astoria. She called her husband at the Hoffman House, where the phone was answered by a press agent named Bess Isbell. This time, she upended her own room, and William Cody paid the bill.[13]

Mistresses aside, their most constant bone of contention was his Scout's Rest Ranch, over which she struggled to gain control, although she refused to live in it. Under pressure from Louisa, William Cody's sister Julia and her husband, Al Goodman, had vacated the premises in 1891, so that Arta and her husband, Horton Boal, could manage the property. Although Goodman returned to manage it again in 1894, he left for good in 1899.[14] Goodman and the other managers and foremen of the ranch took their orders from William Cody, but all of them complained of interference, even hostility, from his wife, who constantly countermanded Cody's orders and imposed demands of her own. As time passed, there may have been confusion about who was in charge. William Cody corresponded with ranch managers and continued to give them advice about how to handle the ranch. "I sent out . . . one of my old dining room tents," he wrote one of them, "to cover the [hay]stacks with . . . to keep the exposed stack from getting wet."[15] He advised them on confrontations with Louisa right up to the time he filed the divorce petition. But in 1900, soon after Al Goodman left, he handed the ranch over to Louisa with a one-line, unpunctuated message: "The ranch is yours take it run it to suit yourself."[16] He returned home to North Platte for a brief Christmas break in 1901. After that, he ceased his visits to the town or to Louisa.[17]

William Cody's petition for divorce rested on two complaints. First, he made the stunning accusation that Louisa had many times threatened to poison him. Second, and more banal, was the charge that she had driven him "from his former home in North Platte, Nebraska, and has at divers times refused" to let him "bring his friends and guests" to that home. At times when he did, Louisa "would make it so unpleasant for him and his guests they were forced to leave." His married life was "unbearable and intolerable" in these conditions.[18]

The nation's newspapers quickly cast the drama as a tongue-in-cheek

Wild West show. "Intrenched in a legal fastness and surrounded by a band of brave attorneys, who know every byepath [sic] of the Wyoming divorce laws, the hero of the thrillers of two generations started today to fight his way to marital freedom," wrote one reporter. On the other side, "Mrs. Cody, surrounded by another brave band of attorneys, is determined to fight to the last ditch, for she asserts the colonel wants the divorce only in order to marry another woman."[19]

The newspaper narrative turned the celebrity divorce trial into entertainment. But understanding how William Cody understood his marriage and his life, and why he lost this case, requires examining a very different story. The divorce trial was in a sense a battle of narratives, and William Cody's charges told a familiar and popular tale. For all the tensions over money and property that checkered their marriage, the heart of his case was the sensational allegation of the poison threat. Wild West show programs had long scripted Buffalo Bill's home, especially Scout's Rest Ranch, as the domesticated triumph of the frontiersman. The poison charge emplotted both Codys into a quite different drama, one in which an evil woman lured her husband to provide home and wealth, and then poisoned him to gain control of the property.

This was, indeed, the plot of *Lucretia Borgia*, a popular melodrama in the nineteenth century, and one which so appealed to William Cody that by the late 1860s he had named his favorite buffalo rifle after the treacherous title character. Whether or not he was aware of the similarities between his accusations and the play, the old showman's complaint resonated with the dark side of the domestic dream, the nightmare of the deceiving woman who strikes out from the heart of the home where the man believes he is safest. As various scholars have observed, this narrative is a mythic trope as old as the home itself, and a powerful undercurrent running against the popular enthusiasm for home and domesticity in the late nineteenth century.[20]

William Cody's first attempt at divorce, more than twenty years before, had halted when little Orra Cody suddenly died. Nothing would stop this one from proceeding, but the couple's bitterness was compounded by another tragedy. Weeks after William Cody filed the petition, daughter Arta suddenly died of "organic trouble." Her life had become a tragedy in itself. Her first husband, Horton Boal, committed suicide in 1902, leaving her with two infant children. She remarried in January 1904, at a small Denver wedding which her father attended. Her new husband, Dr. Charles Thorp, worked as a surgeon for the Northern Pacific railroad. But within a month, she was dead.[21]

With the heartbroken parents locked in a court battle, the funeral was a disaster. Upon hearing of Arta's sudden death, William Cody sent a telegram to Louisa, asking to put "personal differences" aside while they buried their daughter.[22] Louisa herself may have been attempting a reconciliation at the time Arta died. Arta's two children had been visiting Louisa when Arta sent word that she was very ill and was about to have surgery, from which she did not expect to recover. Louisa and the children immediately began journeying to Arta's home in Spokane. She had resented the Cody sisters for many years, but in Denver she asked her husband's youngest sister, May Cody Bradford, to come along and help her, and she may have intended the invitation as a gesture to her husband.

But now, at the Bradford house in Denver, devastated by the telegram announcing Arta's death, Louisa was further hurt and infuriated by her husband's message. She refused to reconcile merely for the duration of the funeral. According to May Cody Bradford, she wanted to send a telegram accusing William Cody of murdering their daughter by breaking her heart with the divorce petition. Relatives persuaded her to soften her language.[23] William Cody, on his way to meet the family funeral procession in Omaha, received a message telling him his wife believed he "broke Arta's heart. Suit entered under false accusation." Louisa would accept no temporary reconciliation. "Never for only a while, forever or not at all."[24]

The couple met in Omaha and did not speak, as they made their way with Arta's body to Chicago and on to its last resting place in Rochester, New York. The procession was tearful and tense. They rode in separate rooms of the sleeper car. As it became clear he would not attempt a reconciliation with her, Louisa threatened to "denounce him as Arta's murderer from the grave of his dead child."[25]

But she was silent as she put her first daughter in the ground, beside the graves of Kit and Orra Cody. At the conclusion of the funeral, William Cody left for New York City. As he left, he turned to his old friend Frank Powell and asked him to see if Louisa was open to a reconciliation. According to Powell, a man for whom Louisa had only contempt, she refused. She made her way back to Nebraska, still accompanied by her sister-in-law. Stopping over in Chicago, she raged at William Cody, shook her fist at his sister, and swore, "I will bring you Codys down so low the dogs won't bark at you."[26]

The divorce trial did not begin until almost a year after Arta's death, by which time William Cody had added two more complaints to his petition. The first was that Louisa refused to sign mortgages, which made it impossible for him to carry on his business. The final charge was that she had subjected him to "extreme cruelty" in charging him with Arta Cody's murder.[27] Testimony was made in depositions, many of them in open court in Cheyenne, before an audience of some three hundred "women, cowboys, and officers from Fort Russell," according to the press.[28] At the close of proceedings, the judge would render his decision.

The opening testimony by William Cody was actually made in a deposition the year before, in which he told the court of his long, unhappy marriage to Louisa—of his fights with her from their earliest days, his venture to "the end of the line" to escape his unhappy home, her discontent with his buffalo hunting and her disappointment in him upon the failure of his town of Rome. She disliked his life in the theater, was jealous of friendly actresses, and was always critical of him. "My home was made disagreeable to such an extent that I am ashamed to say . . . that I chose the saloons and the wine cup at times in preference."[29] In recent years, matters had become worse. "Well, kiss it goodbye, that's gone," she taunted him every time she signed a mortgage to provide cash for the Wild West show. Finally, she "refused to sign her name to any piece of paper at all for me." He had outstanding mortgages he could not pay, and other properties he needed to sell. But "as she will not sign any papers, I find myself unable to conduct my affairs in a businesslike manner."[30]

The allegations of poisoning began to seem almost credible as his witnesses painted a picture of Louisa's generally toxic personality. One seamstress who had worked for Louisa Cody related that she openly disdained her husband.[31] Another, Florence Parker, the daughter of a ranch manager who had departed because of Louisa's constant interference, said that Louise had bragged of beating Irma Cody with a buggy whip and burning her with a match, that she consulted fortune-tellers about her husband "to get power over him so she could get possession of his wealth," that she drank frequently, that "very vulgar" speech was "the most prominent part of her conversation," that she often said she hated her husband, and that she killed his prize greyhound dogs with poison-laced crackers.[32]

Mrs. John Boyer, the wife of another ranch foreman and manager, who lived at Scout's Rest for nine years, said that on her first meeting with Louisa Cody, the wife of America's most famous showman complained that her husband "had ladies traveling with him, or women rather, that made him unloyal to her," and that he was "immoral with any woman that he met." Over subsequent years, "she told me all."[33]

Mrs. Boyer said the woman used "such bad language" in her own home "that ladies could not stay there." She drank heavily—"toddies," wine, and "beer by the case." In years past, "she used to take a drink the first thing in the morning," and when she drank, "you could smell it on her." She refused to entertain his guests, ladies and gentlemen alike, and she accused her husband's friends of stealing household trinkets. The Boyers hired a housemaid, a young woman who had a baby out of wedlock, to work in their quarters at Scout's Rest. Louisa Cody showed up to demand they fire the maid. Mrs. Boyer refused. Louisa "spit in the baby's face," and accused Mrs. Boyer "of keeping that girl in the house for my husband's use." Mrs. Boyer seized Mrs. Cody by the throat and pushed her bodily out the front door.[34]

Mrs. Boyer's testimony was the heart of the poisoning evidence. She recounted how Louisa had bought a concoction called "Dragon's Blood" from a gypsy camp near North Platte and put it in his coffee. Concerned that it would do him harm, "I switched the cups," Mrs. Boyer recalled, "and it made her sick."[35]

One day when William Cody was intoxicated in their home, Louisa Cody told Mrs. Boyer, "I will rule Cody or ruin him." She called him to the top of the stairs and handed him a cup of tea, saying, "Willie, drink this it will do you good." He drank it, then lurched toward the bathroom door and collapsed, vomiting as he fell. "You are a drunken brute," Louisa told him. Some of the hired men put him to bed and called the doctor. "The girl that was working there, Katie Burke, said 'She will surely kill him this time for she has worked on this tea all day.' " Mrs. Boyer claimed that she had confronted Louisa Cody, and been told that nobody would believe her if she said anything. On other occasions Louisa told her that the potion would make him "so weak that she could get him to sign papers" and "she wanted him to make his ranch over to her."[36]

Mrs. Boyer saw Louisa slip more of the potion into a bottle of whiskey on the buffet in their home, just before a banquet honoring her husband. Then she set about "nagging and jawing first about one thing and then another and he said 'Oh Mamma, hush,' and he went over and grabbed the bottle and took a drink and said 'The only way a man can stand you is to drink.' " By the time he rose to speak at the banquet, he was practically incoherent. Moments later, he collapsed at the table, whereupon he was bodily carried from the room.[37]

Cody's banquet speech, or rather his failure to give a coherent speech, became a central moment in the trial narrative. Other witnesses, including his sister May, said that he had complained his legs were numb, and that he felt worse than he ever had in his life, moments before he fainted.[38] Outside, with his stomach in agony, he walked to Guy Laing's saloon, where he climbed onto a billiard table and lay facedown, gripping the railings on both side "in a way as to relieve the agony in my stomach." Half an hour later, he stood up, went to his carriage, and went home.[39]

As riveting as the story of Louisa the Poisoner was for the public, Cody had not reckoned with the powerful countermythology of the home and the domestic order which his show had been entwined with, and in many ways reinforced, for a generation. Very quickly, his wife's attorneys cast William

Cody as an aggressor against his own home. Throughout the trial, Louisa Cody exploited the public's fascination with homemaking as salve to the deleterious influence of nomadism. She played the role of a loyal wife aggrieved by a befuddled, peripatetic husband, whose drinking, infidelities, and unsteady business hand became primary exhibits in the case against him.

The strategy of Louisa's lawyers was to depict the Cody household as loving, warm, and generally happy. In this story of the Cody marriage, William Cody appeared as an affectionate and kind man, but with an unfortunate thirst for alcohol and unrestrained lusts for women. Only through his marriage to Louisa Cody could his anarchic energies and unsavory appetites be contained.

Her attorneys built this case from the most respectable materials. Her witnesses were largely North Platte's middle-class professionals, including bankers, doctors, and lawyers. "She always conducted herself as a loving wife," testified local attorney Beach "Judge" Hinman. "I have never known there to be the least friction between the two."[40] Edith Colvin, who stayed at the Cody household for five weeks in the fall and winter of 1901, described how Louisa headed up a crowd of people who welcomed her husband at the train station when he returned for Christmas, bearing gifts—steel purses and a cut-glass serving set—for his wife and daughters. Their home was decorated with his image in paintings and busts and photographs. She called him "Willie." He called her "Mamma." During Christmas dinner, he treated her "very nicely, indeed."[41]

Others noted that Cody had seemed perfectly happy in 1901, the last time he had been in North Platte. He had discussed plans to build a Masonic temple for the town. He never made any suggestion that he was planning to leave. He ceased to return after that year. Many wondered why.[42]

Still others described Louisa Cody's behavior toward guests as "uniformly courteous," and her conduct toward her husband as "never anything but proper." She was an excellent hostess. "She was always very fully occupied in entertaining his guests. I never heard her say an unkind word to him, or manifest any ill-feeling of any description at any time." Her reputation as wife and mother was "beyond reproach." Another "never saw anything" to indicate trouble and bad feeling. Friends of three decades, including the Grand Master of Nebraska Masons, Frank Bullard, described her as a teetotaler, and the contention that she used "vulgar, obscene, and profane language" was "ridiculous. I never heard of such a thing. . . . I never heard her use a word that even approached that."[43]

Dr. E. B. Warner, fourth-term mayor of North Platte and delegate to the 1892 National Republican Convention, had known the Codys for twenty-five years. He told the court that Louisa Cody was "perfectly ladylike; an ideal hostess," and a loving wife and mother.[44] Said Mrs. W. H. Turpie, a friend of Irma's who was a neighbor of the Codys for several years, "It always seemed to me that she simply idolized him; as much as she could any person. She was very much wrapped up in him, and doing everything for his pleasure, as far as I could see. . . ."[45] Another neighbor who visited often with Louisa testified that Louisa once showed her a newspaper report of her husband's infidelities, but even then, she never said a word against him.[46]

In the strategy of Louisa's attorneys, the public face of the marriage was what mattered. If marriage was by definition a public institution, the foundation of home and civil society, then the judge would have to accept its public face as evidence of how well it ordered the chaotic life of the showman. If a marriage looked happy, it must be happy.

Louisa's attorneys also illuminated the challenges facing the wife and domesticator, by painting William Cody as dissolute and unable to function on his own. Most of the witnesses on this point were longtime friends of both Codys. They proved to be not only enthusiastic in defense of his wife, but so eager to fulminate against Buffalo Bill that one detects a sense of aggrievedness on their part, as if the disgrace of the scandal was only the latest of the old showman's many offenses. Their bewilderment over his abandonment of their town for Cody, Wyoming, apparently added to a popular resentment at being dragged into his marital troubles. To judge by their testimony, they felt their affection for Buffalo Bill was poorly repaid with this self-serving trial. They hit back hard, and their harshest attack was their testimony about Cody's drinking.

Alcohol and its control were major social and political issues in the nineteenth century. To temperance advocates, alcohol was the despoiler of the home, an evil force that corrupted men, broke their marriages, ruined their talents, and left their children destitute. Drink was savagery in a bottle.

Indeed, temperance advocates deployed the symbol of the home and womanly domesticity in much the same way as Buffalo Bill's Wild West did. As we have seen, Cody himself touted his show camp as a temperance community (although even heavy drinking was not unusual when the cast was out on the town) in order to appeal to the respectable middle class. In the minds of many, the home needed to be protected from alcohol, but a faithful wife and a warm domicile were also the best defense against a man's alcohol abuse. Women dominated temperance campaigns, and they depicted the fight to control alcohol as an expression of women's domesticating influence over the public spaces which men traditionally controlled, especially saloons. They were particularly powerful in the West. Carry Nation began chopping her way to glory in 1900 by attacking Kansas saloons with her hatchet. Less spectacularly, campaigns to ban alcohol were often led by, and corresponded with the rising power of, middle-class women. Thus the nation banned alcoholic beverages with the Eighteenth Amendment in

1919, and empowered women with the right to vote in the Nineteenth Amendment of 1921.[47]

The control of alcohol and its influence thus spoke to the containment of savagery and to anxieties about the home which were central to Cody's show and his myth. Charges of habitual drunkenness struck at the heart of his public persona, and he defended himself vigorously. He testified that drinking never interfered with his business, and moreover that he had quit drinking in 1901. He may have. "Oh but I am enjoying this trip—More than I ever did any before," he wrote a friend that year, "because I am not drinking. Everything looks bright and prosperous." Two months later he was still abstaining. In New York, pulling together his show for another season, he was "feeling like new money. [H]ead clear all the time. . . . My prospects never looked brighter."[48] Charles Wayland Towne, a journalist who went hunting with Cody and several of the showman's old drinking partners in 1903, reported that Cody had become a teetotaler on orders from his doctor.[49]

Whether or not Cody had been on the wagon since 1901, residents of North Platte had not seen him since that year, and they had many stories to tell about Cody's drinking from earlier days. "I have seen him frequently when I thought he was very much under the influence of liquor," both "in h[i]s own home and on the streets," said Frank Bullard.[50] William Cody's attorney told Bullard that Cody did not drink during his show season. Bullard shrugged. "He generally waited until he got here to get drunk."[51] A. F. Streitz, the town druggist, concluded that Cody "has been a hard drinker during his stay in North Platte during these years." Streitz had seen Cody intoxicated "many times," and in fact "the first time I met him in North Platte he was intoxicated."[52] C. M. Newton, a merchant who had known the Codys for fifteen years, said he had seen Cody drunk in public many times. William Cody's attorneys suggested that their client was polite and kind even when drunk:

> Q: He always conducted himself gentlemanly, did he not, during the
> times he was drunk, on the streets?
> A: I think at some times he did not act like a gentleman.
> Q: What caused you to think so?
> A: I think he was too much intoxicated.[53]

Louisa Cody's lawyers proved adept at dredging up old acquaintances to testify about his prior habits. Such people were legion in the Platte country. One recalled events two decades before, when William Cody would make his "headquarters" in Dave Perry's bar, a known resort of prostitutes. When

William Cody's lawyers attempted to mitigate the remark by asking if all saloons did not have prostitutes at the time, the witness, Patrick McEvoy, disagreed. Perry's saloon, he pointed out, "was the only saloon in North Platte that allowed women to go into them." The witness was careful to point out that he had never seen Cody with any of these shady women—but he stayed there most days and much of the night, too. "He would be unable to walk, and the boys would have to haul him in a carry-all, or hack, to take him home."[54] One local cowboy turned up to recall Cody bringing wagons of liquor to the Dismal River roundup when he was part owner of the Cody-North Ranch in the Sand Hills.[55] Still another claimed, "I saw him lying drunk myself right at the store building of Mr. Burke's," near Fort McPherson. Even while he had a wife and baby at the fort, he frequented a bordello near Cottonwood Canyon which "stood on a high knoll, and you could not help seeing him."[56]

In this telling, the story of William Cody was of a man who may or may not have been drinking during his show season, but was unable to stop when he was at home. Ira Bare, editor of a North Platte newspaper, who had known the Codys for more than twenty-three years, concluded "as a rule, when the Colonel drank, he kept on drinking . . . during his presence here, he was more or less under the influence of liquor. . . . I do remember instances when he did not drink, but not often."[57]

How much of these stories was true and how much produced by the alchemy of resentment and memory is impossible to say. The self-deprecating humor of his autobiography, in which he often recalled having too much "tanglefoot," buying drink for his detachment and forgetting to buy food, and scouting hostile territory with brandy-filled canteens, suggest either heavy drinking, or playful derision of the era's potent temperance movement, or both.

But however true or false the testimony about Cody's drunkenness was, the stories reflected the barely concealed antitheatricalism of North Platte, a middle-class Nebraska town which had always been uneasy with William Cody's brand of show business patricianism. Charles Iddings, a prominent mill owner and businessman in North Platte, said that whatever shortcomings of temperament or manners Louisa might have, she was simply more honorable, and credible, than her husband, because she was not in show business. While her husband traveled the world in pampered comfort, she stayed home:

> She has not had the extensive travel, she has not mingled with the best people perhaps in the east and the old country. She has not had a press agent to dress up her little stories or to correct her little imperfections of speech. She simply stayed at home. She has not had a ladies maid to mix

her drinks for her or fix her attire to best advantage. She has simply been a *plain body*, stayed at home and taken good care of the children and such property as she had there. . . . She has been at home most of the time during 23 years.[58]

The description of Louisa Cody as a "plain body" suggested she possessed democratic values of sincerity, modesty, and honesty, which William Cody—ornamented, showy, and extravagant—could not have. She was, said Beach Hinman, "a very industrious woman, and I do not know as I have noticed any extravagance in her living or dress." She had a "certain amount of charge at all times over her ranch and farms. She went out and conducted the business of the farm, which was very extensive in later years." Her habits were "exemplary beyond reproach." Hinman had "never heard a mere hint of any source against her reputation or conduct."[59]

In contrast, her husband's style of living was not moral. When William Cody's attorneys tried to put Hinman on the defensive by pointing out that the showman had taken his daughters with him when he traveled, Hinman demurred. "I guess Arta Cody was with him some of the time, but I don't think the truck he had around with him did his daughters any good."[60] At one time, in Hinman's presence, William Cody "got to ridiculing our Lord and Master, and I took exceptions to it. . . ."[61] In these accounts, Cody's debauchery could be attributed equally to an absence of moral regulation along the frontier—which had long since passed into history but which yet coursed through his person—and to the urban theatrical corruptions in which he immersed himself. In fact, the two forces combined in his person, to create a figure who had lost his balance and fallen into the drunkenness and moral lassitude of the savage.

This drunkard, philanderer, and blasphemer was Louisa Cody's husband, and she begged the court to allow her to remain his wife. "He always was kind to me when in North Platte," said Louisa. "He drank a great deal, but he always was pleasant when he came home." Testifying on her own behalf, between sobs, she denied every charge in the divorce petition. She recalled his last visit home, in 1901, when she arranged the Christmas welcome party for him. He seemed delighted. "He embraced me and kissed me," she said. He left on Christmas night. He held her in his arms until the train was about to leave, then kissed her goodbye. That was the last time he had come home. She knew nothing of poisonings, of dragon's blood, of having treated guests badly. Arta had been devastated by the divorce petition. Louisa's attorneys submitted in evidence the last letter she received from her eldest daughter: "About Papa, oh why did he do it? My heart is just broken over it. I cannot find words to express how dreadfully I feel about it."[62]

Louisa said she had been careful with mortgages only to protect him from their many creditors. She had certainly objected to some guests, but never to their faces. She wanted a reconciliation—if only he would retract the allegations of poisoning.[63]

William Cody's case was not helped by the letters he wrote to her, which her attorneys submitted as evidence of his continuing affection. Reading the first of these letters into the record, her attorney stumbled over his crabbed handwriting. "Better let me read it," interrupted William Cody. "That may be one I wrote on horseback."

He read them all, as if he was playing in a drama. "The venerable showman carried off the role with easy grace and due regard to dramatic values," reported the *Chicago Tribune*.[64]

The letters were indeed affectionate, but they also made a powerful case for Louisa's virtues as a wife. The ideal wife of the Gilded Age stayed at home but was capable of assisting her husband in business. One of her witnesses testified that she was "a good business woman, better than the average," and her husband's correspondence substantiated this.[65] One of his letters reminded her of his $50,000 loss with his Canadian tour of 1885, the financial debacle of Ambrose Park in 1894, and the $10,000 lost in *Black America* in 1895, all as a prelude to explaining to her that his "share of the losses" for the 1900 season amounted to another $10,000. "I had a terrible blow this morning. I got all my printing bills in. Our printing was supposed to cost $60,000 a season, but this year it's $80,000 so I have to pay. . . . This makes an unexpected loss to me of $20,000." The show season a bust, he still had to pay half the expenses of sending the cast home and wintering the livestock. For this year, the expense of running Scout's Rest Ranch would have to be paid with hay and grain sales. "Don't you think it can be made to do it?" he asked her. Signing off as "Papa," he scribbled a PS: "Wish you would read this letter and say nothing to any one."[66]

As the ranch prospered, his reliance on her business abilities grew, and his letters expressed his gratitude.

Say you are getting right down to business—why I am delighted—I never believed you could run that big ranch. . . . But you seem to over come business troubles as well as a man who had been used to it—I am really proud of you as a business manager—Wish I had let you have the ranch years ago. May and June will be two busy months for you, then come on and make me a long visit.

With love
Papa[67]

Although he was loath to lose John Boyer as ranch manager, he supported Louisa when she demanded that Mrs. Boyer leave the ranch after the choking incident in the Boyer house.[68] "I have turned the ranch over to Mrs. Cody and she is boss. You look to her for orders," he told Boyer.[69]

By the end of the summer of 1901, the old showman could not have been more pleased with Louisa's success at a job that had for years exhausted the men he hired. "Say you are relieving me of lots of worry and work, by running the ranch and you are making no fuss about it, as though it was nothing to do." His letters were full of his hopes for Cody town and the Irma Hotel and a military college he hoped to found in the town.[70] He complimented her on her liberal food policy for hired men. He confided personal matters to her. "What makes me so poorly outside of the piles is, I have to[o] much on my mind, so many different interests to look after." Thankfully, he had Louisa. "You have relieved me from the ranch worry—and that don't give me a thought any more for you know more about it than I ever did."[71]

Other witnesses substantiated that she had indeed mortgaged her own North Platte properties, which included three houses and four lots, to help him finance his show and other ventures. Moreover, she paid the mortgages from rents on properties she owned.[72]

The final blow to William Cody's case, however, came in the testimony about his infidelities, which her attorneys skillfully dropped on the packed courtroom three days into the trial. Although the name of Katherine Clemmons had floated through press coverage, she split with William Cody in 1894, when the plays he financed for her reportedly lost $35,000. Soon after, Cody and a prominent "sport" named Fred May were in a fistfight in a Washington, D.C., restaurant over insults exchanged concerning the affair. Subsequently, Clemmons married Howard Gould, son of the notorious robber baron Jay Gould. The same year he filed for divorce, Buffalo Bill Cody filed a $10,000 claim against Clemmons for money lost in supporting her show.[73]

But now, the attention of the court, and the public, turned to William Cody's newest lover, twenty-eight-year-old Bess Isbell, reportedly a press agent first hired by the Wild West show in 1899.[74] Isbell seems to have been the woman who was the center of a Buffalo Bill faux pas during the 1903 show season in London. King Edward VII and Queen Alexandra knew Cody well, having ridden in the Deadwood stage during his debut season in London in 1887. They arrived in the show camp again near the end of its 1903 season, and all went well until the end of their visit. Another press agent, Dexter Fellows, recalled: "Just when we in the press department were congratulating ourselves upon the smoothness with which we had entertained our eminent guests, Bill committed a breach of etiquette which just about made us sick." The royal party were leaving the camp when a young woman holding a large bundle of orchids stepped forward. Cody, "with all the nonchalance he could command, said: 'Oh, Your Majesties, permit me to introduce Miss—— ——, my ward.' "

Because nobody is presented to kings and queens except by royal request, the queen turned away, refusing the orchids. Fellows was mortified. "Happily the newsmen present agreed to forget the incident."[75]

But other witnesses to Cody's affection for Isbell trundled forward, telling tales. John Clair, a former valet for the showman, told the court a sensational story of the affair that Buffalo Bill had carried on since Isbell joined the show. The showman and the lady took adjoining rooms on the road. In Sherman, Texas, Cody asked Clair to give him a rubdown in Isbell's room, while Isbell watched, dressed only in "a sort of a kimona ladies generally wear I understand in their private boudoir." They kissed often, but there were troubles between them. She asked to ride in the parade with Cody one day. He refused. She "sat down on the bed which [was] in Col. Cody's tent and began to sob very bitterly." In 1901, while Arta and Irma visited their father in Buffalo, New York, Clair said, Isbell went out to Cody, Wyoming, from where she sent frequent telegrams.[76]

Key facts of Clair's testimony were supported by Ed Clark, a ranch manager who testified that he had built another bedroom onto Cody's small TE ranch home for Isbell's use. The woman stayed there for several weeks in 1901, and William Cody eventually joined her there that year. They rode together frequently. He deeded her forty acres of his spread at the head of Rock Creek, and handed over some of his calves, ordering Clark and several other hands to mark them with her brand, the $\overline{BQ}$ or "bar BQ."[77]

Cody denounced Clair as a liar who was out for revenge after having been fired from the Wild West show for theft, and dismissed Ed Clark as a temporary ranch hand who was only briefly at the TE.[78] He denied that he and Isbell were romantically involved. He did not take a room in Sherman, Texas, in the year in question, he said, because the show was only there for one day (which was true). In any case, on the road, even his private rooms functioned as semipublic business space, where he was surrounded by "from 1 to 10 people" until he went to bed.[79] There had been no kisses between them that he recalled, although his staff was generally an affectionate crowd. As he explained it, Isbell was merely a hardworking, talented press agent. She secured positive reviews for the show in ladies' magazines, a market that the Wild West show's male press agents "did not or could not succeed in reaching."[80] Such coverage, with its appeal to middle-class women, helped maintain the show's appeal as a family attraction. In this regard, Isbell was indispensable.

Unfortunately, the press agent had fallen ill with tuberculosis. "I have sent quite a number of people out to Cody, Wyoming, who were suffering with tuberculosis." The dry climate aided their recovery. He gave her letters of introduction to many people, including the town's finest young women, who accompanied her to his ranch. He did not give her any property. She paid $200 for her forty-acre ranch, and $15 a head for the cattle. When she was at the TE, she stayed in the guest room, like everyone else who visited him.[81]

Whatever the nature of Cody's relationship with Isbell, the scandal of the lady press agent highlighted the contradiction between the domestic imagery of the show and the professionalism and independence of the women performers and publicists, from Annie Oakley to Bess Isbell, who were central to that image. Cody endorsed woman suffrage as early as 1894, and reiterated that support in later years. But for middle-class consumers the presence of unescorted, single women on the stage and in show life generally was one of the most questionable aspects of the theatrical world. William Cody testified that some of the most bitter disputes with Louisa followed farewell kisses bestowed upon him by young actresses at an end-of-the-season party in the mid-1870s. He felt the kisses were as innocent as handshakes. She felt otherwise. Thirty years later, the same issue reared up to separate Cody from his public, as the proximity of an unmarried lady press agent to his bed—whether in his hotel room or in his semipublic tent—became a titillating detail that undermined his assertions of manly self-restraint.

None of his denials could overcome the allure of stories about the love triangle involving the "siren" press agent.[82] In the context of all the other testimony about his drinking and his dalliances with prostitutes, there was enough to persuade the public, and the judge, that Buffalo Bill Cody was in love with a younger woman.

Of all the accusations, Cody fought this one the hardest. "No, no more marriage for me," he told a journalist. "If I get a divorce I'm going to live on the Cody ranch. I'm going to be buried there and have a red granite buffalo, heroic size, put over my grave on the mesa."[83] He wished only for solitude and respite from the domestic war of his marriage, in the peaceful wilderness of the Big Horn Basin. As he explained in his testimony, he went to Wyoming because "I had never had any peace up to this time during my married life, and I wanted to seek a place where I could have peace in my old age; and I went off up into that new wild country to be away from trouble—domestic trouble."[84]

In the narrative combat of the trial, William Cody and his attorneys cast Louisa Cody as Lucretia Borgia and produced a story about a grasping, treacherous wife who attempted to poison her husband and deny him his rightful wealth.

Louisa Cody and her attorneys cast her in a kind of inverted Wild West show, where she retreated to the settler's cabin only to find her pioneer husband had been corrupted by the temptations of the frontier and now attacked her as enthusiastically as any savage. Buffalo Bill had become a renegade.

It was up to the judge to decide which story was true. Then he could choose its ending. If he chose "Lucretia Borgia," he had no choice but to grant William Cody a divorce. But if he chose the inverted Wild West, he could put a stop to the worst excesses of the prairie turncoat and tell him he was still bound to the settler's cabin.

That he chose the latter was, in a sense, not surprising. "Under the laws of this state incompatibility is not a ground for divorce," wrote Judge Scott in his decision. Extreme cruelty and other indignities were cause for ending a marriage, but where William Cody alleged he had been poisoned, the judge averred that Louisa had only administered "some household remedy" to help him sober up before a banquet. In every way, William Cody was the one guilty of inflicting indignities. Louisa and her attorneys had made some charges about Cody's infidelity which remained unproved. But when they withdrew those accusations, the judge found for Louisa. The Codys were still married.

Louisa's victory was the consequence of her story, which was more convincing than her husband's. In this sense, his defeat reflected his failure to extend certain principles of show business into the trial. He had struggled for years to become a middle-class attraction. But in his divorce case, he presented a melodrama cast with a working-class crowd of seamstresses, ranch foremen, and housemaids. His case hinged on sensational tales told by the hired help. The limits of their credibility became apparent when one witness, the wife of ranch manager Henry Parker, testified that Louisa believed her husband had been the lover of Queen Victoria and later Queen Alexandra. The judge, horrified, ruled the testimony "so manifestly unjust, preposterous, false, and brutal" that he expunged it from the record.[85]

Where there was evidence of her inhospitable behavior toward his guests, the court—and the public—sympathized with Louisa. His guests were theater people and besides, with one exception, they did not appear in court. The only testimony against her on this point came from Robert "Pony Bob" Haslam, a former Pony Express rider and booking agent for the show. He related that during a stay at the Cody house in North Platte, he was awoken by William Cody, who told him "things were not very pleasant" in the house, then took him to another of the Cody homes to sleep. The evidence, decided the judge, did not support the charge of mistreatment.[86]

Louisa's case, in contrast, was built on the testimony of North Platte's "better class": bankers, merchants, newspaper editors, and businessmen. There were some lowbrow moments, as when Henry Blake, a bitter retired soldier, related that the scout had a "bevy" of "dusky maidens" in his bed during the Indian wars.[87] But these were the exceptions, and even then the stories were consistent with tales told by North Platte's most esteemed citizens. In the end, Louisa Cody appeared in a middle-class drama as the defender of her own home against the frontier hero gone bad.

This story was nothing if not entertaining, and the press seized upon it even before the trial began. A reporter from the *Chicago Inter-Ocean* interviewed Louisa in North Platte right after her husband filed his petition for divorce. "Less than a week ago a prairie fire raged west of this place, and among the property threatened was the Cody ranch," began the reporter. "North Platte people to the number of nearly 400 went out" to save the ranch Louisa Cody managed, and "for hours fought to save the buildings from the flames."[88] The article went on to warn that North Platte residents would sally to Louisa's defense in her latest trouble, too.

The prairie fire was an old symbol of savage frontier nature, one which Buffalo Bill had reenacted in *The Drama of Civilization*, in fact. Now he had become the prairie fire.

In his decision the judge admonished William Cody and sent a message to Cody himself, advising him to contemplate the reasons for his own unhappiness. During the trial, Louisa's witnesses hinted that Cody's sisters often tried to intervene in the couple's disputes, on their brother's behalf. The judge urged the showman to weigh his own behavior over the years, counseling "that you and Mrs. Cody had been kept apart, not through the workings of your own brain and heart, but through the influence of your relatives."[89]

Inwardly, back in Paris with the show, Cody raged. Judge Scott "has not had to live with her," he fumed to an old friend. "Nor has he any idea of what a man suffers in his mind when he lives with a woman as cold blooded as a frog and who never sees anything good in any one. . . . He has never had to live with a woman like the one he has tied me to. . . . I would far rather die than to live with her. . . . If there is no way to divide the property then it will have to go. But no court can make me live with her."[90]

How much of each story was true? On some issues, the couple's conflicts are easily understood. Their struggle over property had been going on for many years, and had been at the heart of the original petition for divorce in 1883. His income ebbed and flowed like an ocean tide. At high water, Louisa invested in real estate, which left him hurting during low times. In no small measure, the couple's enduring wealth came from her investments.

Disparate accounts of her language and temper are also easily explained. The consistent testimony by ranch hands and hired help regarding Louisa Cody's bad manners suggests she could be coarse and abusive in private with employees. In public, and among people of her own class, she retained a more decorous persona. She resented the presence of "dirty show people," as she called them, and preferred not to play hostess to them.[91] The court found no reason to censure her for reflecting the general view of the middle class.

The most bizarre charge might also be the most revealing. William Cody's testimony about the banquet of 1893 suggests he was ill from something. Perhaps he was especially drunk. Perhaps he had food poisoning. But there is another possibility. Her attorneys suggested the so-called "Dragon's Blood" was "love powders." Louisa consulted astrologers, said one witness, and Mrs. John Boyer said she bought the potion from a gypsy camp.[92] Weird as it sounds, the charge was not outside the realm of possibility: many of North Platte's middle class flocked to a gypsy camp near the town at one point in the early 1890s.

Louisa's prejudices stand out in the trial. But if it was "love powders," and if, as her lawyer implied, she gave her husband a magic potion to make him love her more, this is only another clue to her bitter loneliness. She was married to a profoundly absent man, by whom she had had four children, three of whom were now gone. Much of the divorce testimony concerned the raising of their youngest and sole surviving daughter, Irma. The young woman was now married and living in the Philippines with her army officer husband. But the testimony kept harking back to her treatment as a child, as if by reprising it, something now departed could be restored. William Cody complained that when she was a girl, he placed her in fine boarding schools, from which Louisa promptly removed her. This was the story with Arta, as well. "I furnished the means to send my children to the best schools in the country and paid for their tuitions at these different schools," and with rare exceptions, "the children were never allowed to remain their full term at school."[93] He thought it obstinate and quarrelsome.

But Louisa was lonely. According to one witness, "Mrs. Cody said that Cody could run around the country as he wanted to, but she wasn't going to leave her baby in school, she was all she had and she was going to bring her home."[94]

During William Cody's deposition in 1904, he faced many questions about marriage and children. "Was it while you were living in Rochester that you lost one or more of the children?" asked an attorney.

"Yes, we lost our little son in Rochester," he replied.

"Do you remember his age at the time of his death?"

William Cody seldom spoke of death, or of people who had died. In all his correspondence, there is barely a mention of any deceased friends or acquaintances. He wrote no poignant words about Wild Bill Hickok, Sitting Bull, or Nate Salsbury. No matter how tragic their deaths, he seldom spoke of the loss.

But the death of his son, Kit Carson Cody, was different. The night Kit died, in 1876, William Cody wrote a letter to his sister, Julia. It was 3:00 a.m. "Julia, God has taken from us *our only* little boy," he began. "Lulu is worn out and sick. . . . I was hundreds of miles away when Lulu telegraphed me and I only got home a few hours before Kitty died. He could not speak, but he put his little arms around my neck as much as to say, Papa has come."[95]

Years later, William Cody faced the question of Kit's age at the time of his death. "He was five years and six months old when he died," he answered. Then, almost pensively, he added, "He was five years, six months, and twenty-two days, if I remember rightly."[96]

The little boy was three decades gone, and if Cody's memory reckoned his age wrong by about two months, the error only cast into sharper relief the sense of loss that sent the father backward through the years, trying to number all the child's days. No doubt his mother did the same, for each of their children. There are a few pictures of Louisa and William Cody together, including family portraits with children. But to contemplate them as mother and father, producers of a family, is to weigh the empty spaces between them. Many families lost children in the nineteenth century. But each death eroded the bond between them, and to have lost so many left the Codys precious little to bridge their many differences.

In another sense, William Cody's show business strengths were his marital undoing. His mastery of ambivalence made him a fine icon for a mass audience. His spectacle invited fantasy. His show programs included excerpts from books in which authors made him a veteran of battles he did not fight. Why correct them? Why not reprint them, and let people believe if they wanted? As we have seen over and over again, spectators could project their fantasies upon him in part because he had been in some genuine Plains conflicts, in part because he looked like a frontier hero was supposed to look, and in part because he did so little to dissuade those who credited him with more greatness than he deserved. He lived extravagantly, and hid the costs and losses. He was a shimmering mirage of frontier success.

He brought the same strategy to his marriage, where it proved much less successful. He wrote affectionate letters to Louisa, and simultaneously carried on his affair with Bess Isbell, allowing both women to see him in their future. He avoided open political battle and partisan strife. In private life, he abhorred confrontation too much to inform Louisa, or even to leave her. "I defy any man or woman to swear that they ever heard me speak an unkind word to her," he told the court. "I do not believe in quarreling with either man or woman."[97]

His happy mask was a central issue in the trial. Her lawyers' strategy hinged on a simple rhetorical question: How could a man who was mistreated at home seem so happy in the eyes of his friends and neighbors? Louisa and other North Platte residents puzzled over Buffalo Bill's sudden abandonment of their town in 1901. He had seemed so affable and happy at the Christmas dinner that year. Then he boarded the train and never returned.

In fact, in 1901 he had turned the ranch over to Louisa. That Christmas, he was again in need of cash. He returned home to ask Louisa for a mortgage or for a signature so he could sell some of their land in Wisconsin. She refused. He left angry.

"When you left the home at North Platte the last time did you not leave on friendly and agreeable relations with Mrs. Cody and her friends?" asked Louisa's attorney.

"No," he said, "she knew that I was displeased at being turned down at the ranch." But he would not allow himself to show it: "I used the same tactics as I always have done through life to try and conceal any words or troubles by putting on a smiling face outwardly while my heart might be aching inside. This I have to do in my business as a showman. No matter how bad the business is, we have learned that our capital and stock is a smiling countenance and a buoyant spirit."[98]

Now, his case lost, he headed back to Paris to catch up with the Wild West show. The public backlash against his divorce petition was harsh. The Masonic lodge in North Platte threatened to have a trial to expel him. Cody, a thirty-third-degree Mason who had been a member since 1869, was mortified. Fortunately, the lodge elected not to hold the trial. But Cody did not return to North Platte for years.[99]

The press lampooned him, and criticism was widespread. In North Platte, the Reverend John Gray hailed the judge's decision from the pulpit of the Episcopal church, where the Cody family had long ago donated two stained-glass windows in honor of their deceased children Kit and Orra:

> The careless, licentious and sensual attitude of too many persons in many of our communities has been held up to execration and shame. The pulpit sends back a resounding "Amen" to the judgment of the "righteous judge." It pledges itself anew to teach the rising generation on these boundless plains cleanness of heart and hand the sanctity of the irrevocable holy and indissoluble relation of the marital covenant.[100]

At least one eastern pastor wrote a note of thanks to Judge Scott. "If there were more men of your stamp to preside at divorce suits there would be less scandalous decisions."[101]

The hero of the "Settler's Cabin" was an outcast.

Adele Von Ohl Parker

S HE WAS A VAUDEVILLE PLAYER with a string of stage ponies when she
arrived in Cleveland, Ohio, in 1929, and discovered there was no place
left to show. Keith's Palace Theater had shut its doors for good, finally bowing to the competition of the movies. But Adele Von Ohl Parker never let
anything so trivial as an obstacle get in her way. She found an abandoned
stockyard, opened a riding school, and taught her pupils to handle both
horses and the business, too.

"Something of a gypsy" was the way one former pupil described her.
They say she came from Plainfield, New Jersey, where she was born in 1886,
and grew up teaching herself to stand atop a galloping horse and winning in
horse shows and riding competitions. She clung to the back of a horse as it
dived into a tank of water on the shore in Atlantic City. She claimed to be
the first show cowgirl to perform "picking up." Whether that was true or
not, she rode with Buffalo Bill's Wild West late in his career, in 1908 and for
a few years after that, then took what she learned into silent movies and the
circus, Ringling Brothers and Barnum & Bailey.[1]

Cleveland marked the end of her circus and movie trail, but not of her
performance. Soon after her riding school began, she located property in
nearby North Olmsted and moved her outfit there. Her brochures advertised "Parker's Ranch" as a place to educate children in riding, as well as
archery, crafts, carriage driving, and gardening (students worked her veg-
etable patch). In subsequent decades, her business repeatedly veered toward
insolvency, only to be rescued by friends and neighbors whose generosity
and admiration allowed her to continue teaching crowds of children.

That she attracted so many students requires some explanation. A tall,
imperious, eccentric woman, she lived alone except for her many animals,
the drifters who happened by looking for work, and the down-and-out circus players who came her way, looking for a place to rest, or a place to die.
She raised foals in the living room, chickens in the bathtub. Once, an old

acquaintance arrived with elephants from a lately busted circus. "We had real elephants to ride," recalled a former student. After the animals demolished her stock of hay, Parker and the children took them to the park, where they swam in the river, until "the park commissioner came up screaming about crazy calls he got that there were elephants in his park."

An unmarried old woman from the circus, she opened her house to all; it was a continual shambles that was anything but domestic. But Cleveland parents warmed to her when they saw the magic she worked with children on horseback. Many of her students came back summer after summer. Grown to adulthood, they looked back fondly on her rare blend of stern instruction and whimsy. Robert Hull recalled teenage days playing capture-the-flag on horseback, feeling "so slapdash almighty man and horseman" with the flag in hand until Adele Parker "came busting out of the woods on [that] George Hanover horse of hers and down you went off your animal, kicking in the shale and wondering what hit you and how you lost the flag."[2]

Of all the activities her students adored—the three-day ride to other towns, the overnight stay on her ranch—the most spectacular was her annual Buffalo Bill Wild West show. A thundering spectacle of stagecoach robbery (she kept a coach half repaired for the show), "Custer's Last Stand" (with Parker herself in the title role), and riding stunts, all performed on the high school track. "Complete and utter pandemonium," was the way one woman recalled it many years later. "I rode and shot a bow and arrow. This was part of her training. 'Just hold on with your legs and thighs dear. . . .' "

In 1955, she received a letter from some of Buffalo Bill Cody's descendants, who tracked her down and invited her to come out to Cody, Wyoming, and visit the Buffalo Bill Museum. She wrote back with enthusiasm: "Long time I have been wanting to keep the name of Buffalo Bill alive and loved, he was the father of the West. Have hoped that I could put on a show to play where he played—a very small show but good stuff—to make enough money to pay for a statue—bronze—or picture—to be put in every library. . . . 'The Spirit of Buffalo Bill.' "

As she described it, her life was every bit as happy as her students thought. Like Buffalo Bill, she was an entrepreneur with a colorful outfit, and she kept an eye on the bottom line which seemed always to slip out from under her. "I have 60 horses—and am in great condition—ride harder now than ever. I am alone—and am very comfortable and happy—with a wonderful business—but I would be happy if it would mean business for the both of us to do all I can for the museum."[3]

She went to Cody, rode in the Wild West show parade, and "gave a superb demonstration of horsemanship in the arena at the Wild West Show on Tuesday Evening," reported the town paper.[4]

That fall, she added to her already legendary reputation as teacher and rider with a display of courage. The sixty-nine-year-old horsewoman was driving eighteen Girl Scouts and three women on a hayride when a drunk driver plowed into the wagon. The impact threw Parker into the street. None of the passengers was hurt, but the horses bolted and the wagon lurched forward. Parker, like the professional she was, had clutched the reins even as the collision tossed her from the wagon. Now, as the horses dragged her along on her belly in the street, she could see that the main beam beneath the wagon was broken in half. If the horses continued to pull, the wagon would come apart, and this small accident might become a real tragedy. Without hesitation, she jammed her arm through the spokes of the nearest wheel, stopping the wagon—and shattering her arm. "Don't worry about me," she told a journalist in the hospital, "I'm tough as a pine knot."[5]

She survived that episode, and lived another dozen years. When she died, her funeral was packed with children. Nobody was quite certain how old she was—some said eighty, others eighty-five—and the many stories about this daring western rider swirled through an America transfixed by the civil rights struggle and a failing war in the jungles of Vietnam. Her legend

Adele Von Ohl Parker, "Picking Up," 1919. Courtesy Buffalo Bill Historical Center.

seemed to transcend the real world, until, like Buffalo Bill himself, her public wondered if she had been real, or if they had somehow dreamed her up. "In so many ways, Parker's Ranch was symbolic of a lot of things that don't happen anymore," wrote Robert Hull. "As the years wore on, Mrs. Parker became definitely larger than life—a prodigious teacher, a strangely regal creature, and a character of such darting impulses that half of North Olmsted is less than certain she really existed."[6]

Of Adele Parker's adventure, only some mostly forgotten stories and a few photographs remain. One of these is a magnificent 1919 image of the cowgirl on a galloping horse, doing the "pick up" that was her specialty. She wears a cowboy hat and chaps. Her seat has left the saddle and is now planted on the horse's side. Her thighs clutch the animal with such power, and her body swings from the horse's flanks with such grace, that it looks almost as if gravity has failed. Her right hand grips the pommel, her left arm stretches her opened hand to pluck a handkerchief from the ground. Her face is lit with joy.

CHAPTER EIGHTEEN

End of the Trail

FOR TWO YEARS following the trial, Cody toured Europe, in a figurative exile that largely kept him from the public eye in the United States. In France, where he took up the reins of the Wild West show immediately after Judge Scott rendered his decision, divorce and extramarital affairs were less stigmatized, and details of his personal life were less renowned. In fact, 1905 was the third year of a four-year European tour arranged by managing partner James A. Bailey (whom many suspected of keeping the Wild West show in Europe to protect his American circus, Barnum & Bailey, from competition). In 1903, the Wild West show had opened at the Olympia Theatre in London. After two weeks, the show moved to Manchester for three weeks, then went to Liverpool for three more, and on to a tour of the provinces that lasted until October. The year 1904 saw Buffalo Bill's Wild West and Congress of Rough Riders of the World in Wales, Scotland, and smaller English cities, inscribing the legend of Buffalo Bill in places like Penrith, Rochdale, and Macclesfield. In 1905, the show opened in Paris, then moved into the French countryside—Cholet, Vannes, Chateauroux—finishing in November in Marseilles. There, the Marquis Folco de Baroncelli and the poet Frédéric Mistral met Buffalo Bill and Pedro Esquivel, and Baroncelli began his long friendship with Jacob White Eyes and Sam Lone Bear.

In 1906, Cody—still following Bailey's schedule—stayed clear of the American scene again. Opening in Marseilles, the company toured the south of France, then Italy and Austria-Hungary (with ten days in Budapest and brief appearances in Temesvar, Ungvar, and Brasso). There was a brief foray into today's Ukraine and Poland, with a stop in Kraków, and then a return swing through Germany and Belgium.[1]

These appearances were by no means unsuccessful. Cody donated $5,000 to the survivors of the Mt. Vesuvius eruption in 1906, and $1,000 to the victims of the San Francisco earthquake.[2] But that year, an epidemic of glanders struck the show horses in France. Show handlers had to destroy two hundred animals.

On top of these losses came the death of James A. Bailey, whose heirs found in his papers a note for a $12,000 loan to William F. Cody. The note was several years old, and Cody claimed he had paid it. But if he had, Bailey's heirs insisted he do so again. Buffalo Bill would not be retiring anytime soon.[3]

In 1907, the Wild West show finally returned to the United States, where it played the remainder of its days. The show was still a large draw, and newspaper reviews mostly ignored Cody's scandalous divorce trial. Instead, they portrayed the aging showman as a venerable, fading entertainment. They asked if this was his farewell tour. When he replied it was not, they treated it like one anyway.[4] In part, they responded to his appearance. He looked old. Although journalists still described his hair as long, the tresses were a wig. Outside the arena, he often went without it, his bald pate covered only by a hat.

But the emphasis on Cody's imminent vanishing was also a way of diminishing the controversy around him. He could not be a disruptive force if he was about to disappear, and over the last decade of his life, the dominant theme of his newspaper coverage was his approaching death.

His persona underwent a subtle shift, seemingly at his own direction. After his return from Europe, his show programs dropped all mention of his role as domesticator. There were no references to his family, no illustrations of Scout's Rest Ranch, no poetry about Buffalo Bill and his babies. Indeed, show publicity referred only vaguely to the details of his private life at all. Programs no longer spoke of him as the embodiment of progress. In 1907, audiences read about his frontier heroics, his business and show successes, especially the show's European travels. There was also a two-page spread on Cody town and "The Cody Trail through Wonderland," with "Views of Yellowstone Park—Now Accessible on South via Cody by C. B. & Q. R. R."[5]

The show itself did reprise elements of Cody's old frontier heroics, with his first-ever re-creation of "The Battle of Summit Springs" which both complemented the show finale of the "Attack on the Settler's Cabin" and offered audiences a bridge to a distant, frontier past that preceded the recent scandals. Show programs gave a detailed history of the battle, and the now-aged General Eugene Carr even ventured a personal testimonial in which he averred for the first time that Cody had killed Tall Bull.[6] At some point after 1907, Thomas Edison filmed the tableau, and the clip survives:

Two white women arrive in the arena with the victorious Cheyenne, who sing and thrust their lances at the sky. Tipis go up as the two captives recline nervously on the ground, watching the activity around them. Two Cheyenne women rouse the white women and try to shove them into a tipi. They resist. A chief comes along, and shoves them in. They emerge, arms flailing at their captors. The chief pushes them back inside. Then comes the cavalry charge, the Indians are routed, and Buffalo Bill himself, now an old man, dismounts to shake the hands of the liberated captives.[7]

But the search for an ending which now dominated Cody's life began to permeate the entertainment. Had Cody retired with founding a town he could have made his life correspond to myth, with settlement and fixity succeeding the nomadism of his show career.

Instead, he scripted his now-anticlimactic life back into his show, abruptly abandoning the domestic finale just as he had left Louisa. After twenty-three years of marking the show's climax, the "Attack on the Settler's Cabin" disappeared. Never again would audiences watch the old scout ride through circling Indians to rescue the little pioneer family. The show's culminating attractions in subsequent years included "auto polo," riding tricks of different nations, and, reflecting the rise of collegiate athletics as manly training and entertainment, football games on horseback between cowboys and Indians (with a round ball some five feet in diameter).

As unsatisfying as these finales were, Cody's search for an ending in a sense reflected both his attempted divorce and shifting public attachments to the West which the old performer probably sensed. The show increasingly competed with movies, and among the earliest of these were what became known as "westerns." *The Great Train Robbery* was released in 1903, and was popular enough to generate many imitators. Buffalo Bill's Wild West was among them: the 1907 show included a segment called "The Great Train Hold-Up and Bandit Hunters of the Union Pacific," featuring an automobile mocked up as a locomotive, in front of a giant panorama of Pike's Peak.[8]

Although many assume that western films were merely Wild West shows brought to the screen, there were significant differences between them, which suggest some of the challenges Cody faced in his effort to compete with them. The films built on the literary structure of the western novel, which dates its birth to 1902, the year Owen Wister published *The Virginian*. Wister's novel became the template for the western genre prior to World War II. *The Virginian* made many contributions to western mythology, not the least of them a distancing of western heroes from domesticity. We may attribute the western's antidomestic leanings to a reaction against the domestic novel and reform Christianity, as Jane Tompkins has argued, or we may take the view that Wister sought to reassure men that they remained firmly in charge even in "the Equality State" of Wyoming, where women had the vote, as Lee Clark Mitchell suggests. Either way, *The Virginian*'s plot turns on a new kind of subordination of the independent woman to the novel's hero.[9]

In Buffalo Bill's Wild West, and in many nineteenth-century dime novels, heroes raced to rescue women bodily from the clutches of evil. The woman in the settler's cabin, or the women in the wagon train, supported

William Cody, c. 1915. Almost bald, Cody wore a wig in the arena, probably from the 1890s onward. But he did not try to cover up outside the show and often dressed like the financier and successful capitalist he longed to be. Courtesy Denver Public Library.

the armed combat of their men without hesitation. The alternative was abduction and subordination to a primitive and racially "other" regime.

With *The Virginian*, the central trope of the western becomes a hero who ventures out to battle evil against the wishes of the good woman. In fact, his passage to the showdown is marked by his turning away from the woman, who is left indoors and who has announced that she will leave him if he insists on fighting. By venturing out the door, and into the street, the hero announces that he will forsake the woman and the domestic order she represents in order to defend the honor he embodies. In the western, heroes must renounce domesticity to fight villainy.

Sometimes, this development is resolved by the reassertion of domestic harmony, but only on the hero's terms. After killing the bad man, the Virginian is taken back by his love, Molly Wood. Thus, she validates his violation of her wishes.

In westerns throughout the twentieth century, the climactic scene of *The*

Virginian, with its domestic gender war followed by a showdown, was repeated in various forms. It was vitally different from the climax of the Wild West show. Where the heroes triumphed over nomadic savagery in the Wild West show, they were energized by the domesticating influence of women. Indeed, as we have seen, the presence of white women was the signature "racial" characteristic that allowed white men to vanquish Indians in the first place.

In the western, on the other hand, the protagonist vanquishes not one but two very different adversaries: the woman, who must be refused, and the villain, who must be killed. Indeed, the refusal of the woman's wishes is the necessary precondition for the killing. Thus, the modern western emerges as a symbolic defense of manly honor in ways that require *denial* of the constraining power of home and womanhood. Indeed, the domesticating influence of woman becomes a chief threat to the hero, who needs violence to underscore honor and integrity and—though she does not understand this—to defend the woman's honor, too. Indeed, her moral blindness to the need for killing is a sharp contrast to the moral clarity of the hero's vision.[10]

Of course, in a thousand ways, the picture of western centaurs racing *home* could still resonate with this myth (picture the desperate race to the cabin in John Ford's *The Searchers*). But a symbolic homecoming of western heroes, like the finale of the Wild West show, perhaps brought the scout and his cowboys too close to home to be comfortable after 1907. It certainly clashed with the needs of the western as it developed in the twentieth century: thus the final scene of so many westerns, echoed and reasserted in *The Searchers*, when the hero, having restored the abducted woman to her family, walks away from the cabin and back into the wilderness.

Given his genius for tuning his mythology to national longings, it would be hard to imagine that Cody was completely unaware of these shifting cultural predilections. He practically voiced them himself, when he explained his reasons for wanting a divorce from Louisa in 1904, vowing to make a new home in the solitude, in "that new wild country" where he could "be away from trouble—domestic trouble."[11]

In any case, it was peculiarly fitting that the show which claimed to tell the nation's history *and* the biography of its star and creator ceased to include the "Settler's Cabin" tableau shortly after he made a public, and losing, attack on his own marriage. Even more fitting that the man who had inscribed his life into western myth, and the myth that he reenacted back into his real life, in a sense sought to abandon the old climactic home defense, for a departure into the wilderness. As movies began to find their way into popular consciousness, Cody sought to inscribe what would become the primary denouement of western film into his real life.

THE ABANDONMENT OF the "Settler's Cabin" paralleled his alienation from Louisa and his domestic circle, but it also corresponded with the final failure of his town-founding dreams. The town of Cody had broken free of him with the completion of the money-losing Cody Canal. But back in 1904, the railroad had given him a half interest in the town of Ralston, thirty-five miles east of Cody and on the other side of the Shoshone River, to persuade him to cede the Cody-Salsbury segregation. As soon as the Reclamation Service built its canal, this swath of dry basin soil would become town lots. Although he would have to split the profits with the railroad, Cody anticipated a handsome profit.[12]

But water for the site was slow in coming. Cody wrote dozens of anxious letters from the road, admonishing officials to begin construction of the canal, and to prevent downstream settlements, especially the Mormons at Lovell, from siphoning off water and decreasing the attractions of the north side canal for the government.[13]

With the railroad as his partner and the government promising to build a canal, he was all but certain the town site would flourish. But shortly after the Reclamation Service took over the irrigation project, Ralston's prospects suddenly dimmed, as government authorities began to plan a new town at the site of their headquarters, midway between the railroad town sites of Ralston and Garland.

Rumors of the town's creation preceded the actual staking out of its grid by some years, and Buffalo Bill worked Wyoming's congressional delegation and the governor's office to stop its construction, out of fear it would diminish Ralston's prospects. Initially, the Reclamation Service denied any plans for a permanent settlement.[14]

Not satisfied with the explanations that he was getting and worried by the rumors of a town, Buffalo Bill himself wrote an appeal to President Theodore Roosevelt to request his help in relocating the government's town elsewhere, lest "the old pioneer" again meet with hardship.[15]

But Roosevelt was reluctant to interfere with a government agency. In 1908, the Reclamation Service announced they would begin selling town lots at Camp Colter, which would soon bear the name of Powell (named for the great western surveyor and irrigation advocate, John Wesley Powell). The new town's proximity meant few settlers would be tempted to Ralston. Railroad officials objected. They had anticipated that the Burlington & Missouri—not the government—would be building towns on the new project.[16]

But the most vehement denunciations came from William Cody, who roared his objections in a small flood of letters. He had given up his segregation on the north side of the Shoshone River at great personal expense. "No one at that time had any idea that the Great National Government was going into the townsite business, and if the agents of the National Government contemplated the laying out of a town they did not mention it." Moreover, they had implied the opposite. "They gave me to understand that Ralston should be the townsite and a town should be established there and . . . I perhaps would be able to make back from the sale of town lots some of the money which I had expended on that North Side proposition. . . ."[17]

He pleaded his case as the agent of progress, the man who opened the Big Horn Basin to settlement and who deserved better. The region was a wilderness when he found it, peopled only by a few backward ranchers. "They discouraged the advancement of civilization. They tried to discourage every new home builder whom I brought into the country . . . and in fact discouraged them to such an extent that they would leave the country and the first settlers whom I got to farm and remain I had to keep at my own expense for a year or two, furnishing them teams, farming implements, provisions, etc., until they raised a crop."[18]

He claimed that he and his partners "had to keep lawyers employed at Cheyenne continually to formulate laws under which the Carey Act could be handled." They gave the river a new name to attract settlers, and hired engineers to make the canals possible, and Cody himself persuaded the railroad's president to build a line into the basin (a claim which was at best overstated, as we have seen). He brought English investors in 1903, and then asked them to leave so the government could develop the north side. Had he been allowed to proceed back then, the entire project would have been completed by now. He had spent something like $20,000 on the north side, and he had given up a lucrative partnership with his English capitalists, too. "This project has cost me a fortune, besides years of labor and anxiety saying nothing of hard work, but that is what the pioneer generally gets."[19]

Cody had a point. The federal government built no towns on the railroads. What right had the Reclamation Service to build towns that would compete with his?

But inside the offices of the Reclamation Service, the situation looked very different. What right had the government to stand in the way of settlers who wanted a town at Powell? By 1909, the government had spent over $3 million of the public treasury on the Shoshone project.[20] As an arm of a democratic government, the office was more constrained to side with settlers than railroads and other town builders had been. Cody presented this closing battle of his long career as a fight between an old frontiersman and usurping bureaucrats like Henry Savage, the supervising engineer of the Reclamation Service at Powell, who was "determined to deprive me of any benefits arising from the sale of lots in the town of Ralston," and who "forces all people to accept lands near Powell . . ."[21]

But in reality, Cody's plans for Ralston were not undone by Savage or anyone else in the government. If anyone was to blame for the failure of his last town-site speculation, it was the middle-class settlers of Powell, who wanted a town near the tidy government offices of the officials who provided their water. As Henry Savage pointed out, settlers were spending a lot of money on Reclamation Service water, about $35 per acre. Having a town closer to their homes—at Powell—would keep their other costs down, "and the question to be decided is whether the proceeds from the townsite should go to the benefit of settlers who produce the value, or to others," like William Cody.[22]

In fact, settlers demanded the sale of lots in Powell. Authorities merely gave them what they wanted. "We believe that creditable business houses would be erected here immediately if title to the land could be acquired," wrote these home seekers in a petition to the Reclamation Service, "and we believe that it would greatly encourage prospective settlers if the town were put upon a sure basis. . . ."[23] At the opening auction of Powell property on May 25, 1909, settlers bought twenty-six lots. "Several business houses have been erected since the sale and others are in course of construction," wrote one observer at the end of 1909. "A bank and the usual lines of staple businesses are represented, as well as the principal professions. A commercial club has been organized by the business men to promote the interests of the town. Schools and churches had been established before the opening of the town site and continue in a flourishing condition."[24] Nobody prevented these middle-class, entrepreneurial people from moving to Ralston. They simply refused to go. The government did not betray the old scout. In a sense, his audience did.

In so many ways, their decision reflected the broader trend of middle-class politics. Clashes between monopoly capital and organized labor had so agitated the Gilded Age that by 1900 most Americans believed the partisans needed restraint. Theodore Roosevelt's administration and the two administrations that followed gave it to them, in a form of governance that defined a new age, the Progressive Era.

From 1900 to roughly 1918, reformers and government regulators attacked corporate excess and market irregularities with a host of new commissions, boards, and agencies. In the West, federal agencies, from the Bureau of Reclamation to the U.S. Forest Service, regulated access to resources to guarantee abundance and prevent the clear-cuts, land swindles, and range wars of an earlier day.[25] Railroads still built towns in the West, but on federal reclamation projects, they had far less sway than they had had on the plains of Kansas when they ruined Cody's town of Rome. The day of the railroad town was not yet done. But as Cody's losses in the Big Horn Basin showed, the day of the government town had arrived.

There were powerful economic reasons for Cody's financial failure in the Big Horn Basin. The Reclamation Service had resources no private capital-ist could match, and along with a host of other federal agencies, they reshaped the West into the U.S. region built more than any other on federal dollars. Although reclamation projects seldom met expectations, and disap-pointments soon turned the agency from building country homes to build-ing huge dams for urban reservoirs, Reclamation Service officials were wildly successful compared to the private capitalists who preceded them. In the next six decades, the federal government spent $6 billion on western irrigation projects for farms and cities, bringing unprecedented material wealth and new possibilities to places like the Big Horn Basin, planting small middle-class settlements like Cody and Powell where only wind-whipped sagebrush had grown.[26]

Buffalo Bill's town-site dreams sprang from an earlier American West, in eastern Kansas, where well-watered valleys allowed speculative capitalists like Isaac Cody to found towns without subsidies. William Cody came of age in a West where corporations like the Union Pacific received federal subsidies in the form of land grants and concessions. Now, homeowners were federally subsidized, and they had a voice in where the towns grew. This new West, with its irrigated homes and federal agents anxious to do the bidding of their owners, blew away Cody's dreams like smoke from the embers of a prairie fire.

WITHOUT A MANAGING PARTNER after Bailey's death in 1906, Cody was exhausted by the organizational work of his show. At the end of the 1908 season, Bailey's heirs sold a one-third interest in the show to Gordon "Pawnee Bill" Lillie. Gordon William Lillie was born in 1860, in Illinois, the son of a flour mill owner. When the family moved to Wellington, Kansas, in 1876, the sixteen-year-old boy spent a year as a trapper, then a brief season on a cattle ranch before moving to the Pawnee Agency in Okla-homa, where he became secretary and schoolteacher, and eventually a trans-lator. He was a head shorter than Cody and his own frontier imposture drew heavily on Buffalo Bill's example. A onetime employee of Cody's (he had been a translator for the Pawnees in the Wild West show's debut season of 1883), he created his own Wild West show in 1888, becoming a somewhat uneven competitor for Buffalo Bill's entertainment. This longtime show rival would now take up the reins as Cody's managing partner.[27]

Despite the competition, Lillie idolized Cody. He eagerly bought up Bailey's interest apparently out of desire to work with Buffalo Bill, and to attach himself to the most famous Wild West show of all.

He found Cody anxious and distracted by his financial troubles. "In his business dealings, he was like a child," recalled Lillie. "He apparently cared nothing for money, except when he wanted or needed to spend it. Then, if he did not have it, or could not borrow it, it made him sick—actually sick, so that he would have to go to bed."[28] The Bailey heirs were still demanding payment of Cody's outstanding $12,000 loan. Lillie negotiated a deal, buying out the Bailey heirs and paying off Cody's debt. He then allowed Cody to buy back enough of the show from that year's profits to make him half owner. The move was generous, but also fair. Cody's Wild West comprised most of their joint show and his presence was the main attraction.[29]

The two impresarios then combined their companies to create "Buffalo Bill's Wild West combined with Pawnee Bill's Great Far East." Fans called it the "Two Bills' Show." Virtually every segment of the show was one of Buffalo Bill's standard features, the exception being one segment called "A Dream of the East," in which elephants, camels, belly dancers, and Arab warriors made a circuit of the arena. The array of exotic Oriental wonders dissipated the coherence of the frontier narrative, but it also provided the Wild West show more of a sensual edge, for "oriental" motifs had long been associated with the relaxation of Puritan constraints. The show had some huge successes. In 1908, a two-week stand at Madison Square Garden sold out, and the partners grossed $60,000 in Philadelphia.[30]

In 1910, John Burke proposed advertising Cody's imminent retirement as an inducement to audiences. The partners agreed on a three-year tour that would present Cody one more time to the public, appearing in no place more than once, allowing him to claim each appearance to be "positively" his "last performance" at that location. Kicking off the 1910 season, Cody gave his first of many farewell speeches to a hushed crowd. "Out in the West I have my horses, my buffalo, my staunch old Indian friends, my home, my green fields—but I never see them green. . . . My message to you is one of farewell . . . and I take this opportunity to emphatically state that this will be my last and only professional appearance in the cities selected, as no return dates will be given."[31] "Buffalo Bill Bids You Good Bye," said one program cover. Another leaflet of 1912 announced his retirement with the announcement, "Buffalo Bill, Back to the New West. The Old West I Leave With You." Inside was a list of his many business concerns, especially in the town of Cody.

By no means was the show unprofitable. The 1910 season saw the two owners split a $400,000 profit, and even in 1912, a comparatively weak year, it reportedly made them $125,000.[32]

On these proceeds, perhaps Cody could have retired. Lillie spent $100,000 on a mansion for himself and his wife in Oklahoma, and stashed a like sum into his bank account.[33]

Cody threw his money down a hole. In 1902, Colonel D. B. Dyer, a member of New York's Union League Club, introduced Cody to a prospective gold mine in Arizona, at the Campo Bonito mine works, some forty-three miles from Tucson.[34] Cody began investing. The following year, after seven months of tunneling, his managers reported a gold strike. Cody (who was beginning to realize his Big Horn Basin effort would not pay off) thought his retirement was now secure. "It seemed like a great load had suddenly been taken off me."[35]

Gold continued to appear in smaller quantities, just enough to keep Cody hopeful. But profits from the mine proved as elusive as the proceeds of his towns. The showman emptied something like $200,000 into his Arizona mines.[36] He sought investors and wrote almost as many letters about the shafts as he had about ditches in the Big Horn Basin. Like his other investments, he complained bitterly about managers who failed to keep him informed, and he pretended to supervise the mine as much as he did his show arena.[37]

There was a degree of showmanship in soliciting investors that appealed to him. He led trips to Campo Bonito to convince the parties he brought along to invest their money. The guide and showman understood the value of providing these clients an authentic experience of the mining West. He fixed up his own cabin with western relics, including Yellow Hair's scalp.[38] Letters to his managers instructed them to prepare suitable camping amenities for the travelers, as if Campo Bonito was a new arena for his ongoing show. "Will you have the Mrs. Thomas House sealed with light colored burlap, as it's a rather dark room—two beds like I had in my teepee—nice blankets, pillows &c. A curtain to hide the beds . . . Wash stand—fix it up something like my teepee . . . writing desk &c. . . . Hope you sowed some barley so it will look green like last winter. . . . I wish you would have the Mrs. Thomas house white washed, also the store. It would help the looks greatly. . . . You should get the soft burlap, 56 inches wide, and tack it on the walls—hard burlap goes on with paste."[39]

Cody never deceived investors about his profits. Despite his attention to the entertainment of his guests, he did not hide the fact that the mine consistently failed to turn a profit. There were numerous obstructions to mining and milling, and the promised ore failed to materialize.[40] The show he ran at Campo Bonito was honest, and very unprofitable.

But he was so busy running that show—or maybe he was just credulous—that he failed to realize another show was operating at his mine. Lewis Getchell was the Arizona partner who had lured Cody and Dyer into the operation. Getchell was notorious for promoting worthless commercial properties, and he found an easy mark in Cody, whose faith in the mine sprang from the fraudulent report of a crooked mining engineer (whom Getchell had commissioned, of course). Getchell lived high on Cody's money, sending the showman fake receipts for his expenses and pocketing the money the showman sent. At the same time, he employed forty-five people to scrabble in the tunnels, making the mine look potentially profitable.[41]

Other observers were not fooled. One engineer on a neighboring claim judged the mine "a tremendous swindle and I am very much afraid that Cody is innocent and Getchell is playing him for a sucker."[42]

In a sense, Cody was defrauded by Getchell's show and then constrained by his own public image. In 1912, perplexed by the financial failure of the mine, Cody's partner, D. B. Dyer, requested an evaluation by a qualified mining engineer. The engineer, E. J. Ewing, caught a worker seeding the mill with refined minerals to make the ore look richer than it was, and he uncovered the kickbacks Getchell had engineered. Beyond losing his job, Getchell paid no penalty. Fear of adverse publicity kept Cody from filing charges. After he was taken in by Getchell's staging of a "working" mine, his need to protect his own show reputation as a clear-sighted westerner kept him from seeking legal recourse.[43]

By this time, Cody had spent his great profits from the 1910 season, and even though the mines began making a small profit (mostly from tungsten, used in new electric lightbulbs), it would take many years for them to return the money Cody had spent. Dyer died soon after the fraud was uncovered. Cody, unable to finance more operations, leased the mines to Ewing. For the rest of his life, he searched in vain for buyers.[44]

HIS PRIVATE LIFE was solitary after the scandal of the divorce trial. The fate of Bess Isbell remains mysterious, although documents offer intriguing hints. In 1906, Isbell met Cody at the Hoffman House in New York. There she signed over her power of attorney to W. J. Walls, Cody's lawyer in Wyoming, whom she instructed to sell her forty-acre ranch. After deducting expenses, Walls was to send the proceeds to her mother, Mrs. Julia Isbell, of the St. James Hotel, Denver. Why she wanted the money sent to her mother is not clear. But perhaps, as Cody had testified, she had tuberculosis. Whatever her fate, she disappeared from Cody's life after 1906.[45]

Cody was alone in 1910 when his daughter Irma, now living in North

Platte with her husband and children, persuaded her father to visit the town that had turned against him at his divorce trial. Encouraged by reports from Louisa's friends that she wanted to take him back, town newspapers looked forward eagerly to the return of the old scout. Once again greeted by a large crowd of well-wishers and the town band, Cody was delighted. "Almost one hundred of the best people were out to the ranch for a smoker," he reported to his sisters. "Today at 2 p.m. the Commercial Club gives me a reception. . . . So you can see I am in the lime light again. And hardly know how to meet it."

News flashed along the wires that he and Louisa were reunited. But they were not. "I haven't seen Lulu," Cody wrote. Although Louisa had expressed her longing for a reconciliation to friends and family, when he tried to visit, she refused to come out of her bedroom. He knocked softly. He pleaded. But the door remained closed.[46]

Sometime the following year, she relented. Evidence is thin and contradictory, but the family story is that he stopped in North Platte in July. Daughter Irma, her husband Fred Garlow, their children, and Arta's orphaned children contrived to leave them alone in a room together. When they emerged, Louisa and William Cody were reconciled.[47]

The Codys were not without resources. They still owned Scout's Rest Ranch and Louisa's house in North Platte, called the Welcome Wigwam. They owned the Irma Hotel and the TE Ranch in Wyoming. But the expenses of the Two Bills show were onerous. The partners were supposed to split the $40,000 cost of wintering livestock. Cody, desperate to raise his $20,000 share after a poor season in 1913, took a six-month loan from Henry Tammen, a shady impresario who owned the Sells-Floto Circus. Tammen also owned the sensationalist newspaper the *Denver Post*, which had reported lurid details of Cody's divorce trial in screaming red headlines. Now it reported the loan and a supposed condition: Cody had agreed to a partnership with Tammen's circus instead of with Pawnee Bill Lillie, beginning the next season.[48]

Cody denied he had made any such agreement, but Lillie was furious.[49] Tammen would not likely have been able to enforce the condition even if Cody had agreed to it, since Cody could not unilaterally break his contract with his partner. But Tammen had another scheme for moving Lillie out of the picture. If he could not break the Cody-Lillie partnership, he would break the company.

In 1913, when the show camp arrived in Denver, days from Tammen's deadline for repayment, the Two Bills were already faring poorly from rain and low attendance. The slick publisher had maneuvered a series of foreclosure suits into the courts, and the show was attached for payment of Cody's

$20,000 loan. The sheriff and his deputies arrived on the showgrounds, seized all cash on hand, and then sold all properties at auction. Buffalo Bill's Wild West was bankrupt.[50]

Deprived of his own show, and now under salary to Tammen, Cody toured with the Sells-Floto Circus in 1914 and 1915. The circus had dirty tents and rotting ropes, and at one showing it was nearly flooded out of existence. Still, Cody's life was not all bad. His salary was sizable: $100 a day, plus 40 percent of receipts over $3,000. He rode on horseback to introduce the show, but forsook his shooting acts. He had a private car on the train, a cook, a porter, and a carriage driver. Louisa traveled with him for free. "She has enjoyed the trip immensely," he wrote to sister Julia.[51] Years later, one fellow circus performer recalled, "He kept pretty much to himself in his private dressing tent. Had a certain amount of dignity about him that I admired. Was a handsome man for his age and still looked wonderful on a horse."[52]

The misadventure with Tammen was compounded by Cody's foray into filmmaking, in which he secured the backing of Tammen and Tammen's partner, Frederick G. Bonfils, in the creation of "The Col. W. F. Cody ('Buffalo Bill') Historical Pictures Co." Given the significance of the Wild West for formulating western myth and the spectacle of "moving pictures," making films seemed to many a fitting culmination for Cody's latter years. Cody envisioned a movie, *The Last Indian War,* that was educational and authentic, and thereby secured permission for it from both the army and the Department of Interior, which retained authority over Indians. He then set about gathering actual participants from the Plains campaigns and a slew of younger actors and extras to make his one and only motion picture.

Much of Cody's initial success in the filming came from his friendships with Indians, which he tended carefully. Back in 1909, there had been a flash of the discontent he occasionally encountered at Pine Ridge after one of the show contingent, Good Lance, fell sick and was left in a hospital in Garden City, Kansas, where he died. The tribal council (which included some Indians who had formerly performed with the show) sent a letter to the White House, demanding Wild West shows, including Buffalo Bill's, be banned from hiring Indians. At least some of their anger stemmed from the failure to return Good Lance's body. "We want that dead body to be sen[t] back over here," wrote the council. "So we want him [Buffalo Bill] to do as what the Oglala Council wanted."[53]

For decades, Indians and others who died on tour were buried near their place of death. But in 1913, contracts for Buffalo Bill's Wild West and Pawnee Bill's Far East Combined included a new clause, stipulating that in case an Indian employee died on tour, Cody and Lillie would "make all arrangements and pay all expenses incident to the preparation of the body for burial and transportation of the body to Pine Ridge Agency."[54]

Cody followed on this gesture, the next year, as he began hiring Indians for his film. He hurried to pay back wages owed to those Indians who had been on the lot in Denver the day the sheriff seized the cash box. Since the cast could not be paid until the bankruptcy was settled, Lakotas with the show, like everyone else that year, had gone home without their salaries. So, while filming at Pine Ridge, Cody secured a personal loan and paid some $1,300 in wages to his former employees. Lizzie Sitting Eagle, Alice Running Horse, Peter Stands Up, Ghost Dog, Iron Cloud, and many others received their back wages, as well as small sums for the support of young children who had been with the show in 1913.[55]

His support from the army secured for Cody the services of retired General Nelson A. Miles and three troops of cavalry. Filming began in September 1913. Cody soon expanded the project, from *The Last Indian War*, about the Ghost Dance tragedy, which he had never before reenacted, to *The Indian Wars*, including two battles, Summit Springs and Warbonnet Creek (where he scalped Yellow Hair), that were standards of the Wild West show.[56]

Cody played his moment as film producer for all it was worth. Now he was not only appearing in the film itself. He also heightened the film's authenticity by making himself the arbitrator between hostile forces, telling interviewers from film magazines that the Indians were fearful of the army and that he had talked them out of using live ammunition for the reenactment of the Wounded Knee massacre.[57]

These fictional tales titillated the public, but other attempts at authenticity were more costly and less effective. Miles insisted on reenacting central scenes in places where they actually occurred, forcing a fifty-mile trek out to the Badlands in freezing weather. Cody, who recognized a budget-busting production when he saw one, argued bitterly with the old general about the Badlands filming and other details, to the point that it reportedly ended their friendship.[58]

Ultimately, the film fared poorly at the box office, leading many to speculate that hidden forces conspired to destroy it. Chauncey Yellow Robe, a Lakota who differed with most of his Pine Ridge contemporaries on the usefulness of Wild West shows, denounced Cody and Miles for debasing the sacred burial ground at Wounded Knee "for their own cheap glory."[59] There were rumors of a protest against the film by the tribal council, although it never materialized. Because the release of the film was delayed in Washington (where the army had to approve it for release, as a condition of using real troops in the film), there have been rumors for many years that the film was suppressed, perhaps because the massacre at Wounded Knee was too "realistic" to reflect well on the army, or perhaps because authorities in the Office of Indian Affairs disapproved of the final product.[60]

For all these rumors, it is unlikely the film offended a public once again fond of their army, as World War I raged in Europe. Wounded Knee stands as a black mark on American history, and the dark reputation of the event kept Cody from staging its reenactment during his Wild West show years. But the film evaded this problem by eliminating the massacre altogether, showing no women and children among the bodies in the ravine.

In fact, evidence suggests the film failed for other reasons which are both more conventional and more revealing. In order to secure permission to hire Indians, Cody promised that his film would also illustrate "the advance of the Indians under modern conditions."[61] So, with the battle scenes over, the audience watched clips of Indians in school and performing standard

William F. and Louisa Cody, c. 1915. They traveled together in his later show days. Courtesy Buffalo Bill Historical Center.

farm and business tasks. The Wild West show had never ended with such an anticlimax (which was, of course, why Indian office functionaries so disliked it). The western was still young, but it was already a popular genre, and *The Indian Wars* was no western. Audiences were less than thrilled by the story's prosaic culmination. The authentic, primitive racial energies that spectators usually identified in Indians were erased in a denouement where the Indians became much like people in the audience. Watching Indians resist vanishing was exciting. Watching them after they had symbolically vanished was dull. Cody had turned his narrative over to the Office of Indian Affairs, and their achievement was to bore the public with a didactic lesson in Indian assimilation.

The tedious plot was one factor which undermined the film's appeal. Another was that film was a less than ideal medium for Buffalo Bill Cody. The dispute between Cody and Miles over how best to achieve authentic scenes reminds us of Cody's arena successes and suggests why film worked poorly as a vehicle for his own myth. He had pioneered an art form in which he danced across the line between fake and real, emerging from painted backdrops and then disappearing back into them, surrounding himself with frontier relics and fakery, real frontier people and actors dressed up like them, and begging audiences to separate the two.

Early filmmakers often constructed narratives about real historical figures. Marshall Bill Tilghman, of Oklahoma, made films about his exploits starring himself. To enhance the middle-class appeal of his movies, he toured with them and lectured boys in the audience to stay away from crime. Likewise, Cody toured with *The Indian Wars* for three weeks in 1916, once appearing onstage with Sioux warriors.[62] But Cody was so aged by this time that he appeared less the frontier hero and more the grizzled Plains veteran. He was still interesting. But film was not as effective a form for testing the borders of truth and fiction, simply because it did not allow him to step out of the projection the way that arena performance did. Film worked best when it deployed scenery, lighting, props, and physical types to cue audiences, not necessarily when it showed "real" people on a flat screen.

Unfortunately the film remains a mystery, because the nitrate stock on which it was recorded disintegrated over time. Only a few fragments of it are known to exist.

As he waited for the film to debut, Cody endured more trouble with Tammen. After Cody had toured with the Sells-Floto Circus for two years, Tammen told him his debt was paid, then reneged and told him he still owed $20,000 and that he would have to pay it back with his salary. Cody wrote an old friend, "This man is driving me crazy. I can easily kill him but as I avoided killing in the bad days I don't want to kill him. But if there is no justice left I will."[63]

When Tammen arrived in Lawrence, Kansas, to meet with Cody, he was afraid to go into the old scout's tent. When he finally did, they had a tense conversation, the upshot of which was that Cody agreed to finish the 1915 season with Sells-Floto. Tammen refused to cancel the loan, but he agreed to stop taking payments out of Cody's salary. At the end of the season, Cody was without employment for the first time since entering show business.[64]

Not to be deterred, he scrambled to put together a new show. Tammen claimed ownership of the name "Buffalo Bill's Original Wild West," so Cody combined with the 101 Ranch in Oklahoma to create the "Buffalo Bill (Himself) Pageant of Military Preparedness and 101 Ranch Wild West." He enjoyed the year. His nephew, William Cody Bradford, toured as his assistant. Cody rode in the saddle again, shattering amber balls with his rifle from horseback as he had in days gone by.

Even now he struggled for the ambivalent middle ground. The country was fiercely divided on the subject of American neutrality. Military preparedness was a conservative slogan of those who favored U.S. intervention in World War I, on the side of Britain and France. When the new show played Chicago, home to thousands of German Americans, the proprietors changed the show's name to "Chicago Shan-Kive and Round-Up." ("Shan-Kive" was said to be an "Indian word" for "good time.") The event, which resembled a rodeo and featured bulldogging by the likes of legendary black cowboy Bill Pickett, was a huge success.

Outside of Chicago, the show reverted to its Wild West format, with Pancho Villa's raid on Columbus, New Mexico, as its crowning spectacle.[65]

The show closed in November. Cody was not feeling well. He arrived in Denver on November 17, "sick with a bad cold and played out from the long hard season," according to his nephew. He stayed with his sister May for two weeks, then returned to the TE Ranch, where he hoped to recuperate. He continued to fail, and he returned to Denver to seek medical help in the middle of December. His health "was up and down all the time," recalled Bradford. To the end, he put on a show. "He did not want the papers to get a hold of the news and publish his sickness."

Cody went to Glenwood Springs, hoping a mineral bath would restore his health. But he returned four days later, none the better. He died January 10, 1917. Louisa was with him, as well as his sister May and her family. Johnny Baker, his longtime assistant and virtual foster son, raced from the East where he had been trying to raise money for the next season's show, but arrived too late to say farewell. Six weeks after Cody died, his longtime press agent, John Burke, also passed.

Cody left instructions to have himself buried on a hill overlooking the town of Cody, but Henry Tammen offered to pay for a funeral if the burial occurred in Denver. Some say Louisa took the publisher's offer to revenge herself on the town of Cody, which she resented like one of her husband's mistresses. Others say she had no money to bury him. In any case, the following June, William Cody was interred in a hole blasted into the summit of Lookout Mountain, overlooking the city of Denver and the Great Plains beyond, as a gigantic crowd of journalists, tourists, and sightseers looked on.

———

STILL HE RIDES, across our imagined horizon. In the years since his death, he has become, like so many other symbols, detached from his original context, a free-floating icon that may be, and has been, attached to different causes and ideologies. But this process was evident long before he died. By the time 1916 rolled around, Cody had been a theater and arena performer for forty-four years. His face and image, printed on innumerable posters, programs, and other show ephemera, were ubiquitous. He may have been the most photographed man of the period, and although the currency of the Cody face kept him in the public eye, it had a dark side. A person who has been through a historic event, whether a fight on the Plains, the march on Washington of 1963, or September 11, has more historical meaning and authority than has a mere drawing or photograph of that person or event. Reproduced images of authentic people cannot have the authority of real people. A mechanical reproduction, like a photograph, can be put to practically any use its owner can devise, as somber art or decoration, framed portrait or place mat.

Thus, when images of people or landscapes are mass-produced and widely distributed, the authority of the real is devalued. The face, the hair, the pose become symbols with meanings to spectators, but in the process they are often divorced from the history of the person or their setting. Americans who savored the proximity of the Wild West show's real frontier heroes confronted a paradox. They placed images of Cody and his Wild West show in bedrooms, living rooms, and hallways to bring them closer, to claim some element of their frontier authenticity for themselves. But in substituting copies for the unique people and things in the show, and redistributing them in a private arrangement with private meanings, they diminished the power of the very history and tradition which Cody and other real people conveyed.[66] Many of the fans who bought souvenir photographs, books, and programs, to say nothing of Buffalo Bill toy guns, board games, puzzles, tin whistles, dime novels, buttons, and postcards, knew him more from this show business flotsam than from his arena performances. Inevitably, as his fame mounted, he lost authenticity.[67]

In this sense, William Cody fomented a mountain of representations of his own face and story to draw a following, then represented himself before

crowds who came to watch. The show was not just an adventure of the hinterland. It was a heroic stand of the original against the dead hand of the
copy. Cody's optimistic, forthright confrontation with the artifice of modernity, in day-to-day life and in the painted, landscaped, eye-tricking arena
which resembled the frontier but whose deceptions evoked the city, made
him both the premier symbol of the natural frontier and a hero of artifice
among the most modern people on earth. Reproducing his own image and
selling it widely was a means of reminding audiences of his importance. But
it also meant that by his last decade, the vast majority of his audiences knew
him only as a showman with a putative link to the frontier. His ability to
generate a flood tide of self-promotion helped ensure his renown. Then it
washed him away, like a faded poster in the rain.

The peculiarities of Cody's story, as a popular celebrity who hailed from
the frontier West, so confound show business stereotypes that many have
suspected, or believed, that he must have been the creation of somebody
else. The debate over whether he was a frontiersman or a showman has continued in every Cody biography since he died. But as we have seen, during
Cody's life, even as he advanced to ever greater successes, many rivals and
partners, from Doc Carver to Nate Salsbury, argued that Cody did not fashion his own success. Against these imputations, Cody partisans, then and
now, have maintained that he was a genuine frontier hero who stumbled
into fame, an innocent abroad in the world of modern amusements.

But as I have argued throughout this book, neither of these positions
illuminates the vibrant culture of artful deception and imposture that characterized nineteenth-century American culture and especially that of the
Far West where Cody came of age. True, he was influenced and shaped by
many people and forces, but he was neither a simple creation of publicists
and press agents, nor was he a lifelong ingenue. In his rise to fame and his
long tenure as America's premier showman, his own vision, talents, and
burning ambition played the largest role. Hailing from a West that was
practically a borderland between real and fake, full of charlatans posing as
heroes and of everyday people invited to assume heroic poses, Cody learned
the allure of that tense space between authentic and copy, regeneration and
degeneration.

Americans imbued that space with a story about the ascent of civilization,
and that narrative was so pervasive that settlers easily adopted it as their
own, making themselves the protagonists of upward development, from
hunting, to ranching, to farming, and commerce. Following that story, and
claiming to live it, made Cody's show resonate with public desires, even as
audiences might question how real it actually was. Was he a frontiersman or
a showman? Clearly, he was both.

In the end, we might say that Cody was partly a trickster, a boundary-crossing figure who appears in the myths of many cultures. Tricksters are usually clowns, monsters, ogres, or spirits. As various scholars have observed, they violate sensual taboos, and societies venerate them partly for the vicarious pleasure they provide. They also destroy old institutions and codes as they erect new ones. P. T. Barnum's biographer, Neil Harris, calls Barnum a trickster because of the ways he loosened the grip of elite knowledge and encouraged Americans to enjoy their own powers of discernment. In elevating western history to a respectable show, in allowing Americans to believe that their frontier fantasies were not only real but embodied in his person, and in providing a means for Americans to accept frontier stories as an art form that was as respectable as any European play, Cody did much to destroy older notions of art and performance, and to usher in a new national mythology for the coming American century.

But tricksters are so dangerous they must be contained in the realm of myth and story. As flesh and blood, Cody could not remain a trickster. The failure of his suit for divorce was, among other things, a signal that he could not violate taboos with impunity. At the end of the day, he had to drape his life in standard morals.[68] Louisa Cody died in 1921, shortly after completing her own memoir of her marriage, a deceptive if not artful book in which she recalled no bitterness, no mistresses, only a warm and loving marriage to the man she helped invent the Wild West show.[69]

Many have accepted Cody's publicity that eulogized him as, in his sister's words, "the Last of the Great Scouts." By this estimation, there could be no more like Cody, because the frontier had passed. While he lived, seeing his show became ever more imperative for those who would witness the fading West.

But if the death of William Cody and his generation of Lakota warriors, American fighters, and scouts severed historical connections between modern America and the frontier of history, there was still another, perhaps more powerful reason why there could be no more quite like Buffalo Bill. This was the demise of the story of progress itself. Indian war was never universally accepted among Americans even while it was going on. But progress, the rise of technology over nature and of settlement over the wild, seemed inevitable. Almost until the year of Cody's death, it was yet possible to believe that western industrial society was the apogee of human development, the beginnings of a more peaceful, humane world, and even to fantasize that one person could embody its promise.

But the twentieth century was not kind to the story of progress. The trenches of World War I brimmed with blood, and the holocausts of World War II and the nuclear anxieties that followed made it hard to believe that technology was an unimpeachable wonder and moral boon. The dream of

Buffalo Bill's America, a frontier nation launched from Nature into the bright future of the Machine, suddenly seemed quaint and naive.

And yet, there remained one way in which Buffalo Bill's Wild West show would find enduring resonance, down to the present day. Americans have relegated Indian fighting to that dark space reserved for troubled memories and moral qualms, as they should. (And Cody himself seems to have felt the same way about it, at some points in his latter years even denying he ever killed Yellow Hair. "Bunk! Pure bunk! For all I know Yellow Hand died of old age."[70])

But while the Wild West show was created to tell a story of the Indian wars, its show community itself has long since become Buffalo Bill's myth, a symbolically inclusive congregation that seems to define some bright and optimistic moment in our collective past. If it was a traveling company town, a corporate workforce on the road that subsumed polyglot America under the ruling management of white men, there was a sense among its cast that they were part of something more. The many adventures of its optimistic and forward-looking cowboys, Indians, cowgirls, gauchos, vaqueros, and others stand out as something so surprising, so energetic and benign, that Americans and the world cannot help but find in them some resonance of a modern American promise.

In 1971, the entertainer Montie Montana, Jr., resurrected Buffalo Bill's Wild West show, vowing to imbue "the small fry with the spirit of the Old West as their Grandparents knew it." When the show played Los Angeles, Harry Webb, a cowboy who had ridden in Buffalo Bill's Wild West from 1909 to 1911, was seated in the stands. Webb was astonished at the "fine replica" Montana had assembled. "With a lump the size of an egg in our throat we dug a fist in our eyes and listened to the exact salutation we had heard hundreds of times as Buffalo Bill addressed his audience and introduced his Congress of Rough Riders of the World." Webb laughed and cheered with the sports arena crowd at the bronc riding, the Indian attack on the Deadwood stage, the saloon fight of the cowboys, the wooing of an Indian maiden by her warrior lover, and the trick roping and bullwhip acts.

But as much as Webb wished the new show would succeed, he could not help noticing the absences and gaps in this reenactment of a reenactment.

No longer are there great spreads of canvas, [a] football-[field] sized arena, horse tent housing hundreds of arena and baggage stock and the half acre dining tent. Also, the huge ranges and steam boilers (that poured forth the aroma of breakfasts even before being trundled off a fifty car train . . .) were missing. Nor is there the chant of stake drivers as a circle of sledge hammers sunk hundreds of tent stakes in the earth. The

old ballyhoo around concessions and the shouts of venders are also missing with this new Buffalo Bill Show. Nor will its Indians have their Sunday feasts of dog-stew on the show lot as of old. These scenes are gone
forever.[71]

As a community that developed a history of its own, the Wild West camp
has long since become the larger and more enduring of Cody's legacies.
Even the continuing success of Cody, Wyoming, now home to eight thousand people and the remarkable Buffalo Bill Historical Center (which
houses five state-of-the-art museums), cannot compare to the continuing
fame of William Cody's traveling company town. In the decades since
Cody's death, that "little tented city" has continued to fascinate the public
long after Buffalo Bill's Indian war exploits and the scalping of Yellow Hair
faded into obscurity.

As we have seen, William Cody remains a respected figure among
Lakota people, some of whom remember him as a good employer who provided opportunities which did not long outlive him. Pine Ridge remains one
of America's poorest communities. Although movies hired genuine Indian
actors in the early days of Hollywood, film producers soon discovered that it
was easier and cheaper to hire non-Indians to play Indian roles.[72] Since
then, Indian actors have waged a long and not unsuccessful struggle to win
back their place in Indian performance. In doing so, they carry on the fight
of Lakotas like Standing Bear, No Neck, Black Heart, and Calls the Name,
who allied with Cody to fend off the Indian Service in the 1880s and '90s.

As much as I have been able to explore the participation of Indians and
cowboys and cowgirls in this show, I have attempted to open up what I see as
the often unnoticed power of commodified performance—show business—
as a means to adopt and adapt otherwise pernicious myths. Indians, immigrants, first-generation Americans, and native-born whites all flocked to
Cody's show camp, each with a powerful economic and social rationale for
doing so. Although the Wild West show's ideology was oppressive in its cultural messages of womanly domesticity and Indian subjugation, we have
seen over and over again how performing it brought liberation, or something like it, to Standing Bear, Adele Von Ohl Parker, George Johnson,
Annie Oakley, Broncho Charlie Miller, and a host of others.

The willingness of so many diverse peoples to attach themselves to
Cody's show validates his early recognition that frontier myth had about it
much ambiguity, the necessary precondition for its mass appeal. Cody himself abhorred personal conflict and partisan fights. He found in politically
vague frontier symbols a means to avoid the fierce political contests of his
day. In recent decades, conservatives have appropriated western symbols for

their political ends. In 1986, Wyoming's congressional delegation joined a campaign to have Cody's Congressional Medal of Honor restored to him, something that they achieved in 1989. A primary player in the effort was a taciturn Republican congressman named Dick Cheney, a fact which speaks volumes about the rightward tilt of the Cody legacy in recent years.

Yet during Cody's life, the western myth was the province of no party. As we have seen, conservatives, reformers, and radicals alike found reasons to embrace his show. Buffalo Bill's Wild West was aimed at the broad middle class in ways that allowed audiences to enjoy the amusement without taking sides on the contentious issues it called to mind. By being a show about history, in an age when Americans believed their history followed a course that was largely predetermined, the sense of inevitability allowed them to remain ambivalent about American cruelties, and to celebrate American success, without any consternation about their confidence in the nation, or lack of it.

The amusement both appealed to the mass public and helped to cement it *as* a public, and in so doing, helped create modern America as a functioning political whole. But the costs of this imposture to William Cody himself were considerable. If embodying the frontier myth gave him a continuing hold on America's imagination, it made him peculiarly vulnerable to its narrative constraints as his life continued. Perhaps if he had been merely another businessman or a vaudeville star, his divorce case would have collapsed anyway. But to be a frontiersman and a showman at the same time was to walk a border between dark and light, a kind of lifelong high-wire act that in some sense kept the public on edge. To attack the domestic hearth at the center of the ideology of civilization was to change sides in the war on savagery, to court public condemnation. These were risks he intuited but only half understood. As we have seen, from the army officers who warily appraised their guides in the Indian wars, to Cody's personal acquaintances and partners such as Bram Stoker, Nate Salsbury, and Louisa Frederici Cody, the scout projected a continuing tension between hero and renegade, the figure who ventured over the frontier line to do battle with the darkness, and returned either unstained by it and heroic, or secretly corrupted and malevolent.

The implications of this argument are many, but one important lesson to be drawn, I think, concerns the widespread popular ambivalence about the frontier in the late nineteenth century. For many years now, historians have explained frontier myth, and especially William Cody's brand of it, as an unswervingly triumphalist story. We live in an anxious age, and it would be foolish to assert that the nineteenth century was not more confident than our own in many respects. But if there is one thing William Cody's biography teaches us, it is that the nineteenth century was characterized by doubts about frontier conquest, racial degeneracy, the industrial order, and the failure of the western farm landscape to generate the wealth and security that the story of progress had promised. To construe frontier expansion as a moment of supreme confidence untarnished by reflection or hesitation is to ignore all the dark fears that underlay it.

William Cody could be as defensive and egotistical as any celebrity, but at his apogee he embodied the westward-moving, industrially modern American, who was both optimistic and ambivalent. To be sure, his cheeriness was palpable. He believed fervently in capitalism as his best bet for making lots of money (a bet he seemed to lose consistently). But his simultaneous devotion to Indian friends whose relatives he fought on the Plains, to industrial might and middle-class smallholders, to rural virtue and the ribald world of stage and arena, all suggest his lifelong straddling act, a remarkable unwillingness to choose sides and a talent for creating dramatic spectacle that made it possible for him to avoid doing so.

In so many ways, the show about the triumphant fixity of the settler was Cody's way of calling attention to himself and avoiding the need to settle in one place. Like western film, which allowed generations to believe a frontier promise long after the frontier closed, Buffalo Bill's Wild West generated such powerful mythic images that one could be forgiven for thinking they were real. Cody did not believe all the lies he told, but he did believe in the West as a region that foretold America's bright future. No matter the dismal failures of his town canal systems, the bankruptcy of his mines, the expense of his ranches. The show became his most powerful token of the real West. Much more than a means of telling his story, it became the story. So long as it went on, not only did his life continue, but the story of the West continued, and the drama of onward, upward achievement continued with it.

One author recounts that when Cody's doctor told the showman he had thirty-six hours to live, Cody turned to his brother-in-law, Lew Decker, with a deck of cards, and shrugged off the news. "Let's forget about it and play High Five."[73]

But his nephew, William Cody Bradford, suggests a less sure-footed ending, and one more telling. The doctors had done all they could, and Cody lay dying at his sister May's house in Denver. Johnny Baker was away in the East, looking for money for the next season's show. As if to announce one last time the seamless weave of his life and his show, and his determination to make the story of the West continue, during his last three days, as uremic poisoning sapped his vitality, he returned in his mind to his private railroad car, and imagined he was once more headed to a showground just down the road:

He would send for John Baker and lay down on the bed just as he did in his car and he would have his chair at the head of his bed. He would imagine that he was on the road with his show. He would ask me where we were and what time it was when we got in. He would lay in bed and smoke and read the paper. In fact he lived his life over again. He done just as he did when he was on the road with the show.[74]

NOTES

ABBREVIATIONS

AHC American Heritage Center, University of Wyoming, Laramie, Wyoming
BBDC Buffalo Bill and Dr. Carver Wild West, Rocky Mountain, and Prairie
Exhibition Program 1883 (Hartford, Connecticut: Calhoun Printing)
BBHC McCracken Library, Buffalo Bill Historical Center, Cody, Wyoming
BBM Buffalo Bill Museum, Golden, Colorado
BBWW Buffalo Bill's Wild West
CC *Cody v. Cody*, Civil Case 970, Sheridan County District Court, Wyoming
State Archives, Cheyenne, Wyoming
CHS Colorado Historical Society
DPL Denver Public Library, Denver, Colorado
DPL-WHR Denver Public Library, Western History Room, Denver, Colorado
GAPR General Administrative Project of the Bureau of Reclamation, NARA-
RMR, Denver, Colorado
JCG Julia Cody Goodman
JCGM Julia Cody Goodman memoirs
KSHS Kansas State Historical Society, Topeka, Kansas
NARA National Archives and Records Administration, Washington, D.C.
NARA-CPR National Archives and Records Administration, Central Plains Region,
Kansas City, Missouri
NARA-RMR National Archives and Records Administration, Rocky Mountain Region,
Denver, Colorado
NSHS Nebraska State Historical Society, Lincoln, Nebraska
NSP Nate Salsbury Papers, Yale Collection of American Literature (YCAL),
Beinecke Library, Yale University, New Haven, Connecticut
NSS Nate Salsbury Scrapbooks, W. F. Cody Collection, Western History
Collection, Denver Public Library, Denver, Colorado
WFC William F. Cody
WFC testimony William F. Cody's testimony in *Cody v. Cody*, Civil Case File 970, Folder 2,
Wyoming State Archives, Cheyenne, Wyoming
WSA Wyoming State Archives, Cheyenne, Wyoming
YCAL Yale Collection of American Literature, Yale University, New Haven,
Connecticut

INTRODUCTION

1. Richard J. Walsh and Milton S. Salsbury, *The Making of Buffalo Bill: A Study in Heroics* (1928; rprt. Kissimmee, FL: International Cody Family Association, 1978), 352.

2. *E. E. Cummings: Complete Poems, 1904–1962*, ed. George J. Firmage (New York: Liveright, 1991), 90.

3. Don Russell, *The Lives and Legends of Buffalo Bill* (Norman: University of Oklahoma Press, 1960). The primary debunkers were Richard J. Walsh and Milton S. Salsbury, *The Making of Buffalo Bill*; and Henry Nash Smith, *Virgin Land: The American West as Symbol and Myth* (Cambridge, MA: Harvard University Press, 1950), 103–11.

4. Other biographies, or biographical treatments: Rupert Croft-Cooke and W. S. Meadmore, *Buffalo Bill: The Legend, the Man of Action, the Showman* (London: Sidgwick and Jackson, 1952); Henry Blackman Sell and Victor Weybright, *Buffalo Bill and the Wild West* (New York: Oxford University Press, 1955); Nellie Snyder Yost, *Buffalo Bill: His Family, Fame, Fortunes, Failures, and Friends* (Chicago: Swallow Press, 1979); Joseph G. Rosa and Robin May, *Buffalo Bill and His Wild West: A Pictorial Biography* (Lawrence: University Press of Kansas, 1989), while not comprehensive, offer some useful correctives.

5. Correcting the excesses and dishonesties of myth is a major project of the New Western History, but of earlier scholars, too. Any list of the most helpful recent works would include: William Cronon, Jay Gitlin, George Miles, eds., *Under an Open Sky: Rethinking America's Western Past* (New York: Norton, 1992); Patricia Nelson Limerick, *The Legacy of Conquest: The Unbroken Past of the American West* (New York: Norton, 1985); Patricia Nelson Limerick, Clyde A. Milner, and Charles E. Rankin, eds., *Trails: Toward a New Western History* (Lawrence: University Press of Kansas, 1991); Richard White, *"It's Your Misfortune and None of My Own": A New History of the American West* (Norman: University of Oklahoma, 1991); Don Worster, *Dust Bowl: The Southern Plains in the 1930s* (New York: Oxford, 1982). Predecessors who blazed this trail are also numerous, but include among the most prominent Howard Roberts Lamar, *Dakota Territory, 1861–1889: A Study of Frontier Politics* (New Haven: Yale University Press, 1956), and Henry Nash Smith, *Virgin Land: The American West in Symbol and Myth* (Cambridge, MA: Harvard University Press, 1950).

6. Among the most prominent: Philip J. Deloria, *Indians in Unexpected Places* (Lawrence: University Press of Kansas, 2004), 52–108; Peter H. Hassrick, Richard Slotkin, Vine Deloria, Jr., Howard R. Lamar, William Judson, and Leslie A. Fiedler, *Buffalo Bill and the Wild West* (Brooklyn, NY: Brooklyn Museum, 1984); Joy S. Kasson, *Buffalo Bill's Wild West: Celebrity, Memory, and Popular History* (New York: Hill & Wang, 2000); Paul Reddin, *Wild West Shows* (Chicago: University of Illinois Press, 1999); Richard Slotkin, *Gunfighter Nation: The Myth of the Frontier in Twentieth-Century America* (New York: Atheneum, 1992), 63–87; Jane Tompkins, *West of Everything: The Inner Life of Westerns* (New York: Oxford University Press, 1992); Richard White, "Frederick Jackson Turner and Buffalo Bill," in *The Frontier in American Culture*, ed. James Grossman (Berkeley: University of California Press, 1994), 7–65.

7. For example, see William Cronon, "A Place for Stories: Nature, History, and Narrative," *Journal of American History* 78 (March 1992): 1347–79; Alan S. Taylor, *William Cooper's Town: Power and Persuasion on the Frontier of the Early American Republic* (New York: Alfred A. Knopf, 1995); David Carr, *Time, Narrative, and History* (Bloomington: Indiana University Press, 1986); Ann Fabian, *The Unvarnished Truth: Personal Narratives in Nineteenth-Century America* (Berkeley: University of California Press, 2000).

8. The "progress of civilization" was a common refrain after the Civil War, evoking the triumph of modern, white America—with all its agrarianism, industrialism, literacy, law, Christianity, democracy, capitalism, and the family home—over the dark forces of barbarism and savagery. See Gail Bederman, *Manliness and Civilization: A Cultural History of Gender and Race in the United States, 1880–1917* (Chicago: University of Chicago Press, 1995), 23–44; Raymond Williams, *Keywords: A Vocabulary of Culture and Society*, rev. ed. (New York: Oxford University Press, 1983), 57–60; Charles A. Beard and Mary R. Beard,

The American Spirit: A Study of the Idea of Civilization in the United States (New York: Macmillan, 1942), 62–97.

9. L. G. Moses, *Wild West Shows and the Images of American Indians, 1883–1933* (Albuquerque: University of New Mexico Press, 1996).

10. See, for example, John Mack Faragher, *Daniel Boone* (New York: Henry Holt, 1994); Taylor, *William Cooper's Town;* Laurel Thatcher Ulrich, *A Midwife's Tale: The Life of Martha Ballard, Based on Her Diary, 1785–1812* (New York: Alfred A. Knopf, 1990).

CHAPTER ONE: PONY EXPRESS

1. BBWW 1893 Program (Chicago: Blakely Printing, 1893), 2.

2. *The Free Press* [Ontario, CA], Sept. 2, 1885, in Nate Salsbury Scrapbook (hereafter NSS), vol. 1, 1885–86, W. F. Cody Collection, WH 72, Western History Collection, DPL.

3. BBWW 1893 Program, 7.

4. William F. Cody, *The Life of the Hon. William F. Cody Known as Buffalo Bill the Famous Hunter, Scout and Guide* (1879; rprt. New York: Indian Head Books, 1991), 57–124. Cody, *Life of Buffalo Bill,* 91.

5. Cody, *Life of Buffalo Bill,* 91–92.

6. Cody, *Life of Buffalo Bill,* 93–102.

7. Cody, *Life of Buffalo Bill,* 104.

8. Cody, *Life of Buffalo Bill,* 108.

9. "Buffalo Bill," *New York Herald,* July 21, 1879, 2.

10. The best discussion of the Pony Express in history and legend is Christopher Corbett, *Orphans Preferred: The Twisted Truth and Lasting Legend of the Pony Express* (New York: Broadway Books, 2003). Other literature on the subject is vast, but much of it is antiquarian. The first history of the Pony Express was Frank A. Root and William Elsey Connelley, *The Overland Stage to California* (1901; rprt. Columbus, OH: Long's College Book Co., 1950); followed soon after by William Lightfoot Visscher, *A Thrilling and Truthful History of the Pony Express, or Blazing the Westward Way* (1908; rprt. Chicago: Charles T. Powner, 1946), and Glenn D. Bradley, *The Story of the Pony Express* (Chicago: A. C. McClurg, 1913), reprinted in *The Story of the Pony Express,* ed. Waddell F. Smith, 2nd ed. (San Francisco: Hesperia House, 1960), 27–146. See also Le Roy R. Hafen, *The Overland Mail, 1849–1869: Promoter of Settlement, Precursor of Railroads* (Cleveland: Arthur H. Clark, 1926); Arthur Chapman, *The Pony Express: The Record of a Romantic Adventure in Business* (New York: G. P. Putnam's Sons, 1932); J. V. Frederick, *Ben Holladay: The Stagecoach King* (1940; rprt. Lincoln: University of Nebraska Press, 1989); Roy S. Bloss, *Pony Express—The Great Gamble* (Berkeley, CA: Howell-North, 1959); Robert West Howard, Roy E. Coy, Frank C. Robertson, and Agnes Wright Spring, *Hoofbeats of Destiny: The Story of the Pony Express* (New York: Signet Books, 1960); Raymond W. Settle and Mary Lund Settle, *Saddles and Spurs: The Pony Express Saga* (Harrisburg, PA: Stackpole Books, 1955); M. C. Nathan and W. S. Boggs, *The Pony Express* (New York: The Collector's Club, 1962); Fred Reinfeld, *Pony Express* (1966; rprt. Lincoln: University of Nebraska Press, 1973); W. Turrentine Jackson, "A New Look at Wells Fargo, Stagecoaches, and the Pony Express," *California Historical Society Quarterly* (Dec. 1966): 291–324; Carl H. Scheele, *A Short History of the Mail Service* (Washington, DC: Smithsonian Institution Press, 1970), esp. 83–86.

11. Visscher, *Thrilling and Truthful History;* Corbett, *Orphans Preferred,* 173–99. For an example of the passage of Cody's pony tales from show to history, see Bradley, *Story of the Pony Express,* 127. Bradley lifted his discussion of Cody's exploits almost verbatim from Root and Connelley, *Overland Stage to California,* 129–30. Root and Connelley, in turn, lifted their account almost entirely from Cody himself. Cody, *Life of Buffalo Bill,* 97, 103–7.

12. The closest, most critical analysis is John S. Gray, "Fact Versus Fiction in the Kansas Boyhood of Buffalo Bill," *Kansas History* 8 (Spring 1985): 2–20, esp. 17–19. For contemporary critics, see Luther North, *Man of the Plains: Recollections of Luther North,*

1856–1882, ed. Donald F. Danker (Lincoln: University of Nebraska Press, 1961), 23; Herbert Cody Blake, *Blake's Western Stories: History and Busted Romances of the Old Frontier* (Brooklyn, NY: Herbert Cody Blake, 1929).

13. Russell, *Lives and Legends*, 44–54; Sandra K. Sagala, *Buffalo Bill, Actor: A Chronicle of Cody's Theatrical Career* (Bowie, MD: Heritage Books, 2002), 19–21, 110.

14. Cody, *Life of Buffalo Bill*; Don Russell, ed., "Julia Cody Goodman's Memoirs of Buffalo Bill," *Kansas Historical Quarterly* 28, no. 4 (Winter 1962) (hereafter JCGM): 442–96.

15. Russell, *Lives and Legends*, 272–73. Don Russell and Albert Johannsen make a compelling case that Cody authored several dime novels. See Russell, *Lives and Legends*, 265–73; Albert Johannsen, *The House of Beadle and Adams and Its Dime and Nickel Novels: The Story of a Vanished Literature*, 3 vols. (Norman: University of Oklahoma Press, 1950), 2:59–61. I am not persuaded by the evidence for Cody's authorship of dime novels. Unlike the 1879 autobiography, the Buffalo Bill dime novels I have been able to examine are characterized by flowery, ornate prose nothing like Cody's letters. Johannsen reproduces a Cody letter in which the showman mentions having contributed to the dime novels of a prominent publisher. I suspect Cody was either joking, or referring to the fact that his persona helped boost sales, or both.

16. JCGM, 448; Russell, *Lives and Legends*, 4–10.

17. Russell, *Lives and Legends*, 7.

18. JCGM, 453; Cody, *Life of Buffalo Bill*, 21.

19. JCGM, 457, 461; A. T. Andreas and W. G. Cutler, *History of the State of Kansas* (1883; rprt. Atchison, KS: Atchison Historical Society, 1976), 505, 508.

20. Settlement figures are from Stephen A. Flanders, *Atlas of American Migration* (New York: Facts on File, 1998), 94.

21. D. Jerome Tweton, "Claim Association," in *New Encyclopedia of the American West*, ed. Howard R. Lamar (New Haven, CT: Yale University Press, 1998), 219; Everett Dick, *The Sod-House Frontier, 1854–1890* (Lincoln: University of Nebraska Press, 1937), 21–29; Richard White, *"It's Your Misfortune and None of My Own,"* 141; Allan G. Bogue, "The Iowa Claim Clubs: Symbol and Substance," in *The Public Lands: Studies in the History of the Public Domain*, ed. Vernon Carstensen (Madison: University of Wisconsin Press, 1963), 47–69.

22. Gray, "Fact Versus Fiction," 4; Louise Barry, *The Beginning of the West: Annals of the Kansas Gateway to the American West, 1540–1854* (Topeka: Kansas State Historical Society, 1972), 1266.

23. JCGM, 458; Cody, *Life of Buffalo Bill*, 38; the Fourth of July meeting was announced as a territorial convention. See Martha B. Caldwell, ed., "Records of the Squatter Association of Whitehead District, Doniphan County," *Kansas Historical Quarterly* 13 (Feb. 1944): 23, n. 33.

24. Gray, "Fact Versus Fiction," 4–5. For Indians in the Civil War, Jay Monaghan, *Civil War on the Western Border, 1854–1865* (Boston: Little, Brown and Co., 1955), 209–27; also Ari Kelman, "Deadly Currents: John Ross's Decision of 1861 Sheds Light on Race and Sovereignty in the Cherokee Nation," *Chronicles of Oklahoma* 62 (Spring 1995): 80–103.

25. Gray, "Fact Versus Fiction," 5; JCGM, 459; Cody, *Life of Buffalo Bill*, 42.

26. *The Democratic Platform* [Liberty, Missouri], Sept. 28, 1854, quoted in Russell, *Lives and Legends*, 14.

27. JCGM, 459–60; Cody, *Life of Buffalo Bill*, 41–42.

28. Cody, *Life of Buffalo Bill*, 43.

29. JCGM, 460; Cody, *Life of Buffalo Bill*, 42.

30. Nicole Etcheson, *Bleeding Kansas: Contested Liberty in the Civil War Era* (Lawrence: University Press of Kansas, 2004); Thomas Goodrich, *War to the Knife: Bleeding Kansas, 1854–1861* (Mechanicsburg, PA: Stackpole Books, 1998).

31. Cody, *Life of Buffalo Bill*, 43.

32. JCGM, 460.

33. Cody, *Life of Buffalo Bill*, 48.

34. JCGM, 471.

35. Thomas Goodrich, *Black Flag: Guerrilla Warfare on the Western Border, 1861–65* (Bloomington: Indiana University Press, 1995), 1–5; Etcheson, *Bleeding Kansas,* 109–112.

36. JCGM, 443; for Topeka legislature, and Grasshopper Falls, see Etcheson, *Bleeding Kansas,* 50–88, 150.

37. Cody, *Life of Buffalo Bill,* 47.

38. JCGM, 465–66.

39. JCGM, 465.

40. JCGM, 471.

41. JCGM, 471.

42. JCGM, 475.

43. JCGM, 475.

44. The estimate is from Home E. Socolofsky, "Kansas," in *The New Encyclopedia of the American West,* ed. Howard R. Lamar (New Haven, CT: Yale University Press, 1998), 585. Charles Dunn led an attack on free state voters at Leavenworth in 1855. The Kickapoo Rangers attacked Grasshopper Falls in 1856. Etcheson, *Bleeding Kansas,* 75, 134.

45. JCGM, 475.

46. Daniel C. Fitzgerald, *Faded Dreams: More Ghost Towns of Kansas* (Lawrence: University Press of Kansas, 1994), xi.

47. Maria E. Montoya, "Santa Fe and Chihuahua Trail," in Lamar, *Encyclopedia of the American West,* 1021–22; Elliott West, *The Contested Plains: Indians, Goldseekers, and the Rush to Colorado* (Lawrence: University Press of Kansas, 1998), 8.

48. Merrill J. Mattes, *The Great Platte River Road* (Lincoln: University of Nebraska Press, 1969), 23.

49. Mattes, *Great Platte River Road,* 23.

50. JCGM, 455.

51. West, *Contested Plains,* 145.

52. West, *Contested Plains,* 216.

53. West, *Contested Plains,* 211–12.

54. West, *Contested Plains,* 211–12. The use of this new route did not last long, as the partners acquired a mail contract which required them to deliver along the older government route to the north, along the Platte River, connecting to Denver with a cutoff along the South Platte River.

55. Horace Greeley, *An Overland Journey from New York to San Francisco in the Summer of 1859,* quoted in Corbett, *Orphans Preferred,* 16–17.

56. Mary Cody sued William Russell and several associates in 1860, claiming that after Isaac died they had taken property which belonged to him. See Rosa and May, *Buffalo Bill and His Wild West,* 10.

57. West, *Contested Plains,* 215–25.

58. JCGM, 476.

59. John Willis to WFC, Oct. 4, 1897, in Stella Foote, *Letters from "Buffalo Bill,"* (Billings, MT: Foote Publishing Co., 1954), 46; Gray, "Fact Versus Fiction," 12.

60. Elliott West, *Growing Up with the Country: Childhood on the Far Western Frontier* (Albuquerque: University of New Mexico Press, 1989), 87–91.

61. Norman F. Furniss, *The Mormon Conflict, 1850–1859* (New Haven, CT: Yale University Press, 1960), 109–10.

62. Gray, "Fact Versus Fiction," 13; Otis G. Hammond, ed., *The Utah Expedition, 1857–58: Letters of Capt. Jesse A. Gove, 10th Inf., U.S.A., of Concord, N.H., to Mrs Gove, and Special Correspondence of the New York Herald* (Concord: New Hampshire Historical Society, 1928), 12:28, 70. Leroy and Ann Hafen, eds., "Diary of Captain John W. Phelps," in *The Utah Expedition: A Documentary Account* (Arthur H. Clark, 1958), 8:90–102, 149, esp. 102; "Morehead's Narrative" (with details about the Indian raid) is in William Elsey Connelley, *War with Mexico: Doniphan's Expedition and the Conquest of New Mexico and California* (Topeka, KS: By the author, 1907), 604–5.

63. WFC to Julia Cody Goodman, June 9, 1911, in Stella A. Foote, *Letters from Buffalo Bill,* 72.

64. Gray, "Fact Versus Fiction," 15–17. Crossing the South Platte in Aug. 1857, Captain Jesse Gove remarked, "The water was not over three feet deep in the current." Hammond, *Utah Expedition*, 42.

65. Cody recalls being hired by George Chrisman, who was merely a station tender and had no authority to hire anybody. He later says he rode on "Bill Trotter's division" of the line. But Trotter became division agent for the firm later on. In 1859, he was actually bound for Denver as a teamster. Cody, *Life of Buffalo Bill*, 104; Gray, "Fact Versus Fiction," 17; "William Trotter," *Progressive Men of Montana* (Chicago: A. W. Bowen and Co., 1901), 933.

66. Gray, "Fact Versus Fiction," 19; Joseph G. Rosa, *They Called Him Wild Bill: The Life and Adventures of James Butler Hickok*, 2nd ed. (Norman: University of Oklahoma Press, 1974), 43.

67. JCGM, 488.

68. Gray, "Fact Versus Fiction," 19.

69. Mark Pinney, "Charles Becker: Pony Express Rider and Oregon Pioneer," *Oregon Historical Quarterly* 67, no. 3 (Sept. 1966): 213–56, esp. 228.

70. Gray, "Fact Versus Fiction," 17–19; Alexander Majors, *Seventy Years on the Frontier* (Chicago: Rand McNally, 1893), 243, also 182–93; Russell, *Lives and Legends of Buffalo Bill*, 47–48; Corbett, *Orphans Preferred*, 154–55.

71. Gray, "Fact Versus Fiction," 16; Cody, *Life of Buffalo Bill*, 89; Valentine Devinny, *The Story of a Pioneer* (Denver: Reed Publishing Co., 1904), 11–12, 44–46. For a description of Pony Express riding, see Corbett, *Orphans Preferred*, 82.

72. Sarah Barringer Gordon, *The Mormon Question: Polygamy and Constitutional Conflict in Nineteenth-Century America* (Chapel Hill: University of North Carolina Press, 2002), 55–83; Will Bagley, *Blood of the Prophets: Brigham Young and the Massacre at Mountain Meadows* (Norman: University of Oklahoma Press, 2002), 307–22; see also Sally Denton, *American Massacre: The Tragedy at Mountain Meadows, September 1857* (New York: Alfred A. Knopf, 2003); and Juanita Brooks, *The Mountain Meadows Massacre*, 3rd ed. (1950; Norman: University of Oklahoma Press, 1970).

73. Russell, *Lives and Legends*, 35–36.

74. James W. Cook, *The Arts of Deception: Playing with Fraud in the Age of Barnum* (Cambridge, MA: Harvard University Press, 2001), 224; Roland Barthes, "The Reality Effect," in *The Rustle of Language* (Berkeley: University of California Press, 1989), 141–48.

75. "Camp Sketches—No. IX—John Nelson," *The Topical Times*, Aug. 27, 1887, in Julia Cody Goodman Scrapbook, MS 58, NSHS; Dan L. Thrapp, *Encyclopedia of Frontier Biography*, 3 vols. (Glendale, CA: Arthur H. Clark Co., 1988), 2:1048–49.

76. John Kasson, *Civilizing the Machine: Technology and Republican Values in America, 1776–1900* (New York: Hill & Wang, 1976), 53–136.

77. Quoted in Corbett, *Orphans Preferred*, 121.

78. Malcolm J. Rohrbough, *Days of Gold: The California Gold Rush and the American Nation* (Berkeley: University of California Press, 1997), 32.

79. W. Turrentine Jackson, *Wagon Roads West: A Study of Federal Road Surveys and Construction in the Trans-Mississippi West, 1846–1869* (1952; rprt. New Haven, CT: Yale University Press, 1965), 161–62, 164.

80. Donald C. Biggs, *The Pony Express: Creation of the Legend* (San Francisco: privately printed, 1956), 16–17, quote from 17.

81. Cody, *Life of Buffalo Bill*, 30.

82. Cody, *Life of Buffalo Bill*, 30.

83. Cody, *Life of Buffalo Bill*, 30–37.

84. For the circus in California and the Pacific, see John Culhane, *The American Circus: An Illustrated History* (New York: Henry Holt, 1990), 80–81. For horses: Hubert Howe Bancroft, *California Pastoral* (San Francisco: The History Company, 1888), 336; Dan Flores, *Horizontal Yellow: Nature and History in the Near Southwest* (Albuquerque: University of New Mexico Press, 1999), 81–124.

85. Cody, *Life of Buffalo Bill*, 33.

86. Cody, *Life of Buffalo Bill*, 37.

87. William Webb, *Buffalo Land* (Cincinnati and Chicago: E. Hannaford and Co., 1873), 149.

88. Cody, *Life of Buffalo Bill*, 135.

89. Ned Buntline [E. Z. C. Judson], *Buffalo Bill: The King of Border Men* (1869; rprt. William Roba, Davenport, IA: Service Press, 1987).

90. Sagala, *Buffalo Bill, Actor*, 110.

91. Cody, *Life of Buffalo Bill*, 46.

CHAPTER TWO: THE ATTACK ON THE SETTLER'S CABIN

1. See chapter 9.

2. Cody, *Life of Buffalo Bill*, 139.

3. Thomas Goodrich, *Black Flag: Guerrilla Warfare on the Western Border, 1861–65* (Bloomington: Indiana University Press, 1995), 6–7.

4. Goodrich, *Black Flag*, 16, 24.

5. John Mack Faragher, *Sugar Creek: Life on the Illinois Prairie* (New Haven, CT: Yale University Press, 1986), 86; David P. Handlin, *The American Home: Architecture and Society, 1815–1915* (Boston: Little, Brown, and Co., 1979), 4; David B. Danbom, *The Resisted Revolution: Urban America and the Industrialization of Agriculture, 1900–1930* (Ames: Iowa State University Press, 1979), 9: "Economic exigencies and the American practice of individual land settlement conspired to make the family the preeminent social, economic, and educational institution of rural society."

6. Goodrich, *Black Flag*, frontispiece.

7. Cody, *Life of Buffalo Bill*, 126, 135.

8. Cody, *Life of Buffalo Bill*, 135.

9. JCGM, 488–89.

10. Quoted in Thomas Goodrich, *Black Flag*, 67–70. Mendenhall was recording events from May 1861. In his autobiography, Cody claimed to have joined them in the winter of 1862, but since most of the Red Leg forays occurred in the summer of 1862, he likely has confused dates and seasons, as he frequently did in his autobiography. Julia Cody recalls that her brother "stayed out all summer" with the Red Legs. JCGM, 488–89.

11. Goodrich, *Black Flag*, 69.

12. Goodrich, *Black Flag*, 69.

13. Cody, *Life of Buffalo Bill*, 144–45.

14. Thomas Ewing, commander of the Eleventh Kansas Volunteers, singled out the Red Legs as especially virulent examples of certain Kansans who were "stealing themselves rich in the name of liberty," and "giving respectability to robbery when committed on any whom they declare disloyal." Ewing threatened to meet them "with a rough hand." General James Blunt, the Union officer in charge of Kansas in 1863, ordered the Ninth Kansas Volunteers into western Missouri, with the stated purpose of fighting the Red Legs as well as the bushwhackers. (Captain Tough, whom Cody claimed as his commander, had close ties to Blunt.) Albert Castel, *A Frontier State at War: Kansas, 1861–1865* (Ithaca, NY: Cornell University Press, 1958), 111–13, 137, 214–15.

15. Charles Sellers, *The Market Revolution: Jacksonian America, 1815–1846* (New York: Oxford University Press, 1991), 19–21; Faragher, *Sugar Creek*, 96–99, 199–204, argues that the market penetration of western farming prior to 1850 was slow and uneven.

16. JCGM, 479.

17. JCGM, 490.

18. Cody, *Life of Buffalo Bill*, 125–27.

19. The affidavits are in Box 1, Folder 18, William F. Cody Collection, MS 6 Series I:A., BBHC.

20. Cody, *Life of Buffalo Bill*, 127.

21. Goodrich, *Black Flag* and *War to the Knife: Bleeding Kansas, 1854–1861* (Mechanicsburg, PA: Stackpole Books, 1998); Stephen Z. Starr, *Jennison's Jayhawkers: A Civil War Cavalry Regiment and Its Commander* (Baton Rouge: Louisiana State University Press, 1973), 96–118; T. J. Stiles, *Jesse James: Last Rebel of the Civil War* (New York: Alfred A. Knopf, 2003).

22. JCGM, 489.

23. Goodrich, *Black Flag*, 114.

24. Quoted in Joseph G. Rosa, *They Called Him Wild Bill: The Life and Adventures of James Butler Hickok*, 2nd ed. (Norman: University of Oklahoma Press, 1974), 26.

25. Cody, *Life of Buffalo Bill*, 135.

26. Ibid.

27. See the copies of muster rolls in Box 1/17, William Cody Collection, MS 6, Series I:A, BBHC; also Starr, *Jennison's Jayhawkers*, 356.

28. Charlie Cody's death in JCGM, 491; quote from Goodrich, *Black Flag*, 160.

29. George Miller, quoted in Goodrich, *Black Flag*, 160.

30. Samuel McKee, quoted in Goodrich, *Black Flag*, 162.

CHAPTER THREE: THE VILLAGE . . . THE CYCLONE

1. Scene announcement is in BBWW 1886 programs, M Cody Programs, Folder 2, DPL; quote from "Buffalo Bill in Drama," *New York Times*, Nov. 25, 1886, p. 5.

2. Quote from BBWW 1893 program, p. 4.

3. Lew Parker, *Odd People I Have Met*, (n.p., n.d.), 37–39.

4. Percy MacKaye, *Epoch: The Life of Steele Mackaye*, 2 vols. (New York: Boni and Liveright, 1927), 2:78–79.

5. Parker, *Odd People I Have Met*, 39; BBWW 1887 program, M Cody Programs, Folder 2, DPL.

6. BBWW 1907 Program (Buffalo, NY: Courier, 1907).

7. "Prosperous Kansas," *New York Times*, Nov. 13, 1869, p. 4.

8. John Mack Faragher, *Daniel Boone* (New York: Henry Holt, 1994), 120–23, 241–45; William Cronon, *Nature's Metropolis: Chicago and the Great West* (New York: Norton, 1996); Gunther Barth, *Instant Cities: Urbanization and the Rise of San Francisco and Denver* (New York: Oxford University Press, 1975). For Iowa towns see John W. Reps, *Cities of the Mississippi: Nineteenth-Century Images of Urban Development* (Columbia: University of Missouri Press, 1994), 238–53.

9. Albert D. Richardson, *Beyond the Mississippi* (Hartford, CT: American Publishing Co., 1867), 57–60.

10. JCGM, 461.

11. John Hoyt Williams, *A Great and Shining Road: The Epic Story of the Transcontinental Railroad* (New York: Times Books, 1988), 69–70.

12. Cody, *Life of Buffalo Bill*, 141–42.

13. Louisa Frederici Cody and Courtney Riley Cooper, *Memories of Buffalo Bill, by His Wife* (New York: D. Appleton & Co., 1919), 1–28; William Cody's memory of his mother-in-law is in his divorce testimony, WFC testimony, March 23, 1904, 2, Folder 2, *Cody v. Cody*, Civil Case 970, Sheridan County District Court, Wyoming State Archives, Cheyenne, WY; hereafter WFC testimony.

14. See WFC testimony; also, Cody, *Life of Buffalo Bill*, 144.

15. I infer her desire for a husband in business from the implications of Cody's divorce testimony, and from Cody, *Life of Buffalo Bill*, 144: "Having promised my wife that I would abandon the plains, I rented a hotel in the Salt Creek Valley. . . ."

16. Cody, *Life of Buffalo Bill*, 145; WFC testimony, 2.

17. Russell, *Lives and Legends*, 78; Cody, *Life of Buffalo Bill*, 145.

18. WFC testimony, 4.

19. Russell, *Lives and Legends*, 77–78, 84; Cody, *Life of Buffalo Bill*, 145.

20. Cody, *Life of Buffalo Bill*, 127.

21. "Prosperous Kansas," *New York Times*, Nov. 13, 1869, p. 4.

22. John H. Putnam, "A Trip to the End of the Union Pacific in 1868," *Kansas Historical Quarterly* 13, no. 3 (Aug. 1944): 196–203, at 198.

23. WFC testimony, 3.

24. Hauling goods and dugout is in Russell, *Lives and Legends*, 78; liquor is in Joseph G. Rosa and Robin May, *Buffalo Bill and His Wild West: A Pictorial Biography* (Lawrence: University Press of Kansas, 1989), 16.

25. Rosa and May, *Buffalo Bill and His Wild West*, 17–18.

26. The English traveler likely met Buffalo Bill Cramer, a local settler. Russell, *Lives and Legends*, 90–91.

27. Rosa and May, *Buffalo Bill and His Wild West*, 12; Russell, *Lives and Legends*, 84–85; Cody, *Life of Buffalo Bill*, 149–50.

28. For Cody choosing name, see WFC testimony.

29. Samuel Bowles, *Our New West* (Hartford, CT: Hartford Publishing Co., 1869), 50.

30. "In the East, the railroads are built for the towns; on the border they build the towns." Richardson, *Beyond the Mississippi*, 571.

31. Quiett, *They Built the West*, 85.

32. William A. Bell, *New Tracks in North America* (New York: Scribner, Welford & Co., 1870), 18.

33. Quiett, *They Built the West*, 82–91.

34. Cody, *Life of Buffalo Bill*, 150, says two hundred homes, but his divorce testimony of many years later gives the more credible figure of thirty houses. WFC testimony, 4.

35. WFC testimony, 5.

36. WFC testimony, 5. See also the quote from the *Hays City Sentinel*, Jan. 16, 1877, which states that Cody was a local buffalo hunter throughout 1867–68, in Rosa and May, *Buffalo Bill and His Wild West*, 17–18. Cody's biographers have followed Don Russell's lead in making Cody a hunter for the Kansas Pacific only *after* the failure of his town-building scheme. Russell argued that Cody said eighteen months when he meant eight. He and others have been loath to accept Cody's claims to have been employed as a market hunter in 1867, since the need to deliver twelve buffalo a day would pretty much eliminate any chance that Cody could have been a scout and guide for the army that year. Russell, *Lives and Legends*, 88–89; Rosa and May, *Buffalo Bill and His Wild West*, 17–18. But there can be no doubt Cody hunted buffalo for Goddard Brothers while he promoted the town of Rome. Cody himself recalled that town building and buffalo hunting were contemporaneous, both in his divorce testimony of 1904 and in his autobiography, where he lets slip that he hunted for Goddard Brothers for eighteen months before the railroad ceased construction in May 1868. Cody repeated the eighteen months figure to journalists, too. See Edward Aveling, *An American Journey* (New York: John W. Lovell, 1887), 152. This would mean that he had to be working for Goddard Brothers for all of 1867. How could he have scouted for the army in the same year? The solution to the puzzle is simple: he didn't. The dubious claims of his autobiography aside, there is no evidence that he worked for the military in Kansas until late in 1868.

37. All Cody quotes that follow regarding the town of Rome are in WFC testimony, 4–6.

38. Cody, *Life of Buffalo Bill*, 152; WFC testimony.

39. Daniel C. Fitzgerald, *Faded Dreams: More Ghost Towns of Kansas* (Lawrence: University Press of Kansas, 1994), 49–51. Fitzgerald also mentions Arvonia (p. 69) and Kickapoo City (pp. 7–8).

40. BBWW 1886 program.

41. Frederick Jackson Turner, "The Significance of the Frontier in American History," in *The Frontier in American History* (New York: Holt, Rinehart, and Winston, 1920); see also Ann Fabian, "History for the Masses: Commercializing the Western Past," in *Under an Open Sky: Rethinking America's Western Past*, ed. William Cronon, George Miles, and Jay Gitlin (New York: Norton, 1992), 223; White, "Frederick Jackson Turner and Buffalo Bill."

42. MacKaye, *Epoch*, 2:74, 77.

43. Daniel Justin Herman, *Hunting and the American Imagination* (Washington, DC: Smith-sonian Institution Press, 2001), 41–43; Drew R. McCoy, *The Elusive Republic: Political Economy in Jeffersonian America* (Chapel Hill: University of North Carolina Press, 1980), 19–20.

44. Quoted in Henry Nash Smith, *Virgin Land: The American West as Symbol and Myth* (Cambridge, MA: Harvard University Press), 219.

45. For a sample of settler enthusiasm for wildlife shooting, see Rolf Johnson, *Happy as a Big Sunflower: Adventures in the West, 1876–1880*, ed. Richard E. Jensen (Lincoln: University of Nebraska Press, 2000).

46. Alan Taylor, " 'Wasty Ways': Stories of American Settlement," *Environmental History* 3, no. 3 (1998): 291–310.

47. William Webb, *Buffalo Land*, (Cincinnati and Chicago: E. Hannaford and Co., 1873), 194; see also Theodore R. Davis, "The Buffalo Range," *Harper's New Monthly Magazine* 38, no. 224 (Jan. 1869): 147–63.

48. Rosa and May, *Buffalo Bill and His Wild West*, 17–18.

49. Russell, *Lives and Legends*, 89.

50. David A. Dary, *The Buffalo Book* (1974; rprt. New York: Avon, 1975), 74, 77; Dan Flores, *The Natural West: Environmental History in the Great Plains and Rocky Mountains* (Norman: University of Oklahoma Press, 2001), 50–69.

51. Dary, *Buffalo Book*, 74.

52. Cody, *Life of Buffalo Bill*, 161.

53. Andrew C. Isenberg, *The Destruction of the Bison: An Environmental History, 1750–1920* (New York: Cambridge University Press, 2000), 133. For sitting down, see Stanley Vestal, *Queen of Cowtowns: Dodge City* (Lincoln: University of Nebraska Press, 1952), 41.

54. See, for example, Johnson, *Happy as a Big Sunflower*, 52–74.

55. Vestal, *Queen of Cowtowns*, 41–44.

56. Webb, *Buffalo Land*, 457–58; Dary, *Buffalo Book*, 99.

57. Cody, *Life of Buffalo Bill*, 162; Vestal, *Queen of Cowtowns*, 43–44. The three Clarkson brothers of Hays City killed 22,000 buffalo in brief hunting careers beginning in 1868. "The Matthew Clarkson Manuscripts," ed. Rodney Staab, *Kansas History* 5, no. 4 (1982): 256–87.

58. Elliott West, "Bison R Us: Images of Bison in American Culture," MS in author's possession.

59. Vestal, *Queen of Cowtowns*; West, "Bison R Us."

60. WFC testimony.

61. J. Hector St. John de Crèvecoeur, *Letters from an American Farmer* (1782; rprt. New York: E. P. Dutton, 1957), 42, 47.

62. Carl Ludvig Hendricks, "Recollections of a Swedish Buffalo Hunter, 1871–1873," *Swedish Pioneer Historical Quarterly* 32, no. 3 (1981): 190–204.

63. Joseph W. Snell, ed., "Diary of a Dodge City Buffalo Hunter, 1872–1873," *Kansas Historical Quarterly* 31, no. 4 (1965): 345–95.

64. Gary L. Roberts, "William Matthew Tilghman, Jr." and "Earp Brothers," both in *New Encyclopedia of the American West*, ed. Howard R. Lamar (New Haven, CT: Yale University Press, 1998), 327–29, 1114; Glenn Shirley, *Guardian of the Law: The Life and Times of William Matthew Tilghman* (Austin, TX: Eakin Press, 1988); Casey Tefertiller, *Wyatt Earp: The Life Behind the Legend* (New York: John Wiley, 1997).

65. In the 1870s, William Cody knew John Y. Nelson, Hank and Monte Clifford, Arthur Ruff, and Dick Seymour, all of whom lived with their Sioux wives in western Nebraska, where they hunted buffalo for the market. See Paul A. Hutton, "Introduction," in Henry E. Davies, *Ten Days on the Plains*, ed. Paul A. Hutton (1872; Dallas, TX: DeGolyer Library, 1985), 166, n. 30.

66. See Sylvia Van Kirk, *Many Tender Ties: Women in Fur Trade Society in Western Canada, 1670–1870* (Winnipeg: Watson and Dwyer, 1981); William R. Swagerty, "Marriage and Settlement Patterns of Rocky Mountain Trappers and Traders," *Western Historical Quarterly* 11 (April 1980): 159–80; John Mack Faragher, "The Custom of the Country: Cross-

Cultural Marriage in the Far Western Fur Trade," in *Western Women: Their Land, Their Lives*, ed. Lillian Schlissel, Vicki L. Ruiz, and Janice Monk (Albuquerque: University of New Mexico Press, 1988), 199–215.

67. Dary, *Buffalo Book*, 88–92.
68. Washington Irving, *Astoria*, quoted in Henry Nash Smith, *Virgin Land*, 177.
69. WFC testimony, 7.
70. William A. Dobak, *Fort Riley and Its Neighbors: Military Money and Economic Growth, 1853–1895* (Norman: University of Oklahoma Press, 1998). Among Cody's associates at Fort McPherson were Charles McDonald and Isaac S. Boyer, both of whom profited from military contracts as post traders, and both of whom would parlay these contracts into life-long careers as merchants and local politicians. McDonald would eventually become a prominent banker, on whom Cody relied for many of his Nebraska business dealings. On McDonald as banker, see Mrs. Charles Hendy, Sr., Folder 8, Civil Case 970, *Cody v. Cody* (hereafter CC), pp. 92–96; Yost, *Buffalo Bill*, 171. For Isaac Boyer, see Yost, *Buffalo Bill*, 6, 9, 23.
71. Rosa and May, *Buffalo Bill and His Wild West*, 18; J. G. Rosa, "J. B. Hickok, Deputy U.S. Marshal," *Kansas History: A Journal of the Central Plains* 2, no. 4 (Winter 1979): 239–40.

CHAPTER FOUR: WITH THE PRINCE OF PISTOLEERS

1. Ned Buntline (the pseudonym of E. Z. C. Judson), "Buffalo Bill: The King of Border Men," appeared originally as a serial in the story paper *The New York Weekly* from Dec. 23, 1869, to March 3, 1870. It is reprinted as Ned Buntline, *Buffalo Bill: The King of Border Men*, ed. William Roba (Davenport, IA: Service Press, 1987).
2. Dexter W. Fellows and Andrew A. Freeman, *This Way to the Big Show: The Life of Dexter Fellows* (New York: Viking Press, 1936), 33–34.
3. Cody, *Life of Buffalo Bill*, 70.
4. The story of Hickok's escape first appeared in George Ward Nichols, "Wild Bill," *Harper's New Monthly Magazine* 34, no. 201 (Feb. 1867): 273–85; Cody places himself at the scene in *Life of Buffalo Bill*, 139–40.
5. BBWW 1895 program, p. 16, in Cody Collection, WH 72, Box 2, Folder 27, DPL-WHR.
6. Rosa, *They Called Him Wild Bill*, 17, 34–52.
7. JCGM, 484.
8. Rosa, *They Called Him Wild Bill*, 34–52, 90–93, 103–206, 351–52.
9. Nichols, "Wild Bill," 274.
10. Nichols, "Wild Bill," 279, 285.
11. Nichols, "Wild Bill." The story was published in its entirety in Joseph G. Rosa, *Wild Bill Hickok: The Man and His Myth* (Lawrence: University Press of Kansas, 1996), 215–40.
12. Joseph G. Rosa, *The West of Wild Bill Hickok* (Norman: University of Oklahoma Press, 1982), 87–89.
13. See Ena Raymonde Ballantine Journal, entry for March 6, 1873, MS 1730, Nebraska State Historical Society (hereafter NSHS), Lincoln, Nebraska.
14. John H. Putnam, "A Trip to the End of the Union Pacific in 1868," *Kansas Historical Quarterly* 13, no. 3 (Aug. 1944): 196–203, at 199.
15. Rosa, *They Called Him Wild Bill*, 82–83, 106.
16. Quoted in Rosa, *They Called Him Wild Bill*, 83.
17. Nichols, "Wild Bill," 285.
18. Rosa, *They Called Him Wild Bill*, 205.
19. Rosa, *West of Wild Bill Hickok*, 77; also Rosa, *They Called Him Wild Bill*, 107. Stanley's 1867 account is reproduced in Henry M. Stanley, *My Early Travels and Adventures in America and Asia* (1895; rprt. London: Duckworth, 2001), 29–32, 118.
20. William Elsey Connelley, *Wild Bill and His Era: The Life and Adventures of James Butler Hickok* (New York: Press of the Pioneers, 1933), 18.
21. Rosa, *They Called Him Wild Bill*, 84.

22. Joseph G. McCoy, *Historic Sketches of the Cattle Trade of the West and Southwest* (1874; rprt. Lincoln: University of Nebraska Press, 1985), 203–4.

23. I follow the lead of Hillel Schwartz, who distinguishes "between imposture, the compulsive assumption of invented lives, and impersonation, the concerted assumption of another's public identity." Hillel Schwartz, *The Culture of the Copy: Striking Likenesses, Unreasonable Facsimiles* (New York: Zone Books, 1996), 72.

24. Rosa, *They Called Him Wild Bill*, 120, also 224–25.

25. James F. Meline, *Two Thousand Miles on Horseback. Santa Fe and Back* (1867; rprt. Albuquerque, NM: Horn and Wallace, 1966), 17; also Rosa, *They Called Him Wild Bill*, 92.

26. Neil Harris, *Humbug: The Art of P. T. Barnum* (New York: Little, Brown and Co., 1972), 77–89; Andie Tucher, *Froth and Scum: Truth, Beauty, Goodness, and the Ax Murder in America's First Mass Medium* (Chapel Hill: University of North Carolina Press, 1994), 57; James W. Cook, *The Arts of Deception: Playing with Fraud in the Age of Barnum* (Cambridge, MA: Harvard University Press, 2001), 73–81.

27. Cook, *Arts of Deception*, 30–72, 163–255.

28. Cook, *Arts of Deception*, 73–118; Harris, *Humbug*, 213.

29. Tucher, *Froth and Scum*, 57.

30. Harris, *Humbug*, 21–25, 62–67, 77, 167.

31. See Henry Morton Stanley, *My Early Travels and Adventures in America and Asia* (1895; rprt. London: Duckworth, 2001), 114, 183–86; Robert Dykstra, *The Cattle Towns* (New York: Atheneum, 1976), 112–15.

32. William Cronon, *Nature's Metropolis: Chicago and the Great West* (New York: W. W. Norton, 1991); West, *Contested Plains*.

33. Tall tales were a kind of game for the entertainment of an audience as Carolyn S. Brown explains them. As fictions narrated in the first person, they pretend to be true. At first, the audience believes the ruse, or pretends to, and the narrator designs and manipulates the story's elements to heighten this perception, often by mingling realistic detail and experience with the story's deceptions. Audience members who perceive the fictions—and this might be everyone in the room—often play along, acting as if they believe the narrator is truthful. As the story continues, it begins to challenge the listener with "comic outlandishness," until the punch line or resolution, in which the storyteller makes his deception more or less obvious, undermining his own credibility and allowing the audience to laugh. Carolyn S. Brown, *The Tall Tale in American Folklore and Literature* (Knoxville: University of Tennessee Press, 1987), 58–59.

34. See James H. Wilkins, ed., *The Great Diamond Hoax and Other Stirring Incidents in the Life of Asbury Harpending* (1915; rprt. Norman: University of Oklahoma Press, 1958).

35. In southern Illinois during the era of Hickok's boyhood, the legendary tall-tale narrator Abe Smith attracted hundreds of local people to his town on a given weekend, just waiting to hear his stories. Brown, *Tall Tale*, 37.

36. Brown, *Tall Tale*, 10–11, 32.

37. Brown, *Tall Tale*, 10.

38. Stanley Vestal [Thomas Campbell], *Joe Meek: The Merry Mountain Man* (1952; rprt. Lincoln: University of Nebraska Press, 1963), 292–93.

39. John Mack Faragher, *Women and Men on the Overland Trail* (New Haven, CT: Yale University Press, 1976), 16.

40. The term is ubiquitous in gold rush accounts, but see William H. Goetzmann and William N. Goetzmann, *The West of the Imagination* (New York: Norton, 1986), 131.

41. "Donner Party," in *The New Encyclopedia of the American West*, ed. Howard R. Lamar (New Haven, CT: Yale University Press, 1998), 316–17; also C. F. McGlashan, *History of the Donner Party: A Tragedy of the Sierra*, 2nd ed. (1880; rprt. Stanford, CA: Stanford University Press, 1947).

42. Cody, *Life of Buffalo Bill*, 18.

43. The census of 1880 enumerates 996,096 Kansas settlers. James R. Shortridge, *Peopling the Plains: Who Settled Where in Frontier Kansas* (Lawrence: University Press of Kansas, 1995), 15, 72.

44. Fred A. Shannon, *The Farmer's Last Frontier: Agriculture, 1860–1897* (1945; rprt. New York:, 1966), 74–75; David Emmons, *The Garden in the Grassland: Boomer Literature of the Central Great Plains* (Lincoln: University of Nebraska Press, 1971), 25–46, 99–127; Robert V. Hine and John Mack Faragher, *The American West: A New Interpretive History* (New Haven, CT: Yale University Press, 2000), 335–36; White, *"It's Your Misfortune and None of My Own,"* 43–45.

45. My use of Artifice vs. Nature and their relation to authenticity is inspired by Jennifer Price, *Flight Maps: Adventures with Nature in Modern America* (New York: Basic Books, 1999), 114–24. For further discussion of authenticity, see chapter 6.

46. "Every single one of Barnum's living curiosities was a liminal figure of some sort, a caricatured disruption of the normative boundaries between black and white (albino Negroes), male and female (bearded ladies), young and old (General Tom Thumb), man and animal (dog-faced boys), one self or two (Siamese twins)." Cook, *Arts of Deception,* 121.

47. In London, in 1846, Barnum presented the "Wild Man of the Prairies," an exhibit in which Hervey Leech, a black man from New Jersey, dressed up in a hairy costume, with Barnum claiming that he had been discovered living among Indians in "the wilds of California." Cook, *Arts of Deception,* 133. The showman partnered with the West's own menagerie man, Grizzly Adams, in 1860, as if to reprise some of the themes of his wild man exhibit. Playing on the West as a space for sexual revolution, he invited Brigham Young to become an exhibit in his museum in 1868. Harris, *Humbug,* 195.

48. Indeed, perhaps no Hickok attribute was so pronounced, or so practiced, as his marksmanship. Guns had become such a vital symbol of the frontier that mastery of them was central to any white man's frontier imposture. Guns were mass-produced technological wonders. Central features of the age of mechanical revolution, firearms went from cumbersome, hand-crafted, single-shot instruments to lightweight, mass-produced repeaters during Hickok's lifetime. Their hammers, triggers, chambers, pins, cogs, wheels, and other increasingly standardized parts were emblematic of the "American system" of manufactures, of which they were at the same time products, being made from machined parts, and cogent symbols, "producing" lead slugs—and death—through machinery of their own. The nineteenth century was an age of complex machines, marvels of engineering like the locomotive, the electrical generator, the sewing machine, and an astonishing array of mechanical reapers. Modern guns were at least as intricate as many other machines, but they were more portable, and they were affordable, too. The industrial and technological wizardry which both explained and rationalized the triumph of Anglo-Saxon America could be held in one hand. The frontiersman's mastery of the gun not only empowered him to battle evil. It made him the bearer of civilization, the harbinger of progress. A natural man with a modern weapon, he symbolized America itself.

49. Rosa, *They Called Him Wild Bill,* 339–40. Most of these tales were probably apocryphal, but Hickok and other railside showmen practiced shooting obsessively in the late 1860s and '70s, to provide a vital element of machine authenticity to their frontier pose. As the railroads extended west, they enhanced the value of marksmanship and frontier imposture as a commodity in more remote locations. By the early 1870s, settlers in North Platte, Nebraska, could witness dozens of shooting competitions every week. See the Ena Raymonde Ballantine Journal, MS 1730, NSHS, especially entries for June 7 and July 26. My thanks to Elliott West for calling the Ballantine papers to my attention.

50. According to Luther North, Frank North and Hickok "used to meet about twice a week and shoot at targets at John Talbot's roadhouse between Cheyenne and Fort Russell and Talbot would shoot with them." North claims that his brother Frank would usually come in first, Talbot second, and Hickok third. Luther North, *Man of the Plains: Recollections of Luther North, 1856–1882,* ed. Donald F. Danker (Lincoln: University of Nebraska Press, 1961), 150–51.

51. In 1863, P. T. Barnum's American Museum—which included a lecture hall and performance space—featured a woman spy, identified only as Miss Cushman, a "prettily dressed" speaker who lectured briefly on her duties and then performed a series of quick

changes "to show the power of military disguise." Quote from Harris, *Humbug*, 168. Original source is George D. C. Odell, *Annals of the New York Stage*, 14 vols. (New York: Columbia University Press, 1927–1945), 7:57. Cushman was probably Pauline Cushman, who claimed to have been a spy. See Reneé M. Sentilles, *Performing Menken: Adah Isaacs Menken and the Birth of American Celebrity* (New York: Cambridge, 2003), 169, n. 12.

52. E. C. Downs, *Four Years a Scout and Spy* (Zanesville, OH: Hugh Dunne, 1866), 12, emphasis in original. For other examples of scouts in disguise, see Edward W. Eckert and J. Amato Nicholas, " 'A Long and Perilous Ride': The Memoirs of William W. Averell," part 1, *Civil War Times Illustrated* 16, no. 6 (1977): 22–30. For disguise in the border wars, see Nicholas P. Hardeman, "The Bloody Battle That Almost Happened: William Clarke Quantrill and Peter Hardeman on the Western Border," *Civil War History* 23, no. 3: (1977): 251–58.

53. See Milo Milton Quaife, ed., *Kit Carson's Autobiography* (1926: rprt., Lincoln: University of Nebraska Press, 1966), 152.

54. Quaife, *Kit Carson's Autobiography*, 135.

55. DeBenneville Randolph Keim, *Sheridan's Troopers on the Borders: A Winter Campaign on the Plains* (1870; rprt. Lincoln: University of Nebraska Press, 1985), 38.

56. Also see chapter 7.

57. Dan L. Thrapp, *Encyclopedia of Frontier Biography*, 3 vols. (Glendale: Arthur H. Clark, 1988), I: 281, 297, 385, 403; II: 880; III: 1105; Nat Love, *The Life and Adventures of Nat Love: Better Known in the Cattle Country as Deadwood Dick* (Los Angeles: A. P., 1907). By this time western imposture had become a semilegitimate art form. Cody, Hickok, and others had performed it on eastern stages. In the Black Hills, audiences bought tickets to see it performed in local theaters. In 1879, one traveler recorded meeting "a typical western boy" of "about 16" who looked the quintessential westerner in his "broad brimmed hat and blue woolen shirt." His demeanor was authentic, too, since he "chewed tobacco, smoked, drank, and swore like a bullwhacker." The boy claimed to have spent two years in the Black Hills, where he had been "a miner, muleskinner, bullwhacker, [and] cowboy song and dance boy in the theaters." Like the men and women he was imitating, he had found a way to profit from this alleged life story, in part because its dubious claims were so entertaining. "He is sharp as a steel trap, and had not been with me more than two hours till he had told me over a hundred lies and borrowed half a dollar of me." Johnson, *Happy as a Big Sunflower*, 168–69.

58. Mark Twain, *Roughing It* (1872; rprt. New York: New American Library, 1962); Brown, *Tall Tale*, 89–107.

59. William Webb, *Buffalo Land* (Cincinnati and Chicago: E. Hannaford and Co., 1873), 149.

60. See Webb, *Buffalo Land*, 147.

61. Hickok taunted his opponents, especially southerners, in letters to the press, and he killed several men in Missouri, Kansas, and Nebraska. See Rosa, *They Called Him Wild Bill*, 73–74, 147, 157, 248.

62. Rosa, *They Called Him Wild Bill*, 243–44.

63. Rosa, *They Called Him Wild Bill*, 245. "Wild Bill accuses Buffalo Bill of having given Ned Buntline incidents of his (Wild Bill's) life, and claiming them as his (Buffalo Bill's) own adventures." *Jefferson City (Missouri) People's Tribune*, Aug. 23, 1876.

64. John Burke to Jack Crawford, March 5, 1877 [1878?], M Crawford, Box 1, DPL-WHR.

65. Rosa, *They Called Him Wild Bill*, 156–57, 249.

66. Sagala, *Buffalo Bill, Actor*, 107.

67. Rosa, *They Called Him Wild Bill*, 90–91; Cody made up the expedition in W. F. Cody, *An Autobiography of Buffalo Bill* (New York: Farrar and Rinehart, 1920), 81–90; Robert Athearn writes of Sherman's time in the West, and at Fort Riley, in *William Tecumseh Sherman and the Settlement of the West* (Norman: University of Oklahoma Press, 1956), 46–47.

CHAPTER FIVE: GUIDE AND SCOUT

1. Major Armes of the Tenth Cavalry, *Ups and Downs of an Army Officer* (Washington, DC: By the author, 1900), 272. There is no official record of Cody scouting for the army until Sept.

2. Elbert Huber to Don Russell, Aug. 7, 1953, W. F. Cody 201 File, RG 407, NARA.

3. Russell, *Lives and Legends*, 104.

4. "Scout," *The Compact Edition of the Oxford English Dictionary*, 2 vols. (New York: Oxford University Press, 1971), 2677.

5. Richard Slotkin, *Regeneration Through Violence: The Mythology of the American Frontier, 1600–1860* (Middletown, CT: Wesleyan University Press, 1973), 188, 234–35, 289–91; D. H. Lawrence, *Studies in Classic American Literature* (1923; rprt., New York: Penguin, 1977), 68–69; Henry Nash Smith, *Virgin Land: The American West as Symbol and Myth* (Cambridge, MA: Harvard University Press, 1950), 59–80. For a full discussion of the cultural and political implications of white Indianness in its manifold variations, see Philip J. Deloria, *Playing Indian* (New Haven, CT: Yale University Press, 1998), esp. 11–12, 41–42.

6. Smith, *Virgin Land*, 81–89.

7. Slotkin, *Fatal Environment: The Myth of the Frontier in the Age of Industrialization* (1985; rprt. New York: HarperCollins, 1994), 198–99.

8. Russell, *Lives and Legends*, 480.

9. Colin G. Calloway, *One Vast Winter Count: The Native American West Before Lewis and Clark* (Lincoln: University of Nebraska Press, 2004), 267–312; Frank R. Secoy, *Changing Military Patterns on the Great Plains* (Locust Valley, NY: J. J. Augustin, 1953); Richard White, "The Winning of the West: The Expansion of the Western Sioux in the Eighteenth and Nineteenth Centuries," *Journal of American History* 65, no. 2 (Sept. 1978): 319–43.

10. Richard N. Ellis, "Introduction," xiv–xv, in *Cheyenne Dog Soldiers: A Ledgerbook History of Coups and Combat*, ed. Jean Afton, David Fridtjof Halaas, Andrew E. Masich, and Richard N. Ellis (Niwot CO: Colorado Historical Society and University Press of Colorado, 1997).

11. Eugene F. Ware, *The Indian War of 1864* (1911; rprt. New York: St. Martin's Press, 1960), 114; Louis A. Holmes, *Fort McPherson, Nebraska, Cottonwood, N.T.: Guardian of the Tracks and Trails* (Lincoln, NE: Johnsen Publishing Co., 1963), 6.

12. Figures from Joanna L. Stratton, *Pioneer Women: Voices from the Kansas Frontier* (New York: Simon and Schuster, 1981), 121.

13. Secoy, *Changing Military Patterns*; Richard White, "Winning of the West," 319–43; Preston Holder, *The Hoe and the Horse on the Plains: A Study of Cultural Development Among North American Indians* (Lincoln: University of Nebraska Press, 1970); Andrew Isenberg, *The Destruction of the Bison: An Environmental History, 1750–1920* (New York: Cambridge University Press, 2000), 31–122; Joseph Jablow, *The Cheyenne in Plains Indian Trade Relations, 1795–1840* (Seattle: University of Washington Press, 1950); West, *Contested Plains*.

14. Keim, *Sheridan's Troopers on the Borders*, 134.

15. Custer, "On the Plains," *Turf, Field, and Farm*, Jan. 4, 1868, in *Nomad: George A. Custer in Turf, Field and Farm*, ed. Brian W. Dippie (Austin: University of Texas Press, 1980), 36–37.

16. BBWW program 1887 (London: Allen, Scott, and Co., 1887), 29.

17. Buffalo Bill and Doc Carver Wild West, Rocky Mountain, and Prairie Exhibition 1883 (Hartford, CT: Calhoun Printing Co., 1883), n.p.; BBWW 1893 program (Chicago: Blakely Printing Co., 1893), 6, 17.

18. After his discharge from the Union army in September 1865, he was never a soldier again. Russell, *Lives and Legends*, 61; see also Cody's military records file, MS 6 W. F. Cody, Series I:A, Box 1/17, BBHC.

19. BBWW 1887 program (London: Allen, Scott & Co., 1887), 28. Russell, *Lives and Legends*, 326; for reprinting of the letter and the change of dates, see BBWW 1893 program, 16.

20. Russell, *Lives and Legends*, 160.

21. For a full discussion of Cody's loss of the medal and its restoration in 1989, see Oliver Kennedy, Memo of Jan. 12, 1989, Old Military and Civil Records, Case File of William F. Cody, Restoration of the Congressional Medal of Honor (NWTCB-94-Casefiles-AC88[10374]), NARA, Washington, D.C. The subject of Cody's military record and the Medal of Honor has been exhaustively discussed and documented in 201 File for William Cody, RG 407, Box 219, 370/84/27/03, NARA, Washington, DC (see esp. Lutz Wahl to Richard J. Walsh, Feb. 6, 1928).

22. Cody, *Life of Buffalo Bill*, 271; WFC to "My Dear Friends in Rochester," Aug. 9, 1872 [1874] MS 6, I:B, BBHC. The letter is dated 1872, but since Cody reports his assignment to the Big Horn Expedition of 1874, I have corrected the error in my citation. As chief of scouts for the Fifth Cavalry, a post he ascended to in 1868, Cody would have been entitled to a share of the horses and other property captured from enemy Sioux and Cheyenne. WFC testimony, March 23, 1904, p. 9.

23. Russell, *Lives and Legends*, 103.

24. Philip H. Sheridan, *Personal Memoirs of P. H. Sheridan*, 2 vols. (New York: Charles Webster & Company, 1888), 2:300–1.

25. Cody, *Life of Buffalo Bill*, 188–97.

26. Cody, *Life of Buffalo Bill*, 197; for mules in the army, see Robert Utley, *Frontier Regulars: The United States Army and the Indian, 1868–1891* (Lincoln: University of Nebraska, 1973), 48; also Emmett M. Essin, *Shave Tails and Bell Sharps: The History of the U.S. Army Mule* (Lincoln: University of Nebraska, 1997).

27. Sheridan, *Personal Memoirs*, 2:301.

28. George E. Hyde, *The Life of George Bent, Written from His Letters*, ed. Savoie Lottinville (Norman: University of Oklahoma Press, 1968), 335–39; E. Adamson Hoebel, *The Cheyennes: Indians of the Great Plains* (Fort Worth, TX: Harcourt Brace Jovanovich, 1978), 72–73; West, *Contested Plains*, 198.

29. George F. Price, *Across the Continent with the Fifth Cavalry* (1883; rprt. New York: Antiquarian Press, 1959), 131–33.

30. Russell, *Lives and Legends*, 111.

31. Webb, *Buffalo Land*, 194.

32. George A. Custer, *My Life on the Plains, or Personal Experiences with Indians* (1874; rprt. Norman: University of Oklahoma Press, 1962), 279.

33. Karen Halttunen, *Confidence Men and Painted Women: A Study of Middle Class Culture in America, 1830–1870* (New Haven, CT: Yale University Press, 1982), 1–32.

34. Stanley, *My Early Travels and Adventures*, 114, 183–86.

35. Eugene A. Carr, "Memoirs of Brvt. Major General E. A. Carr," typescript, n.d., p. 195, microfilm MS 2688, Reel 1, NSHS.

36. Utley, *Frontier Regulars*, 65–67.

37. Utley, *Frontier Regulars*, 11–14; also Robert Utley, *Cavalier in Buckskin: George Armstrong Custer and the Western Military Frontier* (Norman: University of Oklahoma Press, 1988), 103; soldiers usually had only partial uniforms—or none at all. See Utley, *Frontier Regulars*, 77; also John F. Finerty, *War-Path and Bivouac: The Big-Horn and Yellowstone Expedition* (1890; rprt. Chicago: R. R. Donnelly & Sons, 1955), 249: "[A]nd as for the uniform the absence thereof is a leading characteristic of the service."

38. Sherry Smith, *The View from Officers' Row: Army Perceptions of Western Indians* (Tucson: University of Arizona Press, 1990), 2.

39. Smith, *View from Officers' Row*, 7–10; Knight, *Life and Manners in the Frontier Army*, 220–26; Utley, *Frontier Regulars*, 59–68. This alienation was traditional. Edward M. Coffman writes that up to 1860, all soldiers shared "the experience of being military men in a country which did not like soldiers and at a time when many also deplored the concept of professionalism in any field." Edward M. Coffman, *The Old Army: A Portrait of the American Army in Peacetime, 1784–1898* (New York: Oxford University Press, 1986), 103.

40. Knight, *Life and Manners in the Frontier Army*, 76.

41. Knight, *Life and Manners in the Frontier Army*, 80.

42. Smith, *View from Officer's Row*, 141. The army reinstituted brevet promotions in 1890.

43. Utley, *Cavalier in Buckskin*, 103; Russell, *Lives and Legends*, 119–20; for jealousy, see Armes, *Ups and Downs of an Army Officer*, 333.

44. For cold, see Armes, *Ups and Downs of an Army Officer*, 208.

45. Custer, *My Life on the Plains*, 49.

46. Among the sternest critics of the Indian wars army were Civil War veterans, who looked down on the struggling Plains campaigns as a series of ill-fought minor skirmishes. Nate Salsbury, Cody's managing partner for many years in the Wild West show and a Union combat veteran, reflected his comrades' consensus when he bitterly remarked that "as a private soldier during the Civil War, I smelled more powder in one afternoon at Chickamauga, than all the 'Great Scouts' that America has ever produced ever did in a lifetime." Nate Salsbury Papers (henceforth cited as NSP), "Long Hair and a Plug Hat," MS 17, Box 2/63, YCAL, Beinecke Library, Yale University, New Haven, CT.

47. Utley, *Frontier Regulars*, 114–21; and *Cavalier in Buckskin*, 47–49.

48. Utley, *Frontier Regulars*, 23. Custer's regiment was plagued by desertion and low morale. Of the 963 enlisted men assigned to the Seventh Cavalry at Fort Riley, Kansas, in 1866, 80—nearly 10 percent—deserted in the next six months. Jeffrey D. Wert, *Custer: The Controversial Life of George Armstrong Custer* (New York: Simon and Schuster, 1996), 233–36, 246–64; Evan S. Connell, *Son of the Morning Star*, 150–51.

49. Coffman, *Old Army*, 339–48. Soldiers voted with their feet. Where fewer than one soldier in ten deserted in 1871, nearly one in three deserted the following year. For six months without pay, see Robert Utley, ed., *Life in Custer's Cavalry: Diaries and Letters of Albert and Jennie Barnitz, 1867–1868* (New Haven, CT: Yale University Press, 1977), 128.

50. Reginald Horsman, *Race and Manifest Destiny: The Origins of American Racial Anglo-Saxonism* (Cambridge, MA: Harvard University Press, 1981), 34–36, 62–97; Slotkin, *Fatal Environment*, 230–31; Smith, *Virgin Land*, 37–38. For contemporary references to Anglo-Saxonism see "The Loss of the Tasmanians," *New York Times*, Jun. 12, 1869, p. 4; "What Anglo-Saxonism Is," *New York Times*, Feb. 8, 1880, p. 7; Walt Whitman meditates on Aryan millennialism and westward expansion in his 1860 poem, "Facing West from California Shores," in Walt Whitman, *Leaves of Grass and Selected Prose*, ed. John Kouwenhoven (New York: Modern Library, 1950), 92. See also Stuart Anderson, *Race and Rapprochement: Anglo-Saxonism and Anglo-American Relations, 1895–1904* (Rutherford, NJ: Fairleigh Dickinson University Press, 1981), 1–70, esp. 39–45, 57–61. General Sherman referred to the Indian wars as "the Battle of Civilization." G. W. Baird, *A Report to the Citizens Concerning Certain Late Disturbances on the Western Frontier Involving Sitting Bull, Crazy Horse, Chief Joseph, and Geronimo* (1891; rprt. Ashland, OR: Lewis Osborne, 1972), 21. In 1868, General Sherman could claim that his soldiers were fighting "enemies of our race and our civilization." William T. Sherman to Philip Sheridan, Oct. 9, 1868, quoted in Utley, *Frontier Regulars*, 145.

51. These were the Thirty-eighth, Thirty-ninth, Fortieth, and Forty-first infantries. Utley, *Frontier Regulars*, 25–26; Coffman, *Old Army*, 331; see also William H. Leckie and Shirley A. Leckie, *The Buffalo Soldiers: A Narrative of the Black Cavalry in the West*, rev. ed. (Norman: University of Oklahoma Press, 2003); Quintard Taylor, *In Search of the Racial Frontier: African Americans in the American West, 1528–1990* (New York: Norton, 1998), 164–91, esp. 165.

52. Oliver Knight, *Following the Indian Wars: The Story of the Newspaper Correspondents Among the Indian Campaigners* (Norman: University of Oklahoma Press, 1960), 23.

53. Custer, in Dippie, *Nomad*, 34; see also Coffman, *Old Army*, 330, 334. For the Irish in Custer's Seventh in 1876, see Utley, *Cavalier in Buckskin*, 168.

54. I am indebted to recent scholarship on whiteness and race for these insights and much of the discussion that follows. See Matthew Frye Jacobson, *Whiteness of a Different Color: European Immigrants and the Alchemy of Race* (Cambridge, MA: Harvard University Press, 1998); Noel Ignatiev, *How the Irish Became White* (New York: Routledge, 1995); David R. Roediger, *The Wages of Whiteness: Race and the Making of the American Working Class* (New York: Verso, 1991), and *Towards the Abolition of Whiteness: Essays on Race, Politics, and Working Class History* (New York: Verso, 1994); Alexander Saxton, *The Rise and Fall of the*

White Republic: Class Politics and Mass Culture in Nineteenth Century America (New York: Verso, 1990).

55. Jacobson, *Whiteness of a Different Color*, 53–55. Germans' ethnic political organization also was a factor in leading some anxious Americans to denounce them for taking opportunities from "white" men. Jacobson, *Whiteness of a Different Color*, 47.

56. Connell, *Son of the Morning Star*, 86.

57. Ignatiev, *How the Irish Became White*, 34–61.

58. Arthur Comte de Gobineau, *The Inequality of Human Races* (1855), quoted in Jacobson, *Whiteness of a Different Color*, 44.

59. Jacobson, *Whiteness of a Different Color*; Ignatiev, *How the Irish Became White*; and Roediger, *Wages of Whiteness*.

60. Coffman, *Old Army*, 332; quote from Utley, *Cavalier in Buckskin*, 120.

61. Armes, *Ups and Downs of an Army Officer*, 288.

62. Armes, *Ups and Downs of an Army Officer*, 247.

63. Cody, *Life of Buffalo Bill*, 158–60, 209.

64. WFC testimony, March 23, 1904, p. 2.

65. Jacobson, *Whiteness of a Different Color*, 47.

66. Knight, *Life and Manners in the Frontier Army*, 223–30. Frontier communities were almost as racially complex as the army. In 1865, more than 14,000 German, Irish, French, and English settlers lived in Kansas. Leavenworth was almost one-third German and Irish, and emigrants from both countries settled in considerable numbers along railroad routes. Over the next decade, they were joined by Russian, Austrian, German, Swedish, and Hungarian emigrants, so that between 15 and 20 percent of the frontier population was so ethnically distinctive as to appear "foreign" to native-born observers. Shortridge, *Peopling the Plains*, 30–33, 92–94.

67. Colin G. Calloway, "Army Allies or Tribal Survival?," in *Legacy: New Perspectives on the Battle of Little Big Horn*, ed. Charles E. Rankin (Helena: Montana Historical Society Press, 1996), 63–81. Fairfax Downey and Jacques Noel Jacobsen Jr., *The Red/Bluecoats* (Fort Collins, CO: Old Army Press, 1973), 193–94; Thomas W. Dunlay, *Wolves for the Blue Soldiers: Indian Scouts and Auxiliaries with the United States Army, 1860–1890* (Lincoln: University of Nebraska Press, 1982).

68. "The Indians—Col. Wyncoop's Letter Resigning His Agency," *New York Times*, Dec. 19, 1868, p. 3.

69. For frontier race degeneracy, see Conevery Bolton Valencius, *The Health of the Country*, 250; Stephen P. Knadler, "Francis Parkman's Ethnography of the Brahmin Caste and the History of the Conspiracy of Pontiac," *American Literature* 65, no. 2 (June 1993): 215–38, esp. 225. Even Francis Parkman's mixed-blood trapper and guide, Henri Chatillon, was without "the restless energy of the Anglo-American." Francis Parkman, *The Oregon Trail* (1847; rprt. New York: Doubleday & Co., 1946), 11. Seminole men, of black, Indian, and white ancestry, frequently scouted for the all-black Ninth and Tenth cavalries (whom Cody also guided). Downey and Jacobsen, *Red/Bluecoats*, 193–94.

70. "Mulatto," *Compact Edition of the Oxford English Dictionary* 1:1872.

71. Robert J. C. Young, *Colonial Desire: Hybridity in Theory, Culture, and Race*, 18.

72. Richard Burton, *The City of the Saints and Across the Rocky Mountains to California* (1861; rprt. New York: Alfred A. Knopf, 1963), 89–90. Francis Parkman referred to mixed-bloods as "a mongrel race," in a few of whom "might be seen the black snaky eye of the Indian half-breed." Parkman, *Oregon Trail*, 61.

73. Anxieties about frontier race mixing were prevalent long before Cody was born, but the abolition of slavery heightened them to a fever pitch after the Civil War. Warnings that the end of slavery would begin a slide into interracial sex and the birth of a mixed-race America gave rise to the term "miscegenation," which was coined only in 1864, replacing the older term "amalgamation," and reflecting the increasing emphasis on race mixing as the "miscasting" or "misbegetting" of people. The word derived from the Latin for "mixed race" but had deep resonances with "miscast," or "misbegotten." "Miscegenation," *Compact Edition of the Oxford English Dictionary*, 1809. See also Gary B. Nash,

"The Hidden History of Mestizo America," *Journal of American History* 82, no. 3 (Dec. 1995): 943.

74. Smith, *Virgin Land*, 177.

75. Rosa, *West of Wild Bill Hickok*, 101.

76. "Unfit amalgamation" is from Joseph G. McCoy, *Historic Sketches of the Cattle Trade of the West and Southwest* (1874; rprt. Lincoln: University of Nebraska Press, 1985), 80. Others who used Mexicans as warnings about frontier race decay include Richard Henry Dana, *Two Years Before the Mast* (1841; rprt. New York: Airmont Publishing Co., 1965), 136–37; Bancroft, *California Pastoral*, 263–65, 284.

77. Bourke, *On the Border with Crook*, 347, quoted in Joe DeBarthe, *The Life and Adventures of Frank Grouard* (1894; rprt. Norman, OK: University of Oklahoma Press, 1958), 88.

78. West, *Contested Plains*, 330; David Fritjof Halaas and Andrew E. Masich, *Halfbreed: The Remarkable True Story of George Bent* (Cambridge, MA: Da Capo Press, 2004), 246–47; Stanley, *My Early Travels and Adventures*, 180.

79. Halaas and Masich, *Halfbreed*, 221–22.

80. Randolph B. Marcy, *The Prairie Traveler* (1859; rprt. Bedford, MA: Applewood Books, n.d.), 173. Custer believed that Indians were superior to even the best white frontiersman when it came to trailing, which was "peculiarly and undeniably an Indian accomplishment." George A. Custer, "On the Plains," Nov. 11, 1867, in *Turf, Farm and Field*, Nov. 23, 1867, in Dippie, *Nomad*, 28, 31.

81. Slotkin, *Regeneration Through Violence*, 289, also 95–98, 114–16; Colin G. Calloway, "Neither White nor Red: White Renegades on the American Indian Frontier," *Western Historical Quarterly* 17, no. 1 (Jan. 1986): 43–66; for an example of how the Boone/Girty, white Indian/renegade confrontation shaped American literature, see Robert Montgomery Bird, *Nick of the Woods, or the Jibbenainosay* (Philadelphia: Carey, Lea, and Blanchard, 1837). From the days of the Puritans, whites abducted by Indians showed a disturbing enthusiasm for Indian life, many of them refusing to return to white society even after they were free to do so. Indian captivity "cannot be, therefore, so bad as we generally conceive it to be," wrote Hector St. John de Crèvecoeur in 1782. "There must be in their social bond something singularly captivating, and far superior to anything boasted of among us; for thousands of Europeans are Indians." J. Hector St. John de Crèvecoeur, *Letters from an American Farmer* (1782; rprt. New York: E. P. Dutton, 1957), 209. Literature on Indian captivity is gigantic. See Roy Harvey Pearce, "The Significance of the Captivity Narrative," *American Literature* 19 (March 1947): 1–20; James Axtell, "The White Indians of Colonial America," *William and Mary Quarterly* 32 (Jan. 1975): 55–88; Slotkin, *Regeneration Through Violence*, esp. 116–45; James Axtell, *The Invasion Within: The Contest of Cultures in Colonial North America* (New York: Oxford University Press, 1985); June Namias, *White Captives: Gender and Ethnicity on American Frontiers* (Chapel Hill: University of North Carolina Press, 1993); John Demos, *The Unredeemed Captive: A Family Story from Early America* (New York: Alfred A. Knopf, 1994).

82. Herman Melville, *Moby-Dick or, The Whale* (1851; rprt. New York: Penguin, 1992), 295.

83. When Cheyenne warriors shouted insults "in plain English" in 1867, they raised suspicions among the Tenth Cavalry's commanders that "many of our own race were with the enemy," whose successes on the battlefield could be attributed to their being led by "the basest of white men, well drilled in war." Armes, *Ups and Downs of an Army Offices*, 249, 252. See also Theodore R. Davis, "A Summer on the Plains," *Harper's New Monthly Magazine* 36 (Feb. 1868): 305–6; Stanley, *My Early Travels and Adventures*, 161.

84. For Carr's views on Hickok, see Rosa, *The West of Wild Bill Hickok*, 101. There is no biography of Frank North, but see George Bird Grinnell, *Two Great Scouts and Their Pawnee Battalion* (1928; rprt. Lincoln: University of Nebraska Press, 1973); Robert Bruce, *The Fighting Norths and Pawnee Scouts* (Lincoln, NE: n.p., 1932); Luther North, *Man of the Plains: Recollections of Luther North, 1856–1882*, ed. Donald F. Danker (Lincoln: University of Nebraska Press, 1961); Frank North, "The Journal of an Indian Fighter: The 1869 Diary of Frank J. North," ed. Donald F. Danker, *Nebraska History* 39, no. 2 (June 1958): 87–178.

85. The story is almost certainly apocryphal, coming as it does from Nate Salsbury, in a particularly bitter memoir written around 1902. See "The Origin of the Wild West Show," NSP, YCAL MSS 17, Box 1/63, Beinecke Rare Book and Manuscript Library, Yale University, New Haven, CT; Walsh and Salsbury, *Making of Buffalo Bill*, 155–56.

86. James T. King, *War Eagle: A Life of General Eugene A. Carr* (Lincoln: University of Nebraska Press, 1963), 276, n. 40; E. A. Carr, "The Combat on Beaver Creek," *Pearson's Magazine* (Aug. 1904): 188.

87. Davis, "Summer on the Plains," 303.

88. DeBarthe, *Life and Adventures of Frank Grouard*, 88, n. 4; Smith, *View from Officers' Row*, 40, 83. Also Hutton, *Phil Sheridan and His Army*, 36.

89. Richard I. Dodge, *Plains of the Great West* (New York: G. P. Putnam's Sons, 1877), 429.

90. North, *Man of the Plains*, 121.

91. Finerty, *War-Path and Bivouac*, 247. Cody, of course, implied that he figured this out on his own, after riding "ahead of the command about ten miles," where he saw a "body of men" marching toward him, "that I at first believed to be the Indians of whom we were in pursuit." Cody, *Life of Buffalo Bill*, 350.

92. Carr, "Memoirs," 30–31; George F. Price, *Across the Continent with the Fifth Cavalry* (1883; rprt. New York: Antiquarian Press, 1959), 133; Russell, *Lives and Legends*, 110.

93. Cody, *Life of Buffalo Bill*, 227.

94. "Mongrels" is in Rosa, *West of Wild Bill Hickok*, 101.

95. Russell, *Lives and Legends*, 114; Luke Cahill, "An Indian Campaign and Buffalo Hunting with 'Buffalo Bill,' " *Colorado Magazine*, 4, no. 4 (Aug. 1927): 125–35.

96. Cody, *Life of Buffalo Bill*, 226–37; Rosa and May, *Buffalo Bill and His Wild West*, 28.

97. WFC testimony, March 23, 1904.

98. H. C. Bonnycastle to Chief, Personnel Division, OQMC, March 20, 1924, in William F. Cody, 201 File, RG 407, NARA, Washington, DC; Russell, *Lives and Legends*, 115.

99. Keim, *Sheridan's Troopers on the Border*, 150.

100. Utley and Washburn, *Indian Wars*, 258; Hutton, *Phil Sheridan and His Army*, 110.

101. Bvt. Maj. Gen. E. A. Carr to Bvt. Brig. Gen. Geo. D. Ruggles, May 22, 1869, and Adj. Gen. E. D. Townsend to Bvt. Maj. Gen. C. C. Augur, June 11, 1869, both in RG 533, U.S. Army Continental Command, Dept. of the Platte, Letters Recd. 1867–69, Microfilm Reel 7, NSHS; Russell, *Lives and Legends*, 122–24; King, *War Eagle*, 99; Rosa and May, *Buffalo Bill and His Wild West*, 29–30.

102. The events leading up to the campaign may be found in James T. King, "The Republican River Expedition, June–July 1869," pt. I, "On the March," *Nebraska History* 41, no. 3 (Sept. 1960): 165–200, esp. 165–70; pt. II, "The Battle of Summit Springs," *Nebraska History* 41, no. 4 (Dec. 1960): 281–99.

103. King, "Republican River Expedition," 170–75.

104. Cody's grocery wagon has been a bone of contention for biographers. Don Russell, believing crass mercantilism below the dignity of a hero-scout, argued that Cody never had such a wagon, and that it was the product of the jealousy of Luther North, whose resentment of Cody's fame had grown to "a positive hatred" by the 1920s. Russell, *Lives and Legends*, 132, 151. But Luther North mentioned the wagon only once, in an account generally complimentary to Cody, though it was incorrect about Cody's role in the battle of Summit Springs. North, *Man of the Plains*, 103. The vital evidence for Cody's grocery wagon comes from his divorce trial, a quarter century before North wrote his memoirs. Eric Ericson explained the wagon and its business origins, in Eric Ericson testimony, Feb. 9, 1905, Folder 8, 21–30; May Cody, who lived with William and Louisa Cody in 1871, says that her brother had the title of "Field Settler Station" (possibly "field sutler"), as which "he furnished goods to the [a]rmy when they were out in the field. . . ." May Cody Bradford Testimony, Feb. 16–20, 1905, File 7-1, 117; William Cody himself claimed, "I had the concession from the commanding officer as a settler [sutler]" for troops in the field, "and I was at the time making a good deal of money out of my sutler store." WFC testimony, March 5, 1905, Folder 13, 14–15, all in CC.

105. North, *Man of the Plains*, 102–3, 126.

106. King, "Republican River Expedition," 174–75; North, *Man of the Plains*, 103–4.

107. "Journal of the March of the Republican River Expedition," entry for June 15, Ra 533 Reel 7, NSHS; King, "Republican River Expedition," 179; Cody, *Life of Buffalo Bill*, 251–53; North, *Man of the Plains*, 107–8. For the Fetterman fight, see Utley, *Frontier Regulars*, 93–110.

108. Cody later claimed to have killed thirty-six buffalo during a hunt at this point in the expedition. No other source confirms that number. Cody, *Life of Buffalo Bill*, 253. Frank North records a hunt in "Journal of an Indian Fighter," 133.

109. King, "Republican River Expedition," 198–99; "Journal of the March," entry for July 10.

110. Cody, *Life of Buffalo Bill*, 255; "Journal of the March," entry for July 11; Bvt. Maj. Gen. E. A. Carr to Bvt. Brig. Gen. Geo. D. Ruggles, July 20, 1869, RG 533, U.S. Army Continental Command, Dept. of the Platte, Letters Recd. 1867–69, Microfilm Reel 6, NSHS; Price, *Across the Continent with the Fifth Cavalry*, 137–41. Also see North, *Man of the Plains*, 113–14; Grinnell, *Two Great Scouts*, 194–95.

111. King, "Republican River Expedition, June–July 1869: pt. II, The Battle of Summit Springs," 289.

112. Pen-and-ink drawing in BBWW 1884 program (Hartford, CT: n.p., 1884); cover illustration on BBWW 1888 program (Hartford, CT: Calhoun, 1888), BBHC.

113. Cody, *Life of Buffalo Bill*, 260–61.

114. Carr to Ruggles, July 20, 1869; North, *Man of the Plains*, 117; Grinnell, *Two Great Scouts*, 198–99; Joyce Szabo, *Howling Wolf and the History of Ledger Art* (Albuquerque: University of New Mexico Press, 1994), 154; Hyde, *Life of George Bent*, 334; also West, *Contested Plains*, 314–15, 378, n. 88, and King, *War Eagle*, 115. The regimental journal recorded Tall Bull "was killed after a desperate personal defence." "Journal of the March," entry for July 11.

115. Price, *Across the Continent with the Fifth Cavalry*, 138.

116. Bvt. Brig. Gen. Thomas Duncan to Lt. Wm. G. Forbush, Dist. of the Republican, Oct. 7, 1869, RG 533, Reel 7, NSHS.

117. *Buffalo Bill: The King of Border Men* originally appeared in serial form between Dec. 23, 1869, and March 3, 1870. See William J. Roba, ed., *Buffalo Bill: The King of Border Men* (Davenport, IA: Service Press, 1987). For Cody's meeting with Buntline, see Cody, *Life of Buffalo Bill*, 263.

118. Michael Denning, *Mechanic Accents: Dime Novels and Working-Class Culture in America*, rev. ed. (New York: Verso, 1998), 10–16.

119. "Memorandum," March 20, 1924, in W. F. Cody 201 File, RG 407, NARA.

120. WFC testimony, March 23, 1904, pp. 9, 27.

121. King, "Republican River Expedition"; North, *Man of the Plains*, 115.

122. Knight, *Life and Manners in the Frontier Army*, 39–70; for an eyewitness account of how much officers' wives shaped fort culture, see Duane Merritt Greene, *Ladies and Officers of the United States Army; or, American Aristocracy* (Chicago: Central Publishing Co., 1880).

123. See the photograph in Rosa and May, *Buffalo Bill and His Wild West*, 41; for carpet, see May Cody Bradford testimony, Folder, 7–1, in CC pp. 106–7.

124. Louisa Burke testimony, Feb. 19, 1905, Civil Case 970, Folder 8, p. 111; Eric Ericson testimony, p. 24; Mrs. Charles Hendy, Sr., testimony, Folder 8, p. 95; all in CC; Kit Carson Cody birthdate in Cody, *Life of Buffalo Bill*, 275; Russell, *Lives and Legends of Buffalo Bill*, 160; quote from Ena Raymonde, entry for July 10, 1872, see also entry for Oct. 11, 1872, Ena Raymonde Ballantine Journal, MS 1730, NSHS.

125. Capt. Charles J. Meinhold, 3rd Cavalry, to Lt. J. B. Johnson, Post Adjutant, April 27, 1872, and attached copies of expedition reports, recommendations, and approvals, in Case File for Correction of Military Record: William Cody, Stack 8W3, 4/8/2, Box 10, RG 94, NARA, Washington, DC; also Adjutant General's Office, document file 377,592 (William Cody), Stack 8W3, 12/1/D, Box 2609, NARA, Washington, DC.

126. "Sharp Pursuit of Indian Thieves," *New York Times*, June 9, 1870.

127. "Sheridan's Buffalo Hunt," *New York Times*, Oct. 7, 1871, p. 11.

128. "The Grand Duke's Hunt—General Sheridan and 'Buffalo Bill' Lead the Way—At Grand Battue on the Plains," *New York Herald,* Jan. 14, 1872, p. 7.

129. Capt. Charles J. Meinhold, 3rd Cavalry, to Lt. J. B. Johnson, Post Adjutant, April 27, 1872, and attached copies of expedition reports, recommendations, and approvals, in Case File for Correction of Military Record: William Cody, Stack 8W3, 4/8/2, Box 10, RG 94, NARA, Washington, DC; also Adjutant General's Office, document file 377, 592 (William Cody), Stack 8W3, 12/1/D, Box 2609, NARA, Washington, DC. Note that Meinhold's report spells the name "Volks," but official records list the man as "Vokes."

130. *The Congressional Medal of Honor: The Names, the Deeds* (Forest Ranch, CA: Sharp & Dunnigan, 1984), 1, 4–5. It was perfectly in keeping with the low status of the award that, even with so colorful a recipient as Buffalo Bill, the press seems not to have noticed. Despite press coverage of various Buffalo Bill hunts and skirmishes, I have yet to find a newspaper report of the commendation.

131. Quote from Cody to Friends in Rochester, Aug. 9, 1872 [1874], MS 6 I:B, BBHC; Anson Mills, *My Story,* 2nd ed. (Washington, DC: Byron S. Adams, 1921), 151; Anson Mills, "Big Horn Expedition, Aug. 15 to Sept. 30, 1874, commanded by Capt. Anson Mills," pamphlet (n.p., n.d.).

132. Quoted in King, *War Eagle,* 154. For departure from stage, see Sagala, *Buffalo Bill, Actor,* 136–37.

133. "The Indian Campaign," *New York Times,* Aug. 17, 1876, p. 5.

134. Description of Cody's costume from Charles King, *Campaigning with Crook* (Milwaukee: The Sentinel Co., 1880), 38; "most reliable account" from Chris Madsen, who gave it to Don Russell, "Buffalo Bill's Fight," MSS in MS 62 Don Russell Collection, Series 1:R, Military, Box 7/4, BBHC. Cody, *Life of Buffalo Bill,* 343–44; see also "Diary of James Frew," MS 58, Box 1, Misc. p. 1, NSHS.

135. Many accounts of the battle incorrectly refer to *southern* Cheyennes. Yellow Hair was from the northern Cheyenne band of Little Wolf, who were then living near Red Cloud Agency, on the Sioux Reserve. Beaver Heart added "Furthermore, Yellow Hair was not killed by any one man as far as I could see, as the whole two troops of soldiers were firing at him. If Buffalo Bill was with those soldiers he stayed with them until Yellow Hair was killed, and he did not come out and engage Yellow Hair single-handed." From E. A. Brininstool, "Who Killed Yellow Hand?," *Outdoor Life—Outdoor Recreation,* Feb. 1930, typescript in MS 62 Don Russell Collection, Series 1:R, Military, Box 7/8, BBHC. See also "Statement of Josie Tangleyellowhair Regarding Killing of Yellow Hair (Yellow Hand) on War Bonnet Creek," May 27, 1929, MS 58, Box 1, Folder 1, NSHS.

136. For army partisans, see Don Russell, *Lives and Legends,* 236; for Cheyenne numbers and Merritt's report, see Paul Hedren, *First Scalp for Custer: The Skirmish at War Bonnet Creek, Nebraska, July 17, 1876,* 58–59, 78; for quote, see Carr, "Memoirs," 127, and King, *War Eagle,* 162.

137. WFC to Louisa Cody, July 18, 1876, on display in the Buffalo Bill Museum, BBHC. The text is reprinted in "Buffalo Bill Yarn Is Verified Here," *Baltimore Sun,* Morning Edition, Dec. 21, 1936, clipping in MS 62 Don Russell Collection, Series 1:R, Military, Box 7/9, BBHC; see also Russell, *Lives and Legends of Buffalo Bill,* 230. The controversy over whether or not Cody killed Yellow Hair has consumed forests. See Don Russell, "Captain Charles King," *The Westerners New York Posse Brand Book* 4, no. 2 (1957): 39; also MS 62 Don Russell Collection, Series 1:R, Box 7, Folders 1–12, BBHC. There is also a file with hundreds of letters on this question in the Cody materials at the NSHS.

138. Cody, *Life of Buffalo Bill,* 355.

139. DeBarthe, *Life and Adventures of Frank Grouard,* xvii; Edgar I. Stewart, "Frank Grouard," in *The Reader's Encyclopedia of the American West,* ed. Howard R. Lamar (New York: Thomas Y. Crowell, 1977), 172; Evan S. Connell evaluates the Grouard controversy in *Son of the Morning Star,* 327–28. See also John S. Gray, "Frank Grouard: Kanaka Scout or Mulatto Renegade," *Chicago Westerner's Brand Book* 16, no. 8 (1959); Russell, *Lives and Legends,* 239–40.

140. Field diary of Gen. A. H. Terry, entry for Aug. 10, 1876, in *The Field Diary of General*

Alfred H. Terry—The Yellowstone Expedition, 1876, ed. Michael J. Koury (Bellevue, NE: Old Army Press, 1970), 31.

141. Burt's authorship is discussed in Sagala, *Buffalo Bill, Actor,* 162; his participation in the 1876 campaign is in Finerty, *War-Path and Bivouac,* 112, 117, 164.

142. King, *Campaigning with Crook,* 32.

143. King, *Campaigning with Crook,* 34. For *New York Herald,* see "The Indian War," *New York Herald,* July 23, 1876, p. 7, col. 3; King's authorship is discussed in Charles King to W. J. Ghent, March 18, 1929, in MS 62 Don Russell Collection, Series 1:R, Military, Box 7/7, BBHC. For King and Cody as drinking partners, see CSS of Don Russell and Paul Hedren in MS 62 Don Russell Collection, Series 1:R Military, Box 7, BBHC.

144. The Buffalo Bill Combination performed *May Cody* and other plays in Milwaukee, Jan. 1–3, 1878. Sagala, *Buffalo Bill, Actor,* 318, 337.

145. King, *Campaigning with Crook,* 36. Merritt's report at the battle says an Indian was killed. See Hedren, *First Scalp for Custer,* 78. King's account was so colorful, and fanciful, that Chris Madsen, a Fifth Cavalry veteran who was at Warbonnet Creek, once wrote, "I can not understand why King would write such stuff about a fight where there was plenty to tell without going Munchauson [*sic*] one better." Chris Madsen to Fred P. Todd, April 8, 1938, MS 62 Don Russell Collection, Series 1:R Military, Box 7/4, BBHC.

146. Emphasis added. The letter is reproduced in *Life of Buffalo Bill,* iv.

147. Carr to Ruggles, July 20, 1869; Carr in Cody, *Life of Buffalo Bill,* vii. For Cody's request for endorsement, Carr's warning against "embroidery," and his attendance at the show, see Carr, "Memoirs," 36–38, also 218; for Carr's career, see King, *War Eagle;* also Russell, *Lives and Legends,* 139–48; for testimonial, see BBWW 1907 program (Buffalo, NY: Courier, 1907), n.p.

148. Charles King (as told to Don Russell), "My Friend, Buffalo Bill," *The Cavalry Journal* 41, no. 173 (Sept.–Oct. 1932): 19. Russell provides an account of his meeting with King, and his research for the article, in Don Russell, "A Very Personal Introduction," in Paul Hedren, *First Scalp for Custer,* 15–21.

149. May Cody Bradford, Folder 7-1, 119, CC.

150. WFC testimony, March 23, 1904, p. 10.

CHAPTER SIX: BUFFALO HUNT

1. From BBWW 1894 program.

2. Cody, *Life of Buffalo Bill,* 253.

3. Buffalo Bill and Dr. Carver Wild West, Rocky Mountain, and Prairie Exhibition 1883 Program (Hartford, CT: Calhoun Printing, 1883), n.p.; also, BBWW 1893 program, 13.

4. Cody, *Life of Buffalo Bill,* 174; William Cody, with John Burke, *Story of the Wild West and Camp-Fire Chats* (Chicago: Historical Publishing, 1888), 511.

5. Cody, *Life of Buffalo Bill,* 156–57.

6. Cody, *Life of Buffalo Bill,* 172.

7. Cody, *Life of Buffalo Bill,* 171–75.

8. Buffalo Bill and Dr. Carver Wild West program, n.p.; BBWW 1893 program, 12–13; also Cody, *Story of the Wild West,* 507–11; 536–37.

9. "Buffalo Bill," n.p., n.d., clipping in WFC Scrapbooks, Stage Play Notices and Reviews, 1875–80, BBHC. See also "That Buffalo Hunt," n.d., n.p., n.p., WFC Scrapbooks.

10. "Both the grown buffalo and the calves, are very frequently driven in this manner to the encampment, where they are readily slaughtered." Lansford W. Hastings, *The Emigrants' Guide to Oregon and California* (1845; rprt. Princeton, NJ: Princeton University Press, 1932), 9; also Elizabeth B. Custer, *Following the Guidon* (1890; rprt. Lincoln: University of Nebraska Press, 1994), 119.

11. The only verification of the Comstock hunt comes from Louisa Frederici Cody's memoirs, which are based entirely on her husband's autobiography and appear even more fictionalized than his. See Cody and Cooper, *Memories of Buffalo Bill, by His Wife,* 122–36; Rosa and May, *Buffalo Bill and His Wild West,* 39–40.

12. Rosa and May, *Buffalo Bill and His Wild West*, 40.
13. William Comstock was killed in a fight with Cheyenne Indians in 1868. See Rosa and May, *Buffalo Bill and His Wild West*, 40; Hutton, *Phil Sheridan and His Army*, 36–38.
14. Richard Slotkin, *Gunfighter Nation*, 32–62.
15. Earl of Dunraven [Windham Thomas Wyndham-Quin], *The Great Divide: Travels in the Upper Yellowstone in the Summer of 1874* (1876; rprt. Lincoln: University of Nebraska Press, 1967), xiii.
16. See Jonathan Culler, "The Semiotics of Tourism," in *Framing the Sign: Criticism and Its Institutions* (Oxford: Basil Blackwell, 1988), 153–67.
17. Roderick Frazier Nash, *Wilderness and the American Mind*, 3rd ed. (New Haven, CT: Yale University Press, 1982), 108–16.
18. "Home Incidents," *Frank Leslie's Illustrated Newspaper*, Nov. 28, 1868, pp. 173–74; see also Theodore R. Davis, "The Buffalo Range," *Harper's New Monthly Magazine* 38, no. 224 (Jan. 1869): 147–63, at 149.
19. Dippie, *Nomad*, 48; E. B. Custer, *Following the Guidon*, 204.
20. Keim, *Sheridan's Troopers on the Borders*, 76.
21. *Kansas State Record* (Topeka), Oct. 20, 1869, quoted in Minnie Dubbs Millbrook, "Big Game Hunting with the Custers, 1869–70," *Kansas Historical Quarterly* 41, no. 4 (Winter 1975): 429–53, at 433.
22. Putnam, "A Trip to the End of the Union Pacific," 197, n. 2.
23. Daniel Justin Herman, *Hunting and the American Imagination* (Washington, DC: Smithsonian Press, 2001), 1–8; Jacoby, *Crimes Against Nature: Settlers, Poachers, Thieves, and the Hidden History of American Conservation* (Berkeley: University of California Press, 2000), 58; Louis S. Warren, *The Hunter's Game: Poachers and Conservationists in Twentieth-Century America* (New Haven, CT: Yale University Press, 1997).
24. I am borrowing the notion of invented traditions from Eric Hobsbawm, "Introduction: Inventing Traditions," in *The Invention of Tradition*, ed. Eric Hobsbawm and Terence Ranger (New York: Cambridge University Press, 1983), 1–14.
25. Elliott West, "Bison R Us: Images of Bison in American History," MS in author's possession.
26. John C. Ewers, "Fact and Fiction in the Documentary Art of the American West," *The Frontier Re-examined*, ed. John Francis McDermott (Urbana: University of Illinois Press, 1967), 79–95, at 84–85.
27. William E. Deahl, Jr., "Nebraska's Unique Contribution to the World of Entertainment," *Nebraska History* 49 (1968): 283–98.
28. Washington Irving, *A Tour on the Prairies* (London: John Murray, 1835), 263–78; William H. Goetzmann, David C. Hunt, Marsha V. Gallagher, and William J. Orr, *Karl Bodmer's America* (Lincoln: Joslyn Art Museum and University of Nebraska Press, 1984); Brian W. Dippie, "The Visual West," 675–705, esp. 682–85, in *The Oxford History of the American West*, ed. Clyde A. Milner, Carol A. O'Connor, and Martha A. Sandweiss (New York: Oxford University Press, 1994); Wayne Gard, *The Great Buffalo Hunt* (New York: Alfred A. Knopf, 1959), 59–74; Ann Hyde, "Tourist Travel," and David C. Hunt, "Alfred Jacob Miller," in *The New Encyclopedia of the American West*, 699–700, 1117–19; for emigrant bison hunting, Herman, *Hunting and the American Imagination*, 200–3, and Faragher, *Women and Men on the Overland Trail*, 84–85, 99–103.
29. *St. Louis Democrat*, Feb. 17, 1868, quoted in Richard J. Walsh and Milton S. Salisbury, *The Making of Buffalo Bill: A Study in Heroics* (rprt. 1978; New York, Bobbs-Merrill, 1928), 113.
30. Warren, *Hunter's Game*, 13–15; Jacoby, *Crimes Against Nature*, 58–62; Herman, *Hunting and the American Imagination*, 122–58. Also, see John Reiger, *American Sportsmen and the Origins of Conservation*, 3rd ed. (Corvallis: Oregon State University Press, 1999), 5–104.
31. Webb, *Buffalo Land*, 149, 453, 458.
32. Davis, "Buffalo Range," 154, 157.
33. Davis, "Buffalo Range," 157.
34. Webb, *Buffalo Land*, 255–56.
35. Davis, "Buffalo Range," 155.

36. Armes, *Ups and Downs of an Army Officer*, 179.

37. Custer, *My Life on the Plains*, 51; Davis, "Buffalo Range," 155–57; Dippie, *Nomad*, 50.

38. David D. Smits, "The Frontier Army and the Destruction of the Buffalo: 1865–1883," *Western Historical Quarterly* 23, no. 3 (Autumn 1994): 313–38; "At that time the War Department encouraged hunting in the army, not only for the game that would help out the company messes, but because the men hunting would learn more about takeng [*sic*] care of themselves and their horses, and how creeks and roads were located in the vicinity of the posts, so that when a call would come in from some ranch that hostile Indians were in the vicinity, some one was able to go direct to the place." Chris Madsen to Don Russell, May 16, 1938, MS 62 Don Russell Collection, Series 1:R Military, Box 7/4, BBHC.

39. Davis, "Buffalo Range," 154. Their wives and daughters occasionally joined these hunts. Patricia Y. Stallard, *Glittering Misery: Dependents of the Indian Fighting Army* (Fort Collins, CO: Old Army Press, 1978), 47.

40. Elizabeth Bacon Custer, *Following the Guidon*, 213–25, and *Tenting on the Plains or, General Custer in Kansas and Texas* (1895; abridged ed., Norman: University of Oklahoma Press, 1994), 342–43.

41. Dippie, *Nomad*.

42. Custer, in Dippie, *Nomad*, 48.

43. George A. Custer, "On the Plains," Oct. 12, 1867, in Dippie, *Nomad*, 13.

44. G. Custer to E. Custer, May 2, 1867, from Ft. Hays, Kansas, in *The Custer Story: The Life and Intimate Letters of General George A. Custer and His Wife Elizabeth*, ed. Marguerite Merington (New York: Devin-Adair Co., 1950), 200.

45. Custer, in Dippie, *Nomad*, 46–47; in Millbrook, "Big Game Hunting," 436–37; Utley, *Cavalier in Buckskin*, 106.

46. Dippie, *Nomad*, 55–57.

47. Barnum quoted in Millbrook, "Big Game Hunting," 447–48.

48. Cody, *Life of Buffalo Bill*, 145.

49. The literature on Custer is enormous but a good place to start is Utley, *Cavalier in Buckskin*, 1–27. See also Jay Monaghan, *Custer: The Life of General George Armstrong Custer* (Boston: Little, Brown and Company, 1959), 237–38.

50. Utley, *Life in Custer's Cavalry*, 98; Utley, *Cavalier in Buckskin*, 52–53. For dogs, see Custer, *My Life on the Plains*, 98.

51. Utley, *Life in Custer's Cavalry*, 128–29.

52. See Elizabeth Custer to Mrs. Sabin, n.d., in Merington, *Custer Story*, 284; also, Robert Winston Mardock, *The Reformers and the American Indian* (Columbia: University of Missouri Press, 1971), 41–42.

53. Utley and Washburn, *Indian Wars*, 256; Russell, *Lives and Legends*, 109–10; Hutton, *Phil Sheridan and His Army*, 67–68, 95–100; Utley, *Cavalier in Buckskin*, 75–78.

54. Utley, *Cavalier in Buckskin*, 106–7; Wert, *Custer*, 26; Connell, *Son of the Morning Star*, 200–2; Smith, *View from Officers' Row*, 83; Hutton, *Phil Sheridan and His Army*, 389, n. 45.

55. Guardhouse in Hays is in Connell, *Son of the Morning Star*, 120–21.

56. Albert Barnitz to Jennie Barnitz, May 15, 1867, in Utley, *Life in Custer's Cavalry*, 50.

57. King, *War Eagle*, 214.

58. Cody, *Life of Buffalo Bill*, 42. Emphasis added.

59. George Custer to Elizabeth Custer, Sept. 11, 1873, in Merington, *Custer Story*, 264: "When the theatrical ventures of Buffalo Bill and Texas Jack were discussed Tom said it might be a good speculation to back our own 'Antelope Jim'—on which Mr C rushed out indignantly from the tent."

60. Davis, "Buffalo Range."

61. Joseph G. Rosa, *Wild Bill Hickok: The Man and His Myth* (Lawrence: University Press of Kansas, 1990), 95–96; John S. Gray, "New Light on Will Comstock, Kansas Scout," in *Custer and His Times*, ed. Paul Hutton (El Paso: Little Big Horn Associates, 1981), 183–207.

62. Custer, *My Life on the Plains*, 144–45.

63. Custer, *My Life on the Plains*, 44.

64. North, *Man of the Plains*, 146–50.
65. Louis A. Holmes, *Fort McPherson, Nebraska, Fort Cottonwood, N.T.: Guardian of the Tracks and Trails* (Lincoln, NE:, Johnsen Publishing Co., 1963), 47.
66. Quoted in Millbrook, "Big Game Hunting," 447.
67. Paul Andrew Hutton, "Introduction," in Davies, *Ten Days on the Plains*, 16–19.
68. Earl of Dunraven [Windham Thomas Wyndham-Quin], *Past Times and Pastimes*, 2 vols. (London: Hodder and Stoughton, 1922), 2: 78.
69. North, *Man of the Plains*, 150.
70. North, *Man of the Plains*, 108.
71. Millbrook, "Big Game Hunting," 451; Cody, *Life of Buffalo Bill*, 153.
72. For significance of Indians, see Deloria, *Playing Indian*, esp. 63–5; for Pawnee scouts in 100th Meridian Expedition, see David Haward Bain, *Empire Express: Building the First Transcontinental Railroad* (New York: Viking, 1999), 292–93; Silas S. Seymour, *Incidents of a Trip Through the Great Platte Valley to the Rocky Mountains and Laramie Plains in the Fall of 1866* (New York: Van Nostrand, 1867).
73. The first Wild West show program included an account of the Hundredth Meridian Expedition. Buffalo Bill and Doc Carver Wild West, Rocky Mountain, and Prairie Exhibition 1883 program (Hartford, CT: Calhoun Printing, 1883), n.p.
74. Donald Danker, in North, *Man of the Plains*, 125; original source is Bruce, *Fighting Norths and Pawnee Scouts*, 19.
75. Webb, *Buffalo Land*, 212.
76. "The Imperial Buffalo Hunter," *New York Herald*, Jan. 16, 1872, p. 7.
77. My interpretation of Cody's tales relies on Carolyn S. Brown, who writes that, generally speaking, tellers of tall tales invent themselves as characters in a performance, a fool or a hero who triumphs over nature, danger, fear, and outsiders through wit and skill. The storyteller holds an audience spellbound in proportion to his ability to fudge the line between truth and fiction, to dance across it and back again, never quite giving away which side is which, suspending the audience over it and allowing them to believe what they will. Brown, *Tall Tale*, 28.
78. My interpretation of guides, dudes, and practical jokes borrows from Tina Loo, "Of Moose and Men: Hunting and Masculinities in British Columbia, 1880–1939," *Western Historical Quarterly* 32, no. 3 (Autumn 2001): 296–319.
79. Webb, *Buffalo Land*, 195.
80. Henry E. Davies, *Ten Days on the Plains*, ed. Paul Andrew Hutton (1872; rprt. Dallas, TX: DeGolyer Library, 1985), 122–23: "A story was told the next day, that, while our camp was buried in repose that night, a small party of Indians roamed among the sleepers, and the appearance of an undersized and ill-favored little squaw, dressed in a complete suit of red flannel, who accompanied the chief in command of the party, was minutely described by those who pretended to have observed these unexpected and unwelcome visitors."
81. Cody, *Life of Buffalo Bill*, 290–91; Millbrook, "Big Game Hunting," 451–53.
82. See Paul A. Hutton's notes in Davies, *Ten Days on the Plains*, 135–49.
83. Cody, *Life of Buffalo Bill*, 282.
84. Davies, *Ten Days on the Plains*, 83.
85. Cody, *Life of Buffalo Bill*, 282–83.
86. Davies, *Ten Days on the Plains*, 113, 123.
87. Davies, *Ten Days on the Plains*, 122.
88. Davies, *Ten Days on the Plains*, 107.
89. William Tucker, *The Grand Duke Alexis in the United States of America* (1872; rprt. New York: Interland Publishing, 1972), 155.
90. Tucker, *Grand Duke Alexis*, 156, 158.
91. Tucker, *Grand Duke Alexis*, 160–62.
92. Tucker, *Grand Duke Alexis*, 163.
93. Tucker, *Grand Duke Alexis*, 164, 167–68.
94. Ambrose, *Crazy Horse and Custer*, 344. Tucker, *Grand Duke Alexis*, 175, 178.
95. Tucker, *Grand Duke Alexis*, 185–89.
96. Joy S. Kasson, *Buffalo Bill's Wild West: Celebrity, Memory, and Popular History* (New York:

Hill and Wang, 2000), 47; at least one of Cody's contemporaries pointed out the fakery. Herbert Cody Blake to Judge Paine, June 6, 1934, Folder 2, WFC Collection, MS 58, NSHS.

97. Cody, *Life of Buffalo Bill*, 305–6.

CHAPTER SEVEN: THEATER STAR

1. Cody, *Life of Buffalo Bill*, 311. The *New York Herald* suggests a different scenario. "When the real Buffalo Bill was recognized on his entrance the audience rose en masse and greeted him with an ovation such as actors at the more aristocratic theatres never received." "Amusements," *New York Herald*, Feb. 21, 1872, p. 5.

2. Paul Hutton, "Introduction," xvii–xviii, in David Crockett, *A Narrative of the Life of David Crockett by Himself* (1834; rprt., Lincoln: University of Nebraska Press, 1987); Carolyn S. Brown, *The Tall Tale in American Folklore and Literature*, 56, 71–72; also, Constance Rourke, *American Humor: A Study of the National Character* (New York: Harcourt, Brace, and Co., 1931), 70–71; James Kirk Paulding, *The Lion of the West*, ed. James N. Tidwell (Palo Alto: Stanford University Press, 1954).

3. Roger A. Hall, *Performing the American Frontier, 1870–1906* (New York: Cambridge University Press, 2001), 28.

4. Russell, *Lives and Legends*, 183.

5. Cody recalled bowing from the box, but the *New York Herald* says only that "strange to say, the hero of the play was present in a box, in company with the writer of the story [Ned Buntline], and the dramatizer, Mr. Fred G. Maeder." "Amusements," *New York Herald*, Feb. 21, 1872, p. 5.

6. Cody, *Life of Buffalo Bill*, 276–78; Russell, *Lives and Legends*, 191.

7. For claims of election to the Nebraska legislature, see Cody, *Life of Buffalo Bill*, 319; BBWW 1895 program, 10; for comparisons to Washington, Jackson, and Lincoln, see BBWW 1909, both in WFC Collection, WH 72, Box 3, DPL-WHR.

8. Cody, *Life of Buffalo Bill*, 311.

9. Cody, *Life of Buffalo Bill*, 324.

10. Cody, *Life of Buffalo Bill*, 324–25.

11. Sagala, *Buffalo Bill, Actor*, 44–46.

12. Hall, *Performing the American Frontier*, 22–48.

13. Cody, *Life of Buffalo Bill*, 327.

14. *Chicago Times*, Dec. 18, 1872, quoted in Sagala, *Buffalo Bill, Actor*, 46.

15. For stage profits, see Sagala, *Buffalo Bill, Actor*, 209.

16. Kit Carson Cody was born on Nov. 26, 1870; Orra Maude on Aug. 15, 1872. See Yost, *Buffalo Bill*, 43.

17. WFC testimony, p. 29.

18. Cody recalls they moved to Rochester in 1873, but he missed the date by a year. According to the *Rochester Democrat and Chronicle*, March 11, 1874, the Cody family moved to Rochester that month. WFC testimony, Folder 2, p. 29; Sagala, *Buffalo Bill, Actor*, 103.

19. "Sharp Pursuit of Indian Thieves," *New York Times*, June 9, 1870; "Sheridan's Buffalo Hunt," *New York Times*, Oct. 7, 1871, p. 11.

20. Webb, *Buffalo Land*, 149.

21. Oliver Knight, *Following the Indian Wars: The Story of the Newspaper Correspondents Among the Indian Campaigners* (Norman: University of Oklahoma Press, 1960), 321; Beau Riffenburgh, *The Myth of the Explorer: The Press, Sensationalism, and Geographic Discovery* (New York: Belhaven, 1993), 58; Hall, *Performing the American Frontier*, 53; David Rains Wallace, *The Bonehunter's Revenge: Dinosaurs, Greed, and the Greatest Scientific Feud of the Gilded Age* (New York: Houghton Mifflin, 1999), 4–10.

22. "The Grand Duke's Hunt—General Sheridan and 'Buffalo Bill' Lead the Way—At Grand Battue on the Plains," *New York Herald*, Jan. 14, 1872, p. 7. See also "The Grand Duke's Buffalo Hunt," *New York Herald*, Jan. 15, 1872, p. 7; "The Imperial Buffalo Hunter," *New York Herald*, Jan. 16, 1872, p. 7; "Alexis' Grand Hunt," *New York Herald*,

Jan. 17, 1872; "Bos Americanus!," *New York Herald,* Jan. 18, 1872, p. 3; "Nimrod Alexis," *New York Herald,* Jan. 22, 1872, p. 7.

23. "The Grand Duke," *New York Herald,* Feb. 13, 1872, p. 3; "Amusements," *New York Herald,* Feb. 13, 1872, p. 4.

24. "Buffalo Bill's Best Shot," *New York Times,* March 9, 1872, p. 5; also "Buffalo Bill's Best Shot," March 10, 1872, p. 5, and "Buffalo Bill's Best Shot," March 11, 1872, p. 5.

25. "An Immense Cattle Drive," *New York Times,* July 21, 1880, p. 1; "Buffalo Bill and Texas Jack," *New York Times,* Oct. 24, 1880, p. 3.

26. Quote from Edwin G. Burrows and Mike Wallace, *Gotham: A History of New York City to 1898* (New York: Oxford University Press, 1999), 947; Mary C. Henderson, *The City and the Theater: New York Playhouses from Bowling Green to Times Square* (Clifton, N.J.: James T. White and Company, 1973), 135.

27. Cody, *Life of Buffalo Bill,* 320.

28. Halttunen, *Confidence Men and Painted Women,* 2; Robert C. Allen, *Horrible Prettiness: Burlesque and American Culture* (Chapel Hill: University of North Carolina Press, 1991), 46–51.

29. David Grimsted, *Melodrama Unveiled: American Theater and Culture, 1800–1850* (Chicago: University of Chicago Press, 1968), 85–86; Allen, *Horrible Prettiness,* 51.

30. Hattie C. Fuller to Nate Salsbury, May 7, 1868, Box 1, Folder 2, Papers, in NSP. In the cousin's hometown, in Iowa, "The People generally—with the exception of the lower classes" were "very bitter against it." Hattie C. Fuller to Nate Salsbury, Jan. 8, 1870, Box 1, Folder 3, NSP.

31. Rosa, *They Called Him Wild Bill,* 162–69. For an account of capturing buffalo for Barnett's show, see Ena Raymonde Ballantine Journal, entry of June 15, 1872.

32. Cody, *Life of Buffalo Bill,* 320.

33. Frank North, "The Journal of an Indian Fighter: The 1869 Diary of Frank J. North," ed. Donald F. Danker, *Nebraska History* 39, no. 2 (June 1958): 87–178.

34. Lawrence Levine, *Highbrow/Lowbrow: The Emergence of Cultural Hierarchy in America* (Cambridge, MA: Harvard University Press, 1988), 21.

35. Melvin Schoberlin, *From Candles to Footlights: A Biography of the Pike's Peak Theatre, 1859–1876* (Denver: Old West Publishing Co., 1941), 50; also Rourke, *American Humor,* 108–15.

36. Schoberlin, *From Candles to Footlights,* 53.

37. Goodrich, *Black Flag,* 114.

38. In *Lives and Legends of Buffalo Bill,* 86, Don Russell speculates that Cody saw the play in St. Louis. The play's staging in Denver is in Schoberlin, *From Candles to Footlights,* 47.

39. C. Robert Haywood, *Victorian West: Class and Culture in Kansas Cattle Towns* (Lawrence: University Press of Kansas, 1991), 174–78.

40. Holmes, *Fort McPherson,* 73.

41. Cody, *Life of Buffalo Bill,* 327.

42. "The Imperial Buffalo Hunter," *New York Herald,* Jan. 16, 1872, p. 7; also Sagala, *Buffalo Bill, Actor,* 64; Philip J. Deloria, *Indians in Unexpected Places* (Lawrence: University Press of Kansas, 2004), 58–60.

43. Undated clipping, "May Cody," Notices of Buffalo Bill Season of 1879–80, BBHC.

44. Richard Slotkin, *Gunfighter Nation,* 70–71; also Peter H. Hassrick, Richard Slotkin, Vine Deloria, Jr., Howard R. Lamar, William Judson, and Leslie Fiedler, *Buffalo Bill and the Wild West* (Brooklyn, NY: Brooklyn Museum, 1981).

45. "Scouts of the Prairie" n.d., New Haven, CT, clipping in WFC Scrapbooks, Stage Play Notices and Reviews, 1875–80, BBHC.

46. Hall, *Performing the American Frontier,* 61.

47. Schwartz, *Culture of the Copy,* 212. My discussion of authenticity borrows from Philip J. Deloria, *Playing Indian,* 101–5; T. J. Jackson Lears, *No Place of Grace: Antimodernism and the Transformation of American Culture* (New York: Pantheon, 1981), 57; Miles Orvell, *The Real Thing: Imitation and Authenticity in American Culture, 1880–1940* (Chapel Hill: University of North Carolina Press, 1989), xv–xix; Dean MacCannell, *The Tourist: A New Theory of the Leisure Class* (New York: Macmillan, 1976), 91–107.

48. Odell, *Annals of the New York Stage*, 9:168, 218, 225–26.

49. Sagala, *Buffalo Bill, Actor*, 329; Odell, *Annals of the New York Stage*, 9:278, 290, 349.

50. Odell, *Annals of the New York Stage*, 9:276.

51. Sagala, *Buffalo Bill, Actor*, 330; Odell, *Annals of the New York Stage*, 9:328.

52. Orvell, *Real Thing*, 50.

53. Orvell, *Real Thing*, 55–56; also Walter Benjamin's "The Work of Art in the Age of Mechanical Reproduction," in Walter Benjamin, *Illuminations: Essays and Reflections*, ed. Hannah Arendt (1955; New York: Schocken Books, 1969), 217–52; see Jennifer Price, *Flight Maps*, for thoughtful essays on this kind of imitation in the late Victorian age and our own.

54. Orvell, *Real Thing*, 57.

55. Odell, *Annals of the New York Stage*, 10:217, 328.

56. Roger Hall maintains that the authentic Cody displaced the faux Cody, and that professional actors ceased to play "Buffalo Bill" by the summer of 1873. Hall, *Performing the American Frontier*, 67. Nevertheless, the play was reprised in New York by Studley and Dowd in 1876 and '77, and presumably elsewhere by others. Odell, *Annals of the New York Stage*, 226, 344.

57. In June 1885, A. H. Sheldon and Co., a vaudeville troupe, performed *Buffalo Bill's Last Shot* at Henry Miner's Theatre in the Bowery (Odell, *Annals of the New York Stage*, 12: 531). From September 7 through 12, 1891, *Buffalo Bill Abroad and at Home* was playing at Bennett's Casino, in Brooklyn, a variety house which featured in subsequent weeks a legless dancer, a male impersonator, and Irish dialect comedians. Odell, *Annals of the New York Stage*, 15:252–53.

58. J. M. Burke to Jack Crawford, March 5, 1877, M Crawford Box 1, DPL-WHR.

59. Odell, *Annals of the New York Stage*, 9:560.

60. Odell, *Annals of the New York Stage*, 9:570.

61. Odell, *Annals of the New York Stage*, 9:560.

62. Cody, *Life of Buffalo Bill*, 335.

63. Grimsted, *Melodrama Unveiled*, 195.

64. John Burke to "Captain Jack" Crawford, March 25, 1877, M Crawford L, DPL-WHR.

65. Role book, "Buffalo Bill in Life on the Border," MS 126, WFC Collection, Box 1, Folder 4, Colorado State Historical Society, Denver, CO.

66. Sagala, *Buffalo Bill, Actor*, 131–33.

67. Sagala, *Buffalo Bill, Actor*, 117, 129.

68. Kit Carson, Jr.'s prospects were not helped by his arrest for striking his wife with intent to kill in 1879. W. F. Cody to Sam Hall, July 5, 1879, Box 1/6, WFC Collection, MS 6 Series I:B, BBHC.

69. The Buffalo Bill Combination took home profits of $13,000 in 1877, and over $50,000 in 1880. Russell, *Lives and Legends*, 257; Sagala, *Buffalo Bill, Actor*, 209.

70. Robert Jenkinson Hicks to A. E. Sheldon, June 21, 1936, MS 58 WFC Collection, NSHS.

71. Richard Slotkin, *Gunfighter Nation*, 11–16, 74–81.

72. "The Indian War," *New York Herald*, July 23, 1876, p. 7; Don Russell, *Lives and Legends*, 224, n. 11.

73. J. M. Burke to Jack Crawford, March 5, 1877, M Crawford Box 1, DPL-WHR.

74. Darlis A. Miller, *Captain Jack Crawford: Buckskin Poet, Scout, and Showman* (Albuquerque: University of New Mexico Press, 1993), 25.

75. Sagala, *Buffalo Bill, Actor*, 143; White, "Frederick Jackson Turner and Buffalo Bill," 35.

76. See R. B. Davenport to Jack Crawford, March 7, 1877, M Crawford Box 1, DPL-WHR; S. R. Shankland to Jack Crawford, Nov. 5, 1877, M Crawford Box 1, DPL-WHR. Darlis Miller says that Crawford's regrets prevented him from capitalizing on the scalp. Miller, *Captain Jack Crawford*, 60–61.

77. WFC to J. Crawford, Aug. 7, 1877, Box 1/3, WFC Collection, WH 72, M Cody L Box 1/3, Western History Collection, DPL-WHR.

78. Jack Crawford to Mrs. Nate Salsbury, March 16, 1907, in NSP.

79. "The Drama of the Future," *New York Times*, April 6, 1873, p. 4.

80. Sagala, *Buffalo Bill, Actor*, 163.

81. Cody, *Life of Buffalo Bill*, 73–77.

82. Grimsted, *Melodrama Unveiled*, 172, 227–28.

83. Cody, *Life of Buffalo Bill*, 362–63; WFC to "Captain Jack" Crawford, April 22, 1879, M Cody L, Box 1, DPL-WHR. Miller, *Captain Jack Crawford*, 210; Rosa, *They Called Him Wild Bill*, 288–89.

84. Cody, *Life of Buffalo Bill*, 306.

85. Jay Monaghan, *The Great Rascal: The Life and Adventures of Ned Buntline* (Boston: Little, Brown, 1951), 147–49.

86. "Prairie Scouts," n.d., n.p., WFC Scrapbooks, Stage Play Notices and Reviews, 1875–80, BBHC.

87. Quoted in Sagala, *Buffalo Bill, Actor*, 235.

88. Sagala, *Buffalo Bill, Actor*, 180–81, 197.

89. Halttunen, *Confidence Men and Painted Women*, 188.

90. Halttunen, *Confidence Men and Painted Women*, 185–88.

91. Jay Monaghan, *Custer: The Life of General George Armstrong Custer* (Boston: Little, Brown and Company, 1959), 358.

92. Ena Raymonde Ballantine Journal, Dec. 30, 1872, MS 1730, NSHS.

93. Ena Raymonde Ballantine Journal, Oct. 4, 1872, MS 1730, NSHS.

94. Everett Dick, *Sod House Frontier*, 367.

95. The quote is Halttunen, summarizing Goffman, in *Confidence Men and Painted Women*, 186.

96. David Nasaw, *Going Out: The Rise and Fall of Public Amusements* (New York: Basic Books, 1993), 13.

97. Nasaw, *Going Out*, 14.

98. Nasaw, *Going Out*, 18.

99. Sagala, *Buffalo Bill, Actor*, 59–60, 132.

100. Untitled clipping, n.d., n.p., WFC Scrapbook, Stage Plays and Theater Reviews, 1875–80, BBHC; for complaints of critics see no title, n.d., n.p., WFC Scrapbook, Stage Play Notices and Reviews, 1875–80, BBHC.

101. "The Scouts at Niblo's," n.d., n.p., WFC Scrapbook, Stage Play Notices and Reviews, 1875–80, BBHC.

102. "Niblo's Garden," n.p., n.d., clipping in WFC Scrapbook, Stage Play Notices and Reviews, 1875–80, BBHC.

103. Denning, *Mechanic Accents*, 47–61; Matthew Frye Jacobson, *Barbarian Virtues: The United States Encounters Foreign Peoples at Home and Abroad, 1876–1917* (New York: Hill and Wang, 2000), 88–97.

104. "Big Indians," n.d., n.p., clipping in WFC Scrapbook, Stage Play Notices and Reviews, 1875–80, BBHC.

105. "The Opera House," n.d., n.p., WFC Scrapbook, Stage Play Notices and Reviews, 1875–80, BBHC.

106. Richard Moody, *The Astor Place Riot* (Bloomington: Indiana University Press, 1958), 12.

107. The significance of Astor Place Riot is in Grimsted, *Melodrama Unveiled*, 67–75; Levine, *Highbrow/Lowbrow*, 63–69; Buntline's sentence is in Moody, *Astor Place Riot*, 236. Quote from "The Great Scalpers on the Warpath—What a Gory Ink-Slinger Considers a 'Gentlemany Intimation'—SCALPS BY THE BALE," *St. Louis Post Dispatch*, n.d., WFC Scrapbooks, BBHC.

108. Entry for March 7, 1874, James Johnson Collection, MSS 1175, Colorado State Historical Society, Denver, CO; WFC testimony, March 23, 1904.

109. "Amphitheatre Play Bill," n.d., n.p., in WFC Scrapbook, Stage Play Notices and Reviews, 1875–80.

110. Rosa, *West of Wild Bill Hickok*, 61.

111. Quoted in Sagala, *Buffalo Bill, Actor*, 130. In important ways, Hickok was heir to an earlier form of violence than Cody. Backcountry brawlers and "rasslers" had long been lower-class heroes, and their better-armed successors in Kansas and Nebraska, Hickok among them, appealed to the same hardscrabble lot. In this sense, he was less suited to be the hero of the predominantly northern and midwestern audience of the mass-market

press. Middle-class readers of *Harper's New Monthly Magazine* enjoyed lurid characters and episodes, but their tastes ran to more reluctant heroes, in part because of gathering anxieties about working-class violence in the exploding cities. Elliot Gorn, "Gouge and Bite, Pull Hair and Scratch: The Social Significance of Fighting in the Southern Back-country," *American Historical Review* 90, no. 1 (Feb. 1985): 18–43. For examples of back-country wrestling and fighting in Kansas, see Nyle H. Miller and Joseph W. Snelly, *Why the West Was Wild* (Topeka: Kansas State Historical Society, 1963); in Nebraska, see Johnson, *Happy as a Big Sunflower*, 102, 107.

112. Cody, *Life of Buffalo Bill*, 333; see also Louisa Frederici Cody and Courtney Riley Cooper, *Memories of Buffalo Bill* (D. Appleton and Co., 1919), 255–56; WFC testimony, March 23, 1904.

113. For Hickok's departure, see entry for March 11, 1874, in James Johnson Collection, MSS 1175, CHS. Cody notes that Hickok left at Rochester in Cody, *Life of Buffalo Bill*, 332–33. For Cody's family moving to Rochester, see Sagala, *Buffalo Bill, Actor*, 102–3. Cody testified in 1904 that Louisa moved to Rochester when the combination played there in 1874, which makes the date of her move March 10–11. See WFC testimony and Sagala, *Buffalo Bill, Actor*, 331.

114. "A Disgrace to Our Civilization," *New York Herald*, Aug. 11, 1876, p. 4.

115. Controversy in King, *Campaigning with Crook*, 39: Slotkin, *Gunfighter Nation*, 73; and Sagala, *Buffalo Bill, Actor*, 142. Madsen's conversation is related in Homer Croy, *Trigger Marshall: The Story of Chris Madsen* (New York: Duell, Sloan and Pearce, 1958), 12; also Homer Croy, "How Buffalo Bill Killed Chief Yellow Hand," *The American Weekly*, June 8, 1958, pp. 11–13, clipping in MS 62 Don Russell Collection, Series 1:R, Military, Box 7/3, BBHC.

116. "Buffalo Bill," n.d., n.p., Notices of Buffalo Bill, 1879–80, BBHC.

117. "The Knight of the Plains," n.d., n.p., Notices of Buffalo Bill, 1879–80, BBHC.

118. "Buffalo Bill," Notices of Buffalo Bill, 1879–80, p. 25, BBHC.

119. Rosa, *They Called Him Wild Bill*, 238; John Culhane, *The American Circus: An Illustrated History* (New York: Henry Holt, 1990), 92; Miller, *Captain Jack Crawford*, 87–111.

120. Grimsted, *Melodrama Unveiled*; Levine, *Highbrow/Lowbrow*; for prices and affordability (or lack thereof) in the theater, see Nasaw, *Going Out*, 13–24.

121. "Another Anti-Rent League," *New York Times*, Aug. 1, 1878, p. 8.

122. "A Notorious Locality," *New York Times*, Sept. 1881, p. 2. Another Buffalo Bill, a man named Horton, ran a boardinghouse and stabbed a man named Grau in a fight over an alleged insult Grau had made to Horton's wife. "A Serious Stabbing Affray," *New York Times*, Sept. 23, 1875, p. 2.

123. Sagala, *Buffalo Bill, Actor*, 97.

124. "Cincinnati," n.d., n.p., "Pike's Opera-House," n.d., n.p., WFC Scrapbook, BBHC.

125. Keim, *Sheridan's Troopers on the Borders*, 3.

126. "Indianapolis," Acadamy [*sic*] of Music, n.p., n.d., WFC Scrapbook, Stage Play Notices and Reviews, 1875–80, BBHC.

127. Reviews of Cody's autobiography are in "Notices of Buffalo Bill Season of 1879–80," BBHC, 60, 61, 64. Typical is the reviewer who writes that Cody tells his experiences "in a plain straight-forward manner and with no effort at braggadacio [*sic*]." Trip to Europe is in Cody, *Life of Buffalo Bill*, 365; and WFC to Robert Haslam, June 20, 1883, Robert Haslam Scrapbook, CHS.

CHAPTER EIGHT: INDIANS, HORSES

1. Cody, *Life of Buffalo Bill*, 297. It is also likely that Cody's friend John Y. Nelson, who was married to a Lakota woman and spoke fluent Lakota, may have played a role. Nelson's home was at the winter village of Whistler's band, not far from the fort; local settlers sometimes called the tipi encampment "Sioux City." Ena Ballantine Papers. Whistler was a leading chief of Spotted Tail's Brulés. George Hyde, *Red Cloud's Folk: A History of the Oglala Sioux Indians* (Norman: University of Oklahoma Press, 1937), 85.

2. Deloria, *Indians in Unexpected Places*, 57–58; Reddin, *Wild West Shows*, 1–52.

3. Cesare Marino, *The Remarkable Carlo Gentile: Pioneer Italian Photographer of the American Frontier* (Nevada City, CA: Carl Mautz Publishing, 1998), 45.

4. Peter Iverson, *Carlos Montezuma and the Changing World of American Indians* (Albuquerque: University of New Mexico Press, 1982).

5. Marino, *Remarkable Carlo Gentile*, 45.

6. Keim, *Sheridan's Troopers on the Borders*, 123–24; Stanley, *My Early Travels and Adventures*, 279; Roger T. Grange, "Fort Robinson, Outpost on the Plains," *Nebraska History* 39, no. 3 (Sept. 1958): 217–18; James T. King, "The Republican River Expedition, June–July 1869," *Nebraska History* 41, no. 3 (Sept. 1960): 173.

7. James R. Walker, *Lakota Society*, ed. Raymond J. DeMallie (Lincoln: University of Nebraska Press, 1982), 65–66; West, *Contested Plains*, 325; Fellows and Freeman, *This Way to the Big Show*, 134.

8. "An Indian Skirmish," *New York Times*, Dec. 11, 1881, p. 13.

9. WFC to Sam Hall, July 5, 1879, MS 6 Series I:B Css, Box 1/6, BBHC: "I did say that I would never again have another Scout or a western man with me that is one [illeg.] I would work up. for just as soon as they see their names in print a few times they git the big head and want to start a company of their own. I will name a few. Wild Bill. Texas Jack. John Nelson. Oregon Bill. Kit Carson. Capt. Jack. etc. all busted flat before they were out a month and wanted to come back because I would not take them then they talked about me."

10. Russell, *Lives and Legends*, 258.

11. Sagala, *Buffalo Bill, Actor*, 163.

12. Spotted Tail's moderate stance toward the United States eventually contributed to his murder at the hands of another Lakota. For Spotted Tail and Sword, see Carl Waldman, *Biographical Dictionary of American Indian History*, rev. ed. (New York: Facts on File, 2001), 369–71; Hyde, *Red Cloud's Folk*, 174, 223, 226. Also for Sword, see Harvey Markowitz, "George Sword," in *Encyclopedia of North American Indians*, ed. Frederick E. Hoxie (New York: Houghton Mifflin, 1996), ⟨http://college.hmco.com/history/readerscomp/naind/html./na037900_swordgeorge.htm⟩ online citation, March 7, 2005. Two Bears was a Hunkpapa who had made a name for himself as a Lakota dissident through his support for U.S. Army officers and the Peace Policy, as well as the missionary Father DeSmet. He would also become a go-between for agent McLaughlin and the Hunkpapa at Standing Rock Reservation in the early 1880s. Robert Utley, *The Lance and the Shield: The Life and Times of Sitting Bull* (New York: Ballantine Books, 1993), 67, 79, 252.

13. Cody, *Life of Buffalo Bill*, 364; Sagala, *Buffalo Bill, Actor*, 320–28.

14. Odell, *Annals of the New York Stage*, 11: 365.

15. Utley, *Lance and the Shield*, 263.

16. Sagala, *Buffalo Bill, Actor*, 163.

17. Moses, *Wild West Shows and the Images of American Indians*.

18. Sagala, *Buffalo Bill, Actor*, 164.

19. Sagala, *Buffalo Bill, Actor*, 223.

20. Robert Berkhofer, *The White Man's Indian: Images of an Idea from Columbus to the Present* (New York: Afred A. Knopf, 1978).

21. Sagala, *Buffalo Bill, Actor*, 139; Sell and Weybright, *Buffalo Bill and the Wild West*, 147.

22. "Buffalo Bill," unattributed clipping, n.d., WFC Scrapbook 1879, BBHC.

23. "Buffalo Bill," unattributed clipping, n.d., WFC Scrapbook 1879, BBHC.

24. Quoted in Sagala, *Buffalo Bill, Actor*, 185.

25. Joe Starita, *The Dull Knifes of Pine Ridge: A Lakota Odyssey* (1995; rprt. Lincoln: University of Nebraska Press, 2002), 150–51, 173.

26. Vine Deloria, Jr., "The Indians," in Hassrick et al., *Buffalo Bill and the Wild West*, 49–50.

27. Untitled clipping, n.d., n.p., in WFC Scrapbook, Stage Play Notices and Reviews, 1875–80, BBHC.

28. Daryl Jones, *The Dime Novel Western* (Bowling Green, OH: Bowling Green State University Popular Press, 1978), 28–34.

29. Jones, *Dime Novel Western*, 28–34.

30. Gail Bederman, *Manliness and Civilization: A Cultural History of Gender and Race in the United States, 1880–1917* (Chicago: University of Chicago Press, 1995); E. Anthony Rotundo, *American Manhood: Transformations in Masculinity from the Revolution to the Modern Era* (New York: Basic Books, 1993); Clyde Griffen, "Reconstructing Masculinity from the Evangelical Revival to the Waning of Progressivism: A Speculative Synthesis," in *Meanings for Manhood: Constructions of Masculinity in Victorian America,* ed. Mark C. Carnes and Clyde Griffen (Chicago: University of Chicago Press, 1990), 183–204; Susan Lee Johnson, *Roaring Camp: The Social World of the California Gold Rush* (New York: Norton, 2000), 151–52.

31. Stanley, *My Early Travels and Adventures,* 154.

32. Fellows and Freeman, *This Way to the Big Show,* 140.

33. Agnes Wright Spring, *Cheyenne and Black Hills Stage and Express Routes* (Glendale, CA: Caxton Press, 1948), 62. Cody met with Sioux diplomats who traveled to Washington about the matter, and likely tried to convince them to sign away the land (p. 64).

34. "An Interview with the Hon. W. F. Cody," *Montreal Herald and Daily Commercial Gazette,* Aug. 17, 1885, clipping in Series VI:G, Box 1, Folder 15, BBHC.

35. See the article on David L. Payne in BBWW 1884 program (Hartford, CT: Calhoun Printing, 1884), n.p.

36. Russell, *Lives and Legends,* 305; Arrell Morgan Gibson, *Oklahoma: A History of Five Centuries,* 2nd ed. (Norman: University of Oklahoma, 1981), 173–78; Carl Coke Rister, *Land Hunger: David L. Payne and the Boomers* (Norman: University of Oklahoma, 1942).

37. Smith, *View from Officers' Row,* 92–93.

38. Smith, *View from Officers' Row,* 92–93; Utley, *Frontier Regulars,* 188–92.

39. Sagala, *Buffalo Bill, Actor,* 82.

40. For quote, see Sagala, *Buffalo Bill, Actor,* 185.

41. Hutton, *Phil Sheridan and His Army,* 180.

42. Quoted in Utley, *Frontier Regulars,* 111.

43. Quotes from Crook, Howard, and Miles from Smith, *View from Officers' Row,* 118–21, 125; Sheridan from Hutton, *Phil Sheridan and His Army,* 182–83.

44. Smith, *View from Officers' Row,* 114.

45. Smith, *View from Officers' Row,* 113–38.

46. *Life on the Border* role book, MS 126, WFC Collection, Box 1, Folder 4, CHS.

47. All quotes from Smith, *View from Officers' Row,* 118–21.

48. Smith, *View from Officers' Row,* 125.

49. Smith, *View from Officers' Row,* 134–35.

50. Cody, *Life of Buffalo Bill,* 280. For Henry A. Ward, see Cody, *Life of Buffalo Bill,* 308. For Sioux hostility to Marsh, see Spring, *Cheyenne and Black Hills Stage and Express Routes,* 45–46.

51. Utley, *Life in Custer's Cavalry,* 72.

52. Richard Irving Dodge, *Our Wild Indians: Thirty-Three Years' Personal Experience of the Red Men of the Great West* (1882; rprt. New York: Books for Libraries Press, 1970), 337.

53. Davis, "Summer on the Plains," 303.

54. Armes, *Ups and Downs of an Army Officer,* 193.

55. Armes, *Ups and Downs of an Army Officer,* 194.

56. Dodge, *Our Wild Indians,* 582.

57. Janet M. Davis, *The Circus Age: Culture and Society Under the American Big Top* (Chapel Hill: University of North Carolina Press, 2002), 16.

58. Davis, *Circus Age,* 17.

59. Fellows and Freeman, *This Way to the Big Show,* 211.

60. Quotes from BBWW 1901 program (Buffalo, NY: Courier, 1901), 3.

61. Cody, *Life of Buffalo Bill,* 172; for buffalo horses, see John Ewers, *The Horse in Blackfoot Indian Culture* (Washington, DC: Smithsonian, 1955).

62. Dodge, *Our Wild Indians,* 341–42.

63. Cody, *Life of Buffalo Bill,* 269.

64. Davis, *Circus Age,* 20.

65. Davis, *Circus Age,* 15–36, 39–46.

66. Davis, *Circus Age*, 93–94.
67. Fellows and Freeman, *This Way to the Big Show*, 106–7, 113–14.
68. Davis, *Circus Age*, 31–32.
69. Fellows and Freeman, *This Way to the Big Show*, 179–80.
70. Davis, *Circus Age*, 7, 21, 39–41, 45.
71. Davis, *Circus Age*, 32.
72. Dan Castello was also part of this partnership, but he soon departed. Fellows and Freeman, *This Way to the Big Show*, 169–70.
73. "Barnum's Roman Hippodrome," *New York Times*, April 25, 1874, p. 7.
74. Davis, *Circus Age*, 40.
75. Elbert R. Bowen, "The Circus in Early Rural Missouri," *Missouri Historical Review* 47, no. 10 (1952): 1–17; Deahl, "Nebraska's Unique Contribution," 283–98.
76. Nellie Snyder Yost, *Buffalo Bill*, 30–33, 41; also the same author's *The Call of the Range: The Story of the Nebraska Stock Growers Association* (Denver, CO: Sage Books, 1966).
77. James C. Olson and Ronald C. Naugle, *History of Nebraska*, 3rd ed. (Lincoln: University of Nebraska Press, 1997), 190–93.
78. Olson and Naugle, *History of Nebraska*, 191–92; John Bratt, *Trails of Yesterday* (Chicago: The University Publishing Co., 1921), 278; lost money is in WFC to Sam Hall, May 9, 1879, MS 6 Series I:B Css Box 1/6, BBHC.
79. Bratt, *Trails of Yesterday*, 279.
80. Cody, *Life of Buffalo Bill*, 363.
81. Bratt, *Trails of Yesterday*, 279.
82. Bratt, *Trails of Yesterday*, 279.
83. Richard W. Slatta, *Cowboys of the Americas* (New Haven, CT: Yale University Press, 1990), 141–42.
84. An 1844 pickup contest between Texas Rangers, Indians, and Hispanics in San Antonio was echoed in a similar contest at the Texas State Fair in 1852. Slatta, *Cowboys of the Americas*, 139.
85. In the first few years of the Wild West show, one act featured a cowboy called Mustang Jack, who leapt over a tall horse from a standing start. Such feats were a range standard, too. Cowboy competition extended to physical feats not necessarily associated with cowboy skills. The Dismal River roundup included swimming races. Throughout Mexico and South America, cowboys eschewed walking or running on foot, but in the United States, cowboys not only ran footraces, but challenged one another to jumping contests, including the high jump, the broad jump, and the triple jump (or "hop, step, and jump" as it was known at the time). Slatta, *Cowboys of the Americas*, 140–41.
86. Cody, *Life of Buffalo Bill*, 362.
87. Yost, *Buffalo Bill*, 118–22.
88. Nate Salsbury, "Cody's Personal Representatives," typescript, YCAL MSS 17, NSP; also Nate Salsbury, "The Origin of the Wild West Show," *Colorado Magazine* 32, no. 3 (July 1955): 205–8, original in YCAL MSS 17, NSP.

CHAPTER NINE: DOMESTICATING THE WILD WEST

1. Yost, *Buffalo Bill*, 132–33.
2. For concerns about unsuitable entertainment, see Allen, *Horrible Prettiness*; John F. Kasson, *Amusing the Million: Coney Island at the Turn of the Century* (New York: Hill and Wang, 1978), 6–7. "Better class of people" in WFC to W. F. Carver, Feb. 11, 1883, WA MSS S-1621, Beinecke Library, New Haven, CT.
3. For middle-class women in audiences, see Nasaw, *Going Out*, 18, 26. For the appeal of the Wild West show to families, see "The Wild West," *Montreal Herald and Commercial Gazette*, Aug. 17, 1885, n.p., clipping in Series VI:G Box 1, folder 15, BBHC.
4. The phrase "Westward the Course of Empire," from an eighteenth-century poem by Bishop Berkeley, was widely used in American painting, and it appeared in Wild West show posters, too. See Jack Rennert, *100 Posters of Buffalo Bill's Wild West* (New York:

Darien House, 1976), foldout A. Anxieties about national decay also inspired art. Between 1835 and 1839, Thomas Cole, America's most famous landscape painter, produced a four-part series of paintings which he titled *The Course of Empire*. The paintings illustrated a people's progress from wilderness savagery, through pastoral and commercial stages to imperial grandeur, before falling into decadence and fiery collapse. Based on the experience of Rome, the paintings suggested America's own passage from wilderness beginnings to nascent imperial grandeur. *The Course of Empire* both celebrated progress and questioned its outcome. All eyes turned westward in the nineteenth century, and most remained optimistic. But Cole's *Course of Empire* might just as well have been titled "Downward the Course of Empire Takes Its Way." See Barbara Novak, *Nature and Culture: American Landscape and Painting, 1825–1875* (New York: Oxford University Press, 1980), 10, 19–20, 110.

5. Quoted in Lears, *No Place of Grace*, 50.

6. Bederman, *Manliness and Civilization*, 84–88; also Lears, *No Place of Grace*, 49–51.

7. Bernard Bailyn, Robert Dallek, David Brion Davis, David Herbert Donald, John L. Thomas, and Gordon S. Wood, *The Great Republic: A History of the American People*, 2 vols. 4th ed. (Lexington, MA: D. C. Heath, 1992), 2:228–29; Matthew Frye Jacobson, *Barbarian Virtues: The United States Encountered Foreign Peoples at Home and Abroad, 1876–1917* (New York: Hill and Wang, 2000), 6: "Between 1870 and 1920, some twenty-six million immigrants entered the United States."

8. See David M. Wrobel, *The End of American Exceptionalism: Frontier Anxiety from the Old West to the New Deal* (Lawrence: University Press of Kansas, 1993); G. Edward White, *The Eastern Establishment and the Western Experience: The West of Frederic Remington, Theodore Roosevelt, and Owen Wister* (Austin: University of Texas Press, 1989).

9. Robert A. Woods, ed., *The City Wilderness: A Settlement Study by Residents and Associates of the South End House* (1898; rprt. New York: Garrett Press, 1970); Burrows and Wallace, *Gotham*, 1174–75; Robert W. Cherny, *American Politics in the Gilded Age, 1868–1900* (Wheeling, IL: Harlan Davidson Press, 1997), 136; Eric Rauchway, *Murdering McKinley: The Making of Theodore Roosevelt's America* (New York: Hill and Wang, 2003), 133–35. Also see Katherine Kish Sklar, *Florence Kelley and the Nation's Work: The Rise of Women's Political Culture, 1830–1902* (New Haven: Yale University Press, 1997); Victoria Brown, *The Education of Jane Addams* (Philadelphia: University of Pennsylvania Press, 2003); Rosalind Rosenberg, *Divided Lives: American Women in the Twentieth Century* (New York: Hill and Wang, 1992), 25–35.

10. Peggy Samuels and Harold Samuels, *Frederic Remington* (Austin: University of Texas Press, 1982), 33; Remington quoted in G. Edward White, *The Eastern Establishment and the Western Experience: The West of Frederic Remington, Theodore Roosevelt, and Owen Wister* (New Haven: Yale University Press, 1968), 109.

11. Remington's painting of Buffalo Bill in 1899 was reproduced in Helen Cody Wetmore's biography of her brother, *Last of the Great Scouts* (1899; rprt. New York: Grosset and Dunlap, 1918), and on the covers of show programs for 1901, with Remington's permission. See BBWW 1901 program (Buffalo, NY: Courier, 1901).

12. Dr. N. Allen, "Changes in Population," *Harper's New Monthly Magazine* 38, no. 225 (Feb. 1869): 386.

13. Theodore Roosevelt, *The Winning of the West*, 6 vols. (New York: G. P. Putnam's Sons, 1889–96); Bederman, *Manliness and Civilization*, 170–215.

14. "Actresses See Cowboys," *New York Advertiser*, July 31, 1894, in NSS, 1894, WH72, Series 7, Box 4, DPL.

15. Brick Pomeroy, quoted in BBWW 1899 program, p. 11. For G. Stanley Hall and educational theory, see Bederman, *Manliness and Civilization*, 88–101.

16. "Women's Kingdom," *Chicago Tribune*, Oct. 20, 1883, p. 12; "Female Suffrage and Woman's Advancement," *Chicago Tribune*, Oct. 21, 1883, p. 4.

17. Jane Tompkins, *West of Everything: The Inner Life of Westerns* (New York: Oxford University Press, 1992), 23–45; Lears, *No Place of Grace*, 103–7; also Halttunen, *Confidence Men and Painted Women*, 56–59.

18. Slotkin, *Gunfighter Nation*, 63–87, esp. 77.

19. Orvell, *Real Thing*, 77, 101.
20. Bachmann, quoted in Rennert, *100 Posters of Buffalo Bill's Wild West*, 4.
21. WFC to Carver, Feb. 11, 1883, WA MSS S-1621, Beinecke Library, Yale University, New Haven, CT.
22. Buffalo Bill and Dr. Carver Wild West, Rocky Mountain, and Prairie Exhibition Program 1883 (Hartford, CT: Calhoun Printing), n.p., [hereafter BBDC]; BBWW 1885 program, n.p., Cody Collection, WH 72, Box 2/19, DPL-WHR.
23. Quotes from Fellows and Freeman, *This Way to the Big Show*, 95, 146; for Matthewson, see "Real Buffalo Bill," *Chicago Post*, July 14, 1894, and "He Met Buffalo Bill," *New York Press*, Sept. 3, 1894, both clippings in NSS, vol. 4; George E. Hyde, *Life of George Bent: Written from His Letters*, ed. Savoie Lottinville (Norman: University of Nebraska Press, 1968), 268; Yost, *Buffalo Bill*, 374–75.
24. See "New Jersey's Farm Work," *New York Times*, Sept. 16, 1884, p. 8.
25. For a survey of competing Wild West shows, see Don Russell, *The Wild West: A History of the Wild West Shows* (Fort Worth, TX: Amon Carter Museum, 1970); Paul Reddin, *Wild West Shows* (Chicago: University of Illinois Press, 1999). For Samuel Franklin Cody, see Garry Jenkins, *"Colonel" Cody and the Flying Cathedral: The Adventures of the Cowboy Who Conquered Britain's Skies* (London: Simon and Schuster, 1999), esp. 8–12.
26. WFC to William Carver, Feb. 11, 1883, WA MSS S-1621, Beinecke Library, Yale University, New Haven, CT.
27. Moses, *Wild West Shows and the Images of American Indians*, 23.
28. Carver's fraudulent biography is in BBDC 1883 program (Hartford, CT: Calhoun, 1883), n.p. Carver paid $200 for 160 acres of North Platte property in 1874. See WA MSS S-1621, Beinecke Library; see also Yost, *Call of the Range*, 106; and Yost, *Buffalo Bill*, 126–27. For a full-length biography of Carver which accepts all of his fabrications uncritically, see Raymond W. Thorp, *Spirit Gun of the West* (Glendale, CA: A. H. Clark, 1957).
29. Cody, *Life of Buffalo Bill*, 337.
30. Salsbury, "The Origins of the Wild West Show," in YCAL MSS 17, NSP, 207. The reference to a piano stool came from Carver's unsuccessful attempt to import a piano to his mother's house near North Platte. See Yost, *Call of the Range*, 106.
31. Fellows and Freeman, *This Way to the Big Show*, 66.
32. "Carver's Big Rifle Feat," *New York Times*, July 14, 1878, p. 12; also, "The Great Rifle Shot," *New York Times*, July 5, 1878, p. 8.
33. James B. Trefethen, "They Were All Sure Shots," *American Heritage* (April 1962): 26–32.
34. WFC to W. F. Carver, Feb. 11, 1883, WA MSS S-1621, Beinecke Library, Yale University, New Haven, CT.
35. WFC to Carver, n.d.; Cody to Carver, Feb. 11, 1883; WFC to Carver, Feb. 28, 1883, in WA MSS S-1621, Beinecke Library, Yale University, New Haven, CT.
36. George Ward Nichols, "Wild Bill," *Harper's New Monthly Magazine* (Feb. 1867): 274; also Webb, *Buffalo Land*, 145.
37. "The Grand Duke's Hunt—General Sheridan and 'Buffalo Bill' Lead the Way—At Grand Battue on the Plains," *New York Herald*, Jan. 14, 1872, p. 7.
38. "Buffalo Bill," undated clipping, BB Scrapbook, 1879, BBHC.
39. Yost, *Buffalo Bill*, 127; Sagala, *Buffalo Bill, Actor*, 265.
40. Yost, *Buffalo Bill*, 128.
41. Roy Harvey Pearce, *The Savages of America: A Study of the Indian and the Idea of Civilization* (Baltimore: Johns Hopkins Press, 1953), 49.
42. The ethnological congress was pioneered by a German circus owner, Carl Hagenbeck, in 1874. Davis, *Circus Age*, 118.
43. BBDC 1883, n.p.
44. BBDC 1883, n.p.
45. This synopsis and quote are from Yost, *Buffalo Bill*, 134–36.
46. BBDC 1883, n.p.
47. Russell, *Lives and Legends*, 295.

48. Clay McShane and Joel A. Tarr, "The Centrality of the Horse in the Nineteenth-Century American City," in *The Making of Urban America*, ed. Raymond Mohl, 2nd ed., (Wilmington, DE: Scholarly Resources, 1997), 109.

49. "Pictures of the Plains," *The World* (New York), July 16, 1886, p. 3. Within months, the tribute was reprinted in the London dramatic publication *The Era* ("The 'Wild West' Show," *The Era*, Sept. 18, 1886, p. 10). Less than two years later, John Burke, Cody's ghostwriter, repeated it for an American readership in *Story of the Wild West and Camp-Fire Chats* (1888; rprt. Freeport, NY: Books for Libraries Press, 1970), 714–15. The description was imitated and plagiarized thereafter, as when Percy MacKaye described Cody as "veritably a Centaur," in 1927, and when Stella Foote recalled him as "the complete restoration of the Centaur," in 1954. MacKaye, *Epoch*, 2:91; Foote, *Letters from "Buffalo Bill,"* 15.

50. "Transatlantic Centaurs," see *The Era*, April 23, 1887, clipping in Johnny Baker Scrapbook, DPL-WHR. For "coming centaur," see Cody, *Story of the Wild West*, 721.

51. Firmage, *E. E. Cummings: Complete Poems, 1904–1962*, 90.

52. J. Michael Padgett, quoted in "Human Fate: Part Beast, Part Angel," *New York Times*, Oct. 31, 2003, p. B42.

53. Page DuBois, *Centaurs and Amazons: Women and the Pre-History of the Great Chain of Being* (Ann Arbor, MI: University of Michigan Press, 1982), 25–42.

54. See Bederman, *Manliness and Civilization*, 16; Deloria, *Playing Indian*, 107–9; Herman, *Hunting and the American Imagination*, 237–69. Remington himself played football at Yale in 1880. See Samuels and Samuels, *Frederic Remington*, 26–27.

55. Yost, *Buffalo Bill*, 135.

56. Handcrafted, individually numbered and named ("The Deadwood," "The Wyoming"), ornamented with hand-painted scrollwork and original landscape paintings on their doors, these coaches were frontier "originals" in two ways: each was unique, and no other company could afford to mimic their master craftsmanship (which was so painstaking that only three thousand of them were ever manufactured). Spring, *Cheyenne and Black Hills Stage Routes*, 88–89, 334; also "Stagecoach," in *New Encyclopedia of the American West*, 1074–75.

57. "Staging in the Far West," *Harper's Weekly*, July 4, 1874, p. 556.

58. In 1884, the owners of the Cheyenne and Black Hills Stage Line sold out when the railroad extended from Cheyenne to the Black Hills. In 1887, the new owner of the line, Russell Thorp, "staged" a final journey of the Deadwood stage for paying customers in Cheyenne, with passengers, driver, and vehicle posing for a famous photograph of "the last coach out" just before they departed. "Days of '49" was a popular miners' song in the Black Hills. See Rodman W. Paul, *Mining Frontiers of the Far West, 1848–1800* (1973; rprt. Albuquerque: University of New Mexico, 1974), 178–79; for "last coach out," see Spring, *Cheyenne and Black Hills Stage Routes*, 334–35. For trolleys, see Wild West Diary of 1896, M. B. Bailey, reprinted in Fellows and Freeman, *This Way to the Big Show*, 352.

59. BBDC 1883 program, n.p.

60. "The Wild West Show," clipping attached to sketch of Deadwood stage pursuit, in WFC Scrapbook, 1887, Buffalo Bill Museum, Lookout Mountain, CO.

61. Russell, *Lives and Legends*, 295; Spring, *Cheyenne and Black Hills Stage and Express Routes*, 359.

62. Cody himself described his route out of the Plains in Cody, *Life of Buffalo Bill*, 359; he recounted it again in WFC testimony, March 6, 1905, Folder 13, 18–19, in CC.

63. In other ways, too, its real history diverged considerably from show accounts. If this coach was named "The Deadwood," it was only one of several dozen to ply the route between Deadwood and Cheyenne. The Cheyenne and Black Hills Stage Line, the original proprietor of this coach, owned thirty Abbot and Downing Concords. When he established the line at the beginning of the Black Hills gold rush in 1874, Luke Voorhees ordered new coaches (not veterans dating from 1863). Later, he outfitted two so-called "treasure coaches," Concord coaches with steel plates bolted to the inside of their compartments, and small portholes for windows—through which guards fired their weapons.

During the Cold Spring holdup, a steel-plated coach named "The Monitor" was attacked by a gang of bandits who killed one guard and wounded others before finally seizing the coach. The famed "Deadwood" of Buffalo Bill's arena had no steel plates, no portholes—and no connection to the Cold Spring holdup. Spring, *Cheyenne and Black Hills Stage and Express Routes,* 248–49, 265–75.

64. Lord Ronald Sutherland Gower, *Old Diaries, 1881–1901* (London: John Murray, 1902), 107–8.

65. Fellows and Freeman, *This Way to the Big Show,* 180.

66. Fellows and Freeman, *This Way to the Big Show,* 180.

67. Although he toyed with the idea of commissioning gamblers to play the crowd, he turned away from it. In future years, whenever small-money shell games and faro dealers became too numerous on the fringes, Cody would send out show cowboys to break their equipment—and their noses, too. Fellows and Freeman, *This Way to the Big Show,* 117–18.

68. "Over the arena proper where the exhibition is given there is nothing but the blue vault of the sky," claimed *Buffalo Bill's Wild West and Congress of Rough Riders of the World 1898 Show Courier* (New York: J. A. Rudolph, 1898), 32.

69. Lears, *No Place of Grace,* 23.

70. Nate Salsbury, "A Card from Nate Salsbury," *The Frontier Express—Buffalo Bill Wild West Courier* 12, no. 95 (1895), BBHC.

71. Buffalo Bill's Wild West, "in no wise partaking of the nature of a 'circus,' will be at once new, startling, and instructive," claimed Wild West show programs, and publicists never tired of contrasting the Wild West with the "old played out circus-menagerie combination." John Burke, "Salutatory" in BBWW 1885 program (Hartford, CT: Calhoun Printing, 1885), n.p.; "played out circus-menagerie" in "The Wild West," *Montreal Herald,* Aug. 12, 1885, in NSS, vol. 1, 1885–86, DPL.

72. Rennert, *100 Posters of Buffalo Bill's Wild West,* 5.

73. Steele Mackaye, quoted in Walter Havighurst, *Annie Oakley of the Wild West* (1954, rprt. Lincoln: University of Nebraska Press, 1992), 86.

74. "The Wild West," *Free Press and Times,* Aug. 6, 1885; in NSS, vol. 1, 1885–86, DPL.

75. Route from Russell, *Lives and Legends,* 295–99; quote from WFC to Julia Cody Goodman, Aug. 16, 1883, in Foote, *Letters from "Buffalo Bill,"* 20.

76. Fellows and Freeman, *This Way to the Big Show,* 68–69;

77. Russell, *Lives and Legends,* 297.

78. Courtney Riley Cooper, quoted in Fellows and Freeman, *This Way to the Big Show,* 69.

79. Cody to Sam Hall, Sept. 2, 1879, MS 6 Series I:B Css Box 1/6, BBHC.

80. "Finding a Fortune," transcript of article from *Denver Tribune,* March 28, 1882, in MSS 126, Box 1, CHS; also WFC to Al Goodman, Feb. 12, 1882, MS 6 Series I:B Css Box 1/7, BBHC. The pattern of legal fights with extended relatives was something of a family tradition. After Isaac Cody died, his brothers, Joseph and Elijah, battled each other in a suit over unpaid debts, tying up Isaac Cody's estate in probate court. See Leavenworth County Probate Court, Case File: *Joseph Cody v. Elijah Cody,* June 8, 1857, KSHS, Topeka, KS.

81. WFC testimony, Denver, March 23, 1904, p. 11; CC Folder 13; also Russell, *Lives and Legends,* 257–58.

82. WFC testimony, March 23, 1904, Folder 2, p. 13.

83. Yost, *Buffalo Bill,* 154–55; Foote, *Letters from "Buffalo Bill,"* 22.

84. WFC to Julia Cody Goodman, Sept. 24, 1883, in Foote, *Letters from "Buffalo Bill,"* 21. For birth of Irma, see Yost, *Buffalo Bill,* 126.

85. Yost, *Buffalo Bill,* 142.

86. McCoy, *Historic Sketches of the Cattle Trade,* 202, 204; Terry Jordan, *North American Cattle Ranching Frontiers: Origins, Diffusion, Differentiation* (Albuquerque: University of New Mexico, 1997), 210–11, 232–34.

87. Robert Zeigler, "The Cowboy Strike of 1883: Its Causes and Meaning," *West Texas Historical Association Year Book* 47 (1971): 33; Don D. Walker, *Clio's Cowboys: Studies in the*

Historiography of the Cattle Trade (Lincoln: University of Nebraska Press, 1981), 141; Hine and Faragher, *American West*, 322.

88. BBWW 1885 program, n.p.; 1893 program, 25–26. Omohundro's article originally appeared as "The Cow-Boy," *Spirit of the Times*, March 24, 1877. See Herschel C. Logan, *Buckskin and Satin* (Harrisburg, PA: Stackpole Co., 1954), 26–30.

89. Robert Utley, *Billy the Kid: A Short and Violent Life* (Lincoln: University of Nebraska Press, 1989); Casey Tefertiller, *Wyatt Earp: The Life Behind the Legend* (New York: John Wiley, 1997).

90. WFC to "Dear Sister and Brother," Sept. 24, 1883, in Foote, *Letters from "Buffalo Bill,"* 21.

91. "The Wild West," *Chicago Tribune*, Oct. 18, 1883, p. 3. On dime novels and crime, see "Sunday Tribune," *Chicago Tribune*, Oct. 20, 1883, p. 4. "The life of 'Red Bill,' alias 'Razor Joe,' a thief who has just died in a Philadelphia prison, is printed in another column. It is recommended to the young as less likely to inspire a criminal inclination than the current histories of Jesse James and 'Cowboy Charley.' " See also Denning, *Mechanic Accents*.

92. "The Wild West," *Chicago Tribune*, Oct. 18, 1883, p. 3.

93. "The Dime Novel," *Chicago Tribune*, Oct. 18, 1883, p. 8.

94. Salsbury, "The Origin of the Wild West Show," in YCAL MSS 17, NSP Box 2/63.

95. Cecil Smith, "The Road to Musical Comedy," *Theatre Arts*, Nov. 1947, pp. 57–58.

96. "Salsbury's Troubadors at the Grand Opera House," *Chicago Tribune*, Oct. 16, 1883, p. 5.

97. BBDC 1883 program, M Cody Box 6, DPL.

98. Nate Salsbury, "Long Hair and a Plug Hat," typescript in YCAL MSS 17, NSP.

99. See, for example, Cody's own celebration of the fact that his show cast was "everywhere acclaimed gentlemen," and "free of impure associations," in "The Wild West," *Montreal Herald and Commercial Gazette*, Aug. 17, 1885, n.p., clipping in Series VI:G, Box 1, Folder 15, BBHC.

100. WFC to Nate Salsbury, n.d., YCAL MSS 17, NSP, Box 1, Folder 4.

101. Sarah J. Blackstone, *Buckskin, Bullets, and Business: A History of Buffalo Bill's Wild West* (Westport, CT: Greenwood Press, 1986), 54.

102. For descriptions of the scene, see "Royalty at the 'Wild West,' " *The Era*, May 7, 1887, p. 15; "Buffalo Bill," *The Globe* (Toronto), Aug. 19, 1885, clipping in Series VI:G, Box 1, Folder 15, BBHC. In those few cases when it was not the show finale, it was almost always included earlier in the program. Alternative finales included a cyclone during parts of the 1886 and 1887 seasons, the battle of Tsien-Tsin in 1901, and an avalanche in 1907. BBWW 1886 (Madison Square Garden Program), Inaugural Invitation Exhibition of Buffalo Bill's Wild West" (Manchester, UK: Guardian Printing Works, 1887), n.p., M Cody Box 6, DPL-WHR; BBWW 1907, various programs, MS 6:VIA, BBHC.

103. Richard White has noted that by the 1890s the log cabin served as an icon of progressive history, the humble origins of a great nation. White, "Frederick Jackson Turner and Buffalo Bill," 19–26.

104. David Nasaw, *Going Out*, 15: "The home—not the club, the saloon, the firehouse, or the theater—was the heart and soul of middle-class existence." Mary Ryan, *Cradle of the Middle Class*, 155–85; Richard Sennett, *Families Against the City: Middle-Class Homes of Industrial Chicago, 1872–1890* (New York, 1974), 52–53, 224.

105. Nate Salsbury, "A Dilemma," typescript, n.d., YCAL MSS 17, NSP, Box 2163; Fellows and Freeman, *This Way to the Big Show*, 70–71.

106. WFC to N. Salsbury, Feb. 14, 1885, YCAL MSS 17, NSP, Box 1/4.

107. WFC to N. Salsbury, March 9, 1885, YCAL MSS 17, NSP, Box 1/4.

108. Russell, *Lives and Legends*, 311–13.

109. Discussion of the merits of shooting skill, as opposed to stage tricks, was widespread. See "The Referee," n.d., n.p., clipping in Annie Oakley Scrapbook, 1887, BBHC.

110. Russell, *Lives and Legends*, 315.

111. Allen, *Horrible Prettiness*.

112. Nasaw, *Going Out*, 26.

113. Glenda Riley, *The Life and Legacy of Annie Oakley* (Norman: University of Oklahoma Press, 1994), 22–26.

114. See the advertisement for the Wild West show in the *Cincinnati Commercial Gazette*, Oct. 19, 1884, p. 12.

115. Russell, *Lives and Legends*, 314.

116. The theory of "male essence" was articulated by George H. Naphey, *The Transmission of Life: Counsels on the Nature and Hygiene of the Masculine Function*, 2nd ed. (Philadelphia: H. C. Watts, 1878). For further discussion, see Bram Dijkstra, *Evil Sisters: The Threat of Female Sexuality and the Cult of Manhood* (New York: Alfred A. Knopf, 1996). Bederman, *Manliness and Civilization*, 48–49, 80–90; see also Michel Foucault, *History of Sexuality*, vol. 1: *An Introduction* (New York: Vintage, 1978); Cynthia Eagle Russett, *Sexual Science: The Victorian Construction of Womanhood* (Cambridge, MA: Harvard University Press, 1989), 112–16.

117. Nell Irvin Painter, *Standing at Armageddon: The United States, 1877–1919* (New York: W. W. Norton, 1987), 15–18.

118. Painter, *Standing at Armageddon*, 22; Paul Avrich, *The Haymarket Tragedy* (Princeton, NJ: Princeton University Press, 1984), 33–35.

119. "Marksmanship of the Militia," *New York Times*, Sept. 12, 1877, p. 4.

120. Cody, *Life of Buffalo Bill*, 202; Utley, *Frontier Regulars*, 147–48.

121. Warren, *Hunter's Game*, 45, 71–105.

122. BBWW 1884 program (Hartford, CT: Calhoun Printers, 1884), n.p.; James W. Wojtowicz, *The W. F. Cody Buffalo Bill Collector's Guide with Values* (Paducah, KY: Collector Books, 1998), 13.

123. Mexican displays of skill were restricted to rope tricks. Indians were marvelous riders, and seem to have carried guns some of the time, but had no room to display marksmanship in the show. In the buffalo hunt they carried lances. For buffalo hunt and Custer's Last Stand photos, see Isabelle S. Sayers, *Annie Oakley and Buffalo Bill's Wild West* (New York: Dover Publications, 1981), 65–66.

124. BBWW 1884 program; Wojtowicz, *Buffalo Bill Collector's Guide*, 13.

125. See the ad in *Cincinnati Commercial Gazette*, Oct. 19, 1884, p. 12.

126. Walter Havighurst, *Annie Oakley of the Wild West*, 9; Annie Fern Swartout, *Missie: An Historical Biography of Annie Oakley* (Blanchester, OH: Brown Publishing Co, 1947), 3–34; see also Riley, *Life and Legacy of Annie Oakley*; Sayers, *Annie Oakley and Buffalo Bill's Wild West*. For much of the discussion that follows, I am indebted to Christine Bold, "Introduction," in Walter Havighurst, *Annie Oakley of the Wild West*, ix–xvii.

127. "Camp Sketches No. IV: Annie Oakley," *The Topical Times* (UK), June 23, 1887, clipping in Julia Cody Goodman Scrapbook, MS 58 Box 1, NSHS.

128. Even Oakley's niece, Annie Fern Swartout, in a loving biography, refers to Oakley's fixation with the name as "an obsession," and concludes "my dear aunt was utterly in the wrong" to expunge it from family records. Swartout, *Missie*, 41–42. Also Russell, *Lives and Legends*, 312.

129. Not even family members could explain why Oakley chose this name. Swartout, *Missie*, 68.

130. Indeed, her extended family reviled her for becoming an entertainer. Swartout, *Missie*, 68.

131. Russell, *Lives and Legends*, 315.

132. Fellows and Freeman, *This Way to the Big Show*, 73.

133. Caroll Smith-Rosenberg, *Disorderly Conduct: Visions of Gender in Victorian America* (New York: Alfred A. Knopf, 1985), 181. For wives and the restraint of male sexuality, see John D'Emilio and Estelle B. Freedman, *Intimate Matters: A History of Sexuality in America* (New York: Harper & Row, 1988), 179.

134. "Women and the home represented stability in a rapidly changing society, and women were forced into a more circumscribed position to facilitate the transition to an industrial society." Joyce Warren, quoted in Tracy Davis, "Annie Oakley and Her Ideal Husband of No Importance," p. 302, in *Critical Theory and Performance*, ed. Janelle G. Reinelt and Joseph R. Roach (Ann Arbor: University of Michigan Press, 1992), 229–312.

135. Other scholars have argued that Annie Oakley's act was in fact a conservative spectacle

for being a complete inversion of domestic norms, therein heightening awareness and sensitivity to the "normal" domestic order. See Tracy C. Davis, "Shotgun Wedlock: Annie Oakley's Power Politics in the Wild West," p. 153, in *Gender in Performance: The Presentation of Difference in the Performing Arts*, ed. Laurence Senelick (Hanover, NH: University Press of New England, 1992), 140–53.

136. *The Courier of London*, n.d., Annie Oakley Scrapbook, 1887, BBHC.

137. Unattributed clipping, n.d., MS 126 WFC Collection, Box 2, Folder 19, CHS. For a sample of how reformers saw the bicycle, see Frances E. Willard's 1895 memoir of bicycle riding and social advocacy. Originally published under the title *A Wheel Within a Wheel*, it is available in revised form as *How I Learned to Ride the Bicycle*, ed. Carol O'Hare (Sunnyvale, CA: Fair Oaks Publishing, 1991).

138. Bold, "Introduction," xii.

139. Fellows and Freeman, *This Way to the Big Show*, 72–73.

140. C. L. Daily to "Dear Folks," n.d., Neuilly, France, 22nd (no month), 1889, copy in BBHC; there is a photo of Princess Winona in William Cody Bradford Scrapbook, P. 6.612.20A, BBHC.

141. For Smith's years with the show, see BBWW, 1886–89, BBHC; Wojtowicz, *Buffalo Bill's Collector's Guide*, 14–17. Georgia Duffy was with the show as early as 1886. She was married to Tom Duffy, one of the show's cowboys. See "Pictures of the Plains," *The World* (NY), July 16, 1886, p. 3; and berth assignments for the 1887 trip to London in "W. F. Cody Scrapbook, 1883–1886–1888," BBHC.

142. For family, see Swartout, *Missie*, 79–80; for resentments, see Bold, "Introduction," xv: "She seems to have regarded the other white female performers in the Wild West . . . as rivals to be vanquished, not sisters to be embraced."

143. Cody, *Story of the Wild West*, 737.

144. Havighurst, *Annie Oakley of the Wild West*, 207–8.

145. Rennert, *100 Posters of Buffalo Bill's Wild West*, 8, 46.

146. Burrows and Wallace, *Gotham*, 1072.

147. "The Wild West," (illegible attribution) clipping in WFC Scrapbook, 1887, Buffalo Bill Museum, Lookout Mountain, CO.

148. See the show programs, 1886–1916, in BBHC and DPL, or see the show program summaries in Wojtowicz, *Buffalo Bill Collector's Guide*, 14–47. The frequency of the Virginia reel or quadrille on horseback scene is difficult to judge, given that it was often incorporated into the "Attack on the Emigrant Train" scene and not mentioned separately. For connection of the dance and emigrant train scenes, see BBWW programs for 1886, 1888, 1898, 1902, 1903, 1910. Wojtowicz, *Buffalo Bill Collector's Guide*, 15–16.

149. See for example "Programme, Subject to Changes and Additions," in the opening pages of BBWW 1885 program (Hartford, CT: Calhoun Printers), n.p.; also Rocky Bear, quoted in Kasson, *Buffalo Bill's Wild West*, 212.

150. For Ma Whittaker in the Wild West show, see "The Wild West's 'Mamma,'" *Brooklyn Citizen*, Sept. 15, 1894; "City Camp Life," *Brooklyn Citizen*, May 20, 1894; "With 'Marm' Whittaker," *New York Commercial Advertiser*, June 16, 1894; all in NSS, vol. 4, CC, Series 7, Box 4.

151. Judith R. Walkowitz, *City of Dreadful Delight: Narratives of Sexual Danger in Late-Victorian London* (Chicago: University of Chicago Press, 1992).

152. In this sense the scene harkened to traditions of American melodrama. See Grimstead, *Melodrama Unveiled*; also Allen, *Horrible Prettiness*, 81–87. Thanks to Karen Halttunen for the insight.

153. In the words of one study, "Population movement was ubiquitous" in the nineteenth century. Michael Katz, Michael J. Doucet, and Mark J. Stern, *The Social Organization of Early Industrial Capitalism* (Cambridge, MA: Belknap Press of Harvard University Press, 1982), 113, 119.

154. The fact that the settler's cabin itself occupied a prominent place in the arena throughout the show, so that all other acts swirled around it, suggested too that the home anchored the drama, and that all of the movement and energy on display in the arena would in fact end up there. See the arena photos, Series XI:J, Box 2, BBHC.

155. Rauchway, *Murdering McKinley*, 133–35.
156. Margaret Marsh, *Suburban Lives* (New Brunswick, NJ: Rutgers University Press, 1990), 67–74; also Margaret Marsh, "Suburban Men and Masculine Domesticity, 1870–1915," in *Meanings for Manhood: Constructions of Masculinity in Victorian America*, ed. Mark C. Carnes and Clyde Griffen (Chicago: University of Chicago Press, 1990), 111–28.
157. Marsh, *Suburban Lives*, 79.
158. In other ways, the show was at pains to remind people that the white people were only temporary nomads. Thus, in the 1887 season, the wagons were loaded with white families, as well as furniture and household effects, the very stuff of domesticity. For families, see "The Wild West Show," *The Era*, May 14, 1887, Annie Oakley Scrapbook, 1887, BBHC. For furniture, see "Royal Visit to the Wild West," *The Sporting Life*, May 12, 1887, Annie Oakley Scrapbook, BBHC.
159. For Cody's correspondence requesting Sitting Bull for his show, see WFC to J. O. Lamar, April 29, 1885, Letters Received, 1881–1907, Box 239, no. 9492, RG 75, NARA; WFC to Secretary Lamar, May 2, 1885, Letters Received, 1881–1907, no. 10488, Box 241, RG 75, NARA. Sherman's endorsement—"Sitting Bull is a humbug but has a popular fame on which he has a natural right to 'bank' "—is in Utley, *Lance and the Shield*, 264.
160. Swartout, *Missie*, 91–92; "Camp Sketches—No. VII," *Topical Times* (London), Aug. 13, 1887, in Annie Oakley Scrapbook, 1887, BBHC.
161. "Greek Meets Greek," *Buffalo Courier*, n.d., reprinted in BBWW 1885 program, n.p. For sitting Bull's adoption of Salsbury, "The Wild West," *Boston Daily Advertiser*, July 28, 1885, NSS, vol. 1, 1885–86.
162. *The Daily Witness*, Aug. 12, 1885, clipping in NSS, vol. 1, 1885–86, DPL; the cabinet photograph is in BBHC, p. 69. 1844.
163. Utley, *Lance and the Shield*, 266.
164. Untitled clipping, *New York Herald*, July 12, 1886; "Happy Wild West Redmen," *The Sun*, July 11, 1886; "The Sioux Dog Feast," *The Mail and Express*, July 7, 1886; "Sioux Hymn Singers," *The Morning Journal*, July 5, 1886; "A Fire on the Plains," *Telegram*, June 28, 1886; all NSS, vol. 1, 1885–86, Microfilm 18, Reel 1, in WFC Collection, Western History Collection, DPL.
165. Havighurst, *Annie Oakley of the Wild West*, 85.

CHAPTER TEN: *THE DRAMA OF CIVILIZATION:* VISUAL PLAY AND MORAL AMBIGUITY

1. For "Burning of Moscow," see "Amusements," *The World* (New York), July 17, 1886, p. 5; "Amusements This Evening," *New York Times*, July 16, 1886, p. 4. For London precursors, see Henry Llewellyn Williams, *Buffalo Bill: A Full Account of His Adventurous Life with the Origins of His "Wild West Show"* (London: George Routledge and Sons, 1887), 191; also Rupert Croft-Cooke and W. S. Meadmore, *The Sawdust Ring* (London: Odhams Press, 1951).
2. My treatment of panorama paintings is based on the following sources: Martha A. Sandweiss, *Print the Legend: Photography and the American West* (New Haven, CT: Yale University Press, 2002), 48–86; Cook, *Arts of Deception*, 227–30; Stephan Oetterman, *The Panorama: History of a Mass Medium*, trans. Deborah Lucas Schneider (New York: Zone Books, 1997); Bernard Comment, *The Panorama*, trans. Anne-Marie Glasheen (London: Reaktion Books, 1999).
3. Sandweiss, *Print the Legend*, 57.
4. Oetterman, *Panorama*, 339–40.
5. Sandweiss, *Print the Legend*, 52.
6. William Cody Collection, WH 72, Box 2/2, Brighton Beach, Coney Island, DPL-WHR.
7. These striking similarities of presentation matched, and perhaps required, similar methods of production. The paintings took years to produce, with artists and support staff traveling, sketching, or even daguerreotyping, then painting and refining the separate

"scenes," before conjoining them and emblazoning the final result on thousands of square feet of canvas. The final work subsequently went on tour, sometimes across the Atlantic. Thus moving panorama, like the Wild West show, required corporate organization of investors who put up large amounts of capital to see it through. (Consequently, the panorama industry, like Wild West shows, was characterized by widespread allegations of conceptual theft among impresarios, various of whom claimed they originated ideas for the most popular depictions.) Moving panorama, like the Wild West show, depended on notices and advertising in the mass press to draw audiences, and it depended on modern transportation to make its progress through the amusement world and bring audiences to it. In a remarkable precursor to Wild West show organization, some impresarios even arranged special excursion fares on the railroad for their audiences, thereby expanding their appeal beyond the city and capturing the amusement traffic of a whole region. Sandweiss, *Print the Legend*, 49; Oetterman, *Panorama*, 334, 342.

8. Oettermann, *Panorama*, 335.

9. Oetterman, *Panorama*, 341.

10. BBWW 1885 program (Hartford, CT: Calhoun Printing).

11. Cook, *Arts of Deception*, 229.

12. The most influential of these was William Harnett, who produced four versions of *After the Hunt* between 1883 and 1885. The work of a Harnett disciple suggests the thrill of visual play and historical representation which connected trompe l'oeil and the Wild West. George W. Platt's *Vanishing Glories* was a rendering of a buffalo skull fastened to an old barn door, on which hung a lariat, pistols, a Winchester, and a large hat, "all that was once the necessary outfit of the Western cowboy," in the words of one reviewer. As with Harnett's work, observers gathered in front of Platt's painting to debate his method and the reliability of their own sense of sight. Of the thousands of paintings and other items on display at the St. Louis Exposition of 1888, *Vanishing Glories* became one of the most controversial—and popular. "A great many people think the picture is painted on an old barn door, and others think that the artist has simply painted well the old weather beaten pine." The painting was, in fact, on canvas. Cook, *Arts of Deception*, 238–42.

13. Cook, *Arts of Deception*, 225.

14. Cody himself admired trompe l'oeil painting enough to hang a work that resembled Platt's *Vanishing Glories* in his Wyoming hotel in 1902. Titled *Relics of the Past*, it depicted a buffalo head mounted on a board, above which was tacked a calling-card photograph of Cody himself, and around which were arrayed Indian war clubs and more photographs, of Wild Bill Hickok, Red Cloud, Gall, and scout Frank Grouard. *Relics of the Past* is in the collection of the Whitney Gallery of Western Art, BBHC. Artists incorporated trompe l'oeil techniques into the cyclorama paintings of the 1880s, in which the most popular subjects were historical, as in Paul Philippotteaux's *Siege of Paris* and his gigantic *Battle of Gettysburg*. This last work appeared in Chicago as Cody's show made its first appearance in that city in 1883, and it may have been the cyclorama visited by show Indians and cowboys in Philadelphia in 1885. Havighurst, *Annie Oakley of the Wild West*, 74–75. Visitors made their way through "a narrow wooden labrynth" to a small platform where they found themselves "in the clouds," smack in the middle of the fifty-foot-high painting, a "circular wall of canvas" four hundred feet in circumference, which presented the dramatic, bloody action of the Civil War's greatest battle. Adjacent stage props augmented the visual effects of paint and perspective. "Where it touches the ground theatrical properties are joined on in a way that defies discovery by the eye of the place where, say a rail-fence loses the essence of reality and becomes simply a painting." Untitled editorial, *Chicago Tribune*, Oct. 21, 1883, p. 4; also, "Gettysburg," *Chicago Tribune*, Oct. 21, 1883, p. 14; see also Oetterman, *Panorama*, 343.

15. BBWW 1885 program, frontispiece.

16. "Buffalo Bill's Wild West Drama," *Brick Pomeroy's Democrat*, Jan. 5, 1887, p. 16.

17. "The Wild West Show," *The Era*, May 14, 1887, p. 9; "The American Exhibition," *The Penny Illustrated Paper*, May 7, 1887, p. 298; see also "Buffalo Bill's Wild West from the Plains of America," M Cody Box 6, DPL-WHR. "The arena in front of this stand is about one-third of a mile in circumference. The scenery which surrounds this is painted

on canvas, and extends to a great height, shutting out the neighboring houses. It is merged at the bottom into rocks, trees and shrubbery, giving a realistic representation of a rocky pass in the mountains through which the scouts and Indians defile upon the plains, represented by the arena."

18. Cody, *Story of the Wild West*, 751; also, "Inaugural Invitation Exhibition of Buffalo Bill's Wild West," Dec. 17, 1887, in M Cody Programs, Folder 2, DPL.

19. The combination of panorama painting and live action was reprised so often before such large crowds—at Paris in 1889, at Glasgow in 1891, at Chicago in 1893, at Ambrose Park, Brooklyn in 1894, at annual Madison Square Garden shows in the 1890s, at the Olympia Theater in London in 1903, and even as late as 1916, when Cody was reduced to appearing with the Miller Brothers' 101 Ranch Wild West—that it created a visual memory of a kind of trompe l'oeil show, begging observers to parse the line between history and the present, the arena and the West. For Glasgow, see "Buffalo Bill's Wild West," *Glasgow Herald*, Nov. 17, 1891, p. 3. For other dates, see Reddin, *Wild West Shows*, 90; and P. 69.1300, in Series XI:I, Arena Photos, Box 4, BBHC.

20. Sayers, *Annie Oakley and Buffalo Bill's Wild West*, 66; dimensions are in "Buffalo Bill's Great Show," unattributed clipping, Salsbury Scrapbooks, 1894, p. 29, in WH 72, Series 7, Box 4, DPL.

21. Slotkin, *Fatal Environment*, 14; in 1968, Don Russell turned up 848 different pictures of the fight, in a search he described as "by no means exhaustive." Don Russell, *Custer's Last* (Fort Worth, TX: Amon Carter, 1968), 3–5; see also Brian W. Dippie, *Custer's Last Stand: The Anatomy of an American Myth* (1976; rprt. Lincoln: University of Nebraska Press, 1999), esp. 32–61, and " 'What Valor Is': Artists and the Mythic Moment," in *Legacy: New Perspectives on the Battle of Little Big Horn*, ed. Charles Rankin (Helena: Montana Historical Society, 1999), 209–30; Kasson, *Buffalo Bill and the Wild West*, 245–46.

22. P.6.513 Series XI: H Group Photos, Box 2; Series XI:J Arena Photos, Box 3, P.69.885, P.69.884, P.69.883, P.69.882, BBHC. Paintings by Moran hung beside those of Albert Bierstadt, the nation's most popular landscape artist, in the art gallery of the American Exhibition, next door to the Wild West arena in London in 1887. Bierstadt's paintings had become popular in the 1860s, and they were practically passé by 1887; indeed, his work was rejected from the Paris exposition, two years later, for precisely this reason. They were large—seven feet by ten feet—and they so mimicked panoramas that one critic thought audiences would wonder just when "*the thing was going to move.*" Bierstadt painted both background and foreground in total focus, so that spectators could examine them with opera glasses, as if they were looking at a distant mountain peak (or a theatrical stage). His mountains loomed up so dramatically that upon visiting the real peaks viewers were sometimes underwhelmed. Hassrick, "The Artists," in Hassrick et al., *Buffalo Bill and the Wild West*, 22–23.

23. The same peak featured often in "stereographs," specially produced photographs which, when viewed through a small device known as a stereoscope, appeared to be three-dimensional, and which were popular as middle-class home entertainment by the 1850s. Andrew Anker, "Projecting into Space: American Looks Through the Stereoscope," master's thesis, School of Architecture, Yale University, 1995; Sandweiss, *Print the Legend*, 136–37.

24. In 1885, he vanquished Doc Carver in a court battle over the rights to the name "Wild West." In London, he sued a circus impresario, George Sanger, for naming a segment of his show "Scenes from Buffalo Bill." Back in New York the following year, he took competing shows to court for pirating his posters. Over decades, he dueled with his imitators by commissioning the highest-quality poster art, then covering their advertisements with his posters, billboards, and flyers depicting his Indians, buffalo, cowboys, and especially his face, forcing competitors far afield in search of audiences. Sanger claimed that he was showing this imitation Wild West show for a full year before Cody arrived. "Lord" George Sanger, *Seventy Years a Showman* (London: J. M. Dent, 1927), 229–33. WFC to Julia Cody Goodman, Aug. 19, 1905, MS 6 Series I:B Css Box 1/21, BBHC.

25. Strike figures from Alan Trachtenberg, *The Incorporation of America: Culture and Society in*

the Gilded Age (New York: Hill and Wang, 1982), 91; quote from Richard Slotkin, *Gunfighter Nation*, 77.

26. Frederic Remington, "Chicago Under the Mob," *Harper's Weekly*, July 21, 1894; "Buffalo Bill in London," *Harper's Weekly*, Sept. 3, 1892; "A Gallop Through the Midway," *Harper's Weekly*, Oct. 7, 1893; also, "Chicago Under the Law," *Harper's Weekly*, July 28, 1894; "The Withdrawal of U.S. Troops," *Harper's Weekly*, Aug. 11, 1894; "The Affair of the -th July," *Harper's Weekly*, Feb. 2, 1895, all reprinted in *The Collected Writings of Frederic Remington*, ed. Peggy and Harold Samuels (New York: Doubleday, 1979), 96–98, 111–13, 152–54, 155–59, 164–66, 176–83.

27. "Among the Rough Riders," *Hamilton (Ontario) Spectator*, July 17, 1897, clipping in WFC Collection, MS 6, Series VI:G, Box 1, Folder 15, BBHC.

28. For participation in the march, see "Wild with Enthusiasm," *New York Times*, Oct. 28, 1888, p. 13; for Harrison inaugural, see "The Ball," unattributed clipping, n.d., in WFC Scrapbook, 1883–1886–1888, BBHC. Partisan division of the period is in Cherny, *American Politics in the Gilded Age*, 86.

29. For McKinley inaugural, see Yost, *Buffalo Bill*, 275. For Democratic Party organization, see Beck to WFC, July 29, 1896, in G. T. Beck Papers, MS 59, Box 25, 1896 Letterpress Book, American Heritage Center, University of Wyoming, Laramie, WY.

30. Painter, *Standing at Armageddon*, 40–44.

31. Rauchway, *Murdering McKinley*, 17, 89–96; Avrich, *Haymarket Tragedy*, 35–36, 45–51, 59.

32. Painter, *Standing at Armageddon*, 48–49; Avrich, *Haymarket Tragedy*, 215–39.

33. Avrich, *Haymarket Tragedy*, 3–14.

34. Labor unions opposed federal appropriations to the National Guard on the grounds that their own tax dollars were being used to oppress them. See "Education, Not Force," *New York Herald*, Jan. 12, 1887, p. 5.

35. Jacobson, *Barbarian Virtues*, 90–91; Slotkin, *Fatal Environment*, 480–89; Avrich, *Haymarket Tragedy*, 215–19; Richard Drinnon, " 'My Men Shoot Well': Theodore Roosevelt and the Urban Frontier," in *The Haymarket Scrapbook*, ed. David Roediger and Franklin Rosemont (Chicago: Charles H. Kerr Publishing Co., 1986), 129–30.

36. For orator, see Blackstone, *Buckskin, Bullets, and Business*, 21.

37. All quotes from "Buffalo Bill in Drama," *New York Times*, Nov. 25, 1886, p. 5.

38. Lears, *No Place of Grace*, 98–139.

39. "Custer's Fate Illustrated," *New York Times*, Jan. 4, 1887, p. 4.

40. Odell, *Annals of the New York Stage*, 13:537.

41. Edmund Morris, *The Rise of Theodore Roosevelt*, rev. ed. (New York: Modern Library, 2001), 379.

42. Painter, *Standing at Armageddon*, 47–50; Avrich, *Haymarket Tragedy*, 301.

43. Unless otherwise indicated, show programs may be found in collections in MS 6, BBHC, or in M Cody Programs, DPL-WHR. "Programme of Exhibition Before the Queen," 1887, in *Souvenir Album of the Visit of Her Majesty Queen Victoria to the American Exhibition* (London, 1887), also BBWW 1887 program, BBHC. After its appearance in New York in early 1887, the Custer fight was not staged again until December, in Manchester, England. See the program for "Inaugural Invitation Exhibition" of Buffalo Bill's Wild West, "under the patronage and presence of His Worship the Mayor of Salford," on Dec. 17, 1887, at 2:30, in the "New Colossal Building at the Manchester Race Track," BBHC; BBWW 1888 program, BBHC; the Custer reenactment did not appear in the Paris shows of 1889. See BBWW 1889 program, *L'Ouest Sauvage de Buffalo Bill* (Paris: Imprimerie Parrot et Cie, 1889), in MS 62 Don Russell Collection, Series I:G, Box 2, Folder 27, BBHC; for the years 1890–94, see the collections of programs in BBHC and DPL-WHR, also Warren Vincent to H. H. Vincent, March 1, 1890, M Cody L Box 1, DPL; BBWW 1895 program, DPL; BBWW 1896 program, DPL and Huntington Library, San Marino, CA; BBWW 1897 program and BBWW 1898 program in BBHC; programs for 1899–1916 in BBHC and DPL. The scene reenacting Custer's demise was no more common in Europe, where Cody staged it in only three seasons out of ten, and never during its most famous and well-attended stands. After all the work historians have

done to connect Custer and Cody, it can be startling to realize who did *not* see the Custer segment in Cody's show. The huge London audiences of 1887, which included Queen Victoria, did not see it, nor did the Paris audiences in 1889. The Germans flocked to the show in enormous numbers in 1890, as did the Italians and the Austrians—but not to see "Custer's Last Rally." And when Frederick Jackson Turner gave his famous essay at the American Historical Association meeting in a hot tent at the World's Fair in July of 1893, none of the historians who might have sneaked out of the session to see Buffalo Bill's Wild West would have seen Cody's Custer. The segment was not added to the show until August. See Wojtowicz, *Buffalo Bill Collector's Guide*, 10–47, esp. 19–20; for Chicago shows, see Kasson, *Buffalo Bill's Wild West*, 113. The Custer reenactment was a feature during the show's 1896 weeklong stay in St. Louis, but the act does not appear in extant programs. "It Has Made a Hit," *St. Louis Republic*, May 21, 1896, clipping in Beck Family Papers, #10386, Box 15/13, American Heritage Center, University of Wyoming, Laramie, WY; Wojtowicz, *Buffalo Bill Collector's Guide*, 28–29.

44. See above note 43.

45. Painter, *Standing at Armageddon*, 121–25; BBWW 1894 program.

46. The New York Society of Decorative Arts was an organization of wealthy New York women—including Mrs. John Jacob Astor; Caroline Belmont, the wife of August Belmont; and Julia Bryant, daughter of poet and *New York Evening Post* editor William Cullen Bryant—devoted to teaching poor New York women how to make and sell fine needlework at home. Shirley A. Leckie, *Elizabeth Bacon Custer and the Making of a Myth* (Norman: University of Oklahoma Press), 216, 245.

47. Leckie, *Elizabeth Bacon Custer*, 233–35. When the Boston Cyclorama Company commissioned E. Pierpont and staff to paint a "Cyclorama of Custer's Last Fight," in 1888, they also consulted Mrs. Custer, and she endorsed the project in the twenty-page pamphlet that spectators carried. The painting was displayed in Boston in 1889, then in Detroit, and possibly in Chicago, before it moved on to its last owner in Hollywood. Russell, *Custer's Last*, 37.

48. Leckie, *Elizabeth Bacon Custer*, 242.

49. "Elks at the Wild West," *New York Times*, July 15, 1886, p. 8; also "At the Wild West," *The Sentinel*, July 17, 1886, and "Mrs. Custer Visits Buffalo Bill," unattributed clipping, July 17, 1886, both in NSS, 1885–86, WH72, Microfilm 18, Reel 4, Cody Collection, DPL.

50. WFC to Elizabeth Bacon Custer, Aug. 13, 1886, quoted in Leckie, *Elizabeth Bacon Custer*, 246–47.

51. Steele Mackaye to Salsbury, Oct. 31, 1886, in MacKaye, *Epoch*, 2:80.

52. Havighurst, *Annie Oakley of the Wild West*, 93; MacKaye, *Epoch*, 2:90.

53. Custer family cartoon in Robert Utley and Wilcomb Washburn, *The Indian Wars* (New York: American Heritage, 1977), 276; Connell, *Son of the Morning Star*, 122; E. Custer, *Following the Guidon*, 188.

54. Fellows and Freeman, *This Way to the Big Show*, 133.

55. Elizabeth Bacon Custer, *Tenting on the Plains: General Custer in Kansas and Texas* (1887; rprt. Norman: University of Oklahoma Press, 1971), 47. Libbie Custer tried to confirm Cody's claim to having been a scout for George Custer, but inadvertently she undermined it. Eliza, she wrote, "went to Mr. Cody's tent after the exhibition, to present my card of introduction, *for he had served as General Custer's scout after Eliza left us, and she was, therefore, unknown to him except by hearsay*" (p. 46, emphasis added). As we have seen, Cody claimed that he scouted for the Boy General only once, in 1867. Eliza was with the Custers on the Plains in 1867, and did not leave them until 1869. Leckie, *Elizabeth Bacon Custer*, 122. For other references to Cody's impersonation of Custer, see "Custer's Last Rally," *New York Herald*, Jan. 4, 1887, p. 2; "Custer's Fate Illustrated," *New York Times*, Jan. 4, 1887, p. 4.

56. Elizabeth Custer to WFC, May 9, no year [1893?], photocopy in WFC Collection, No. 264, American Heritage Center, Box 1, Folder 2, original from William C. Garlow collection, in BBHC.

57. When some critics began to question the propriety of casting Indians in the drama, Cody

responded that "there is no law in the land that can prevent an Indian, like any other man, from making his own living and earning money." "Too Realistic for Comfort," *New York Times*, Jan. 16, 1887, p. 3.

58. "Buffalo Bill's Wild West Drama," *Brick Pomeroy's Democrat*, Jan. 5, 1887, p. 16. Emphasis added.

59. "Buffalo Bill's Wild West," 16.

60. Henry Wadsworth Longfellow, "The Revenge of Rain-in-the-Face," in *Buffalo Bill's Wild West and Congress of Rough Riders of the World*, 1898 Show Courier (Buffalo, NY: Courier, 1898), 15.

61. "An Interview with the Hon. W. F. Cody," *Montreal Herald and Daily Commercial Gazette*, Aug. 17, 1885, clipping in MS 6, Series VI:G, Box 1, Folder 15, BBHC.

62. MacKaye, *Epoch*, 2:96–97, 127. In 1887, Mackaye debuted a new play, *Anarchy*, in which he used a story of the French Revolution to advance his argument that only justice could stem both the violent mobs (strikers) and the excesses of elites (capitalists) that incited them. The hero of his play denounces one villainous aristocrat: "Anarchists are monsters your race bred when it brutalized their mothers." Steele Mackaye, *Paul Kauvar; or, Anarchy,"* in *Representative Plays by American Dramatists, 1856–1911*, ed. Montrose J. Moses (New York: Benjamin Blom, n.d., microfilm), 329. Where Longfellow, the poet, blamed Indian war on American moral failure—"our broken faith"—Mackaye, the playwright, attributed anarchist violence to the excesses of wealthy industrialists. Nate Salsbury was so impressed with the drama that he offered to produce it. *Epoch*, 15, 24; 2:67–70. Others in the Wild West show's orbit shared Mackaye's sentiment. When Cody and Salsbury became partners in 1883, a prominent Illinois lawyer, John P. Altgeld, drew up the paperwork. In 1893, Altgeld became the governor of Illinois, in which position, against a tidal wave of conservative anger, he pardoned the surviving Haymarket suspects and denounced their persecution by police and courts. Avrich, *Haymarket Tragedy*, 417–27; for Altgeld's role in Wild West partnership, see Nate Salsbury, "The Origin of the Wild West Show," typescript, n.d., YCAL MSS 17, Box 2/63, NSP; Russell, *Lives and Legends*, 300.

63. "Our History," unattributed clipping, April 17, 1897, in NSS, 1897, DPL-WHR.

64. Aveling, *American Journey*, 136.

65. Aveling, *An American Journey*, 146.

66. Aveling's impressions of proletarianism came mostly from his meeting with "Broncho John," a cowboy who appeared in a Cincinnati dime museum, where he lectured passionately on "the gross treatment of his class by their bosses, the ranch owners." In Aveling, *An American Journey*, 154–55.

67. "[I]t was our business," Aveling reported, "and we made it our business, to speak at every meeting held in America in favor of a new trial for the condemned anarchists of Chicago." Aveling, *American Journey*, 121, 127.

68. Eleanor Marx and Edward Aveling, *The Working Class Movement in America*, ed. Paul Le Blanc, 2nd ed. (1891; rprt. Amherst, NY: Humanity Books, 2000).

69. Aveling, *American Journey*, 146.

70. Aveling, *American Journey*, 147. Cody's rise was contemporaneous with the emergence of professional anthropology. One of the field's seminal studies was by Lewis Henry Morgan, whose *Ancient Society*, in 1877, argued that Indians were primitive communists whose "advancement" occurred in part through the privatization of communal property. Morgan's vision of communist Indians—and his millenarian faith that Progress would someday return all the world's peoples to the peace and harmony Indians once enjoyed— made Indians (and, indeed, Morgan) into powerful symbols for leftists like Aveling. "The Indians," *The Alarm*, Nov. 8, 1884; Franklin Rosemont, "Anarchists and the Wild West," in Roediger and Rosemont, *Haymarket Scrapbook*, 101–2.

71. Buffalo Bill's Wild West became a legal corporation in Feb. 1887. " 'Buffalo Bill's Wild West Company' Incorporated Under the Laws of New Jersey, February 1887," in YCAL MSS 17, Box 1, Folder 22, NSP.

72. Aveling, *American Journey*, 150. Emphasis added.

73. Aveling, *American Journey*, 154.

74. Aveling, *American Journey*, 150.

75. Nate Salsbury to Steele Mackaye, Nov. 1, 1886, reproduced in MacKaye, *Epoch*, 2:81.
76. Nate Salsbury to Steele Mackaye, Dec. 17, 1886, reproduced in MacKaye, *Epoch*, 2:86–87.
77. MacKaye, *Epoch*, 2:92–93.
78. "Buffalo Bill in Drama," *New York Times*, Nov. 25, 1886, p. 5; "Madison Square Garden Thronged," *New York Times*, Nov. 30, 1886, p. 2.
79. "Buffalo Bill's Wild West Drama," *Brick Pomeroy's Democrat*, Jan. 5, 1887, p. 16.
80. "The Last of the Wild West," *New York Times*, Feb. 23, 1887, p. 2.
81. "Buffalo Bill as General Custer," *New York Times*, Jan. 2, 1887, p. 7.
82. "Still Attracting Crowds," *New York Times*, Jan. 23, 1887, p. 3.
83. Anonymous, *A Peep at Buffalo Bill's Wild West* (New York: McLoughlin Bros., 1887), copy in BBHC.
84. Levine, *Highbrow/Lowbrow*, 171–242, esp. 192–93.
85. "Buffalo Bill's Wild West Drama," *Brick Pomeroy's Democrat*, Jan. 5, 1887, p. 16.

CHAPTER ELEVEN: WILD WEST LONDON

1. Quote from "Buffalo Bill's Goodbye," *New York Times*, April 1, 1887. This account says there were 133 Indians. Source for my count is the passenger list of the *State of Nebraska*, in NSP, YCAL 17, Box 1, Folder 13. Also Russell, *Lives and Legends*, 327; Cody, *Story of the Wild West*, 701–4.
2. For holes in deck, see Parker, *Odd People I Have Met*, 3; for deaths of buffalo and elk, see Ray DeMallie, ed., *The Sixth Grandfather: Black Elk's Teachings Given to John G. Neihardt* (Lincoln: University of Nebraska Press, 1984), 248; also Nicholas Black Elk and John G. Neihardt, *Black Elk Speaks* (Lincoln: University of Nebraska, 1972), 219–20. Cody, *Story of the Wild West*, 706, says there were no animal deaths but for one horse.
3. *Illustrated Bits* (UK), no. 120, May 14, 1887, p. 4; Alan Gallop, *Buffalo Bill's British Wild West* (Thrupp, UK: Sutton Publishing, 2001), 67.
4. The visit of the Prince of Wales is in "Royalty at the Wild West," *The Era*, May 7, 1887, p. 15; "Princess and Princesses Among the Squaws," *Pall Mall Gazette*, May 6, 1887, p. 10; "The Showman," *Penny Illustrated Paper*, May 14, 1887, p. 316.
5. Cody, *Story of the Wild West*, 734.
6. Cody, *Story of the Wild West*, 736–37.
7. Cody, *Story of the Wild West*, 742.
8. The story is widespread, in many versions: Cody, *Story of the Wild West*, 742–43; Parker, *Odd People I Have Met*, 92; Russell, *Lives and Legends*, 331. Agnes Wright Spring, *Cheyenne and Black Hills Stage Routes*, 359.
9. Admittedly, these retellings seem only to have mentioned the four kings, but not the alleged joke. See "Clydeside Echoes," *Glasgow Evening News*, Nov. 6, 1891, p. 4; "The Mild West," *The Million*, Sept. 3, 1892, p. 246.
10. For Londoners telling the joke, see J. B. Booth, *London Town* (London: T. Werner Laurie, 1929), 182.
11. George Gilbertson to WFC, May 26, 1887, Letters and Invitations, 1887–88, BBHC.
12. Clippings, "Jack and Jill at Play," n.p., n.d., and "Opening of the American Exhibition. Buffalo Bill's Wild West," *Lloyd's Weekly London Newspaper*, n.d. Both in Annie Oakley Scrapbook, 1887, BBHC.
13. "Buffalo Bill was requested by the Prince of Wales to give a special morning performance. . . . The prince was very much pleased at the exhibition, and according to the gossipers, this is what he said." Unattributed clipping, n.p., n.d., BBM.
14. Untitled clipping, *Nottingham Daily Express*, JCG Scrapbook, MS 58, NSHS: " 'Cody's social success,' the *Nation* observes, 'like that of Fred. Archer, the jockey, marks the enormous space which pure amusement now occupies in the life of the well-to-do classes in England'; and it adds that 'Americans who can contribute to this are especially successful in London society. Their stories, their jokes, their songs, their new card tricks, their skill in poker and euchre, supply the place in giving them social consideration of nearly every-

thing else which makes a human being respectable. This is biting, but true; as if sated with our own social follies, we must go out of the way to import those of our Yankee cousins.' "

15. "Circus and Sideshow—At Last!," title illegible (Eurati?), June 10, 1887, JCG Scrapbook, MS 58, NSHS. Contrasting the fortune Cody amassed during his first British tour with the lesser amounts received by the American tours of Charles Dickens and several other leading British intellectuals, a *Chicago Times* correspondent remarked, "England cannot point the finger of scorn at America on this account, however. The fact is as discreditable to her as to the people of the United States." Clipping in E. H. Leog to WFC, May 29, 1888, in WFC Scrapbooks, 1883–1886–1888, BBHC.

16. For historians who have made this claim, see Russell, *Lives and Legends*, 330; Kasson, *Buffalo Bill's Wild West*, 77, 79–81; Gallop, *Buffalo Bill's British Wild West*, 96–102; Sell and Weybright, *Buffalo Bill and the Wild West*, 170, 172. The catalogue of the Royal Armouries Exhibit of 1999 states that the royal appearance of May 11, 1887, was "the first attendance by Queen Victoria at any public event since the death of Prince Albert twenty-six years before." Martin Pegler and Graeme Rimer, *Buffalo Bill's Wild West* (Leeds, UK: Royal Armouries Museum, 1999), 24; Walsh and Salsbury, *Making of Buffalo Bill*, 267, point out that Victoria had been seen at other public functions.

17. Cody, *Story of the Wild West*, 735.

18. *The World* (UK), June 22, 1887, p. 17.

19. See "Royalty at the Wild West," *Penny Illustrated Paper*, June 25, 1887, p. 407; also "The Daily Telegraph," n.d., Annie Oakley Scrapbook, 1887, BBHC.

20. Ian Bevan, *Royal Performance: The Story of Royal Theatregoing* (London: Hutchinson, 1954), 187–89.

21. Quoted in Gallop, *Buffalo Bill's British Wild West*, 101.

22. Quotation from *The World* (UK), May 18, 1887, p. 15; placement of the flag presentation is in "The Queen in London," *Daily Telegraph*, May 12, 1887, and "Royal Visit to the Wild West," *Sporting Life*, May 12, 1887, both in Annie Oakley Scrapbook, 1887, BBHC; see also "The Queen at the American Exhibition," *The Standard*, May 12, 1887, clipping in Johnny Baker 1886–87 Scrapbook, WH 72, Box 4, DPL; "The Queen at 'Buffalo Bill's,' " *Penny Illustrated Paper*, May 21, 1887, p. 334; "Victoria at the Wild West Show," account of the *London Daily News*, reprinted in *New York Times*, May 22, 1887, p. 12; also Gower, *Old Diaries*, 55–56.

23. *The Graphic* (London), May 21, 1887, p. 544.

24. Show locations in 1895 from BBWW Routes 1883–1916, BBHC; posters from Rennert, *100 Posters of Buffalo Bill's Wild West*, 7, 27, 30, 34–35.

25. Jacobson, *Barbarian Virtues*, 105–21.

26. The best example is Don Russell, whose *Lives and Legends of Buffalo Bill* set out to prove the truth of Cody's frontier biography, then assumed that the legends of the Wild West show were mostly, perhaps entirely, true.

27. Harris, *Humbug*, 94–95; Hassrick, "The Artists," in Hassrick et al., *Buffalo Bill and the Wild West*, 21; Reddin, *Wild West Shows*, 35–36.

28. Reddin, *Wild West Shows*, 112; Russell, *Wild West*, 37; " 'Mexican Joe' at Battersea," *The Era*, Jan. 7, 1888, p. 14; Harris, *Humbug*, 274–75.

29. " 'Mexican Joe' at Battersea," *The Era*, Jan. 7, 1888, p. 14.

30. C. L. Daily to "Dear Folks" [no month] 22, 1889, copy in BBHC; Webb, "Buffalo Bill, Saint or Devil?," 6.

31. For an account of Cody's remonstrations with his cooks, see Luther Standing Bear, *My People the Sioux* (1928; rprt. Lincoln: University of Nebraska Press, 1975), 260–61.

32. "Scene at the Liverpool Exhibition," *The Era*, Sept. 3, 1887, p. 7.

33. Untitled, *The Era*, Oct. 1, 1887, p. 13.

34. Harris, *Humbug*, 274–75.

35. Rennert, *100 Posters of Buffalo Bill's Wild West*, 9, 48.

36. By 1887, the United States produced machine tools of comparable quality to those in Britain, at half the cost; the small arms industry (for which the Wild West was practically a living advertisement) had been using interchangeable parts since the mid-1800s, and

the British had only just begun to do so; the rate of new technology adoption and innovation was much higher in the United States than in Britain, and the United States had a much higher volume of capital investment than Britain. See H. J. Habakkuk, *American and British Technology in the Nineteenth Century: The Search for Labour-Saving Inventions* (Cambridge: Cambridge University Press, 1967), 106, 151, 202–3, 207–8, 212.

37. Grimsted, *Melodrama Unveiled*, 138.

38. Quoted in Grimsted, *Melodrama Unveiled*, 137.

39. As late as 1923, D. H. Lawrence [*Studies in Classic American Literature* (1923; rprt. New York: Penguin, 1977), 3] felt it necessary to argue the case for American literature in the court of European opinion, where the attitude toward American culture was as follows:

> Where *is* this new bird called the true American? Show us the homunculus of the new era. Go on, show us him. Because all that is visible to the naked eye, in America, is a sort of recreant European.

40. Nash, *Wilderness and the American Mind.* Summarizing the reports, photographs, and paintings from western surveys, one newspaper editor concluded, "Every day seems to bring forth a new wonder, and the time is coming quickly when the tides of health-desiring and wonder-seeking travel will be from Europe to America." "The Splendor of the West," *New York Herald*, Feb. 11, 1872, p. 6.

41. WFC to "My Dear General," June 15, 1882, MS 6 Series I:B Css Box 1/7, BBHC.

42. Harris, *Humbug*, 282.

43. The letter was printed in show programs and in advertisements almost immediately after it was received. See the advertisement in *Cincinnati Commercial Gazette*, Oct. 19, 1884, p. 4.

44. Twain, *Roughing It*, 66.

45. Grimsted, *Melodrama Unveiled*, 57.

46. *Illustrated Bits* (UK), no. 115, April 9, 1887, p. 7.

47. "Palette and Brush," *Court and Society*, July 13, 1887, p. 42.

48. "Palette and Brush," *Court and Society*, July 12, 1887, p. 43.

49. See "Mohawk Minstrels," *The Era*, Nov. 13, 1886, p. 7; also "Musical and Dramatic," *Scottish Sport*, Sept. 29, 1891; on minstrels and black performers, Robert C. Toll, *Blacking Up: The Minstrel Show in Nineteenth-Century America* (New York: Oxford University Press, 1974), 195–263.

50. Orvell, *Real Thing*, 59–65.

51. Erik Larson, *The Devil in the White City: Murder, Magic, and Madness at the Fair That Changed America* (New York: Crown Publishers, 2003), 312.

52. Crèvecoeur, *Letters from an American Farmer;* Smith, *Virgin Land;* Deloria, *Playing Indian*, 10.

53. John M. Burke, *Buffalo Bill from Prairie to Palace* (Chicago: Rand McNally & Co., 1893), 247.

54. See Nate Salsbury, "At the Vatican," typescript, n.d., in YCAL MSS 17, Box 2/63, NSP.

55. "Wild West at the Vatican," *New York Herald*, March 4, 1890, reprinted in Burke, *Buffalo Bill from Prairie to Palace*, 245.

56. WFC to "My Dear Doctor," Feb. 15, 1890, MS 6 Series I:B Css Box 1/11, BBHC.

57. "Wild West at the Vatican," *New York Herald*, March 4, 1890, reprinted in Burke, *Buffalo Bill from Prairie to Palace*, 246.

58. Bram Stoker, *Personal Reminiscences of Henry Irving*, 2 vols. (New York: Macmillan, 1906), 2: 142; Stoker recalls the outing occurred in the fall, but Irving made the invitation for June, and both he and Stoker were touring the United States after July. See Henry Irving to WFC, May 1887, "Invitations and Letters 1887–95," Microfilm Reel, BBHC; "Mr. Irving's Farewell," *The Era*, July 16, 1887, p. 13; "Henry Irving's Farewell," *The Era*, July 23, 1887, p. 12.

59. Maurice Hindle, "Introduction," in Bram Stoker, *Dracula* (1897; rprt. ed., New York: Penguin Books, 1993), edited and with notes by Maurice Hindle, vii; David J. Skal, *Hol-*

lywood Gothic: The Tangled Web of "Dracula" from Novel to Stage to Screen (London: Andre Deutsch, 1990), 28.

60. Christopher Frayling, "Lord Byron to Count Dracula," 69–74, in *Vampyres: Lord Byron to Count Dracula*, ed. Christopher Frayling (Boston: Faber and Faber, 1991), 1–84.

61. Stephen Arata, *Fictions of Loss in the Victorian Fin de Siecle* (New York: Cambridge University Press, 1996), 107–32, esp. 108; Stoker, *Dracula*, 8; also, Stephen Arata, "The Occidental Tourist: *Dracula* and the Anxiety of Reverse Colonization," 463–64, in Bram Stoker, *Dracula*, ed. Nina Auerbach and David J. Skal (1897; rprt. New York: Norton, 1997), 462–70.

62. "The Effect of Town Life on the Human Body," *Islington News* (London), Sept. 10, 1887, p. 6.

63. Arata, *Fictions of Loss*; Daniel Pick, " 'Terrors of the Night': *Dracula* and Degeneration in the Late Nineteenth Century," *Critical Quarterly* 30, no. 4 (Winter 1988): 71–87, and *Faces of Degeneration: A European Disorder, c. 1848–c. 1918* (Cambridge: Cambridge University Press, 1989), esp. 155–75; J. Edward Chamberlin and Sander Gilman, *Degeneration: The Dark Side of Progress* (New York: Columbia University Press, 1985). Matthew Frye Jacobsen expounds on what he calls "variegated whiteness" of Europeans in his *Whiteness of a Different Color,* 41–52.

64. Bram Stoker, *A Glimpse of America* (London: Sampson Low, Marston & Co., 1886).

65. Franco Moretti, *Signs Taken for Wonders: Essays in the Sociology of Literary Forms* (London: Verso, 1983), 84–96; Clive Leatherdale, *Dracula: The Novel and the Legend*, rev. ed. (Brighton, UK: Desert Island Books, 1993), 129–36.

66. Slotkin, *Gunfighter Nation;* Jane Tompkins, *West of Everything: The Inner Life of Westerns* (New York: Oxford University Press, 1988); Robin Wood, *Hollywood from Vietnam to Reagan* (New York: Columbia University Press, 1986); Cynthia A. Freeland, *The Naked and the Undead: Evil and the Appeal of Horror* (Boulder, CO: Westview Press, 2000).

67. Richard White, "Trashing the Trails," in *Trails: Toward a New Western History*, ed. Patricia Nelson Limerick, Clyde A. Milner II, and Charles E. Rankin (Lawrence: University Press of Kansas, 1991), 26–39; Patricia Nelson Limerick, *The Legacy of Conquest: The Unbroken Past of the American West* (New York: Norton, 1987); White, *"It's Your Misfortune and None of My Own"*; James R. Grossman, ed., *The Frontier in American Culture: Essays by Richard White and Patricia Nelson Limerick* (Berkeley: University of California Press, 1994); William Truettner, ed., *The West as America: Reinterpreting Images of the Frontier* (Washington, DC: National Museum of American Art, 1991); Smith, *Virgin Land;* Slotkin, *Regeneration Through Violence.*

68. Richard Davenport-Hines, *Gothic: Four Hundred Years of Excess, Evil, Horror, and Ruin* (New York: North Point, 1998), 257.

69. Stoker, *Personal Reminiscence,* 1:31.

70. Hindle, "Introduction," xvii–xxx; Barbara Belford, *Bram Stoker: A Biography of the Author of Dracula* (New York: Alfred A. Knopf, 1996), esp. 48–78; Daniel Farson, *The Man Who Wrote Dracula: A Biography of Bram Stoker* (London: Michael Joseph, 1975).

71. Quotes from J. B. Booth, *London Town* (London: T. Werner and Laurie Ltd., 1929), 43; Phyllis A. Roth, *Bram Stoker* (Boston: Twayne Publishers, 1982), 136. Also Farson, *Man Who Wrote Dracula,* 215–16; David J. Skal, *Hollywood Gothic: The Tangled Web of Dracula from Novel to Stage to Screen* (New York: Norton, 1990), 31. During his career with Irving, Stoker collected what is still the largest body of Irving ephemera. See the Papers of Henry Irving and Ellen Terry, Shakespeare Birthplace Trust, Stratford-on-Avon, UK.

72. Roth, *Bram Stoker,* 136; Belford, *Bram Stoker,* 121, 173–74; Leatherdale, *Dracula,* 70; Maggie Kilgour, "Stoker's Defence of Poetry," 50, in *Bram Stoker: History, Psychoanalysis, and the Gothic,* ed. William Hughes and Andrew Smith (New York: St. Martin's, 1998), 47–61.

73. Belford, *Bram Stoker,* 178–79; Farson, *Man Who Wrote Dracula,* 84–87.

74. Belford, *Bram Stoker,* 270.

75. Farson, *Man Who Wrote Dracula,* 164–65. Also Hindle, "Introduction," xvi–xvii; Kilgour, "Stoker's Defence of Poetry," 49–50; Jerrold E. Hogle, "Stoker's Counterfeit Gothic," 210, in Hughes and Smith ed., *Bram Stoker,* 205–24; Nina Auerbach, *Romantic Imprison-*

ment: Women and Other Glorified Outcasts (New York: Columbia University Press, 1985), 269–70; Belford, *Bram Stoker,* 5, 106, 270; Leatherdale, *Dracula,* 82–83.

76. "Henry Irving," *Chicago Tribune,* Oct. 22, 1883, p. 1; "Henry Irving in America," *The Era,* Sept. 11, 1886, p. 19; "The 'Wild West' Show," *The Era,* Sept. 18, 1886, p. 10; Russell, *Lives and Legends,* 328; Sell and Weybright, *Buffalo Bill and the Wild West,* 151; Horace Porter to William Cody, Feb. 10, 1887, "Invitations and Letters 1887–1891," Microfilm Reel, BBHC.

77. For Cody's plans to visit the UK, see Cody, *Life of Buffalo Bill,* 364. For Irving's social stature: "Address by Mr. Henry Irving," *Glasgow Evening News,* Nov. 10, 1891, p. 7; Jeffrey Richards, ed., *Sir Henry Irving: Theatre, Culture, and Society—Essays, Addresses, and Lectures* (Keele, UK: Ryburn Publishers, 1994), esp. 7.

78. Belford, *Bram Stoker,* 71.

79. Untitled clipping, *The Era,* April 23, 1887, Johnny Baker Scrapbook, DPL-WHR.

80. For Irving at opening day, see "What the World Says," *The World* (UK), April 27, 1887, p. 17; "The American Exhibition and Wild West Show," *Pall Mall Gazette* (UK), May 10, 1887, p. 11; Irving's private box is in *The World* (UK), May 11, 1887, p. 16; for dinner see *Illustrated Bits* (UK), May 7, 1887, p. 11; Cody also attended dinner backstage during the last night of the Lyceum run in 1887; see "Court and Society," *Court and Society* (UK), July 20, 1887, p. 52. For another gathering attended by Irving, Cody, and Stoker, see "Mansion House Dramatic Luncheon, Wednesday, June 15, 1887, Plan of Tables," in Papers of Henry Irving and Ellen Terry, Reel 21, 52/48–49. For invitations, see E. Yates to WFC, June 7, 1887, "Letters and Invitations, 1887–88," BBHC; photograph in Papers of Henry Irving and Ellen Terry; also Gallop, *Buffalo Bill's British Wild West,* 65.

81. For burlesque and melodrama, see "Yesterday's Amusements," *Lloyds,* Dec. 6, 1887, and untitled clipping, *American Register,* n.d., and untitled clipping, *Penny Illustrated News,* June 25, 1887, all in Julia Cody Goodman (henceforth JCG) Scrapbook, MS 58, NSHS; for Gilbert and Sullivan, see *Illustrated Bits* (UK), Sept. 10, 1887, p. 6.

82. "Buffalo Bill as a Leader of Fashion," *Birmingham Daily Mail,* clipping in JCG Scrapbook, Aug. 15, 1887, MS 58, NSHS.

83. "The American Exhibition and Wild West Show," *Pall Mall Gazette* (UK), May 10, 1887, p. 11.

84. *Illustrated Bits* (UK), March 26, 1887, p. 7; *Illustrated Bits* (UK), May 21, 1887, 3.

85. "Texan cow-boy" is in *Illustrated Bits* (UK), May 28, 1887, p. 4; Cody as Faust in "Waiting Verification," *Punch,* May 7, 1887, n.p., clipping in Papers of Henry Irving and Ellen Terry, Reel 21, Item 52/19.

86. Henry Irving to Cody, May [date illegible] 1887, "Invitations and Letters, 1887–1895," Microfilm Reel, BBHC.

87. See note 58 above.

88. "The Wild West at Horfield," *Bristol (UK) Evening News,* Sept. 28, 1891, Crager Scrapbook, 1891–92, BBHC.

89. "The Lorgnette," *Glasgow Evening News* (UK), Nov. 28, 1891, p. 1.

90. WFC to Stoker, July 25, 1887; WFC to Stoker, May 6, 1892; WFC to Stoker, n.d., Brotherton Collection, Leeds University; Stoker to Nate Salsbury, Oct. 30, 1893, YCAL MSS 17, NSP.

91. The story, "The Squaw," appeared in 1893. Bram Stoker, *Midnight Tales,* ed. Peter Haining (London: Peter Owen, 1990), 85–97. Both the 1887 London program and Cody's calling card, which was in Stoker's possession, informed the public about Cody's Nebraska home. "Buffalo Bill's Wild West from the Plains of America," n.p., M Cody Box 6 Misc., DPL-WHR; WFC to Stoker, n.d., Brotherton Collection, Leeds University. For the connection of "The Squaw" to Quincey Morris, Leatherdale, *Dracula,* 130; Belford, *Bram Stoker,* 178.

92. Bram Stoker, *The Shoulder of Shasta,* ed. Alan Johnson (1895; rprt. Westcliff-on-Sea, UK: Desert Island Books, 2000), 27–28, 99–100.

93. See Alan Johnson's annotations in Stoker, *Shoulder of Shasta,* 27, 115–17.

94. Alan Johnson, "Introduction," in Stoker, *Shoulder of Shasta,* 15, 17, also 118 n. 1.

95. Bederman, *Manliness and Civilization;* Lears, *No Place of Grace;* G. Edward White, *The*

Eastern Establishment and the Western Experience: The West of Frederic Remington, Theodore Roosevelt, and Owen Wister (Austin: University of Texas Press, 1989); Alex Nemerov, *Frederic Remington and Turn-of-the-Century America* (New Haven, CT: Yale University Press, 1995); Truettner, *The West as America*.

96. See chapter 9.

97. See programs for these and other years in DPL-WHR, M Cody Programs, and at BBHC. For composition of show in London, see "The Queen in London. Visit to Westminster and the American Exhibition," *Daily Telegraph* (London), May 12, 1887, clipping in Annie Oakley Scrapbook, BBHC, and "Programme of Exhibition Before the Queen," 1887, in *Souvenir Album of the Visit of Her Majesty Queen Victoria to the American Exhibition* (London, 1887), copy in BBHC.

98. Walkowitz, *City of Dreadful Delight;* Hindle, "Introduction," x.

99. Untitled, *The World* (UK), May 11, 1887, p. 10.

100. Richard White compares the frontiers of Turner and Cody in White, "Frederick Jackson Turner and Buffalo Bill." For Anglo-Saxonism: Anderson, *Race and Rapprochement,* 1–70, esp. 39–45, 57–61; Frank N. Hankins, *The Racial Basis of Civilization: A Critique of the Nordic Doctrine* (New York: Alfred A. Knopf, 1926), 159–63; Horsman, *Race and Manifest Destiny,* 62–97; Roosevelt, *Winning of the West;* Owen Wister, "The Evolution of the Cow-Puncher," *Harper's Magazine* 91 (1895): 610, reprinted in Ben Merchant Vorpahl, *My Dear Wister: The Frederic Remington–Owen Wister Letters* (Palo Alto, CA: American West Publishing Co., 1972), 77–96.

101. The late Victorian scholarship on Aryanism is enormous. The best history of the myth itself is Leon Poliakov, *The Aryan Myth: A History of Racist and Nationalist Ideas in Europe,* trans. Edmund Howard (London: Chatto Heinemann for Sussex University Press, 1974). Other sources consulted include Isaac Taylor, *The Origin of the Aryans* (New York: Humboldt Publishing Co., 1890); Charles Morris, *The Aryan Race: Its Origin and Its Achievements* (Chicago: S. C. Griggs and Company, 1888); V. Gordon Childe, *The Aryans: A Study of Indo-European Origins* (New York: Alfred A. Knopf, 1926); Joseph P. Widney, *Race Life of the Aryan Peoples* (New York: Funk & Wagnalls, 1907), 2 vols., esp. vol. 1, 10–25; Madison Grant, *The Passing of the Great Race, or the Racial Basis of European History* (New York: Charles Scribner's Sons, 1918), esp. 169–70, 233; Hankins, *Racial Basis of Civilization,* esp. 20–32. For the impact of the Asian origins thesis on American thought generally, see Horsman, *Race and Manifest Destiny,* 34–36; and Smith, *Virgin Land,* 37. Walt Whitman's Aryanism is expressed in his 1860 poem "Facing West from California Shores," in Whitman, *Leaves of Grass,* 92. Stoker was a devoted reader and defender of Whitman from his college days, particularly *Leaves of Grass.* "Bram Stoker's Correspondence with Walt Whitman," in Stoker, *Dracula,* 487–97. For views of Arthur MacArthur, see Richard Drinnon, *Facing West: The Metaphysics of Indian-Hating and Empire-Building,* rev. ed. (1980; New York: Schocken Books, 1990), 317–18.

102. "The Jubilee," *The World* (UK), June 22, 1887, p. 5. The theory was a common rationalization for the British acquisition of India. Thomas R. Metcalf, *Ideologies of the Raj* (New York: Cambridge University Press, 1995), 81–86.

103. Stoker was acquainted with premier Aryanists of his day, including Max Muller and Armenius Vambery. For Muller, see Frayling, *Vampyres,* 343; Clemens Ruthner, "Bloodsuckers with Teutonic Tongues: The German-Speaking World and the Origins of Dracula," 60–61, in *Dracula: The Shade and the Shadow,* ed. Elizabeth Miller (Westcliff-on-Sea, UK: Desert Island Books, 1998), 54–65. For Vambery: Stoker, *Dracula,* 309, 518, n. 125; Belford, *Bram Stoker,* 260. For Anglo-Saxonism: Quincey Morris is hailed as "a moral Viking" in the pages of *Dracula,* and Harold An Wolf, the English hero of Stoker's 1905 novel, *The Man,* finds that sea voyages in stormy weather revive "the old Berserker spirit." Stoker endorsed the theories of the period's most popular Anglo-Saxonists, John Fiske and Edward Freeman, in Bram Stoker, *A Glimpse of America* (London: Sampson Low and Marston, 1886), 30–31. For Viking fixations in Britain, see Poliakov, *Aryan Myth,* 39; Andrew Wawn, *The Vikings and the Victorians: Inventing the Old North in Nineteenth-Century Britain* (Rochester, NY: D. S. Brewer, 2000); Paul C. Sinding, *The Northmen* (New York: published for the author, 1880), 19–20. For Stoker and storms,

Belford, *Bram Stoker*, 194. To Stoker, racial alliance could mitigate racial decay. Thus, in his novels *Lady Athlyne*, *The Mystery of the Sea*, *The Lady of the Shroud*, and *The Man*, and in *Dracula*, we find Stoker's English, German, American, and Dutch characters reenergizing their flagging bloodlines through infusions of "pioneer blood," often Viking blood, from racial relatives. William Hughes, *Beyond Dracula: Bram Stoker's Fiction and Its Cultural Context* (New York: St. Martins Press, 2000), 59. Stoker's beliefs in the advantages of miscegenation between "the right races" were in keeping with contemporary racial thought, which held that race mixing among purer Aryan descendants was one way of ensuring the continued viability of Aryan civilization. Thus, the English themselves were a mix of Viking, Celt, and other white races, as were the Americans in the works of Frederick Jackson Turner and Theodore Roosevelt. Bederman, *Manliness and Civilization*, 179; Roosevelt, *Winning of the West*, vol. 1.

104. Horsman, *Race and Manifest Destiny*, 34–36; Smith, *Virgin Land*; Poliakov, *Aryan Myth*, 197–99.

105. George Earle Buckle, ed. *The Letters of Queen Victoria, 1886–1901*, 3rd series, 3 vols. (London: John Murray, 1930), 1: 308.

106. "Mistaken Identity," untitled cartoon, in JCG Scrapbook, MS 58, Box 1, NSHS.

107. Untitled clipping, *The Times*, Nov. 1, 1887, "Letters and Invitations, 1887–88," BBHC; "The Wild West Show," *The Era*, April 23, 1887, Johnny Baker Scrapbook, DPL-WHR.

108. George Stocking, *Victorian Anthropology* (New York: The Free Press, 1987), 64, 106; Anderson, *Race and Rapprochement*, 67; Bederman, *Manliness and Civilization*, 179; Roosevelt, *Winning of the West*, 1:23. Even before he began writing *Dracula*, Stoker's thought about Americans was informed by a sense that the American environment had formed them into a new race. In his 1886 essay, "A Glimpse of America," he outlined the "social conditions" that brought about "distinct methods of race development," making Americans a more inventive and energetic race than the British. Stoker, *Glimpse of America*, 12–23, 47–48.

109. "The Wild West Show," *The Era*, April 23, 1887, Johnny Baker Scrapbook, DPL-WHR.

110. "Round the Coast with Buffalo Bill," *Hull News* (UK), May 12, 1888, copy of clipping in Association Files, "Europe: BBWW," BBHC.

111. DeMallie, *Sixth Grandfather*, 251–52.

112. Stephen Knight, *Jack the Ripper: The Final Solution* (London: Panther Books, 1976), 59; also Tom A. Cullen, *When London Walked in Terror* (Boston: Houghton Mifflin, 1965), 106.

113. "A 'Wild West' Cowboy," *The Era*, Aug. 20, 1887, p. 11; "The Giant Cowboy at the Middlesex Sessions," *Islington News* (London), Aug. 27, 1887, p. 3; "Our Weekly Whirligig," *Ally Sloper's Half-Holiday*, Sept. 3, 1887, p. 285; Gallop, *Buffalo Bill's British Wild West*, 122–23.

114. "Incognita," *Court and Society Review*, July 6, 1887, p. 12; Stoker saved a cartoon of "The American Invasion of England," *Funny Folks*, Oct. 7, 1886, in Papers of Henry Irving and Ellen Terry, Reel 21, 51/57.

115. Russell, *Lives and Legends*, 328.

116. "The Worship of Yankeedom," *Moonshine*, Oct. 22, 1887, clipping in JCG Scrapbook, MS 58, Box 1, NSHS.

117. Reinhold Wagnleitner, *Coca-Colonization and the Cold War: The Cultural Mission of the United States in Austria after the Second World War*, trans. Diana M. Wolf (Chapel Hill: University of North Carolina Press, 1994), 20–21.

118. "Topics of the Week," *The Graphic*, May 14, 1887, p. 502; F. C. Burnand, *Records and Reminiscences*, 2 vols. (London: Methuen and Co., 1904), 1:238. I am indebted to Bruce Rosen for the vital source on Jung Bahadur's significance. Bruce Rosen, "Love for Sale: Victorian Paramours and the Marriage Market," paper given at the Victorian Studies Association Conference, Canterbury University, Christchurch, N2, Feb. 1997.

119. R. D. Blumenfeld, *R. D. B.'s Diary, 1887–1914* (London: Heinemann, 1930), 3.

120. WFC to Stoker, n.d., Brotherton Collection, Leeds University.

121. *Illustrated Bits* (UK), May 28, 1887, p. 4.

122. Ian Bevan, *Royal Performance: The Story of Royal Theatregoing* (London: Hutchinson, 1954), 187–89; Gallop, *Buffalo Bill's British Wild West*, 103.

123. Gallop, *Buffalo Bill's British Wild West*, 102.

124. *Illustrated Bits* (UK), May 28, 1887, p. 4.

125. "The Jubilee," *The World* (UK), June 22, 1887, p. 5.

126. David Cannadine, "The Context, Performance, and Meaning of Ritual: The British Monarchy and the 'Invention of Tradition,' c. 1820–1977," in *The Invention of Tradition*, ed. Eric Hobsbawm and Terence Ranger (New York: Cambridge University Press, 1983), 101–64.

127. "Respectful Remonstrance," *Illustrated Bits* (UK), June 25, 1887, p. 10. The editorial appeared earlier, as "Respectful Remonstrance," in *The World*, May 18, 1887, p. 8.

128. "Jubilation," *The World* (UK), June 15, 1887, p. 5.

129. "What the World Says," *The World* (UK), May 18, 1887, p. 10.

130. "Buffalo Bill on His Visit to London," *The Era*, Aug. 27, 1887, p. 13.

131. *Illustrated Bits* (UK), May 21, 1887, p. 3.

132. Contemporaries commented occasionally on Cody's infidelities. See Kasson, *Buffalo Bill's Wild West*, 137–41. For Englishmen's fears: Ben Shephard, "Showbiz Imperialism: The Case of Peter Lobengula," 102, in *Imperialism and Popular Culture*, ed. John Mackenzie (Dover, NH: Manchester University Press, 1985), 94–112; Fraser Harrison, *The Dark Angel: Aspects of Victorian Sexuality* (London: Sheldon Press, 1977), 123.

133. *Illustrated Bits* (UK), July 9, 1887, p. 3.

134. Arata, *Fictions of Loss*, 2–3.

135. Untitled clipping, *Sunday Chronicle*, July 24, 1887, Annie Oakley Scrapbook, 1887–1925, BBHC.

136. "The American Exhibition and the Wild West," *Sporting Life*, May 10, 1887, Annie Oakley Scrapbook, 1887–1925, BBHC.

137. Arata, *Fictions of Loss*; also, David Cannadine, *The Decline and Fall of the British Aristocracy* (New Haven, CT: Yale University Press, 1990); Gareth Stedman Jones, *Outcast London: A Study in the Relationship Between Classes in Victorian Society* (1971; rprt. New York: Pantheon Books, 1984); Richard A. Soloway, *Demography and Degeneration: Eugenics and the Declining Birthrate in Twentieth-Century Britain* (1990; rprt. Chapel Hill: University of North Carolina Press, 1995).

138. Paul Reddin, *Wild West Shows* (Chicago: University of Illinois Press, 1999), 92.

139. "Our Drawing-Room Pets," *Punch*, July 2, 1887, 322, clipping in JCG Scrapbook, MS 58, Box 1, NSHS.

140. "Buffalo Bill," unattributed clipping, n.d., in Johnny Baker Scrapbook, 1886–87, WH 72, DPL.

141. At least two columnists made the connection between WFC and Cetshwayo. See "General Chatter," *The People*, May 22, 1887, Annie Oakley Scrapbook, 1887–1925, BBHC; also "Topics of the Week," *The Graphic* (UK), May 14, 1887, p. 502.

142. Anderson, *Race and Rapprochement*, 62; Arata, *Fictions of Loss*, 216, n. 44; Stoker, *Glimpse of America*, 8–9.

143. *The Times*, Nov. 1, 1887, "Letters and Invitations, 1887–88," BBHC.

144. In the original notes for the novel, Stoker intended the posse to carry a Maxim gun, but dropped it for the American weapon. For Maxim gun, see Bram Stoker, "Dracula" MS, p. 34b, Rosenbach Museum, Philadelphia. For Winchester in the Wild West show, see "Buffalo Bill's Wild West, from the Plains of America," 1887, M Cody Box 6, DPL-WHR, and the longer 1887 program, including an ad for Winchester guns, in "Buffalo Bill's Wild West," 1887 program, DPL-WHR.

145. Leatherdale, *Dracula*, 129–36.

146. Moretti, *Signs Taken for Wonders*, 84–96; Leatherdale, *Dracula*, 130–31; Stoker, "Dracula" MS, Rosenbach Museum, Philadelphia.

147. Moretti, *Signs Taken for Wonders*, 84–96; Arata, *Fictions of Loss*, 129.

148. Stoker, *Dracula*, 225.

149. Russell, *Lives and Legends*, 162–84.

150. Stoker wrote "The Squaw" in the mid-1890s, shortly before publishing *Dracula*, based on notes made years before. Charles Osborne, ed., *The Bram Stoker Bedside Companion* (London: Victor Gollancz, 1973), 11.

151. Stoker, *Dracula*, 309.

152. Frederick Jackson Turner, "The Significance of the Frontier in American History," 33, in *Rereading Frederick Jackson Turner*, ed. John Mack Faragher (New Haven, CT: Yale University Press, 1998), 31–60; Kerwin Lee Klein, *Frontiers of Historical Imagination: Narrating the European Conquest of Native America, 1890–1990* (Berkeley: University of California Press, 1997), 18–20; William Cronon, "Revisiting Turner's Vanishing Frontier: The Legacy of Frederick Jackson Turner," *Western Historical Quarterly* 18 (April 1987): 157–76; John T. Juricek, "American Usage of the Word 'Frontier' from Colonial Times to Frederick Jackson Turner," *Proceedings of the American Philosophical Society* 110 (Feb. 1966). For European concepts of frontier, see Anderson, *Race and Rapprochement*, 18–19; Horsman, *Race and Manifest Destiny*, 35. Jack D. Forbes pointed out the similarity between Turner's frontier and European frontiers forty years ago. Jack D. Forbes, "Frontiers in American History," *Journal of the West* 1 (July 1962): 63–71; also Jack D. Forbes, "Frontiers in American History and the Role of the American Historian," *Ethnohistory* 15 (Spring 1968): 203–35.

153. "Our London Letter," and "Arrest of M. Schnaebele of the Franco-German Frontier," in *Penny Illustrated Paper*, May 7, 1887, pp. 290, 292–93; see also "France and Germany on the Frontier," *Pall Mall Gazette*, April 29, 1887, p. 11.

154. Transylvania was well-known to the English public from newspaper coverage about the "Eastern Question," the issue of how Britain should respond to the endemic racial strife of the Carpathians and the region of Europe adjoining the Ottoman Empire. Arata, *Fictions of Loss*, 113. For wilderness, see a book that Stoker consulted in his research for *Dracula:* Anonymous (A Fellow of the Carpathian Society), *Magyarland: Being the Narrative of Our Travels Through the Highlands and Lowlands of Hungary*, 2 vols. (London: Sampson Low, 1881), esp. 1:25–27. As late as the 1870s, English observers suggested an English diaspora as a way of wresting Transylvania from the twin scourges of barbarism and inefficiency. See Andrew F. Crosse, *Round About the Carpathians* (Edinburgh: W. Blackwood, 1878), esp. 197–98, but also 141–42, 156, 229, 287, 352–53. Some of the more telling references to racial segmentation and race strife from other works Stoker consulted: E. C. Johnson, *On the Track of the Crescent: Erratic Notes from the Piraeus to Pesth* (London: Hurst and Blackett, 1885), 149; Emily Gerard, *The Land Beyond the Forest: Facts, Figures, and Fancies from Transylvania*, 2 vols. (London: William Blackwood and Sons, 1888), 2: 86–87, 112–13.

155. "Cupid at Wild West," unattributed clipping, Thursday, April 15, 1897, "These People Make History," *Brooklyn Daily Times*, April 12, 1897, clipping, in NSS, 1897, DPL-WHR.

156. Bram Stoker, "Dracula" MS, Rosenbach Museum, Philadelphia. Stoker, *Dracula*, 9, 59.

157. Stoker, *Dracula*, 42–43.

158. Stoker, *Dracula*, 43.

159. BBWW 1885 program (Hartford, CT: Calhoun Co., 1885), n.p.; "every phase of border life" is in "Buffalo Bill's Wild West, from the Plains of America," 1887, M Cody Box 6, DPL-WHR; Slotkin, *Gunfighter Nation*, 75–76.

160. Hindle, "Introduction," ix.

161. Stoker, *Dracula*, 43.

162. The quotation is from the character of Dr. Van Helsing. Stoker, *Dracula*, 308.

163. BBWW 1893 program, 6, 18.

164. *The Era*, April 23, 1887, clipping in Johnny Baker Scrapbook (microfilm), DPL-WHR.

165. Stoker, *Dracula*, 42–43.

166. Stoker, *Dracula*, 309.

167. David Mogen, "Wilderness, Metamorphosis, and Millennium: Gothic Apocalypse from the Puritans to the Cyberpunks," 94, in *Frontier Gothic: Terror and Wonder at the Frontier in American Literature*, ed. David Mogen, Scott P. Sanders, and Joanne B. Karpinski (Rutherford, NJ: Fairleigh Dickinson University Press, 1993), 94–108.

168. Slotkin, *Regeneration Through Violence;* 116–45, 219–22.

169. Slotkin, *Regeneration Through Violence*, esp. 219–22. Racial degeneracy was only part of a wider anxiety about the inherent political, social, and economic degeneracy of colonial societies. See Anthony Pagden, "Identity Formation in Spanish America," 76, in *Colonial Identity in the Atlantic World, 1500–1800*, ed. Nicholas Canny and Anthony Pagden (Princeton, NJ: Princeton University Press, 1987), 51–93.

170. "Unfit amalgamation" from McCoy, *Historic Sketches of the Cattle Trade*, 80. Dana, *Two Years Before the Mast*, 136–37; Bancroft, *California Pastoral*, 263–65, 284. For Philippines: Kristin L. Hoganson, *Fighting for American Manhood: How Gender Politics Provoked the Spanish-American and Philippine-American Wars* (New Haven, CT: Yale University Press, 1998), 180–99.

171. Stoker, *Dracula*, 79, 417.

172. At the time Stoker wrote *Dracula*, the Huns were still recalled as Asiatic barbarians who invaded the West. "Hun," *Compact Edition of the Oxford English Dictionary* (New York: Oxford University Press, 1971), 3993.

173. Arata, "Occidental Tourist," 466.

174. Stoker, *Dracula*, 25, 28.

175. So linked was the American frontier to the original frontier of Anglo-Saxon expansion that scholars on both sides of the Atlantic split their studies of Anglo-Saxon race history into two volumes: one for Europe, the other for America. For Theodore Roosevelt, the conquest of the American West essentially began on "the day when the keels of the Low-Dutch sea-thieves first grated on the British coast." Roosevelt, *Winning of the West*, 6:4.

176. Stocking, *Victorian Anthropology*, 169–79; Frederick Jackson Turner's frontier thesis is perhaps the clearest example. Turner, "Significance of the Frontier in American History."

177. See the chart in Frayling, *Vampyres*, 42–63.

INTERLUDE: BRONCHO CHARLIE MILLER

1. Sources for this account are as follows: The earliest account of Charlie Miller's life is from "Camp Sketches No. X, Broncho Charlie," *Topical Times*, Sept. 3, 1887, clipping in JCG Scrapbook, MS 58, NSHS, in which readers will note that Miller claims 1860 as his year of birth and makes no mention of being a Pony Express rider; Miller's tall autobiography is Gladys Shaw Erskine, *Broncho Charlie: A Saga of the Saddle—The Life Story of Broncho Charlie Miller, the Last of the Pony Express Riders* (1935; rprt. New York: Thomas Crowell, 1939). For parade participation, see Greater Astoria Historical Society website, "Daily Star," March 1944, ⟨*http://www.astorialic.org/starjournal/1940s/1944march.shtm*⟩. Boy Scout reminiscence is in L. I. "Rusty" Heale [actually Haak], "Broncho Charlie Whip-lit Match," in "Letters to the Editor," *Cody Enterprise* (Wyoming), May 26, 1997; family lore of Charlie Miller is in tape transcript of interview with Walter Miller, 1987, in "Broncho Charlie Miller," Association Files, BBHC; also Lois Miller Ellsworth, *Tales of Broncho Charlie: Youngest Rider of the Pony Express* (Greenfield, MA: Hollis Books, 1999); "just like gettin' home" is in Erskine, *Broncho Charlie*, 248. For a measured account of Miller's life, see Christopher Corbett, *Orphans Preferred: The Twisted Truth and Lasting Legend of the Pony Express* (New York: Broadway Books, 2003), 231–45. My suggestion that Miller may have inspired Berger's Jack Crabb comes from my reading of Miller's frequent press, which places him, much like Berger's Crabb, at 104 years of age in 1954, seated in a wheelchair in a rest home, puffing away on cigarettes and telling tall tales. See Charlie Duprez, "Last of the Pony Express Riders," typescript, n.d., in M206 Broncho Charlie Miller file, DPL-WHR.

CHAPTER TWELVE: WILD WEST EUROPE

1. "BBWW Routes, 1883–1916," BBHC; Russell, *Lives and Legends*, 352–53.

2. JCG testimony, March 11, 1905, CC.

3. Arta Cody to WFC, Nov. 1, 1885, Plaintiff's Exhibit 1, in CC. Arta Cody attended

Brownell Hall in Omaha, an exclusive girls' school, as well as eastern finishing schools. Yost, *Buffalo Bill*, 148.

4. WFC to Mollie Moses, March 1, 1886; WFC to Mollie Moses, April 26, 1886, and other letters in file; also "Bare Buffalo Bill's Love for Kentucky Girl," *Evansville Press* (KY), n.d. [1927], all in WFC Collection, MS 6, Series I:B, Box 1/9, BBHC.

5. Threat of divorce in Ed Goodman to Al Goodman, March 17, 1887, WFC Collection, MS 6, Series VI:H, Box 1, BBHC; lack of letters in Mary Cody Bradford testimony, March 11, 1905, in Folder 4, CC. My research has revealed no known letters between Louisa and William Cody in 1887–88. In her memoirs, Louisa Cody claimed she received a letter on the day he drove four kings in the Deadwood coach. Whether that was her story or an invention of her collaborator, Courtney Riley Cooper, the incident itself was invented, and the style of the letter is not in keeping with William Cody's prose. See Cody and Cooper, *Memories of Buffalo Bill by His Wife*, 296.

6. Arta with him at public functions is in "Mansion House Dramatic Luncheon, Wednesday, June 15, 1887, Plan of Tables," in Papers of Henry Irving and Ellen Terry, Reel 21, 52/48–49; tour of continent is in Ed Goodman to "Uncle Will," Sept. 16, 1887, and Ed Goodman to "My dear Ma and Pa," Aug. 27, 1887, WFC Collection, MS 6, Series VI:H, Box 1, BBHC; Cody, *Story of the Wild West*, 749.

7. "Some Early Experiences of Katherine Clemmons," unattributed clipping, 1898; "For Her Reputation This Woman Fights," unattributed clipping, n.d. [1909], in Robert Haslam Scrapbook, Colorado Historical Society, Denver, CO.

8. Gallop, *Buffalo Bill's British Wild West*, 126–27, 179–83.

9. WFC to Al Goodman, July 7, 1887, in Foote, *Letters from Buffalo Bill*, 31.

10. Four-in-hand is in Yost, *Buffalo Bill*, 217–20.

11. WFC to Al Goodman, July 12, 1888, Plaintiff's Exhibit 2, and WFC to Al Goodman, July 17, 1888, Plaintiff's Exhibit 3, in Folder 4, CC.

12. Yost, *Buffalo Bill*, 213–16.

13. Yost, *Buffalo Bill*, 213–14, 223.

14. JCG testimony, March 11, 1905, Folder 4, p. 6 (of J. C. Goodman testimony), CC.

15. Judy Greaves Rainger, "Buffalo Bill, Boulanger, and Bonheur: Trans-Atlantic Cultural Exchanges in the *Fin-de-Siecle*," *Proceedings of the Western Society for French History: Selected Papers of the 1998 Annual Meeting* (Greeley: University Press of Colorado, 2000), 243.

16. Quoted in Dore Ashton and Denise Brown Hare, *Rosa Bonheur: A Life and Legend* (New York: Viking, 1981), 152–53.

17. Robert Hughes, *The Shock of the New: The Hundred-Year History of Modern Art* (New York: Alfred A. Knopf, 1980), 127–32.

18. Hughes, *Shock of the New*, 276.

19. Hughes, *Shock of the New*, 277.

20. WFC to Charles Stobie, March 12, 1903, CHS.

21. " 'Horse Fair' Takes at the Wild West," *Chicago Evening Post*, June 9, 1896, in NSS 1896, WH 72, DPL-WHR.

22. For Bonheur, see Ashton and Hare, *Rosa Bonheur*, 144–57.

23. See Deloria, *Playing Indian*, 100.

24. A file of letters from Esquivel to Baroncelli is in the Palais du Roure, Avignon.

25. The most thorough and intriguing treatment of Baroncelli's regionalism and the influence of Cody's show upon him is Rob Zaretsky, *Cock and Bull Stories: Folco de Baroncelli and the Invention of the Camargue* (Lincoln: University of Nebraska Press, 2005), esp. 61–84. Quotes from Baroncelli to Jacob White Eyes, June 6, 1906, Palais du Roure, Avignon.

26. "Buffalo-Bill en Avignon," *La Femaille*, July 19, 1905, clipping in Palais du Roure, Avignon.

27. Quoted in Tudor Edwards, *The Lion of Arles: A Portrait of Mistral and His Circle* (New York: Fordham University Press, 1964), 161. Baroncelli once sought to sacrifice a bull in the crypt of the church of Les Saintes at his hometown of Les-Saintes-Marie-de-la-Mer, and was crushed when the curate refused. Edwards, *Lion of Arles*, p. 160.

28. Translation of letter, Baroncelli to White Eyes, June 6, 1906, Palais du Roure, Avignon.

29. Jacques Nissou, "Autour de Joe Hamman: Les Amerindiens, la Camargue, et le Western francais," in *Les Indiens de Buffalo Bill et la Camargue*, ed. Thierry Lefrancois (Paris: Editions de Lat Martinière, 1994), 104–5, 123–25; Rainger, "Buffalo Bill, Boulanger, and Bonheur," 250.

30. Rainger, "Buffalo Bill, Boulanger, and Bonheur," 249–50.

31. Eric Hobsbawm, "Mass Producing Traditions," in *The Invention of Tradition*, ed. Hobsbawm and Ranger, 263–308.

32. My discussion of western mythology in Germany is drawn from Peter Bolz, "Indians and Germans: A Relationship Riddled with Clichés," in *Native American Art: The Collections of the Ethnological Museum Berlin*, ed. Peter Bolz and Hans-Ulrich Sanner (Seattle: University of Washington Press, 1999), 9–21.

33. Karl Markus Kreis, "Indians Playing, Indians Praying: Native Americans in Wild West Shows and Catholic Missions," in *Germans and Indians: Fantasies, Encounters, Projections*, ed. Colin G. Calloway, Gerd Germunden, and Susanne Zantop (Lincoln: University of Nebraska Press, 2003), 200.

34. Kreis, "Indians Playing, Indians Praying," 195; Bolz, "Indians and Germans," 15–16.

35. Sam Lone Bear to Marquis Baroncelli, Aug. 22, 1929, Palais du Roure, Avignon.

36. Bolz, "Indians and Germans," 12.

37. Kreis, "Indians Playing, Indians Praying," 202–3.

38. Jeffrey Sammons, "Nineteenth-Century German Representation of Indians from Experience," in *Germans and Indians*, 190–92; Bolz, "Indians and Germans," 13; also Richard H. Cracroft, "The American West of Karl May," *American Quarterly* 19, no. 2, pt. 1 (Summer 1967): 249–58.

39. Kreis, "Indians Playing, Indians Praying," 201.

40. Deloria, *Playing Indian*, 95–153.

41. Stocking, *Victorian Anthropology*, 169–79; Frederick Jackson Turner's frontier thesis is perhaps the clearest example. Turner, "Significance of the Frontier in American History."

42. In remote regions of Europe, British and other writers recounted stagecoaches pursued by Gypsies. "They were completely naked, of dark copper colour, with shaggy black hair, and pearly white teeth, and ran after the carriage, yelling and throwing up their arms." Johnson, *On the Track of the Crescent*, 148–49. American magazines that covered the Indian wars also featured accounts in which outlaws "worse than Bedouins or Indians" waylaid stagecoaches on the "Uralian steppes," and their victims were either killed or "borne away into a captivity worse than death." "Uralian Steppe Robbers," *Harper's Weekly*, Nov. 7, 1874, p. 921.

43. Folco de Baroncelli-Javon, *La Camargue de Baroncelli du Marquis Folco de Baroncelli-Javon* (Nîmes, France: Editions Camarguo, 1984 [privately printed]), 159–66.

44. Edwards, *Lion of Arles*, 160–63; Remi Venture, "La defense d'une identité, fondement de l'amitie baroncello-amerindienne," in *Les Indiens de Buffalo Bill at la Camargue*, ed. Lefrancois, 35–36.

CHAPTER THIRTEEN: GHOST DANCE

1. V. Deloria, "The Indians," in Hassrick et al., *Buffalo Bill and the Wild West*, 54, 56.

2. DeMallie, *Sixth Grandfather*, 245.

3. DeMallie, *Sixth Grandfather*, 251.

4. DeMallie, *Sixth Grandfather*, 254.

5. Guy Dull Knife, Sr., quoted in Starita, *Dull Knifes of Pine Ridge*, 173.

6. For Pratt, see White, *"It's Your Misfortune and None of My Own,"* 113. For assimilation, see Frederick E. Hoxie, *A Final Promise: The Campaign to Assimilate the Indians, 1880–1920* (Lincoln: University of Nebraska Press, 1984), 1–39.

7. Deloria, *Indians in Unexpected Places*, 69.

8. Starita, *Dull Knifes of Pine Ridge*, 150–51.

9. For ban on dances, see Robert M. Utley, *Last Days of the Sioux Nation* (New Haven, CT:

Yale University Press, 1963), 49; for sweat lodges among show Indians, see Parker, *Odd People I Have Met*, 54; "The Mild West," *The Million*, Sept. 3, 1892, p. 245. For religiosity of the sweat lodge, see William K. Powers, *Oglala Religion* (Lincoln: University of Nebraska Press, 1977), 89–91, 134–36; Raymond A. Bucko, *The Lakota Ritual of the Sweat Lodge: History and Contemporary Practice* (Lincoln: University of Nebraska Press, 1998).

10. Ed Goodman to Parents, May 29, 1886, in WFC Collection, MS 6 Series VI:B.

11. Davis, *Circus Age*, 52, 187–88; Trachtenberg, *Incorporation of America*, 91.

12. The song comes from Calvin Jumping Bull. Juti Winchester, "Buffalo Bill and the Indians: Pine Ridge Remembers William F. Cody," paper delivered at the Western History Association Meeting, Oct. 12, 2000, San Antonio, TX; also Severt Young Bear and R. D. Theisz, *Standing in the Light: A Lakota Way of Seeing* (Lincoln: University of Nebraska Press, 1994), 97.

13. Calvin Jumping Bull, presentation to Consulting Committee for Buffalo Bill Museum, July 8, 2004, and July 9, 2004, BBHC; see also Moses, *Wild West Shows and the Images of American Indians*, 272; Young Bear and Theisz, *Standing in the Light*, 97–98.

14. Thomas Biolsi, *Organizing the Lakota*, 18–20, 24.

15. Commissioner of Indian Affairs, *Report of the Commissioner of Indian Affairs, 1886* (Washington, DC: Government Printing Office, 1886), 77; *Report of the Commissioner of Indian Affairs, 1887* (Washington, DC: Government Printing Office, 1887), xxxvii; *Report of the Commissioner of Indian Affairs, 1890* (Washington, DC: Government Printing Office, 1890), xc, 469.

16. See contracts for 1888 in Bonds and Contracts 1888, no. 22362, Box 480, LR 1881–1907, RG 75, NARA; 1889 in "Contract and Bond to Take Certain Indians into Their Show," no. 9526, Box 513, Letters Received 1881–1907, RG 75, NARA; and 1906 contracts in RG 75, Box 162, 047 Fairs and Expositions, Buffalo Bill's Wild West, 1906 Contracts, NARA-CPR.

17. See the extensive archive of show contracts in RG 75, Box 162, 047 Fairs and Expositions, Buffalo Bill's Wild West, 1906 Contracts, NARA-CPR: also "1906–11 Contracts" folder, in Box 162, RG 75, NARA-CPR; and "BBWW Show Contracts 1912–13," RG 75, Pine Ridge Box 162, 047 Fairs and Expositions, NARA-CPR.

18. Ella Bissonett's salary is in A. C. Belt to Sec. of Interior, Nov. 18, 1890, Correspondence Land Division, Letters Sent, vol. 104, Letter Book 207, pp. 191–201, NARA.

19. See Samuel D. Oliphant to Major John R. Brennan, Jan. 13, 1916, in 047 Fairs and Expositions, Box 162, BBWW Bankruptcy, Folder 2 of 2, RG 75, NARA-CPR.

20. WFC to Captain C. Penney, May 2, 1891, RG 75, Pine Ridge, Misc. Css. Received, 1891–95, A–C, Folder Jan. 26, 1891–Dec. 25, 1891, NARA-CPR.

21. WFC to Captain C. Penney, Sept. 30, 1891, RG 75, Pine Ridge, Misc. Css. Received, 1891–95, A–C, Folder Jan. 26, 1891–Dec. 25, 1891, NARA-CPR. See also, in the same file: WFC to Capt. C. G. Penney, Dec. 18, 1891.

22. WFC to Nelson Miles, Nov. 12, 1891, RG 75, Pine Ridge, Misc. Css. Received, 1891–95, A–C, Folder Jan. 26, 1891–Dec. 25, 1891, NARA-CPR.

23. For show calculations, see Jule Keen to Anonymous, June 6, 1891, in 047 Fairs and Expositions, Box 162, BBWW, 1891–95, RG 75, NARA-CPR. Freighting figures from *Annual Report of the Commissioner of Indian Affairs, 1889*, 151–58. Even in 1905, per capita payments disbursed to the Oglala by the Pine Ridge Agency amounted only to $30,767; per diem labor ($73,213) and purchase of beef cattle ($34,686) paid more. Biolsi, *Organizing the Lakota*, 28.

24. Cowboy wages: Ed Goodman to Parents, May 29, 1886, MS 6 Series VI:B, BBHC; Blackstone, *Buckskin, Bullets, and Business*, 97; for Indian wages see contracts for various dates, and list of names, April 12, 1895, in 047 Fairs and Expositions, Box 162, BBWW, 1891–95, RG 75, NARA-CPR.

25. Nasaw, *Going Out*, 43.

26. Davis, *Circus Age*, 30.

27. See Moses, *Wild West Shows and the Images of American Indians*, 101–3; Clyde Ellis, *A Dancing People: Powwow Culture on the Southern Plains* (Lawrence: University Press of Kansas, 2003), 79–101.

28. Nasaw, *Going Out*, 15–18.
29. Sagala, *Buffalo Bill, Actor*, 163.
30. Unattributed clipping (New Orleans?), n.d. (received in Interior/Indian office on May 19, 1885), in Cody to Bureau, no. 11212, Letters Received, 1881–1907, Box 242, RG 75, NARA.
31. See Nasaw, *Going Out*, 13; U.S. Department of Commerce, Bureau of the Census, *Historical Statistics of the United States: Colonial Times to 1970*, part 1 (Washington, DC: Government Printing Office, 1975), 165, 168.
32. John Burke to "The Honorable Commissioner," n.d. (Letter Received Feb. 20, 1886), Letters Received, 1881–1907, no. 5564, Box 290, RG 75, NARA. In 1886, several New York dailies ran articles poking fun at show Indians who allegedly fell asleep during a sermon at Henry Ward Beecher's Plymouth Church. George Bates, who was in charge of the Indians during this season, responded with a letter arguing that "there was not a white man or woman in Plymouth church on the occasion referred to, that was more reverent, more respectful or more attentive to the service than were these red men from the far West." Perhaps the entire congregation fell asleep. John Burke was careful to send the published letter to the commissioner of Indian affairs, assuring him that "we have many instructive expeditions planned" for the Indians. G. H. Bates enclosure in WFC to Lamar, no date 1886, Letters Received, 1881–1907, no. 34611, Box 364, RG 75, NARA; Burke to Gen. Upshaw, Commissioner of Indian Affairs, Dec. 13, 1886, Letters Received, 1881–1907, Box 361, no. 33319.
33. Bonds and Contract, April 14, 1887, no. 9855, Box 388, Letters Received, 1881–1907, RG 75, Bureau of Indian Affairs, NARA.
34. G. H. Bates to LCQ Lamar, Jan. 11, 1887, no. 1124, Box 367; also, WFC to Upshaw, Jan. 12, 1887, no. 1157, Box 368; W. R. Maul to Commissioner of Indian Affairs, Jan. 28, 1887, no. 3054, Box 372; G. H. Bates to Commissioner of Indian Affairs, Feb. 7, 1887, no. 3637, Box 374, all in Letters Received, 1881–1907, RG 75, NARA.
35. Box 574, no. 34459, Rosebud Agency—J. Geo. Wright to CIA, Nov. 23, 1887, Letters Received, 1881–1907, RG 75, NARA.
36. Box 575, no. 34973, from Company River Agency, Henry George to CIA, Nov. 25, 1889, Letters Received, 1881–1907, RG 75, NARA.
37. Box 578, no. 35938, from Devil's Lake Agency, John W. Cransic to CIA, Dec. 10, 1889, Letters Received, 1881–1907, RG 75, NARA.
38. Box 579, no. 36269, John Blair to CIA, 1889, Letters Received, 1881–1907, RG 75, NARA.
39. Rev. John F. Copley of the Omaha Mission, quoted in Robert Ashley to CIA, Jan. 9, 1890, no. 1239, Box 586, Letters Received, 1881–1907, RG 75, NARA.
40. There were rumors, too, of several Indian deaths from smallpox or influenza in Spain. See Moses, *Wild West Shows and the Images of American Indians*, 86–87, 94.
41. "Three Hungry Indians," unattributed clipping, n.d., in G. C. Crager Scrapbook, 1891–92, BBHC.
42. James O'Beirne to H. D. Gallagher, July 4, 1890, Pine Ridge, Misc. Css. Received, Folder Feb. 18, 1889–Dec. 29, 1890, RG 75, NARA-CPR.
43. G. C. Crager Scrapbook, 1891–92, BBHC, includes a smattering of the news coverage.
44. A. C. Belt to Secretary of Interior, Nov. 18, 1890, RG 75, Correspondence Land Division, Letters Sent, vol. 104, Letterbook 207, pp. 191–201, NARA.
45. "Three Hungry Indians," unattributed clipping, n.d., G. C. Crager Scrapbook, 1891–92, BBHC.
46. For Rocky Bear, see WFC to George LeRoy Brown, April 22, 1892, RG 75, Pine Ridge, Misc. Css. Received, 1891–95, A–C, Folder Jan. 4–May 10, 1892, NARA-CPR; Standing Bear, *My People the Sioux*, 253.
47. For twenty-five-cent fee, see Red Cloud to Nate Salsbury, July 18, 1889, NSP, YCAL 17, Box 1, Folder 6, July 18, 1889; interference, see Cody to LCQ Lamar, March 20, 1887, no. 7592, Box 383, Letters Received, 1881–1907, RG 75, NARA.
48. "Memorial of Sioux Indians," Senate Doc. No. 90, 55th Congress, 1st Session, May 17, 1897.

49. Petition from the Tribal Council, May 10, 1901, "Petitions, ca. 1875–1907," Box 780, RG 75, Pine Ridge, NARA-CPR. Thanks to Thomas Andrews for the citation.

50. Chauncey Yellow Robe, "The Menace of the Wild West Show," address to the Fourth Annual Conference of the Society of American Indians, Oct. 6–11, 1914, in *Quarterly Journal of the Society of American Indians*, no. 2 (1914): 223–24.

51. WFC to George LeRoy Brown, April 22, 1892, RG 75, Pine Ridge, Misc. Css. Received, 1891–95, A–C, Folder Jan. 4, 1892–May 10, 1892, NARA-CPR.

52. Sam Madra, *Glasgow's Ghost Shirt* (Glasgow: Glasgow Museums, 1991); George Crager to H. Q. C. Lamar, June 21, 1890, no. 19021, Box 634, Letters Received, 1881–1907, Records of the Bureau of Indian Affairs, RG 75, NARA; Nate Salsbury to Commissioner of Indian Affairs, enclosing affidavit of G. C. Crager, March 1, 1892, no. 9249, Box 834, Letters Received, 1881–1907, RG 75, NARA.

53. Rex Alan Smith, *Moon of Popping Trees: The Tragedy at Wounded Knee and the End of the Indian Wars* (New York: Crowell, 1975), 48.

54. Emily Greenwald, *Reconfiguring the Reservation: The Nez Perces, Jicarilla Apaches, and the Dawes Act* (Albuquerque: University of New Mexico Press, 2002); also Wilcomb E. Washburn, *The Assault on Indian Tribalism: The General Allotment Law (Dawes Act) of 1887* (Philadelphia: Lippincott, 1975).

55. Smith, *Moon of Popping Trees*, 61–62; Starita, *Dull Knifes of Pine Ridge*, 91; Utley, *Last Days of the Sioux Nation*, 40–59.

56. These were the conclusions of the Merriam Report of 1928. See Philip Weeks, ed., *The American Indian Experience: A Profile, 1524 to the Present* (Arlington Heights, IL: Forum Press, 1988), 240.

57. Note in Letters Received, 1881–1907, Box 551, no. 24780, Sept. 2, 1889, RG 75, NARA.

58. Starita, *Dull Knifes of Pine Ridge*, 91–92; Utley, *Last Days of the Sioux Nation*, 40–59; Jeffrey Ostler, *The Plains Sioux and U.S. Colonialism from Lewis and Clark to Wounded Knee* (New York: Cambridge, 2004), 235–39; Raymond J. DeMallie, "Teton," in *Handbook of North American Indians*, ed. William C. Sturtevant. 17 vols. (Washington DC: Smithsonian Institution, 1990–2001), vol. 13, pt. 2: 815.

59. Utley, *Last Days of the Sioux Nation*, 57.

60. Utley, *Last Days of the Sioux Nation*, 69.

61. Smith, *Moon of Popping Trees*, 75, 103–6; Starita, *Dull Knifes of Pine Ridge*, 100. Other sources for my discussion of the Ghost Dance include James Mooney, *The Ghost-Dance Religion and the Sioux Outbreak of 1890* (1896; abridged ed., Chicago: University of Chicago Press, 1965); Utley, *Last Days of the Sioux Nation*.

62. James Mooney: "The Sioux nation numbers over 25,000, with between 6,000 and 7,000 warriors. Hardly more than 700 warriors were concerned altogether, including those of Big Foot's band and those who fled to the Bad Lands. None of the Christian Indians took any part in the disturbance." Mooney, *Ghost-Dance Religion*, 98.

63. Starita, *Dull Knifes of Pine Ridge*, 102. See also Commissioner Morgan, quoted in Mooney, *Ghost-Dance Religion*, 98.

64. Smith, *Moon of Popping Trees*, 118–45.

65. Starita, *Dull Knifes of Pine Ridge*, 103; Utley, *Last Days of the Sioux Nation*, 110–11.

66. Smith, *Moon of Popping Trees*, 119.

67. Utley, *Last Days of the Sioux Nation*, 126. See also Jeffrey Ostler, "Conquest and the State: Why the United States Employed Massive Military Force to Suppress the Lakota Ghost Dance," *Pacific Historical Review* 1996, 65 (2): 217–48.

68. Smith, *Moon of Popping Trees*, 146; Russell, *Lives and Legends*, 359. On the back of his calling card, which he gave to Cody, General Miles also wrote "Com'd'g officers will please give Col. Cody transportation for himself and party and any protection he may need for a small party." Russell, *Lives and Legends*, 359. Typescript of orders is in WFC Collection, MS 6, Series I:B Correspondence, Box 2/23, BBHC.

69. Russell, *Lives and Legends*, 307–8, 423–24; "Dr. Frank D. Powell as Manager," *Wyoming Stockgrower and Farmer*, March 22, 1904, in Robert Haslam Scrapbook, CHS.

70. Corbett, *Orphans Preferred*, 198–99; and see the testimony of Haslam in CC, File 7-1,

p. 133; WFC to Robert Haslam, Jan. 20, 1883; "Soldiers' Hospital Train Is Expected," *Dayton Daily* [no state] clipping, n.d., and " 'Pony Bob' Is Dead," unattributed clipping, Feb. 29, 1912, all in Robert Haslam Scrapbook, CHS.

71. "The Messiah Found," *Rocky Mountain News*, Nov. 25, 1890, p. 1.

72. "Buffalo Bill Ready," unattributed clipping, n.d., in Robert Haslam Scrapbook, CHS.

73. See Smith, *Moon of Popping Trees*, 146–49; and David Humphreys Miller, *Ghost Dance* (Lincoln: University of Nebraska Press, 1959), 159–61.

74. James McLaughlin, *My Friend the Indian* (1910; rprt. Lincoln: University of Nebraska Press, 1989), 209–11; Peter E. Traub, "The First Act of the Last Sioux Campaign," *Journal of the United States Cavalry Association*, no. 15 (1905): 872–79.

75. Smith, *Moon of Popping Trees*, 146–49; Traub, "First Act of the Last Sioux Campaign."

76. Clipping from *Chicago Herald*, Dec. 13, in BBWW 1893 program (Chicago: Blakely Printing), 50.

77. Quote from Traub, "First Act of the Last Sioux Campaign," 874. See also Maj. M. F. Steel, "Buffalo Bill's Bluff," *South Dakota Historical Collections* 9 (1918): 475–85; E. A. Brininstool, "Buffaloing Buffalo Bill," *Hunter-Trader-Trapper* 76, no. 4 (April 1938): 17–18; also Utley, *Lance and the Shield*, 294; Ostler, *Plains Sioux*, 313–16.

78. Utley, *Lance and the Shield*, 265; Stanley Vestal, *Sitting Bull* (Norman: University of Oklahoma, 1932), 251.

79. Stanley Vestal, *New Sources of Indian History, 1850–1891* (Norman: University of Oklahoma Press, 1934), 2–3.

80. Smith, *Moon of Popping Trees*, 157–60.

81. Smith, *Moon of Popping Trees*, 180–200; Utley, *Last Days of the Sioux Nation*, 209–30.

82. BBWW 1893 program, 53.

83. Thayer's office was inundated with requests from western Nebraska for food and drought relief through much of the fall. Those requests shifted abruptly, to urgent demands for guns and ammunition, in November. See for example: J. M. Thayer to A. D. Cole, Nov. 21, 1890; "A Homesteader" to John Thayer, Nov. 24, 1890; J. M. Thayer to George M. Sheldon, Nov. 26, 1890; L. P. Sudden to J. M. Thayer, Nov. 26, 1890; J. T. Sumny to John Thayer, Nov. 27, 1890, and Nov. 28, 1890; Neil Brennan to J. M. Thayer, Nov. 29, 1890; J. M. Thayer to Capt. Sidney B. Higgins, Nov. 29, 1890; J. M. Thayer to C. W. Worth, Dec. 13, 1890; J. M. Thayer to S. A. Daly, Dec. 1, 1890; J. M. Thayer to Capt. A. L. Field, Dec. 1, 1890, all in Record Group 1, SG14, Box 7/64, NSHS.

84. Oliver Knight, *Following the Indian Wars: The Story of the Newspaper Correspondents Among the Indian Campaigners* (Norman: University of Oklahoma Press, 1960), 313–15.

85. William J. Adelman, "The Road to Fort Sheridan," in David Roediger and Franklin Rosemont, *The Haymarket Scrapbook* (Chicago: Charles H. Kerr, 1986), 130.

86. Utley, *Last Days of the Sioux Nation*, 271–72; Moses, *Wild West Shows and the Images of American Indians*, 110–11.

87. Utley, *Last Days of the Sioux Nation*, 271–72; "Prisoners of War on Exhibition," *Harper's Weekly*, May 30, 1891, p. 399.

88. Smith, *Moon of Popping Trees*, 201–4; Utley, *Last Days of the Sioux Nation*, 230, 249.

89. For the egregious propaganda that passed as journalism in the Ghost Dance troubles, see Elmo Scott Watson, "The Last Indian War, 1890–91: A Study of Newspaper Jingoism," *Journalism Quarterly* 20 (1943): 205–19.

90. The letters were widely reprinted in show publicity. See for example BBWW 1893 program; and Burke, *Buffalo Bill from Prairie to Palace*, 258–59. Emphasis added.

91. BBWW 1893 program, 51; Burke, *Buffalo Bill from Prairie to Palace*, 257.

92. BBWW 1893 program, 44; James Mooney, *The Ghost-Dance Religion and the Sioux Outbreak of 1890*, 14th Annual Report of the Bureau of American Ethnology, 1892–93, Part 2 (Washington, DC: Government Printing Office, 1896), p. 657.

93. BBWW program 1893, 61–62. Emphasis in the original.

94. For military officer at Pine Ridge, see Utley, *Last Days of the Sioux Nation*, 282; for Brown, see George LeRoy Brown to WFC, May 21, 1891, RG 75 Pine Ridge, Misc. Letters Sent, 1887–1891, vol. 7, Box 342, NARA-CPR.

95. They remained at Fort Niobrara until 1906. Biolsi, *Organizing the Lakota*, 23.
96. A. C. Belt to Secretary of Interior, Nov. 18, 1890, Correspondence Land Division, Letter Sent, vol. 104, Letter Book 207, pp. 191–201, RG 75, NARA.
97. D. F. Royer to T. J. Morgan, Jan. 10, 1891, no. 3186, Box 699, Letters Received, 1881–1907, RG 75, NARA; Burke, *Buffalo Bill from Prairie to Palace*, 257.
98. DeMallie, *Sixth Grandfather*, 277–78.
99. DeMallie, *Sixth Grandfather*, 281.
100. In 1890, bricklayers made on average $3.55 a day: plasterers $3.50 per day. Indian wages amounted to $0.96 per day (assuming a six-day workweek; the Wild West show did not perform on Sundays). Wage information from Scott Derks, *The Value of a Dollar: Prices and Incomes in the United States, 1860–1989* (Washington, DC: Gale Research, 1994), 15.

INTERLUDE: STANDING BEAR

1. DeMallie, *Sixth Grandfather*, 101, 106, 184–89. Quote from 106.
2. Standing Bear left behind is in D. F. Royer to Commissioner of Indian Affairs, Jan. 10, 1891, no. 3186, Box 699, Letters Received, 1881–1907, RG 75, NARA.
3. DeMallie, *Sixth Grandfather*, 254.
4. Even while traveling, Indians with Buffalo Bill often received notes about the latest family news from the reservation. I discuss the phenomenon of Lakota correspondence in the next chapter.
5. "Standing Bear Information as compiled by Adrienne DeArmas for the Lakota section of the Changing Cultures in Changing World Exhibition, Dec. 13, 1993," typescript, copy in author's possession, courtesy of Arthur Amiotte; author interview with Arthur Amiotte, June 21, 2003, tapes in author's possession.
6. Interview with Arthur Amiotte, June 21, 2003 tapes.
7. Family tradition tells of how Louise and others adapted to a temporary shortage of tanned soft leather by sewing canvas tops onto rawhide soles, making "the first sneakers." Interview with Arthur Amiotte, personal communication to author, March 24, 2005; Arthur Amiotte, June 21, 2003.
8. Industrial Status Report for Standing Bear, Wounded Knee District, Allotment No. 936, 1913, Pine Ridge archives, copy in author's possession. My thanks to Arthur Amiotte for these documents. For a description of the cabin see Hilda Neihardt, *Black Elk and Flaming Rainbow: Personal Memories of the Lakota Holy Man and John Neihardt* (Lincoln: University of Nebraska, 1995), 50–51. Average income statistic from Derks, *Value of a Dollar*, 123.
9. "Even today, among the Lakotas, relatives are people who *act* like relatives and consider themselves to be related." Raymond J. DeMallie, in James R. Walker, *Lakota Society* (Lincoln: University of Nebraska Press, 1982), 5–7. Quote from p. 6.
10. Charles Eastman, *From the Deep Woods to Civilization* (1916; rprt. Lincoln: University of Nebraska Press, 1977), 125.
11. Amiotte interview, June 21, 2003; Amiotte, personal communication to author, March 24, 2005.

CHAPTER FOURTEEN:
COWBOYS, INDIANS, AND THE ARTFUL DECEPTIONS OF RACE

1. Standing Bear, *My People the Sioux*, 259.
2. M. B. Bailey, ed., *Official Souvenir, Buffalo Bill's Wild West and Congress of Rough Riders of the World 1896* (Buffalo, NY: Courier Co., 1896).
3. Warren G. Vincent to H. H. Vincent, March 1, 1890, M Cody L Box 1, DPL-WHR.
4. Walker, *Clio's Cowboys*, 131.
5. Harry Webb, "Buffalo Bill, Saint or Devil?," typescript, BBHC.
6. Webb, "Buffalo Bill, Saint or Devil?," 9.
7. Webb, "Buffalo Bill, Saint or Devil?," 10–11.

8. Webb, "Buffalo Bill, Saint or Devil?," 6.

9. C. L. Daily to "Dear Folks," [no month] 22, 1889, copy in BBHC.

10. Standing Bear, *My People the Sioux*, 261.

11. Standing Bear, *My People the Sioux*, 264.

12. BBWW 1893 program, 27–28.

13. Arthur Frank Wertheim and Barbara Bair, eds., *The Papers of Will Rogers* (Norman: University of Oklahoma Press, 1996), 1: 222–23.

14. C. L. Daily to "Dear Folks," n.d. [1889], BBHC.

15. For Pedro Esquivel, see Bailey, *Official Souvenir*, 14; for gauchos, BBWW 1893 program, 55.

16. Clara Esquivel Parker, "Anthony 'Tony' Esquivel," Oct. 1, 1969, in Clara Esquivel Parker Papers, MS 92 DPL-WHR; Russell, *Lives and Legends*, 317, 332, 340, 372, 377; also Yost, *Call of the Range*.

17. Bailey, *Official Souvenir*, 18; for Tony Esquivel as Mexican, see Yost, *Buffalo Bill*, 208; Russell, *Lives and Legends*, 377; "Serious Shooting Accident at the 'Wild West,' " *Evening News* (London), July 14, 1887, clipping in JCG Scrapbook, MS 58, NSHS.

18. Bailey, *Official Souvenir*, 14, 18; *Route Book, Buffalo Bill's Wild West 1899* (Buffalo: Matthews-Northrup Co., 1899), 7; *Official Route and Roster of the Buffalo Bill's Wild West Season of 1902* (Los Angeles: Los Angeles Printing Co., 1902), 9, BBHC; Russell, *Lives and Legends*, 442.

19. Vincente Oropeza to Frank Hammitt, Feb. 16, 1895, Misc. Files, "Hammett," BBHC; Russell, *Lives and Legends*, 377.

20. Clara Esquivel Parker, "Anthony 'Tony' Esquivel."

21. George Johnson to "Dear Brother Justus and Sister Gussie," June 21, 1892, Nebraska Prairie Museum, Holdredge, NE.

22. Standing Bear, *My People the Sioux*, 264; BBWW 1903 program (London: Weiners, 1903), 4.

23. Irving told a fabulous story about running away from home as a little boy with the army and ending up at Pine Ridge. Yost, *Buffalo Bill*, 186–87.

24. For W. G. Bullock, see Hyde, *Red Cloud's Folk*, 174, 183; and Spring, *Cheyenne and Black Hills Stage and Express Routes*, 24–25, 34, 108. Billy Bullock gives a concise and apparently truthful account of his life in "Camp Sketches—No. 5, Billy Bullock," *Topical Times*, July 30, 1887, clipping in JCG Scrapbook, MS 58, NSHS. Also, Russell, *Lives and Legends*, 308, 317.

25. Russell, *Lives and Legends*, 308.

26. Bennie Irving photograph is in J. Wojtowicz, *Buffalo Bill Collector's Guide*, 68.

27. Havighurst, *Annie Oakley of the Wild West*, 57.

28. "Camp Sketches—No. 9, John Nelson," *Topical Times*, Aug. 27, 1887, clipping in JCG Scrapbook, 54, MS 58, NSHS.

29. "Camp Sketches—No. 5, Billy Bullock," *Topical Times*, July 30, 1887, clipping in JCG Scrapbook, MS 58, NSHS.

30. Rocky Bear's history is in Hyde, *Red Cloud's Folk*, 114, 259. His relationship to Ella Bissonett is in Yost, *Buffalo Bill*, 186. He was in the show contingent in 1888, 1889, 1893, and other years. See Supplemental Agreement, April 10, 1888, in Misc. Letters Sent, 1887–89, vol. 5, pp. 30–32, Pine Ridge, RG 75, NARA-CPR; George LeRoy Brown to WFC and Salsbury, April 19, 1893, Misc. Css. Received, 1891–95 A–C, Folder B May 2–Nov. 23, 1895, Pine Ridge, RG 75, NARA-CPR; Yost, *Buffalo Bill*, 211.

31. BBDC 1883; BBWW 1883 program, n.p.; BBWW 1888 program (Hartford, CT: Calhoun, 1888), 28.

32. Eric Lott, *Love and Theft: Blackface Minstrelsy and the American Working Class* (New York: Oxford University Press, 1993); Toll, *Blacking Up*, 200.

33. "Won a White Bride," *New York Times*, Aug. 19, 1886, p. 3; "Pushaluck's Romance," *New York Times*, Aug. 15, 1886; "Refused to Tie the Knot," *New York Times*, Dec. 10, 1886, reports on the refusal of Jersey City's "Justice Weed" to marry a Wild West show Indian named Cloud Foot and Annette Copeland, 17, of Brooklyn.

34. "Glasgow," *Glasgow Weekly Mail*, Jan. 9, 1892, p. 2.

35. Clara Esquivel Parker, "Anthony (Tony) Esquivel."

36. "Camp Sketches—No. 5, Billy Bullock," in *Topical Times*, July 30, 1887, clipping in JCG Scrapbook, MS 58, NSHS.

37. For Black Elk see DeMallie, *Sixth Grandfather,* 252–54; for White Eyes, see Jacob White Eyes to Folco Baroncelli, Aug. 24, 1906, Palais du Roure, Avignon.

38. Jacob White Eyes to Folco Baroncelli, Aug. 24, 1906, Palais du Roure, Avignon.

39. There is one account that disputes the authenticity of show Indians. Gordon "Pawnee Bill" Lillie, who became a showman rival to Cody, began his entertainment career with Buffalo Bill's Wild West in 1883. According to Lillie, his job was "to do all the interpreting" for the Pawnees, "and even to make up as an Indian myself and go on with them." Glenn Shirley, *Pawnee Bill: A Biography of Major Gordon W. Lillie* (Albuquerque: University of New Mexico Press, 1958), 99.

40. Standing Bear, *My People the Sioux,* 252.

41. Standing Bear, *My People the Sioux,* 254.

42. Amos Bad Heart Bull and Helen H. Blish, *A Pictographic History of the Oglala Sioux* (Lincoln: University of Nebraska Press, 1967), 450–61; Gordon MacGregor, with Royal B. Hassrick and William H. Henry, *Warriors Without Weapons: A Study of the Society and Personality Development of the Pine Ridge Sioux* (Chicago: University of Chicago Press, 1946), 38; DeMallie, "Teton," 816.

43. Peter Iverson, *When Indians Became Cowboys: Native Peoples and Cattle Reaching in the American West* (Norman: University of Oklahoma Press, 1994), 59.

44. Iverson, *When Indians Became Cowboys,* 73–76.

45. Iverson, *When Indians Became Cowboys,* 73.

46. George LeRoy Brown to T. J. Morgan, June 17, 1893, in RG 75, Pine Ridge, Misc. Letters Sent, 1892, vol. 13, p. 119, NARA-CPR; H. D. Gallagher to Charles Foster, Oct. 19, 1889, RG 75, Pine Ridge, Misc. Letters Sent, 1887–91, vol. 5, pp. 291–92, NARA-CPR; "Col. Cody's Motley Crowd," *The Times* (Kansas City, Missouri), Oct. 19, 1896, NSS, 1896, DPL.

47. George LeRoy Brown to Kicking Bear, May 13, 1892, in RG 75, Pine Ridge, Misc. Letters Sent, 1892, vol. 12, pp. 325–26, NARA-CPR; George LeRoy Brown to John Shangrau, Aug. 9, 1892, RG 75, Pine Ridge, Misc. Letters Sent, 1892, vol. 14, p. 227, NARA-CPR; G. L. Brown to WFC, Sept. 14, 1892, and G. L. Brown to WFC, Sept. 15, 1892, both in RG 75, Pine Ridge, Misc. Letters Sent, 1892, vol. 15, first one on p. 82, other on p. 97, NARA-CPR.

48. Nate Salsbury to the Hon. Commissioner of Indian Affairs, March 1, 1892, in no. 9249, Box 834, Letters Received, 1881–1907, RG 75, NARA.

49. In 1906, Jacob White Eyes sold a beaded vest to a French acquaintance for ninety francs. Jacob White Eyes to Folco Baroncelli, Aug. 24, 1906, Palais du Roure, Avignon.

50. See exhibit 2 and exhibit 3 in Nate Salsbury to the Hon. Commissioner of Indian Affairs, March 1, 1892, in no. 9249, Box 834, Letters Received, 1881–1907, RG 75, NARA.

51. See Register 1883–1892, 226–28, Kelvin Grove Museum, Glasgow, Scotland. Also George C. Crager to Curator Paton, Dec. 17, 1891, in files of the Kelvin Grove Museum, Glasgow, Scotland.

52. After his sentencing, his sister, who was also with the show but who unfortunately remains anonymous in press accounts, handed him a bundle of apples. "The Assault on Buffalo Bill's Interpreter," *Glasgow Evening News,* Jan. 4, 1892, p. 4; "Glasgow," *Glasgow Weekly Mail,* Jan. 9, 1892, p. 2; " 'Charging Thunder' Gets Thirty Days. 'His Lemonade Was Mixed,' " *Glasgow Evening News,* Jan. 12, 1892, p. 5; "Glasgow," *Glasgow Weekly Mail,* Jan. 16, 1892, p. 2; " 'Charging Thunder' Sent to Prison," *Glasgow Weekly Herald,* Jan. 16, 1892, p. 7.

53. Madra, *Glasgow's Ghost Shirt.*

54. Biolsi, *Organizing the Lakota,* 20.

55. Standing Bear, *My People the Sioux,* 242.

56. F. E. Leupp to U.S. Indian Agent, May 14, 1908, in 047 Fairs and Expositions, Box 162, RG 75, NARA-CPR; copy in "Petitions by BBWW Indians," Association Files, BBHC.

57. Utley, *Lance and the Shield*, 225–33. Nick Black Elk, who originally joined the show hoping to see the Holy Land whence Jesus came, recalled that when Queen Victoria met the Lakota performers, she said that they had "a Grandfather over there who takes care of you over there, but he shouldn't allow" the white people "to take you around as beasts to show the people." DeMallie, *Sixth Grandfather*, 250. Black Elk's version of the meeting is highly dubious, but the point is less what Victoria said than how much Indians remembered and appreciated her words as a critique of U.S. Indian policy, something that had considerable weight coming from the sovereign of the world's largest empire.

58. For Red Cloud's request of a flag, see Red Cloud to Nate Salsbury, July 18, 1889, Box 1/6, NSP, YCAL 17.

59. U.S. Indian Agent to Commissioner of Indian Affairs, May 18, 1908, in 047 Fairs and Expositions, Box 162, BBWW, RG 75, NARA-CPR; copy in "Petitions from BBWW Indians," Association Files, BBHC.

60. Charles S. McNichols to Commissioner of Indian Affairs, Nov. 16, 1903, in "Encounter Between Sioux Indians of the Pine Ridge Agency, S. Dak, and a Sheriff's Posse of Wyoming," Senate Document 128, 59th Congress, Jan. 27, 1904, 14. For a provocative analysis of the events at Lightning Creek, see Deloria, *Indians in Unexpected Places*, 15–51.

61. A. P. Putnam to Governor Fenimore Chatterton, Nov. 10, 1903, in "Encounter Between Sioux Indians," 5–7.

62. Two of the most outspoken critics of the government's failure to punish the murderers of Lightning Creek were veterans of Buffalo Bill's theatrical show and the Wild West, too: George Sword, Jack Red Cloud, "Statement to the Public by Pine Ridge Indians Relating to Late Trouble in Wyoming," in "Encounter Between Sioux Indians," 16. Bull and Blish, *A Pictographic History of the Oglala Sioux*, 500–1; Roberta Carkeek Cheney, *Sioux Winter Count: A 131-Year Calendar of Events* (Happy Camp, CA: Naturegraph, 1998), 44; James R. Walker, *Lakota Society*, ed. Raymond J. DeMallie (Lincoln: University of Nebraska Press, 1982), 155.

63. U.S. Indian Agent to Commissioner of Indian Affairs, May 18, 1908, "Petitions by BBWW Indians," Association Files, BBHC.

64. For Brown's education, see H. D. Gallagher to U.S. Indian Agent, Rosebud Agency, March 20, 1889, RG 75, Pine Ridge, Misc. Letters Sent, 1887–91, vol. 5, p. 193, NARA-CPR.

65. Warren G. Vincent to H. H. Vincent, March 1, 1890, M Cody L Box 1, DPL-WHR.

CHAPTER FIFTEEN: BUFFALO BILL'S AMERICA

1. Russell, *Lives and Legends*, 370–71.

2. Arabs from the Paris Hippodrome, then appearing at the Olympia Theater, visited the Wild West camp in London in 1887; Cossacks, or the Georgian horsemen who pretended to be Cossacks, were appearing in European circuses by the late 1880s. "Buffalo Bill's Wild West," *Pictorial News*, Nov. 5, 1887, in WFC Scrapbook, Buffalo Bill Museum, Golden, CO; for Cossacks, see Irakli Makharadze and Akaki Chkhaidze, *Wild West Georgians* (Tbilisi Georgia: New Media, n.d.), 1–2.

3. Oakley's memory is in Russell, *Lives and Legends*, 372; U.S. Army and circuses in Davis, *Circus Age*, 78.

4. Burke, *Buffalo Bill from Prairie to Palace*, 266.

5. WFC to Al Goodman, Aug. 25, 1891, in Foote, *Letters from Buffalo Bill*, 37–38.

6. Foote, *Letters from Buffalo Bill*, 40.

7. Nate Salsbury, "Wild West at Windsor," typescript, n.d., in YCAL MSS 17, NSP.

8. Davis, *Circus Age*, 10. In 1891, while the Wild West show was in Glasgow, Salsbury and Cody briefly installed "educated" elephants and a group of "Schuli warriors" from Africa. "Musical and Dramatic," *Scottish Sport* (Glasgow), Jan. 22, 1892, p. 14.

9. "The Ladies Expedition," unattributed clipping, n.d.; also "Brussels Gossip—From Wounded Knee to Waterloo" unattributed clipping, n.d. in G. C. Crager Scrapbook, 1891–92, BBHC.

10. The scholarship on world's fairs and exhibitions is huge. A good summary of it may be found in Robert W. Rydell, John E. Findling, and Kimberly D. Pelle, *Fair America: World's Fairs in the United States* (Washington, DC: Smithsonian Institution Press, 2000), esp. 1–13. Other sources consulted here include Robert W. Rydell, *All the World's a Fair: Visions of Empire at American International Expositions, 1876–1916* (Chicago: University of Chicago Press, 1984), and *World of Fairs: The Century of Progress Expositions* (Chicago: University of Chicago Press, 1993); Burton Benedict, *The Anthropology of World's Fairs* (Berkeley, CA: Scolar Press, 1983); Karal Ann Marling, *Blue Ribbon: A Social and Pictorial History of the Minnesota State Fair* (St. Paul: Minnesota Historical Society, 1990). For the World's Columbian Exposition of 1893, see also Erik Larson, *The Devil in the White City: Murder, Magic, and Madness at the Fair That Changed America* (New York: Crown, 2003); and Neil Harris, Wim de Wit, James Gilbert, and Robert W. Rydell, *Grand Illusions: Chicago's World's Fair of 1893* (Chicago: Chicago Historical Society, 1993).

11. Larson, *Devil in the White City*, 117; Harris et al., *Grand Illusions*, 81–84.

12. Stanley Applebaum, *The Chicago World's Fair of 1893* (New York: Dover, 1980), 103; Larson, *Devil in the White City*, 250.

13. See Slotkin, *Gunfighter Nation*, 80–82; White, "Frederick Jackson Turner and Buffalo Bill," 7–65; Fabian, "History for the Masses," 223–39, esp. 223–26.

14. Larson, *Devil in the White City*, 236; gondolas in Harris et. al., *Grand Illusions*, 65; J. W. Buel, *The Magic City: A Massive Portfolio of the Original Photographic View of the World's Fair* (St. Louis, MO: Historical Publishing Co., 1894), n.p.

15. Swimming races and "Ball of the Midway Freaks" in Larson, *Devil in the White City*, 311–15; prune rider in Claire Perry, *Pacific Arcadia: Images of California, 1600–1915* (New York: Oxford University Press, 1999), 94–95.

16. Amy Leslie [Lilian West Brown Buck], *Amy Leslie at the Fair* (Chicago: W. B. Conkey, 1893), 20.

17. "The Last of the Wild West," *New York Times*, Feb. 23, 1887, p. 2.

18. Burrows and Wallace, *Gotham*, 1228–29.

19. Kasson, *Amusing the Million*, 34.

20. Nate Salsbury, "Contract with Bailey," typescript, n.d., Box 1/63, YCAL MSS 17, NSP.

21. Jacobson, *Barbarian Virtues*, 14.

22. "Cossack and Cowboy," unattributed clipping, July 29, 1888, WFC Scrapbook 1883–1886–1888, BBHC.

23. Remington, "Buffalo Bill in London," 96–98; for an example of the comparison, see Leslie, *Amy Leslie at the Fair*, 24–25.

24. Burke, *Buffalo Bill from Prairie to Palace*, 250–51.

25. BBWW 1893 program, 27–28.

26. Quote from Blackstone, *Buckskin, Bullets, and Business*, 82; Thomas M. Barrett, "Cowboys or Indians? Cossacks and the Internationalization of the American Frontier," *Journal of the West* 42: 1 (Winter 2003): 52–59; Makharadze and Chkhaidze, *Wild West Georgians*.

27. Burke, *Buffalo Bill from Prairie to Palace*, 50, 55. For horse purchases, see WFC to Frank Hammitt, Dec. 21, 1892, and WFC to Frank Hammitt, Dec. 21, 1894, MS 6, Series I:B, Box 1, BBHC.

28. In 1895, western author Owen Wister published his "Evolution of the Cow-Puncher," which argued the cowboy was the advance guard of Anglo-Saxon expansion. Owen Wister, "The Evolution of the Cow-Puncher," *Harper's New Monthly Magazine*, 1895, in Vorpahl, *My Dear Wister*, 77–96. Quote from p. 80.

29. Nasaw, *Going Out*, 1–46.

30. Harold Coffin Syrett, *The City of Brooklyn, 1865–1898: A Political History* (1944; rprt. New York: Ams Press, 1968), 235–36; there were 89,722 Irish in Kings County (Brooklyn) in 1890, according to "The Historical Census," online database at ⟨http://fisher.lib.virginia.edu/collections/stats/hlistcensus⟩. Nov. 1, 2004.

31. Vaudeville theaters charged a dime for admission, and drew immigrant crowds. The cheapest theaters, the so-called "ten-twenty-thirties," charged ten cents for their upper

balcony seats and thirty cents for the best seats in the house. These were popular destinations for laborers and low-level clerks, too. Nasaw, *Going Out*, 40–42.

32. For Germans, see M. B. Bailey, *Original Souvenir*, 151; "George Hamid," *Philadelphia Bulletin*, June 14, 1971, clipping in MS 6, WFC Collection Series VI:B BBWW Personnel Box 1/6, BBHC.

33. Shanton from "How Shantor [*sic*] Rode the Bear," *Chicago Herald*, July 10, 1894, and "The Laramie Kid's Career," *New York Press*, July 8, 1894; McPhee from "Cody's Bold Cowboys," *New York Advertiser*, May 20, 1894, all in NSS, vol. 4, 1894, WH 72, DPL-WHR; these names are drawn from George H. Gooch, ed., *Route-Book Buffalo Bill's Wild West 1899* (Buffalo, NY: Matthews Northrup, 1899), 3–4.

34. "Our Unique Idea," *Morning Journal*, May 20, 1894, in NSS, vol. 4, 1894, WH 72, DPL-WHR.

35. Clipping from *Deutsche Eindrucke*, Aug. 20, 1896, in NSS, 1896, DPL, translation by Warren Dym.

36. Wetmore, *Last of the Great Scouts*, ix–x. Deloria, *Playing Indian*, 39–41, 46–47; Fintan O'Toole, *The Lie of the Land: Irish Identities* (New York: Verso, 1997), 26–28; for jokes, see "Lebkuecher's Levee," *New Jersey Times*, June 23, 1891, clipping in Crager Scrapbook, BBHC; for Tammany members at Wild West show, see "Wild West Open," *Brooklyn Citizen*, May 5, 1894, clipping in NSS, vol. 4, 1894, WH 72, DPL-WHR. For Croker's career with Tammany Hall, see Burrows and Wallace, *Gotham*, 1104–10.

37. Nate Salsbury, "At Police Headquarters" typescript, n.d., in YCAL MSS 17, Box 2/63, NSP.

38. "The Historical Census," Nov. 1, 2004.

39. E. J. Hobsbawm, *The Age of Empire: 1875–1914*, (London: Weidenfeld and Nicolson, 1987), 180. Census figures on American-born children of immigrants are as follows: according to the 1890 census, native-born males of foreign parents in Kings County, New York, numbered 157,204; native-born females numbered 164,653. "The Historical Census," Nov. 1, 2004; Nasaw, *Going Out*, 43–44.

40. Syrett, *City of Brooklyn*, 129, 220.

41. Ellen M. Snyder-Grenier, *Brooklyn! An Illustrated History* (Philadelphia: Temple University Press, 1996), 35. For Forefather's Day, see "City and Suburban News," *New York Times*, Dec. 19, 1886, p. 7. Other historical associations were no more inclusive. The Brooklyn Historical Society began as the Long Island Historical Society in 1863, with quarters in the exclusive Brooklyn Heights neighborhood which was home to most of Brooklyn's New England descendants. Snyder-Grenier, *Brooklyn!*, 36.

42. Nasaw, *Going Out*, 44–45.

43. Nasaw, *Going Out*, 52–53.

44. "Old-Time Actors with the Indians," *New York Telegram*, June 21, 1894, in NSS, vol. 4, 1894, WH 72, DPL-WHR; Keen's "Dutchman" act is mentioned in various places. See "Rubbart at the 'Wild West,' " *The Bailie* (Glasgow), Nov. 25, 1891, p. 7.

45. BBWW 1893 program; BBWW 1894 program; Wojtowicz, *Buffalo Bill Collector's Guide*, 24–25.

46. BBWW 1894 program; Wojtowicz, *Buffalo Bill Collector's Guide*, 25.

47. Roosevelt, *Winning of the West*, 1: 4.

48. Turner, "Significance of the Frontier in American History"; Klein, *Frontiers of Historical Imagination*, 13–31; Cronon, "Revisiting the Vanishing Frontier," 157–76.

49. Herbert Baxter Adams, *Saxon Tithing-Men in America* (Baltimore: Johns Hopkins University Press, 1882), and *The Germanic Origin of New England Towns* (Baltimore: Johns Hopkins University Press, 1882).

50. Quoted in William Cronon, "Turner's First Stand: The Significance of Significance in American History," in *Writing Western History: Essays on Major Western Historians*, ed. Richard W. Etulain (Albuquerque: University of New Mexico Press, 1991), 77.

51. For American history departments, Lawrence Levine, "Clio, Canons, and Culture," *Journal of American History* 80, no. 3 (Dec. 1993): 849–67, esp. 855–56; for show business, Nasaw, *Going Out*, 43, n.

52. Gooch, ed., *Route-Book Buffalo Bill's Wild West 1899*, 21; George H. Gooch, ed., *Route-Book Buffalo Bill's Wild West 1900* (Kansas City, MO: Hudson-Kimberley Publishing, 1900), 42, in BBHC.

53. Fellows and Freeman, *This Way to the Big Show*, 119–20.

54. NSP, YCAL MSS 17, Box 1, Folder 21, Beinecke Library, Yale University, New Haven, CT; for African Americans in the actual West see Quintard Taylor, *In Search of the Racial Frontier*, 17–221.

55. Quoted in Yost, *Buffalo Bill*, 263–64.

56. WFC to George T. Beck, March 26, 1895, in WFC Letters, No. 9972, Box 1/1, AHC. Census figures from "Historical Census," March 7, 2005.

57. "These People Making History," *Brooklyn Daily Times*, April 12, 1897, in NSS, 1897, DPL-WHR. See also Nate Salsbury to WFC, Oct. 10, 1899, in YCAL MSS 17, Box 1/11, NSP. Nina Silber writes that *Black America* attracted 200,000 people in Brooklyn, and that it showed in London by the end of 1895. Nina Silber, *The Romance of Reunion: Northerners and the South, 1865–1900* (Chapel Hill: University of North Carolina Press, 1993), 135.

58. I owe this idea of place to William Cronon.

59. "Indians See 'The World,' " *The World*, June 4, 1894; "New for the Boulevardiers," *New York Herald*, June 1, 1894; "Invaded by Riffian Moors," *Brooklyn Eagle*, n.d.: "Eleven Texans with Guns," *New York Sun*, May 9, 1894. All in NSS, 1894, Microfilm 18, Reel 1, DPL.

60. See tickets to Chicago show and Ambrose Park show, in YCAL MSS 17, Box 1, Folder 23, NSP.

61. "Buffalo Bill 'At Home' to Friends," *New York Herald*, May 10, 1894, NSS, 1894, p. 30, Series 7, Box 4, DPL.

62. "Buffalo Bill's Wild West Expanded," *New York Telegram*, May 5, 1894, p. 28; and "Buffalo Bill in Brooklyn," *New York Mercury and America*, May 6, 1894, p. 27, of NSS, 1894, WH 72, Series 7, Box 4, DPL.

63. Remington, "Buffalo Bill in London," 98.

64. Jacob A. Riis, *How the Other Half Lives: Studies Among the Tenements of New York*, ed. David Leviatin (1893; rprt. New York: St. Martin's, 1996), 60; also David Leviatin, "Introduction," in Riis, *How the Other Half Lives*, 28.

65. Leviatin, "Introduction," 48, n. 78.

66. Riis, *How the Other Half Lives*, 73.

67. "City Camp Life," *Brooklyn Citizen*, May 20, 1894, clipping in NSS, vol. 4, Series 7, Box 4, DPL.

68. Untitled clipping, *American Hebrew*, Aug. 24, 1894, NSS.

69. "Buffalo Bill's Wild West," *Recorder*, May 10, 1894, in NSS, 1894, p. 29, WH 72, Series 7, Box 4, DPL. BBWW 1910 program (New York: Southern & Co. Publishers), n.p.

70. Riis, *How the Other Half Lives*, 179.

71. For parks movement, see Jon C. Teaford, *The Unheralded Triumph: City Government in America, 1870–1900* (Baltimore: Johns Hopkins University Press, 1984), 252–58. Quotation from "An Army from All Nations," *New York Tribune*, May 10, 1894, NSS, vol. 4, Series 7, Box 4, DPL.

72. Remington, "Buffalo Bill in London," 98.

73. "City Camp Life," *Brooklyn Citizen*, May 20, 1894. At least one columnist wrote in 1897 that the show was "Stirring Up Savage Passions in the Rising Generation," a remark that suggested the show's usefulness for inoculating boys against neurasthenia. "The Wild West Show," unattributed clipping, April 14, [no year], NSS, vol. 7, 1897, Series 7, Box 7, DPL.

74. Although not entirely positive. Boys who committed acts of serious violence while playing "Buffalo Bill's Wild West" also appeared in the press. "Played Wild West," *New York Commercial Advertiser*, Aug. 29, 1894, NSS, vol. 4, Series 7, Box 4, DPL.

75. "New Wild West Show," *New York Recorder*, Aug. 23, 1894, NSS, vol. 4, 1894, Series 7, Box 4, DPL.

76. Deloria, *Playing Indian*.
77. M. B. Bailey, *Official Souvenir*, 274; Blackstone, *Buckskins, Bullets, and Business*, 42–43.
78. See, for example, "Buffalo Bill at Portsmouth," unattributed clipping, n.d., G. C. Crager Scrapbook, BBHC.
79. Both men claimed the vaccinations were absolutely "not necessary." "Virus for Heap Big Injun," *Evening World* (New York), May 16, 1894, NSS, 1894, Series 7, Box 4, DPL. For the history of urban public health campaigns and the response of immigrant communities, see Charles Rosenberg, *The Cholera Years: The United States in 1832, 1849, and 1866*, rev. ed. (Chicago: University of Chicago Press, 1982), esp. 33–34.
80. David E. Nye, *Electrifying America: Social Meanings of a New Technology 1880–1940* (Cambridge, MA: MIT Press, 1990), 29–39, and passim.
81. David Nasaw, *Going Out*, 8.
82. Harold Coffin Syrett, *The City of Brooklyn, 1865–1898* ([1944] New York: AMS Press), 166–72, 208–12; David Nye, *Electrifying America*.
83. Nye, *Electrifying America*, 96.
84. Ellen M. Snyder-Grenier, *Brooklyn! An Illustrated History* (Philadelphia: Temple University Press, 1996), 103–4; untitled clipping, *Electrical Review*, May 23, 1894, in NSS, vol. 4, Series 7, Box 4, DPL.
85. Quote from "Electricity at the Wild West Show," *The Electrical World* 24 (1) Sept. 15, 1894, 255; see also "Scientists Visit the Wild West," *New York Times*, Sept. 7, 1894; "Electricians at the Wild West," *New York Tribune*, Sept. 7, 1894; "Electricians at the Wild West," *New York Press*, Sept. 7, 1894; "Electricians Pleased," *New York Recorder*, Sept. 7, 1894; "Camp Cody Invaded," *New York Advertiser*, Sept. 7, 1894; "Electricians at the Wild West," *Brooklyn Eagle*, Sept. 7, 1894; "New York Electrical Society," *New York Electricity*, Sept. 12, 1894; "The New York Electrical Society," *The New York Electrical Age*, Sept. 15, 1894, all in NSS, vol. 4, 1894, Series 7, Box 4, DPL.
86. "Electricity Is Life," *Brooklyn Weekly*, Aug. 18, 1894, in NSS, Microfilm 18, Reel 4, DPL.
87. See the program materials for the Coney Island appearances in WFC Collection, Denver Public Library, WH 72, Box 2/2, DPL.
88. BBWW 1898 Show Courier (New York: Fless and Ridge, 1898), 14; M. B. Bailey, *Official Souvenir*, 24.
89. Order of parade in M. B. Bailey, *Official Souvenir*, 37; BBWW 1899 program, n.p.; for electricity in circuses, see Janet Davis, *The Circus Age*, 251, n. 43.
90. David E. Nye, *American Technological Sublime* (Cambridge, MA: MIT Press, 1994), esp. xiii, 1–16; also John Kasson, *Civilizing the Machine: Technology and Republican Values in America, 1776–1900* (New York: Penguin, 1977), 162–72; Leo Marx, *The Machine in the Garden: Technology and the Pastoral Ideal in America* (New York: Oxford University Press, 1970), 195–207; Perry Miller, *The Life of the Mind in America* (Harcourt Brace Jovanovich, 1965), 295–306.
91. Burrows and Wallace, *Gotham*, 1038; Davis, *Circus Age*, 39; Trachtenberg, *The Incorporation of America*.
92. "How He Does It," *Brooklyn Standard Union*, Aug. 20, 1894, in NSS, vol. 4, Series 7, Box 4, DPL.
93. "Great Managers Join Hands," in *The Frontier Express and Buffalo Bill Wild West Courier*, (1895), 7–8; BBWW 1898 Show Courier, 3.
94. "A Happy Strike at the Wild West," *Freemason New York*, Aug. 4, 1894, in NSS, WH 72, Series 7, Box 4, DPL.
95. Slotkin, *Gunfighter Nation*.
96. Fellows and Freeman, *This Way to the Big Show*, 140.
97. "Big family" from "The Wild West's 'Mama,' " *Brooklyn Citizen*, Sept. 15, 1894; "Farewell to Ambrose Park," *New York Times*, Oct. 7, 1894, in NSS, vol. 4, Series 7, Box 4, DPL.
98. "Little Irma Cody," *New York Journal*, Aug. 26, 1894, NSS, vol. 4, Series 7, Box 4, DPL.
99. See, for example, "Farewell to Ambrose Park," *New York Times*, Oct. 7, 1894, NSS, vol. 4, Series 7, Box 4, DPL.
100. See the illustration in "Little Irma Cody," *New York Journal*, Aug. 26, 1894.

101. "The Wild West's 'Mama,' "; "City Camp Life."

102. "The Wild West's 'Mama.' "

103. "With 'Marm' Whittaker," *New York Commercial Advertiser,* June 16, 1894, NSS, vol. 4, Series 7, Box 4, DPL; for Pop Whittaker, see "Pop Whittaker Buried," Feb. 16, 1887, *New York Times,* Feb. 16, 1887, p. 2.

104. "Little Irma Cody."

105. "The Wild West's 'Mama.' "

106. "The Wild West's 'Mama.' "

107. Quotation from "The Wild West's 'Mama.' " See also "City Camp Life"; "With 'Marm' Whittaker." Whittaker's intimacy with Indians was potentially subversive, and in some ways it bucked against the dark fears of miscegenation that energized the "Settler's Cabin" rescue and the show's many messages of white female vulnerability and Indian savagery. At the same time, the notion of white woman leading Indian man to civilization was a powerful idea with resonances in missionary work and assimilation campaigns as they unfolded both on the reservation and in immigrant ghettoes. When asked what could ensure the "gradual amalgamation" of Indians "with the superior white race," John Burke raised the example of an unnamed Lakota man who some years before had traveled with the show and married "a Viennese German widow." Burke was referring to Standing Bear, and he told the press that his example should be followed by recruiting five hundred German peasant women to marry Sioux men, bringing about "the crossing of healthy breeds, the raising of new citizens, who would be imbued with the spirit of arbitration, under the direction of that best of instructors, mother." See "Major John M. Burke, A Notable Character in Buffalo Bill's Wild West Camp," *New York Recorder,* June 24, 1894, NSS, 1894, Microfilm 18, Reel 4, DPL.

The suggestion at once embraced arbitration as the union of races and contradicted the show's teachings of racial segregation as the bulwark against decay. But Burke contained the subversions of his suggestion by proposing union between Indians and *lower-class Germans,* not Indians and native whites. In some quarters, these were roughly parallel social classes. At one point, the Indian agent at Pine Ridge requested that a Chicago postal inspector track down the parents of Louise Rieneck, who were lost in the city. By this time, many German Americans had become members of the middle class. Nonetheless, the inspector still relegated these recent immigrants to America's steerage. "I just returned from Chicago where, after two days' search through the squallor [*sic*], I found the balance of the relatives of the Standing-Bear-of-the-German-Wife." Where he located them is not clear, but he judged them "good subjects for a teepee. The old gent is not bad looking if he were polished up somewhat, but, alas! soap and water in anything like a necessary quantity are unknown to the family." Perceptions of immigrants as filthy savage aliens made them candidates for assimilation campaigns that in some ways resembled those directed at Indians: missionary efforts, sanitation and literacy and civics lessons, and educational programs to stamp out indigenous language. Burke's proposal—doubly ironic for its origination with an Irish Catholic—reflected the contradictory impulses of the assimilation movement which sought to remove the threat of "primitive" races from civilization, but simultaneously to avoid embracing them too closely through marriage and sexual intimacy with the middle or upper classes. See E. C. Clement to George LeRoy Brown, Feb. 26, 1892, Pine Ridge, Misc. Css. Received, 1891–95, A–C, Jan. 4–May 10, 1892, RG 75, NARA-CPR.

108. Leslie, *Amy Leslie at the Fair,* 148–49.

109. "Yesterday Was Women's Professional League Day at the Wild West," *New York Advertiser,* July 31, 1894, in NSS, 1894, WH72, Series 7, Box 4, DPL.

110. "Colonel Cody Talks," *New York Recorder,* May 22, 1894, clipping in Robert Haslam Scrapbook, CHS.

111. "Lo, the Dry Indian," unattributed clipping; "Mustn't Sell Firewater to the Braves," *New York World,* June 15, 1894; "Feared Drunken Indians," *New York Evening World,* June 17, 1894; "This Is the Toughest Yet," *Brooklyn Times,* June 4, 1894, all in NSS, vol. 4, Series 7, Box 7, DPL.

112. George R. Scott, "Prohibition in Brooklyn, N.Y.," *New York Witness,* June 20, 1894, NSS, vol. 4, Series 7, Box 4, DPL.

113. All from "Wild West's Kitchen," *Chicago Evening Post*, June 6, 1896, in NSS, 1896, Series 7, Box 4, DPL.
114. Eric Rauchway, *The Refuge of Affections: Family and American Reform Politics* (New York: Columbia University Press, 2001).

INTERLUDE: THE JOHNSON BROTHERS

1. Richard E. Jensen, "Introduction," in Johnson, *Happy as a Big Sunflower*, xiii–xxiv, 227, n. 2; Owen Wister, "Evolution of the Cow-Puncher," 80.
2. There were 115,747 foreign-born white males in Nebraska in 1890, and 86,497 foreign-born white females. Native-born white males of foreign parentage numbered 130,246, while native-born white females of foreign parentage numbered 120,174. The total population of Nebraska was 1,058,910. "The Historical Census," cited Nov. 1, 2004.
3. Johnson, *Happy as a Big Sunflower*, 53, 159.
4. Johnson, *Happy as a Big Sunflower*, 54, 57, 187–89.
5. Robert Johnson to "My Dear Robins," May 4, 1959; Grace Capron Johnson, "George William Johnson," n.d.; Grace Capron Johnson to Paul Fees, Sept. 3, 1992, in "WW Show Personnel," Association Files, BBHC. There is another copy of Grace Capron Johnson's MSS in the Nebraska Prairie Museum, Holdredge, NE.

CHAPTER SIXTEEN: EMPIRE OF THE HOME

1. Painter, *Standing at Armageddon*, 116–17; on industrial armies, see Todd Depastino, *Citizen Hobo: How a Century of Homelessness Shaped America* (Chicago: University of Chicago Press, 2003), 58–62; Carlos Schwentes, *Coxey's Army: An American Odyssey* (Lincoln: University of Nebraska Press, 1985); Lucy Barber, *Marching on Washington: The Forging of an American Political Tradition* (Berkeley: University of California Press, 2002), 11–43.
2. BBWW 1899 program; Gooch, ed., *Route-Book Buffalo Bill's Wild West 1899*, 7.
3. Theodore Roosevelt, *The Rough Riders* (1899; rprt. New York: New American Library, 1961), 14–15.
4. Slotkin, *Gunfighter Nation*, 101–6; Buck Taylor was one of TR's Rough Riders, see Roosevelt, *Rough Riders*, 26; Tom Isbell was a cowboy in Cody's Wild West and Roosevelt's Rough Riders, too. See Roosevelt, *Rough Riders*, 181. For "Theater" Roosevelt, see Aaron Hoffman, "The Speaker of the House: A Monologue," Pt. 3 1914, in the Library of Congress, on line at ⟨*http://memory.loc.gov*⟩.
5. BBWW 1900 program, 36, WFC Collection, WH 72, Box 2/34, DPL-WHR.
6. Edmund Morris, *The Rise of Theodore Roosevelt*, rev. ed. (New York: Modern Library, 2001), 379.
7. Cherny, *American Politics in the Gilded Age*, 128, 141; Hoganson, *Fighting for American Manhood*; Slotkin, *Gunfighter Nation*, 106–7.
8. BBWW 1898 program, BBWW 1899 program, BBWW 1900 program; BBWW 1901 Program (Buffalo, NY: Courier Co); Wojtowicz, *Buffalo Bill Collector's Guide*, 30–32.
9. BBWW 1899 program, 63, WFC Collection, WH 72, Box 2/34, DPL-WHR.
10. Richard Hofstadter, *The Age of Reform: From Bryan to FDR* (New York: 1955), 90–93, 273–74.
11. Painter, *Standing at Armageddon*, 141–69.
12. Hoganson, *Fighting for American Manhood*, 180–99.
13. Havighurst, *Annie Oakley of the Wild West*, 203; Reddin, *Wild West Shows*, 136; Slotkin, *Gunfighter Nation*, 86.
14. WFC to George Everhart, April 29, 1898, quoted in Russell, *Lives and Legends*, 417.
15. Nate Salsbury pencil notes re: complaints about Buffalo Bill Cody, n.d., in NSP, YCAL MSS 17, Box 1/12.
16. WFC to Moses Kerngood, Aug. 3, 1898, WFC Collection, MS 6 Series I:B Correspondence, Box 1/14, BBHC.

17. Russell, *Lives and Legends*, 417–19.

18. Painter, *Standing at Armageddon*, 154–57.

19. For 1903 show, see "The Wild West," *Manchester Courier*, April 28, 1903, clipping in NSS 1903; quote from BBWW 1907 program (Buffalo, NY: Courier Co., 1907), 6.

20. Foote, *Letters from Buffalo Bill*, 42–43.

21. Russell, *Lives and Legends*, 255–56.

22. David Carr, *Time, Narrative, and History*, 7.

23. Trachtenberg, *Incorporation of America*, 91; Davis, *Circus Age*, 52.

24. Coffee is in Beck Family Papers, No. 10386, Box 15/17, AHC; for guiding services, see Foote, *Letters from Buffalo Bill*, 41–42. Short Line railroad in Gallop, *Buffalo Bill's British Wild West*, 203–5.

25. See the ads in BBWW 1898 program, and BBWW 1899 program, both in Huntington Library, San Marino, CA. Program advertisements varied from one locality to another. For advertising and its significance, see Trachtenberg, *Incorporation of America*, 135–39; Jackson Lears, *Fables of Abundance: A Cultural History of Advertising in America* (New York: Basic Books, 1994).

26. Yost, *Buffalo Bill*, 170–71, 217.

27. Yost, *Buffalo Bill*, 259.

28. George Beck, autobiography MSS, in G. T. Beck Papers, No. 59, Box 7/4, AHC, 103.

29. George Beck, autobiography MSS, 104.

30. G. T. Beck to F. W. Mondell, July 26, 1896, in G. T. Beck Papers, No. 59, Box 25, Book 12, Beck Css, AHC.

31. WFC to Mike Russell, July 13, 1895, WA-MSS, S-197, Box 1/5, Beinecke Library, Yale University, New Haven, CT. For contributions of Blestein and others, see Beck, autobiography MSS, 103–5.

32. WFC to Mike Russell, July 13, 1895. For Cody's partnership with Salsbury on the north side, see Robert E. Bonner, "Buffalo Bill Cody and Wyoming Water Politics," *Western Historical Quarterly* 32, no. 4 (Winter 2002): 437.

33. BBWW 1896 program; BBWW 1897 program, WFC Collection, WH 72, Box 2/29, DPL.

34. BBWW 1901 program, WFC Collection, WH 72, Box 2/29, DPL.

35. BBWW 1901 program, WFC Collection, WH 72, Box 2/29, DPL. At this point, according to the advertisement, the water rights could be had for $10 per acre, payable in five annual installments at 6 percent interest. City names from "BBWW Routes, 1883–1916," BBHC.

36. *Cody Enterprise*, May 5, 1905.

37. "Buffalo Bill," *Manchester Sunday Chronicle* (UK), April 19, 1903, clipping in NSS, 1903, DPL. As an example of how much Cody's irrigation efforts enhanced his reputation and advanced him along a mythic narrative trajectory in the public eye, consider this description of his irrigation efforts in the Big Horn Basin: "The most notable recent enterprise in Wyoming is that undertaken in the Bighorn Basin by the famous scout, William F. Cody. . . . This energetic and ambitious man, who has twice won fame, first as a daring and successful scout, and then as exhibitor to two continents of the life, people, and customs of the Wild West—has laid broad and deep the foundations of a *still stronger claim to remembrance*. He conceived the idea of planting civilization in one of the wildest regions which he had first known as hunter and Indian-fighter." The passage goes on to describe the irrigation project and the promise of the Big Horn Basin: "In time the region must acquire a large population, supporting a many-sided life, and form a very substantial monument to William F. Cody and his work for the West." William Ellsworth Smythe, *The Conquest of Arid America*, 2nd ed. ([1899]; Norwood, MA: Norwood Press, 1905), 227–28. Emphasis added. Note that the trajectory here is "scout, exhibitor, planter of civilization."

38. WFC to W. A. Richards, Sept. 25, 1903, MS 6 Series I:B Css, Box 1/19, BBHC.

39. Gold mines: "We have located four thousand acres of placer mines on the line of our ditch." WFC to Mike Russell, Feb. 17, 1896, in WA-MSS, S-197, Beinecke Library, Yale University, New Haven, CT.

40. Photo p. 6.246, MS 6, Series XI, I, Box 4, BBHC; BBWW 1907 program, 14.

41. Alva Adams, a former governor of Colorado, speaking in 1911, quoted in Karen Merrill, *Public Lands and Political Meaning* (Berkeley: University of California Press, 2002), 202, n. 10.

42. Quoted in Danbom, *Resisted Revolution*, 22; see also Marx, *The Machine in the Garden*.

43. Emmons, *Garden in the Grassland*, 137.

44. Lawrence M. Woods, *Wyoming's Big Horn Basin to 1901: A Late Frontier* (Spokane, WA: Arthur H. Clarke, 1997), 10.

45. Frederic Remington describes it in Samuels and Samuels, *Frederic Remington*, 411.

46. William A. Jones, *Report upon the Reconnaissance of Northwestern Wyoming Including Yellowstone National Park Made in the Summer of 1873* (Washington, DC: Government Printing Office, 1875), 16–17.

47. George Beck, autobiography MSS, 109; for climate, see Woods, *Wyoming's Big Horn Basin*, 10.

48. WFC to Beck, Oct. 27, 1895, WFC Letters, No. 9972, Box 1/1, AHC.

49. See Beck to WFC, Aug. 23, 1896; Beck to WFC, Aug. 26, 1896; Beck to H. C. Alger, Aug. 26, 1896, G. T. Beck Papers, No. 59, Box 25, 1896 Letterpress Book, Beck Css, AHC.

50. Beck to WFC, Aug. 31, 1896, G. T. Beck Papers, No. 59, Box 25, 1896 Letterpress Book, Beck Css, AHC; also for Populists, see Nate Salsbury to George Beck, Oct. 8, 1896, Beck Family Papers, No. 10386, Box 1/8, AHC.

51. Beck to WFC, Oct. 2, 1896, G. T. Beck Papers, No. 59, Box 25, 1896 Letterpress Book, Beck Css, AHC.

52. "William A. Cody and George T. Beck to Phebe A. Hearst, Bond," Feb. 4, 1897, and "William F. Cody and George T. Beck to Phebe Hearst, Indemnity Bond," July 12, 1901, in G. T. Beck Papers, No. 59, Doc. 6, Folder 12, AHC. The indemnity bond reveals that they could not pay it off and had to carry the bond over to July 1904.

53. John Erwin Price, "A Study of Early Cody, Wyoming, and the Role of William F. Cody in Its Development," MA thesis, University of Denver, 1956, 139–41.

54. WFC to Mike Russell, April 9, 1896, in WA-MSS, S-197, Beinecke Library, Yale University, New Haven, CT; for Beck loan to Cody and Salsbury, see Beck, autobiography MSS, 117.

55. In 1870, farms made up 407,735,000 acres; by 1900, 838,592,000 acres were converted to farm. Hofstadter, *Age of Reform*, 56.

56. For crop prices, see Cherny, *American Politics in the Gilded Age*, 139; Hine and Faragher, *American West*, 347–48; Jeff Ostler, *Prairie Populism: The Fate of Agrarian Radicalism in Kansas, Nebraska, and Iowa, 1880–1892* (Lawrence: University Press of Kansas, 1993), 18; see also Shannon, *The Farmer's Last Frontier*; for drought in Nebraska, see Olson and Naugle, *History of Nebraska*, 235.

57. Laurence Goodwyn, *The Populist Moment*, 271.

58. Nate Salsbury to George Beck, Aug. 14, 1896, Beck Family Papers, No. 10386, Box 1/8, AHC.

59. Salsbury to Beck, Aug. 14, 1896, Beck Family Papers, No. 10386, Box 1/8, AHC. For corporate perceptions of Bryan generally, see Robert H. Wiebe, *The Search for Order, 1877–1920* (New York: Hill and Wang, 1967), 103.

60. Yost, *Buffalo Bill*, 267, 275.

61. Michael P. Malone and F. Ross Peterson, "Politics and Protests," 510–11, in *The Oxford History of the American West*, ed. Clyde A. Milner II, Carol A. O'Connor, and Martha A. Sandweiss (New York: Oxford University Press, 1994), 501–33.

62. "The Historical Census," cited Sept. 28, 2004.

63. For the Johnson County War, see Helena Huntington Smith, *The War on Powder River: The History of an Insurrection* (Lincoln: University of Nebraska Press, 1966), 183–242; A. S. Mercer, *The Banditti of the Plains; or the Cattlemen's Invasion of Wyoming in 1892 (The Crowning Infamy of the Ages)* (1894; rprt. Norman: University of Oklahoma Press, 1954); Merrill, *Public Lands and Political Meaning*, 49.

64. Karen Merrill, *Public Lands and Political Meanings*, 49: ". . . the turn-of-the-century livestock owner was seen as anything but a homebuilder, and before the early 1900s, ranch-

ing and homebuilding were culturally and politically viewed as antithetical categories in stories of western development."

65. T. A. Larson, *History of Wyoming* (Lincoln: University of Nebraska, 1965), 121.

66. "The Historical Census" lists 29,347 native-born females and 5,000 foreign-born females in the census of 1900.

67. In the words of one rural historian: "It was in these millions of tiny commonwealths that everything important in life took place." Danbom, *Resisted Revolution*, 9.

68. Beck, autobiography MSS, 93.

69. Paul Wallace Gates, "Land Reform Movement" and "Safety Valve Theory," in *The New Encyclopedia of the American West*, ed. Howard R. Lamar (New Haven: Yale University Press, 1998), 614–16, 998–99. The most trenchant critic of the safety valve theory is Shannon, *The Farmer's Last Frontier*, 356–59; see also his two essays, "A Post-Mortem on the Labor-Safety-Valve Theory," in *Agricultural History*, 19 Jan. 1945: 31–37; and "The Homestead Act and the Labor surplus," in *The Public Lands: Studies in the History of the Public Domain*, ed. Vernon Carstenson (Madison: University of Wisconsin, 1963), 297–313.

70. Smythe, *Conquest of Arid America*, 1–47; for more on reclamation and irrigation campaigns, see White, *"It's Your Misfortune and None of My Own,"* 402–6; Donald Worster, *Rivers of Empire: Water Acidity and the Growth of the American West* (New York: Oxford University Press, 1985); Donald Pisani, *Water and American Government: The Reclamation Bureau, National Water Policy, and the West, 1902–1935* (Berkeley: University of California Press, 2002), 1–31.

71. For the Carey Act, and how it operated in Cody, see Bonner, "Buffalo Bill Cody and Wyoming Water Politics," 433–51; also Donald Worster, *River of Empire*, 157; Donald J. Pisani, *Water and American Government*, xiv, 66–67; Price, "Study of Early Cody, Wyoming," 209–10.

72. Price, "Study of Early Cody, Wyoming," 131–32; Jerry Bales, personal communication to the author, July 22, 2005.

73. Price, "Study of Early Cody, Wyoming," 142.

74. Price, "Study of Early Cody, Wyoming," 157. The average laborer earned $438 per year in 1900. Derks, *Value of a Dollar*, 63.

75. Price, "Study of Early Cody, Wyoming," 134; Jeannie Cook, Lynn Johnson Houze, Bob Edgar, and Paul Fees, *Buffalo Bill's Town in the Rockies: A Pictorial History of Cody, Wyoming* (Virginia Beach, VA: Donning, 1996), 49.

76. Nate Salsbury, "The Pan-American Exposition," typescript, n.d., in NSP, YCAL MSS 17, Box 2/63.

77. D. H. Elliott to WFC, June 26, 1897; D. H. Elliott to WFC, July 8, 1897, G. T. Beck Papers, No. 59, Box 25, Book 12, Beck Css, AHC.

78. Howard Martin to G. T. Beck, June 27, 1904; C. M. Stewart to Beck, July 5, 1904, Folder 2; A. C. Fowler to Beck, Oct. 14, 1904, Folder 7; C. L. Goodwin to Beck, Dec. 3, 1904, Folder 7, 41 in Beck Family Papers, Box 2, AHC.

79. WFC to James R. Garfield, Jan. 29, 1909, in Gen'l Administrative and Project Records (Shoshone), Entry 3, Box 899, Folder 448-A1 (1909), RG 115, NARA-RMR.

80. Bonner, "Buffalo Bill and Wyoming Water Politics," 439, n. 15; Edward Gillette, *Locating the Iron Trail* (Boston: Christopher Publishing House, 1925), 117–24; Price, "Study of Early Cody, Wyoming," 124.

81. WFC to G. T. Beck, Sept. 25, [1898?], G. T. Beck Papers, No. 59, Doc. 6, Folder 12, AHC.

82. They handed the land over to the railroad's town-building subsidiary, the Lincoln Land Company. Price, "Study of Early Cody, Wyoming," 185.

83. Bonner, "Buffalo Bill and Wyoming Water Politics," 439; Cook et al., *Buffalo Bill's Town in the Rockies*, 51.

84. "Boom Town of the West Which Was Built Up in a Single Year," *Boston Herald*, Jan. 4, 1903, in Beck Family Papers, No. 10386, Box 15/20, AHC.

85. Bonner, "Buffalo Bill and Wyoming Water Politics," 435.

86. For a sample of the vigorous social scene in early Cody, see Agnes Chamberlin Scrapbook, Park County Historical Society, Cody, WY.

87. " 'The Irma,' " unattributed clipping, Nov. 22, 1902, Agnes Chamberlin Scrapbook, Park County Historical Society, Cody, WY.

88. "A Window to the Past: Nana Haight's Letters from Cody, 1910–1914," typescript, n.d., 1–5, Local History Collection, BBHC.

89. Price, "Study of Early Cody, Wyoming," 153–56.

90. WFC to Beck, Oct. 21, 1895, in G. T. Beck Papers, No. 59, Doc. 5, Folder 12, AHC.

91. For complaints, see WFC to Beck, June 8, 1898; "This is discouraging . . ." from WFC to Beck, Aug. 7, 1897, "It was neglect . . ." from WFC to Beck, Aug. 21, 1898, G. T. Beck Papers, No. 59, Doc. 6, Folder 12, AHC.

92. WFC to Beck, Aug. 19, 1896, in G. T. Beck Papers, No. 59, Doc. 6, Folder 12, AHC.

93. WFC to Beck, n.d., in G. T. Beck Papers, No. 59, Doc. 6, Folder 12, AHC.

94. WFC to JCG, April 12, 1903, MS 6 Series I:B Css, Box 1/19, BBHC.

95. WFC to JCG, July 19, 1903, MS 6 Series I:B Css, Box 1/19, BBHC.

96. The minimum cost for building the main canal from the river was more than $300,000; for getting that water to distributing ditches across the proposed settlement, another $245,000; for the waterworks to the town of Cody, which would provide water for up to 10,000 people, a minimum of $32,000; for the power plant to generate the town's electricity, a minimum expenditure of $165,000 was required. Frank C. Kelsey to WFC and Salsbury, Sept. 20, 1901, Engineering and Research Center Project Reports, Box 782 (Old Box), 520 SHO 10-52–530-SHO-22, Records of the Bureau of Reclamation, RG 115, Records of the Bureau of Reclamation, NARA-RMR.

97. D. F. Richards to A. O. Woodruff, May 19, 1902, in Papers of D. F. Richards, Wyoming State Archives, Cheyenne; D. R. Richards to WFC, June 21, 1902; Papers of Acting Governor Fenimore Chatterton, General Css.-Incoming, Box 2, WSA.

98. Worster, *Rivers of Empire*, 157; Pisani, *Water and American Government*, xiv–xv, 90.

99. Governor DeForest Richards offered the Cody-Salsbury tract to the Reclamation Service in a letter of Jan. 26, 1903, telling federal officials that the state board of land commissioners "will be glad to relinquish this land to the United States." See U.S. Department of the Interior, U.S. Geological Survey, *Second Annual Report of the Reclamation Service* (Washington, DC: Government Printing Office, 1904), 507, see also 508–9. The government estimated that it could reclaim 125,000 acres of land and irrigate it for farming at a cost to farmers of $25 per acre. ". . . opposite the railroad station at Ralston, is the 24,000 acres of first-class land segregated by the State under the Carey Act, which may be relinquished to the Secretary of the Interior." U.S. Department of the Interior, U.S. Geological Survey, *Third Annual Report of the Reclamation Service* (Washington, DC: Government Printing Office, 1905), 617–18, quote from 618; also U.S. Department of the Interior, U.S. Geological Survey, *Fourth Annual Report of the Reclamation Service, 1904–5* (Washington, DC: Government Printing Office, 1906), 346–50.

100. Fenimore Chatterton to Charles D. Walcott, Jan. 4, 1904; and see also the indenture of Dec. 12, 1902, between Cody and Salsbury and the State of Wyoming, both in General Administrative and Project Records (Shoshone), 1902–1919, Entry 3, Box 912, Folder 958, in RG 115, Records of the Bureau of Reclamation, NARA-RMR.

101. "Cody Has the $3,500,000," *New York Times*, Dec. 23, 1903, p. 2; quote from WFC to James Garfield, Jan. 24, 1909, in General Administrative and Project Records (Shoshone), Entry 3, Box 899, Folder 448-A1 (1909), RG 115, Records of the Bureau of Reclamation, NARA-RMR.

102. For settler discontent with the absence of a town waterworks, see "Why Not an Artesian Well?" *Wyoming Stockgrower and Farmer*, Dec. 15, 1903; also see "Large Irrigation Works," *Wyoming Stockgrower and Farmer*, Dec. 15, 1903; the town raised their own money to pay for a new waterworks by selling bonds. See "Accepted the Bid," *Wyoming Stockgrower and Farmer*, Dec. 29, 1903.

103. WFC to James R. Garfield, Jan. 24, 1909.

104. Republican Club of Northern Big Horn County to Chatterton, n.d., in Papers of Acting Governor Fenimore Chatterton, General Css.-Incoming, Box 2, WSA.

105. WFC to James R. Garfield, Jan. 29, 1909, in General Administrative and Project Records

(Shoshone), Entry 3, Box 899, Folder 448-A1 (1909), RG 115, Records of the Bureau of Reclamation, NARA-RMR.

106. C. H. Morrill to C. A. Guernsey, July 1, 1908, in General Administrative and Project Records (Shoshone), Entry 3, Box 899, Folder 448-A1 (1909), RG 115, Records of the Bureau of Reclamation, NARA-RMR.

107. WFC testimony, March 23, 1904.

108. Cody signed relinquishment, WFC to Fenimore Chatterton, Feb. 15, 1904, but then he recalled and annulled it before finally relinquishing it again; in Papers of Acting Governor Fenimore Chatterton, General Css.-Incoming, Box 2, WSA.

CHAPTER SEVENTEEN: SHOWDOWN IN CHEYENNE

1. Nate Salsbury, "Contract with Bailey," typescript, n.d., in YCAL MSS 17, NSP. For Bailey: see Davis, *The Circus Age*, 54–56.

2. Nate Salsbury, "Long Hair and a Plug Hat," typescript, n.d., NSP. "Many people may imagine I am inspired by a spirit of malice in writing these things. Not at all. I am only giving those who are dear to me a club to pound him with if he ever attempts to blacken me in support of his overweening vanity."

3. Nate Salsbury, "Secret Service," typescript, n.d., in YCAL MSS 17, NSP.

4. "Tin Jesus on horseback" from Nate Salsbury; "Long Hair and a Plug Hat," typescript, n.d.; "abused every man" from Nate Salsbury, "Cody's Personal Representatives," typescript, n.d., both in NSP.

5. Nate Salsbury, "Long Hair and a Plug Hat," typescript, n.d., NSP.

6. Nate Salsbury, "Cody's Personal Representatives," typescript, n.d., NSP.

7. Nate Salsbury, "American Exhibition," typescript, n.d., NSP.

8. Nate Salsbury, "Cody, Manager," typescript, n.d., NSP.

9. Nate Salsbury, "At the Vatican," typescript, n.d., NSP. Nate Salsbury, "Long Hair and a Plug Hat," typescript, n.d., NSP.

10. Home illustrated in BBWW 1885 program (Hartford, CT: Calhoun Printing, 1885), n.p.; quote from 1885 Buffalo Bill's Wild West Show Courier, in WH 72, Box 2/19, DPL.

11. BBWW 1893 program, 19; for masculine domesticity, see Marsh, *Suburban Lives*, 67–74.

12. Mrs. John Boyer testimony, Folder 7-1, 73, CC.

13. Russell, *Lives and Legends*, 432–33.

14. Russell, *Lives and Legends*, 425.

15. WFC to Henry Parker, June 9, 1901, Henry Parker Collection, Accession No. 388, Box 1, AHC.

16. WFC to Mrs. W. F. Cody, Aug. 21, 1900, MS 6 Series I:B Css, Box 1/15, BBHC.

17. For confrontations between ranch foremen/managers and Louisa Cody, see Henry Parker testimony, CC, Folder 7-2, 170–8; John Boyer testimony, CC, Folder 7-2, 179–89.

18. The divorce petition is reprised in "Wife to Fight 'Buffalo Bill,' " *Chicago Daily Tribune*, Feb. 15, 1905, p. 2.

19. "Buffalo Bill at Last Stand," *Chicago Daily Tribune*, Feb. 17, 1905, p. 1.

20. Bram Dijkstra, *Evil Sisters: The Threat of Female Sexuality and the Cult of Manhood* (New York: Alfred A. Knopf, 1996); Smith-Rosenberg, *Disorderly Conduct*, 181.

21. "The Sad Death of Horton S. Boal," *Cody Enterprise*, Nov. 6, 1902, clipping in Agnes Chamberlin Scrapbook, Park County Historical Society, Cody, WY; Yost, *Buffalo Bill*, 320.

22. May Cody Bradford testimony, CC, Folder 7-1, 89–90.

23. May Cody Bradford testimony, CC, Folder 7-1, 92.

24. May Cody Bradford testimony, CC, Folder 7-1, 94.

25. May Cody Bradford testimony, CC, Folder 7-1, 97; quote from D. Franklin Powell testimony, CC, Folder 7-2, 228. Louisa refused to speak to William Cody or sit with him in the carriage that transferred the coffin from one depot to another in Chicago. Robert Haslam testimony, CC, Folder 7-1, 137–38.

26. May Cody Bradford testimony, CC, Folder 7-1, 100, 105; reconciliation attempt is in D. Franklin Powell testimony, CC, Folder 7-2, 228.

27. "Buffalo Bill at Last Stand," *Chicago Daily Tribune*, Feb. 17, 1905, p. 1.

28. "Buffalo Bill Reads of Love," *Chicago Daily Tribune*, Feb. 19, 1905, p. 5.

29. WFC testimony, March 23, 1904, Folder 2, p. 14.

30. WFC testimony, March 23, 1904, Folder 2, pp. 18, 56, 57.

31. Mrs. C. P. Davis testimony, CC, Folder 7-1, 79–80.

32. Florence Parker testimony, CC, Folder 7-1, 153–60; another witness testified to the "horse-whipping" Irma received. See Mrs. C. P. Davis testimony, CC, Folder 7-1, 83.

33. Mrs. J. Boyer testimony, CC, 6–9.

34. Mrs. J. Boyer testimony, CC, 10–12, 24, 32, 34, 64–66, 69–72. Louisa Cody demanded that Mr. Boyer put his wife off the ranch or leave. Mrs. J. Boyer testimony, CC, 33.

35. Mrs. J. Boyer testimony, CC, 26, 41.

36. Mrs. J. Boyer testimony, CC, 29, 30, 50–54.

37. Mrs. J. Boyer testimony, CC, 48, 57.

38. May Cody Bradford testimony, CC, Folder 7-1, 114–15; also WFC testimony, March 6, 1905, Folder 13, 40.

39. WFC testimony, March 6, 1905, Folder 13, 41.

40. Beach Hinman testimony, CC, Feb. 9, 1905, Folder 8, 4.

41. Edith Colvin testimony, CC, Feb. 16–20, 1905, Folder 7-2, 356–60.

42. John Sorenson testimony, CC, Folder 7-2, 354–55.

43. Frank Bullard testimony, CC, Folder 7-2, 347–48, Folder 8, 83–84.

44. E. B. Warner testimony, CC, Folder 8, 12–20, esp. 13.

45. W. H. Turpie testimony, CC, Folder 8, 48.

46. Mrs. Florence M. Hershey, testimony, CC, Folder 8, 74–80.

47. For Carry Nation, see Homer E. Socolofsky, "Carry Amelia Nation," in Lamar, *The New Encyclopedia of the American West*, 760. For alcohol and temperance, see W. J. Rorabaugh, *The Alcoholic Republic: An American Tradition* (New York: Oxford University Press, 1979); Ian R. Tyrell, *Sobering Up: From Temperance to Prohibition in Ante-Bellum America, 1800–1860* (Westport, CT: Greenwood Press, 1979).

48. WFC to Mike Russell, Jan. 22, 1901; WFC to Mike Russell, March 14, 1901, MS 6 Series I:B Css, Box 1/17, BBHC.

49. Charles Wayland Towne, "Preacher's Son on the Loose with Buffalo Bill Cody," *Montana: The Magazine of Western History* 18, no. 4 (Fall 1968): 49.

50. Frank R. Bullard testimony, CC, Folder 7-2, 348.

51. Frank R. Bullard testimony, CC, Feb. 10, 1905, Folder 8, 90.

52. A. F. Streitz testimony, CC, Feb. 10, 1905, Folder 8, 106.

53. C. M. Newton testimony, CC, Folder 8, 44.

54. Patrick McEvoy testimony, CC, Feb. 11, 1905, Folder 8, 122.

55. Loren Sturgis testimony, CC, Feb. 10, 1905, Folder 8, 97–103.

56. Mrs. Louisa Burke testimony, CC, Feb. 10, 1905, Folder 8, 110–12, 120.

57. Ira L. Bare testimony, CC, Feb. 10, 1905, Folder 8, 65.

58. Charles Iddings testimony, CC, Folder 7-2, 329, 334–35. Emphasis added.

59. Beach Hinman testimony, CC, Feb. 9, 1905, Folder 8, 4–5. My analysis of Louise Cody as a "plain body" relies on Halttunen, *Confidence Men and Painted Women*.

60. Beach Hinman testimony, CC, Feb. 9, 1905, Folder 8, 8.

61. Beach Hinman testimony, CC, Feb. 9, 1905, Folder 8, 5.

62. The letter is not in the other defendant's exhibit, but Judge Scott quoted from it in his decision. See CC, Opinion of the Court, Folders 14 and 15, 2.

63. Louisa Cody's deposition does not survive in the case file at the Wyoming State Archives, so I have resorted to newspaper accounts of her testimony. "Loves Cody, Swears It," *Chicago Daily Tribune*, March 1, 1905, 2.

64. "Buffalo Bill Reads of Love," *Chicago Daily Tribune*, Feb. 19, 1905, 5; also, WFC testimony, Feb. 19, 1905, Folder 7-2, 272–86.

65. Charles Idding testimony, CC, Folder 7-2, 329.

66. WFC to Louisa Cody, Oct. 5, [1900], CC, Def. Ex. 2, Folder 7-2. The letter has no year,

but it written from Joplin, Missouri. The Wild West show was in Joplin on Oct. 5, 1900; see "BBWW Routes, 1883–1916," BBHC.

67. WFC to Louisa Cody, May 1, 1900, CC, Def. Ex. 3, Folder 7-2.

68. WFC to Louisa Cody, May 20, 1900, CC, Def. Ex. 4, and WFC to Louisa Cody, May 28, 1900, Def. Ex. 5, Folder 7-2.

69. WFC to Louisa Cody, May 20, 1900, CC, Folder 7-2; also WFC to Louisa Cody, May 29, 1900, Folder 7-2.

70. WFC to Louisa Cody, May 22, [1901], CC, Folder 7-2. No year on letter, but it was written from Richmond, Indiana, where the Wild West show performed on May 22, 1900. See "BBWW Routes List, 1883–1916," BBHC.

71. WFC to Louisa Cody, June 28, 1901, CC, Folder 7-2.

72. Mary M. Harrington testimony, CC, Feb. 21, 1905, Folder 10, pp. 10, 12.

73. "Fred May's Last Mistake," unattributed clipping, n.d., "Frederick May Dies After Life of Much Turmoil," unattributed clipping, 1918, "Mrs. Gould Wins Decree," unattributed clipping, 1909, in Robert Haslam Scrapbook, CHS; "Why Katherine and Cody Parted," *New York Herald*, April 17, 1894; "Fred May Meets Col. Cody," *New York Sun*, Feb. 17, 1894; "Is it Puff or Pouff?" *New York World*, Feb. 19, 1894; "Where Is Col. 'Buffalo Bill'?," *New York World*, Feb. 19, 1894; for losses of Clemmons's plays, see "Losses of the Year," *Dramatic Times*, April 21, 1894, all in NSS, 1894.

74. Her age is in WFC testimony, March 6, 1905, Folder 13, 51.

75. Fellows and Freeman, *This Way to the Big Show*, 150.

76. John W. Clair testimony, CC, April 1904, Folder 11, 9, 17.

77. Louis "Ed" Clark testimony, CC, Nov. 5, 1904, Folder 12.

78. WFC testimony, March 6, 1905, Folder 13, 12–13; William McCune supported Cody's testimony on this point. See William McCune testimony, Folder 7-1, 152.

79. WFC testimony, March 6, 1905, Folder 13, 7.

80. WFC testimony, March 6, 1905, Folder 13, 12.

81. WFC testimony, March 6, 1905, 11.

82. "Cody's Heart Won by Press Agent?," *Chicago Daily Tribune*, Feb. 20, 1905, 3.

83. "Buffalo Bill at Last Stand," *Chicago Daily Tribune*, Feb. 20, 1905, 3.

84. WFC testimony, March 23, 1904, 15.

85. See the judge's ruling, which he made the following day, also Lester Walker testimony, Folder 7-2, 263; and "Buffalo Bill's Suit for Divorce Recalled by Henning," *Chicago Daily Tribune*, Jan. 8, 1954, 7.

86. CC, Opinion of the Court, Folders 14 and 15, 2.

87. Henry Blake testimony, CC, Jan. 30, 1905, Folder 9, 17.

88. "Mrs. Cody the Josephine in a Suit for Divorce," *Chicago Inter-Ocean*, March 20, 1904, pp. 6–7, clipping in Beck Family Papers, No. 10386, Box 15, Folder 18, AHC.

89. The message was sent in a letter from Frank Powell, who met with the judge after the trial. See D. Franklin Powell to WFC, March 28, 1905, Hon. Richard H. Scott Collection, No. 2627, Box 1, AHC.

90. WFC to D. Franklin Powell, April 12, 1905, Hon. Richard H. Scott Collection, No. 2627, Box 1, AHC.

91. William Whelan testimony, CC, March 4, 1905, Folder 6.

92. Mrs. J. Boyer testimony, CC, 41.

93. WFC testimony, March 6, 1905, Folder 13, 27.

94. William Whelan testimony, CC, March 4, 1905, Folder 6, 4.

95. WFC to JCG, April 22, 1876, MS 6 I:B Correspondence, Box 1/5, BBHC.

96. WFC testimony, March 23, 1904, Folder 2, 30.

97. WFC testimony, March 23, 1904, Folder 2, 16.

98. WFC testimony, March 23, 1904, Folder 2, 70.

99. Yost, *Buffalo Bill*, 337. Hints of discontent caused by the trial appear in comments about Cody, in "Mike Taguin [?]" to "Old Pard," April 7, 1904, MS 126, William Cody Collection, Box 1, Folder 1, CHS: "I tell you the North Platte people and the Denverites are all down on him also the Masons and the Millitaries [*sic*]. The North Platte People says for him to keep away from there for it can't be healthy for him to go there."

100. "Pulpit Praises the Court," unattributed clipping, 1905, Hon. Richard H. Scott Collection, No. 2627, Box 1, Correspondence, AHC.
101. Henry J. Nicholas to Richard H. Scott, March 24, 1905, Hon. Richard H. Scott Collection, No. 2627, Box 1, Correspondence, AHC.

INTERLUDE: ADELE VON OHL PARKER

1. Robert Hull, "Adele Von Ohl Parker: 'Something of a Gypsy,' " *Cleveland Plain Dealer Magazine*, Nov. 4, 1973, 24–39.
2. Hull, "Adele Von Ohl Parker."
3. Adele Von Ohl Parker to "My Dears," Jan. [no day], 1955, in MS 6 WFC Collection VI:B, BBWW Personnel, Box 1/4, BBHC.
4. "Noted Rider with Buffalo Bill Wild West Show, Here," *Cody Enterprise*, Aug. 25, 1955, p. 1, clipping in MS 6 WFC Collection VI:B, BBWW Personnel, Box 1/4, BBHC.
5. "Wagon Hit, Woman Is Heroine," unattributed clipping, n.p., n.d., in MS 6 WFC Collection VI:B, BBWW Personnel, Box 1/4, BBHC.
6. Hull, "Adele Von Ohl Parker," 24–25.

CHAPTER EIGHTEEN: END OF THE TRAIL

1. "BBWW Routes, 1883–1916," BBHC; Russell, *Lives and Legends*, 441–43.
2. Russell, *Lives and Legends*, 444.
3. Russell, *Lives and Legends*, 443.
4. See "Old Scout Is Writing Life Story," *Sacramento Bee*, Oct. 1, 1907, p. 5.
5. BBWW 1907 program (Buffalo, NY: Courier Co., 1907), WH 72, Box 2/39, DPL.
6. BBWW 1907 program, WH 72, Box 2/39, DPL.
7. "Buffalo Bill's Wild West 'Live!' Original Film Footage, 1898–1912," Buffalo Bill Historical Center, Cody, WY, 1998, 15 min., videocassette.
8. BBWW 1907 program, 11; Russell, *Lives and Legends*, 445.
9. Tompkins, *West of Everything*, esp. 23–45; Lee Clark Mitchell, *Westerns: Making the Man in Fiction and Film* (Chicago: University of Chicago Press, 1996), 113–19.
10. Mitchell, *Westerns*, 28–54.
11. WFC testimony, March 23, 1904, 15.
12. Like his claim at the town of Cody itself, Buffalo Bill's claim at Ralston was now split with the Burlington Railroad's Lincoln Land Company. C. H. Morrill to C. A. Guernsey, July 1, 1908, and H. N. Savage to Chief Engineer, U.S. Reclamation Service, Dec. 6, 1905, RG 115, GAPR (Shoshone), Entry 3, Box 899, Folder 448-A1 (1909), FARC-Denver.
13. Thus, when the Mormon stake downstream filed for a water permit, Cody scribbled anxious letters from California and, later, from Britain urging against its approval. Repeatedly, the showman recommended that the government or a private individual take up the challenge: "If you know of any private individuals who wish to build the canal, I am perfectly willing to turn my interests over to them as no one is more anxious to see the canal completed than myself; but when the canal is built it should be started in the canyon above Cody so as to furnish water to the bench lands opposite the town and around the foot of Hart Mountain." But "if the Mormons or anyone else is permitted to take out canals to irrigate cheaply the lower end of this tract of land it will not pay the government or any private individuals to take a canal out of the canyon." WFC to Acting Governor Fenimore Chatterton, May 24, 1903, Gen'l Correspondence—Incoming, Acting Governor Fenimore Chatterton, RG 1.16, Box 2, WSA.
14. The buildings going up alongside the railroad at the location known as Camp Colter were merely "a temporary headquarters" midway between the stations of Garland and Ralston, which were eleven miles apart and therefore remote from survey crews working between them. "No definite arrangements have been made for townsite at this point, although it would seem a proper location for one." Chief Engineer to Hon. F. W. Mon-

dell, Aug. 8, 1906; F. W. Mondell to F. H. Newell, Aug. 3, 1906; Director to Secretary of Interior, Sept. 13, 1907, all in RG 115, GAPR (Shoshone), Entry 3, Box 899, Folder 448-A1 (1909), FARC-Denver.

15. WFC to Theodore Roosevelt, March 10, 1905, in RG 115, GAPR (Shoshone), 1902–1919, Entry 3, Box 912, Folder 958-A, NARA-RMR.

16. C. H. Morrill to C. A. Guernsey, July 1, 1908, GAPR (Shoshone), Entry 3, Box 899, Folder 448-A1 (1909), RG 115, FARC-Denver. Under the terms of the reclamation act, the government irrigated 278 farms by June 30, 1910; those farms covered a total of 16,552 acres. The town site of Powell opened with lots for sale on May 25, 1909, and by June 30, 1910, fifty-nine lots had been sold. U.S. Department of the Interior, U.S. Geological Survey, *Ninth Annual Report of the Reclamation Service, 1909–1910* (Washington, DC: Government Printing Office, 1911), 317.

17. WFC to James R. Garfield, Jan. 29, 1909, GAPR (Shoshone), Entry 3, Box 899, Folder 448-A1 (1909), RG 115, FARC-Denver.

18. WFC to James R. Garfield, Jan. 29, 1909.

19. WFC to James R. Garfield, Jan. 29, 1909.

20. Between 1902 and 1909, the Reclamation Service spent $3,678,000 on the Shoshone Project alone. See U.S. Department of the Interior, U.S. Geological Survey, *Eighth Annual Report of the Reclamation Service, 1908–1909* (Washington, DC: Government Printing Office, 1910), 21.

21. WFC to James R. Garfield, Jan. 29, 1909.

22. Director to Secretary of the Interior, Sept. 13, 1907, GAPR (Shoshone), Entry 3, Box 899, Folder 448-A1 (1909), RG 115, NARA-RMR.

23. Petition to Jeremiah Ahern, District Engineer, May 23, 1908, in GAPR (Shoshone), Entry 3, Box 899, Folder 448-A1 (1909), RG 115, NARA-RMR.

24. U.S. Department of the Interior, *Eighth Annual Report of the Reclamation Service*, 214.

25. For the Progressive Era, see Eric Rauchway, *Murdering McKinley*, 89–96, 184–96; Hofstadter, *Age of Reform;* Robert Wiebe, *The Search for Order, 1877–1920;* Pisani, *Water and American Government* 1–122.

26. White, *"It's Your Misfortune and None of My Own,"* 523; Pisani, *Water and the American State,* 272–95.

27. Shirley, *Pawnee Bill,* 176; Russell, *Wild West,* 32, and *Lives and Legends,* 296–98.

28. Shirley, *Pawnee Bill,* 193.

29. Russell, *Lives and Legends;* Shirley, *Pawnee Bill,* 186–90.

30. Shirley, *Pawnee Bill,* 186, 191; for oriental imagery and sensualism, see Lears, *Fables of Abundance,* 103–4.

31. Quoted in Yost, *Buffalo Bill,* 363.

32. For "Buffalo Bill Back to the New West," see Frank Winch, "How Buffalo Bill Is to Spend His Time," n.d., MS 6 Series IA, Box 119, BBHC. Shirley, *Pawnee Bill,* 199.

33. Shirley, *Pawnee Bill,* 199.

34. See E. J. Ewing. "Operations of the Cody-Dyer Milling Co. and Campo Bonito and Southern Belle Properties, Oracle, Arizona, 1912–1916, and a History of the Properties," May 3, 1945, MS 6 I:G, Box 1/17, BBHC.

35. WFC to JCG, March 13, 1903, MS 6 Series I:B Css, Box 1/19, BBHC. See also WFC to JCG, April 12, 1903, MS 6 Series I:B Css, Box 1/19, BBHC.

36. He owned 157,000 shares of the company, and gave thousands more to his sisters and to Louisa. See stockholder certificates in MS 6 I:G, Box 1, BBHC. Figures on Cody's investments are hard to come by. Lillie said that Cody claimed expenses of $125,000 to $150,000. Shirley, *Pawnee Bill,* 192.

37. For seeking investment, see WFC to My Dear Old Pard, Sept. 7, 1911, copy in MS 6 I:G, Box 1, "1911," BBHC; for complaints about managers, see WFC to My Dear Getchell, Oct. 9, 1911, copy in MS 6 I:G, Box 1, "1911," BBHC.

38. See the map in E. Hobart Molson to Richard I. Frost, Feb. 15, 1974, in MS 6, I:G, Box 1, BBHC.

39. WFC to Noble Getchell, Oct. 13, 1911, copy in MS 6 I:G, Box 1, "1911," BBHC.

40. WFC to Dear Pard, Sept. 20, 1911, copy in MS 6 I:G, Box 1, "1911," BBHC.

41. According to Lillie, Getchell once persuaded Cody to send him $25,000 to buy out rival claims that had cost Getchell a total of $2,500. Shirley, *Pawnee Bill*, 192.

42. Eugene Sawyer to Mother, Feb. 6, 1912, MS 360, Arizona Historical Society, copies in MS 6 I:G, Box 1/36, BBHC.

43. "Operations of the Cody-Dyer Milling Co."; Shirley, *Pawnee Bill*, 192.

44. See WFC to JCG, June 14, 1913; WFC to JCG, July 10, 1914; WFC to JCG, Aug. 22, 1915; in Foote, *Letters from Buffalo Bill*, 74–76. In 1918, soon after Cody's death, courts transferred the mines to heirs of Barney Link, a poster printer to whom Cody left an unpaid debt of $10,000. Ewing, "Operations of the Cody-Dyer Milling Co."

45. See Bess Isbell to W. J. Walls, Feb. 10, 1906, accession no. 74.0360, and 74.0361; also, WFC to W. J. Walls, Feb. 10, 1906, accession no. 74.0362; WFC to Judge Walls, Feb. 28, 1906, no. 74.0368, in BBM.

46. WFC to Dear Ones, March 28, [1910], MS 6 Series I:B, Box 1/3, BBHC; Yost, *Buffalo Bill*, 362.

47. Russell says they were reconciled on July 28, 1910, after William Cody visited when the Wild West was in the area, but cites no evidence. *Lives and Legends*, 435; also Yost, *Buffalo Bill*, 365. The problem with the account is that the Wild West show was in South Bend, Indiana, on that date, and nowhere near North Platte at any time during that season. "BBWW Show Routes, 1883–1916," BBHC.

48. Shirley, *Pawnee Bill*, 206.

49. Shirley, *Pawnee Bill*, 207.

50. Russell, *Lives and Legends*, 452–57; Gene Fowler, *Timberline: A Story of Bonfils and Tammen* (Garden City, NY: Garden City Books, 1933), 371–81.

51. WFC to JCG, May 27, 1915, in Foote, *Letters from Buffalo Bill*, 76.

52. WFC to JCG, May 27, 1915, in Foote, *Letters from Buffalo Bill*, 76; Karl King, quoted in Don Russell, *Lives and Legends*, 459.

53. Oglala Council to William H. Taft, Dec. 23, 1911, RG 75, Box 162, 047 Fairs and Expositions, BBWW Bankruptcy, Folder 1 of 2, NARA-CPR.

54. See the extensive contracts in RG 75, Box 162, 047 Fairs and Expositions, BBWW Bankruptcy, Contracts, 1912–13, NARA-CPR.

55. Superintendent to Samuel D. Oliphant, Jan. 17, 1916, and Superintendent to Samuel D. Oliphant, Nov. 16, 1916; names from list of payees in Samuel D. Oliphant to Major John R. Brennan, Jan. 13, 1916, all in 047 Fairs and Expositions, Box 162, BBWW Bankruptcy, 1913, RG 75, NARA-CPR; also Kevin Brownlow, *The War, the West, and the Wilderness* (New York: Knopf, 1979), 233.

56. Moses, *Wild West Shows and the Images of American Indians*, 227–48.

57. Moses, *Wild West Shows*, 234.

58. Brownlow, *The War, the West, and the Wilderness*, 232–33.

59. Moses, *Wild West Shows* 239.

60. Brownlow, *The War, the West, and the Wilderness*, 228. See the discussion of this matter in Moses, *Wild West Shows*, 238–48.

61. Franklin K. Lane to Frederick G. Bonfils, Aug. 28, 1913, RG 48, Department of the Interior, Office of the Secretary, Central Classified File 1907–1936, 5-2, "Indians, Moving Pictures," copies in WFC Collection, MS 6 I:A, Biographical Box 2/24, BBHC.

62. Russell, *Lives and Legends*, 461; Brownlow, *The War, the West, and the Wilderness*, 233, 275–83.

63. Quoted in Walsh and Salsbury, *Making of Buffalo Bill*, 352.

64. Russell, *Lives and Legends*, 461; Walsh and Salsbury, *Making of Buffalo Bill*, 353–54.

65. Russell, *Lives and Legends*, 464; *Buffalo Bill (Himself) and 101 Ranch 1916 Program*, n.p., BBHC.

66. Walter Benjamin, *Illuminations*, 220–21. Benjamin refers to the historical tradition conveyed in the authentic as its "aura," a term I avoid because of its astrological, New Age associations.

67. For a sampling of the range of Buffalo Bill memorabilia, see Wojtowicz, *Buffalo Bill Collector's Guide*, esp. 187–261.

68. I am relying, heavily, on Neil Harris, *Humbug*, 230–31; and Roger D. Abrahams, "Trick-

ster, Our Outrageous Hero," in *Our Living Traditions: An Introduction to American Folk-lore*, ed. Tristram Peter Coffin (New York: Basic Books, 1968), 171–72.

69. Yost, *Buffalo Bill*, 411; Louisa Frederici Cody and Riley Cooper, *Memories of Buffalo Bill*.
70. Harry Webb, "Buffalo Bill's Goodbye," typescript, n.d., BBHC.
71. Webb, "Buffalo Bill's Goodbye," 46.
72. Moses, *Wild West Shows*, 251.
73. Walsh and Salsbury, *Making of Buffalo Bill*, 359.
74. "Col. Cody's Last Year," narrative in William Cody Bradford Scrapbook, BBHC.

ACKNOWLEDGMENTS

This book began as a social history of the Wild West show, but I soon realized that cast members' accounts of life in the show were so inflected with the mythology of William Cody himself that it became impossible to evaluate them without first understanding him. The resulting project took much longer than I anticipated, and it took me much further afield, too. I have many debts, and I know the list below is incomplete.

I have been the beneficiary of much institutional support, beginning with faculty research grants at the University of San Diego and the University of California, Davis. Early on, my research received a major boost from a summer seminar, "Social Historians Write Biography," sponsored by the National Endowment for the Humanities at the Newberry Library (ably taught by James Grossman and Elliott Gorn, who gave me some of the first and most helpful advice on following Cody's trail). I subsequently was honored to receive a W. M. Keck Fellowship at the Huntington Library in San Marino, California, and a fellowship from the Albert and Lois P. Graves Fund, which generously financed my research trip to France and Britain. A Fred Garlow Grant from the Buffalo Bill Historical Center provided valuable travel support for my research at the Buffalo Bill Historical Center, during which I also was treated to the center's wonderful hospitality at the Paul Stock House. A University of California President's Research Fellowship in the Humanities, a fellowship from the UC Davis Humanities Institute, and sabbatical leave from UC Davis provided me with time to begin drafting this book.

Portions of chapter 9 first appeared in "Cody's Last Stand: Masculine Anxiety, the Custer Myth, and the Frontier of Domesticity in Buffalo Bill's Wild West Show," *Western Historical Quarterly* 35 (Spring 2003): 49–69 (copyright Western History Association; reprinted by permission). Portions of Chapter 11 and Chapter 12 appeared in "Buffalo Bill Meets Dracula: William F. Cody, Bram Stoker, and the Frontiers of Racial Decay," *American*

Historical Review 107: 4 (October 2002): 1124–57. My thanks to both publications for allowing me use of the material here.

At Alfred A. Knopf, Jane Garrett, my editor, recognized the value of the project early on and has been a strong supporter ever since. I am indebted also to Emily Molanphy for the prompt and cheerful editorial assistance, and Susanna Sturgis for the excellent copyediting.

Out in Cody, I owe special thanks to Paul Fees, a scholar as distinguished by his remarkable generosity as by his vast knowledge of Buffalo Bill Cody and the Far West. Time and again, Paul steered me to sources and offered the benefit of his own Cody scholarship, and his sense of humor, too. Our talks alone made my annual visits to the town of Cody well worth the trip.

Arthur Amiotte welcomed me to his home, where he shared family history, as well as documents and photographs of adventurous ancestors who went to Europe with Buffalo Bill. My thanks to him for generosity with time and his family heritage, and also for his insights and our many great conversations during the writing of this book.

With many others, I mourned the passing of Calvin Jumping Bull shortly before this book was completed. I am indebted to Calvin for sharing the history of his family's involvement with Buffalo Bill's Wild West, and also for explaining the show's long-term legacy for Lakota performers. My thanks to him for the stories, and the wisdom.

At research libraries and archives I discovered not only great staff, but good friends. At the Buffalo Bill Historical Center, Juti Winchester and Bob White were extremely helpful and encouraging; Frances Clymer and Ann Marie Donoghue fielded numerous questions and, late in the game, urgent requests for lots of photographs. Steve Frieson was enthusiastic in his assistance with materials in the Buffalo Bill Museum, in Golden, Colorado. Bruce Hanson and Janice Prater at the Denver Public Library were always welcoming and extremely helpful. On this as on several other projects over the last fifteen years, George Miles has steered me through the wonders of western history at Yale's Beinecke Rare Book and Manuscript Library. I remain grateful for his help and his friendship. Alan Perry, at the National Archives branch in Kansas City, offered much assistance and made certain I did not miss out on his hometown's barbeque ribs. I have also been fortunate to work with the staff of the Nebraska State Historical Society, the National Archives in Washington, D.C., and the National Archives regional center in Denver, Colorado. In Europe, I received much assistance from the staff of the Kelvin Grove Museum, Glasgow, the staff of the British Library, London, and Sabine Barnicaud, at the Palais du Roure, Avignon, France.

In the UK, thanks to John and Noni Cordingley, Jeremy and Rosemary Cordingley, Mark and Sally Hobbs, Alan and Elizabeth Megahey, Ken and Polly Anderson, and Karina Upton and Paul Kelland for the support and hospitality. On the Continent, Rupert and Josiene Buxton not only opened their home, but saved my research agenda with a spate of last-minute travel bookings that got me across France, and in time.

At the University of San Diego, where I was teaching when I began this project, Jim Gump first proposed that I tackle Buffalo Bill. His advice was strongly seconded by Iris Engstrand and Lisa Cobbs Hoffman. My thanks to all.

Colleagues and friends have been unstinting in their willingness to read drafts of chapters, to comment on the work, and to listen to my (often lengthy) musings. Phil Deloria provided thoughtful criticism and coaching on cultural history, nineteenth-century America, and William Cody's career. Early in the work, Mike Saler pointed me toward issues of race decay, national expansion, and popular entertainments, and gave me a sounding board for many of the ideas which found their way into the final work (and talked me out of some that did not). Stephen Arata, Steve Aron, Ann Fabian, Todd DePastino, Mark Fiege, Dan Flores, Karen Halttunen, Catherine Robson, David Simpson, and Elliott West read draft chapters and dispensed helpful criticism and advice. Alan Taylor and Emily Albu, Bill Ainsworth and Kathy Olmsted, Andrew Anker and Nancy Leroy, and Ted and Jo Burr Margadant provided conceptual advice, criticism of drafts, and much emotional support—and many dinners. Also, I have been enlightened by many conversations with Thomas Andrews, Bob Bonner, David Biale, William Cronon, William Hagen, Jack Hicks, Drew Isenberg, Susan Johnson, Cathy Kudlick, Norma Landau, Howard Lamar, David Rich Lewis, Ming-Cheng Lo, Sally McKee, Barbara Metcalf, Tom Metcalf, Clyde Milner, George Moses, Louis Owens, Andres Resendez, Kevin Rozario, Marni Sandweiss, Suzana Sawyer, John Smolenski, Krystyna Von Henneberg, Clarence Walker, and Li Zhang. In addition to my faculty colleagues in the UC Davis Department of History, I would like to thank my research assistants for their cheerful, relentless pursuit of sources: Robert Chester, Phil Garone, Emily Hanawalt, David Hickman, Ben Perez, and Josh Reid.

Thanks to my parents, Claude and Elizabeth Warren, who have long encouraged me to follow the paths I most enjoy and stay on them to the end. My in-laws, Robert and Mary Streeter, have provided encouragement and a lovely retreat in the high country of Wyoming for many years now.

I reserve my greatest debt for last. During the research and writing of this book, my family has exhibited both stalwart patience with being ignored for long stretches of time, and enthusiasm for the sometimes weird travel itinerary. Much as my boys enjoyed the trip to Disneyland Paris—where they watched the live reenactment of the Wild West show, "La Legende de Buffalo Bill"—they have not been wild about Buffalo Bill. Not long ago, my son Sam spoke for himself and his big brother, Jesse, when he informed me that this must be my last book, "because writing keeps us from having fun with you." To both my boys, I can only say that I am even happier than you are that this book is finished.

For eight years, through all the ups and downs of this project, and the many thousands of miles we've logged in completing it, my wife, Spring, has believed in it and seen me through all my doubts, disruptions, and setbacks. She edited every chapter (more than once) and provided me the best and most consistent advice on history, narrative, and literary style. I could not have done it without her. Her good-natured observation about how enthusiastically I turn almost any conversation back toward the subject of this book—"All roads lead to Buffalo Bill"—has long become a standing joke among friends and family. Now that we've reached our destination, there are a thousand new roads waiting. Which one we choose does not concern me, so long as I share it with you.

INDEX

Page numbers in *italics* refer to illustrations.

A NOTE ON THE TYPE

This book was set in Janson, a typeface long thought to have been made by the Dutchman Anton Janson, who was a practicing typefounder in Leipzig during the years 1668–1687. However, it has been conclusively demonstrated that these types are actually the work of Nicholas Kis (1650–1702), a Hungarian, who most probably learned his trade from the master Dutch typefounder Dirk Voskens. The type is an excellent example of the influential and sturdy Dutch types that prevailed in England up to the time William Caslon (1692–1766) developed his own incomparable designs from them.

Composed by North Market Street Graphics, Lancaster, Pennsylvania

Printed and bound by Berryville Graphics, Berryville, Virginia

Designed by Robert C. Olsson